CALIFORNIA
REAL ESTATE PRINCIPLES

9th Edition

Sherry Shindler Price

This publication is designed to provide accurate and current information regarding the subject matter covered. The principles and conclusions presented are subject to local, state and federal laws and regulations, court cases, and revisions of same. If legal advice or other expert assistance is required, the reader is urged to consult a competent professional in that field.

Director of Publishing: *Lars Jentsch*
Real Estate Publisher: *Leigh Conway*
Technical Advisor: *Ignacio Gonzalez*
Creative Editor: *Judy Hobbs*
Editor: *Joan Manno*
Assistant Editor: *Sue Carlson*
Graphic Designer: *Dria Kasunich*

©1997, 1998, 1999, 2000, 2001, 2002, 2003, 2005, 2006 by Ashley Crown Systems, Inc.

Ashley Crown Systems, Inc.
22952 Alcalde Drive
Laguna Hills, California 92653

Printed in the United States of America
ISBN 0-934772-32-0

CONTENTS

PREFACE

Whether your purpose is to increase your knowledge as a buyer or seller, or to pass the California Real Estate License Exam, you will find the information presented in this book to be useful. This textbook is written primarily for the beginning real estate student; however, inquiring consumers and investors will also find answers to their real estate questions.

New design features have been created to give the 9th edition structure. A new page layout was designed for ease of reading and note-taking. Chapters have been edited and reorganized to more closely follow a real estate transaction.

Each chapter in this textbook has been divided into topics. Topic content is reinforced through real-life examples, photographs, illustrations, charts, and tables. Important terms are highlighted in **bold type** in each chapter. Each chapter ends with a summary.

The 9th edition has been revised to include the following:

- updated information on eminent domain.
- updated real estate forms.

Review exercises have been designed for each chapter. The quiz exercises feature real estate terms and multiple-choice questions. The multiple-choice questions at the end of each chapter will help the student prepare for the real estate exam. These challenging questions were designed to test higher-level concepts and will often require the student to combine information they have learned in different chapters.

After completing a quiz exercise, students can check their answers by reviewing the Answer Key in the Appendix. Students should be encouraged to review their work often to make sure they understand what they have read.

ABOUT THE AUTHOR

Sherry Shindler Price has been a California Community College real estate instructor since 1986. Her twenty-six years in the real estate profession include eight years of specialization in investment properties and residential sales. She has authored *Escrow Principles and Practices* and *Real Estate Finance*. In addition, Ms. Price has reviewed numerous real estate textbooks for major publishers and has written a series of continuing education courses for private real estate schools. Her extensive knowledge in real estate was used to write test questions for state licensing examinations in Nevada, Wisconsin, Minnesota, Maryland, and Iowa.

Ms. Shindler Price has a Bachelor of Science degree in Education from Long Beach State College.

ABOUT THE TECHNICAL ADVISOR

Ignacio Gonzalez is a Real Estate Coordinator with Mendocino Community College in Ukiah, California. He has over twelve years in real estate education and has taught classes in Real Estate Principles, Real Estate Practices, Appraisal, Finance, Property Management, and Real Estate Economics. In 1999, he received a Mendocino College President's Award for Outstanding Teacher as an Adjunct Instructor. He has authored *California Real Estate Economics*.

Mr. Gonzalez is a Land Use Planner whose specialization is in urban and rural land use planning. This expertise includes subdivision review, zoning administration, community general planning, redevelopment, environmental analysis, transportation planning, coastal review, and natural resource administration.

Mr. Gonzalez has a Bachelor of Arts degree in Planning from Sonoma State University.

RESEARCH AND DEVELOPMENT

Judy Hobbs is the creative editor and production coordinator for Ashley Crown Systems, Inc. She also manages textbook research and development for new products as well as improvement to existing products. This ensures that higher education materials are accurate and current.

Ms. Hobbs has over 10 years experience in textbook publishing from State University of New York at Buffalo and Buffalo State College. She has a Bachelor of Science Degree from Empire State College with graduate studies from Cornell University.

ACKNOWLEDGMENTS

The author would like to thank the real estate professionals and educators who contributed to the earlier editions of this textbook. Contributors to earlier editions include Jeff Tiss, Tom Dahl, Carol Gerber, Bob Hunt, Evelyn Winkel, and Becky Thompson, Cynthia Simone Communications, Meagan Jones, Susan Mackessy, Karen Achenbach, and Mary Achenbach.

The *Principles, 9th edition* was the result of teamwork from the publisher, educators, and other professionals to make this introductory textbook the best in *California Real Estate Principles*. Special thanks to Leigh Conway, Joan Manno, Sue Carlson, Verity Fletcher, Eric Sharkey, Laura Dearman, and Lisa Schoenle for their experience and skill in bringing together the material content, photographs, illustrations, and layout.

The author especially would like to thank reviewer Ignacio Gonzalez, Adjunct Instructor from Mendocino Community College, whose expertise and experience has been invaluable.

Finally, the author would like to acknowledge the California Department of Real Estate, California Association of REALTORS®, and others for the forms and contracts printed throughout the textbook.

California's Diversity

1

Chapter

Introduction

In this chapter you will learn about California and why it is called the "Golden State". We will discuss how the diversity in California's economic base and population sustains California's economic growth. Also we will look at California's continued economic prosperity and how it influences the national economy. Finally we will touch on the brokerage business and opportunities in the real estate industry.

Learning Objectives

After reading this chapter, you will be able to:

- describe the impact real estate has on the economy in California and in the U.S.
- summarize how California's economy influences the national economy.
- list three major careers in real estate.
- name two types of real estate licenses.

Only in California

Location! Location! Location! Most of you have seen this phrase in a real estate ad describing the perfect neighborhood. All of you reading this, no matter what city you live in, are experiencing the perfect location. No...we are not referring to your specific street, town or county...we are talking about California. California has everything, and usually it is the best! Whoever said, "Less is more" just never lived in California.

California's natural and man-made wonders can only be described with superlatives. California has the 5th largest economy in the world—after the United States, Japan, Germany, and the United Kingdom. Additionally, it is the first state to ever reach a trillion-dollar economy in gross state product. At over 37 million people, California is the most culturally diverse and the most populous state in the country, and has been since 1962. In fact, one out of every eight United States residents lives in California. California is called "The Golden State." Some say it is due to its long association with gold mining made famous by the Gold Rush. Others point to the golden grasses that cover our hills in the summer and fall, or the fields of golden poppies that bloom in the springtime. You might call California golden because of our fabulous, golden sunshine and warm climate. In any event, gold has been intertwined with the history and development of California.

Climate and Geography

Where but California could you surf in the morning, play 18 holes of golf, and then enjoy a torch-lit night ski run—all in the same day? California is a beautiful place, blessed with phenomenal natural beauty and a climate free from hurricanes, tornadoes, and blizzards. We definitely enjoy a relatively mild climate.

California has a relatively mild climate.

Climate

Our basic climate is called Mediterranean, characterized by general sun and warmth with rain mainly in the winter. Of course there are variations based on the distance from the ocean and the elevation. Average rainfall varies from 80 inches in Del Norte County (north coast) to as low as 3 inches in Imperial County (desert).

We have five main zones: coastal, desert, foothill, valley, and mountain.

Coastal climate is characterized by mild temperatures with minor annual variations. Most of the state's population lives along the coast.

Desert climate is characterized by high summer temperatures, extremely low humidity, and very little rainfall.

Valley climate is characterized by high temperature and low humidity in the summer and low temperature and high humidity in the winter. Both the Sacramento and San Joaquin Valleys have this weather pattern.

Foothill climate (1,000 to 3,000 feet in elevation) is similar to the valley regions but with more rain and less fog.

Mountain climate is the only area that gets heavy snow in the winter. Winters are very cold and summers are bright and sunny.

Geography

California is the third largest state in land area (158,693 square miles) with 1,264 miles of coastline and an average width of 175 miles. We have everything here: beautiful beaches, deserts, valleys, foothills, towering mountains, and even a delta with levees.

There are still three active volcanoes in California. In the Cascade Mountain Range are Mt. Lassen (elevation 10,457 feet) and Mt. Shasta (elevation 14,162 feet). Mt. Mammoth (elevation 11,000 feet) is located in the Sierra Nevada Mountain Range.

California—the "People Magnet"

California, with its mild climate and seemingly unending opportunities, continues to draw immigrants today just as it did 150 years ago. We shouldn't be surprised. A Harris Poll® conducted online in July 2003 among a nationwide cross section of 2,215 adults showed, that for the second year running, more Americans would like to live here than in any other state. They were asked, "If you could live in any state in the country, except the state you live in now, what state would you choose to live in?" California was the first choice with Florida second and Hawaii third.

Finding California

California was already inhabited by Native Americans in villages and tribes when early explorers touched our coastline and made new claims for foreign countries. Portuguese-born Juan Rodriguez Cabrillo explored the California coastline from San Diego to Santa Barbara and claimed it for Spain. Sir Francis Drake landed north of San Francisco Bay and claimed the territory for England. The Russians established Fort Ross, a trading post near Bodega Bay, and claimed the territory north of San Francisco for Russia.

A few hardy settlers in covered wagons took the perilous trek across the deserts to reach the promise of a better future. But when gold was discovered in Sutter's Mill in 1849, the "FortyNiners" flocked here with "strike-it-rich" dreams. When Southern Pacific Railroad finally extended its rail system into Los Angeles, it hired real estate developers to tout Southern California as a Mediterranean-like paradise. They were very successful because over 12,000 eager tourists and settlers arrived by railroad each month. In just 20 short years, the population in Los Angeles grew from 11,000 in 1880 to more than 100,000 by 1900. During World War II, the government spent billions of dollars each year in government contracts to build liberty ships and thousands of warplanes. Lured by the promise of work, more than 700,000 workers had come to California by 1943. They located by the defense plants in Los Angeles, Santa Monica, Burbank, Long Beach, El Segundo, and San Diego.

After the war, the California economy continued to boom drawing yet more people. In 1962, California, with a population of more than 17 million, officially surpassed that of New York. Since then people have come here from all parts of the world, drawn to our wonderful climate, stunning landscapes, and economic opportunities.

As of the 2000 Census, Los Angeles County was the nation's most populous county, with 9.8 million residents. In addition, it experienced the largest population growth, with an increase of 129,000. Both Orange County and San Diego County were also in the top five counties in the country for most populous county and the largest population increase.

This large population corridor interconnected by economic activity, transportation, and communication linkages creates a megalopolis. A megalopolis is a large, densely populated metropolitan area consisting of a number of major urban areas and smaller surrounding cities. The Southern California **megalopolis** stretches from Santa Barbara to the Mexican border, and is centered around the city of Los Angeles. It is the **largest population center and industrial center in the western United States**, and the second largest in the nation.

Multicultural California

Because people everywhere have viewed California as a land of opportunity, California has become one of the most ethnically diverse regions of the world. Our population reflects virtually every area of the globe, as new arrivals continue to stake their claims to the California dream. Victorian homes in Eureka, New England-style cottages in Mendocino, a houseboat in Sausalito, and Spanish-style homes in southern California remind us of the diversity of our grandparents.

The largest group (more than half of the population) is made up of people whose ancestors came from the British Isles; European countries such as Germany, France, Poland and Italy; and Scandinavian countries such as Norway and Sweden. More than 25% of Californians are Hispanic. Most of them have ethnic roots in

California has become one of the most ethnically diverse regions of the world.

Spain and Latin America, especially in Mexico and Central America. The Golden State has more people who speak Spanish than any other state.

Asian Americans (Chinese, Japanese, Filipino, Korean, and Vietnamese ancestry) and Pacific Islanders are about one-tenth of the state's population. The Tien Hau Temple in San Francisco is the oldest Chinese temple in the United States. The Bok Kai Taoist temple in Marysville is over 121 years old. African Americans are about 7% of the state's population.

Although Native Americans make up less than one percent of the total population, California has about 250 Native American tribes, more than exist in any other state.

Native American
dancer

One of the best ways to learn about California's ethnic diversity is to enjoy the many festivals and celebrations held up and down the state. In February, the annual San Francisco Chinese New Year Festival and Parade features a huge dancing dragon and brightly lit floats. In early May, Mexican Americans throughout the state celebrate Cinco de Mayo with large fiestas. Native American tribes gather from across the country to perform ceremonial dancing, drumming, and singing at the annual Indian Fair held each June in San Diego. Each July, the French Festival in Santa Barbara celebrates the music, art, dancing, and food of France. The Los Angeles African Marketplace and Cultural Faire celebrate African culture around the world in late summer. The Japanese Cultural Bazaar is held every August in Sacramento and features Japanese food, dancing, art, and Taiko drummers. Every July 4th, Americans, regardless of ethnic ancestry, join together to celebrate our nation's birthday with parades, picnics, and fireworks.

Asian drummer

California's Strong Economy

The economic system in America, and therefore California, is a mixed capitalistic system. **Capitalism** is an economic system in which most of the economy's resources are privately owned and managed. The government is asked by its citizens to influence the general economic direction, and to assure reasonable, stable competition. Currently, California has the fifth largest economy in the world. California generates 13% of the United States Gross Domestic Product (GDP) and is the nation's number one exporting state. California produces more than $1 trillion worth of goods and services each year.

More than 2.6 million small businesses account for 98% of all employers in California. If you've ever eaten at a Denny's, Carl's Jr., Taco Bell, A&W, or Bob's Big Boy, you've eaten at a restaurant chain that started in California. Dick and Mac McDonald opened the first McDonald's restaurant in San Bernardino, California.

Oil pump jack

The early California economy was based primarily on agriculture, mining, and drilling for oil and gas. Gold and silver mining brought wealth to Northern California. The "black gold" of our oil wells brought capital investment and unbridled growth to Southern California.

The Golden Era of Hollywood captured the imagination of all Americans with movie making and star building and brought more wealth into Southern California. Northern California experienced a new Gold Rush when computer technology made the Silicon Valley a "buzz word" around the world.

Currently, California's top industries include: tourism, manufacturing, construction, agriculture, oil and gas production, telecommunications, engineering services, aerospace, and entertainment (including motion pictures, TV, and recording). The state is geared for the future with continuing advances in microelectronics, bio-technology, and environmental technology.

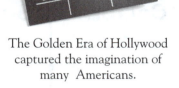
The Golden Era of Hollywood captured the imagination of many Americans.

California... where dreams are rewarded.

With the opportunity to work in such a diverse society and robust economy, no wonder California has such a strong appeal. Where else are dreams so welcomed and so often rewarded?

Economic Firsts

1853 - Levi Strauss made denim blue jeans for the prospectors. Levi Strauss & Co. of San Francisco is the largest clothing manufacturer in the world.

1860 - California's famous mail courier service, the Pony Express, was the first of its kind, connecting California's communication system with the Midwest.

1873 - The world's first cable car rumbled down the streets of San Francisco. Cable cars are still popular today with visitors and residents.

1905 - Eleven-year-old Frank Epperson accidentally invented "Popsicles" in San Francisco. He applied for the patent in 1923.

1908 - The "Sultan's Power" was the first complete film made in Los Angeles.

1927 - Lindbergh's plane, "The Spirit of St. Louis", was built in San Diego.

1934 - The first mass-produced commercial aircraft, the DC-2, was built by McDonald Douglas in Santa Monica.

1935 - A statewide irrigation system was started. Irrigation turned the vast land of the Great Central Valley from semi-arid plains to green croplands. This project is the world's largest water project. Allegedly, according to Susan Sward writing in the Santa Barbara News-Press in March, 1977, "...the astronauts who landed on the moon reported they could see the California project, the only man-made item they could identify from that distance." Today, California is the leading agricultural economy of the United States.

1970 - Security National Bank activated the first automated teller bank in Los Angeles.

1970s - Mountain biking was invented in Mill Valley and first tested on Mount Tamalpais in Marin County.

1977 - The Apple II computer was developed in Silicon Valley.

The Importance of Real Estate in the Economy

The real estate industry is so large that it influences both the state and the national economies. The major roles that real estate plays in our economy are creating net worth, increasing income flow, creating jobs, and helping control appreciation and inflation.

Net Worth

Real estate in the form of land and improvements makes up a very large portion of the total net worth of the United States as a nation (not to be confused with the government). **Net worth** is the value of all assets minus all liabilities.

Income Flow

The circular flow chart of our economy—money is paid for the use of real estate and for the raw materials, labor, capital, and management used in construction work of all kinds.

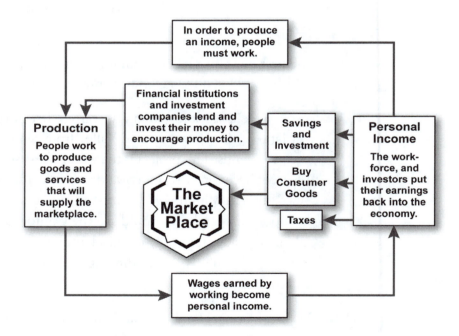

The circular flow of the national economy.

Major Employer

The real estate industry (brokerage, construction, management, finance) is a major employer in this country. It provides employment for a large segment of the population, accounting for billions of dollars in national income.

Appreciation and Inflation

In recent years appreciation in the value of real estate has overtaken the annual rate of inflation and is the single largest indicator of inflation. **Appreciation** is the increase in market value of real estate. **Inflation** is increase in the general price level of goods and services, or as a decrease in purchasing power of the dollar. As the value of the dollar has decreased, passbook savings accounts and other forms of financial savings have lost their appeal as ways to save and invest for the future. Real estate has become a major means by which people save. Particularly in California where property has historically appreciated at such an alarmingly fast rate, it has been common for homeowners to consider their home as "money in the bank."

California Housing Market

The housing market is shaped mainly by the inventory of available housing, by housing affordability, and by mortgage interest rates. California's **inventory** of housing units is not enough to meet the demand because our population increases faster than our supply of housing. Nearly 250,000 new households are formed every year and about 190,000 new housing units are built—creating a shortfall of about 60,000 units. With a shortage of housing, we know there is demand. The next thing to look at is the affordability index. The **affordability** index shows how many households will be able to afford a median-priced home in California. As the affordability index gets lower it means fewer households will be able to buy a home. For example, if the affordability index falls to 19, less than one-in-five households will be able to purchase a median-priced home in California. The higher the affordability index, the more households are able to purchase homes. And finally, we need to look at current **mortgage interest rates**. Interest rates determine the amount of a loan a borrower can get. The higher the interest, the lower the loan amount, and conversely, the lower the interest, the higher the loan amount.

Based on this, the best housing market would be created with adequate housing inventory, a high affordability index and low interest rates.

Median Home Prices

The **median home price** is the price that is midway between the least expensive and most expensive home sold in an area during a given period of time. It is used by economists to compare home sale prices and measure increases and decreases. For example, the median home price in the second quarter of 2004 was $461,730, an increase of nearly $100,000 over the second quarter 2003 median of $368,620. The housing market fluctuates with time and location. Over the last 20 years all areas of California have shown dramatic increases in the median home price. Some areas, however, have increased far more than others.

The **California Association of REALTORS®** (C.A.R.) is a **trade association** with more than 165,000 members and is dedicated to the advancement of professionalism in real estate. C.A.R. tracks the median home sales price for several geographic areas. The following table shows some of the areas and the increase in the median home sales price.

As we can see from the following table, the median price of a single-family home in California continues to increase. In spite of the increase in prices, home sales in California continue to be strong.

Median Home Prices, by County

California Counties	1983	2005	% Increase	Average Per Year
Kern	92,700	615,000	663%	30%
Los Angeles	118,545	495,000	418%	19%
Monterey	112,585	609,750	542%	25%
Napa	94,725	577,000	609%	28%
Nevada	85,650	475,000	555%	25%
Orange	131,455	616,000	469%	21%
Riverside	94,910	412,500	435%	20%
Sacramento	76,140	375,000	493%	22%
San Bernardino	80,425	358,500	446%	20%
San Diego	103,080	510,000	495%	22%
San Francisco	133,730	750,000	561%	25%
San Luis Obispo	104,150	499,000	479%	22%
Santa Barbara	131,745	504,000	383%	17%
Santa Clara	134,000	665,000	496%	23%
Ventura	128,665	599,500	466%	21%

C.A.R. economists also track other statistics about California. For example, the unemployment rate, job growth, and population change. The unemployment rate is the percentage of the people classified as unemployed as compared to the total labor force. All of these factors affect the real estate market by affecting the demand for housing and the ability to pay for it.

CALIFORNIA ECONOMY			
	2003	2004	2005
Unemployment Rate	6.8%	6.2%	5.4%
Job Growth	-0.3%	1.0%	1.3%
Population Change	1.5%	1.5%	1.2%

Getting Started in Real Estate

You may also have heard the saying, "Success Breeds Success". Well, California is highly successful. When you combine that proven success with our fabulous climate and natural beauty, we become a "people magnet". Over 25,000 people move here every month. Each person will need housing and that is where you come in. As a licensed real estate broker or salesperson you are in the unique position to help our current and incoming residents to buy homes, rent apartments, get loans, buy businesses, manage properties or buy investments—to help them achieve their dreams.

A licensed real estate broker or salesperson is in a unique position to help people achieve their dreams.

In California, if you want to work in a real estate brokerage business you must have a real estate license. There are two types of real estate licenses: a salesperson's license and a broker's license. We will learn more about the licenses and the work that you will do during the course of this book. For now, it is enough to know that a salesperson must put his or her license with a licensed broker who will help you as you get started in the business. Think of it as being a sort of apprenticeship.

This book is designed to help you understand the concepts you need to start your career in real estate. As you read through the chapters, you will be introduced to real estate concepts and laws regarding real estate transactions. Additionally, it offers practical information and useful tips to help you pass the state exam. You will learn property law, agency law, required disclosures, and contract law. You will study how property is owned and how ownership can be limited; how title is held and how title is transferred. Of course, we will learn about getting financing, valuing property, and the role that escrow and title play in a transaction. Once the basics are covered, we will go over residential real estate brokerage and specialty fields. Finally, we will go over the steps needed to get and keep your real estate license.

After passing the state examination and receiving your license you will probably enter one of the new licensee training programs offered by larger real estate firms. With consistent marketing, persistent prospecting, dedication to client satisfaction, and a strong dose of hard work you can make a good career in real estate.

In 2004, over 600,000 housing units were sold—the majority through a licensed real estate agent. By the time you have finished this book, another 25,000 people will have come to California, and all these newcomers will need help from a real estate professional.

Uniquely California

Floor mosaic of the seal of the state of California, created in the late 1800s. Located in San Francisco's ferry building.

Economy

- California has a vibrant, healthy economy which ranks 5th largest in the world. There are only four other countries, including the United States, ahead of California in economic production.

- Los Angeles International Airport (LAX) claims to be the world's third busiest airport with 67.3 million passengers in 2000.

- California is the first state to ever reach a trillion dollar economy in gross state product.

LAX Control Tower

- The city of Los Angeles is ranked the fourth largest economy in the country compared to other states.

- The Port of Los Angeles located in San Pedro Bay is one of the world's largest, busiest, and most successful seaports.

- California has the most major military bases and installations in the country.

- Tarzana is named after Edgar Rice Burroughs' Tarzana Ranch, the home of "Tarzan".

Demographics

- At over 37 million people, California is the most culturally diverse and the most populous state in the country, and has been since 1962.

More than four million seniors reside in California.

- California has the largest number of senior citizens living within its borders, with more than four million residents over 60 years of age.

- At only 10 feet wide, the Kaweah Post Office in Tulare is the smallest post office still in operation.

- One out of every eight United States residents lives in California.

- The Little Red Schoolhouse in Solvang, the Danish Capital of America, was built in 1883, and is the oldest schoolhouse still in use.

- The Chinese hamlet of Locke is the only rural community in the country built and occupied by Chinese.

- Totaling nearly three million acres, San Bernardino County is the largest county in the country.

Natural Wonders

- Lake Tahoe is the highest lake of its size in the country and the largest alpine lake in North America. It is the second deepest lake in the country and the tenth deepest in the world.

- Sutter Buttes (2,132 feet high) is a mountain range near Sutter and is the world's smallest mountain range.

- The oldest living thing in the world, the Bristlecone Pine tree, grows at an altitude of 11,000 feet in California's White Mountains. Aged at nearly 5,000 years, it is as old as the Great Pyramids of Egypt.

Lake Tahoe

- Yosemite Falls, with its drop of 2,425 feet, has the longest drop for any waterfall in the country.

- At 14,495 feet, Mt. Whitney in Sequoia National Park is the highest elevation point in the contiguous United States. From there you can see Badwater, in Death Valley National Park, which at 282 feet below sea level is the lowest elevation point in the United States.

- California Caverns claims the distinction of being the most extensive system of caverns and passageways in the Mother Lode region of the state.

- The San Francisco Bay is the largest natural harbor on the West Coast of the United States.

- The world's tallest living tree (367.5 feet) is the California Redwood found along the North and Central Coast area.

- The largest trees in the world are the Sequoias and grow in the high Sierra Nevadas. The General Grant Tree in Kings Canyon National Park is famous as "The Nation's Christmas Tree". Its trunk measures 40 feet around at its base and is wider than a three-lane freeway. The General Sherman Tree, in Sequoia National Park, is the biggest living thing on earth. At almost 2.7 million pounds, it would make enough lumber to build 40 five-room houses.

Tunnel log in Sequoia National Park

- The area around Geyserville, just north of San Francisco, is the largest geothermal area in the world.

- Death Valley is recognized as the hottest, driest place in the United States. It isn't uncommon for the summer temperatures to reach more than 115 degrees.

- In the center of California, the California Delta has over 1,000 miles of navigable waterways forming a triangle of channels and sloughs from Sacramento (north) to Stockton (south) to Pittsburg (west).

- Once again, Coronado Beach was named among America's Top Ten Beaches.

Death Valley National Park

Ecology

- The Monterey Marine Sanctuary encompasses 5,312 square feet making it the largest marine sanctuary in the country.

- Lake Merritt, a natural saltwater lake in the middle of Oakland, became the country's first state wildlife refuge in 1870.

- Lava Beds National Monument and the adjoining Klamath Basin National Wildlife Refuge in Northeastern California have the most bald eagles in the contiguous United States.

- Anza Borrego Desert State Park is the largest state park in the Southwest, covering 600,000 acres from the edge of the coastal mountains east to the Salton Sea and south almost to the U.S./Mexico border.

- The Salton Sea north of El Centro has the most diverse bird species of any National Wildlife Refuges in the west.

- California Condors are the largest flying birds in North America.

- The Joshua Tree is the largest of the yuccas and grows only in the Mojave Desert.

The Joshua Tree

Agriculture

- Castroville is known as the Artichoke Capital of the World. In 1947 a young woman named Norma Jean was crowned Castroville's first Artichoke Queen. She went on to become actress Marilyn Monroe.

- California has been the number one agricultural state in the country for more than 50 years.

Orchid

- The largest orchid farm (over 1.5 million square feet of greenhouse space) in the country is in Carpenteria.

- California is the only U.S. producer of almonds, artichokes, dates, figs, kiwifruit, olives, persimmons, pistachios, prunes, raisins, and walnuts.

- California is the second most important rice state in the country, producing about 20% of the nation's crop in a typical year. California supplies about half of Japan's imports of rice.

- California has by far the highest per capita avocado consumption in the country and produces the most, as well.

- Southern California produces over 90% of all lemons grown in the country.

- California leads the nation in tree nut production, accounting for over three-quarters of the total value of U.S. tree nut production in 2000. Virtually all U.S. almonds, pistachios, and walnuts are California produced.

- The Coachella Valley in Southern California remains the unrivaled date capital of the United States.

- California's most famous farm is probably Knott's Berry Farm, a popular tourist attraction. A new berry, the boysenberry, was created. It is a cross between the red raspberry, blackberry, and loganberry.

- California is the nation's leading dairy state, producing more milk than any other state. In fact with over 740,000 cows, Tulare County is the country's No. 1 dairy county.

Dairy cows

- California produces the most wine of any other state in the country. In fact, California is the fourth leading wine-producer in the world behind Italy, France, and Spain. Wine grapes are grown in 45 of California's 58 counties.

- Fresno is the Raisin Capital of the World.

- California is the largest producer of grapes, strawberries, peaches, nectarines, and kiwifruit. It is a major producer of a variety of other noncitrus fruit like apples, pears, plums, and sweet cherries.

- The most turkeys in the country are raised in California.

Natural Resources

- The Mojave Desert is the most important source of boron in the world.

- The tourmaline deposits in Riverside and San Diego Counties have produced more tourmaline, and of greater value, than any other deposits in the Northern Hemisphere.

- The Kennedy Mine, located in Jackson, was one of the richest gold mines in the world and the deepest mine in North America.

Mojave Desert

- By the spring of 1849, California experienced the largest gold rush in American history.

- Redding is the nation's second-sunniest city (Tucson, AZ is first) with an average of more than 320 days of sunshine per year.

Engineering Marvels

Golden Gate Bridge

- Named one of the "Seven Wonders of the Modern World" by the American Society of Civil Engineers, the Golden Gate Bridge in San Francisco is one of the longest single-span suspension bridges ever built. Its two massive towers are the highest bridge towers in the country at 746 feet above the water.

- The longest runway in the world (7.5 miles) is located at Edwards Air Force Base near Lancaster and is used for space shuttle landings.

- The Long Beach Harbor is the world's largest man-made harbor.

- The Palm Springs Arial Tramway is the world's largest rotating tramcar, rising up the sheer cliffs of Chino Canyon (2,643 ft.) to the Mountain Station at 8,516 ft. on Mt. San Jacinto.

- The world famous Tehachapi Loop is a feat of civil engineering genius allowing trains from the Central Valley to cross an exceptionally steep section of the Tehachapi mountains in order to reach Los Angeles. It is one of the seven wonders of the railroad world.

- The Shasta Dam spillway, at 487 feet tall, is the world's highest man-made waterfall and is three times the height of Niagara Falls.

- The Altamont Pass by San Francisco still contains the world's largest concentration of wind turbines; however, the wind turbines in the Tehachapi Pass are the largest producers of wind-generated electricity in the country. This is enough electricity to meet the residential needs of more than 500,000 Southern Californians or nearly one million Europeans.

Wind Turbines in Tehachapi Pass

- The first cable car in the world went into service in San Francisco.

Entertainment

- California has the most theme parks and amusement parks in the country.

- The largest permanent archery range in North America is at the ARCO Olympic Training Center, Chula Vista.

- The largest private zoo in the world was created by William Randolph Hearst on his ranch at San Simeon. Hearst Castle is one of the world's greatest showplaces and one of the largest historic house museums (90,080 square feet) in the country.

- The Hollywood Bowl is the world's largest outdoor amphitheater.

- San Francisco had the first municipally owned opera house in the country.

- Furnace Creek Inn, built in Death Valley in 1927, has the lowest grass golf course in the world, at 214 feet below sea level.

- Gold Mountain Ski Area, near Graeagle is the oldest reported sport-skiing area in the western hemisphere.

- The largest three-day rodeo in the country is held on the Tehama County Fairgrounds in Red Bluff.

- The world's largest display of sharks is the 700,000 gallon Shark Encounter exhibit at Sea World in San Diego.

- The "Perilous Plunge" water slide at Knott's Berry Farm in Buena Park is the world's steepest, tallest, and wettest water slide.

- Grauman's Chinese Theatre in Hollywood is the most famous movie theatre in the world. Millions of tourists visit each year to see the footprints of the stars. Since opening, it has had more gala Hollywood movie premieres than any other theatre.

- Valencia is home to Six Flags Magic Mountain where "Superman: The Escape", which is the world's fastest and tallest thrill ride, reaching 100 mph in seven seconds and standing 41 stories high, is located.

Grauman's Chinese Theatre

- The tallest and biggest thermometer in the world is in Baker.

- The largest roadside dinosaur in the country is a 150-foot long, 150-ton brontosaurus (nicknamed "Dinny") off Interstate 10 in Cabazon. Next to "Dinny" is "Rexxie", a 65-foot tall, 100-ton tyrannosaurus housing a date shop and an observation tower in his jaws.

- For his presidential inauguration, former California Governor Ronald Reagan ordered 3.5 tons of Jelly Belly candies from the Jelly Belly factory in Fairfield. A large portrait of President Reagan made out of jelly beans is displayed at the factory.

Summary

California is a diverse state in geography, economic base, and population. There are five main climate zones: coastal, desert, foothill, valley, and mountain.

The strong economy in California is a mixed capitalistic system. Top industries in this state include tourism, manufacturing, construction, agriculture, oil and gas production, telecommunications, engineering services, aerospace, and entertainment.

California's population is a mixed blend of European/Scandinavian/Great Britain Americans, Hispanic Americans, Asian/Pacific Islander Americans, African Americans, and Native Americans.

Real Estate is important to California's economy.

Real estate is an important part of California's economy, contributing to its **net worth**, income flow, major employers, and its **appreciation** and **inflation**. California's current housing is not enough to meet the demand because the state's population is increasing faster than its supply of housing. Affordability is a concern because less than one-in-five households will be able to purchase a **median-priced home** in California.

A California real estate license is required in the state of California to sell property. This license can be obtained by passing the state real estate licensing examination.

Chapter 1 Review Exercises

Matching Exercise

Instructions: Look up the meaning of the terms in the Glossary, then write the letter of the matching term on the blank line before its definition. Answers are in Appendix B.

Terms

a. affordability index

b. appreciation

c. black gold

d. C.A.R.

e. capitalism

f. demographics

g. diversity

h. gold rush

i. housing inventory

j. inflation

k. median home price

l. mortgage interest rate

m. net worth

n. trade association

o. unemployment rate

Definitions

1. __E__ An economic system in which most of the economy's resources are privately owned.

2. __M__ The value of all assets minus all liabilities.

3. __B__ The increase in market value of real estate.

4. __J__ The increase in the general price level of goods and services.

5. __K__ The price that is midway between the least expensive and most expensive home sold in an area during a given period of time.

6. __F__ Information from a variety of sources used to create a broad profile of any community.

7. __H__ A large migration of people to a newly discovered gold field.

8. __I__ Housing units that are available for sale or in the process of being made ready for sale.

9. __D__ A California trade association representing more than 165,000 REALTORS® statewide.

10. __O__ The percentage of the people classified as unemployed as compared to the total labor force.

▉ Multiple Choice Questions

Instructions: Circle your response and go to Appendix B to read the complete explanation for each question.

1. California has the 5th largest economy in the world. Which of following countries have economies larger than California's?
   a. United States, Japan, China, and France
   b. United States, Japan, Germany, and the United Kingdom
   c. United States, the United Kingdom, Japan, and France
   d. United Kingdom, United States, Japan, and China

2. The most populous state in the country is:
   a. New York.
   b. Ohio.
   c. Florida.
   d. California.

3. In California, 98% of the employers are:
   a. small business owners.
   b. large corporations.
   c. military installations.
   d. federal institutions.

4. An economic system in which most of the economy's resources are privately owned and managed is called:
   a. capitalism.
   b. socialism.
   c. communism.
   d. Marxism.

5. The increase in market value of real estate defines:
   a. inflation.
   b. net worth.
   c. purchasing power.
   d. appreciation.

6. A decrease in purchasing power of the dollar describes:
   - a. inflation.
   - b. appreciation.
   - c. net worth.
   - d. median.

7. The real estate housing market is influenced by:
   - a. the inventory of available housing.
   - b. the affordability of housing.
   - c. mortgage interest rates.
   - d. all of the above

8. The best housing market would be created by all of the following, except:
   - a. adequate housing inventory.
   - b. a low affordability index.
   - c. a high affordability index.
   - d. low interest rates.

9. The price that is midway between the least expensive and most expensive home sold in an area during a given period of time is called:
   - a. affordability index.
   - b. inflation.
   - c. median home price.
   - d. appreciation.

10. In California, to work as a real estate salesperson or broker you must have:
   - a. a college degree.
   - b. a real estate license issued by the California Department of Real Estate.
   - c. a driver license.
   - d. all of the above

Property, Estates, and Ownership

2
Chapter

Introduction

Ownership is the basic element of real estate. Owning real estate is considered a basic right in our culture. However, the right to own property did not always exist. Our laws of property ownership began with English Common Law at a time when all property was owned by the current monarch or an appointed noble. No one else was allowed to own property. Upset by their lack of rights, people set powerful forces of change in motion. Eventually, all people gained the right to own real property, now called real estate. Each owner of real estate acquired certain rights along with property ownership. In fact, ownership of real estate is legally described in terms of these rights, and not in terms of what is owned.

Historically, the question has been: "Who owns this property, and what is their interest in it?" As a real estate agent, you will explain to your clients (sellers) and customers (buyers) the ways property may be owned, what kind of ownership may be taken, how ownership is measured, the duration of that ownership and how much is owned.

This section answers these questions about titles and estates, with information that will be used every time you are involved in the transfer of real property.

Learning Objectives

After reading this chapter, you will be able to:

- describe the "bundle of rights" and name each right.
- explain the three-part definition of real property.
- define the characteristics of personal property.
- identify the five legal tests of a fixture and explain each legal test.
- identify freehold estates and less-than-freehold estates characteristics.
- discuss the historical background of land ownership in California.
- describe the process of recording evidence of title or interest.

Bundle of Rights

When you buy real estate, you might think you are buying the property. What you are buying are the rights to use that property. Property rights are the rights someone has in something and are known collectively as the **bundle of rights**. This important package includes: the right to own, possess, use, enjoy, borrow against, and dispose of real property. An owner may choose to sell or give away one of the rights and keep the rest. For example, an owner may give away the right of use for a period of time to a tenant, under a lease agreement.

Use:	The right use of property, within the law, in any way, or for any purpose.
Possession:	The right to live on the property and the right to keep others out.
Transfer:	The right to sell property, give it as a gift, or dispose of it in any way permitted by law.
Encumber:	The right to borrow money and use property as security for the loan.
Enjoyment:	The right to peace and quiet enjoyment without aggravation by others.

Bundle of Rights: Property rights are the rights someone has in something. Remember the mnemonic "UPTEE" – Use, Possession, Transfer, Encumber, and Enjoyment.

Anything that may be owned and gained lawfully is known as **property**. Property can be real or personal. Anything that is not real property is personal property.

Real property

Personal property

Real property

Property can be real or personal.

Personal Property

Personal property, sometimes known as **chattel** (from "cattle" an early form of personal property), is movable and transferred or sold using a bill of sale. Personal property may be **pledged** as a security for a loan. Personal property includes money, movable goods such as trade fixtures, evidences of debt such as a promissory note, and some growing things such as crops.

Real Property

Real property may be described as land, anything permanently attached to the land, anything appurtenant to the land or anything immovable by law. Real property is immovable and is usually transferred or sold by a deed. When real property is sold, anything that has become attached to it goes to the buyer as part of the sale unless other arrangements have been made.

Real property is transferred by deed, and personal property is transferred by a bill of sale.

Land

Land includes airspace, surface rights, mineral rights, and water rights.

Airspace is considered real property to a reasonable height. An owner or developer of high-rise condominiums may sell the airspace as real property.

Minerals are owned as real property unless they are fugitive substances, that is, non-solid, migratory minerals such as oil or gas. These may not be owned until taken from the ground and then become the personal property of whoever removed them.

Water on the surface, flowing in a stream or underground **(percolating)** is real property. If it is taken and bottled, then it becomes personal property. Surface water rights depend on whether or not the water is flowing or in a defined channel. **A defined channel** is any natural watercourse, even if it is dry. Water that overflows a defined channel is called **floodwater.** The three types of floodwater are **inundation, sheet overflow**, and **ponding.**

Land As Real Property
- Airspace
- Surface Rights
- Mineral Rights
- Water Rights

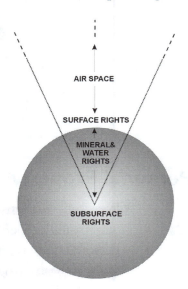

- The right to use the earth's surface is surface rights.

- The right to use natural resources lying below the earth's surface is referred to as subsurface rights.

Land includes airspace, surface rights, mineral rights, and water rights.

Certain **water rights** go with the land and are considered real property. A person's water rights do not exceed the amount reasonably needed for one's own personal use. Because of the many disputes over the use of water, the law is very clear about the rights of owners. Water cannot be owned, nor can it be channeled or dammed for the benefit of one landowner to the detriment of other property owners. Under the **Doctrine of Correlative User**, an owner may take only a reasonable share of underground waters (not to exclude adjoining owners).

The owner of property bordering a stream or river has **riparian rights** (a riparian owner). Riparian property owners have reasonable use of flowing water, providing it does not injure other riparian landowners. Owners of land bordering a lake (**littoral owners**) generally own to the average low water mark or the edge of the lake. The boundary line of land touching the ocean is the ordinary high tide mark.

Riparian Rights

When there is a need for the government to divert water for public use, its right of appropriation is applied. **Appropriation** is the right to use water for a beneficial use by diverting surface water. Typically beneficial uses include: domestic, municipal, agricultural, mining, stock watering, recreation, wildlife, or power generation.

Anything Permanently Attached to the Land

Items permanently attached to the land are real property and belong to the owner. **Improvements** such as houses, garages, fences, swimming pools or anything resting on the land to become permanent are owned as a part of the property. Anything permanently attached to the building, such as a fixture, is owned as real property. A **fixture** is real property that used to be personal property. It has become a fixture because it is permanently attached to real property. Any **growing thing** attached by roots, such as trees, shrubs and flowers are real property except emblements.

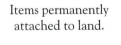
Items permanently
attached to land.

Fixtures

Disputes about real and personal property have caused the courts to adopt a set of tests to help them decide ownership rights of disagreeing parties. The five tests to determine a fixture are: method of attachment, adaptation, relationship of the parties, intent of the parties, and agreement of the parties.

Method of Attachment

How is the disputed item attached to the property? If it is permanently attached, it is real property. A chandelier wired into the electrical system makes it a fixture, or real property. It would be included in

Five Tests of a Fixture: Mnemonic = "MARIA"	
M	ethod of attachment
A	daptation
R	elationship of the parties
I	ntention
A	greement of the parties

the sale of the house as something attached or affixed to the land unless the sellers specifically mentioned they wanted to take it with them.

Adaptation

Has the item been made especially for the property? For example, have the drapes been custom-made for the windows? Has the carpet been cut especially to fit the rooms? Is the stove built into the counter? If so, each has become a fixture and has lost its status as personal property.

Relationship of the Parties

In a dispute about fixtures, when there is no convincing evidence of the right of one party, courts will look at whether the parties are landlord-tenant, lender-borrower, or buyer-seller. The court then makes a decision based on the relationship of the parties in the case. Usually the court will favor the tenant over the landlord, the lender over the borrower, and the buyer over the seller.

Intention

If apparent, either in writing or by the actions of either party involved, this is considered to be the most important test of a fixture. Let's look at the tenant who wired special cosmetic lights into the bathroom wall, telling the landlord he intended the lights to remain his personal property. He said he would repair the wall when he moved and would take the lights with him. This was a clear case of a tenant's intention to keep the lights as his personal property. A fixture may remain personal property if all parties are informed. Intention should always be put in writing.

Agreement of the Parties

When there has been a clear agreement between the parties in a dispute about fixtures, the courts will apply this test to determine who is in the right.

> Example: Now that you know what real property is—and is not—let's examine what that means to the consumer. Imagine that you are a prospective buyer. You walk into a house and fall in love with the chandelier hanging from the ceiling in the dining room. You make an offer to buy the house, it is accepted and the escrow goes through smoothly. The sellers get their money and you get the deed to the house.
>
> When you arrive with your moving van, your anticipation turns to hostility when you discover a lonely light bulb hanging where the elegant chandelier had been. The former owners wonder why you are annoyed when you call to arrange the return of your chandelier. They tell you it is not your chandelier; it has been in the family for generations. They never intended it to go with the house.

If you didn't know the difference between real and personal property, you might think the sellers had a right to the chandelier.

Part of a real estate agent's job is to make sure all parties involved in a sale know what goes and what stays. In the above case, the listing agent should have asked the sellers if they wanted to keep the chandelier, and notified prospective buyers that it did not go with the house.

Since it was not excluded from the listing, it was reasonable for the buyer to assume it was real property. It had become a fixture and therefore should have gone with the sale.

When a buyer makes an offer on a property, there is a section in the offer-to-purchase contract where he or she may request any item of real or personal property such as the chandelier, washer and dryer, a refrigerator or a bedspread that matches the custom drapes. The buyer should always put an intention in writing to make sure the seller is informed and agrees.

Trade Fixtures

Trade fixtures are items of personal property, such as shelves, cash registers, room partitions or wall mirrors, used to conduct a business. Tenants retain ownership of the items as personal property when they vacate the premises, but are responsible for repairing any damage that results from replacing the trade fixtures.

Growing Things

Real property includes anything **growing** attached by its roots, such as trees, shrubs, and flowers. When a home is sold, the planted trees and landscaping are real property and go with the sale. Naturally occurring plant growth (such as grasses) are called **fructus naturales.**

Emblements

An exception may exist with the transfer of farm property, because the crops may belong to a tenant farmer and not the owner. Grow-ing crops that are cultivated annually for sale and orchards in a commercial grove are called **emblements**. Emblements or **fructus industriales** are crops produced by human labor (lettuce, grapes, etc.). Emblements are personal property, owned by tenants as well as fee owners. Remember, the crops are the personal property, not the trees or plants they grow on.

> Example: Real and personal property can change from one to the other. A tree is real property until it is cut as timber; then it becomes the personal property of whoever cut it. If that timber is milled into lumber, sold and used to build a house, it becomes real property. As the house ages and deteriorates, is torn down and hauled away as scrap lumber, it becomes personal property once again.

Anything Appurtenant to the Land

An **appurtenance** is anything used with the land for its benefit. Appurtenance means "belonging to" so an appurtenance does not exist apart from the land to which it belongs. Easements and stock rights in a mutual water company are the two most common appurtenances to real property.

An **easemen**t is a right-of-way across a parcel of land, and is transferred automatically with the property whenever it is sold. The easement is appurtenant to the property.

Stock in a mutual water company is real property owned by water users who have organized to form a water company for their mutual benefit. The shares in this water company are appurtenant to the land and go with the sale of the property.

Anything Immovable by Law

Established trees are considered immovable by law and must be sold with the property. A seller may not sell the property and exclude the orange grove from the sale. The

> **Review - Real Property**
> - Land
> - Attached to land
> - Appurtenances to land
> - Immovable by law

seller may have sold the crop resulting from the trees as personal property, but the trees remain real property and may not be excluded from the sale.

Types of Estates

An **estate** is the ownership interest or claim a person has in real property. There are two types of estates that may be owned: freehold and less-than-freehold. A **freehold estate** is an estate of indefinite duration and can be sold or inherited. The freehold estate is a real property estate of an owner, whose *hold* on the estate is *free* of anyone else's restrictions.

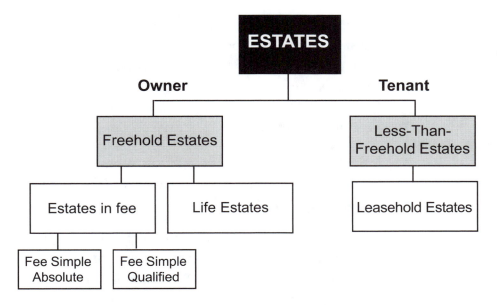

Types of estates

A **less-than-freehold estate** is an estate owned by a tenant who rents real property. The tenant has temporary and limited right of use in a real property estate. The rights are described by a lease, which is personal property. The less-than-freehold estate is a personal property estate of a tenant, and is also known as a **leasehold estate**.

The type of estate determines the extent of the claim. Each type of estate is described in terms of its duration and rights.

Freehold Estates

Freehold estates are real property estates of ownership. This type of estate continues for an indefinite period of time and is sometimes called an estate of inheritance. The two types of freehold estates are estates in fee and life estates.

Estates in Fee

An estate in fee, sometimes known as a **fee** or **fee simple estate,** is the most complete form of ownership. Since an owner of an estate in fee may dispose of it in his or her lifetime or after death by will, it is also known as an **estate of inheritance** or a **perpetual estate.** This is commonly the kind of estate that is transferred in a normal real estate transaction. If the property is transferred or sold with no conditions or limitations on its use, it is known as an estate in **fee simple absolute.**

A property owner may impose qualifications, conditions, or restrictions when transferring title to property. Property restrictions are created by deed or written agreement. If a seller imposes qualifications or conditions that the buyer must do or not do, this is known as a **fee simple qualified** or **fee simple defeasible** estate. The conditions are classified as a condition subsequent or a condition precedent.

If a fee simple estate has a **condition subsequent**, there is something that the owner must not do. If the owner breaks the condition, the property will go back to the former owner.

> Example: A seller may require the property to be used for a specified purpose such as a church or a rehabilitation center. The owner sells the property with the condition that this requirement be met. If the buyer breaches this condition subsequent after the sale, the seller may take possession of the property and regain title.
>
> In another example of a condition subsequent, the seller may place special limitations on the use of the property after the sale. A buyer may be denied the right to sell alcoholic beverages on the property or allow a board and care use. If either of those events occurs, ownership of the property reverts to the seller or his or her heirs.

The parties to a contract may also impose a restriction known as a **condition precedent**. In this case, something must occur before a transaction becomes absolute and final. For example, a sale may be contingent on the buyer obtaining financing or qualifying for a VA or FHA loan.

Life Estates

A **life estate** is one that is limited in duration to the life of its owner or the life of another designated person. The term used to describe a life estate created on the life of a designated person is **pur autre vie** (for another's life).

Since a life estate is a type of freehold, or fee estate, the holder of a life estate has all the rights that go with fee ownership except disposing of the estate by will. Remember, the life estate is tied to a designated life, and when that party dies, the estate goes either to the person in reversion or the person in remainder, or their heirs.

Life estate holders must pay the taxes and maintain the property. They may collect all rents and keep all profits for the duration of the life estate. They may encumber the property or dispose of it in any way except by will. Any interest the life estate holders may create in the property—extending beyond the life of the person used to measure the estate—will become invalid when that designated person dies.

Types of Life Estates

Estate in reversion. Amy grants to Bob a life estate with the provision that upon Bob's death, the property reverts to Amy. Bob is then the life tenant, or the designated party on whom the life estate is based. Amy holds an estate in reversion.

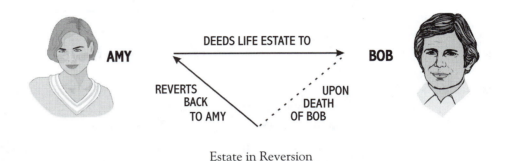

Estate in Reversion

Reserving a life estate. Tom grants to Susan a life estate for the life of Elizabeth, with the provision that it goes to Laura when Elizabeth dies. Susan may enjoy the benefits of the life estate as long as Elizabeth is alive. Upon Elizabeth's death, the estate goes to Laura or her heirs. That is called reserving a life estate.

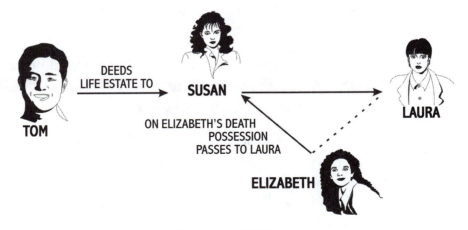

Reserving a Life Estate

Estate in remainder. Greg grants to Linda a life estate, with the provision that upon Linda's death, the property goes to a third party, Charles. The interest that Charles holds is known as an estate in remainder.

Estate in Remainder

Review - A Life Estate Holder
1. Must pay the taxes and maintain the property
2. May collect all rents and keep all profits for the duration of the life estate
3. May encumber the property or dispose of it in any way except by will

---

Less-Than-Freehold Estates

Freehold estates are the most complete form of ownership, and include the most rights. The **less-than-freehold estate** (also called a leasehold estate) is owned by renters or tenants. Leasehold estates are also called **chattels real** because the lease is personal property (*chattel*) that concerns real property (*real*).

Remember, anything movable becomes personal property. The **lease is a movable document describing the temporary possession and use of the property, and thus is personal property.**

The owner of the leasehold (tenant) has exclusive possession and use of real property for a fixed period of time including the right to the use and quiet enjoyment of the premises during the term of the lease. They have the right to the exclusive use of the rented property and to live quietly without privacy invasion.

Types of Leasehold Estates

The duration of leasehold is known as a tenancy. Each of the four types of leaseholds is distinctive because of its duration:

1. Estate for years
2. Estate at will
3. Estate from period to period
4. Estate at sufferance

Estate for Years

An **estate for years** is for a fixed term. It does not have to be for only a year, but if a definite end date is stated, it nevertheless is known as an estate for years. The lease of office space or a commercial center is commonly an estate for years. It is not automatically renewable and does not require notice to quit at the end of the lease (must be renegotiated). It is a less-than-freehold estate.

When an apartment lease mentions an end date, it is considered an estate for years. Increasingly, owners of residential income property (apartment buildings) are using this type of an agreement to guarantee that a tenant will stay, at least until the lease expires.

The benefit of an estate for years to the landlord is that a desirable, long-term tenant may be attracted to the apartment or house. The benefit to the renter is assurance that the rent will remain the same over the period of the lease. At the expiration of the lease, terms must be mutually renegotiated.

Estate from Period to Period

Another kind of lease or rental agreement, probably the most common for residential use, is the **estate from period to period**, also known as periodic tenancy. This is the typical month-to-month tenancy that requires 30-days notice to quit. It automatically renews itself unless terminated by landlord or tenant.

Estate at Will

When there is no written agreement between the landlord and tenant, the tenancy is known as an **estate at will.** The tenancy may be ended by the unilateral decision of either party. There is no agreed-upon termination date; however, and either party must give 30-days notice before ending the tenancy.

Estate at Sufferance

An **estate at sufferance** occurs when a tenant occupies the property without paying rent and without the permission of the landlord.

Ownership of Real Property

Ownership of land in California began with Spanish explorers who claimed it for the king of Spain in the early 16th Century. Since the king technically owned everything, all land was granted to private parties by the military representatives of Spanish rule. Ownership and transfer of land and property rights were determined by local authorities operating under a strict set of civil laws that were given to them by the Spanish king.

This continued until 1822, when Mexico began colonizing California and took over governing the territory. In 1848, the **Treaty of Guadalupe Hidalgo** ended the war with Mexico, and California became a possession of the United States. Land claims that had been granted by Mexico were honored, and confirmed with **patents** to the land, by the U.S. government, to those with proven ownership. Even though Spain or Mexico granted ownership, according to the Roman Civil Law they followed, the laws changed after California became a state in 1850. England's Common Law principles now governed the title of real property.

Title Vesting

All property has an owner, either the government, or a private institution or an individual. **Tenancy** refers to a mode or method of ownership or holding title to property. **Title** is the evidence that the owner of land is in lawful possession. It is the proof of ownership. Separate ownership and concurrent ownership are the two ways a person or other entity can take title to or own real estate. **Paramount title** is a right to real property which prevails over any other person's claim of title.

Separate Ownership

Separate property means ownership by one person or one entity, such as a city or corporation. Property owned by one person or entity is known as sole and separate, or **ownership in severalty.** With separate ownership the ownership rights are severed from everyone else. A corporation is known to hold title in **severalty**, because it is a sole entity.

Ownership by one entity (ABC Company) or one person.

Concurrent Ownership

When property is owned by two or more persons or entities at the same time, it is known as **concurrent ownership**, or co-ownership. They hold title jointly and severally. Concurrent ownership comes in several forms such as joint tenancy, tenancy in common, community property, and tenancy in partnership.

> **Four Types of Concurrent Ownership**
> 1. Tenancy in common
> 2. Joint tenancy
> 3. Community property
> 4. Tenancy in partnership

Tenancy in Common

When two or more persons, whose interests are not necessarily equal, are owners of **undivided interests** in a single estate, a **tenancy in common** exists. Whenever some other form of ownership or vesting is not mentioned specifically, and there are co-owners, title is assumed to be a tenancy in common. It is created when a deed does not specify that the interest is acquired in joint tenancy or a community property.

The only requirement of **unity** (equality) for tenants in common is the equal right of possession or undivided interest—as it is called. That means each owner has a certain equitable interest in the property (such as one-half interest, or one-fourth interest), but has the right to use the whole property. None of the owners may exclude any co-owner from the property, nor claim any portion of the property for exclusive use.

> **The Four Characteristics of Tenants in Common**
> 1. Tenants in common may take title at different times.
> 2. Tenants in common may take title on separate deeds.
> 3. Tenants in common may have unequal interests.
> 4. Tenants in common have an undivided interest or equal right of possession (one unity).

Any tenant in common may sell, encumber or will his or her interest, with heirs simply becoming a tenant in common among the others. One tenant in common cannot create an easement on the property without the consent of the other co-owners. A tenant in common must pay a proportionate share of any expenses incurred on the property, including money spent for repairs, taxes, loan payments, and insurance.

This is an example of tenancy
in common – have equal possession.

When tenants in common do not agree on matters pertaining to the property, any of the co-owners may file a **partition action** which asks the court to decide the fate of the investment.

> Example: Stacey, Ken, Catherine, and Dan are joint tenants. Dan sells his interest to Eva. The joint tenancy has been broken regarding the interest Dan had in the property. The new vesting, after the sale of Dan's interest, is Stacey, Ken, and Catherine as joint tenants with equal interests, and the right of survivorship, with Eva as a tenant in common.
>
> Stacey, Ken, Catherine, and Eva, in the above property, wish to restore a joint tenancy with each of the four having the right of survivorship. Eva holds a tenancy in common, so she will have to be added to the joint tenancy. Since all joint tenants must take title at the same time, on the same document, Stacey, Ken, Catherine, and Eva must sign a new deed that lists Stacey, Ken, and Catherine as joint tenants and Eva as a tenant in common. Then the property can be deeded to all four parties as joint tenants. All requirements for a joint tenancy—time, title, interest, and possession—will then be fulfilled.

Joint Tenancy

When two or more parties own real property as co-owners, with the right of survivorship, it is called **joint tenancy**. The **right of survivorship** means that if one of the joint tenants dies, the surviving joint tenant automatically becomes sole owner of the property.

Time   Title   Interest   Possession

This is an example of joint tenancy.

The deceased's share does not go to his or her estate or heirs, but becomes the property of the co-tenant without becoming involved in probate. Also, the surviving joint tenant is not liable to creditors of the deceased who hold liens on the joint tenancy property.

In order to have a joint tenancy, there are four unities that must be in existence: time, title, interest, and possession. If any one of the unities is missing, a tenancy in common is created.

> **The Four Unities of Joint Tenancy**
> **Mnemonic = "T" Tip**
> **T ime** All parties must become joint tenants at the same time.
> **T itle** All parties must take title on the same deed.
> **I nterest** All parties must have an equal undivided interest in the property.
> **P ossession** All parties have equal right of possession.

All four items must occur to have a joint tenancy. Co-owners may sell their interest, give it away or borrow money against it, without consent of the other joint tenants. A joint tenant may sever his or her interest in the joint tenancy by selling it. The new co-owner would become a tenant in common with the remaining joint tenants. The joint tenancy is not severed (broken) if a lien is put against the interest of one of the co-owners. However, a foreclosure on the lien would sever that interest from the joint tenancy.

Due to the right of survivorship, a joint tenant may not will his or her share. Joint tenancy is terminated when any one of the four unities ends, such as by sale, gift or by mutual agreement.

> Example: Audrey, Bob, Carol, and David are joint tenants. David dies and his interest automatically goes to Audrey, Bob and Carol as joint tenants with equal one-third interests.
>
> Kelly and Roger own a house as joint tenants. Roger dies and Kelly now owns the house as her sole and separate property without probate. Roger's heirs are not entitled to his share because of the right of survivorship. If Kelly wishes to convey title after Roger's death, she will need to record an affidavit of "Death of Joint Tenant" and then record a new deed removing Roger from title. This would allow her to convey the title to the property without Roger.

Community Property

All property acquired by a husband and wife during a valid marriage—except for certain separate property—is called **community property**. Community property excludes property acquired before marriage or during marriage by gift or inheritance. Any income, including wages from either spouse, is considered community property, unless it is income derived from separate property. Community property has one unity— equal interest, with each spouse owning 50%. The one similarity between community property and joint tenancy is the unity of equal interests.

Interest is equal (50/50) in community property.

In 2001, California enacted a law allowing a husband and wife to hold title to their property as **community property with right of survivorship**. Holding title as community property provides a "stepped-up" tax basis for both halves of the property upon the death of the first spouse. Holding title as joint tenants provides for the immediate and automatic transfer of title to the surviving spouse upon the death of the first spouse. This new form of holding title combines the desirable tax features of community property with the right of survivorship of joint tenancy.

Separate property includes all:
* property owned before marriage.
* property acquired by either of the parties during marriage by gift or inheritance.
* income derived from separate property.

If spouses want to maintain the status of their separate property, they must be very careful not to commingle it with their community property. For example, if community property funds are used to offset the negative cash flow of an apartment building that is separate property, the apartment building will become community property.

Community property cannot be sold or encumbered by only one of the partners. Either spouse may lease community property for up to one year or may sign a listing agreement to put a property "on the market". Although a listing agreement signed by the husband or wife is enforceable, both must accept and sign any contract to actually sell the community property (**deposit receipt**). Either spouse may buy real or personal property without the consent of the other; both are bound by the contract made by either one, unless the new property is bought specifically as separate property with funds from a separate property account.

A married couple in California has three choices when it comes to how they may take title. However, unless otherwise stated, title is presumed community property. The first is joint tenancy, which includes the right of survivorship if one of the spouses dies but also may include a tax liability for the surviving spouse. The second is community property, which does include the right of survivorship, but also includes probate after a spouse dies and all the costs involved in that process. The third type of vesting is community property with the right of survivorship, which includes the better of the first two types of vesting. There is no particular tax liability because of the death of a spouse and there is also no probate with its seemingly endless costs.

When title is taken simply as community property, either party may will one-half of the community property. When vesting is community property, if there is no will, the surviving spouse inherits all community property by **intestate** succession. This is important to know, particularly with multiple marriages, for estate planning. Property may be owned with the intention that it go to one's children, only to learn after the parent's death that children of the first marriage are no longer natural heirs. If there is a subsequent husband or wife and no will has been made, the new spouse will become the natural heir to any property owned or community property.

Regarding separate property, if there is no will, the surviving spouse gets one-half and one child gets one-half. If there is more than one child, the surviving spouse gets one-third and the children get two-thirds.

Do All States Recognize Community Property Law?

Nine states—Arizona, California, Idaho, Louisiana, Nevada, New Mexico, Texas, Washington, and Wisconsin—use the community property system to determine the interest of a husband and wife in property acquired during marriage. If you now live or previously lived in one of these states, you should be aware that some special rules apply to community property. Any property you may have acquired while living in one of these nine states is probably community property even today.

Tenancy in Partnership

Ownership by two or more persons who form a partnership for business purposes is known as tenancy in partnership. The rights of each of the partners are subject to a partnership agreement and are described therein.

Concurrent Ownership				
	Joint Tenancy	Tenancy in Common	Community Property	Partnership
Parties	Any number	Any number	Spouses only	Any number
Interest	Must be equal	Equal or unequal	Must be equal	Mutual consent
Possession	Equal right	Equal right	Equal right	Equal right
Death	Survivorship	No survivorship	Survivorship (no will)	No survivorship

Recording Safeguards Ownership

In a move that was strictly an American device for safeguarding the ownership of land, the California legislature adopted a system of recording **evidence of title** or interest. This system meant records could be collected in a convenient and safe public place, so that those purchasing land would be more fully informed about the ownership and condition of the title. Even then, California was a leader in consumer friendly legislation. Citizens were protected against secret **conveyance**s and liens, and title to real property was freely transferable.

Acknowledgment

The Recording Act of California provides that, after acknowledgment, any instrument or **judgment** affecting the title to—or possession of—real property may be recorded. **Acknowledgment** is a formal declaration before a notary public or certain public officials, by the person (grantor) who signed (executed) the instrument (deed) that he or she in fact did execute (sign) the document.

A **notary public** (notary) is a licensed public officer who takes or witnesses the acknowledgment. A notary cannot acknowledge any document in which the notary is named a principal. A notary who is an employee of a corporation may notarize a deed involving the corporation so long as he or she does not have a personal interest in the subject matter of the transaction.

Acknowledgment acts as a safeguard against forgery and once acknowledged, a document is accepted as **prima facie** (on its face) evidence in court.

A deed must be acknowledged to be recorded. Recording permits, rather than requires, documents that affect title to real property to be filed.

Recording Process

The process consists of copying the instrument to be recorded in the proper index, and filing it in alphabetical order, under the names of the parties, without delay. Documents must be recorded by the county recorder in the county within which the property is located to be valid there.

When the recorder receives a document to be filed, he or she notes the time and date of filing and at whose request it was filed. After the contents of the document are copied into the record, the original document is marked "filed for record", stamped with the proper time and date of recording, and returned to the person who requested the recording.

Constructive Notice

Recording a document as well as possession of the property give **constructive notice** of an interest in real property. Recording gives public notice (constructive notice) of the content of any instrument recorded to anyone who cares to look into the records. Possession is also considered constructive notice. Even the act of taking possession of an unrecorded deed gives constructive notice. A buyer should always check to be sure there is no one living on the property who might have a prior claim to ownership. It is the buyer's duty to conduct proper inquiry before purchasing any property. Failure to do so does not relieve the buyer of that responsibility.

> Example: Ann bought a property through her broker, sight unseen. The escrow closed and the deed was recorded. When Ann tried to move into her new home; however, she found George living there. He told her he had bought the property a year ago and had not bothered to record the deed, but had moved in and considered it his home. When she consulted her attorney, Ann found that indeed George—because he was in possession of the property—had given notice to anyone who might inquire. One remedy for the situation would be legal action against the grantor who sold the property to both George and Ann. However, at the moment, George does have legal title because of his possession of the property.

Actual Notice

If a person has direct, express information about the ownership interest of a property it is called **actual notice**. Actual notice is a fact, such as seeing the grant deed or knowing that a person inherited a property by will.

Priorities in Recording

As we have seen, recording laws are meant to protect citizens against fraud and to give others notification of property ownership. The first valid deed that is recorded determines the owner, unless that person, prior to recording, had either actual or constructive notice of the rights of others. Other information that might influence ownership can be recorded also, such as liens and other encumbrances. **Priority** means the order in which deeds are recorded. Whether or not it is a grant deed, trust deed or some other evidence of a lien or encumbrance, the priority is determined by the date stamped in the upper right-hand corner of the document by the county recorder. To obtain priority through recording, a buyer must be a good faith purchaser, for a valuable **consideration**, and record the deed first.

If there are several grant deeds recorded against the property, the one recorded first is valid. In a case where there are several trust deeds recorded against a property, no mention will be made about which one is the first trust deed, which is the second, and so forth.

A person inquiring about the priority of the deeds should look at the time and date the deed was recorded for that information. You will see, as we proceed in our study, the importance of the date and time of recording.

There are certain instruments not affected by the priority of recording rule. Certain liens, such as tax liens and mechanic's liens, take priority even though they are recorded after a deed. We will discuss liens and encumbrances later in detail, but it is helpful to note here the impact of the recording laws on this subject.

Summary

Property is anything lawfully owned and is either real or personal. **Real property** is immovable; **personal property** is movable. Real property is land, anything attached to land or anything lawfully immovable, and is transferred or sold with a deed. **Land** as real property includes surface rights, airspace, mineral rights, and water rights. **Airspace** is considered real property to a reasonable height. **Minerals** are owned as real property unless they are fugitive substances such as oil or gas. Water flowing in a stream or underground is real property. **Water** that overflows its banks is floodwater. There are three types of **floodwater**: inundation, sheet overflow, and ponding. The owner of property bordering on a stream or river has **riparian rights**. When there is a need for the government to divert water for public use, the right of **appropriation** is applied.

Fixtures are an example of real property because they are attached permanently to the real estate. There are five tests used to decide whether an item is a fixture: method of attachment, adaptation, relationship of the parties, intent of the parties, and agreement of the parties ("MARIA"). **Trade fixtures** such as shelves, business signs, cash registers, room partitions, or wall mirrors are personal property of the business owner; even though they are temporarily attached to a building.

Bundle of rights is an ownership understanding that describes all the legal rights attached to real property. These are: possess, use, enjoy, encumber, and transfer. Legally, ownership is described by the bundle of rights one owns, not the property one owns.

An **estate** is the ownership interest or claim a person has in real property. There are two types of estates: freehold estates and less-than-freehold estates. A **freehold estate** is a real property estate of an owner, is of indefinite duration and can be sold or inherited. Freehold estates are also known as **estates of inheritance** (the estate continues for an indefinite time) except life estates (the estate continues for tenant's own life or lives of one or more persons).

There are two types of freehold estates: (1) estates in fee and (2) life estates. An estate in fee is the most complete and common form of ownership. A property owner may impose qualifications, conditions or restrictions when transferring title to property. Property restrictions are created by deed or written agreement. This type of property is transferred or sold with no conditions or limitations on its use. **Fee simple qualified** or **defeasible** occurs when the seller imposes qualifications or conditions that may apply before or after the transaction. A seller can impose two types of conditions when selling property: condition subsequent and condition precedent. Condition subsequent involves the owner selling property with the stipulation that certain requirements need to be met after the sale, or the property needs to be used for a certain purpose. Condition precedent involves parties to a contract who may impose a restriction in which something must occur before a transaction becomes final. **Life estate** is limited in duration to the life of a designated person. There are three types of life estates: (1) **estate in reversion**, (2) estate in remainder, and (3) reserving a life estate. Life estate holders are required to pay taxes and maintain the property. The life estate holder may collect all rents and keep all profits for the duration of the life estate.

Less-than-freehold estate is property held by tenants who rent or lease property. Less-than-freehold estates are also known as leasehold estates or chattel. The renter or tenants have the right to use the property (lease) for a fixed time. A lease is a movable document describing the temporary possession and use of the property, and is personal property.

Personal property, also known as **chattel**, is movable property and can be transferred or sold using a bill of sale. The seller keeps all personal property unless special arrangements are made when real estate is sold. Personal property also may be **pledged** as a security for a loan.

The government or an individual can own property under separate ownership or **concurrent ownership**. There are four types of concurrent ownership: (1) joint tenancy, (2) tenancy in common, (3) community property, and (4) tenancy in partnership. There are four entities of joint tenancy: (1) time, (2) title, (3) interest, and (4) possession ("T" Tip). A **tenancy in common** forms when two or more persons own undivided interest in property. There are four characteristics of tenants in common: (1) may take title at different times, (2) take title on separate deeds, (3) have unequal interests, and (4) have an undivided interest or equal right of possession.

Chapter 2   Review Exercises

Matching Exercise

Instructions: Look up the meaning of the terms in the Glossary, then write the letter of the matching term on the blank line before its definition. Answers are in Appendix B.

Terms

a. acknowledgment

b. appurtenance

c. bundle of rights

d. chattel

e. constructive notice

f. easement

g. emblements

h. estate

i. estate in fee

j. fee simple absolute

k. fee simple qualified

l. fixture

m. freehold estate

n. less-than-freehold estate

o. life estate

p. littoral

q. patents

r. personal property

s. pur autre vie

t. quiet enjoyment

u. real property

v. riparian rights

w. severalty

x. title

y. trade fixture

Definitions

1. ___*A*___   A formal declaration to a public official (notary) by a person who has signed an instrument which states that the signing was voluntary.

2. ___*b*___   Those rights, privileges, and improvements that belong to and pass with the transfer of real property but are not necessarily a part of the actual property.

3. ___*C*___   An ownership concept describing all the legal rights that attach to the ownership of real property.

4. ___*F*___   The right to use another's land for a specified purpose, sometimes known as a right-of-way.

5. ___*H*___   A legal interest in land; defines the nature, degree, extent, and duration of a person's ownership in land.

6. ___*y*___   An article of personal property affixed to leased property by the tenant as a necessary part of the business; may be removed by tenant as personal property upon termination of the lease.

7. __V__   The rights of a landowner whose land is next to a natural watercourse to reasonable use of whatever water flows past the property.

8. __M__   An estate in real property which continues for an indefinite period of time.

9. __G__   Annual crops produced for sale.

10. __R__   Anything movable that is not real property.

11. __P__   Land bordering a lake, ocean, or sea.

12. __L__   Personal property that has become affixed to real estate.

13. __U__   Land, anything affixed to the land, anything appurtenant to the land, anything immovable by law.

14. __W__   Ownership of real property by one person or entity.

15. __D__   Personal property.

16. _____   A leasehold estate; considered to exist for a definite period of time or successive periods of time until termination.

17. __O__   An estate that is limited in duration to the life of its owner or the life of some other chosen person.

18. __X__   Evidence of ownership of land.

19. __E__   Notice given by recording a document or taking physical possession of the property.

20. __T__   The right to peace without aggravation by others.

Multiple Choice Questions

Instructions: Circle your response and go to Appendix B to read the complete explanation for each question.

1. In a technical sense, the term "property" refers to:
    - a. rights or interests in the thing owned.
    - b. a freehold estate.
    - c. personal property only.
    - d. land and buildings only.

2. It is often difficult to determine ownership rights of personal property because personal property can:
    a. become real property.
    b. be hypothecated.
    c. be pledged.
    d. all of the above

3. Which of the following is considered real property?
    a. Timber
    b. Airspace above the land
    c. Unharvested crops under a prior sales contract
    d. Landfill soil being hauled

4. Which of the following is considered personal property?
    a. Mineral rights
    b. Leasehold estates
    c. All improvements to land
    d. Trees growing in a natural forest

5. A running stream is considered:
    a. personal property.
    b. real property.
    c. a fixture.
    d. a chattel.

6. Which of the following statements concerning riparian rights is **not** correct?
    a. A riparian owner may convey any part of his or her land that is not immediately adjacent to the river.
    b. If a riparian owner conveys part of his or her land that is not immediately adjacent to the river, riparian rights are not conveyed with that property.
    c. Riparian rights may not be severed from the property by prescription or condemnation.
    d. The owner of adjacent land may not lawfully divert all available water and thereby deprive a riparian owner of water.

7. Which of the following is considered personal property?
    a. An easement
    b. Mineral rights
    c. Trees growing in a forest
    d. An existing mortgage

8. Which of the following is considered appurtenant to land?
   a. Something acquired by legal right and used with the land for its benefit
   b. A right-of-way over another's adjoining land
   c. Stock in a mutual water company
   d. All of the above

9. Of the following, which is not one of five general tests of a fixture?
   a. Method of attachment
   b. Time of attachment
   c. Adaptability of the item
   d. Intention of the parties

10. Which of the following is considered real property?
   a. A bearing wall in a single-family residence
   b. A maturing grape crop that will be harvested later and is governed by a sales contract
   c. Trade fixtures installed by a tenant that are removable without damage
   d. A built-in refrigerator in a mobile home that is not attached to a permanent foundation

11. "Of indefinite duration" is a phrase that describes a(n):
   a. estate for years.
   b. estate from period to period.
   c. estate of inheritance.
   d. less-than-freehold estate.

12. If Jones conveys to Ford a portion of Jones' fee estate for a term less than his own, Jones' own interest would be:
   a. remainder.
   b. reversion.
   c. vested sufferance.
   d. fee defeasible.

13. Which of the following is a less-than-freehold estate?
   a. Life estate
   b. Estate of inheritance
   c. Estate for years
   d. Estate in remainder

14. An uncle left his nephew 2/3 interest and left his nephew's wife 1/3 interest in real property jointly and without the right of survivorship. They will assume title to an estate that is classified as:
    a. community property.
    b. joint tenancy.
    c. tenancy in common.
    d. partnership.

15. Ownership in severalty would most likely involve:
    a. a fee simple defeasible estate.
    b. tenancy in common.
    c. ownership with other parties.
    d. sole ownership.

16. Three people own equal interests in a parcel of land as tenants in common. Without the consent of the others, one of the co-tenants leased the entire parcel to another party for agricultural purposes. Such a lease would be:
    a. valid and binding for all three co-tenants.
    b. invalid because land owned by multiple owners may not be leased.
    c. valid, provided that the term did not exceed 51 years.
    d. invalid, because one co-tenant cannot obligate the other co-tenants for a lease of the whole property without their consent.

17. The words "time, title, interest, and possession" are most closely related to which of the following concepts?
    a. Severalty
    b. Survivorship
    c. Sole ownership
    d. Adverse possession

18. Concerning real property, a joint tenancy of interest and a community property interest are alike in which of the following ways?
    a. Ownership interests are equal
    b. Only a husband and wife are involved
    c. Both owners must join in any conveyance
    d. Both provide the right of survivorship

19. Chris, Jordan, and Logan took title to a property as joint tenants. Chris sold her share to Payton, and then Jordan died. Who owns the property now?

   a. Logan owns 2/3 and Payton owns 1/3 as tenants in common.

   b. Logan, Payton, and Jordan's heirs own the property 1/3 each as joint tenants.

   c. Logan owns 2/3 and Payton owns 1/3 as joint tenants.

   d. Logan, Payton, and Jordan's heirs own the property 1/3 each as tenants-in-common.

20. An agreement for the sale of community property made by one spouse only is considered:

   a. valid.

   b. illegal.

   c. enforceable.

   d. unenforceable.

Encumbrances and Transfer of Ownership

3 Chapter

Introduction

You need an organized system for keeping track of property ownership to determine who owns what, and how ownership can be transferred. Of course, the system—which serves you as a real estate agent and a consumer—must be completely reliable.

In this chapter, you will learn how real property can be transferred and the types of deeds that are used to transfer ownership from one person to another.

Learning Objectives

After reading this chapter, you will be able to:

- define encumbrances and liens.
- explain the California homestead law.
- list the different ways real estate is conveyed.
- name the requirements for valid deeds.
- discuss the transfer of title and when the courts may get involved.
- discuss the advantages and disadvantages of title insurance.

Encumbrances: Limitations on Real Property

An **encumbrance** is an interest in real property that is held by someone who is not the owner. Anything that burdens or affects the title or the use of the property is an encumbrance. A property is encumbered when it is burdened with legal obligations against the title. Most buyers purchase encumbered property.

Encumbrances fall into two categories: those that affect the title, known as **money encumbrances**, and those that affect the use of the property, known as **non-money encumbrances**. The encumbrances that create a legal obligation to pay are known as **liens**. A lien uses real property as security for the payment of a debt (lein$ - Memory aid: the dollar sign is to show liens involve money).

Common types of liens are trust deeds and mortgages, mechanic's liens, tax liens, and special assessments, attachments, and judgments. The types of encumbrances that affect the physical use of property are easements, building restrictions, and zoning requirements and encroachments.

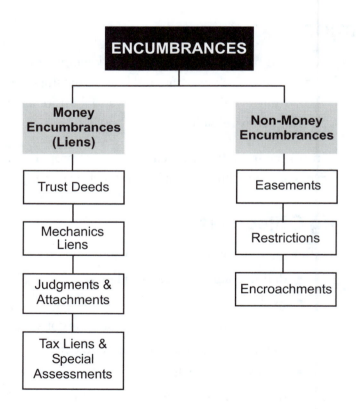

Money Encumbrances

A lien is an obligation to pay a money encumbrance that may be voluntary or involuntary. An owner may choose to borrow money, using the property as security for the loan, creating a **voluntary lien**. A voluntary lien does not have to be recorded.

Typical voluntary liens include trust deeds and mortgages. On the other hand, if the owner does not pay taxes or the debt owed, a lien may be placed against his or her property without permission, creating an **involuntary lien**. Typical involuntary liens include mechanic's liens, judgments, tax liens, and attachments.

A lien may be specific or general. A **specific lien** is one that is placed against a certain property, such as a mechanic's lien, trust deed, attachment, property tax lien, and lis pendens. A **general lien** affects all property of the owner such as a judgment lien or federal or state income tax liens.

All liens are encumbrances but not all encumbrances are liens.

Trust Deeds and Mortgages

Trust deeds and mortgages are both instruments used in real estate financing to create voluntary, specific liens against real property. They will be discussed in Chapter 9.

Mechanic's Lien

Mechanic's liens may be placed against a property by anyone who supplies labor, services, or materials used for **improvements** on real property and who did not receive payment for the improvements. Therefore, a contractor, a subcontractor, a laborer on a job, any person who furnishes materials such as lumber, plumbing or roofing, or anyone who furnishes services such as an architect, engineer, teamster, or equipment lessor is eligible to file a mechanic's lien.

A mechanic's lien must be verified and recorded. The law is very time specific about the recording. The **statutory** procedure must be followed exactly if the mechanic's lien is to be valid. The four steps to be taken include: (1) the preliminary notice, (2) the notice of completion, (3) no notice of completion, and (4) foreclosure action.

1. **Preliminary Notice:** A preliminary notice is a written notice that must be given to the owner within 20 days of first furnishing labor or materials

for a job by anyone eligible to file a mechanic's lien. This document gives owners notice that their property may be liened if they do not pay for work completed.

2. **Notice of Completion**: If the owner records a notice of completion within 10 days after the project is finished, the original contractors have 60 days after the notice is filed, and all others have 30 days after the notice is filed, to record a mechanic's lien.

3. **No Notice of Completion**: If the owner does not record a notice of completion when work is finished, all claimants have a maximum of 90 days from the day work was finished to record a mechanic's lien.

4. **Foreclosure Action**: After a mechanic's lien is recorded, the claimant has 90 days to bring foreclosure action to enforce the lien. If he or she does not bring action, the lien will be terminated and the claimant loses the right to foreclose.

If an owner discovers unauthorized work on the property, he or she must file a **notice of nonresponsibility.** This is a notice that must be recorded and posted on the property to be valid, stating the owner is not responsible for work being done. This notice releases the owner from the liability for work done without permission. The owner must record this notice within 10 days after discovering the unauthorized work. The notice normally is posted with a commercial lease at the beginning of a job, if a tenant is ordering the job.

Mechanic's Lien Time Line

Here are the major events to be followed, in a timely manner, whenever improvement of real property is done.
1. Work Commences
2. Preliminary 20-Day Notice
3. Work Completed
4. Notice of Completion Recorded
5. Lien Recorded
6. Foreclosure Action and Lis Pendens Recorded
7. Service of Process
8. Court Decision
   a) Judgment
   b) Release of Lien
   c) Dismissed
   d) Foreclosure

RECORDING REQUESTED BY

WHEN RECORDED MAIL TO

NAME

ADDRESS

CITY

STATE&ZIP

Title Order No.   **Escrow No.**

SPACE ABOVE THIS LINE FOR RECORDER'S USE

MECHANICS LIEN

The undersigned, _____ , claimant
(name of person or firm claiming mechanics lien. Contractors use name exactly as it appears on the contractors license.)

Claims a mechanics lien upon the following described real property:

City of _____ , County of _____ , California.
_____ (General description of property where the work or

materials were furnished. A street address is sufficient, but if possible, use both street address and legal description.)

The sum of $ _____ together with interest thereon at the rate of 0.00% _____
(Amount of Claim due and unpaid.)

percent per annum from _____, is due claimant (after deducting all just credits and offsets) for
(date when balance became due)

the following work and material furnished by claimant :

_____
(insert general description of the work or materials furnished)

Claimant furnished the work and materials at the request of, or under contract, with _____

_____
(name of the person or firm who ordered or contract for the work or materials.)

The owners or reputed owners of the property are : _____

_____

(Insert name of owner of real property. This can be obtained from the county recorder or by checking the building permit application at

the building department.)

Firm Name _____

By: _____
(Signature of claimant or authorized agent)

VERIFICATION

I, the undersigned, say: I am the _____ the claimant of the forgoing
("President of", "Manager of", "A partner of", "Owner of", etc.)

mechanic's lien; I have read said claim of mechanic's lien and know the contents thereof: the above is true of my own knowledge.

I declare under perjury that the forgoing is true and correct.

Executed on _____, at _____, California.
(Date of signature)   (City where signed)

_____

(Personal signature of the individual who is swearing that the contents of the claim of mechanic's lien are true.)

Determining the starting date for a mechanic's lien is very important. Mechanic's liens have priority as of the date work began or materials were first furnished for the job. A mechanic's lien has priority over any other liens filed after the commencement of labor or delivery of materials with the exception of government liens (taxes and special assessments). That means if there is a foreclosure action, the mechanic's lien would be paid before any other liens that were recorded after work started on the job.

That includes trust deeds or mortgages recorded prior to the filing of the mechanic's lien, but after the start of the work. Lenders will make a physical inspection of the property to determine that no materials have been delivered and no work has been done before recording a construction loan to assure the priority of their trust deed or mortgage.

In the following example, the mechanic's lien has the priority:

> **Mechanic's Lien has Priority over Trust Deed**
> 1. Start of work June 15
> 2. Trust Deed recorded June 18
> 3. Notice of completion Sept 1
> 4. Mechanic's Lien recorded September 28

Tax Liens and Special Assessments

If any government taxes, such as income or property taxes are not paid, they become a **tax lien** against the property. **Special assessments** are levied against property owners to pay for local improvements, such as underground utilities, street repair, or water projects. Payment for the projects is secured by a special assessment which becomes a lien against real property. Property taxes and special assessments are specific liens, whereas other government taxes are general liens.

Lis Pendens

A **lis pendens** (also called a pendency of action) is a recorded notice that indicates pending litigation affecting the title on a property. It clouds the title, preventing the sale or transfer of the property until the lis pendens is removed, the action is dismissed, or final judgment is rendered. A pendency of action gives the least protection against a mechanic's lien.

Attachments and Judgments

An **attachment lien** or writ of attachment is the process by which the court holds the real or personal property of a defendant as security for a possible judgment pending the outcome of a lawsuit. An attachment lien is an involuntary, specific lien which is valid for three years. It does not terminate upon death and may be extended in certain cases.

A **judgment** is the final determination of the rights of parties in a lawsuit by the court. A judgment does not automatically create a lien. A summary of the court decision, known as an abstract of judgment, must be recorded with the county recorder. When the **abstract of judgment** is recorded, it is a general lien on all non-exempt property owned or acquired by the judgment debtor for 10 years, in the county in which the abstract is filed. The court may force the sale of the property to satisfy the judgment by issuing a **writ of execution**. The sale is called an **execution sale.**

Non-Money Encumbrances

A non-money encumbrance is one that affects the use of property such as an easement, a building restriction, an encroachment, or a lease (discussed in Chapter 6).

Easements

An **easement** is the right to enter or use someone else's land for a specified purpose. An interest in an easement is non-possessory. That means the holder of an easement can use it only for the purpose intended and may not exclude anyone else from using it. The right to enter onto a property using an easement is called **ingress** (enter). The right to exit from a property using an easement is called **egress** (exit).

Appurtenant Easement

As you recall, an appurtenance is anything used for the benefit of the land. An easement appurtenant has a servient and a dominant tenement. The owner whose land is being used is the one giving the easement and the land is the **servient tenement.** The servient tenement is the one encumbered by the easement. The person's land receiving the benefit of the easement is known as the **dominant tenement.**

Appurtenant Easement

An easement appurtenant automatically goes with the sale of the dominant tenement. To be valid, the dominant and servient tenements of an appurtenant easement do not have to be mentioned in the deed, nor do they have to touch each other (abut).

Easement in Gross

Since an unlocated easement is valid, it is possible to have an easement that is not appurtenant to any particular land. Thus, Jacob—who owns no land—may have an easement over Sal's land for the purpose of getting to the stream where he regularly fishes. The easement for the path to cross the land does not need to specify where the path is actually located. A commercial camping enterprise may use an easement over private property to take clients to remote sites, which may otherwise be inaccessible.

Public utilities also have easements that are not appurtenant to any one parcel. These easements are known as **easements in gross,** and only have a servient tenement (no dominant tenement). Easements in gross are the most common type of easement.

Make sure you understand the difference between an easement in gross and a license. An easement may not be terminated arbitrarily, as you will see in the following section. A **license** is permission to use property. However, a license to use may be revoked at any time.

Creating an Easement

Easements are created in various ways—commonly by express grant or reservation in a grant deed or by a written agreement between owners of adjoining land. An easement always should be recorded to assure its continued existence. It is recorded by the party benefiting from the easement as the dominant tenement.

Express Grant

The servient tenement, or the giver of the easement, grants the easement by deed or express agreement.

Express Reservation

The seller of a parcel who owns adjoining land reserves an easement or right-of-way over the former property. It is created at the time of the sale with a deed or express agreement.

Implied Grant or Reservation

The existence of an easement is obvious and necessary at the time a property is conveyed, even though no mention is made of it in the deed.

Necessity

An easement is created when a parcel is completely land locked and has no access. It is automatically terminated when another way to enter and leave the property becomes available.

Prescription

Prescription is the process of acquiring an interest, not ownership, in a certain property.

An **easement by prescription** may be created by continuous and uninterrupted use, by a single party, for a period of five years. The use must be against the owner's wishes and be open and notorious. No confrontation with the owner is required and property taxes do have to be paid. The party wishing to obtain the prescriptive easement must have some reasonable claim to the use of the property.

The method used for acquiring property rights through prescription is similar to **adverse possession**. The main difference is the payment of taxes. Adverse possession requires the payment of taxes for five continuous years, while prescription does not. Also, remember one acquires title to property through adverse possession, but only a specified interest in property through prescription.

Terminating an Easement

The owner of the property with the servient tenement cannot revoke or terminate the easement. Easements may be terminated or extinguished in eight ways:

1. **Abandonment:** Abandonment is the obvious and intentional surrender of the easement. **Non-use:** If a prescriptive easement is not used for a period of five years, the easement is terminated.

2. **Destruction of the servient tenement:** If the government takes the servient tenement for its use, as in eminent domain, the easement is terminated.

3. **Adverse possession:** The owner of the servient tenement may, by his or her own use, prevent the dominant tenement from using the easement for a period of five years, thus terminating the easement.

4. **Merger:** If the same person owns both the dominant and servient tenements, the easement is terminated.

5. **Express release:** The owner of the dominant tenement is the only one who can release an easement. A usual way would be to sign a quitclaim deed.

6. **Legal proceedings:** In order to terminate an easement, the owner of the servient tenement would bring an action to quiet title against the owner of the dominant tenement. A lawsuit to establish or settle title to real property is called a **quiet title action** or an action to quiet title.

7. **Estoppel:** Unless created by express grant, an easement may be terminated by non-use and the property owner has reason to believe that no further use is intended.

   > Example: John is a farmer who owns some land. Bob, the son of a neighboring farmer, cuts through John's field on the way to high school. Upon graduation, Bob leaves for college and stops taking the shortcut through John's field. Farmer John, seeing that the easement was no longer in use, fenced his field. John's action showed that he relied on Bob's conduct (no longer taking the shortcut). Therefore, the easement terminates through the estoppel.

8. **Excessive use:** Depending on the terms of the easement, excessive use can terminate the easement.

   > Example: Dan Smith, the owner of a Victorian style 6-bedroom, 2-story house, has an easement to cross Betty's property to get to his home. In order to pay for an upcoming trip, Dan decided to rent out all the bedrooms in his home to college students. He calculated he could rent each room to two or three students. Therefore, the traffic across the easement increased dramatically. Betty, understandably upset, terminated Dan's easement due to excessive use.

**The Requirements for Terminating an Easement
Mnemonic = "ADAM E. LEE"**

A bandonment
D estruction of the servient tenement
A dverse possession
M erger
E xpress release
L egal proceedings
E stoppel
E xcessive

Restrictions

Another type of encumbrance is a restriction. A **restriction** is a limitation placed on the use of property and may be placed by a private owner, a developer or the government. It is usually placed on property to assure that land use is consistent and uniform within a certain area. **Private restrictions** are placed by a present or past owner and affect only a specific property or development, while **zoning (public restriction)** is an example of government restrictions that benefit the general public.

Private Restrictions

Private restrictions are created in the deed at the time of sale or in the general plan of a subdivision by the developer. For example, a developer may use a height restriction to ensure views from each parcel in a subdivision.

CC&Rs

Restrictions are commonly known as **CC&Rs** or covenants, conditions, and restrictions. The CC&Rs for a new subdivision are listed in a recorded **Declaration of Restrictions** which gives each owner the right to enforce the CC&Rs.

A **covenant** is a promise to do or not do certain things. The penalty for a breach of a covenant is usually money damages or an injunction. An **injunction** is a court order forcing a person to do or not do an act, such as violating a private restriction. An example of a covenant might be that the tenant agrees to make certain repairs, or that a property may be used only for a specific purpose.

A **condition** is much the same as a covenant, a promise to do or not do something (usually a limitation on the use of the property), except the penalty for breaking a condition is return of the property to the grantor. A **condition subsequent** is a restriction, placed in a deed at the time of conveyance, upon future use of the property. It is a condition placed on the property that comes into play subsequent to the transaction. Upon breach of the condition subsequent, the grantor may take back the property. A **condition precedent** requires that a certain event, or condition, occur before title can pass to the new owner. It is a condition that must be taken care of preceding the transaction.

Covenants, conditions, and restrictions are **void** if they are unlawful, impossible to perform, or in restraint of alienation. Therefore, a deed restriction prohibiting "For Sale" signs is illegal, but the signs may be limited to a reasonable size.

Public Restrictions

Public restrictions are primarily zoning laws (zoning) which promote public health or general public welfare. Zoning regulates land use with regard to lot sizes, types of structures permitted, building heights, setbacks, and density.

Zoning departments use zoning symbols to show types of property use. For example, R-3 is multiple family, R-1 is single family, M-1 is light industrial and C-1 stands for commercial property.

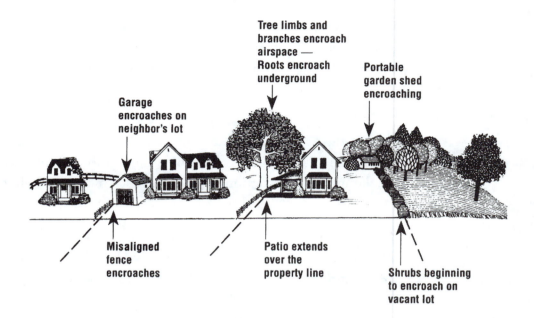

Common Encroachments

Changes in zoning may be initiated by a single property owner, developer, or government entity. Commonly, zoning is changed from a high density use to a lower density use, such as commercial (C-1) or light manufacturing (M-1) to residential (R-1), or from residential to conservation. This is called **downzoning.** Sometimes developers ask for higher density, such as changing from low density residential (R-1) to high density (R-3) in order to build condominiums.

Zoning changes can create **non-conforming** use, for example, farm land rezoned for residential use. All new structures must conform to the new zoning and be for residential use. Existing farms are now non-conforming properties, but may continue to operate because a **grandfather clause** allows an owner to continue to use structures which are now non-conforming with the new zoning laws.

If a person wants to use property in a way that is currently prohibited by zoning laws, he or she may petition to rezone the entire area or petition for a variance for the single piece of land. A **variance** is an allowable difference to the zoning laws for a structure or land use.

Whenever there is a conflict between zoning and deed restrictions, the more restrictive of the two must be followed.

Encroachments

Placing a permanent improvement such as a fence, wall, driveway or roof, so that it extends over the lot line into adjacent property owned by another, is known as an **encroachment**. This unauthorized intrusion on the adjoining land can limit its use and reduce it in size and **value**. An owner has three years in which to sue the neighbor to have the unauthorized encroachment removed.

Declared Homestead

California and many other states have homestead laws to protect families. Some or all of the land that is occupied by a family as their home is exempt from the claims of, or eviction by, unsecured creditors. A **homestead** is not truly an encumbrance, but it does limit the amount of liability for certain debts against which a home can be used to satisfy a judgment. A **Declaration of Homestead** is the recorded document that protects a homeowner from foreclosure by certain judgment creditors.

The first $75,000 of a home's value may not be used to satisfy a judgment against the head of a household. A mentally or physically disabled person, or someone over the age of 65, is entitled to protection up to $150,000. All others have a homestead exemption of $50,000. A

A homestead

homestead does not protect an owner against foreclosure on a trust deed, mechanic's lien, or lien recorded prior to the filing of the homestead.

Requirements for a Valid Homestead

Certain requirements must be met before a homestead is valid. The claimant must be living on the property at the time of filing, must state his or her status as head of household or other, must describe the property and give an estimate of value. Only one homestead can be valid at any one time.

RECORDING REQUESTED BY

WHEN RECORDED MAIL TO

NAME

ADDRESS

CITY

STATE&ZIP

Title Order No.   **Escrow No.**

_____

SPACE **ABOVE** THIS LINE FOR RECORDER'S USE

HOMESTEAD DECLARATION

I._____

(Full Name of Declarant)

do hereby certify and declare as follows:

(1)I hereby claim as a declared homestead the premises located in the City of _____,

County of _____ , State of California, commonly known as _____

_____,

(Street Address)

and more particularly described as follows: [Give complete legal description]

(2) I am the declared homestead owner of the above declared homestead.

(3) I own the following interest in the above declared homestead:

(4) The above declared homestead is: ☐ my principal dwelling, or, ☐ the principal dwelling of my spouse, and

I am, or,   my spouse is currently residing on that declared homestead.

(5) The facts stated in this Declaration are true as of my personal knowledge.

Dated: _____, 20___   _____

(Signature of Declarant)

STATE OF CALIFORNIA

COUNTY OF _____   } SS

On _____ , before me, the

undersigned, _____ , a Notary Public in and for

said State, personally appeared _____

_____

personally known to me (or proved to me on the basis of satisfactory
evidence) to be the person whose name (s) is/are subscribed to the
within instrument and acknowledged to me that he/she/they executed
the same in his/her/their authorized capacity(ies), and that by his/her/
their signature(s) on the instrument the person(s), or the entity upon
behalf of which the person(s) acted, executed the instrument.

WITNESS my hand and official seal

_____

Notary Public in and for said State.

Termination of a Homestead

An owner must file an **Abandonment of Homestead** form in order to obtain a homestead on a new property. Sale of the property automatically causes the homestead to terminate. However, if the owner moves from the homesteaded property and does not wish to file a new one, the original homestead remains valid. Destruction of the property does not terminate the homestead.

How Title to Real Estate Is Acquired or Conveyed

Acquisition and conveyance is also defined as "buying and selling". If one person is buying, someone must be selling. This section studies the two functions together. Real property may be acquired or conveyed in the following ways: **will, succession, accession, occupancy, and transfer.**

Will

A **will** disposes of property after death. A **testator** is a person who makes a will. If a person died **testate** it means the person left a valid will. If a person died **intestate** it means the person did not leave a will. A gift of real property by will is a **devise**, while a gift of money or personal property by will is a **bequest** or legacy. The maker may, before death, change a will by a **codicil**.

One type of will is a **witnessed will**, usually prepared by an attorney and signed by the maker (testator) and two witnesses. A **holographic will** is written in the maker's writing, dated, and signed by the maker.

Probate

Probate is the legal process to prove a will is valid. Probate proceedings are held in the superior court to determine creditors' claims and beneficiaries' interests in an estate upon the owner's death. A hearing is held to appoint a representative to handle the estate of the deceased. If that person is named in a will, he or she is referred to as an **executor** or **executrix**. If there is no will or someone named in a will to administer the estate, the court will appoint an **administrator** or **administratrix**.

Estate property may be sold during the probate period at a public or private auction. An administrator or executor may list the property for up to 90 days with court permission. The court confirms the final sale and sets the broker's commission. The first offer must be for at least 90% of the appraised value, and a subsequent offer at least 10% of the first $10,000 original bid, plus 5% of the remainder.

Sample Probate Bid	
Appraised value	100,000
1. First bid: at least 90% of appraised value	90,000
2. Second bid: at least 10% of first $10,000	1,000
Plus 5% of the remainder ($80,000)	4,000
Total minimum second bid required:	95,000

Succession

Succession is the legal transfer of a person's interests in real and personal property under the laws of descent and distribution. When a person inherits property as a result of someone dying without a will, it is called **intestate succession**. An intestate decedent's property passes to his or her heirs according to the laws of descent in the state where such real property is located. The law provides for disposition of the deceased's property by statute.

If the deceased was married, and died intestate, the surviving spouse receives all community property. Separate property is divided between a surviving spouse and any children. If there is only one child, the separate property is split equally. If there is more than one child, the surviving spouse receives one-third and the children, two-thirds.

Accession

Accession is a process by which there is an addition to property by the efforts of man or natural forces. An example of accession is alluvial deposits. When property is adjacent to a flow of water, accession may occur. Ownership is extended to include the property that has been gained.

Accession can occur by the addition of personal property to land so that it becomes a fixture or by improvements to land made in error. If an improvement was made innocently, the person responsible may remove it, provided he or she pays for any damage to the property.

The gradual build-up of soil, or **alluvium**, by natural causes on property bordering a river, lake, or ocean is called **accretion**. **Erosion** is the gradual wearing away of land by natural processes. The gradual wearing away of land is by the act of water, wind, or glacial ice. The sudden washing or tearing away of land by water action is known as **avulsion**. Accession can occur by **reliction** when land covered by water becomes uncovered because of alluvial deposits along the banks of streams.

Occupancy

Ownership of real property can be acquired by using (occupying) it. The property must be occupied without the owner's knowledge. It cannot be publicly owned (national and state parks, government buildings, public beaches, and the like). There are three ways to acquire property by occupancy: 1) abandonment, 2) adverse possession, and 3) prescription.

Adverse Possession

Adverse possession also can affect a transfer. It is accomplished by acquiring title to property through continued possession and payment of taxes. There are six requirements: (1) possession must be actual occupation, (2) adverse, (3) notorious, (4) continuous and uninterrupted for five years, (5) hostile to the present owner's title and wishes, and (6) open.

> **Review - Six Ways for Adverse Possession**
> **Mnemonic = "PANCHO"**
> **P** ossession
> **A** dverse
> **N** otorious
> **C** ontinuous
> **H** ostile
> **O** pen

Transfer

Property is acquired by transfer when, by an act of the parties or law, title is **conveyed**, or transferred, from one person to another by means of a written document. The transfer may be voluntary, such as the sale of a home, or involuntary by act of law, such as a foreclosure sale. Real property may be transferred, or **alienated**—by private grant, public grant, public dedication or operation of law (court action).

Private Grant

When property is transferred by **private grant** a written instrument is used. An **instrument** is a formal legal document such as a contract, deed or will. The kinds of deeds commonly used for private grants include: grant deed, quitclaim deed, gift deed, and warranty deed.

Grant Deed

In California, the **grant deed** is the most frequently used instrument to transfer title. The parties involved in the grant deed are the grantor and grantee. The **grantor** is the person conveying the property, and the **grantee** is the person receiving the property or to whom it is being conveyed.

A grant deed must have a "granting clause" and has two implied warranties by the grantor. One is that the grantor has not already conveyed title to any other person, and the other is that the estate is free from encumbrances other than those disclosed by the grantor. If you see the words **"et ux."** on a grant deed, it means "and wife".

> **Review - Grant Deed**
> - A written instrument (document) that transfers title to real property.
> - Must contain a "granting clause".

The grantor also promises to deed any rights he or she might acquire to the property after conveying it to the grantee. This is called **after-acquired title** which means any benefits that come to the property after a sale must follow the sale and accrue to the new owner. For example, oil or mineral rights might revert to the property at some time in the future, after the present owner has sold the property.

A grant deed must contain certain basics in order to be legally binding.

Requirements for a Valid Grant Deed

- According to the Statute of Frauds a deed must be in writing.
- The parties to the transfer (grantor and grantee) must be sufficiently identified and described.
- The grantor must be competent to convey the property (not a minor or incompetent).
- The grantee must be capable of holding title (must be a real living person, not fictitious).
- The property must be adequately described but it does not require a legal description.
- Words of granting such as grant or convey must be included.
- The deed must be executed (signed) by the grantor. The deed may be signed by a witnessed mark "X".
- The deed must be delivered to and accepted by the grantee.

A deed is **void** (invalid) if the grantor is a minor or incompetent or if the grantee does not exist. A deed to a deceased person or fictitious person, like ABC Company is void; however, a deed to an actual person using a fictitious name or DBA is valid. A **fictitious business name** or assumed name is a business name other than the name of the person who has registered the business. For example, "ABC Real Estate Brokerage" owned by Jill Jones or "South Coast Property Management" owned by Bill Hernandez. The acronym DBA means "doing business as". An example is, Bill Hernandez, DBA "South Coast Property Management".

A grant deed is not effective until it is delivered. It must be the intention of the grantor that the deed is delivered and title be transferred during his or her lifetime. For example, a deed would not be valid if signed and put in a safe place until the death of the grantor, and then recorded. **Recording** a deed is considered the same as delivery. After a deed has been acknowledged by the grantor, it may be filed with the county recorder, giving **constructive notice** of the sale. An **acknowledgment** is a signed statement, made before a notary public, by a named person confirming that the signature on a document is genuine and that it was made of free will. A deed does not have to be acknowledged to be valid, but must be acknowledged to be recorded.

The purpose of recording a deed is to protect the **chain of title**. This is a sequential record of changes in ownership showing the connection from one owner to the next. A complete chain of title is desirable whenever property is transferred and required by **title insurance** companies if they are writing a policy on a property.

> Example: Jane Borden, a single woman, owned the house in which she lived, as her sole and separate property. After marrying Sam Jones, she decided to sell the house. However, because the chain of the title showed that Jane Borden owned it, reference had to be made, in the grant deed to the buyer, that Jane Jones, a married woman, previously known as Jane Borden, was conveying her interest in the property. In that way the chain of title remained unbroken.

The priority of a deed is determined by the date it is recorded. In other words, recording establishes a claim of ownership which has priority over any deeds recorded after it. The first to record a deed is the first in right.

RECORDING REQUESTED BY

WHEN RECORDED MAIL TO

NAME
ADDRESS
CITY
STATE & ZIP

Title Order No.   Escrow No.

SPACE ABOVE THIS LINE FOR RECORDER'S USE

GRANT DEED

The undersigned declares that the documentary transfer tax is   and is

☐ Computed on the full value of the interest or property conveyed, or is

☐ Computed on the full value less the value of liens or encumbrances remaining at time of sale. The land, tenements realty is located in

☐ Unincorporated area of: ☐ City of: and

FOR A VALUABLE CONSIDERATION, receipt of which is hereby acknowledged.

hereby GRANT(S) to

the following described real property in the

County of: , State of:

Dated:

STATE OF:

COUNTY OF: }ss

On _____ before me, the undersigned, a Notary Public in and for State, personally appeared

_____

personally known to me or proved to me on the basis of satisfactory evidence to be the person(s) whose name(s) is/are subscribed to the within instrument and acknowledged to me that he/she/they executed the same in his/her/their authorized capacity(ies), and that by his/her/their signature(s) on the instrument the person(s), or the entity upon behalf of which the person(s) acted, executed the instrument.

WITNESS my hand and official seal

Signature _____   (This area for official notary seal)

MAIL TAX STATEMENTS AS DIRECTED ABOVE

Example: Cal sells his house to Margaret, and, without telling Margaret, also sells it to Anita. Anita records her deed before Margaret has a chance to record hers. Anita is the owner of record and gets the house. Margaret has a definite cause for a lawsuit against Cal.

However, there are some exceptions to the "first to record is first in right" rule. If the same property is sold to two parties, and the second party knows of the first sale and is aware of the fraud intended by the seller, the original sale is valid, even if it was not recorded first.

Also, as you recall, possession is considered constructive notice, just like recording. So, if a deed is not recorded, but the buyer moves in, that sale has priority over later recorded deeds.

Example: Greta sells her house to Victor, who moves in without recording the deed. Greta also sells the house to Alex, telling him to record the deed quickly, making him aware that she had previously sold it to Victor. In this case, Victor gets the house because of Alex's knowledge of the prior sale and also because of Victor's possession of the property (he had moved in), which established his right of ownership.

A grantee must accept a deed before it is considered effective. Acceptance is automatic if the grantee is an infant or incompetent person. Acceptance may be shown by the acts of the grantee, such as moving onto the property.

The grant deed need not be signed by the grantee. An undated, unrecorded and unacknowledged grant deed may be valid as long as it contains the essential items required for a valid deed. Here is a list of non-essentials for a grant deed to be valid:

Review - Not Necessary for Valid Grant Deed
- Acknowledgment
- Recording
- Competent grantee; may be a minor, felon or incompetent
- Date
- Mention of the consideration
- Signature of grantee
- Habendum clause (to have and to hold)
- Seal or witnesses
- Legal description, an adequate description is sufficient

RECORDING REQUESTED BY

AND WHEN RECORDED MAIL TO

NAME
ADDRESS
CITY
STATE & ZIP

MAIL TAX STATEMENTS TO

NAME
ADDRESS
CITY
STATE & ZIP

Title Order No. _____ Escrow No. _____

SPACE ABOVE THIS LINE FOR RECORDER'S USE

QUITCLAIM DEED

The undersigned grantor(s) declares(s) that the documentary transfer tax is _____ and is

☐ Computed on the full value of the interest or property conveyed, or is

☐ Computed on the full value less the value of liens or encumbrances remaining at time of sale.

☐ Unincorporated area of: _____ ☐ City of: _____ and

FOR A VALUABLE CONSIDERATION, receipt of which is hereby acknowledged.

hereby REMISE(S), RELEASE(S) AND FOREVER QUITCLAIM(S) to

the following described real property in the

County of: _____ , State of:

Dated: _____

STATE OF: _____

COUNTY OF: _____ }ss

_____

On _____ before me, the
undersigned, a Notary Public in and for State,
personally appeared

_____

_____

_____

personally known to me or proved to me on the basis of satisfactory evidence to be the person(s) whose
name(s) is/are subscribed to the within instrument and acknowledged to me that he/she/they executed the
same in his/her/their authorized capacity(ies), and that by his/her/their signature(s) on the instrument the
person(s), or the entity upon behalf of which the person(s) acted, executed the instrument.

WITNESS my hand and official seal

Signature _____ (This area for official notary seal)

MAIL TAX STATEMENTS AS DIRECTED ABOVE

Quitclaim Deed

A **quitclaim deed** contains no warranties and transfers any interest the grantor may have at the time the deed is signed. It is often used to clear a cloud on the title. A cloud on title is any condition that affects the clear title of real property or minor defect in the chain of title which needs to be removed. A quitclaim is used to transfer interests between husband and wife or to terminate an easement. If a buyer defaults on a loan carried back by the seller, the fastest way to clear title would be for the defaulting buyer to sign a quitclaim deed to the seller.

Gift Deed

A **gift deed** is used to make a gift of property to a grantee, usually a close friend or relative. The consideration in a gift deed is called **love and affection.**

Warranty Deed

A **warranty deed** is a document containing express covenants of title and is rarely used in California because title companies have taken over the role of insuring title to property.

Financing Instruments

Since the **deed of trust** and **deed of reconveyance** are primarily financing instruments, they will be discussed in Chapter 9.

Public Grant

Real property can be transferred by **public grant**, which is the transfer of title by the government to a private individual. In the last century many people moved west and improved land by building and planting crops. As they qualified for ownership under the homestead laws, they received a patent from the government as proof of ownership. A **patent** is the document used by the government to transfer title to land instead of using a deed.

Public Dedication

When real property is intended for public use, it may be acquired as a **public dedication**. There are three means of public dedication: (1) common law dedication, (2) statutory dedication and (3) deed.

In a **common law dedication**, a property owner implies through his or her conduct the intent that the public use the land. In order to be effective, the dedication must be accepted by public use or local ordinance.

A **statutory dedication** is a dedication made by a private individual to the public. An owner follows procedures outlined in the Subdivision Map Act—commonly used by developers to dedicate streets and common areas to the public.

A **deed** is a formal transfer by a party as in a gift deed where there is no consideration.

Operation of Law

Sometimes property is transferred by the operation of law. It is usually an involuntary transfer involving foreclosure or is the result of a judgment or some other lien against the title. There are a variety of situations in which courts establish legal title regardless of the desires of the record owners.

Foreclosure

The legal process used by a lender to seize property of a homeowner, usually due to the homeowner not making timely payments on the mortgage is called **foreclosure**. This will be discussed in greater detail in Chapter 9.

Bankruptcy

The court proceeding to relieve a person's or company's financial insolvency is called **bankruptcy**. A person whose debts exceed assets and who is unable to pay current liabilities is financially insolvent.

In a "Chapter 7" bankruptcy, known as a "liquidation bankruptcy", title to all of the debtor's real property is **vested** in a court-appointed **trustee**. The debtor lists (schedules) all of the debts he or she owes. The bankruptcy judge may discharge the debts or may sell the debtor's property to satisfy the claims of the creditors. Creditors' claims are discharged as of the date of the filing. Although most of the person's or company's debts are forgiven, not all debts can be discharged through bankruptcy. Nondischargeable debts include: income taxes, child support, alimony, student loans, gambling debts, and criminal fines.

Quiet title action

Quiet title action is a court proceeding to clear a cloud on the title of real property. It is frequently used to clear tax titles, titles based on adverse possession, and the seller's title under a forfeited, recorded land contract.

Execution sale

An execution sale is a forced sale of property under a "writ of execution" with the proceeds used to satisfy a money judgment. A sheriff's deed is given to a buyer when property is sold through court action in order to satisfy a judgment for money or foreclosure of a mortgage.

Partition action

Partition action is a court proceeding to settle a dispute between co-owners (joint tenants or tenants in common) about dividing their interests in real property. The court can physically divide either the property or the money derived from its sale.

Partition action is a court proceeding to settle a dispute between co-owners (joint tenants or tenants in common) about dividing their interests in real property.

Escheat

Escheat is a legal process in which property reverts to the state because the deceased owner left no will and has no legal heirs. The state must wait five years before trying to claim the property.

Eminent domain

The power of **eminent domain** is the power of the government to take private property for the public use after paying "just compensation" to the owner. **Just compensation** is fair and reasonable payment due to a private property owner when his or her property is condemned under eminent domain.

Condemnation is the process by which the government acquires private property for public use, under its right of eminent domain. This right is based on the **Fifth Amendment** of the U. S. Constitution and is not an example of **police power** or zoning.

Inverse condemnation is the opposite of eminent domain. With inverse condemnation, a private party forces the government to pay just compensation if the property value or use has been diminished by a public entity. For example, if part of a farmer's land is condemned for freeway construction, leaving an unusable piece which is cut off from the rest of the farm, the farmer could sue for inverse condemnation since the small piece has been effectively taken without "just compensation".

Review - Five Ways to Acquire or Convey Property
Mnemonic = "WASTO"
W ill
A ccession
S uccession
T ransfer
O ccupancy

Summary

Ownership of real property requires a title. A **title** is evidence that a person has a legal right in the land. An **encumbrance** is anything that affects or limits title to property such as a mortgage. There are two types of encumbrances: (1) those that affect the title to the property (money encumbrances, called liens) and (2) those that affect the use of the property (non-money encumbrances).

A **lien** is a claim that a person has on the property as security for a debt or obligation. **Trust deeds** or **mortgages** used in real estate financing create voluntary, specific liens against real property. Anyone who supplies labor or materials for improvements and remains unpaid by the property owner can place a **mechanic's lien** against the property. There are four steps to verify and record a lien: (1) **preliminary notice**, (2) **notice of completion**, (3) **no notice of completion**, and (4) **foreclosure action**.

A **lis pendens** is a recorded notice that indicates pending litigation affecting the title on a property. The lis pendens clouds the title, preventing the sale or transfer of the property. A property owner initiates proceedings to remove the **cloud on the title** by a **quitclaim deed** or court action.

A **non-money encumbrance** affects the use of property. Types of non-money encumbrances are **easements**, building restrictions, and **encroachments**. There are two types of easements: **servient tenement**, and **dominant tenement**. **Abandonment, destruction** of the servient tenement, and **adverse possession**, can also terminate easements. CC&Rs can place restrictions on the use of property. There are two types of CC&Rs: **condition subsequent** and **condition precedent**. **Encroachment** is the placement of permanent improvements on adjacent property owned by another.

A **Declaration of Homestead** is the recorded document that protects a homeowner from foreclosure by certain judgment creditors.

Chapter 3   Review Exercises

Matching Exercise

Instructions: Look up the meaning of the terms in the Glossary, then write the letter of the matching term on the blank line before its definition. Answers are in Appendix B.

Terms

a. abandonment

b. accession

c. accretion

d. alienate

e. avulsion

f. bequest

g. codicil

h. easement in gross

i. encroachment

j. executor

k. grantee

l. grantor

m. homestead

n. instrument

o. intestate

p. license

q. lis pendens

r. quiet title action

s. reliction

t. succession

Definitions

1. _____ An easement that is not appurtenant to any one parcel. For example, the rights given to public utilities to install power lines.

2. _____ Permission to use a property which may be revoked at any time.

3. _____ The unauthorized placement of permanent improvements that intrude on adjacent property owned by another.

4. _____ Status provided to a homeowner's principal residence that protects the home against judgments up to specified amounts.

5. _____ A gift of personal property by will.

6. _____ Dying without leaving a will.

7. _____ The acquisition of title to additional land or to improvements as a result of annexing fixtures, or as a result of natural causes such as alluvial deposits along the banks of streams by accretion.

8. _____ A buildup of soil by natural causes on property bordering a river, lake, or ocean.

9. _____ Occurs when land that has been covered by water is exposed by receding of the water.

10. _____ The act of transferring ownership, title, or interest.

11. _____ The person receiving the property, or to whom it is being conveyed.

12. _____ The person conveying or transferring the property.

13. _____ A document in real estate.

14. _____ It is a court proceeding to clear a cloud on the title of real property.

15. _____ A recorded notice that indicates pending litigation affecting title on a property, preventing a conveyance or any other transfer of ownership until the lawsuit is settled and the lis pendens removed.

Multiple Choice Questions

Instructions: Circle your response and go to Appendix B to read the complete explanation for each question.

1. Which of the following is the best definition of encumbrance?
   a. The degree, quantity, nature, and extent of interest that a person has in real property.
   b. Anything that affects or limits the fee simple title to or value of property.
   c. The use of property as security for a debt.
   d. Any action regarding property, other than acquiring or transferring title.

2. The form of encumbrance that makes specific property the security for the payment of a debt or discharge of an obligation is called a:
   a. reservation.
   b. fief.
   c. lien.
   d. quitclaim.

3. A recorded judgment is usually classified as a(n) _____ lien.
   a. equitable
   b. involuntary
   c. inferior
   d. superior

4. Recording a lis pendens:
    a. does not affect the title.
    b. clouds the title but does not affect marketability.
    c. clouds the title and affects marketability.
    d. affects the current owner but not a subsequent owner.

5. The owner of an apartment building does not declare the income from the rental units. The IRS filed a government tax lien as a result of the omission. This is called a:
    a. voluntary lien.
    b. general lien.
    c. judgment lien.
    d. none of the above

6. The personal, revocable, unassignable permission to use the property of another without a possessory interest in it is called a(n):
    a. license.
    b. easement.
    c. encroachment.
    d. option.

7. Roger, who owns a ranch, gave Sam who owns no property, a non-revocable right to cross his ranch to fish in the stream. Sam has a(n):
    a. easement in gross.
    b. license.
    c. easement appurtenant.
    d. easement by prescription.

8. Private restrictions on land can be created by deed:
    a. only.
    b. or written agreement.
    c. or zoning ordinance.
    d. or written agreement or zoning ordinance.

9. Alienation of title to real property most nearly means to:
    a. cloud the title.
    b. encumber the title.
    c. record a homestead.
    d. convey or transfer title and possession.

10. To be binding on a buyer and a seller, a deed to transfer real property must be:
    a. recorded.
    b. delivered and accepted.
    c. acknowledged.
    d. all of the above.

11. A grant deed is considered executed when it is:
    a. recorded by the grantee.
    b. signed by the grantor.
    c. acknowledged by the grantee.
    d. delivered by the grantor.

12. Effective delivery of a deed depends on:
    a. the intention of the grantor.
    b. recording the deed.
    c. knowledge of its existence by the grantee.
    d. acknowledgment of the grantor's signature before a Notary Public.

13. Dana sold a property to Kim, who did not record the deed but did occupy the premises. Dana then sold the same property to Lee, who did not inspect the property but did record the deed. After the second sale, who would have legal title to the property?
    a. The title would revert to Dana as the remainderman.
    b. The title would remain with Kim.
    c. The title would be Lee's due to Kim's failure to record his deed.
    d. Lee would be able to sue Kim for his failure to record his deed.

14. An owner of a parcel of real property gave his neighbor a deed conveying an easement for ingress and egress. The easement was not specifically located in the deed. Under the circumstances, the neighbor's right to use the easement is:
    a. enforceable because the location of the easement does not need to be specified.
    b. enforceable only if the easement is an easement in gross.
    c. unenforceable because the location of the easement must be specified.
    d. unenforceable because easements are never created by deed, only by written agreement.

15. Which of the following actions is a quiet title action?
    a. Court action to foreclose
    b. Court action in ejectment
    c. Police action to quiet a noisy neighbor
    d. Court action to remove a cloud on title

Contracts: The Basics

4

Chapter

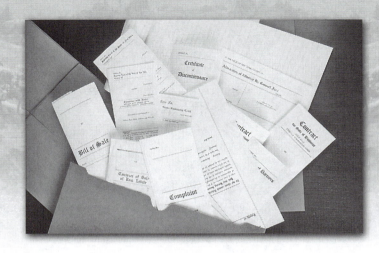

Introduction

Every time you are involved in a real estate transaction, you will use a contract that transfers or indicates an interest in the property. It is important that you understand the nature of legal agreements, so you are able to explain them to your **clients** and **customers** as part of your role as a real estate agent. This chapter explains what a contract is and how contracts are used to assure the understanding and approval of all parties to an agreement.

Learning Objectives

After reading this chapter, you will be able to:

- define contract.
- discuss the legal requirements for an enforceable contract.
- describe performance of contracts and give two examples.
- explain Statute of Frauds.
- identify the remedies for breach of contract.

Contracts in General

A **contract** is a legally enforceable agreement made by competent parties, to perform or not perform a certain act. It may be an **express contract**, where the parties declare the terms and put their intentions in words, either oral or written. A lease or rental agreement, for example, is an express contract. The landlord agrees to allow the tenant to live in the apartment and the renter agrees to pay rent in return.

A contract may be an **implied contract** in which agreement is shown by act and conduct rather than words. When we go into a restaurant and order food, go to a movie or have a daily newspaper delivered, we create a contract. By showing a desire to use a service, we imply that we will pay for it.

Contracts may be bilateral or unilateral. A **bilateral contract** is an agreement in which each person promises to perform an act in exchange for another person's promise to perform. In other words, both parties must keep their agreement for the contract to be completed. An example might be a promise from a would-be pilot to pay $2,500 for flying lessons, and a return promise from the instructor to teach him or her to fly.

A **unilateral contract** is a contract where a party promises to perform without expectation of performance by the other party. The second party is not bound to act, but if he or she does, the first party is obligated to keep the promise. An example might be a radio station offering $1,000 to the 100th caller. Some lucky person makes the call and the station pays the money. An option is another example of a unilateral contract.

A contract may be executory or executed. In an **executory contract**, something remains to be performed by one or both parties. An escrow that is not yet closed or a contract not signed by the parties are examples of executory contracts. In an **executed contract**, all parties have performed completely. One of the meanings of execute is to sign, or complete in some way. An executed contract may be a sales agreement that has been signed by all parties.

Contracts may be void, voidable, unenforceable or valid. A **void contract** is no contract at all or no legal effect (example: due to lack of capacity, illegal subject matter). A **voidable contract** is valid and enforceable on its face, but may be rejected by one or more of the parties (example: induced by fraud, menace, duress). An **unenforceable contract** is valid, but for some reason cannot be proved by one or both of the parties (example: an oral agreement should be in writing because of the Statute of Frauds). A **valid contract** that is binding and enforceable has all the basic elements required by law.

Basic Elements of All Contracts

In order for a contract to be legally binding and enforceable, there are four requirements: (1) legally competent parties, (2) mutual consent between the parties, (3) lawful objective, and (4) sufficient consideration.

Legally Competent Parties

Parties entering into a contract must have legal capacity to do so. Almost anyone is capable, with a few exceptions. A person must be at least 18 years of age, unless married, in the military or declared emancipated by the court.

A minor is not capable of appointing an agent, or entering into an **agency** agreement with a broker to buy or sell. Brokers dealing with minors should proceed cautiously and should seek an attorney's advice. A contract with a minor is considered voidable by the minor.

When it has been determined judicially that a person is not of sound mind, the contract made by the incompetent person is terminated. If it is obvious that a person is completely without understanding there can be no contract. In the case of an incompetent, a court-appointed guardian would have legal capacity to contract. Both minors and incompetents may acquire title to real property by gift or inheritance. However, any transfer of acquired property must be court approved.

A contract made by a person who is intoxicated or under the influence of legal or illegal drugs can be cancelled when the individual sobers up. Or the contract may be **ratified** (approved after the fact) depending on the parties.

Any person may give another the authority to act on his or her behalf. The legal document that does this is called a **power of attorney.** The person holding the power of attorney is an attorney-in-fact. When dealing with real property, a power of attorney must be recorded to be valid, and is good for as long as the **principal** is competent. A power of attorney can be cancelled by the principal at any time by recording a **revocation**. A power of attorney is useful, for example, when a buyer or seller is out of town and has full trust in that **agent** to operate in his or her behalf.

Mutual Consent Between the Parties

In a valid contract, all parties must mutually agree. **Mutual consent** (or mutual assent), is sometimes called a "**meeting of the minds**". It is an offer by one party and acceptance by the other party.

Offer

An **offer** shows the contractual intent of the **offeror**, or the person making the offer, to enter into a contract. That offer must be communicated to the **offeree**, or the person to whom the offer is being made. Unconditional acceptance of the offer is necessary for all parties to be legally bound. The offer must be definite and certain in its terms, and the agreement must be genuine or the contract may be voidable by one or both parties.

Acceptance

One party must offer and another must accept, without condition. An acceptance is an unqualified agreement to the terms of an offer. The offeree must agree to every item of the offer for the acceptance to be complete. If the original terms change in any way in the acceptance, the offer becomes a **counteroffer**, and the first offer terminates. The person making the original offer is no longer bound by that offer, and may accept the counteroffer or not. The counteroffer becomes a new offer, made by the original offeree. Acceptance of an offer must be communicated to the offeror, in the manner specified, before a contract becomes binding between the parties. The seller may rescind an offer prior to acceptance. Silence is not considered to be acceptance.

Termination

An offeror is hopeful that his or her offer is accepted in a **timely manner** and a contract created. An offer is specific, and an offeror does not have to wait indefinitely for an answer.

> **Review - An offer may be terminated by:**
> - lapse of time: an offer is revoked if the offeree fails to accept it within a prescribed period.
> - communication of notice of revocation: notice is filed by the offeror anytime before the other party has communicated acceptance.
> - failure of offeree to fulfill a condition of acceptance prescribed by the offeror.
> - a qualified acceptance, or counteroffer by the offeree.
>   - rejection by the offeree.
>   - death or insanity of the offeror or offeree.
>   - unlawful object of the proposed contract.

Genuine Assent

A final requirement for mutual consent is that the offer and acceptance be genuine and freely made by all parties. Genuine assent does not exist if there is fraud, misrepresentation, mistake, duress, menace, or undue influence involved in reaching an agreement.

Fraud

An act meant to deceive in order to get someone to part with something of value is called **fraud**. An outright lie, or making a promise with no intention of carrying it out, can be fraud. Lack of disclosure—causing someone to make or accept an offer—is also fraud. For example, failure to tell a prospective buyer who makes an offer to purchase on a sunny day that the roof leaks is fraud. It can make the contract voidable.

Innocent Misrepresentation

When the person unknowingly provides wrong information, **innocent misrepresentation** occurs. Even though no dishonesty is involved, a contract may be rescinded or revoked by the party who feels misled. The **"hold harmless" clause** protects the broker from incorrect information.

Mistake

In contract law, **mistake** means an agreement was unclear or there was a misunderstanding in the facts. Mistake does not include ignorance, incompetence or poor judgment. For example, you accepted an offer to purchase a home on what you thought was an all cash offer. Later you found that you had agreed to carry a second trust deed. Even though you made a "mistake" in reading the sales contract, you now have a binding agreement.

There are times when ambiguity creates a misunderstanding, and ultimately you void the contract. For instance, you were given directions to a friend's beach house, went there on your own, and fell in love with the home. You immediately made an offer, which was accepted, only to discover you had gone to the wrong house. Because you thought you were purchasing a different property than the one the seller was selling, this "mistake" is a "major misunderstanding of a material fact", and therefore would void any signed contract.

Duress

Use of force, known as **duress** or **menace**, which is the threat of violence, cannot be used to get agreement.

Undue Influence

Undue influence or using unfair advantage is also unacceptable. All can result in a contract to be **voidable** by the injured party.

> **Review - No Genuine Assent If The Contract Involves:**
> - fraud
> - misrepresentation
> - mistake
> - duress or menace
> - undue influence

Lawful Objective

Even though the parties are capable, and mutually agreeable, the object of the contract must be lawful. A contract requiring the performance of an illegal act would not be valid, nor would one where the consideration was stolen.

The contract also must be legal in its formation and operation. For example, a note bearing an **interest** rate in excess of that allowed by law would be void. Contracts contrary to good morals and general public policy are also unenforceable.

Sufficient Consideration

There are several types of consideration one can use in a contract. Generally, consideration is something of value such as a promise of future payment, money, property, or personal services. For example, there can be an exchange of a promise for a promise, money for a promise, money for property, or goods for services. Legally, all contracts require **acceptable consideration**. Terms that denote acceptable consideration include "valuable", "adequate", "good", or "sufficient" consideration.

Forbearance, or forgiving a debt or obligation, or giving up an interest or a right, qualifies as valuable consideration. Gifts such as real property based solely on love and affection are "good consideration". They meet the legal requirement that consideration be present in a contract.

In an option, the promise of the offeror is the consideration for the forbearance desired from the offeree. In other words, the person wanting the option promises to give something of value in return for being able to exercise the option to purchase at some specifically named time in the future.

In a bilateral contract, a promise of one party is consideration for the promise of another. For example, in the sale of real property, the buyer promises to pay a certain amount and the seller promises to transfer title.

Note: The earnest money given at the time of an offer is not the consideration for the sale. It is simply an indication of the buyer's intent to perform the contract, and may be used for damages, even if the buyer backs out of the sale.

Contracts That Must Be In Writing

In California, the Statute of Frauds requires that certain contracts be in writing to prevent fraud in the sale of land or an interest in land. Included in this are offers, acceptances, loan assumptions, land contracts, deeds, escrows, and options to purchase. Trust deeds, promissory notes and leases for more than one year also must be in writing to be enforceable.

The following contracts must be in writing:
- Listings
- Offers
- Deeds
- Options
- Promissory Notes
- Trust Deeds
- Leases for More Than a Year

Statute of Frauds

Most contracts required by law to be in writing are under the **Statute of Frauds**. The statute adopted in England in 1677 became part of English common law. Later, it was introduced to this country and is now part of California's law. The statute's primary purpose is to prevent forgery, perjury and dishonest conduct on the part of unethical people against citizens. Thus, it improves the existence and terms of certain important types of contracts.

The law provides that certain contracts are invalid unless they are in writing and signed by either the parties involved or their agents. The California Civil Code lists the contracts that must be in writing to be enforceable.

Contracts That Must Be In Writing

- Any agreement where the terms are not to be performed within a year from making the contract

- A special promise to answer for the debt, default or no performance of another, except in cases covered by the Civil Code

- An agreement made upon the consideration of marriage, other than a mutual promise to marry

- An agreement to lease real property for a period longer than one year, or to sell real property or an interest therein; also, any agreement authorizing an agent to perform the above acts

- An agreement employing an agent, broker or any other person to purchase, sell or lease real estate for one year; or find a buyer, seller, lessee or lessor for more than one year in return for compensation

- An agreement, which by its terms is not to be performed during the lifetime of the promisor, or an agreement that devises or bequeaths any property, or makes provisions for any reason by will

- An agreement by a purchaser of real estate to pay a debt secured by a trust deed or mortgage on the property purchased, unless assumption of that debt by the purchaser is specifically designated in the conveyance of such property

The Statute of Frauds also affects personal property. The sale of personal property with a value of more than $500 must be accompanied by a bill of sale in writing.

Parol Evidence Rule

When two parties make oral promises to each other, and then write and sign a contract promising something different, the written contract will be considered the valid one. Parol means "oral", or by "word of mouth". The **parol evidence rule** extends this meaning and prohibits introducing any kind of outside evidence to vary or add to the terms of deeds, contracts or other writings once executed. Under the parol evidence rule, when a contract is intended to be the parties' complete and final agreement, no further outside promises, oral or written, are allowed. Occasionally a contract is ambiguous or vague. Then the courts will allow use of prior agreements to clarify an existing disputed contract.

One of a **real estate agent**'s major duties is to make sure all contract language conveys the parties' wishes and agreements. Oral agreements have caused much confusion and bad feelings over the years, particularly in real estate. Even a lease for less than one year should be in writing, though the Statute of Frauds does not require it. (A lease for one or more years must be in writing). It is easy to forget verbal agreements. A written contract is the most reasonable way to ensure mutual assent.

Discharge of Contracts

Discharge of contract refers to the cancellation or termination of a contract. Contracts are discharged by performance, release, assignment, novation, and breach.

Performance

Commonly the discharge of a contract occurs when the contract has been fully performed.

Tender of Performance

A **tender** of performance is an **offer** by one of the parties to carry out his or her part of the contract. Usually, a tender is made at the time to close escrow. The person to whom the tender is made must state any objections at that time or they are **waived**. A **waiver** is the relinquishment or refusal to accept a right. A person must take advantage of his or her rights at the proper time. If they do not, they give up (waive) their rights. A tender of performance by the buyer, for example, by depositing the purchase money into escrow, places the seller in default, if the seller refuses to accept it and deliver a deed. The buyer could rescind the transaction, or sue for breach of contract or for **specific performance.**

Release

The person in the contract to whom an obligation is owed may release the other party from the obligation to perform the contract.

Mutual Rescission

A **mutual rescission** occurs when all parties to a contract agree to cancel the agreement.

Assignment

An assignment will transfer all the interests of the assignor (principal) to the **assignee**. The assignee takes over the assignor's rights, remedies, benefits and duties in the contract. In this situation, the assignor is not completely released from the obligations for the contract and remains secondarily liable.

Novation

If the assignor wants to be released entirely from any obligation for the contract, it may be done by **novation**. That is the substitution, by agreement, of a new obligation for an existing one, with the intent to extinguish the original contract. For example, novation occurs when a buyer assumes a seller's loan, and the lender releases the seller from the loan contract by substituting the buyer's name on the loan.

Breach

Occasionally the result is a breach of contract, where someone does not fulfill the agreement. A breach of contract is a failure to perform on

> **Three Remedies for Breach of Contract**
> - Unilateral Rescission
> - Lawsuit for money damages
> - Lawsuit for specific performance

part or all of the terms and conditions of a contract. A person harmed by non-performance can accept the failure to perform or has a choice of three remedies: unilateral rescission, lawsuit for money damages or lawsuit for specific performance.

Unilateral Rescission

Unilateral rescission is available to a person who enters a contract without genuine assent because of fraud, mistake, duress, menace, undue influence, or faulty consideration. Rescission may be used as a means of discharging a contract by agreement, as we have mentioned.

If one of the parties has been wronged by a breach of contract that innocent party can stop performing all obligations as well, therefore unilaterally rescinding the contract. It must be done promptly, restoring to the other party everything of value received as a result of the breached contract, on condition that the other party shall do the same.

Lawsuit for Money Damages

When a party is a breach-of-contract victim, a second remedy is a **lawsuit for money damages**. If damages to an injured party are expressed in a dollar amount, the innocent party could sue for money damages to include: the price paid by the buyer, the difference between the contract price and the value of the property, title and document expenses, consequential damages and interest.

Lawsuit for Specific Performance

A third remedy for breach of contract is a **lawsuit for specific performance**. This is an action in court by the injured party to force the breaching party to carry out the remainder of the contract according to the agreed-upon terms, price, and conditions. Generally, this remedy occurs when money cannot restore an injured party's position. This is often the case in real estate because of the difficulty in finding a similar property.

> **Review - Discharge of Contracts**
> - Full performance
> - Release by one or all of the parties
> - Assignment
> - Novation
> - Breach of contract

Preprinted Forms

What about using and changing preprinted real estate forms? If the parties involved want to make handwritten changes and initial them, those changes control the document.

Generally, when using preprinted forms:

- specific information takes precedence over general information.

- typed clauses and insertions take precedence over the preprinted material.

Many real estate forms are now electronic and can be downloaded.

- handwritten clauses and insertions take precedence over the typed and preprinted material.

Statute of Limitations

Under California law, any person seeking relief for a breach of contract must do so within the guidelines of the **Statute of Limitations**. This set of laws determines that civil actions start only within the time periods prescribed by law. Filing lawsuits within the allowed time prevents this right from expiring. Here are some actions of special interest to real estate agents, with the time frames required.

Actions Which Must Be Brought Within:

90 Days—Civil actions to recover personal property such as suitcases, clothing or jewelry alleged to have been left at a hotel or in an apartment; must begin within 90 days after the owners depart from the personal property.

Six Months—An action against an officer to recover property seized in an official capacity—such as by a tax collector.

One Year—Libel or slander, injury or death caused by wrongful act, or loss to depositor against a bank for the payment of a forged check.

Two Years—Action on a contract, not in writing; action based on a policy of title insurance.

Three Years—Action on a liability created by statute; action for trespass on or injury to real property, such as encroachment; action for relief on the grounds of fraud or mistake; attachment.

Four Years—An action on any written contract; includes most real estate contracts.

10 Years—Action on a judgment or decree of any court in the United States.

Summary

A **contract** is a legally enforceable agreement to perform or not perform a certain act. There are five types of contracts: (1) **express contracts,** (2) **implied contracts,** (3) **bilateral contracts,** (4) **unilateral contracts**, and (5) **executory contracts.** A contract may be executory or executed. Contracts are void, voidable, unenforceable or valid.

There are four requirements for a contract to be legally binding and enforceable: (1) legally competent parties, (2) mutual consent between the parties, a (3) lawful objective, and (4) sufficient consideration.

In a valid contract, all parties must mutually agree ("meeting of the minds"). One party must offer and another must accept unconditionally. An **acceptance** is an unqualified agreement to the terms of an offer. The offer must be definite and certain in its terms, and the agreement must be genuine or the contract may be voidable by one or both parties. A **counteroffer** becomes a new offer, made by the original party (offeree).

Parties must take advantage of their rights at the proper time. For example, a person must state any objections at the time of contract performance.

Parties can terminate a contract by performance, release, assignment, novation, and breach.

All contracts require acceptable consideration. Types of **acceptable consideration** are valuable, adequate, good, or sufficient consideration. **Forbearance** (forgiving a debt) also qualifies as consideration.

The **California Statute of Frauds** requires that certain contracts be in writing to prevent fraud in the sale of land or an interest in land. Seven contracts are under the umbrella of the Statute of Frauds. Written contracts are valid and enforceable.

When using preprinted forms, make sure the document focuses on specific information. Typed or handwritten clauses and insertions take priority over the preprinted material.

Chapter 4   Review Exercises

Matching Exercise

Instructions: Look up the meaning of the terms in the Glossary, then write the letter of the matching term on the blank line before its definition. Answers are in Appendix B.

Terms

a. abrogation
b. addendum
c. assignee
d. assignor
e. consideration
f. counteroffer
g. executory contract
h. express contract
i. forbearance
j. novation

k. offer
l. offeree
m. offeror
n. rescission
o. revocation
p. specific performance
q. Statute of Frauds
r. Statute of Limitations
s. tender
t. waiver

Definitions

1. _____ The rejection of an original offer that becomes a new offer.

2. _____ A presentation or proposal for acceptance to form a contract.

3. _____ Something of value-such as money, a promise, property or personal services.

4. _____ An offer by one of the parties to carry out his or her part of the contract.

5. _____ The law that requires contracts to be in writing.

6. _____ The relinquishment or refusal to accept a right.

7. _____ The person transferring a claim, benefit, or right in property to another.

8. _____ A court action brought to compel a party to carry out the terms of a contract.

9. _____ A contract in which obligation to perform exists on one or both sides.

10. _____ The canceling of an offer to contract by the person making the original offer.

11. _____ Party to whom a lease is assigned or transferred.

12. _____ Legal action taken to repeal a contract either by mutual consent of the parties or by one party when the other party has breached a contract.

13. _____ The party making an offer.

14. _____ The substitution by agreement of a new obligation for an existing one.

15. _____ Parties declare the terms and put their intentions in oral or written words.

Multiple Choice Questions

Instructions: Circle your response and go to Appendix B to read the complete explanation for each question.

1. An agreement to do or not to do a certain thing is called:
   a. a contract.
   b. forbearance.
   c. mutual consent.
   d. negotiation.

2. When a promise is given by both parties with the expectation of performance by the other party, it is known as a(n) _____ contract.
   a. unilateral
   b. bilateral
   c. implied
   d. express

3. A minor cannot hire a real estate broker using a listing agreement because a minor:
   a. can disaffirm the contract.
   b. is legally incapable.
   c. is incapable of making an adult decision.
   d. cannot do so without parental approval.

4. All of the following are necessary for a valid contract, **except**:
   a. sufficient writing.
   b. genuine consent.
   c. lawful object.
   d. capable parties.

5. All of the following are necessary for a valid contract **except**:
    a. payment of money.
    b. genuine consent.
    c. lawful object.
    d. adequate mental capacity of the contracting parties.

6. The following are necessary elements to create a valid contract, **except**:
    a. consideration.
    b. acceptance.
    c. offer.
    d. performance.

7. Another name for mutual assent is:
    a. unilateral agreement.
    b. meeting of the minds.
    c. implied agreement.
    d. executory agreement.

8. A contract signed under duress is:
    a. void.
    b. voidable.
    c. illicit.
    d. enforceable.

9. Consideration is one of the necessary elements of a valid contract. Which of the following is consideration?
    a. A promise to perform an act
    b. An exchange of money
    c. A service rendered
    d. All of the above

10. An oral agreement for the sale of a business is:
    a. valid.
    b. void.
    c. voidable.
    d. unenforceable.

11. The essential element needed to create a binding employment contract for the sale of any right, title or interest in real property is a(n):
    a. written instrument.
    b. written authorization to accept offers on the property.
    c. written agreement as to the amount of commission.
    d. authorization to accept a deposit.

12. A written contract takes precedence over oral agreements. This principle is expressed by the:
    a. Statute of Limitations.
    b. Statute of Frauds.
    c. parol evidence rule.
    d. rule of previous evidence.

13. The relinquishment or refusal to accept a right is known as:
    a. tender.
    b. waiver.
    c. novation.
    d. forbearance.

14. A synonym for rescind is:
    a. abate.
    b. annul.
    c. abolish.
    d. abrogate.

15. The substitution of an obligation or contract with a new one is called:
    a. rescission.
    b. subordination.
    c. novation.
    d. conversion.

Agency Relationships

5 Chapter

Introduction

As a real estate licensee, your main job will be to represent someone else in a real estate transaction. When that person gives you the authority to act on his or her behalf, it creates a special legal relationship called agency, which is defined, within real estate law, by a body of laws called agency law. This chapter will outline the different types of relationships you as a licensee can form with a client. These relationships are called agency relationships. Agency law affects all of your dealings as a licensee—all of your agency relationships.

The purpose of agency law is to make sure you know who you are representing and what your obligations are when you act for another person. Your success in real estate sales will depend on your knowledge of agency law. Consumers rely on you to explain the law as well as to make sure it is carried out. They want to be assured that you are representing their best interests.

Learning Objectives

After reading this chapter, you will be able to:

- define agency and list two reasons for creating an agency.
- describe the fiduciary relationship between the principal and real estate broker.
- name two real estate agency violations and the appropriate legal action.
- explain the responsibilities of a broker and real estate sales associates.
- explain an agency disclosure document and use the document.
- discuss termination of agency.

What is Agency?

Agency is a legal relationship in which a principal authorizes an agent to act as the principal's representative when dealing with third parties. This creates a **fiduciary** relationship between the agent and the principal. A fiduciary relationship implies a position of trust or confidence. The agent is in a position of trust or confidence with the principal and owes the principal certain fiduciary duties. The agent has the fiduciary duty of loyalty, integrity, and utmost care to the principal. This means that the agent bound by agency law acts in the best interests of the principal. There is an obligation always to act fairly and honestly with third parties. The law compares the fiduciary duties owed by the agent to the principal, as to the **trustee** to a **beneficiary**, or like a **mortgagee** to **mortgagor**.

> **The agent works for the principal and with third parties.**

An agent is either a special agent or **general agent**. This depends on the scope of authority delegated to the agent by the principal. A **special agent** is employed to perform a specific task, whereas any other agent would be a **general agent**. A real estate broker, for example, who has a contract is a special agent authorized to perform certain acts for a specified time.

The authority given an agent is determined by the principal. If described in a written agreement, it is called **actual authority**. A principal is not responsible for the acts of the agent if those acts are beyond the agent's actual authority. If the principal has not given the agent actual or ostensible (apparent) authority to do the act, a third party cannot hold the principal responsible. An agent may have authority under a power of attorney, allowing him or her to conduct certain business for a principal. A **power of attorney** is a written document that gives a person legal authority to act on behalf of another person. Typically there are two types used in real estate: special and general. A **special power of attorney** authorizes the agent to do certain specific acts. A **general power of attorney** allows the agent to transact all the business of the principal. The agent is then known as an attorney-in-fact.

Agency Relationships in Real Estate

As we just learned, every agency relationship has a principal, an agent, and a third party. In a real estate transaction the **principal** (buyer or seller), **agent** (real estate broker) and **third party** (customer) are bound together in a legal relationship, with all the duties and rights that go with that connection. Most frequently, the principal is a seller who employs an agent to find a buyer for his or her property. Sometimes the principal is a buyer who employs an agent to locate a property.

The Broker is the Agent

The agent is always a licensed real estate broker. That is why a listing broker is also called a listing agent; a selling broker is also called a selling agent; and a buyer's broker is also called a buyer's agent. When a broker represents only the buyer or the seller in the transaction, it is called single agency. A dual agency exists if one broker represents both principals in the transaction.

Review - Agency Relationships

Agent (Broker)	Principal (Client)	Third Party (Customer)
Listing Agent	Seller	Buyer
Subagent	Seller	Buyer
Buyer's Agent	Buyer	Seller
Selling Agent	Seller or Buyer	Buyer or Seller
Cooperating Broker	Seller or Buyer	Buyer or Seller
Dual Agent	Seller & Buyer	No Third Party

Listing Agent

A **listing agent** is a broker who obtains a listing from a seller to act as an agent for compensation. A **listing** is a contract between an owner of real property and an agent who is authorized to obtain a buyer.

Subagent

A **subagent** is a broker delegated by the listing agent (*if authorized by the seller*) who represents the seller in finding a buyer for the listed property.

Buyer's Agent

A **buyer's agent** is a broker employed by the buyer to locate a certain kind of real property.

Dual Agent

A **dual agent** is a broker acting as agent for both the seller and the buyer in the same transaction. A broker can legally be the agent of both the seller and the buyer in a transaction, but the broker must have the informed, written consent of both the seller and the buyer. The dual agent is a broker who may be working independently or through an associate licensee. A real estate broker who has a listing agreement with a seller may establish an agency with a buyer as well. In this case, whether the broker is the actual agent of both the seller and the buyer, or the agent of the seller and the ostensible or implied agent of the buyer, the broker is acting as a dual agent. Dual agency commonly occurs when two associate licensees employed by the same broker represent two or more parties to a transaction. The real estate broker is then a dual agent.

A real estate broker who represents both buyer and seller must act with extreme care because the broker owes fiduciary duties to both principals. The broker would have conflict with the negotiation of price and terms between seller and buyer and the negotiation of loan amount and terms between lender and borrower. A real estate broker functioning as a dual agent may not disclose to the seller that the buyer is willing to pay more than the buyer's written offer to purchase. A dual agent cannot disclose to the buyer that the seller will take less than the listing agreement, without the express written consent of the party authorizing the disclosure.

Selling Agent

A **selling agent** is the broker who finds a buyer and obtains an offer for the real property. Usually a cooperating broker, the selling agent (broker) may act as a subagent of the seller, as an agent of the buyer, or as a dual agent.

Cooperating Broker

A **cooperating broker** is a selling agent who assists another broker by finding a buyer. A cooperating broker participates in the multiple listing service (MLS), and finds a buyer for a property listed in MLS. A cooperating broker may represent either the seller or the buyer.

Is the Cooperating Broker a Subagent?

Most property is sold through a local association of brokers called a multiple listing service. A **multiple listing service (MLS)** is a cooperative listing service conducted by a group of brokers, usually members of a real estate association. Listings are submitted to a central bureau where they are entered into a computerized system and printed regularly in a multiple listing book that is available to the members. The MLS maintains an inventory of all the available, listed properties in the area. Any MLS member may view the listed properties and obtain offers from buyers for these properties even though he or she is not the listing broker.

A broker who brings an offer to the listing broker in this way is called a cooperating broker. The cooperating broker receives a part of the commission at the close of escrow.

Since a cooperating broker finds the buyer, an issue that can be confusing is the question of whether the cooperating broker represents the seller or the buyer. Buyers commonly believe that the cooperating broker represents the buyer. Others assume that the cooperating broker is a subagent of the listing broker and represents the seller.

A **subagent** is defined as the agent of someone who is already the agent of the principal. If authorized by the seller, the listing agent can delegate another broker to be a subagent who will also represent the seller. Therefore, subagents take on the same fiduciary duties as primary agents. If the cooperating broker is a subagent for the seller, then the cooperating broker owes a fiduciary duty and loyalty to the seller. If the cooperating broker represents the buyer, the fiduciary duty is to the buyer.

Nothing in the listing agreement compels the cooperating broker to represent the seller. A seller authorizes the listing broker to cooperate in any manner with other brokers in showing the property, but the seller must give specific authorization for subagency. If authorized, the listing broker may offer subagency to a cooperating broker, and the cooperating broker may accept or decline the offer. (Acceptance could be in writing or by the conduct of the cooperating broker).

Thus, a cooperating broker does not automatically become a subagent when he or she shows a listed property. As long as complete disclosure is made about agency relationships, the cooperating broker can represent either the seller or the buyer.

Cooperating brokers should choose to be either the seller's agent or the buyer's agent, and make sure their actions conform to their choice. They should be aware of the practical and legal consequences of this choice to avoid a conflict of loyalties or a violation of **real estate law.**

In general, if the cooperating broker is acting like the agent of the buyer, he or she is the agent of the buyer. An agency relationship is created between the broker and the buyer by implication. The buyer becomes the cooperating broker's principal, and the seller becomes the **third party.** When the buyer makes an offer, he or she signs the Confirmation of Agency form and confirms the agency relationship in writing. Until that point, there is no clear rule about when the fiduciary relationship starts between the cooperating broker and the buyer. It is safe to assume that the agency relationship starts as soon as the cooperating broker begins acting in the best interest of the buyer.

The Orange County Association of Realtors addresses the optional nature of subagency in Rule 7.12

Rule 7.12 Unilateral Contractual Offer; Subagency Optional. In filing a property with the MLS, the broker participant makes a blanket unilateral contractual offer of compensation to the other MLS broker participants for their services in selling the property. A broker participant must specify some compensation to be paid to either a buyer's agent or a subagent and the offer of compensation must be stated in one, or a combination of the following forms (1) a percentage of the gross selling price; or (2) a definite dollar amount. At the broker participant's option, a broker participant may limit his or her offer of compensation to buyer's agents only, to subagents only, or make the offer of compensation to both. Any such limitations must be specified on the property data form and in the MLS. The amount of compensation offered to buyer's agents or subagents may be the same or different but must be clearly specified on the property data profile sheet. Broker participants wishing to offer subagency to the other MLS participants must so specify on the property data profile sheet and on the MLS; otherwise, the offer of compensation does not constitute an offer of subagency.

Agents Working for the Broker

A **sales associate** (also called an **associate licensee**) is a licensed real estate salesperson or broker whose license is held by an employing licensed broker. The sales associate works for an employing broker, and the employing broker is responsible for the acts of the sales associate. A sales associate is the agent of his or her employing broker and must deal fairly with the broker's customers. Sales associates are not agents of the buyer or seller in a real property transaction.

> Example: Rose, a sales associate in the employ of broker Dan, listed a property owned by Jose Miranda. Under the law, the agency has been created between Jose Miranda and broker Dan. Rose is bound by the agency because she represents Dan.

Review - Agency
- **In a real estate transaction, the agent is always a broker.**
- **In a listing agreement:**
  - the agent of the seller (principal) is the listing agent or listing broker.
  - a subagent represents the seller.
  - a broker who works with the buyer (third party) can be the selling agent or cooperating broker.
- **A broker who represents both buyer and seller is a dual agent.**
- **In a buyer representation agreement:**
  - the agent of the buyer is the buyer's agent or buyer broker.

Disclosing the Agency Relationship

Traditionally, the principal in a real estate transaction was a seller, represented by the listing broker. The selling broker might have represented the principal as a subagent. Then, as now, the selling broker was legally bound by a fiduciary duty to the seller. So who represented the buyer when the listing broker wrote up the offer? Who represented the buyer when a selling broker wrote up the offer and presented it to the seller? The answer is—no one. Legally, the buyer had no representation, even though it appeared to be the licensed agent showing the property and writing up the offer.

The requirement to disclose agency and reveal what relationship the parties have with each other came out of public demand for assurance of representation in all real estate dealings.

As of January 1, 1988, the **Agency Relationship Disclosure Act** became effective in an attempt to clarify the agency relationships between sellers, agents and buyers. It applies to every residential property transaction of one-to-four units. The law requires that an agent supply a written document, called Disclosure Regarding Real Estate Agency Relationships, explaining the nature of agency. This disclosure must be made **prior** to taking a listing or writing an offer.

Disclosure Process

The steps in the disclosure process are: disclose, elect, and confirm. (Mnemonic "DEC").

Disclose the Relationship

The Disclosure Regarding Real Estate Agency Relationships document describes the obligations of an agent as "seller's agent", "buyer's agent", or "dual agent". At this point, all parties are made aware that they do have a choice of who is to represent them as their own agent. A written disclosure must be presented by a:

- listing agent (or his or her sales associate) who must deliver the form to the seller before entering into a listing agreement.

- selling agent (who may also be the listing agent) who must provide the form to the buyer before the buyer makes an offer to purchase.

- selling agent (if different from the listing agent) who must provide the form to the seller before the offer to purchase is accepted.

Elect the Agency

The second part of the agency disclosure form requires all parties involved to confirm that they understand the agent's role. In other words, the first part of the disclosure reveals that the agent may represent only the buyer, only the seller, or both. All parties acknowledge their understanding at this point.

Confirm the Agency

All parties to the transaction (buyer, seller, and agents) are required to acknowledge that they understand who is representing whom, and sign the agency confirmation form. One more time, the relationship will be confirmed in the sales contract, which is signed by all parties.

**CALIFORNIA
ASSOCIATION
OF REALTORS®**

DISCLOSURE REGARDING
REAL ESTATE AGENCY RELATIONSHIPS
(As required by the Civil Code)
(C.A.R. Form AD, Revised 10/04)

When you enter into a discussion with a real estate agent regarding a real estate transaction, you should from the outset understand what type of agency relationship or representation you wish to have with the agent in the transaction.

SELLER'S AGENT
A Seller's agent under a listing agreement with the Seller acts as the agent for the Seller only. A Seller's agent or a subagent of that agent has the following affirmative obligations:
To the Seller:
    A Fiduciary duty of utmost care, integrity, honesty, and loyalty in dealings with the Seller.
To the Buyer and the Seller:
    (a) Diligent exercise of reasonable skill and care in performance of the agent's duties.
    (b) A duty of honest and fair dealing and good faith.
    (c) A duty to disclose all facts known to the agent materially affecting the value or desirability of the property that are not known to, or within the diligent attention and observation of, the parties.
An agent is not obligated to reveal to either party any confidential information obtained from the other party that does not involve the affirmative duties set forth above.

BUYER'S AGENT
A selling agent can, with a Buyer's consent, agree to act as agent for the Buyer only. In these situations, the agent is not the Seller's agent, even if by agreement the agent may receive compensation for services rendered, either in full or in part from the Seller. An agent acting only for a Buyer has the following affirmative obligations:
To the Buyer:
    A fiduciary duty of utmost care, integrity, honesty, and loyalty in dealings with the Buyer.
To the Buyer and the Seller:
    (a) Diligent exercise of reasonable skill and care in performance of the agent's duties.
    (b) A duty of honest and fair dealing and good faith.
    (c) A duty to disclose all facts known to the agent materially affecting the value or desirability of the property that are not known to, or within the diligent attention and observation of, the parties.
An agent is not obligated to reveal to either party any confidential information obtained from the other party that does not involve the affirmative duties set forth above.

AGENT REPRESENTING BOTH SELLER AND BUYER
A real estate agent, either acting directly or through one or more associate licensees, can legally be the agent of both the Seller and the Buyer in a transaction, but only with the knowledge and consent of both the Seller and the Buyer.

In a dual agency situation, the agent has the following affirmative obligations to both the Seller and the Buyer:
    (a) A fiduciary duty of utmost care, integrity, honesty and loyalty in the dealings with either the Seller or the Buyer.
    (b) Other duties to the Seller and the Buyer as stated above in their respective sections.

In representing both Seller and Buyer, the agent may not, without the express permission of the respective party, disclose to the other party that the Seller will accept a price less than the listing price or that the Buyer will pay a price greater than the price offered.

The above duties of the agent in a real estate transaction do not relieve a Seller or Buyer from the responsibility to protect his or her own interests. You should carefully read all agreements to assure that they adequately express your understanding of the transaction. A real estate agent is a person qualified to advise about real estate. If legal or tax advice is desired, consult a competent professional.

Throughout your real property transaction you may receive more than one disclosure form, depending upon the number of agents assisting in the transaction. The law requires each agent with whom you have more than a casual relationship to present you with this disclosure form. You should read its contents each time it is presented to you, considering the relationship between you and the real estate agent in your specific transaction.

This disclosure form includes the provisions of Sections 2079.13 to 2079.24, inclusive, of the Civil Code set forth on the reverse hereof. Read it carefully.

I/WE ACKNOWLEDGE RECEIPT OF A COPY OF THIS DISCLOSURE AND THE PORTIONS OF THE CIVIL CODE PRINTED ON THE BACK (OR A SEPARATE PAGE).

☐ BUYER ☐ SELLER _____ Date _____ Time _____ ☐ AM ☐ PM

☐ BUYER ☐ SELLER _____ Date _____ Time _____ ☐ AM ☐ PM

AGENT _____ By _____ Date _____
           (Please Print)   (Associate-Licensee or Broker Signature)

THIS FORM SHALL BE PROVIDED AND ACKNOWLEDGED AS FOLLOWS (Civil Code §2079.14):
• When the listing brokerage company also represents Buyer, the Listing Agent shall have one AD form signed by Seller and one signed by Buyer.
• When Buyer and Seller are represented by different brokerage companies, the Listing Agent shall have one AD form signed by Seller and the Buyer's Agent shall have one AD form signed by Buyer and one AD form signed by Seller.

The System for Success™

Published and Distributed by:
REAL ESTATE BUSINESS SERVICES, INC.
a subsidiary of the California Association of REALTORS®
525 South Virgil Avenue, Los Angeles, California 90020

Reviewed by _____ Date _____

⌂ EQUAL HOUSING OPPORTUNITY

AD REVISED 10/04 (PAGE 1 OF 1)

DISCLOSURE REGARDING REAL ESTATE AGENCY RELATIONSHIPS (AD PAGE 1 OF 1)

Agent:	Phone:	Fax:	Prepared using WINForms® software
Broker:			

CIVIL CODE SECTIONS 2079.13 THROUGH 2079.24 (2079.16 APPEARS ON THE FRONT)

2079.13 As used in Sections 2079.14 to 2079.24, inclusive, the following terms have the following meanings:
(a) "Agent" means a person acting under provisions of title 9 (commencing with Section 2295) in a real property transaction, and includes a person who is licensed as a real estate broker under Chapter 3 (commencing with Section 10130) of Part 1 of Division 4 of the Business and Professions Code, and under whose license a listing is executed or an offer to purchase is obtained. **(b)** "Associate licensee" means a person who is licensed as a real estate broker or salesperson under Chapter 3 (commencing with Section 10130) of Part 1 of Division 4 of the Business and Professions Code and who is either licensed under a broker or has entered into a written contract with a broker to act as the broker's agent in connection with acts requiring a real estate license and to function under the broker's supervision in the capacity of an associate licensee. The agent in the real property transaction bears responsibility for his or her associate licensees who perform as agents of the agent. When an associate licensee owes a duty to any principal, or to any buyer or seller who is not a principal, in a real property transaction, that duty is equivalent to the duty owed to that party by the broker for whom the associate licensee functions. **(c)** "Buyer" means a transferee in a real property transaction, and includes a person who executes an offer to purchase real property from a seller through an agent, or who seeks the services of an agent in more than a casual, transitory, or preliminary manner, with the object of entering into a real property transaction. "Buyer" includes vendee or lessee. **(d)** "Dual agent" means an agent acting, either directly or through an associate licensee, as agent for both the seller and the buyer in a real property transaction. **(e)** "Listing agreement" means a contract between an owner of real property and an agent, by which the agent has been authorized to sell the real property or to find or obtain a buyer. **(f)** "Listing agent" means a person who has obtained a listing of real property to act as an agent for compensation. **(g)** "Listing price" is the amount expressed in dollars specified in the listing for which the seller is willing to sell the real property through the listing agent. **(h)** "Offering price" is the amount expressed in dollars specified in an offer to purchase for which the buyer is willing to buy the real property. **(i)** "Offer to purchase" means a written contract executed by a buyer acting through a selling agent which becomes the contract for the sale of the real property upon acceptance by the seller. **(j)** "Real property" means any estate specified by subdivision (1) or (2) of Section 761 in property which constitutes or is improved with one to four dwelling units, any leasehold in this type of property exceeding one year's duration, and mobilehomes, when offered for sale or sold through an agent pursuant to the authority contained in Section 10131.6 of the Business and Professions Code. **(k)** "Real property transaction" means a transaction for the sale of real property in which an agent is employed by one or more of the principals to act in that transaction, and includes a listing or an offer to purchase. **(l)** "Sell," "sale," or "sold" refers to a transaction for the transfer of real property from the seller to the buyer, and includes exchanges of real property between the seller and buyer, transactions for the creation of a real property sales contract within the meaning of Section 2985, and transactions for the creation of a leasehold exceeding one year's duration. **(m)** "Seller" means the transferor in a real property transaction, and includes an owner who lists real property with an agent, whether or not a transfer results, and who receives an offer to purchase real property of which he or she is the owner from an agent on behalf of another. "Seller" includes both a vendor and a lessor. **(n)** "Selling agent" means a listing agent who acts alone, or an agent who acts in cooperation with a listing agent, and who sells or finds and obtains a buyer for the real property, or an agent who locates property for a buyer or who finds a buyer for a property for which no listing exists and presents an offer to purchase to the seller. **(o)** "Subagent" means a person to whom an agent delegates agency powers as provided in Article 5 (commencing with Section 2349) of Chapter 1 of Title 9. However, "subagent" does not include an associate licensee who is acting under the supervision of an agent in a real property transaction.

2079.14 Listing agents and selling agents shall provide the seller and buyer in a real property transaction with a copy of the disclosure form specified in Section 2079.16, and, except as provided in subdivision (c), shall obtain a signed acknowledgement of receipt from that seller or buyer, except as provided in this section or Section 2079.15, as follows: **(a)** The listing agent, if any, shall provide the disclosure form to the seller prior to entering into the listing agreement. **(b)** The selling agent shall provide the disclosure form to the seller as soon as practicable prior to presenting the seller with an offer to purchase, unless the selling agent previously provided the seller with a copy of the disclosure form pursuant to subdivision (a). **(c)** Where the selling agent does not deal on a face-to-face basis with the seller, the disclosure form prepared by the selling agent may be furnished to the seller (and acknowledgement of receipt obtained for the selling agent from the seller) by the listing agent, or the selling agent may deliver the disclosure form by certified mail addressed to the seller at his or her last known address, in which case no signed acknowledgement of receipt is required. **(d)** The selling agent shall provide the disclosure form to the buyer as soon as practicable prior to execution of the buyer's offer to purchase, except that if the offer to purchase is not prepared by the selling agent, the selling agent shall present the disclosure form to the buyer not later than the next business day after the selling agent receives the offer to purchase from the buyer.

2079.15 In any circumstance in which the seller or buyer refuses to sign an acknowledgement of receipt pursuant to Section 2079.14, the agent, or an associate licensee acting for an agent, shall set forth, sign, and date a written declaration of the facts of the refusal.

2079.17 (a) As soon as practicable, the selling agent shall disclose to the buyer and seller whether the selling agent is acting in the real property transaction exclusively as the buyer's agent, exclusively as the seller's agent, or as a dual agent representing both the buyer and the seller. This relationship shall be confirmed in the contract to purchase and sell real property or in a separate writing executed or acknowledged by the seller, the buyer, and the selling agent prior to or coincident with execution of that contract by the buyer and the seller, respectively. **(b)** As soon as practicable, the listing agent shall disclose to the seller whether the listing agent is acting in the real property transaction exclusively as the seller's agent, or as a dual agent representing both the buyer and seller. This relationship shall be confirmed in the contract to purchase and sell real property or in a separate writing executed or acknowledged by the seller and the listing agent prior to or coincident with the execution of that contract by the seller.

(c) The confirmation required by subdivisions (a) and (b) shall be in the following form.

_____ **(DO NOT COMPLETE, SAMPLE ONLY)** _____ is the agent of (check one): ☐ the seller exclusively; or ☐ both the buyer and seller.
(Name of Listing Agent)

_____ **(DO NOT COMPLETE, SAMPLE ONLY)** _____ is the agent of (check one): ☐ the buyer exclusively; or ☐ the seller exclusively; or
(Name of Selling Agent if not the same as the Listing Agent) ☐ both the buyer and seller.

(d) The disclosures and confirmation required by this section shall be in addition to the disclosure required by Section 2079.14.

2079.18 No selling agent in a real property transaction may act as an agent for the buyer only, when the selling agent is also acting as the listing agent in the transaction.

2079.19 The payment of compensation or the obligation to pay compensation to an agent by the seller or buyer is not necessarily determinative of a particular agency relationship between an agent and the seller or buyer. A listing agent and a selling agent may agree to share any compensation or commission paid, or any right to any compensation or commission for which an obligation arises as the result of a real estate transaction, and the terms of any such agreement shall not necessarily be determinative of a particular relationship.

2079.20 Nothing in this article prevents an agent from selecting, as a condition of the agent's employment, a specific form of agency relationship not specifically prohibited by this article if the requirements of Section 2079.14 and Section 2079.17 are complied with.

2079.21 A dual agent shall not disclose to the buyer that the seller is willing to sell the property at a price less than the listing price, without the express written consent of the seller. A dual agent shall not disclose to the seller that the buyer is willing to pay a price greater than the offering price, without the express written consent of the buyer. This section does not alter in any way the duty or responsibility of a dual agent to any principal with respect to confidential information other than price.

2079.22 Nothing in this article precludes a listing agent from also being a selling agent, and the combination of these functions in one agent does not, of itself, make that agent a dual agent.

2079.23 A contract between the principal and agent may be modified or altered to change the agency relationship at any time before the performance of the act which is the object of the agency with the written consent of the parties to the agency relationship.

2079.24 Nothing in this article shall be construed to either diminish the duty of disclosure owed buyers and sellers by agents and their associate licensees, subagents, and employees or to relieve agents and their associate licensees, subagents, and employees from liability for their conduct in connection with acts governed by this article or for any breach of a fiduciary duty or a duty of disclosure

(AD BACKER)

CALIFORNIA
ASSOCIATION
OF REALTORS®

CONFIRMATION REAL ESTATE
AGENCY RELATIONSHIPS
(As required by the Civil Code)

Subject Property Address _____
The following agency relationship(s) is/are hereby confirmed for this transaction:

LISTING AGENT: _____   **SELLING AGENT:** _____
  is the agent of (check one):   (if not the same as Listing Agent)
  ☐ the Seller exclusively; or   is the agent of (check one):
  ☐ both the Buyer and Seller   ☐ the Buyer exclusively; or
                                                  ☐ the Seller exclusively; or
                                                  ☐ both the Buyer and Seller

I/WE ACKNOWLEDGE RECEIPT OF A COPY OF THIS CONFIRMATION.

Seller _____ Date _____   Buyer _____ Date _____

Seller _____ Date _____   Buyer _____ Date _____

Listing Agent _____ By _____ Date _____
                  (Please Print)   (Associate Licensee or Broker-Signature)

Selling Agent _____ By _____ Date _____
                  (Please Print)   (Associate Licensee or Broker-Signature)

A REAL ESTATE BROKER IS QUALIFIED TO ADVISE ON REAL ESTATE. IF YOU DESIRE LEGAL ADVICE, CONSULT YOUR ATTORNEY.

This form is available for use by the entire real estate industry. It is not intended to identify the user as a REALTOR®. REALTOR® is a registered collective membership mark which may be used only by members of the NATIONAL ASSOCIATION OF REALTORS® who subscribe to its Code of Ethics.

The copyright laws of the United States (17 U.S. Code) forbid the unauthorized reproduction of this form by any means, including facsimile or computerized formats. Copyright © 1987-1997, CALIFORNIA ASSOCIATION OF REALTORS®

┌─── OFFICE USE ONLY ───┐
Reviewed by Broker
or Designee _____
Date _____
└────────────────────────┘

EQUAL HOUSING
OPPORTUNITY

FORM AC-6 REVISED 1987

Phone: _____ Fax: _____   T6073385.ZFX

Review - Basic Requirements of the Agent in the Disclosure of Agency
- A fiduciary duty of utmost care, integrity, honesty, and loyalty in dealings with the agent's principal
- Reasonable skill and care in performance of agent's duties
- A duty of honesty, fair dealing, and good faith
- A duty to disclose all facts known to the agent materially affecting the value or desirability of the property not known to the other parties

In case you are wondering why all this repetition and paperwork, the agency disclosure is probably one of the most important documents available to the consumer. After years of ambiguity, the law is clear about who is legally representing whom. Buyers or sellers can be confident that their best interests are being represented by an agent on their side in the negotiations.

As a licensee, you must use the Disclosure Regarding Real Estate Agency Relationships form and be able to explain it to your clients and customers. The law is very clear about your responsibility for full disclosure. Misunderstanding or ignorance of the law is not a defense. A real estate license may be revoked or suspended for violation of the agency disclosure law.

Steps in the Disclosure Process
Mnemonic = "DEC"
- **D** isclosure
- **E** lect
- **C** onfirm

Review - Disclosure of Agency Law
- An agent is either the agent of the seller, the buyer, or both buyer and seller.
- A listing broker who is also a selling broker is a dual agent and may not be the agent for the buyer only.
- A dual agent may not tell the seller that the buyer is willing to pay more, nor may a dual agent tell the buyer that the seller will take less without the express written consent of the parties.
- An agency relationship can exist even though no compensation is received from the party with whom the agency relationship is established.

Creating an Agency Relationship

An agency relationship is created between an agent and principal, by **agreement**, **ratification**, or **estoppel**. It is created by an express or implied, written or oral contract. Brokers are fiduciaries whether the agency is created by **oral agreement** or by **express** (written) **agreement**.

> **Review - Creation of Agency Relationship**
> - Agreement
> - Ratification
> - Estoppel (*Ostensible or Implied Agency*)

Agency by Agreement

An agency relationship may be created by agreement, with or without a written contract. However, a real estate agreement must be in writing to be enforceable in a court of law. The two common ways to create agency with a written real estate contract are through a listing agreement or a buyer representation agreement.

Listing Agreements

A **listing agreement** is a written contract by which a principal, or seller, employs a broker to sell real estate. When the seller signs a listing agreement promising payment for service by the listing broker and the broker promises to "use due diligence" in finding a buyer, it is a **bilateral contract**—in that a promise is given in exchange for a promise.

> **Review - A listing agreement is the most common way to create an agency relationship.**

The listing agreement is where the seller promises to pay a commission upon presentation of a "ready, willing, and able" buyer who meets all the terms of the listing. A **"ready, willing, and able"** buyer is prepared to enter into a purchase contract, is ready to buy, and meets the financing requirements of purchase. A listing agreement gives the broker the right to be paid only after doing the job, or producing results. Think of it as simply an employment contract between the seller and the broker.

Under agency law, the listing broker is a **special agent** who deals in the name of the principal to negotiate the sale of property. The broker does not have control over the property itself, while acting within the course of a special agency, but only has the right to represent that principal. The seller is not promising to sell the house, nor can the seller be forced to sell even after signing a listing agreement. The seller is promising to pay a commission to the broker if he or she brings a "ready, willing, and able" buyer.

> Example: Ellen, a licensed real estate broker, spoke to everyone in her area at least once a month. Since she was well known, when owners wanted to sell their homes, they called Ellen. She would then meet with the owners to complete the listing agreement. An agency by express, written agreement had been created.

Buyer Representation Agreements

As a single agency becomes more prevalent, more brokers represent the buyer to locate a property rather than represent the seller. Typically, an agency relationship is created through the Exclusive Right to Represent Buyer Agreement. The listing agreement is to the seller as the buyer representation agreement is to the buyer. As with all exclusive agreements, a definite termination date is specified. Also, the manner of the broker's compensation is described, stating that all real estate commissions are negotiable.

Agency by Ratification

Ratification means acceptance of an act already performed. Ratification of an agency relationship is created by approving acts after they are done. For example, a seller can accept an offer presented by a licensee and agree to pay a commission, even though no agency has been approved. The seller is creating an agency by ratification by accepting the actions of the agent, after the fact.

> Example: As Ellen walked through the neighborhood talking to people, she became familiar with most of the homes in the area. One day, she answered the office phone and talked to a caller who described the type of home he wanted to buy. She knew of one just like his description, but it was not listed for sale. She called the owner of the house, who told her she could show it to the prospective buyer. Afterward, she presented an offer from the buyer which included a request to pay Ellen a commission. The owner accepted the offer and agreed to pay Ellen a commission—thus an agency by ratification was created.

Agency by Estoppel

Finally, an agency relationship can be created by estoppel. **Estoppel** is a legal bar that prevents a person from asserting facts or rights that are not consistent with what was implied by the person's previous behavior. That's why this is also called an **implied** or **ostensible** (apparent) agency. Agency is created when the principal causes a third party to believe another person is the principal's agent. What the principal has implied by his or her behavior is barred, or estopped, from being denied. Authority is given when a principal allows a third party to believe that another person is the agent, even if the third party is unaware of the appointment.

Example: If a seller allows a buyer to believe a broker represents the seller, and the buyer believes that to be so, the existence of an agency cannot be denied by the seller, who will be bound by the actions of the broker. This is known as the Doctrine of Estoppel.

Ostensible or Implied Agency

A licensee must be aware that an agency relationship can result from one's conduct, even though no express employment contract has been signed, or possible payments established. This is a subject where great care must be taken to assure that the agent is operating correctly, under the law.

When a listing is taken by a broker, he or she promises to represent the seller while finding a buyer. The broker has a **fiduciary** duty to conduct negotiations in the best interest of the seller in dealing with buyers who are interested in the property. However, in California, the distinction of who represents whom can get blurred unintentionally.

As the seller's agent, a broker has the duty of utmost care, integrity, honesty, and loyalty in dealings with the seller. Yet the law also requires that the broker exercise reasonable skill and care, honest and fair dealing, and full disclosure of all material facts to all parties. It is difficult for an agent to live up to fiduciary duty to a seller and at the same time meet general obligations to a buyer.

A seller's agent may provide the following services to a buyer without becoming the ostensible or implied agent of the buyer.

Seller's agent may:
- show the buyer properties meeting the buyer's requirements and describe to the buyer a property's amenities, attributes, condition, and status.

- complete a standard purchase contract by inserting the terms of the buyer's offer in the form's blanks and transmit all offers of the buyer to the seller on a timely basis.

- inform the buyer about the availability of financing, legal service, inspection companies, title companies, or other related services desired or required by the buyer to complete the transaction.

While performing the above tasks, it is very difficult not to establish an implied agency with the buyer. A seller's agent must be very alert and conscious of his or her role at all times to avoid becoming a dual agent by implication or conduct.

Listing brokers would violate their agency relationships with their sellers if they made these types of comments to buyers:

- "Leave it all up to me. I can get you the house at the price you want."

- "I'm sure I can get the seller to agree to this price and get the financing you need."

- "I know the seller personally, and I'm sure they won't counter at that price."

- "The house has been for sale for more than eight months and I think it is listed too high. Let's make a lower offer to see if they take it."

- "If the sellers insist on their asking price, I'll remind them that the heating system is old; the carpet is not exactly designer quality; and the whole place needs repainting. That should convince them to reduce their price."

- "I'll write up the offer for you and present it to the seller. If they don't like it, I can always try to find out their bottom line and we can go from there."

Terminating an Agency Relationship

At any time during the agency, the principal or agent may terminate the agency, except in an agency coupled with an interest. An agency is also terminated by the expiration of its term, the full performance of the terms of the agency, the destruction of the property, or the death or incapacity of either principal or agent.

Review - Termination of Agency Relationship
- Full performance
- Expiration of its term
- Agreement of the parties
- Acts of the parties
- Destruction of the property
- Death, incapacity, or insanity of the broker or principal
- Bankruptcy of the principal

Since the relationship between a principal and agent is a personal one, the principal has the right to revoke the agency at any time. If the cancellation is without good reason, the seller may be liable for breach of contract and may be liable to pay a commission to the listing broker. A seller cannot terminate a listing agreement if it is coupled with an interest. An **agency coupled with an interest** is one in which the agent gets an interest in the subject of the agency, which is the property. For example, a broker might advance funds to pay for a defaulted loan on the property to keep it out of foreclosure. The seller cannot revoke the listing after the broker has cured the loan.

An agency agreement must be in writing for the agent to enforce a commission claim based upon a breach of contract.

Types of Listing Agreements

In California, there are four commonly used listing agreements: exclusive right to sell listing, exclusive agency listing, open listing, and net listing.

The California Association of REALTORS® (C.A.R.), a dominant provider of real estate forms, has renamed its listing forms to the following:

- **Residential Listing Agreement - Exclusive (Form RLA)**, formerly named Exclusive Authorization and Right to Sell Agreement

- **Residential Listing Agreement - Agency (Form RLAA)**, formerly named Exclusive Agency Listing Agreement

- **Residential Listing Agreement - "Open" (Form RLAN)**, formerly named Non-Exclusive ("Open") Agency Residential Listing Agreement

Exclusive Authorization and Right-to-Sell Listing

An **exclusive authorization and right-to-sell listing** is an exclusive contract where the seller must pay the listing broker a commission if the property is sold within the time limit by the listing broker, any other broker, or even by the owner. If the broker brings the seller a "mirror offer", or an offer that matches exactly all terms in the listing, the seller does not have to accept the offer. However, under the terms of the listing, the seller must pay the broker a commission. In this listing, the phrase "right to sell" means "right to find a buyer". It does not authorize the broker the right to convey any property belonging to the principal unless the agent has a power of attorney to do so.

> **Every exclusive listing must specify a definite termination date.**

Exclusive Agency Listing

An **exclusive agency listing** is an exclusive contract where the seller must pay the listing broker a commission if any broker sells the property. However, the seller has the right to sell the property without a broker, and pay no commission. Every exclusive listing must specify a definite termination date.

Open Listing

An **open listing** is a listing agreement that gives any number of brokers the right to sell a property. It is not exclusive and may be given to any number of agents at the same time. The first broker to obtain a buyer who meets the terms of the listing, and whose offer is accepted by the seller, earns the commission. That agent is known as the procuring cause of the sale. **Procuring cause** refers to a broker who produces a buyer "ready, willing, and able" to purchase the property for the price and on the terms specified by the seller, regardless of whether the sale is completed. Unlike an exclusive listing agreement, an open listing does not require a specific termination date. The owner may sell the property without an agent, owing no commission.

Net Listing

A **net listing** is a listing agreement in which the commission is not definite. Instead, the broker receives all the money from the sale of the property that is in excess of the selling price set by the seller. The broker must disclose the selling price to both buyer and seller within 30 days after closing the transaction.

Option Listing

An option listing gives the broker the right to purchase the property that is listed. A broker with an option is acting as a principal as well as an agent. Prior to exercising the option, the seller must be informed of the full amount of the broker's profit and agree to it in writing.

Obligations and Rights of Agents and Principals

Agency law binds listing brokers and sellers. In a real estate agency relationship, both parties have legal obligations.

Duties an Agent Owes to a Principal

A real estate agent owes loyalty and confidentiality to his or her principal. The agent is a fiduciary and may not personally profit from the agency relationship except through the agreed-upon commission. As a fiduciary, the agent is bound by law to show good faith, loyalty, and honesty to the principal. Remember the mnemonic "COALD" — Care, Obedience, Accounting, Loyalty, and Disclosure.

CALIFORNIA ASSOCIATION OF REALTORS®

RESIDENTIAL LISTING AGREEMENT - EXCLUSIVE
(Exclusive Authorization and Right to Sell)
(C.A.R. Form RLA, Revised 4/05)

1. **EXCLUSIVE RIGHT TO SELL:** _____ ("Seller")
   hereby employs and grants _____ ("Broker")
   beginning (date) _____ and ending at 11:59 P.M. on (date) _____ ("Listing Period")
   the exclusive and irrevocable right to sell or exchange the real property in the City of _____ ,
   County of _____ , Assessor's Parcel No. _____
   California, described as: _____ ("Property").

2. **ITEMS EXCLUDED AND INCLUDED:** Unless otherwise specified in a real estate purchase agreement, all fixtures and fittings that are attached to the Property are included, and personal property items are excluded, from the purchase price.
   ADDITIONAL ITEMS EXCLUDED: _____
   ADDITIONAL ITEMS INCLUDED: _____ .
   Seller intends that the above items be excluded or included in offering the Property for sale, but understands that: **(i)** the purchase agreement supersedes any intention expressed above and will ultimately determine which items are excluded and included in the sale; and **(ii)** Broker is not responsible for and does not guarantee that the above exclusions and/or inclusions will be in the purchase agreement.

3. **LISTING PRICE AND TERMS:**
   A. The listing price shall be: _____ Dollars ($ _____).
   _____
   B. Additional Terms: _____
   _____

4. **COMPENSATION TO BROKER:**
   Notice: The amount or rate of real estate commissions is not fixed by law. They are set by each Broker individually and may be negotiable between Seller and Broker (real estate commissions include all compensation and fees to Broker).
   A. Seller agrees to pay to Broker as compensation for services irrespective of agency relationship(s), either ☐ _____ percent of the listing price (or if a purchase agreement is entered into, of the purchase price), or ☐ $ _____
   AND _____ , as follows:
      (1) If Broker, Seller, cooperating broker, or any other person procures a buyer(s) who offers to purchase the Property on the above price and terms, or on any price and terms acceptable to Seller during the Listing Period, or any extension.
   OR **(2)** If Seller, within _____ calendar days **(a)** after the end of the Listing Period or any extension, or **(b)** after any cancellation of this Agreement, unless otherwise agreed, enters into a contract to sell, convey, lease or otherwise transfer the Property to anyone ("Prospective Buyer") or that person's related entity: **(i)** who physically entered and was shown the Property during the Listing Period or any extension by Broker or a cooperating broker; or **(ii)** for whom Broker or any cooperating broker submitted to Seller a signed, written offer to acquire, lease, exchange or obtain an option on the Property. Seller, however, shall have no obligation to Broker under paragraph 4A(2) unless, not later than **3 calendar days** after the end of the Listing Period or any extension or cancellation, Broker has given Seller a written notice of the names of such Prospective Buyers.
   OR **(3)** If, without Broker's prior written consent, the Property is withdrawn from sale, conveyed, leased, rented, otherwise transferred, or made unmarketable by a voluntary act of Seller during the Listing Period, or any extension.
   B. If completion of the sale is prevented by a party to the transaction other than Seller, then compensation due under paragraph 4A shall be payable only if and when Seller collects damages by suit, arbitration, settlement or otherwise, and then in an amount equal to the lesser of one-half of the damages recovered or the above compensation, after first deducting title and escrow expenses and the expenses of collection, if any.
   C. In addition, Seller agrees to pay Broker: _____ .
   D. Seller has been advised of Broker's policy regarding cooperation with, and the amount of compensation offered to, other brokers.
      (1) Broker is authorized to cooperate with and compensate brokers participating through the multiple listing service(s) ("MLS"):
         (i) by offering MLS Brokers: either ☐ _____ percent of the purchase price, or ☐ $ _____ ;
         OR (ii) (if checked) ☐ as per Broker's policy.
      (2) Broker is authorized to cooperate with and compensate brokers operating outside the MLS as per Broker's policy.
   E. Seller hereby irrevocably assigns to Broker the above compensation from Seller's funds and proceeds in escrow. Broker may submit this Agreement, as instructions to compensate Broker pursuant to paragraph 4A, to any escrow regarding the Property involving Seller and a buyer, Prospective Buyer or other transferee.
   F. **(1)** Seller represents that Seller has not previously entered into a listing Agreement with another broker regarding the Property, unless specified as follows: _____ .
      (2) Seller warrants that Seller has no obligation to pay compensation to any other broker regarding the Property unless the Property is transferred to any of the following individuals or entities: _____
      _____
      (3) If the Property is sold to anyone listed above during the time Seller is obligated to compensate another broker: **(i)** Broker is not entitled to compensation under this Agreement; and **(ii)** Broker is not obligated to represent Seller in such transaction.

Seller acknowledges receipt of a copy of this page.
Seller's Initials (_____) (_____)

| Reviewed by _____ Date _____ |

EQUAL HOUSING OPPORTUNITY

RLA REVISED 4/05 (PAGE 1 OF 3)

RESIDENTIAL LISTING AGREEMENT - EXCLUSIVE (RLA PAGE 1 OF 3)

| Agent: | Phone: | Fax: | Prepared using WINForms® software |
| Broker: | | | |

Property Address _____ Date: _____

5. **OWNERSHIP, TITLE AND AUTHORITY:** Seller warrants that: **(i)** Seller is the owner of the Property; **(ii)** no other persons or entities have title to the Property; and **(iii)** Seller has the authority to both execute this Agreement and sell the Property. Exceptions to ownership, title and authority are as follows: _____

6. **MULTIPLE LISTING SERVICE:** All terms of the transaction, including financing, if applicable, will be provided to the selected MLS for publication, dissemination and use by persons and entities on terms approved by the MLS. Seller authorizes Broker to comply with all applicable MLS rules. MLS rules allow MLS data to be made available by the MLS to additional Internet sites unless Broker gives the MLS instructions to the contrary. MLS rules generally provide that residential real property and vacant lot listings be submitted to the MLS within 48 hours or some other period of time after all necessary signatures have been obtained on the listing agreement. However, Broker will not have to submit this listing to the MLS if, within that time, Broker submits to the MLS a form signed by Seller (C.A.R. Form SEL or the locally required form) instructing Broker to withhold the listing from the MLS. Information about this listing will be provided to the MLS of Broker's selection unless a form instructing Broker to withhold the listing from the MLS is attached to this listing Agreement.

7. **SELLER REPRESENTATIONS:** Seller represents that, unless otherwise specified in writing, Seller is unaware of: **(i)** any Notice of Default recorded against the Property; **(ii)** any delinquent amounts due under any loan secured by, or other obligation affecting, the Property; **(iii)** any bankruptcy, insolvency or similar proceeding affecting the Property; **(iv)** any litigation, arbitration, administrative action, government investigation or other pending or threatened action that affects or may affect the Property or Seller's ability to transfer it; and **(v)** any current, pending or proposed special assessments affecting the Property. Seller shall promptly notify Broker in writing if Seller becomes aware of any of these items during the Listing Period or any extension thereof.

8. **BROKER'S AND SELLER'S DUTIES:** Broker agrees to exercise reasonable effort and due diligence to achieve the purposes of this Agreement. Unless Seller gives Broker written instructions to the contrary, Broker is authorized to order reports and disclosures as appropriate or necessary and advertise and market the Property by any method and in any medium selected by Broker, including MLS and the Internet, and, to the extent permitted by these media, control the dissemination of the information submitted to any medium. Seller agrees to consider offers presented by Broker, and to act in good faith to accomplish the sale of the Property by, among other things, making the Property available for showing at reasonable times and referring to Broker all inquiries of any party interested in the Property. Seller is responsible for determining at what price to list and sell the Property. **Seller further agrees to indemnify, defend and hold Broker harmless from all claims, disputes, litigation, judgments and attorney fees arising from any incorrect information supplied by Seller, or from any material facts that Seller knows but fails to disclose.**

9. **DEPOSIT:** Broker is authorized to accept and hold on Seller's behalf any deposits to be applied toward the purchase price.

10. **AGENCY RELATIONSHIPS:**
    A. **Disclosure:** If the Property includes residential property with one-to-four dwelling units, Seller shall receive a "Disclosure Regarding Agency Relationships" form prior to entering into this Agreement.
    B. **Seller Representation:** Broker shall represent Seller in any resulting transaction, except as specified in paragraph 4F.
    C. **Possible Dual Agency With Buyer:** Depending upon the circumstances, it may be necessary or appropriate for Broker to act as an agent for both Seller and buyer, exchange party, or one or more additional parties ("Buyer"). Broker shall, as soon as practicable, disclose to Seller any election to act as a dual agent representing both Seller and Buyer. If a Buyer is procured directly by Broker or an associate-licensee in Broker's firm, Seller hereby consents to Broker acting as a dual agent for Seller and such Buyer. In the event of an exchange, Seller hereby consents to Broker collecting compensation from additional parties for services rendered, provided there is disclosure to all parties of such agency and compensation. Seller understands and agrees that: **(i)** Broker, without the prior written consent of Seller, will not disclose to Buyer that Seller is willing to sell the Property at a price less than the listing price; **(ii)** Broker, without the prior written consent of Buyer, will not disclose to Seller that Buyer is willing to pay a price greater than the offered price; and **(iii)** except for (i) and (ii) above, a dual agent is obligated to disclose known facts materially affecting the value or desirability of the Property to both parties.
    D. **Other Sellers:** Seller understands that Broker may have or obtain listings on other properties, and that potential buyers may consider, make offers on, or purchase through Broker, property the same as or similar to Seller's Property. Seller consents to Broker's representation of sellers and buyers of other properties before, during and after the end of this Agreement.
    E. **Confirmation:** If the Property includes residential property with one-to-four dwelling units, Broker shall confirm the agency relationship described above, or as modified, in writing, prior to or concurrent with Seller's execution of a purchase agreement.

11. **SECURITY AND INSURANCE:** Broker is not responsible for loss of or damage to personal or real property, or person, whether attributable to use of a keysafe/lockbox, a showing of the Property, or otherwise. Third parties, including, but not limited to, appraisers, inspectors, brokers and prospective buyers, may have access to, and take videos and photographs of, the interior of the Property. Seller agrees: **(i)** to take reasonable precautions to safeguard and protect valuables that might be accessible during showings of the Property; and **(ii)** to obtain insurance to protect against these risks. Broker does not maintain insurance to protect Seller.

12. **KEYSAFE/LOCKBOX:** A keysafe/lockbox is designed to hold a key to the Property to permit access to the Property by Broker, cooperating brokers, MLS participants, their authorized licensees and representatives, authorized inspectors, and accompanied prospective buyers. Broker, cooperating brokers, MLS and Associations/Boards of REALTORS® are **not** insurers against injury, theft, loss, vandalism or damage attributed to the use of a keysafe/lockbox. Seller does (or if checked ☐ does not) authorize Broker to install a keysafe/lockbox. If Seller does not occupy the Property, Seller shall be responsible for obtaining occupant(s)' written permission for use of a keysafe/lockbox.

13. **SIGN:** Seller does (or if checked ☐ does not) authorize Broker to install a FOR SALE/SOLD sign on the Property.

14. **EQUAL HOUSING OPPORTUNITY:** The Property is offered in compliance with federal, state and local anti-discrimination laws.

15. **ATTORNEY FEES:** In any action, proceeding or arbitration between Seller and Broker regarding the obligation to pay compensation under this Agreement, the prevailing Seller or Broker shall be entitled to reasonable attorney fees and costs from the non-prevailing Seller or Broker, except as provided in paragraph 19A.

16. **ADDITIONAL TERMS:** _____
_____
_____
_____

Seller acknowledges receipt of a copy of this page.
Seller's Initials (_____) (_____)

Reviewed by _____ Date _____

x.zfx

Property Address _____ Date: _____

17. MANAGEMENT APPROVAL: If an associate-licensee in Broker's office (salesperson or broker-associate) enters into this Agreement on Broker's behalf, and Broker or Manager does not approve of its terms, Broker or Manager has the right to cancel this Agreement, in writing, within **5 Days** after its execution.

18. SUCCESSORS AND ASSIGNS: This Agreement shall be binding upon Seller and Seller's successors and assigns.

19. DISPUTE RESOLUTION:

    A. MEDIATION: Seller and Broker agree to mediate any dispute or claim arising between them out of this Agreement, or any resulting transaction, before resorting to arbitration or court action, subject to paragraph 19B(2) below. Paragraph 19B(2) below applies whether or not the arbitration provision is initialed. Mediation fees, if any, shall be divided equally among the parties involved. If, for any dispute or claim to which this paragraph applies, any party commences an action without first attempting to resolve the matter through mediation, or refuses to mediate after a request has been made, then that party shall not be entitled to recover attorney fees, even if they would otherwise be available to that party in any such action. THIS MEDIATION PROVISION APPLIES WHETHER OR NOT THE ARBITRATION PROVISION IS INITIALED.

    B. ARBITRATION OF DISPUTES: (1) Seller and Broker agree that any dispute or claim in Law or equity arising between them regarding the obligation to pay compensation under this Agreement, which is not settled through mediation, shall be decided by neutral, binding arbitration, including and subject to paragraph 19B(2) below. The arbitrator shall be a retired judge or justice, or an attorney with at least 5 years of residential real estate law experience, unless the parties mutually agree to a different arbitrator, who shall render an award in accordance with substantive California Law. The parties shall have the right to discovery in accordance with Code of Civil Procedure §1283.05. In all other respects, the arbitration shall be conducted in accordance with Title 9 of Part III of the California Code of Civil Procedure. Judgment upon the award of the arbitrator(s) may be entered in any court having jurisdiction. Interpretation of this agreement to arbitrate shall be governed by the Federal Arbitration Act.

    (2) EXCLUSIONS FROM MEDIATION AND ARBITRATION: The following matters are excluded from mediation and arbitration hereunder: **(i)** a judicial or non-judicial foreclosure or other action or proceeding to enforce a deed of trust, mortgage, or installment land sale contract as defined in Civil Code §2985; **(ii)** an unlawful detainer action; **(iii)** the filing or enforcement of a mechanic's lien; and **(iv)** any matter that is within the jurisdiction of a probate, small claims, or bankruptcy court. The filing of a court action to enable the recording of a notice of pending action, for order of attachment, receivership, injunction, or other provisional remedies, shall not constitute a waiver of the mediation and arbitration provisions.

        "NOTICE: BY INITIALING IN THE SPACE BELOW YOU ARE AGREEING TO HAVE ANY DISPUTE ARISING OUT OF THE MATTERS INCLUDED IN THE 'ARBITRATION OF DISPUTES' PROVISION DECIDED BY NEUTRAL ARBITRATION AS PROVIDED BY CALIFORNIA LAW AND YOU ARE GIVING UP ANY RIGHTS YOU MIGHT POSSESS TO HAVE THE DISPUTE LITIGATED IN A COURT OR JURY TRIAL. BY INITIALING IN THE SPACE BELOW YOU ARE GIVING UP YOUR JUDICIAL RIGHTS TO DISCOVERY AND APPEAL, UNLESS THOSE RIGHTS ARE SPECIFICALLY INCLUDED IN THE 'ARBITRATION OF DISPUTES' PROVISION. IF YOU REFUSE TO SUBMIT TO ARBITRATION AFTER AGREEING TO THIS PROVISION, YOU MAY BE COMPELLED TO ARBITRATE UNDER THE AUTHORITY OF THE CALIFORNIA CODE OF CIVIL PROCEDURE. YOUR AGREEMENT TO THIS ARBITRATION PROVISION IS VOLUNTARY."

        "WE HAVE READ AND UNDERSTAND THE FOREGOING AND AGREE TO SUBMIT DISPUTES ARISING OUT OF THE MATTERS INCLUDED IN THE 'ARBITRATION OF DISPUTES' PROVISION TO NEUTRAL ARBITRATION."

Seller's Initials _____ / _____	Broker's Initials _____ / _____

20. ENTIRE AGREEMENT: All prior discussions, negotiations and agreements between the parties concerning the subject matter of this Agreement are superseded by this Agreement, which constitutes the entire contract and a complete and exclusive expression of their agreement, and may not be contradicted by evidence of any prior agreement or contemporaneous oral agreement. If any provision of this agreement is held to be ineffective or invalid, the remaining provisions will nevertheless be given full force and effect. This Agreement and any supplement, addendum or modification, including any photocopy or facsimile, may be executed in counterparts.

By signing below, Seller acknowledges that Seller has read, understands, accepts and has received a copy of this Agreement.

Seller _____ Date _____
Address _____ City _____ State _____ Zip _____
Telephone _____ Fax _____ E-mail _____

Seller _____ Date _____
Address _____ City _____ State _____ Zip _____
Telephone _____ Fax _____ E-mail _____

Real Estate Broker (Firm) _____
By (Agent) _____ Date _____
Address _____ City _____ State _____ Zip _____
Telephone _____ Fax _____ E-mail _____

SURE TRAC
The System for Success™

Reviewed by _____ Date _____

EQUAL HOUSING OPPORTUNITY

RLA REVISED 4/05 (PAGE 3 OF 3)

x.zfx

RESIDENTIAL LISTING AGREEMENT - EXCLUSIVE (RLA PAGE 3 OF 3)

A broker must present all offers to his or her principal before closing unless expressly instructed otherwise or unless the offer is patently frivolous.

A real estate broker is usually an independent contractor. Under the law of agency, the listing broker is a special agent who deals in the name of the principal to negotiate the sale of property. The broker does not have control over the property itself. He or she acts within the course of a special agency, and only has the right to represent that principal.

A listing contract does not give the listing broker the right to convey any property belonging to the principal unless the agent has a power of attorney to do so.

Listing Violations

If an agent does not comply with the following obligations, the punishment may be suspension or revocation of the real estate license:

- Every exclusive listing must specify a definite termination date.

- A listing broker must give a copy of the listing to the seller at the time the seller signs it.

- A listing broker cannot accept a deposit from a buyer unless specifically authorized to do so in the listing agreement. When a listing broker does so without authorization from the seller, he or she is acting as an agent of the buyer and not the seller. Any misappropriation of these funds by the listing broker would result in loss to the buyer and not the seller. Most listing agreements, however, do allow the broker to receive the buyer's deposit on behalf of the seller. This authority given to the broker also applies to any **subagents**, unless the subagent is working as the agent of the buyer.

- A listing broker may not return a buyer's deposit after the seller accepts the offer, without the consent of the seller.

- The acceptance of a check, rather than cash or a promissory note, as an earnest money deposit must be disclosed to the seller at the time the offer is presented.

- Also, if the buyer instructs the listing broker to hold the check uncashed until the offer is accepted, the fact must be disclosed to the seller when the offer is presented.

- Any agent who puts a client's money in his or her own personal bank account is guilty of commingling. **Commingling** is the illegal practice of depositing client's funds in a broker's personal or general business account. Checks must be deposited within three-business days after receiving them, either into a trust account or a neutral escrow account. If a broker uses the client's money, it is known as **conversion**.

Duties an Agent Owes to Third Parties

In addition to those duties to the seller, the listing broker owes a duty of fair and honest dealing to the buyer, including the duty of full disclosure. The duty to disclose requires that the listing broker conduct a reasonably competent and diligent inspection of the property and note anything that would affect its value or desirability.

A listing broker may not withhold any material facts that are known to the seller or broker, from a prospective buyer. A **material fact** is any fact that would seem likely to affect the judgment of the principal in giving consent to the agent to enter into the particular transaction on the specified terms. As a result of the Easton decision (*Easton v. Strassburger*, 1984), real estate agents can be held liable, not only for defects they know about, but for defects about which they should have known as a result of careful investigation.

Occasionally, the line between truth and fiction is blurred, sometimes innocently, sometimes with malice intended. It is easy for an agent to misrepresent a fact to a third party if the agent is not careful.

Misrepresentation

Misrepresentation is making a false statement or concealing a material fact. There are three types of misrepresentations: (1) innocent misrepresentations, (2) negligent misrepresentations, and (3) fraudulent misrepresentations.

Innocent Misrepresentations

Innocent misrepresentations are statements not known to be untrue at the time they are made, and usually carry no legal liability for an agent. However, a buyer or seller could cancel a contract as a result.

Negligent Misrepresentations

Negligent misrepresentations are untrue statements made without facts to back them up. The agent is not aware of the falseness of the statement at the time, but is liable for them.

Fraudulent Misrepresentations

Untrue statements made by an agent who knows that he or she is not telling the truth. The agent may be liable for committing fraud.

Puffing

Puffing is a statement of opinion, that is not factual, about a piece of property. Puffing describes an opinion made by an agent who honestly believes that the inflated statement about the condition of a property is just another innocent way to make a sale. If a prospective buyer believes the statement to be true, the agent may be guilty of misrepresentation and may be held liable.

Tort

A **tort** is a violation of a legal right, or a civil wrong such as negligence, libel or nuisance. An agent is not liable for torts committed by the principal only his or her own torts.

> Example: If a seller does not disclose to the listing broker that the shower floor has dry rot or that the roof leaks, the listing broker is not responsible for lack of disclosure by the seller.

Duties a Principal Owes to an Agent

A seller cannot be forced to sell, even after signing a listing agreement. However, he or she can be forced to pay a commission if the broker finds a buyer (even if the seller refuses to sell to that buyer). When the broker has fulfilled the obligations of the listing agreement, he or she is entitled to the agreed-upon commission.

Negotiating the Commission

The amount of commission is decided by the seller and the broker, and included in the listing agreement. Usually it is a percentage of the sales price, but does not necessarily have to be mentioned in this manner. The amount of commission is not set by law and is always negotiable between sellers and brokers.

Agreements between cooperating brokers for dividing commissions are normally made. Usually the listing broker is the one who receives the commission as a result of his or her contract with the seller. Commonly, the broker agrees to a 50-50 split with the cooperating, or selling, broker. The payment ordinarily is made through escrow at the closing.

> **Review - Commissions**
> - The amount of commission is not set by law and is always negotiable.
> - It is a violation of the Sherman Anti-Trust Law for brokers to discuss or set commission rates in a community.

When Does the Agent Earn the Commission?

Actually, a seller can opt out of a sale but must still pay a commission. A broker has earned a commission once the above tasks are accomplished. If the broker brings about a "meeting of the minds" of the buyer and seller on price and other terms for the transaction, the broker has earned the commission. Thus, if buyer and seller enter into a valid contract, the broker is entitled to a commission even though the sale is never completed.

During the term of the listing, if a broker presents an accepted offer to the seller, the broker has earned the commission. If, after a listing has expired, a buyer and seller complete a sale on the exact terms of those presented and rejected during the term of the listing, the broker has earned a commission.

Procuring Cause

Procuring cause refers to a broker who produces a buyer "ready, willing, and able" to purchase the property for the price and on the terms specified by the seller, regardless of whether the sale is completed. A "procuring cause" is that which produces the desired results. The broker must be the procuring cause of the sale to earn a commission.

Occasionally, determining who the procuring cause of a sale is becomes a matter of great dispute between real estate agents. When more than one agent has shown a prospective buyer a property, with or without the knowledge of the other agent's involvement, each may feel they have earned the commission when the buyer finally authorizes one of them to write up an offer which is accepted by the seller.

The law states that the broker who is the procuring cause of the sale, or the one who actually wrote the offer and presented it to the seller for acceptance, has earned the commission. The others were unable to bring the buyer to the point of sale and, therefore, did not earn a commission.

Safety Clause

Most listing agreements have a safety clause, sometimes called a protection clause. The **safety clause** protects the listing broker's commission, if the owner personally sells the property to someone who was shown the property or made an offer during the term of the listing. At the time the listing is signed, the seller and broker need to agree on a length of time for the protection period. The protection clause applies only if the broker has given the seller a list containing the names of the "protected" buyers within three calendar days of expiration of the listing. This prevents a seller from waiting for a listing to end before accepting an offer and then refusing to pay the original broker (the procuring cause), a commission.

The agent produces a "ready, willing, and able" buyer to purchase on the seller's terms and asking price.

Review - An Agent's Commission is Earned When:
- The agent produces a "ready, willing, and able" buyer to purchase on the terms and at the price asked by the seller.
- The agent secures from a prospective buyer a binding contract with terms and conditions that are accepted by the seller.

CALIFORNIA
ASSOCIATION
OF REALTORS®

COMMISSION AGREEMENT

1. **COMPENSATION: Notice: The amount or rate of real estate commissions is not fixed by law. They are set by each broker individually and may be negotiable between the Seller/Buyer ("Principal") and Broker.**

_____ ("Principal"),
agrees to pay to _____ , ("Broker(s)"),
as compensation for services, irrespective of agency relationships, the sum of either ☐ _____ percent of the transaction price, or
☐
Dollars ($ _____), for property situated in the City of _____ , County of
_____ , California, described as: _____

Compensation is payable as follows: (a) On recordation of the deed or other evidence of title; or (b) If completion of the transaction is prevented by default of Principal, then upon such default; or (c) If completion of the transaction is prevented by a party to the transaction other than Principal, then only if and when Principal collects damages by suit, settlement, or otherwise, and then in an amount equal to the lesser of one-half of the damages recovered, or the above compensation, after first deducting title and escrow expenses and the expenses of collection, if any. Broker may cooperate with other brokers, and divide with other brokers such compensation in any manner acceptable to Broker. Principal hereby irrevocably assigns to Broker the above compensation from Principal's funds and proceeds in escrow.

2. **ATTORNEY FEES:** In any action, proceeding, or arbitration between Principal and Broker(s) arising out of this Agreement, the prevailing party shall be entitled to reasonable attorney fees and costs.

3. **DISPUTE RESOLUTION:**

A. **MEDIATION:** Principal and Broker agree to mediate any dispute or claim arising between them out of this Agreement, or any resulting transaction, before resorting to arbitration or court action, subject to paragraph 3C below. Mediation fees, if any, shall be divided equally among the parties involved. If any party commences an action based on a dispute or claim to which this paragraph applies, without first attempting to resolve the matter through mediation, then that party shall not be entitled to recover attorney's fees, even if they would otherwise be available to that party in any such action. THIS MEDIATION PROVISION APPLIES WHETHER OR NOT THE ARBITRATION PROVISION IS INITIALED.

B. **ARBITRATION OF DISPUTES: Principal and Broker agree that any dispute or claim in law or equity arising between them regarding the obligation to pay compensation under this Agreement, which is not settled through mediation, shall be decided by neutral, binding arbitration, subject to paragraph 3C below. The arbitrator shall be a retired judge or justice, or an attorney with at least five years of residential real estate law experience, unless the parties mutually agree to a different arbitrator, who shall render an award in accordance with substantive California Law. In all other respects, the arbitration shall be conducted in accordance with Part III, Title 9 of the California Code of Civil Procedure. Judgment upon the award of the arbitrator(s) may be entered in any court having jurisdiction. The parties shall have the right to discovery in accordance with Code of Civil Procedure §1283.05.**

"**NOTICE: BY INITIALING IN THE SPACE BELOW YOU ARE AGREEING TO HAVE ANY DISPUTE ARISING OUT OF THE MATTERS INCLUDED IN THE 'ARBITRATION OF DISPUTES' PROVISION DECIDED BY NEUTRAL ARBITRATION AS PROVIDED BY CALIFORNIA LAW AND YOU ARE GIVING UP ANY RIGHTS YOU MIGHT POSSESS TO HAVE THE DISPUTE LITIGATED IN A COURT OR JURY TRIAL. BY INITIALING IN THE SPACE BELOW YOU ARE GIVING UP YOUR JUDICIAL RIGHTS TO DISCOVERY AND APPEAL, UNLESS THOSE RIGHTS ARE SPECIFICALLY INCLUDED IN THE 'ARBITRATION OF DISPUTES' PROVISION. IF YOU REFUSE TO SUBMIT TO ARBITRATION AFTER AGREEING TO THIS PROVISION, YOU MAY BE COMPELLED TO ARBITRATE UNDER THE AUTHORITY OF THE CALIFORNIA CODE OF CIVIL PROCEDURE. YOUR AGREEMENT TO THIS ARBITRATION PROVISION IS VOLUNTARY.**"

"**WE HAVE READ AND UNDERSTAND THE FOREGOING AND AGREE TO SUBMIT DISPUTES ARISING OUT OF THE MATTERS INCLUDED IN THE 'ARBITRATION OF DISPUTES' PROVISION TO NEUTRAL ARBITRATION.**"

| Principal's Initials _____ / _____ | Broker's Initials _____ / _____ |

C. **EXCLUSIONS FROM MEDIATION AND ARBITRATION:** The following matters are excluded from Mediation and Arbitration hereunder: (a) A judicial or non-judicial foreclosure or other action or proceeding to enforce a deed of trust, mortgage, or installment land sale contract as defined in Civil Code §2985; (b) An unlawful detainer action; (c) The filing or enforcement of a mechanic's lien; (d) Any matter that is within the jurisdiction of a probate, small claims, or bankruptcy court; and (e) An action for bodily injury or wrongful death, or for latent or patent defects to which Code of Civil Procedure §337.1 or §337.15 applies. The filing of a court action to enable the recording of a notice of pending action, for order of attachment, receivership, injunction, or other provisional remedies, shall not constitute a violation of the mediation and arbitration provisions.

4. **OTHER TERMS AND CONDITIONS:** _____
_____
_____

Prinicpal has read and acknowledges receipt of a copy of this Agreement.

Principal _____   Principal _____
Address _____   Address _____
_____   _____
Date _____ Phone/Fax/Email _____   Date _____ Phone/Fax/Email _____

Real Estate Broker agrees to the foregoing:
Broker _____   By _____ Date _____

The copyright laws of the United States (Title 17 U.S. Code) forbid the unauthorized reproduction of this form, or any portion thereof, by photocopy machine or any other means, including facsimile or computerized formats. Copyright © 1986-2003, CALIFORNIA ASSOCIATION OF REALTORS®, INC. ALL RIGHTS RESERVED.
THIS FORM HAS BEEN APPROVED BY THE CALIFORNIA ASSOCIATION OF REALTORS® (C.A.R.). NO REPRESENTATION IS MADE AS TO THE LEGAL VALIDITY OR ADEQUACY OF ANY PROVISION IN ANY SPECIFIC TRANSACTION. A REAL ESTATE BROKER IS THE PERSON QUALIFIED TO ADVISE ON REAL ESTATE TRANSACTIONS. IF YOU DESIRE LEGAL OR TAX ADVICE, CONSULT AN APPROPRIATE PROFESSIONAL.
This form is available for use by the entire real estate industry. It is not intended to identify the user as a REALTOR®. REALTOR® is a registered collective membership mark which may be used only by members of the NATIONAL ASSOCIATION OF REALTORS® who subscribe to its Code of Ethics.

SURE TRAC
The System for Success™

Published by the
California Association of REALTORS®

| Reviewed by _____ Date _____ |

EQUAL HOUSING
OPPORTUNITY

CA 10/00 (PAGE 1 OF 1)   **COMMISSION AGREEMENT (CA PAGE 1 OF 1)**

Phone: ( )   Fax: ( )   T6073385.ZFX

Summary

Agency is a legal relationship created when a principal (seller or buyer) gives an agent (licensed broker) the authority to represent them in a real estate transaction. A broker representing either a buyer or a seller is a **single agent**, representing both, a **dual agent**.

A real estate agency can be created by express agreement, ratification, and estoppel. Usually an **agency relationship** is created by a listing contract between the seller and broker. A contract between a broker and a buyer is called the **buyer representation agreement**.

An agent must disclose to both the buyer and seller who the agent is representing and the duties involved in that representation. California requires that all parties read and sign the Disclosure Regarding Real Estate Agency Relationships document.

The agent has the duties of full disclosure and loyalty to the principal, and the duties of honesty and good-faith dealing with all parties. The principal's duties include good-faith dealing with the agent, as well as responsibility for all the actions the agent takes within the agency relationship.

Common agency violations include: incomplete disclosure, commingling, **misrepresentation**, false promise, trust fund problems, and problems with commissions.

Termination of agency can be made at any time by the principal or the agent, unless it is an agency coupled with an interest. Agency can also be terminated by expiration of terms, full performance of terms, destruction of the property, or death or incapacity of either principal or agent.

Chapter 5 Review Exercises

Matching Exercise

Instructions: Look up the meaning of the terms in the Glossary, then write the letter of the matching term on the blank line before its definition. Answers are in Appendix B.

Terms

a. agency relationship

b. agent

c. associate licensee

d. attorney-in-fact

e. commingling

f. conversion

g. customer

h. dual agent

i. fiduciary relationship

j. general agent

k. listing agreement

l. misrepresentation

m. net listing

n. principal

o. procuring cause

p. puffing

q. ratification

r. ready, willing, and able

s. real estate salesperson

t. RLA - exclusive form

u. safety clause

v. single agency

w. special agent

x. subagent

y. third party

Definitions

1. _____ The approval of a previously authorized act, performed on behalf of a person, which makes the act valid and legally binding.

2. _____ When a broker represents only the buyer or the seller in the transaction.

3. _____ A person employed to perform a specific task.

4. _____ A buyer who is prepared to enter a purchase contract, who really wants to buy, and who meets the financing requirements of purchase.

5. _____ A relationship that implies a position of trust or confidence.

6. _____ Another term used for a licensed real estate salesperson employed by a licensed real estate broker.

7. _____ A broker who represents both parties in a transaction.

8. _____ Depositing client funds in the broker's personal account or general business account.

9. _____ A listing agreement in which the commission is not definite.

10. _____ Exaggerated comments or opinions not made as representations of fact, thus not grounds for misrepresentation.

11. _____ The appropriation of property belonging to another as in a broker using a client's funds.

12. _____ A person with a real estate license and employed by a real estate broker—agent of the broker—not the seller or buyer.

13. _____ In a real estate transaction, the one (seller) who hires the broker to represent him or her in the sale of the property.

14. _____ A person who acts for and in the place of another, called a principal, for the purpose of affecting the principal's legal relationship with third persons.

15. _____ A prospective buyer of real estate; not to be confused with a property seller, who is the listing broker's client.

16. _____ A written contract by which a principal, or seller, employs a broker to sell real estate.

17. _____ Clause that protects the listing broker's commission, if the owner personally sells the property to someone who was shown the property or made an offer during the term of the listing.

18. _____ The new C.A.R. name for the Exclusive Authorization and Right to Sell Listing Agreement.

19. _____ A person who would be considered the customer in an agency relationship.

20. _____ The broker who produces a buyer "ready, willing, and able" to purchase the property for the price and on the terms specified by the seller, regardless of whether the sale is completed.

Multiple Choice Questions

Instructions: Circle your response and go to Appendix B to read the complete explanation for each question.

1. Which of the following is **not** one of the tests of agency?
   a. Confirmation
   b. Compensation
   c. Disclosure
   d. Election

2. Weiss hired Horning to sell a property through a 90-day exclusive agency listing. Thirty (30) days later the house had not sold, so Weiss sent Horning a certified letter ending the agency listing. A few days later, another broker sold the house through an open listing. Under such circumstances:
    a. Weiss has the right to release Horning, and Horning is not owed a commission.
    b. only the open agent is owed a commission.
    c. Weiss was not entitled to cancel the exclusive agency listing.
    d. the exclusive agent and the open agent are both entitled to a commission.

3. An agent receives an offer. The agent gives the offer to the seller, who asks to consider it for 24 hours. At 6 p.m. the same day, the agent receives two more offers. The agent believes the seller will not accept any of the three offers. The agent must convey the two new offers:
    a. in the order in which they were received.
    b. by 10 a.m. the next day.
    c. at the same time.
    d. none of the above

4. A listing agreement is a(n):
    a. bilateral contract.
    b. promise for a promise.
    c. employment contract.
    d. all of the above

5. Which of the following is a fiduciary duty of the buyer's agent, according to the law of agency in the Civil Code?
    a. Acting with utmost care, integrity, honesty, and loyalty in dealings with the buyer
    b. Giving the buyer advice about how to hold title
    c. Telling the buyer which escrow company to use
    d. Acting as a subagent

6. Which of the following is not essential to the creation of an agency relationship?
    a. Fiduciary relationship of the agent and principal
    b. Competency on the part of the principal
    c. Payment of consideration
    d. Agreement of the parties to an agency

7. An agency is deemed to be created by:
   a. express contract.
   b. ratification.
   c. estoppel.
   d. all of the above

8. An agency relationship may be terminated by all of the following **except**:
   a. a fire destroying the property that is the subject of the agency contract.
   b. the principal's refusal of an offer to purchase that was presented in the name of a third party.
   c. mutual agreement of both the principal and the agent before the original term expires.
   d. the renunciation of the agency by the agent.

9. Broker Davis signed an exclusive agency listing to sell Johnson's $365,000 house. Davis diligently advertised the sale of the house. One week before the listing was to expire, the house was sold through Johnson's own efforts to a friend. Under current rules and regulations, Davis is most likely to receive:
   a. no commission.
   b. half of the commission.
   c. the costs of advertising the house.
   d. all of the commission.

10. An enforceable listing contract for the sale of real property must be:
    a. in writing.
    b. acknowledged.
    c. recorded.
    d. all of the above

11. An agency relationship can be created by all of the following **except**:
    a. oral authorization.
    b. necessity or emergency.
    c. implied contract.
    d. voluntary offer by the agent.

12. To be entitled to a commission, a broker must show that he or she was the procuring cause of the sale under all of the following types of listings **except** a(n) _____ listing.
    a. net
    b. open
    c. exclusive agency
    d. exclusive right-to-sell

13. In an exclusive agency listing, as a matter of law, the duration of the listing between the broker and seller:
    a. is whatever term that is agreeable to both parties.
    b. is three months.
    c. is 90 days after the listing agreement is signed.
    d. has no specified term.

14. A licensed broker obtained an exclusive right-to-sell listing from an owner. During the listing period, the broker found a buyer who made an offer on the property that was accepted by the seller. Neither the offer nor the escrow instructions mentioned: (a) the broker as the agent, or (b) terms for payment of a commission. Under these circumstances the broker:
    a. has no legal right to a commission.
    b. must prove that the broker was the "procuring cause" to be able to collect a commission.
    c. is legally entitled to a commission.
    d. is subject to disciplinary action by the Real Estate Commissioner for negligence.

15. Seller Jordan signs a memorandum for an open listing with a broker authorizing the sale of her house for $65,000. The broker expends considerable time and money advertising and showing the house and obtains several offers. However, Jordan rejects the offers and instead sells the house to a friend. The broker:
    a. is not entitled to a commission because of the open listing.
    b. would be entitled to half the agreed commission.
    c. could probably collect the full commission in a civil lawsuit.
    d. should file for arbitration with the Real Estate Commissioner.

16. A listing contract that does not include a complete legal description of the subject property is:
    a. void.
    b. unenforceable.
    c. a violation of the Real Estate Law.
    d. none of the above

17. To be entitled to a commission, a broker must show that he or she was the procuring cause of the sale under all of the following types of listing agreements except a(n) _____ listing.
    a. net
    b. open
    c. exclusive agency
    d. exclusive right-to-sell

18. A broker received a bona fide offer and a personal check as a deposit. The prospective buyer asked the broker to hold the check uncashed until the end of the week. The broker must:
    a. deposit the check within 24 hours.
    b. inform the seller.
    c. follow the buyer's instructions to the letter.
    d. refuse even to accept the check.

19. When is a broker relieved of the obligation to present an offer to purchase real property to the principal?
    a. When the offer contains more than three contingency clauses
    b. When the offer is for the purchase of nonresidential property
    c. When the broker is acting on written instructions from the principal or the offer is patently frivolous
    d. When the broker notifies the seller in writing of his or her decision not to present the offer

20. During an inspection of a seller's residence when taking the listing on a property, the agent noticed cracks in the walls and slab floors. Moreover, some of the doors and windows were jammed and would not open properly. In view of these observations, the agent has a duty to advise the owner to:
    a. order an inspection from a licensed Structural Pest Control Operator.
    b. obtain a soil report from a licensed engineer.
    c. contact the city for a zoning map.
    d. purchase a Home Protection Plan

21. The usual listing contract authorizes a broker to:
    a. find a purchaser and bind his or her principal to a contract to sell.
    b. find a purchaser and accept an offer to purchase accompanied by a deposit.
    c. assure a prospective purchaser that an offer meeting the terms of the listing will be accepted by his or her principal.
    d. convey the real property that is being listed.

22. A broker made a sale to an interested buyer based on false information the seller had provided to the broker. The broker had acted in good faith and in a reasonable manner in relying on the false information. The buyer rescinded the sales contract on grounds of fraud. Given these circumstances, the broker would normally be entitled to:
    a. reimbursement only for out-of-pocket expenses incurred in connection with the transaction.
    b. a full commission and indemnity for losses caused by related legal action by the defrauded buyer against the broker.
    c. one-half of the full commission.
    d. no commission because the broker is guilty of fraud through commission.

23. If a broker acts as an agent, the broker owes to the seller a fiduciary duty. What does the broker owe to the buyer?
    a. The same fiduciary duty
    b. A duty of fair and honest dealing
    c. A duty to answer all questions
    d. A duty to disclose all information regarding the selling price only

24. A seller is not responsible for actions and representations made by which of the following?
    a. Seller's agent
    b. Buyer's agent
    c. Seller's subagents
    d. Agents employed by the seller's agent

25. A broker is most likely to earn a commission when the broker:
    a. attempts to bind the principal to the contract.
    b. secures an offer with a substantial deposit.
    c. communicates the buyer's offer to the seller.
    d. communicates the seller's acceptance to the buyer.

Real Estate Contracts

6
Chapter

Introduction

In this chapter, you will review the basic elements of a contract and learn about real estate contracts. Real estate contracts discussed include:

- agreements employing a broker to market and sell real estate for compensation (discussed in Chapter 5).

- agreements employing a broker to locate real estate for compensation (discussed in Chapter 5).

- contracts for the purchase of real property, or of an interest therein.

- contracts for the option of real property, or of an interest therein.

- agreements for leasing realty for more than a year.

Real estate contracts must have all the elements of a valid contract. Additionally, they must be in writing, according to the Statute of Frauds, and must be signed by the parties.

Learning Objectives

After reading this chapter, you will be able to:

- discuss real estate contracts.
- explain performance and discharge of real estate contracts.
- describe Statute of Frauds and breach of a real estate contract.
- name the provisions of a real estate contract.
- summarize the responsibilities of a landlord and a tenant.
- discuss the importance of a deposit receipt (purchase agreement).

Listing and Buyer Representation Agreements

Listing agreements and buyer representation agreements were discussed in the previous chapter. As a review:

A listing is a contract by which a principal, or seller, employs a broker to sell real estate. Primarily, a listing agreement is an employment contract between a seller and a broker. It is a bilateral agreement where the seller agrees to pay a commission if the broker finds a buyer, and the broker promises to use due diligence to procure a buyer.

A buyer representation agreement is an employment contract between a buyer and a broker. It is a single agency agreement where the broker agrees to represent a buyer in purchasing a property.

Offer to Purchase

In California, most real estate agents use the Residential Purchase Agreement and Joint Escrow Instructions, commonly known as a **deposit receipt** or **purchase offer** because it is an offer to purchase real property. The deposit receipt acts as the receipt for earnest money given by the buyer to secure an offer, as well as being the basic contract, or agreement, between the buyer and seller. Once the seller agrees to the offer and the buyer is informed of the seller's acceptance, the deposit receipt is a legally binding contract. Once all parties **execute**, or sign, the deposit receipt it becomes a bilateral contract.

Upon writing an offer to purchase real property, a buyer may give some consideration such as a personal check, commonly in the amount of 1% of the purchase price, as a sign that he or she is serious about making the offer. The check is made out to an escrow company or the listing broker. The real estate agent holds the check. If the seller refuses the offer, the check is returned to the buyer. If the seller accepts the offer, the buyer's check is deposited into an escrow account or into the broker's trust account within three business days after receiving it.

The deposit receipt includes all terms of the sale, including agreements about financing. The buyer and seller are bound by the contract when the buyer receives notification of the seller's acceptance of the offer, without any changes. The deposit receipt, as the original agreement between the buyer and seller, may become the actual escrow instructions or simply the basic agreement for escrow instructions which will follow when escrow is opened. Usually there are terms in the contract that must be met during the escrow period; therefore, the contract is considered executory until all the terms are completed and escrow closes.

California Residential Purchase Agreement and Joint Escrow Instructions

In most cases, a standard California Residential Purchase Agreement and Joint Escrow Instructions (RPA-CA) contract is used by real estate agents when a buyer makes an offer anywhere in California. It was created by the California Association of REALTORS® (C.A.R.). The Department of Real Estate does not officially recommend this form; nor is any type of specific form required by law. Real estate agents do have an alternative, however, among the standard C.A.R. forms, depending on the custom in their area of the state. Real estate practices differ significantly in different parts of California and some of those differences are not reflected in the commonly used deposit receipt. An alternate form, Area Edition Residential Purchase Agreement (AERPA11) is available to real estate agents who desire features not included in the other form.

The Main Clauses Included in the Deposit Receipt

- Date of the agreement
- Names and addresses of the parties to the contract
- Description of the property
- The consideration or price
- Financing and terms
- Date and place of closing
- Signatures of buyer and seller

CALIFORNIA
ASSOCIATION
OF REALTORS®

CALIFORNIA
RESIDENTIAL PURCHASE AGREEMENT
AND JOINT ESCROW INSTRUCTIONS
For Use With Single Family Residential Property — Attached or Detached
(C.A.R. Form RPA-CA, Revised 1/06)

Date _____ , at _____ , California.

1. OFFER:
   A. THIS IS AN OFFER FROM _____ ("Buyer").
   B. THE REAL PROPERTY TO BE ACQUIRED is described as _____
      _____ , Assessor's Parcel No. _____ , situated in
      _____ , County of _____ , California, ("Property").
   C. THE PURCHASE PRICE offered is _____
      _____ Dollars $ _____ .
   D. CLOSE OF ESCROW shall occur on _____ (date) (or ☐ _____ **Days** After Acceptance).

2. FINANCE TERMS: Obtaining the loans below **is a contingency** of this Agreement unless: **(i)** either 2K or 2L is checked below; or **(ii)** otherwise agreed in writing. Buyer shall act diligently and in good faith to obtain the designated loans. Obtaining deposit, down payment and closing costs **is not a contingency.** Buyer represents that funds will be good when deposited with Escrow Holder.
   A. INITIAL DEPOSIT: Buyer has given a deposit in the amount of . . . . $ _____
      to the agent submitting the offer (or to ☐ _____), by personal check
      (or ☐ _____), made payable to _____ ,
      which shall be held uncashed until Acceptance and then deposited within **3 business days** after Acceptance
      (or ☐ _____), with
      Escrow Holder, (or ☐ into Broker's trust account).
   B. INCREASED DEPOSIT: Buyer shall deposit with Escrow Holder an increased deposit in the amount of . . . . . $ _____
      within _____ **Days** After Acceptance, or ☐ _____ .
   C. FIRST LOAN IN THE AMOUNT OF . . . . $ _____
      (1) NEW First Deed of Trust in favor of lender, encumbering the Property, securing a note payable at maximum
         interest of _____ % fixed rate, or _____ % initial adjustable rate with a maximum interest rate
         of _____ %, balance due in _____ years, amortized over _____ years. Buyer shall
         pay loan fees/points not to exceed _____ . (These terms apply whether the designated loan
         is conventional, FHA or VA.)
      (2) ☐ FHA ☐ VA: (The following terms only apply to the FHA or VA loan that is checked.)
         Seller shall pay _____ % discount points. Seller shall pay other fees not allowed to be paid by Buyer,
         ☐ not to exceed $ _____ . Seller shall pay the cost of lender required Repairs (including
         those for wood destroying pest) not otherwise provided for in this Agreement, ☐ not to exceed
         $ _____ . (Actual loan amount may increase if mortgage insurance premiums, funding
         fees or closing costs are financed.)
   D. ADDITIONAL FINANCING TERMS: ☐ Seller financing, (C.A.R. Form SFA); ☐ secondary financing, ... $ _____
      (C.A.R. Form PAA, paragraph 4A); ☐ assumed financing (C.A.R. Form PAA, paragraph 4B)
      _____
      _____
   E. BALANCE OF PURCHASE PRICE (not including costs of obtaining loans and other closing costs) in the amount of . . $ _____
      to be deposited with Escrow Holder within sufficient time to close escrow.
   F. PURCHASE PRICE (TOTAL): . . . . $ _____
   G. LOAN APPLICATIONS: Within **7 (or ☐** _____ **) Days** After Acceptance, Buyer shall provide Seller a letter from lender or mortgage loan broker stating that, based on a review of Buyer's written application and credit report, Buyer is prequalified or preapproved for the NEW loan specified in 2C above.
   H. VERIFICATION OF DOWN PAYMENT AND CLOSING COSTS: Buyer (or Buyer's lender or loan broker pursuant to 2G) shall, within **7 (or ☐** _____ **) Days** After Acceptance, provide Seller written verification of Buyer's down payment and closing costs.
   I. LOAN CONTINGENCY REMOVAL: (i) Within **17 (or ☐** _____ **) Days** After Acceptance, Buyer shall, as specified in paragraph 14, remove the loan contingency or cancel this Agreement; **OR (ii)** (if checked) ☐ the loan contingency shall remain in effect until the designated loans are funded.
   J. APPRAISAL CONTINGENCY AND REMOVAL: This Agreement is **(OR,** if checked, ☐ is **NOT)** contingent upon the Property appraising at no less than the specified purchase price. If there is a loan contingency, at the time the loan contingency is removed (or, if checked, ☐ within **17 (or** _____ **) Days** After Acceptance), Buyer shall, as specified in paragraph 14B(3), remove the appraisal contingency or cancel this Agreement. If there is no loan contingency, Buyer shall, as specified in paragraph 14B(3), remove the appraisal contingency within **17 (or** _____ **) Days** After Acceptance.
   K. ☐ NO LOAN CONTINGENCY (If checked): Obtaining any loan in paragraphs 2C, 2D or elsewhere in this Agreement is NOT a contingency of this Agreement. If Buyer does not obtain the loan and as a result Buyer does not purchase the Property, Seller may be entitled to Buyer's deposit or other legal remedies.
   L. ☐ ALL CASH OFFER (If checked): No loan is needed to purchase the Property. Buyer shall, within **7 (or ☐** _____ **) Days** After Acceptance, provide Seller written verification of sufficient funds to close this transaction.

3. CLOSING AND OCCUPANCY:
   A. Buyer intends (or ☐ does not intend) to occupy the Property as Buyer's primary residence.
   B. Seller-occupied or vacant property: Occupancy shall be delivered to Buyer at _____ ☐ AM ☐ PM, ☐ on the date of Close Of Escrow;
      ☐ on _____ ; or ☐ no later than _____ **Days** After Close Of Escrow. (C.A.R. Form PAA, paragraph 2.) If transfer of title and occupancy do not occur at the same time, Buyer and Seller are advised to: **(i)** enter into a written occupancy agreement; and **(ii)** consult with their insurance and legal advisors.

Buyer's Initials (_____) (_____)
Seller's Initials (_____) (_____)

Reviewed by _____ Date _____

EQUAL HOUSING OPPORTUNITY

RPA-CA REVISED 1/06 (PAGE 1 OF 8)
CALIFORNIA RESIDENTIAL PURCHASE AGREEMENT (RPA-CA PAGE 1 OF 8)

Agent:	Phone:	Fax:	Prepared using WINForms® software
Broker:			

Property Address: _____ Date: _____

  C. **Tenant-occupied property: (i)** Property shall be vacant at least **5 (or** ☐ _____ **) Days** Prior to Close Of Escrow, unless otherwise agreed in writing. **Note to Seller: If you are unable to deliver Property vacant in accordance with rent control and other applicable Law, you may be in breach of this Agreement.**

  OR (ii) (if checked) ☐ **Tenant to remain in possession.** The attached addendum is incorporated into this Agreement (C.A.R. Form PAA, paragraph 3.);

  OR (iii) (if checked) ☐ **This Agreement is contingent** upon Buyer and Seller entering into a written agreement regarding occupancy of the Property within the time specified in paragraph 14B(1). If no written agreement is reached within this time, either Buyer or Seller may cancel this Agreement in writing.

  D. At Close Of Escrow, Seller assigns to Buyer any assignable warranty rights for items included in the sale and shall provide any available Copies of such warranties. Brokers cannot and will not determine the assignability of any warranties.

  E. At Close Of Escrow, unless otherwise agreed in writing, Seller shall provide keys and/or means to operate all locks, mailboxes, security systems, alarms and garage door openers. If Property is a condominium or located in a common interest subdivision, Buyer may be required to pay a deposit to the Homeowners' Association ("HOA") to obtain keys to accessible HOA facilities.

4. **ALLOCATION OF COSTS** (If checked): Unless otherwise specified here, this paragraph only determines who is to pay for the report, inspection, test or service mentioned. If not specified here or elsewhere in this Agreement, the determination of who is to pay for any work recommended or identified by any such report, inspection, test or service shall be by the method specified in paragraph 14B(2).

  A. **WOOD DESTROYING PEST INSPECTION:**

   (1) ☐ Buyer ☐ Seller shall pay for an inspection and report for wood destroying pests and organisms ("Report") which shall be prepared by _____ , a registered structural pest control company. The Report shall cover the accessible areas of the main building and attached structures and, if checked: ☐ detached garages and carports, ☐ detached decks, ☐ the following other structures or areas _____ . The Report shall not include roof coverings. If Property is a condominium or located in a common interest subdivision, the Report shall include only the separate interest and any exclusive-use areas being transferred and shall not include common areas, unless otherwise agreed. Water tests of shower pans on upper level units may not be performed without consent of the owners of property below the shower.

  OR (2) ☐ **(If checked)** The attached addendum (C.A.R. Form WPA) regarding wood destroying pest inspection and allocation of cost is incorporated into this Agreement.

  B. **OTHER INSPECTIONS AND REPORTS:**

   (1) ☐ Buyer ☐ Seller shall pay to have septic or private sewage disposal systems inspected _____ .

   (2) ☐ Buyer ☐ Seller shall pay to have domestic wells tested for water potability and productivity _____ .

   (3) ☐ Buyer ☐ Seller shall pay for a natural hazard zone disclosure report prepared by _____ .

   (4) ☐ Buyer ☐ Seller shall pay for the following inspection or report _____ .

   (5) ☐ Buyer ☐ Seller shall pay for the following inspection or report _____ .

  C. **GOVERNMENT REQUIREMENTS AND RETROFIT:**

   (1) ☐ Buyer ☐ Seller shall pay for smoke detector installation and/or water heater bracing, if required by Law. Prior to Close Of Escrow, Seller shall provide Buyer a written statement of compliance in accordance with state and local Law, unless exempt.

   (2) ☐ Buyer ☐ Seller shall pay the cost of compliance with any other minimum mandatory government retrofit standards, inspections and reports if required as a condition of closing escrow under any Law. _____ .

  D. **ESCROW AND TITLE:**

   (1) ☐ Buyer ☐ Seller shall pay escrow fee _____ .
    Escrow Holder shall be _____ .

   (2) ☐ Buyer ☐ Seller shall pay for **owner's** title insurance policy specified in paragraph 12E _____ .
    Owner's title policy to be issued by _____ .
    (Buyer shall pay for any title insurance policy insuring Buyer's **lender,** unless otherwise agreed in writing.)

  E. **OTHER COSTS:**

   (1) ☐ Buyer ☐ Seller shall pay County transfer tax or transfer fee _____ .

   (2) ☐ Buyer ☐ Seller shall pay City transfer tax or transfer fee _____ .

   (3) ☐ Buyer ☐ Seller shall pay HOA transfer fee _____ .

   (4) ☐ Buyer ☐ Seller shall pay HOA document preparation fees _____ .

   (5) ☐ Buyer ☐ Seller shall pay the cost, not to exceed $ _____ , of a one-year home warranty plan, issued by _____ ,
    with the following optional coverage: _____ .

   (6) ☐ Buyer ☐ Seller shall pay for _____ .

   (7) ☐ Buyer ☐ Seller shall pay for _____ .

5. **STATUTORY DISCLOSURES (INCLUDING LEAD-BASED PAINT HAZARD DISCLOSURES) AND CANCELLATION RIGHTS:**

  A. **(1)** Seller shall, within the time specified in paragraph 14A, deliver to Buyer, if required by Law: **(i)** Federal Lead-Based Paint Disclosures and pamphlet ("Lead Disclosures"); and **(ii)** disclosures or notices required by sections 1102 et. seq. and 1103 et. seq. of the California Civil Code ("Statutory Disclosures"). Statutory Disclosures include, but are not limited to, a Real Estate Transfer Disclosure Statement ("TDS"), Natural Hazard Disclosure Statement ("NHD"), notice or actual knowledge of release of illegal controlled substance, notice of special tax and/or assessments (or, if allowed, substantially equivalent notice regarding the Mello-Roos Community Facilities Act and Improvement Bond Act of 1915) and, if Seller has actual knowledge, an industrial use and military ordnance location disclosure (C.A.R. Form SSD).

   (2) Buyer shall, within the time specified in paragraph 14B(1), return Signed Copies of the Statutory and Lead Disclosures to Seller.

   (3) In the event Seller, prior to Close Of Escrow, becomes aware of adverse conditions materially affecting the Property, or any material inaccuracy in disclosures, information or representations previously provided to Buyer of which Buyer is otherwise unaware, Seller shall promptly provide a subsequent or amended disclosure or notice, in writing, covering those items. **However, a subsequent or amended disclosure shall not be required for conditions and material inaccuracies disclosed in reports ordered and paid for by Buyer.**

Buyer's Initials (_____)(_____)
Seller's Initials (_____)(_____)

Copyright © 1991-2006, CALIFORNIA ASSOCIATION OF REALTORS®, INC.
RPA-CA REVISED 1/06 (PAGE 2 OF 8)

Reviewed by _____ Date _____

CALIFORNIA RESIDENTIAL PURCHASE AGREEMENT (RPA-CA PAGE 2 OF 8)

EQUAL HOUSING OPPORTUNITY

x.zfx

Property Address: _____ Date: _____

(4) If any disclosure or notice specified in 5A(1), or subsequent or amended disclosure or notice is delivered to Buyer after the offer is Signed, Buyer shall have the right to cancel this Agreement within **3 Days** After delivery in person, or **5 Days** After delivery by deposit in the mail, by giving written notice of cancellation to Seller or Seller's agent. (Lead Disclosures sent by mail must be sent certified mail or better.)

(5) **Note to Buyer and Seller: Waiver of Statutory and Lead Disclosures is prohibited by Law.**

B. **NATURAL AND ENVIRONMENTAL HAZARDS:** Within the time specified in paragraph 14A, Seller shall, if required by Law: **(i)** deliver to Buyer earthquake guides (and questionnaire) and environmental hazards booklet; **(ii)** even if exempt from the obligation to provide a NHD, disclose if the Property is located in a Special Flood Hazard Area; Potential Flooding (Inundation) Area; Very High Fire Hazard Zone; State Fire Responsibility Area; Earthquake Fault Zone; Seismic Hazard Zone; and **(iii)** disclose any other zone as required by Law and provide any other information required for those zones.

C. **DATA BASE DISCLOSURE:** Notice: Pursuant to Section 290.46 of the Penal Code, information about specified registered sex offenders is made available to the public via an Internet Web site maintained by the Department of Justice at www.meganslaw.ca.gov. Depending on an offender's criminal history, this information will include either the address at which the offender resides or the community of residence and ZIP Code in which he or she resides. (Neither Seller nor Brokers are required to check this website. If Buyer wants further information, Broker recommends that Buyer obtain information from this website during Buyer's inspection contingency period. Brokers do not have expertise in this area.)

6. **CONDOMINIUM/PLANNED UNIT DEVELOPMENT DISCLOSURES:**

A. **SELLER HAS: 7 (or ☐ _____) Days** After Acceptance to disclose to Buyer whether the Property is a condominium, or is located in a planned unit development or other common interest subdivision (C.A.R. Form SSD).

B. If the Property is a condominium or is located in a planned unit development or other common interest subdivision, Seller has **3 (or ☐ _____) Days** After Acceptance to request from the HOA (C.A.R. Form HOA): **(i)** Copies of any documents required by Law; **(ii)** disclosure of any pending or anticipated claim or litigation by or against the HOA; **(iii)** a statement containing the location and number of designated parking and storage spaces; **(iv)** Copies of the most recent 12 months of HOA minutes for regular and special meetings; and **(v)** the names and contact information of all HOAs governing the Property (collectively, "CI Disclosures"). Seller shall itemize and deliver to Buyer all CI Disclosures received from the HOA and any CI Disclosures in Seller's possession. Buyer's approval of CI Disclosures is a contingency of this Agreement as specified in paragraph 14B(3).

7. **CONDITIONS AFFECTING PROPERTY:**

A. Unless otherwise agreed: **(i) the Property is sold (a) in its PRESENT physical condition as of the date of Acceptance and (b) subject to Buyer's Investigation rights; (ii)** the Property, including pool, spa, landscaping and grounds, is to be maintained in substantially the same condition as on the date of Acceptance; and **(iii)** all debris and personal property not included in the sale shall be removed by Close Of Escrow.

B. **SELLER SHALL, within the time specified in paragraph 14A, DISCLOSE KNOWN MATERIAL FACTS AND DEFECTS affecting the Property, including known insurance claims within the past five years, AND MAKE OTHER DISCLOSURES REQUIRED BY LAW (C.A.R. Form SSD).**

C. **NOTE TO BUYER: You are strongly advised to conduct investigations of the entire Property in order to determine its present condition since Seller may not be aware of all defects affecting the Property or other factors that you consider important. Property improvements may not be built according to code, in compliance with current Law, or have had permits issued.**

D. **NOTE TO SELLER: Buyer has the right to inspect the Property and, as specified in paragraph 14B, based upon information discovered in those inspections: (i)** cancel this Agreement; or **(ii)** request that you make Repairs or take other action.

8. **ITEMS INCLUDED AND EXCLUDED:**

A. **NOTE TO BUYER AND SELLER:** Items listed as included or excluded in the MLS, flyers or marketing materials are **not** included in the purchase price or excluded from the sale unless specified in 8B or C.

B. **ITEMS INCLUDED IN SALE:**

(1) All EXISTING fixtures and fittings that are attached to the Property;

(2) Existing electrical, mechanical, lighting, plumbing and heating fixtures, ceiling fans, fireplace inserts, gas logs and grates, solar systems, built-in appliances, window and door screens, awnings, shutters, window coverings, attached floor coverings, television antennas, satellite dishes, private integrated telephone systems, air coolers/conditioners, pool/spa equipment, garage door openers/remote controls, mailbox, in-ground landscaping, trees/shrubs, water softeners, water purifiers, security systems/alarms; and

(3) The following items: _____
_____ .

(4) Seller represents that all items included in the purchase price, unless otherwise specified, are owned by Seller.

(5) All items included shall be transferred free of liens and without Seller warranty.

C. **ITEMS EXCLUDED FROM SALE:** _____
_____

9. **BUYER'S INVESTIGATION OF PROPERTY AND MATTERS AFFECTING PROPERTY:**

A. Buyer's acceptance of the condition of, and any other matter affecting the Property, is a contingency of this Agreement as specified in this paragraph and paragraph 14B. Within the time specified in paragraph 14B(1), Buyer shall have the right, at Buyer's expense unless otherwise agreed, to conduct inspections, investigations, tests, surveys and other studies ("Buyer Investigations"), including, but not limited to, the right to: **(i)** inspect for lead-based paint and other lead-based paint hazards; **(ii)** inspect for wood destroying pests and organisms; **(iii)** review the registered sex offender database; **(iv)** confirm the insurability of Buyer and the Property; and **(v)** satisfy Buyer as to any matter specified in the attached Buyer's Inspection Advisory (C.A.R. Form BIA). Without Seller's prior written consent, Buyer shall neither make nor cause to be made: **(i)** invasive or destructive Buyer Investigations; or **(ii)** inspections by any governmental building or zoning inspector or government employee, unless required by Law.

B. Buyer shall complete Buyer Investigations and, as specified in paragraph 14B, remove the contingency or cancel this Agreement. Buyer shall give Seller, at no cost, complete Copies of all Buyer Investigation reports obtained by Buyer. Seller shall make the Property available for all Buyer Investigations. Seller shall have water, gas, electricity and all operable pilot lights on for Buyer's Investigations and through the date possession is made available to Buyer.

Buyer's Initials (_____) (_____)
Seller's Initials (_____) (_____)

RPA-CA REVISED 1/06 (PAGE 3 OF 8)

Reviewed by _____ Date _____

EQUAL HOUSING OPPORTUNITY

CALIFORNIA RESIDENTIAL PURCHASE AGREEMENT (RPA-CA PAGE 3 OF 8)

x.zfx

Property Address: _____ Date: _____

10. REPAIRS: Repairs shall be completed prior to final verification of condition unless otherwise agreed in writing. Repairs to be performed at Seller's expense may be performed by Seller or through others, provided that the work complies with applicable Law, including governmental permit, inspection and approval requirements. Repairs shall be performed in a good, skillful manner with materials of quality and appearance comparable to existing materials. It is understood that exact restoration of appearance or cosmetic items following all Repairs may not be possible. Seller shall: **(i)** obtain receipts for Repairs performed by others; **(ii)** prepare a written statement indicating the Repairs performed by Seller and the date of such Repairs; and **(iii)** provide Copies of receipts and statements to Buyer prior to final verification of condition.

11. BUYER INDEMNITY AND SELLER PROTECTION FOR ENTRY UPON PROPERTY: Buyer shall: **(i)** keep the Property free and clear of liens; **(ii)** Repair all damage arising from Buyer Investigations; and **(iii)** indemnify and hold Seller harmless from all resulting liability, claims, demands, damages and costs. Buyer shall carry, or Buyer shall require anyone acting on Buyer's behalf to carry, policies of liability, workers' compensation and other applicable insurance, defending and protecting Seller from liability for any injuries to persons or property occurring during any Buyer Investigations or work done on the Property at Buyer's direction prior to Close Of Escrow. Seller is advised that certain protections may be afforded Seller by recording a "Notice of Non-responsibility" (C.A.R. Form NNR) for Buyer Investigations and work done on the Property at Buyer's direction. Buyer's obligations under this paragraph shall survive the termination of this Agreement.

12. TITLE AND VESTING:
   A. Within the time specified in paragraph 14, Buyer shall be provided a current preliminary (title) report, which is only an offer by the title insurer to issue a policy of title insurance and may not contain every item affecting title. Buyer's review of the preliminary report and any other matters which may affect title are a contingency of this Agreement as specified in paragraph 14B.
   B. Title is taken in its present condition subject to all encumbrances, easements, covenants, conditions, restrictions, rights and other matters, whether of record or not, as of the date of Acceptance except: **(i)** monetary liens of record unless Buyer is assuming those obligations or taking the Property subject to those obligations; and **(ii)** those matters which Seller has agreed to remove in writing.
   C. Within the time specified in paragraph 14A, Seller has a duty to disclose to Buyer all matters known to Seller affecting title, whether of record or not.
   D. At Close Of Escrow, Buyer shall receive a grant deed conveying title (or, for stock cooperative or long-term lease, an assignment of stock certificate or of Seller's leasehold interest), including oil, mineral and water rights if currently owned by Seller. Title shall vest as designated in Buyer's supplemental escrow instructions. THE MANNER OF TAKING TITLE MAY HAVE SIGNIFICANT LEGAL AND TAX CONSEQUENCES. CONSULT AN APPROPRIATE PROFESSIONAL.
   E. Buyer shall receive a CLTA/ALTA Homeowner's Policy of Title Insurance. A title company, at Buyer's request, can provide information about the availability, desirability, coverage, and cost of various title insurance coverages and endorsements. If Buyer desires title coverage other than that required by this paragraph, Buyer shall instruct Escrow Holder in writing and pay any increase in cost.

13. SALE OF BUYER'S PROPERTY:
   A. This Agreement is NOT contingent upon the sale of any property owned by Buyer.
   OR B. ☐ (If checked): The attached addendum (C.A.R. Form COP) regarding the contingency for the sale of property owned by Buyer is incorporated into this Agreement.

14. TIME PERIODS; REMOVAL OF CONTINGENCIES; CANCELLATION RIGHTS: The following time periods may only be extended, altered, modified or changed by mutual written agreement. Any removal of contingencies or cancellation under this paragraph must be in writing (C.A.R. Form CR).
   A. **SELLER HAS: 7 (or ☐ _____) Days** After Acceptance to deliver to Buyer all reports, disclosures and information for which Seller is responsible under paragraphs 4, 5A and B, 6A, 7B and 12.
   B. **(1) BUYER HAS: 17 (or ☐ _____) Days** After Acceptance, unless otherwise agreed in writing, to:
      (i) complete all Buyer Investigations; approve all disclosures, reports and other applicable information, which Buyer receives from Seller; and approve all matters affecting the Property (including lead-based paint and lead-based paint hazards as well as other information specified in paragraph 5 and insurability of Buyer and the Property); and
      (ii) return to Seller Signed Copies of Statutory and Lead Disclosures delivered by Seller in accordance with paragraph 5A.
      (2) Within the time specified in 14B(1), Buyer may request that Seller make repairs or take any other action regarding the Property (C.A.R. Form RR). Seller has no obligation to agree to or respond to Buyer's requests.
      (3) By the end of the time specified in 14B(1) (or 2I for loan contingency or 2J for appraisal contingency), Buyer shall, in writing, remove the applicable contingency (C.A.R. Form CR) or cancel this Agreement. However, if **(i)** government-mandated inspections/ reports required as a condition of closing; or **(ii)** Common Interest Disclosures pursuant to paragraph 6B are not made within the time specified in 14A, then Buyer has **5 (or ☐ _____) Days** After receipt of any such items, or the time specified in 14B(1), whichever is later, to remove the applicable contingency or cancel this Agreement in writing.
   C. **CONTINUATION OF CONTINGENCY OR CONTRACTUAL OBLIGATION; SELLER RIGHT TO CANCEL:**
      (1) Seller right to Cancel; Buyer Contingencies: Seller, after first giving Buyer a Notice to Buyer to Perform (as specified below), may cancel this Agreement in writing and authorize return of Buyer's deposit if, by the time specified in this Agreement, Buyer does not remove in writing the applicable contingency or cancel this Agreement. Once all contingencies have been removed, failure of either Buyer or Seller to close escrow on time may be a breach of this Agreement.
      (2) Continuation of Contingency: Even after the expiration of the time specified in 14B, Buyer retains the right to make requests to Seller, remove in writing the applicable contingency or cancel this Agreement until Seller cancels pursuant to 14C(1). Once Seller receives Buyer's written removal of all contingencies, Seller may not cancel this Agreement pursuant to 14C(1).
      (3) Seller right to Cancel; Buyer Contract Obligations: Seller, after first giving Buyer a Notice to Buyer to Perform (as specified below), may cancel this Agreement in writing and authorize return of Buyer's deposit for any of the following reasons: **(i)** if Buyer fails to deposit funds as required by 2A or 2B; **(ii)** if the funds deposited pursuant to 2A or 2B are not good when deposited; **(iii)** if Buyer fails to provide a letter as required by 2G; **(iv)** if Buyer fails to provide verification as required by 2H or 2L; **(v)** if Seller reasonably disapproves of the verification provided by 2H or 2L; **(vi)** if Buyer fails to return Statutory and Lead Disclosures as required by paragraph 5A(2); or **(vii)** if Buyer fails to sign or initial a separate liquidated damage form for an increased deposit as required by paragraph 16. **Seller is not required to give Buyer a Notice to Perform regarding Close Of Escrow.**
      (4) Notice To Buyer To Perform: The Notice to Buyer to Perform (C.A.R. Form NBP) shall: **(i)** be in writing; **(ii)** be signed by Seller; and **(iii)** give Buyer at least **24 (or ☐ _____) hours** (or until the time specified in the applicable paragraph, whichever occurs last) to take the applicable action. A Notice to Buyer to Perform may not be given any earlier than **2 Days** Prior to the expiration of the applicable time for Buyer to remove a contingency or cancel this Agreement or meet a 14C(3) obligation.

Buyer's Initials (_____) (_____)
Seller's Initials (_____) (_____)

Reviewed by _____ Date _____

RPA-CA REVISED 1/06 (PAGE 4 OF 8)

CALIFORNIA RESIDENTIAL PURCHASE AGREEMENT (RPA-CA PAGE 4 OF 8)

EQUAL HOUSING OPPORTUNITY

x.zfx

Property Address: _____ Date: _____

   D. EFFECT OF BUYER'S REMOVAL OF CONTINGENCIES: If Buyer removes, in writing, any contingency or cancellation rights, unless otherwise specified in a separate written agreement between Buyer and Seller, Buyer shall conclusively be deemed to have: **(i)** completed all Buyer Investigations, and review of reports and other applicable information and disclosures pertaining to that contingency or cancellation right; **(ii)** elected to proceed with the transaction; and **(iii)** assumed all liability, responsibility and expense for Repairs or corrections pertaining to that contingency or cancellation right, or for inability to obtain financing.

   E. EFFECT OF CANCELLATION ON DEPOSITS: If Buyer or Seller gives written notice of cancellation pursuant to rights duly exercised under the terms of this Agreement, Buyer and Seller agree to Sign mutual instructions to cancel the sale and escrow and release deposits to the party entitled to the funds, less fees and costs incurred by that party. Fees and costs may be payable to service providers and vendors for services and products provided during escrow. **Release of funds will require mutual Signed release instructions from Buyer and Seller, judicial decision or arbitration award. A party may be subject to a civil penalty of up to $1,000 for refusal to sign such instructions if no good faith dispute exists as to who is entitled to the deposited funds (Civil Code §1057.3).**

15. **FINAL VERIFICATION OF CONDITION:** Buyer shall have the right to make a final inspection of the Property within **5 (or _____) Days** Prior to Close Of Escrow, NOT AS A CONTINGENCY OF THE SALE, but solely to confirm: **(i)** the Property is maintained pursuant to paragraph 7A; **(ii)** Repairs have been completed as agreed; and **(iii)** Seller has complied with Seller's other obligations under this Agreement.

16. **LIQUIDATED DAMAGES: If Buyer fails to complete this purchase because of Buyer's default, Seller shall retain, as liquidated damages, the deposit actually paid. If the Property is a dwelling with no more than four units, one of which Buyer intends to occupy, then the amount retained shall be no more than 3% of the purchase price. Any excess shall be returned to Buyer. Release of funds will require mutual, Signed release instructions from both Buyer and Seller, judicial decision or arbitration award.**
   BUYER AND SELLER SHALL SIGN A SEPARATE LIQUIDATED DAMAGES PROVISION FOR ANY INCREASED DEPOSIT. (C.A.R. FORM RID)

Buyer's Initials _____ / _____	Seller's Initials _____ / _____

17. **DISPUTE RESOLUTION:**

   A. MEDIATION: Buyer and Seller agree to mediate any dispute or claim arising between them out of this Agreement, or any resulting transaction, before resorting to arbitration or court action. Paragraphs 17B(2) and (3) below apply to mediation whether or not the Arbitration provision is initialed. Mediation fees, if any, shall be divided equally among the parties involved. If, for any dispute or claim to which this paragraph applies, any party commences an action without first attempting to resolve the matter through mediation, or refuses to mediate after a request has been made, then that party shall not be entitled to recover attorney fees, even if they would otherwise be available to that party in any such action. THIS MEDIATION PROVISION APPLIES WHETHER OR NOT THE ARBITRATION PROVISION IS INITIALED.

   B. ARBITRATION OF DISPUTES: (1) Buyer and Seller agree that any dispute or claim in Law or equity arising between them out of this Agreement or any resulting transaction, which is not settled through mediation, shall be decided by neutral, binding arbitration, including and subject to paragraphs 17B(2) and (3) below. The arbitrator shall be a retired judge or justice, or an attorney with at least 5 years of residential real estate Law experience, unless the parties mutually agree to a different arbitrator, who shall render an award in accordance with substantive California Law. The parties shall have the right to discovery in accordance with California Code of Civil Procedure §1283.05. In all other respects, the arbitration shall be conducted in accordance with Title 9 of Part III of the California Code of Civil Procedure. Judgment upon the award of the arbitrator(s) may be entered into any court having jurisdiction. Interpretation of this agreement to arbitrate shall be governed by the Federal Arbitration Act.
   (2) EXCLUSIONS FROM MEDIATION AND ARBITRATION: The following matters are excluded from mediation and arbitration: (i) a judicial or non-judicial foreclosure or other action or proceeding to enforce a deed of trust, mortgage or installment land sale contract as defined in California Civil Code §2985; (ii) an unlawful detainer action; (iii) the filing or enforcement of a mechanic's lien; and (iv) any matter that is within the jurisdiction of a probate, small claims or bankruptcy court. The filing of a court action to enable the recording of a notice of pending action, for order of attachment, receivership, injunction, or other provisional remedies, shall not constitute a waiver of the mediation and arbitration provisions.
   (3) BROKERS: Buyer and Seller agree to mediate and arbitrate disputes or claims involving either or both Brokers, consistent with 17A and B, provided either or both Brokers shall have agreed to such mediation or arbitration prior to, or within a reasonable time after, the dispute or claim is presented to Brokers. Any election by either or both Brokers to participate in mediation or arbitration shall not result in Brokers being deemed parties to the Agreement.
   "NOTICE: BY INITIALING IN THE SPACE BELOW YOU ARE AGREEING TO HAVE ANY DISPUTE ARISING OUT OF THE MATTERS INCLUDED IN THE 'ARBITRATION OF DISPUTES' PROVISION DECIDED BY NEUTRAL ARBITRATION AS PROVIDED BY CALIFORNIA LAW AND YOU ARE GIVING UP ANY RIGHTS YOU MIGHT POSSESS TO HAVE THE DISPUTE LITIGATED IN A COURT OR JURY TRIAL. BY INITIALING IN THE SPACE BELOW YOU ARE GIVING UP YOUR JUDICIAL RIGHTS TO DISCOVERY AND APPEAL, UNLESS THOSE RIGHTS ARE SPECIFICALLY INCLUDED IN THE 'ARBITRATION OF DISPUTES' PROVISION. IF YOU REFUSE TO SUBMIT TO ARBITRATION AFTER AGREEING TO THIS PROVISION, YOU MAY BE COMPELLED TO ARBITRATE UNDER THE AUTHORITY OF THE CALIFORNIA CODE OF CIVIL PROCEDURE. YOUR AGREEMENT TO THIS ARBITRATION PROVISION IS VOLUNTARY."
   "WE HAVE READ AND UNDERSTAND THE FOREGOING AND AGREE TO SUBMIT DISPUTES ARISING OUT OF THE MATTERS INCLUDED IN THE 'ARBITRATION OF DISPUTES' PROVISION TO NEUTRAL ARBITRATION."

Buyer's Initials _____ / _____	Seller's Initials _____ / _____

RPA-CA REVISED 1/06 (PAGE 5 OF 8)

Buyer's Initials (_____) (_____)
Seller's Initials (_____) (_____)
Reviewed by _____ Date _____

CALIFORNIA RESIDENTIAL PURCHASE AGREEMENT (RPA-CA PAGE 5 OF 8)

x.zfx

Property Address: _____ Date: _____

18. **PRORATIONS OF PROPERTY TAXES AND OTHER ITEMS:** Unless otherwise agreed in writing, the following items shall be PAID CURRENT and prorated between Buyer and Seller as of Close Of Escrow: real property taxes and assessments, interest, rents, HOA regular, special, and emergency dues and assessments imposed prior to Close Of Escrow, premiums on insurance assumed by Buyer, payments on bonds and assessments assumed by Buyer, and payments on Mello-Roos and other Special Assessment District bonds and assessments that are now a lien. The following items shall be assumed by Buyer WITHOUT CREDIT toward the purchase price: prorated payments on Mello-Roos and other Special Assessment District bonds and assessments and HOA special assessments that are now a lien but not yet due. Property will be reassessed upon change of ownership. Any supplemental tax bills shall be paid as follows: **(i)** for periods after Close Of Escrow, by Buyer; and **(ii)** for periods prior to Close Of Escrow, by Seller. TAX BILLS ISSUED AFTER CLOSE OF ESCROW SHALL BE HANDLED DIRECTLY BETWEEN BUYER AND SELLER. Prorations shall be made based on a 30-day month.

19. **WITHHOLDING TAXES:** Seller and Buyer agree to execute any instrument, affidavit, statement or instruction reasonably necessary to comply with federal (FIRPTA) and California withholding Law, if required (C.A.R. Forms AS and AB).

20. **MULTIPLE LISTING SERVICE ("MLS"):** Brokers are authorized to report to the MLS a pending sale and, upon Close Of Escrow, the terms of this transaction to be published and disseminated to persons and entities authorized to use the information on terms approved by the MLS.

21. **EQUAL HOUSING OPPORTUNITY:** The Property is sold in compliance with federal, state and local anti-discrimination Laws.

22. **ATTORNEY FEES:** In any action, proceeding, or arbitration between Buyer and Seller arising out of this Agreement, the prevailing Buyer or Seller shall be entitled to reasonable attorney fees and costs from the non-prevailing Buyer or Seller, except as provided in paragraph 17A.

23. **SELECTION OF SERVICE PROVIDERS:** If Brokers refer Buyer or Seller to persons, vendors, or service or product providers ("Providers"), Brokers do not guarantee the performance of any Providers. Buyer and Seller may select ANY Providers of their own choosing.

24. **TIME OF ESSENCE; ENTIRE CONTRACT; CHANGES:** Time is of the essence. All understandings between the parties are incorporated in this Agreement. Its terms are intended by the parties as a final, complete and exclusive expression of their Agreement with respect to its subject matter, and may not be contradicted by evidence of any prior agreement or contemporaneous oral agreement. If any provision of this Agreement is held to be ineffective or invalid, the remaining provisions will nevertheless be given full force and effect. **Neither this Agreement nor any provision in it may be extended, amended, modified, altered or changed, except in writing Signed by Buyer and Seller.**

25. **OTHER TERMS AND CONDITIONS,** including attached supplements:
    A. ☐ Buyer's Inspection Advisory (C.A.R. Form BIA) _____
    B. ☐ Purchase Agreement Addendum (C.A.R. Form PAA paragraph numbers: _____)
    C. ☐ Statewide Buyer and Seller Advisory (C.A.R. Form SBSA) _____
    D. _____

26. **DEFINITIONS:** As used in this Agreement:
    A. **"Acceptance"** means the time the offer or final counter offer is accepted in writing by a party and is delivered to and personally received by the other party or that party's authorized agent in accordance with the terms of this offer or a final counter offer.
    B. **"Agreement"** means the terms and conditions of this accepted California Residential Purchase Agreement and any accepted counter offers and addenda.
    C. **"C.A.R. Form"** means the specific form referenced or another comparable form agreed to by the parties.
    D. **"Close Of Escrow"** means the date the grant deed, or other evidence of transfer of title, is recorded. If the scheduled close of escrow falls on a Saturday, Sunday or legal holiday, then close of escrow shall be the next business day after the scheduled close of escrow date.
    E. **"Copy"** means copy by any means including photocopy, NCR, facsimile and electronic.
    F. **"Days"** means calendar days, unless otherwise required by Law.
    G. **"Days After"** means the specified number of calendar days after the occurrence of the event specified, not counting the calendar date on which the specified event occurs, and ending at 11:59PM on the final day.
    H. **"Days Prior"** means the specified number of calendar days before the occurrence of the event specified, not counting the calendar date on which the specified event is scheduled to occur.
    I. **"Electronic Copy"** or **"Electronic Signature"** means, as applicable, an electronic copy or signature complying with California Law. Buyer and Seller agree that electronic means will not be used by either party to modify or alter the content or integrity of this Agreement without the knowledge and consent of the other.
    J. **"Law"** means any law, code, statute, ordinance, regulation, rule or order, which is adopted by a controlling city, county, state or federal legislative, judicial or executive body or agency.
    K. **"Notice to Buyer to Perform"** means a document (C.A.R. Form NBP), which shall be in writing and Signed by Seller and shall give Buyer at least 24 hours **(or as otherwise specified in paragraph 14C(4))** to remove a contingency or perform as applicable.
    L. **"Repairs"** means any repairs (including pest control), alterations, replacements, modifications or retrofitting of the Property provided for under this Agreement.
    M. **"Signed"** means either a handwritten or electronic signature on an original document, Copy or any counterpart.
    N. **Singular and Plural** terms each include the other, when appropriate.

Buyer's Initials (_____)(_____)
Seller's Initials (_____)(_____)

RPA-CA REVISED 1/06 (PAGE 6 OF 8)

Reviewed by _____ Date _____

EQUAL HOUSING OPPORTUNITY

CALIFORNIA RESIDENTIAL PURCHASE AGREEMENT (RPA-CA PAGE 6 OF 8)

x.zfx

Property Address: _____ Date: _____

27. **AGENCY:**

    A. **DISCLOSURE:** Buyer and Seller each acknowledge prior receipt of C.A.R. Form AD "Disclosure Regarding Real Estate Agency Relationships."

    B. **POTENTIALLY COMPETING BUYERS AND SELLERS:** Buyer and Seller each acknowledge receipt of a disclosure of the possibility of multiple representation by the Broker representing that principal. This disclosure may be part of a listing agreement, buyer-broker agreement or separate document (C.A.R. Form DA). Buyer understands that Broker representing Buyer may also represent other potential buyers, who may consider, make offers on or ultimately acquire the Property. Seller understands that Broker representing Seller may also represent other sellers with competing properties of interest to this Buyer.

    C. **CONFIRMATION:** The following agency relationships are hereby confirmed for this transaction:

    Listing Agent _____ (Print Firm Name) is the agent

    of (check one): ☐ the Seller exclusively; or ☐ both the Buyer and Seller.

    Selling Agent _____ (Print Firm Name) (if not same

    as Listing Agent) is the agent of (check one): ☐ the Buyer exclusively; or ☐ the Seller exclusively; or ☐ both the Buyer and Seller. Real Estate Brokers are not parties to the Agreement between Buyer and Seller.

28. **JOINT ESCROW INSTRUCTIONS TO ESCROW HOLDER:**

    A. **The following paragraphs, or applicable portions thereof, of this Agreement constitute the joint escrow instructions of Buyer and Seller to Escrow Holder,** which Escrow Holder is to use along with any related counter offers and addenda, and any additional mutual instructions to close the escrow: 1, 2, 4, 12, 13B, 14E, 18, 19, 24, 25B and 25D, 26, 28, 29, 32A, 33 and paragraph D of the section titled Real Estate Brokers on page 8. If a Copy of the separate compensation agreement(s) provided for in paragraph 29 or 32A, or paragraph D of the section titled Real Estate Brokers on page 8 is deposited with Escrow Holder by Broker, Escrow Holder shall accept such agreement(s) and pay out from Buyer's or Seller's funds, or both, as applicable, the Broker's compensation provided for in such agreement(s). The terms and conditions of this Agreement not set forth in the specified paragraphs are additional matters for the information of Escrow Holder, but about which Escrow Holder need not be concerned. Buyer and Seller will receive Escrow Holder's general provisions directly from Escrow Holder and will execute such provisions upon Escrow Holder's request. To the extent the general provisions are inconsistent or conflict with this Agreement, the general provisions will control as to the duties and obligations of Escrow Holder only. Buyer and Seller will execute additional instructions, documents and forms provided by Escrow Holder that are reasonably necessary to close the escrow.

    B. A Copy of this Agreement shall be delivered to Escrow Holder within **3** business days after Acceptance (or ☐ _____). Buyer and Seller authorize Escrow Holder to accept and rely on Copies and Signatures as defined in this Agreement as originals, to open escrow and for other purposes of escrow. The validity of this Agreement as between Buyer and Seller is not affected by whether or when Escrow Holder Signs this Agreement.

    C. Brokers are a party to the escrow for the sole purpose of compensation pursuant to paragraphs 29, 32A and paragraph D of the section titled Real Estate Brokers on page 8. Buyer and Seller irrevocably assign to Brokers compensation specified in paragraphs 29 and 32A, respectively, and irrevocably instruct Escrow Holder to disburse those funds to Brokers at Close Of Escrow or pursuant to any other mutually executed cancellation agreement. Compensation instructions can be amended or revoked only with the written consent of Brokers. Escrow Holder shall immediately notify Brokers: **(i)** if Buyer's initial or any additional deposit is not made pursuant to this Agreement, or is not good at time of deposit with Escrow Holder; or **(ii)** if Buyer and Seller instruct Escrow Holder to cancel escrow.

    D. A Copy of any amendment that affects any paragraph of this Agreement for which Escrow Holder is responsible shall be delivered to Escrow Holder within **2** business days after mutual execution of the amendment.

29. **BROKER COMPENSATION FROM BUYER:** If applicable, upon Close Of Escrow, **Buyer** agrees to pay compensation to Broker as specified in a separate written agreement between Buyer and Broker.

30. **TERMS AND CONDITIONS OF OFFER:**

This is an offer to purchase the Property on the above terms and conditions. All paragraphs with spaces for initials by Buyer and Seller are incorporated in this Agreement only if initialed by all parties. If at least one but not all parties initial, a counter offer is required until agreement is reached. Seller has the right to continue to offer the Property for sale and to accept any other offer at any time prior to notification of Acceptance. Buyer has read and acknowledges receipt of a Copy of the offer and agrees to the above confirmation of agency relationships. If this offer is accepted and Buyer subsequently defaults, Buyer may be responsible for payment of Brokers' compensation. This Agreement and any supplement, addendum or modification, including any Copy, may be Signed in two or more counterparts, all of which shall constitute one and the same writing.

RPA-CA REVISED 1/06 (PAGE 7 OF 8)

Buyer's Initials (_____) (_____)
Seller's Initials (_____) (_____)

Reviewed by _____ Date _____

CALIFORNIA RESIDENTIAL PURCHASE AGREEMENT (RPA-CA PAGE 7 OF 8)

x.zfx

Property Address: _____ Date: _____

31. EXPIRATION OF OFFER: This offer shall be deemed revoked and the deposit shall be returned unless the offer is Signed by Seller and a Copy of the Signed offer is personally received by Buyer, or by _____ , who is authorized to receive it by 5:00 PM on the third Day after this offer is signed by Buyer (or, if checked, ☐ by _____ (date), at _____ ☐ AM ☐ PM).

Date _____   Date _____
BUYER _____   BUYER _____
_____   _____
(Print name)   **(Print name)**
_____
(Address)

32. BROKER COMPENSATION FROM SELLER:
    A. Upon Close Of Escrow, **Seller** agrees to pay compensation to Broker as specified in a separate written agreement between Seller and Broker.
    B. If escrow does not close, compensation is payable as specified in that separate written agreement.

33. ACCEPTANCE OF OFFER: Seller warrants that Seller is the owner of the Property, or has the authority to execute this Agreement. Seller accepts the above offer, agrees to sell the Property on the above terms and conditions, and agrees to the above confirmation of agency relationships. Seller has read and acknowledges receipt of a Copy of this Agreement, and authorizes Broker to deliver a Signed Copy to Buyer.
    ☐ (If checked) **SUBJECT TO ATTACHED COUNTER OFFER, DATED** _____ .

Date _____   Date _____
SELLER _____   SELLER _____
_____   _____
(Print name)   **(Print name)**
_____
(Address)

(_____ / _____) **CONFIRMATION OF ACCEPTANCE:** A Copy of Signed Acceptance was personally received by Buyer or Buyer's authorized
      (Initials) agent on (date) _____ at _____ ☐ AM ☐ PM. **A binding Agreement is created when a Copy of Signed Acceptance is personally received by Buyer or Buyer's authorized agent whether or not confirmed in this document. Completion of this confirmation is not legally required in order to create a binding Agreement; it is solely intended to evidence the date that Confirmation of Acceptance has occurred.**

REAL ESTATE BROKERS:
A. **Real Estate Brokers are not parties to the Agreement between Buyer and Seller.**
B. **Agency relationships are confirmed as stated in paragraph 27.**
C. If specified in paragraph 2A, Agent who submitted the offer for Buyer acknowledges receipt of deposit.
D. **COOPERATING BROKER COMPENSATION:** Listing Broker agrees to pay Cooperating Broker **(Selling Firm)** and Cooperating Broker agrees to accept, out of Listing Broker's proceeds in escrow: **(i)** the amount specified in the MLS, provided Cooperating Broker is a Participant of the MLS in which the Property is offered for sale or a reciprocal MLS; or **(ii)** ☐ (if checked) the amount specified in a separate written agreement (C.A.R. Form CBC) between Listing Broker and Cooperating Broker.

Real Estate Broker (Selling Firm) _____ License # _____
By _____ License # _____ Date _____
Address _____ City _____ State _____ Zip _____
Telephone _____ Fax _____ E-mail _____

Real Estate Broker (Listing Firm) _____ License # _____
By _____ License # _____ Date _____
Address _____ City _____ State _____ Zip _____
Telephone _____ Fax _____ E-mail _____

ESCROW HOLDER ACKNOWLEDGMENT:
Escrow Holder acknowledges receipt of a Copy of this Agreement, (if checked, ☐ a deposit in the amount of $ _____), counter offer numbers _____ and _____ , and agrees to act as Escrow Holder subject to paragraph 28 of this Agreement, any supplemental escrow instructions and the terms of Escrow Holder's general provisions.

Escrow Holder is advised that the date of Confirmation of Acceptance of the Agreement as between Buyer and Seller is _____
Escrow Holder _____ Escrow # _____
By _____ Date _____
Address _____
Phone/Fax/E-mail _____
Escrow Holder is licensed by the California Department of ☐ Corporations, ☐ Insurance, ☐ Real Estate. License # _____

(_____ / _____) **REJECTION OF OFFER:** No counter offer is being made. This offer was reviewed and rejected by Seller on
(Seller's Initials) _____ (Date)

Published and Distributed by:
REAL ESTATE BUSINESS SERVICES, INC.
a subsidiary of the California Association of REALTORS®
525 South Virgil Avenue, Los Angeles, California 90020

SURE TRAC
The System for Success™

Reviewed by _____ Date _____

EQUAL HOUSING OPPORTUNITY

RPA-CA REVISED 1/06 (PAGE 8 OF 8)
CALIFORNIA RESIDENTIAL PURCHASE AGREEMENT (RPA-CA PAGE 8 OF 8)   x.zfx

Remember, the deposit receipt is probably the most important real estate document you—as an agent—will have to understand. Consumers rely on your knowledge, and your commission depends on your ability to explain a sometimes difficult transaction to them. It is important that you read through the entire California Residential Purchase Agreement and Joint Escrow Instructions (deposit receipt).

The offer covers more than just the purchase price and closing date. It covers contingencies, various inspections, mandatory disclosures, buyer's rights to investigate the property, how the buyer will take title, damages and dispute resolution, escrow instructions, compensation to the brokers, and acceptance of the offer.

The first line on the contract to be filled in is the date and place the contract is signed by the buyer. As you read through the contract pay particular attention to the clauses listed below:

Offer: This paragraph shows the name of the buyer, describes the property to be purchased, the offered purchase price, and the closing date for escrow.

Finance Terms: This section addresses whether the purchase will be an all cash offer or an offer based on obtaining financing. If the buyer must obtain financing to complete the transaction, the finance terms should state if the purchase of the property is contingent upon the buyer's ability to get financing. The amounts of the **initial deposit**, any **increased deposit** and the loans are listed and added to total the amount of the purchase price. Remember, any earnest money or deposits received by an agent are trust funds and handled as prescribed by the Commissioner's Real Estate Law and Regulations.

Closing and Occupancy: This section covers the intent of the buyer to occupy the property as a primary residence, the date the seller (or tenant) will turn over possession of the property to the buyer, and if the buyer is allowed to take possession of the property prior to close of escrow. In order to protect the rights and obligations of both seller and buyer, an **Interim Occupancy Agreement** should be used if a buyer wants early possession of the property. The new C.A.R. form contains wording that prohibits a landlord from demanding that rent be paid in cash.

Allocation of Costs: Since there are many inspections, reports, and tests associated with purchasing a property, it is important for both buyer and seller to agree about who will be responsible for their payment. Also, buyer and seller select the escrow and title provider and allocate the payment responsibility.

Statutory Disclosures: A seller is required by law to give a buyer several disclosures about the property and surrounding area which may affect the buyer's decision to purchase the property. These disclosures are discussed in detail in Chapter 7.

Personal Property Included or Excluded from the Sale: We learned about fixtures in Chapter 2. Sometimes sellers plan to take an appliance, window coverings, and light fixtures with them when they sell the property. Unless personal property items are excluded in the listing agreement, buyers may assume that what they see in the property is included in the sale. Some buyers will list items to be sure that they are included in their offering price. Listing agents need to discuss which personal property, if any, sellers may want to exclude from the sale.

Title and Vesting: Explain the importance of reviewing the preliminary title report with the buyer. Check for any undisclosed liens or easements that may affect the use of the property. Because the property is still owned by the seller, any existing trust deeds will be shown with the seller as the trustor. Once the property is sold, the new title insurance policy will show the buyer's loan. The manner in which a buyer takes title to real property (**vesting**) can have unforeseen legal and tax ramifications. Always direct the buyer to an attorney and/or tax professional to get advice on vesting.

Contingencies: Buyers and sellers are given specific amounts of time to meet the various conditions written in the contract.

Liquidated Damages: Parties to a contract may decide in advance the amount of damages to be paid, should either party breach the contract. In fact, the offer to purchase, or sales contract, usually contains a printed clause that says the seller may keep the deposit as liquidated damages if the buyer backs out without good reason. In the event the buyer defaults on the contract, the liquidated damages cannot exceed 3% of the purchase price if the property is a single family residence.

Dispute Resolution: Even when the utmost care is taken in a transaction, disputes may arise. To try to settle any disputes amicably, the contract offers both mediation and arbitration. Both buyer and seller must agree to be bound by mutual arbitration in order for the clause to be effective.

Prorations: Since most real estate offices use the C.A.R. Purchase Agreement and Joint Escrow Instruction contract, this clause tells escrow the buyers' and sellers' wishes regarding the prorations (allocation) of property tax, interest, assessments, and any other charge normally prorated in escrow.

Time is of the Essence: Time is often significant in a contract; indeed, its performance may be measured by the passage of time. By law, if no time is required by the contract, a reasonable time is allowed. If the act can be done instantly—as in the payment of money—it must be done at once.

Expiration of the Offer: If the offer is not accepted by the seller within the time frame, the offer is revoked and any deposit is returned to the buyer. A deposit may be refunded by agreement, judgment, or arbitration.

Acceptance of the Offer: Once the deposit receipt is accepted and signed by the seller it becomes a legally binding contract. Death or incapacity does not automatically cancel a contract. After acceptance of the offer, if the seller dies or becomes incapacitated, the seller's heirs must complete the sale.

Termination of Offer

An offer may be terminated for a number of reasons. The buyer may withdraw the offer before the seller accepts it. Since the seller has not accepted the offer, there is no contract, so the buyer would get his or her deposit back. An offer ends when the time limit given in the offer for acceptance expires. If the buyer dies before the seller accepts the offer, the offer terminates. The original offer expires if the seller gives the buyer a counteroffer.

Counteroffer

In a real estate transaction, a **counteroffer** is the rejection of an original purchase offer and the submission of a new and different offer. If a seller rejects the offer and submits a counteroffer, the original offer automatically terminates.

Option

An **option** is a contract to keep open, for a set period of time, an offer to purchase or lease real property. The person who owns the property (seller, lessor) is the **optionor**. The person who wants to purchase or lease (lessee) the property is called the **optionee**. An optionor is to an optionee as an assignor is to an assignee. An option is a written, unilateral contract between the owner of real property and a prospective buyer, stating the right to purchase, a fixed price, and time frame. The price and all other terms should be stated clearly, as the option may become the sales agreement when the optionee exercises the right to purchase. If the option is exercised by the optionee, it does not necessarily require a separate sales contract. A real estate broker earns commission on an option when it is exercised.

CALIFORNIA
ASSOCIATION
OF REALTORS®

COUNTER OFFER No. _____

For use by Seller or Buyer. May be used for Multiple Counter Offer.
(C.A.R. Form CO, Revised 10/04)

Date _____ , at _____ , California.

This is a counter offer to the: ☐ California Residential Purchase Agreement, ☐ Counter Offer, or ☐ Other _____ ("Offer"),

dated _____ , on property known as _____ ("Property"),

between _____ ("Buyer") and

_____ ("Seller").

1. **TERMS:** The terms and conditions of the above referenced document are **accepted subject to the following:**
   A. Paragraphs in the Offer that require initials by all parties, but are not initialed by all parties, are excluded from the final agreement unless specifically referenced for inclusion in paragraph 1C of this or another Counter Offer.
   B. Unless otherwise agreed in writing, down payment and loan amount(s) will be adjusted in the same proportion as in the original Offer.
   C. _____
      _____
      _____
      _____
      _____
      _____
      _____
   D. The following attached supplements are incorporated into this Counter Offer: ☐ Addendum No. _____
      ☐ _____   ☐ _____

2. **RIGHT TO ACCEPT OTHER OFFERS:** Seller has the right to continue to offer the Property for sale or for other transaction, and to accept any other offer at any time prior to notification of acceptance, as described in paragraph 3. If this is a Seller Counter Offer, Seller's acceptance of another offer prior to Buyer's acceptance and communication of notification of this Counter Offer, shall revoke this Counter Offer.

3. **EXPIRATION:** This Counter Offer shall be deemed revoked and the deposits, if any, shall be returned unless this Counter Offer is signed by the Buyer or Seller to whom it is sent and a Copy of the signed Counter Offer is personally received by the person making this Counter Offer or _____ ,
   who is authorized to receive it, by 5:00 PM on the third Day After this Counter Offer is made or, (if checked) by ☐ _____
   (date), at _____ ☐ AM ☐ PM. This Counter Offer may be executed in counterparts.

4. ☐ **(If checked:) MULTIPLE COUNTER OFFER:** Seller is making a Counter Offer(s) to another prospective buyer(s) on terms that may or may not be the same as in this Counter Offer. Acceptance of this Counter Offer by Buyer shall **not** be binding unless and until it is subsequently re-Signed by Seller in paragraph 7 below and a Copy of the Counter Offer Signed in paragraph 7 is personally received by Buyer or by _____ , who is authorized to receive it, by 5:00PM
   on the third Day after this Counter Offer is made or, (if checked) by ☐ _____ (date), at _____ ☐ AM ☐ PM.
   Prior to the completion of all of these events, Buyer and Seller shall have no duties or obligations for the purchase or sale of the Property.

5. **OFFER:** ☐ BUYER OR ☐ SELLER MAKES THIS COUNTER OFFER ON THE TERMS ABOVE AND ACKNOWLEDGES RECEIPT OF A COPY.
   _____ Date _____
   _____ Date _____

6. **ACCEPTANCE: I/WE** accept the above Counter Offer (If checked ☐ **SUBJECT TO THE ATTACHED COUNTER OFFER**) and acknowledge receipt of a Copy.
   _____ Date _____ Time _____ ☐ AM ☐ PM
   _____ Date _____ Time _____ ☐ AM ☐ PM

7. **MULTIPLE COUNTER OFFER SIGNATURE LINE:** By signing below, Seller accepts this Multiple Counter Offer.
   NOTE TO SELLER: Do NOT sign in this box until after Buyer signs in paragraph 6. (Paragraph 7 applies only if paragraph 4 is checked.)
   _____ Date _____ Time _____ ☐ AM ☐ PM
   _____ Date _____ Time _____ ☐ AM ☐ PM

8. (_____ / _____) (Initials) **Confirmation of Acceptance:** A Copy of Signed Acceptance was personally received by the maker of the Counter Offer, or that person's authorized agent as specified in paragraph 3 (or, if this is a Multiple Counter Offer, the Buyer or Buyer's authorized agent as specified in paragraph 4) on (date) _____ , at _____ ☐ AM ☐ PM. A binding Agreement is created when a Copy of Signed Acceptance is personally received by the the maker of the Counter Offer, or that person's authorized agent (or, if this is a Multiple Counter Offer, the Buyer or Buyer's authorized agent) whether or not confirmed in this document. Completion of this confirmation is not legally required in order to create a binding Agreement; it is solely intended to evidence the date that Confirmation of Acceptance has occurred.

Published and Distributed by:
REAL ESTATE BUSINESS SERVICES, INC.
a subsidiary of the California Association of REALTORS®
525 South Virgil Avenue, Los Angeles, California 90020

Reviewed by _____ Date _____

CO REVISED 10/04 (PAGE 1 OF 1)

COUNTER OFFER (CO PAGE 1 OF 1)

Agent: _____ Phone: _____ Fax: _____ Prepared using WINForms® software
Broker: _____

Elements of a Valid Option

An option must be in writing and must have actual monetary consideration paid to the owner (optionor). The consideration may be in the form of cash, a check, or something else of value. In a lease option, payment of rent and the provisions of the lease are acceptable as the consideration.

Rights of the Optionor and Optionee

An option contract actually restricts the rights of the seller (optionor) because he or she cannot sell or lease the property during the option period. If the optionee decides not to buy the property during the term of the option, the consideration remains with the optionor.

The buyer (optionee) is the only one who has a choice, once the contract is signed and the consideration given. The option does not bind the optionee to any performance—he or she does not have to exercise the option. It merely provides the right to demand performance from the optionor, who must sell if the optionee decides to buy the property during the course of the option. The option does not give the optionee a legal interest in the title and the optionee does not have any right to use the land. The optionee may assign or sell the option without the permission of the optionor during the term of the option. The optionee may find another buyer for the property to exercise the option.

Leases

A lease lists the rights and options of the property manager and the lessee.

A **lease** is a contract between an owner, (lessor or landlord) and a lessee (tenant) which gives the tenant a tenancy. Tenancy is an arrangement, by formal lease or informal agreement, in which the owner (landlord) allows another (tenant) to take exclusive possession of land in consideration for rent. **Tenancy** is also defined as the interest of a person holding property by any right or title. Normally, under a lease, the tenant takes possession and use of a property in return for rent payment. The lease is usually a written agreement which transfers the right of exclusive possession and use of real estate for a definite time period. Another name for lease is **rental agreement**.

CALIFORNIA
ASSOCIATION
OF REALTORS®

OPTION AGREEMENT
To be used with a purchase agreement. May also be used with a lease.
(C.A.R. Form OA, Revised 10/05)

Date _____ , at _____ , California

_____ ("Optionor"), grants to

_____ , ("Optionee"),

on the following terms and conditions, an option ("Option") to purchase the real property and improvements situated in

(City) _____ , County of _____ ,

California, described as _____ ("Property") on the terms and

conditions specified in the attached: ☐ Real Estate Purchase Agreement ☐ Other _____ ,

which is incorporated by reference as a part of this Option.

1. **OPTION CONSIDERATION:**
   A. _____ Dollars ($ _____),
      payable upon acceptance of this Option, or, if checked, ☐ _____ ,
      by ☐ cash, ☐ cashier's check, ☐ personal check, or ☐ _____
      made payable to _____ .

OR B. ☐ (If checked) Mutual execution of the attached lease specified in paragraph 2A.

OR C. ☐ (If checked) Both 1A and 1B.

2. ☐ **LEASE (If checked):**
   A. The attached lease agreement, dated _____ , between Optionee as Tenant and Optionor as Landlord, is incorporated by reference as part of this Option.
   B. If the Option is exercised, the lease shall terminate on the earliest of (i) the date scheduled for close of escrow under the purchase agreement, or as extended in writing, (ii) the close of escrow of the purchase agreement, or (iii) mutual cancellation of the purchase agreement.

3. **OPTION PERIOD:** The Option shall begin on (date) _____ , and shall end at 11:59 p.m.
   (or at ☐ _____), on (date) _____ .

4. **MANNER OF EXERCISE:** Optionee may exercise the Option **only** by delivering a written unconditional notice of exercise, signed by Optionee, to Optionor, or _____ , who is authorized to receive it.
   A copy of the unconditional notice of exercise shall be delivered to the Brokers identified in this Agreement.

5. **NON-EXERCISE:** If the Option is not exercised in the manner specified, within the option period or any written extension thereof, or if it is terminated under any provision of this Option, then:
   A. The Option and all rights of Optionee to purchase the Property shall immediately terminate without notice; and
   B. All Option Consideration paid, rent paid, services rendered to Optionor, and improvements made to the Property, if any, by Optionee, shall be retained by Optionor in consideration of the granting of the Option; and
   C. Optionee shall execute, acknowledge, and deliver to Optionor, within **5 (or ☐ _____ calendar Days** of Optionor's request, a release, quitclaim deed, or any other document reasonably required by Optionor or a title insurance company to verify the termination of the Option.

6. **EFFECT OF DEFAULT ON OPTION:**
   A. Optionee shall have no right to exercise this Option if Optionee has not performed any obligation imposed by, or is in default of, any obligation of this Option, any addenda, or any document incorporated by reference.
   B. In addition, if a lease is incorporated by reference in paragraph 2A, Optionee shall have no right to exercise this Option if Optionor, as landlord, has given to Optionee, as tenant, two or more notices to cure any default or non-performance under that lease.

7. **OPTIONOR DISCLOSURE:**
   A. Unless exempt, if the Property contains one-to-four residential dwelling units, Optionor shall provide to Optionee (i) a Real Estate Transfer Disclosure Statement , a Natural Hazard Disclosure Statement and other disclosures required by Civil Code §§1102 and 1103 et seq., (ii) ☐ a preliminary title report, and (iii) ☐ _____ .
   B. If any disclosure or notice specified in 7A is delivered to Optionee after the Option is Signed, Optionee shall have the right to cancel this Option within **3 Days After** delivery in person or **5 Days After** delivery by deposit in the mail by giving written notice of cancellation to Optionor or Optionor's agent.

Optionee and Optionor acknowledge receipt of copy of this page, which constitutes Page 1 of _____ Pages.
Optionee's Initials (_____) (_____) Optionor's Initials (_____) (_____)

OA REVISED 10/05 (PAGE 1 OF 3)

Reviewed by _____ Date _____

EQUAL HOUSING
OPPORTUNITY

OPTION AGREEMENT (OA PAGE 1 OF 3)

Produced with ZipForm™ by RE FormsNet, LLC 18025 Fifteen Mile Road, Clinton Township, Michigan 48035 www.zipform.com

123 main zfx

The **lessor (landlord)** owns the property and signs the lease to give possession and use to the lessee (tenant). The lessor keeps the right to retake possession of the property after the lease term expires. The right of the landlord to reclaim the property is known as the **reversionary right**. The lessor's interest is called a **leased fee estate**. The **lessee** (tenant) has the use, possession and the right of quiet enjoyment of the property for the duration of the lease. The lessee's interest is a **less-than-freehold estate** in real property.

A lease can be described in any number of ways, as long as the names of the parties, description of the property, rent amount, and duration of lease are included. Sometimes the words "to let" or "to **demise**", (another way to say "to rent"), will be found in a rental agreement, but those words are optional.

Leases for longer than one year (1 year plus 1 day) must be in writing, according to the California Statute of Frauds. However, it is common practice, and makes common sense to produce all lease agreements in writing. It must be signed by the lessor, but not necessarily by the lessee. Again, it is common practice for the lessee to sign the lease, but the law requires only that the lease be delivered to the lessee for it to be binding. The tenant's acceptance of the lease signed by the landlord or the tenants paying rent and taking possession of the property binds both parties to the terms of the agreement.

> **Review - Requirements of a Lease**
> **Mnemonic = "LAND"**
>   **L** ength of time
>   **A** mount of rental payments
>   **N** ames of parties
>   **D** escription of the property

Facts About Leases

- If more than 1 year, must be in writing
- Signed by lessor (landlord)
- Lessee (tenant) does not have to sign lease
- Reversionary right belongs to the lessor
- Possessory right belongs to the lessee
- A rental is presumed to be month to month unless specified otherwise
- Agricultural lease limited to maximum of 51 years
- Urban lease limited to maximum of 99 years
- Mineral, oil, and gas leases are limited to a maximum of 99 years

Classifications of Leases

There are many varieties of lease contracts. If a lessee and lessor agree on terms that differ from the law, both will be required to meet the terms of their written agreement. For example, a new two-page lease agreement adopted by the California Association of REALTORS® only requires a four-hour notice for a landlord to inspect a leased property. California statutory law states that 24 hours is necessary, unless landlord and tenant have a different written agreement.

Leases are generally classified in one of the following three ways: (1) type of real estate, (2) length of term, or (3) method of payment.

Type of Real Estate

Leases based on type of real estate would include office leases, ground leases, proprietary leases, and residential leases. A **ground lease** is a lease for only the land. A **proprietary lease** is used in co-op apartment buildings. The lessee is also a stockholder in the corporation that owns the building. A **residential lease** is used for all residential property including single-family homes, duplexes, and multiple-family dwellings.

Length of Time

Leases based on length of time would include short-term and long-term leases. An apartment lease is an example of a short-term lease. An example of a long-term lease is a major tenant in a shopping center that has multiple-renewal rights.

Method of Rent Payments

Leases are also classified by method of rent payments, such as gross, net, and percentage leases.

Gross lease: A gross lease is also called a flat, fixed, or straight lease. The tenant pays an agreed-upon sum as rent and the landlord pays any other expenses such as taxes, maintenance, or insurance.

Net lease: In a net lease, the tenant pays an agreed-upon sum as rent, plus certain agreed-upon expenses per month (i.e., taxes, insurance, and repairs). The benefit of a net lease to the lessor is that it creates a fixed income.

Percentage lease: A percentage lease is a lease in which the tenant pays a percentage of gross monthly receipts in addition to a base rent. Usually the higher the gross receipts, the lower the percentage **rate**. An example of a percentage lease is a commercial parking lot. It would typically pay the highest percentage in a percentage lease.

CALIFORNIA
ASSOCIATION
OF REALTORS®

RESIDENTIAL LEASE OR
MONTH-TO-MONTH RENTAL AGREEMENT
(C.A.R. Form LR, Revised 10/04)

_____ ("Landlord") and
_____ ("Tenant") agree as follows:

1. PROPERTY:
    A. Landlord rents to Tenant and Tenant rents from Landlord, the real property and improvements described as: **xxx,** _____
    _____ ("Premises").
    B. The Premises are for the sole use as a personal residence by the following named person(s) **only:** _____
    _____ .
    C. The following personal property, maintained pursuant to paragraph 11, is included: _____
    _____ or ☐ (if checked) the personal property on the attached addendum.

2. TERM: The term begins on (date) _____ ("Commencement Date"), **(Check A or B):**
    ☐ **A. Month-to-Month:** and continues as a month-to-month tenancy. Tenant may terminate the tenancy by giving written notice at least 30 days prior to the intended termination date. Landlord may terminate the tenancy by giving written notice as provided by law. Such notices may be given on any date.
    ☐ **B. Lease:** and shall terminate on (date) _____ at _____ ☐ AM/ ☐ PM. Tenant shall vacate the Premises upon termination of the Agreement, unless: **(i)** Landlord and Tenant have in writing extended this agreement or signed a new agreement; **(ii)** mandated by local rent control law; or **(iii)** Landlord accepts Rent from Tenant (other than past due Rent), in which case a month-to-month tenancy shall be created which either party may terminate as specified in paragraph 2A. Rent shall be at a rate agreed to by Landlord and Tenant, or as allowed by law. All other terms and conditions of this Agreement shall remain in full force and effect.

3. RENT: "Rent" shall mean all monetary obligations of Tenant to Landlord under the terms of the Agreement, except security deposit.
    A. Tenant agrees to pay $ _____ per month for the term of the Agreement.
    B. Rent is payable in advance on the **1st (or** ☐ _____ **) day** of each calendar month, and is delinquent on the next day.
    C. If Commencement Date falls on any day other than the day Rent is payable under paragraph 3B, and Tenant has paid one full month's Rent in advance of Commencement Date, Rent for the second calendar month shall be prorated based on a 30-day period.
    D. PAYMENT: Rent shall be paid by ☐ personal check, ☐ money order, ☐ cashier's check, ☐ other _____ , to
    (name) _____ (phone) _____ at
    (address) _____ ,
    (or at any other location subsequently specified by Landlord in writing to Tenant) between the hours of _____ and _____
    on the following days _____ . If any payment is returned for non-sufficient funds ("NSF") or because tenant stops payment, then, after that: **(i)** Landlord may, in writing, require Tenant to pay Rent in cash for three months and **(ii)** all future Rent shall be paid by ☐ money order, or ☐ cashier's check.

4. SECURITY DEPOSIT:
    A. Tenant agrees to pay $ _____ as a security deposit. Security deposit will be ☐ transferred to and held by the Owner of the Premises, or ☐ held in Owner's Broker's trust account.
    B. All or any portion of the security deposit may be used, as reasonably necessary, to: **(i)** cure Tenant's default in payment of Rent (which includes Late Charges, NSF fees or other sums due); **(ii)** repair damage, excluding ordinary wear and tear, caused by Tenant or by a guest or licensee of Tenant; **(iii)** clean Premises, if necessary, upon termination of the tenancy; and **(iv)** replace or return personal property or appurtenances. **SECURITY DEPOSIT SHALL NOT BE USED BY TENANT IN LIEU OF PAYMENT OF LAST MONTH'S RENT.** If all or any portion of the security deposit is used during the tenancy, Tenant agrees to reinstate the total security deposit within five days after written notice is delivered to Tenant. Within 21 days after Tenant vacates the Premises, Landlord shall: **(1)** furnish Tenant an itemized statement indicating the amount of any security deposit received and the basis for its disposition and supporting documentation as required by California Civil Code § 1950.5(g); and **(2)** return any remaining portion of the security deposit to Tenant.
    C. Security deposit will not be returned until all Tenants have vacated the Premises. Any security deposit returned by check shall be made out to all Tenants named on this Agreement, or as subsequently modified.
    D. No interest will be paid on security deposit unless required by local law.
    E. If the security deposit is held by Owner, Tenant agrees not to hold Broker responsible for its return. If the security deposit is held in Owner's Broker's trust account, **and** Broker's authority is terminated before expiration of this Agreement, **and** security deposit is released to someone other than Tenant, **then** Broker shall notify Tenant, in writing, where and to whom security deposit has been released. Once Tenant has been provided such notice, Tenant agrees not to hold Broker responsible for the security deposit.

5. MOVE-IN COSTS RECEIVED/DUE: Move-in funds made payable to _____
    shall be paid by ☐ personal check, ☐ money order, or ☐ cashier's check.

Category	Total Due	Payment Received	Balance Due	Date Due
Rent from _____ to _____ (date)				
*Security Deposit				
Other				
Other				
Total				

*The maximum amount Landlord may receive as security deposit, however designated, cannot exceed two months' Rent for unfurnished premises, or three months' Rent for furnished premises.

LR REVISED 10/04 (PAGE 1 OF 6)

Tenant's Initials (_____) (_____)
Landlord's Initials (_____) (_____)

Reviewed by _____ Date _____

EQUAL HOUSING
OPPORTUNITY

RESIDENTIAL LEASE OR MONTH-TO-MONTH RENTAL AGREEMENT (LR PAGE 1 OF 6)

Agent:	Phone:	Fax:	Prepared using WINForms® software
Broker:			

Premises: _____ Date: _____

6. LATE CHARGE; RETURNED CHECKS:

    A. Tenant acknowledges either late payment of Rent or issuance of a returned check may cause Landlord to incur costs and expenses, the exact amounts of which are extremely difficult and impractical to determine. These costs may include, but are not limited to, processing, enforcement and accounting expenses, and late charges imposed on Landlord. If any installment of Rent due from Tenant is not received by Landlord within **5 (or ☐ _____) calendar days** after the date due, or if a check is returned, Tenant shall pay to Landlord, respectively, an additional sum of $ _____ or _____ % of the Rent due as a Late Charge and $25.00 as a NSF fee for the first returned check and $35.00 as a NSF fee for each additional returned check, either or both of which shall be deemed additional Rent.

    B. Landlord and Tenant agree that these charges represent a fair and reasonable estimate of the costs Landlord may incur by reason of Tenant's late or NSF payment. Any Late Charge or NSF fee due shall be paid with the current installment of Rent. Landlord's acceptance of any Late Charge or NSF fee shall not constitute a waiver as to any default of Tenant. Landlord's right to collect a Late Charge or NSF fee shall not be deemed an extension of the date Rent is due under paragraph 3 or prevent Landlord from exercising any other rights and remedies under this Agreement and as provided by law.

7. PARKING: (Check A or B)

    ☐ **A.** Parking is permitted as follows: _____

        The right to parking ☐ is ☐ is not included in the Rent charged pursuant to paragraph 3. If not included in the Rent, the parking rental fee shall be an additional $ _____ per month. Parking space(s) are to be used for parking properly licensed and operable motor vehicles, except for trailers, boats, campers, buses or trucks (other than pick-up trucks). Tenant shall park in assigned space(s) only. Parking space(s) are to be kept clean. Vehicles leaking oil, gas or other motor vehicle fluids shall not be parked on the Premises. Mechanical work or storage of inoperable vehicles is not permitted in parking space(s) or elsewhere on the Premises.

    OR ☐ **B.** Parking is not permitted on the Premises.

8. STORAGE: (Check A or B)

    ☐ **A.** Storage is permitted as follows: _____

        The right to storage space ☐ is ☐ is not included in the Rent charged pursuant to paragraph 3. If not included in the Rent, storage space fee shall be an additional $ _____ per month. Tenant shall store only personal property Tenant owns, and shall not store property claimed by another or in which another has any right, title or interest. Tenant shall not store any improperly packaged food or perishable goods, flammable materials, explosives, hazardous waste or other inherently dangerous material, or illegal substances.

    OR ☐ **B.** Storage is not permitted on the Premises.

9. UTILITIES: Tenant agrees to pay for all utilities and services, and the following charges: _____ except _____ , which shall be paid for by Landlord. If any utilities are not separately metered, Tenant shall pay Tenant's proportional share, as reasonably determined and directed by Landlord. If utilities are separately metered, Tenant shall place utilities in Tenant's name as of the Commencement Date. Landlord is only responsible for installing and maintaining one usable telephone jack and one telephone line to the Premises. Tenant shall pay any cost for conversion from existing utilities service provider.

10. CONDITION OF PREMISES: Tenant has examined Premises and, if any, all furniture, furnishings, appliances, landscaping and fixtures, including smoke detector(s).

    (Check all that apply:)

    ☐ **A.** Tenant acknowledges these items are clean and in operable condition, with the following exceptions: _____

    ☐ **B.** Tenant's acknowledgment of the condition of these items is contained in an attached statement of condition (C.A.R. Form MIMO).

    ☐ **C.** Tenant will provide Landlord a list of items that are damaged or not in operable condition within **3 (or ☐ _____) days** after Commencement Date, not as a contingency of this Agreement but rather as an acknowledgment of the condition of the Premises.

    ☐ **D.** Other: _____ .

11. MAINTENANCE:

    A. Tenant shall properly use, operate and safeguard Premises, including if applicable, any landscaping, furniture, furnishings and appliances, and all mechanical, electrical, gas and plumbing fixtures, and keep them and the Premises clean, sanitary and well ventilated. Tenant shall be responsible for checking and maintaining all smoke detectors and any additional phone lines beyond the one line and jack that Landlord shall provide and maintain. Tenant shall immediately notify Landlord, in writing, of any problem, malfunction or damage. Tenant shall be charged for all repairs or replacements caused by Tenant, pets, guests or licensees of Tenant, excluding ordinary wear and tear. Tenant shall be charged for all damage to Premises as a result of failure to report a problem in a timely manner. Tenant shall be charged for repair of drain blockages or stoppages, unless caused by defective plumbing parts or tree roots invading sewer lines.

    B. ☐ Landlord ☐ Tenant shall water the garden, landscaping, trees and shrubs, except: _____

    C. ☐ Landlord ☐ Tenant shall maintain the garden, landscaping, trees and shrubs, except: _____

    D. ☐ Landlord ☐ Tenant shall maintain _____

    E. Tenant's failure to maintain any item for which Tenant is responsible shall give Landlord the right to hire someone to perform such maintenance and charge Tenant to cover the cost of such maintenance.

    F. The following items of personal property are included in the Premises without warranty and Landlord will not maintain, repair or replace them: _____

Tenant's Initials (_____) (_____)
Landlord's Initials (_____) (_____)

Reviewed by _____ Date _____

EQUAL HOUSING OPPORTUNITY

RESIDENTIAL LEASE OR MONTH-TO-MONTH RENTAL AGREEMENT (LR PAGE 2 OF 6)

Premises: _____ Date: _____

12. **NEIGHBORHOOD CONDITIONS:** Tenant is advised to satisfy him or herself as to neighborhood or area conditions, including schools, proximity and adequacy of law enforcement, crime statistics, proximity of registered felons or offenders, fire protection, other governmental services, availability, adequacy and cost of any speed-wired, wireless internet connections or other telecommunications or other technology services and installations, proximity to commercial, industrial or agricultural activities, existing and proposed transportation, construction and development that may affect noise, view, or traffic, airport noise, noise or odor from any source, wild and domestic animals, other nuisances, hazards, or circumstances, cemeteries, facilities and condition of common areas, conditions and influences of significance to certain cultures and/or religions, and personal needs, requirements and preferences of Tenant.

13. **PETS:** Unless otherwise provided in California Civil Code § 54.2, no animal or pet shall be kept on or about the Premises without Landlord's prior written consent, except: _____ .

14. **RULES/REGULATIONS:**
    A. Tenant agrees to comply with all Landlord rules and regulations that are at any time posted on the Premises or delivered to Tenant. Tenant shall not, and shall ensure that guests and licensees of Tenant shall not, disturb, annoy, endanger or interfere with other tenants of the building or neighbors, or use the Premises for any unlawful purposes, including, but not limited to, using, manufacturing, selling, storing or transporting illicit drugs or other contraband, or violate any law or ordinance, or commit a waste or nuisance on or about the Premises.
    B. **(If applicable, check one)**
        ☐ 1. Landlord shall provide Tenant with a copy of the rules and regulations within _____ days or _____ .
        OR ☐ 2. Tenant has been provided with, and acknowledges receipt of, a copy of the rules and regulations.

15. ☐ (If checked) **CONDOMINIUM; PLANNED UNIT DEVELOPMENT:**
    A. The Premises is a unit in a condominium, planned unit development, common interest subdivision or other development governed by a homeowners' association ("HOA"). The name of the HOA is _____ .
    Tenant agrees to comply with all HOA covenants, conditions and restrictions, bylaws, rules and regulations and decisions. Landlord shall provide Tenant copies of rules and regulations, if any. Tenant shall reimburse Landlord for any fines or charges imposed by HOA or other authorities, due to any violation by Tenant, or the guests or licensees of Tenant.
    B. **(Check one)**
        ☐ 1. Landlord shall provide Tenant with a copy of the HOA rules and regulations within _____ days or _____ .
        OR ☐ 2. Tenant has been provided with, and acknowledges receipt of, a copy of the HOA rules and regulations.

16. **ALTERATIONS; REPAIRS:** Unless otherwise specified by law or paragraph 27C, without Landlord's prior written consent, **(i)** Tenant shall not make any repairs, alterations or improvements in or about the Premises including: painting, wallpapering, adding or changing locks, installing antenna or satellite dish(es), placing signs, displays or exhibits, or using screws, fastening devices, large nails or adhesive materials; **(ii)** Landlord shall not be responsible for the costs of alterations or repairs made by Tenant; **(iii)** Tenant shall not deduct from Rent the costs of any repairs, alterations or improvements; and **(iv)** any deduction made by Tenant shall be considered unpaid Rent.

17. **KEYS; LOCKS:**
    A. Tenant acknowledges receipt of (or Tenant will receive ☐ prior to the Commencement Date, or ☐ _____):
        ☐ _____ key(s) to Premises,   ☐ _____ remote control device(s) for garage door/gate opener(s),
        ☐ _____ key(s) to mailbox,   ☐ _____ ,
        ☐ _____ key(s) to common area(s),   ☐ _____ .
    B. Tenant acknowledges that locks to the Premises ☐ have ☐ have not, been re-keyed.
    C. If Tenant re-keys existing locks or opening devices, Tenant shall immediately deliver copies of all keys to Landlord. Tenant shall pay all costs and charges related to loss of any keys or opening devices. Tenant may not remove locks, even if installed by Tenant.

18. **ENTRY:**
    A. Tenant shall make Premises available to Landlord or Landlord's representative for the purpose of entering to make necessary or agreed repairs, decorations, alterations, or improvements, or to supply necessary or agreed services, or to show Premises to prospective or actual purchasers, tenants, mortgagees, lenders, appraisers, or contractors.
    B. Landlord and Tenant agree that 24-hour written notice shall be reasonable and sufficient notice, except as follows: 48-hour written notice is required to conduct an inspection of the Premises prior to the Tenant moving out, unless the Tenant waives the right to such notice. Notice may be given orally to show the Premises to actual or prospective purchasers provided Tenant has been notified in writing within 120 days preceding the oral notice that the Premises are for sale and that oral notice may be given to show the Premises. No notice is required: **(i)** to enter in case of an emergency; **(ii)** if the Tenant is present and consents at the time of entry or **(iii)** if the Tenant has abandoned or surrendered the Premises. No written notice is required if Landlord and Tenant orally agree on an entry for agreed services or repairs if the date and time of entry are within one week of the oral agreement.
    C. ☐ (If checked) Tenant authorizes the use of a keysafe/lockbox to allow entry into the Premises and agrees to sign a keysafe/lockbox addendum (C.A.R. Form KLA).

19. **SIGNS:** Tenant authorizes Landlord to place FOR SALE/LEASE signs on the Premises.

20. **ASSIGNMENT; SUBLETTING:** Tenant shall not sublet all or any part of Premises, or assign or transfer this Agreement or any interest in it, without Landlord's prior written consent. Unless such consent is obtained, any assignment, transfer or subletting of Premises or this Agreement or tenancy, by voluntary act of Tenant, operation of law or otherwise, shall, at the option of Landlord, terminate this Agreement. Any proposed assignee, transferee or sublessee shall submit to Landlord an application and credit information for Landlord's approval and, if approved, sign a separate written agreement with Landlord and Tenant. Landlord's consent to any one assignment, transfer or sublease, shall not be construed as consent to any subsequent assignment, transfer or sublease and does not release Tenant of Tenant's obligations under this Agreement.

21. **JOINT AND INDIVIDUAL OBLIGATIONS:** If there is more than one Tenant, each one shall be individually and completely responsible for the performance of all obligations of Tenant under this Agreement, jointly with every other Tenant, and individually, whether or not in possession.

Tenant's Initials (_____)(_____)
Landlord's Initials (_____)(_____)

LR REVISED 10/04 (PAGE 3 OF 6)

Reviewed by _____ Date _____

RESIDENTIAL LEASE OR MONTH-TO-MONTH RENTAL AGREEMENT (LR PAGE 3 OF 6)

Premises: _____ Date: _____

22. ☐ **LEAD-BASED PAINT (If checked):** Premises was constructed prior to 1978. In accordance with federal law, Landlord gives and Tenant acknowledges receipt of the disclosures on the attached form (C.A.R. Form FLD) and a federally approved lead pamphlet.

23. ☐ **MILITARY ORDNANCE DISCLOSURE:** (If applicable and known to Landlord) Premises is located within one mile of an area once used for military training, and may contain potentially explosive munitions.

24. ☐ **PERIODIC PEST CONTROL:** Landlord has entered into a contract for periodic pest control treatment of the Premises and shall give Tenant a copy of the notice originally given to Landlord by the pest control company.

25. **DATABASE DISCLOSURE:** NOTICE: The California Department of Justice, sheriff's departments, police departments serving jurisdictions of 200,000 or more, and many other local law enforcement authorities maintain for public access a database of the locations of persons required to register pursuant to paragraph (1) of subdivision (a) of Section 290.4 of the Penal Code. The data base is updated on a quarterly basis and a source of information about the presence of these individuals in any neighborhood. The Department of Justice also maintains a Sex Offender Identification Line through which inquiries about individuals may be made. This is a "900" telephone service. Callers must have specific information about individuals they are checking. Information regarding neighborhoods is not available through the "900" telephone service.

26. **POSSESSION:**
   A. Tenant is not in possession of the premises. If Landlord is unable to deliver possession of Premises on Commencement Date, such Date shall be extended to the date on which possession is made available to Tenant. If Landlord is unable to deliver possession within **5 (or ☐_____) calendar days** after agreed Commencement Date, Tenant may terminate this Agreement by giving written notice to Landlord, and shall be refunded all Rent and security deposit paid. Possession is deemed terminated when Tenant has returned all keys to the Premises to Landlord.
   B. ☐ Tenant is already in possession of the Premises.

27. **TENANT'S OBLIGATIONS UPON VACATING PREMISES:**
   A. Upon termination of the Agreement, Tenant shall: **(i)** give Landlord all copies of all keys or opening devices to Premises, including any common areas; **(ii)** vacate and surrender Premises to Landlord, empty of all persons; **(iii)** vacate any/all parking and/or storage space; **(iv)** clean and deliver Premises, as specified in paragraph C below, to Landlord in the same condition as referenced in paragraph 10; **(v)** remove all debris; **(vi)** give written notice to Landlord of Tenant's forwarding address; and **(vii)** _____.
   B. All alterations/improvements made by or caused to be made by Tenant, with or without Landlord's consent, become the property of Landlord upon termination. Landlord may charge Tenant for restoration of the Premises to the condition it was in prior to any alterations/improvements.
   C. **Right to Pre-Move-Out Inspection and Repairs as follows: (i)** After giving or receiving notice of termination of a tenancy (C.A.R. Form NTT), or before the end of a lease, Tenant has the right to request that an inspection of the Premises take place prior to termination of the lease or rental (C.A.R. Form NRI). If Tenant requests such an inspection, Tenant shall be given an opportunity to remedy identified deficiencies prior to termination, consistent with the terms of this Agreement. **(ii)** Any repairs or alterations made to the Premises as a result of this inspection (collectively, "Repairs") shall be made at Tenant's expense. Repairs may be performed by Tenant or through others, who have adequate insurance and licenses and are approved by Landlord. The work shall comply with applicable law, including governmental permit, inspection and approval requirements. Repairs shall be performed in a good, skillful manner with materials of quality and appearance comparable to existing materials. It is understood that exact restoration of appearance or cosmetic items following all Repairs may not be possible. **(iii)** Tenant shall: **(a)** obtain receipts for Repairs performed by others; **(b)** prepare a written statement indicating the Repairs performed by Tenant and the date of such Repairs; and **(c)** provide copies of receipts and statements to Landlord prior to termination. Paragraph 27C does not apply when the tenancy is terminated pursuant to California Code of Civil Procedure § 1161(2), (3) or (4).

28. **BREACH OF CONTRACT; EARLY TERMINATION:** In addition to any obligations established by paragraph 27, in the event of termination by Tenant prior to completion of the original term of the Agreement, Tenant shall also be responsible for lost Rent, rental commissions, advertising expenses and painting costs necessary to ready Premises for re-rental. Landlord may withhold any such amounts from Tenant's security deposit.

29. **TEMPORARY RELOCATION:** Subject to local law, Tenant agrees, upon demand of Landlord, to temporarily vacate Premises for a reasonable period, to allow for fumigation (or other methods) to control wood destroying pests or organisms, or other repairs to Premises. Tenant agrees to comply with all instructions and requirements necessary to prepare Premises to accommodate pest control, fumigation or other work, including bagging or storage of food and medicine, and removal of perishables and valuables. Tenant shall only be entitled to a credit of Rent equal to the per diem Rent for the period of time Tenant is required to vacate Premises.

30. **DAMAGE TO PREMISES:** If, by no fault of Tenant, Premises are totally or partially damaged or destroyed by fire, earthquake, accident or other casualty that render Premises totally or partially uninhabitable, either Landlord or Tenant may terminate this Agreement by giving the other written notice. Rent shall be abated as of the date Premises become totally or partially uninhabitable. The abated amount shall be the current monthly Rent prorated on a 30-day period. If the Agreement is not terminated, Landlord shall promptly repair the damage, and Rent shall be reduced based on the extent to which the damage interferes with Tenant's reasonable use of Premises. If damage occurs as a result of an act of Tenant or Tenant's guests, only Landlord shall have the right of termination, and no reduction in Rent shall be made.

31. **INSURANCE:** Tenant's or guest's personal property and vehicles are not insured by Landlord, manager or, if applicable, HOA, against loss or damage due to fire, theft, vandalism, rain, water, criminal or negligent acts of others, or any other cause. **Tenant is advised to carry Tenant's own insurance (renter's insurance) to protect Tenant from any such loss or damage.** Tenant shall comply with any requirement imposed on Tenant by Landlord's insurer to avoid: **(i)** an increase in Landlord's insurance premium (or Tenant shall pay for the increase in premium); or **(ii)** loss of insurance.

32. **WATERBEDS:** Tenant shall not use or have waterbeds on the Premises unless: **(i)** Tenant obtains a valid waterbed insurance policy; **(ii)** Tenant increases the security deposit in an amount equal to one-half of one month's Rent; and **(iii)** the bed conforms to the floor load capacity of Premises.

Tenant's Initials (_____) (_____)
Landlord's Initials (_____) (_____)

Reviewed by _____ Date _____

LR REVISED 10/04 (PAGE 4 OF 6)

RESIDENTIAL LEASE OR MONTH-TO-MONTH RENTAL AGREEMENT (LR PAGE 4 OF 6)

EQUAL HOUSING OPPORTUNITY

Premises: _____ Date: _____

33. **WAIVER:** The waiver of any breach shall not be construed as a continuing waiver of the same or any subsequent breach.

34. **NOTICE:** Notices may be served at the following address, or at any other location subsequently designated:
Landlord: _____ Tenant: _____
_____ _____
_____ _____

35. **TENANT ESTOPPEL CERTIFICATE:** Tenant shall execute and return a tenant estoppel certificate delivered to Tenant by Landlord or Landlord's agent within 3 days after its receipt. Failure to comply with this requirement shall be deemed Tenant's acknowledgment that the tenant estoppel certificate is true and correct, and may be relied upon by a lender or purchaser.

36. **TENANT REPRESENTATIONS; CREDIT:** Tenant warrants that all statements in Tenant's rental application are accurate. Tenant authorizes Landlord and Broker(s) to obtain Tenant's credit report periodically during the tenancy in connection with the modification or enforcement of this Agreement. Landlord may cancel this Agreement: **(i)** before occupancy begins; **(ii)** upon disapproval of the credit report(s); or **(iii)** at any time, upon discovering that information in Tenant's application is false. A negative credit report reflecting on Tenant's record may be submitted to a credit reporting agency if Tenant fails to fulfill the terms of payment and other obligations under this Agreement.

37. **MEDIATION:**
   A. Consistent with paragraphs B and C below, Landlord and Tenant agree to mediate any dispute or claim arising between them out of this Agreement, or any resulting transaction, before resorting to court action. Mediation fees, if any, shall be divided equally among the parties involved. If, for any dispute or claim to which this paragraph applies, any party commences an action without first attempting to resolve the matter through mediation, or refuses to mediate after a request has been made, then that party shall not be entitled to recover attorney fees, even if they would otherwise be available to that party in any such action.
   B. The following matters are excluded from mediation: **(i)** an unlawful detainer action; **(ii)** the filing or enforcement of a mechanic's lien; and **(iii)** any matter within the jurisdiction of a probate, small claims or bankruptcy court. The filing of a court action to enable the recording of a notice of pending action, for order of attachment, receivership, injunction, or other provisional remedies, shall not constitute a waiver of the mediation provision.
   C. Landlord and Tenant agree to mediate disputes or claims involving Listing Agent, Leasing Agent or property manager ("Broker"), provided Broker shall have agreed to such mediation prior to, or within a reasonable time after, the dispute or claim is presented to such Broker. Any election by Broker to participate in mediation shall not result in Broker being deemed a party to this Agreement.

38. **ATTORNEY FEES:** In any action or proceeding arising out of this Agreement, the prevailing party between Landlord and Tenant shall be entitled to reasonable attorney fees and costs, except as provided in paragraph 37A.

39. **CAR FORM:** C.A.R. Form means the specific form referenced or another comparable form agreed to by the parties.

40. **OTHER TERMS AND CONDITIONS; SUPPLEMENTS:** _____
_____

The following ATTACHED supplements are incorporated in this Agreement: ☐ Keysafe/Lockbox Addendum (C.A.R.Form KLA); ☐ Interpreter/Translator Agreement (C.A.R. Form ITA); ☐ Lead-Based Paint and Lead-Based Paint Hazards Disclosure (C.A.R. Form FLD)

41. **TIME OF ESSENCE; ENTIRE CONTRACT; CHANGES:** Time is of the essence. All understandings between the parties are incorporated in this Agreement. Its terms are intended by the parties as a final, complete and exclusive expression of their Agreement with respect to its subject matter, and may not be contradicted by evidence of any prior agreement or contemporaneous oral agreement. If any provision of this Agreement is held to be ineffective or invalid, the remaining provisions will nevertheless be given full force and effect. Neither this Agreement nor any provision in it may be extended, amended, modified, altered or changed except in writing. This Agreement is subject to California landlord-tenant law and shall incorporate all changes required by amendment or successors to such law. This Agreement and any supplement, addendum or modification, including any copy, may be signed in two or more counterparts, all of which shall constitute one and the same writing.

42. **AGENCY:**
   A. **CONFIRMATION:** The following agency relationship(s) are hereby confirmed for this transaction:
   Listing Agent: (Print firm name) _____
   is the agent of (check one): ☐ the Landlord exclusively; or ☐ both the Landlord and Tenant.
   Leasing Agent: (Print firm name) _____
   (if not same as Listing Agent) is the agent of (check one): ☐ the Tenant exclusively; or ☐ the Landlord exclusively; or ☐ both the Tenant and Landlord.
   B. **DISCLOSURE:** ☐ (If checked): The term of this lease exceeds one year. A disclosure regarding real estate agency relationships (C.A.R. Form AD) has been provided to Landlord and Tenant, who each acknowledge its receipt.

43. ☐ **TENANT COMPENSATION TO BROKER:** Upon execution of this Agreement, Tenant agrees to pay compensation to Broker as specified in a separate written agreement between Tenant and Broker.

44. ☐ **INTERPRETER/TRANSLATOR:** The terms of this Agreement have been interpreted for Tenant into the following language: _____. Landlord and Tenant acknowledge receipt of the attached interpretor/translator agreement (C.A.R. Form ITA).

45. **FOREIGN LANGUAGE NEGOTIATION:** If this Agreement has been negotiated by Landlord and Tenant primarily in Spanish, Chinese, Korean or Vietnamese. Pursuant to the California Civil Code Tenant shall be provided a translation of this Agreement in the language used for the negotiation.

Tenant's Initials (_____) (_____)
Landlord's Initials (_____) (_____)
Reviewed by _____ Date _____

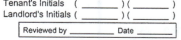

EQUAL HOUSING OPPORTUNITY

RESIDENTIAL LEASE OR MONTH-TO-MONTH RENTAL AGREEMENT (LR PAGE 5 OF 6)

Premises: _____ Date: _____

> Landlord and Tenant acknowledge and agree Brokers: **(a)** do not guarantee the condition of the Premises; **(b)** cannot verify representations made by others; **(c)** cannot provide legal or tax advice; **(d)** will not provide other advice or information that exceeds the knowledge, education or experience required to obtain a real estate license. Furthermore, if Brokers are not also acting as Landlord in this Agreement, Brokers: **(e)** do not decide what rental rate a Tenant should pay or Landlord should accept; and **(f)** do not decide upon the length or other terms of tenancy. Landlord and Tenant agree that they will seek legal, tax, insurance and other desired assistance from appropriate professionals.

Tenant _____ Date _____
Address _____ City _____ State _____ Zip _____
Telephone _____ Fax _____ E-mail _____

Tenant _____ Date _____
Address _____ City _____ State _____ Zip _____
Telephone _____ Fax _____ E-mail _____

46. ☐ **GUARANTEE:** In consideration of the execution of the Agreement by and between Landlord and Tenant and for valuable consideration, receipt of which is hereby acknowledged, the undersigned ("Guarantor") does hereby: **(i)** guarantee unconditionally to Landlord and Landlord's agents, successors and assigns, the prompt payment of Rent or other sums that become due pursuant to this Agreement, including any and all court costs and attorney fees included in enforcing the Agreement; **(ii)** consent to any changes, modifications or alterations of any term in this Agreement agreed to by Landlord and Tenant; and **(iii)** waive any right to require Landlord and/or Landlord's agents to proceed against Tenant for any default occurring under this Agreement before seeking to enforce this Guarantee.

Guarantor (Print Name) _____
Guarantor _____ Date _____
Address _____ City _____ State _____ Zip _____
Telephone _____ Fax _____ E-mail _____

47. OWNER COMPENSATION TO BROKER: Upon execution of this Agreement, Owner agrees to pay compensation to Broker as specified in a separate written agreement between Owner and Broker (C.A.R. Form LCA).

48. RECEIPT: If specified in paragraph 5, Landlord or Broker, acknowledges receipt of move-in funds.

Landlord _____ Date _____
(Owner or Agent with authority to enter into this Agreement)
Landlord _____ Date _____
(Owner or Agent with authority to enter into this Agreement)
Landlord Address _____ City _____ State _____ Zip _____
Telephone _____ Fax _____ E-mail _____

> **REAL ESTATE BROKERS:**
> **A.** Real estate brokers who are not also Landlord under the Agreement are not parties to the Agreement between Landlord and Tenant.
> **B.** Agency relationships are confirmed in paragraph 42.
> **C.** **COOPERATING BROKER COMPENSATION:** Listing Broker agrees to pay Cooperating Broker (Leasing Firm) and Cooperating Broker agrees to accept: **(i)** the amount specified in the MLS, provided Cooperating Broker is a Participant of the MLS in which the Property is offered for sale or a reciprocal MLS; or **(ii)** ☐ (if checked) the amount specified in a separate written agreement between Listing Broker and Cooperating Broker.

Real Estate Broker (Leasing Firm) _____
By (Agent) _____ Date _____
Address _____ City _____ State _____ Zip _____
Telephone _____ Fax _____ E-mail _____

Real Estate Broker (Listing Firm) _____
By (Agent) _____ Date _____
Address _____ City _____ State _____ Zip _____
Telephone _____ Fax _____ E-mail _____

Reviewed by _____ Date _____

LR REVISED 10/04 (PAGE 6 OF 6)

RESIDENTIAL LEASE OR MONTH-TO-MONTH RENTAL AGREEMENT (LR PAGE 6 OF 6)

123 main.zfx

Rent and Security Deposits

Rent is payment for the use of a property, generally under a lease agreement. The rent becomes due at the end of the term, unless otherwise agreed upon in the lease. If the rent is not paid when due, the tenant may be evicted. Rent received by the owner is taxable in the year received. Frequently rent adjustments on commercial leases are tied to increases in the **Consumer Price Index** for Urban Wage Earners and Clerical Workers (CPI-W).

In addition to the first month's rent, most leases require security deposits. A **security deposit** is money given to a landlord to prepay for any damage that might occur to a property during a lease term that is more than just normal wear and tear. Effective January 1, 2005, a landlord may not require tenants to pay rent in cash except if the tenant has defaulted on the rent. If the landlord first gives a tenant written notice that the rent must be paid in cash, the landlord can only require up to three payments to be paid in cash.

The maximum deposit allowed on an unfurnished property may not exceed the amount of two months rent. The maximum deposit allowed on a furnished property is not more than the amount of three months rent. A security deposit also includes any charges imposed at the beginning of the tenancy to reimburse the landlord for costs associated with processing a new tenant, other than application screening fees.

> Example: If rent on an unfurnished 2-bedroom apartment is $900 per month and the landlord charged the tenant a $20 general processing fee, the maximum the landlord could collect up front is $2,700. The landlord can charge $900 for the first month's rent, $1,800 for the security deposit and nothing for the general processing fee because it is considered part of the security deposit.

The law is specific on the handling of residential security deposits. A security deposit must be refundable. The landlord has 21 days after the tenant has moved out to return all unused portions of the security deposit, with a written statement showing how the remainder was used (to clean, repair damage, replace windows, etc.). A landlord may only deduct from the security deposit the cleaning cost "necessary to return the unit to the same level of cleanliness it was in at the beginning of the tenancy". A landlord who keeps deposits without reason for more than three weeks after the tenant has moved may be subject to damages up to $600.

Responsibilities of a Landlord

In every lease the law implies a promise on the part of the lessor to the quiet enjoyment and possession of the property by the lessee during the term of the lease. In exchange for rent, a landlord gives up the use and possession of the property to a tenant.

The landlord also has certain duties and responsibilities:

- A landlord guarantees that health and safety codes are being met. With residential property, a landlord is usually liable for injuries occurring as a result of unsafe conditions in common areas such as hallways, stairwells, or surrounding grounds. There is an **implied warranty of habitability** from the landlord to the tenant that the property will be maintained to meet bare living requirements.

- Periodic inspection of the property is allowed by a landlord, who must give reasonable notice of intent to enter, and then only during normal business hours. Twenty-four hours is considered reasonable notice. Some rental agreements only require a four-hour notice of entry to be given by the landlord. All leases are not the same and should be read carefully by both landlord and tenant before signing.

- A landlord must obey federal and state fair housing laws. Refer to Chapter 13 for a complete discussion of fair housing rules and regulations.

- California renters under month-to-month leases must be given 30-day notices to move out. The tenant does have recourse if the **eviction** is unfair, based on fair housing laws, or if the eviction is retaliatory. A **retaliatory eviction** is an eviction that occurs in revenge for some complaint made by the tenant.

- Tenants have the right to a "Pre-Move-Out" inspection of the rental unit, no earlier than two weeks prior to the termination of the tenancy. The landlord provides to the tenant a written notice of the right to inspect the premises within a reasonable time. The landlord also informs the tenant of his or her right to be present at the inspection. If no agreement can be made for the inspection time, the landlord must give the tenant written notice 48 hours prior of the time of inspection and then may proceed with the inspection whether the tenant is there or not. Based on the inspection, the landlord must give the tenant an itemized statement listing of any proposed repairs or cleaning. The cost of the cleaning and repairs is the basis for deductions taken from the security deposit.

- The landlord has 21 days after the tenant has moved out to return all unused portions of the security deposit, with a written statement showing how the remainder was used.

Responsibilities and Rights of a Tenant

In return for the payment of rent, a tenant has certain obligations and rights by law:

- A tenant must pay the rent when it is due.

- A tenant must give proper written notice before moving out, unless there is an agreement stating otherwise. The notice is based on the number of days between rent payments. For example, a tenant who pays monthly must give 30-days written notice or weekly at least 7-days written notice.

- A tenant may not interfere with the rights of other tenants.

- If there is a repair problem involving the tenant's health, welfare, or safety, the landlord has a duty to make needed repairs. If the landlord refuses, under the law, a tenant may spend up to one-month's rent to make repairs, and subtract the amount from the rent. The tenant may do this only two times in any 12-month period. A landlord may not retaliate by eviction or raising the rent for 180 days after this rent offset is used by the tenant to make lawful repairs. If the landlord does not correct the problem, the tenant may abandon the premises and break the lease.

Review - Landlord & Tenant Responsibilities

Landlord Must:
- provide habitable dwelling units.
- give 24-hours notice before entering.
- obey fair housing laws.
- give a 30-day written notice to the tenant before ending a month-to-month tenancy.
- return deposit within 21 days after tenant moves out.

Tenant Must:
- pay rent when due.
- give 30-days notice before ending month-to-month tenancy.
- not interfere with the rights of other tenants.

Tenant May:
- make needed repairs twice yearly and deduct from rent.

Transfer of a Lease

If the lease does not prohibit it, a lessee (tenant) may assign or sublease his or her interest in the property to another person.

Assignment

An **assignment** is the transfer of the entire leasehold estate to a new person, called an **assignee**. The original lessee (**assignor**) steps out of primary responsibility for the lease and a new lessee (assignee) becomes responsible to the landlord for all the terms of the original rental agreement.

> Example: Brad leases a two-bedroom apartment from Al and lives there for six months until he is transferred to another part of the country. The term of the lease is one year and he has six months left before it expires. Melissa accepts Brad's offer of assignment of his lease and moves into the apartment when Brad moves out. Melissa is responsible directly to the landlord (Al) who also collects the rent. Brad no longer has any interest in the lease.

Sublease

A **sublease** transfers possession of a leased property to a new person called the **sublessee**. The original tenant, who is now the **sublessor**, is still primarily liable for paying the rent to the owner. The sublessee is liable only to the sublessor. This type of lease is called a **sandwich lease**.

> Example: Bruce leases a two-bedroom apartment at $1,000 per month on a two year lease from Al. He lives there for six months until he is transferred to another part of the country. He has 18 months left on the lease before it expires. Bruce knows the transfer is temporary and wants to return to his apartment at some time in the future.
>
> Shawn accepts Bruce's offer to sublease the apartment for one year at $1,200 per month and moves in. Since Shawn's sublease is with Bruce, not the landlord, he sends his rent check in the amount of $1,200 to Bruce each month. Bruce pays rent of $1,000 to his landlord, Al.
>
> Bruce is still responsible for his original agreement with the lessor and keeps his interest as lessee in the property. Bruce holds a **sandwich lease** or a position in between the original lessor (Al) and the sublessee (Shawn).

Termination of a Lease

The majority of leases end by the expiration of the agreed-upon lease term or by mutual agreement between the landlord and tenant. Other ways to terminate a lease are destruction of the premises, breach of conditions by either lessor or lessee, or eviction. A sale of the property during the term of the lease does not usually terminate the lease.

When a tenant voluntarily gives up a lease before the expiration of its term, it is known as **surrender**. The tenant gives up any rights of possession, and has surrendered the property back to the landlord. If the landlord accepts the surrender, the tenant is no longer liable for rent. Sometimes a tenant just moves out or abandons the premises without doing a formal surrender. In this instance, the landlord has the option of demanding the balance of the rent due or rent due until the landlord finds another tenant.

Violations of the Terms or Conditions

If a landlord fails to make needed repairs to property after repeated requests by the tenant, the tenant may terminate the lease.

If a tenant fails to meet the terms of the rental agreement, or has not paid the rent, the landlord only has to give a three-day notice in writing, asking the tenant to conform. The tenant then must move out within three days or meet the landlord's requirements. The **notice to pay rent** or **quit** is an **eviction notice.** The landlord can sue for each installment of rent when it is due, re-let the premises and sue for damages, or serve a three-day notice to pay or quit to the tenant.

What a landlord may not do is give in to frustration about the delinquent or remiss tenant by committing unlawful acts, such as removing the tenant's belongings, changing the locks, shutting off the utilities or bullying the tenant with threats of bodily harm. Under the **right of replevin**, a tenant has the legal right to recover personal property unlawfully taken by the landlord.

Review - Unlawful Acts by a Landlord (Lessor)

- Tenant Lockout
- Taking Tenant Property
- Removing Doors and Windows
- Shutting Off Utilities
- Trespassing

Eviction Process

If the tenant defaults on the rent or refuses to give up the premises, the landlord may have to resort to the operation of law for removal. The legal remedy to remove a tenant is called **unlawful detainer action** or **action in ejectment.**

Steps in the Eviction Process

1. Notice to Pay or Quit served

2. Tenant has three days to respond

3. Unlawful Detainer filed

4. Tenant has five days to respond after being served

5. Writ of Possession granted

6. Sheriff sends eviction notice and physically removes tenant if no response within five days

The landlord may file an unlawful detainer action in the municipal court if a tenant ignores or fails to respond to the notification to pay or quit. This document lists the charges against the tenant, who then has five days to respond after being served; otherwise, a default hearing is set. A **writ of possession** is granted by the court to the landlord if the tenant does not move out or answer the lawsuit. This authorizes the sheriff to send an eviction notice to the tenant, and then after five days, physically remove the tenant from the premises.

The landlord must store any belongings left behind by the tenant after the eviction for 30 days, charging the tenant a reasonable storage fee. After that time, a public sale may be held and the proceeds used by the owner to pay costs of storage and sale. Any balance remaining after payment of these costs must be returned to the tenant.

Review - Termination of a Lease
- Expiration of the Term
- Mutual Agreement
- Violations of Terms and Conditions
- Destruction of the Premises
- Eviction

CALIFORNIA
ASSOCIATION
OF REALTORS®

NOTICE OF TERMINATION OF TENANCY
(C.A.R. Form NTT, Revised 1/06)

To: _____ ("Tenant")

and any other occupant(s) in possession of the premises located at:

(Street Address) _____ (Unit/Apartment #) _____

(City) _____ (State) _____ (Zip Code) _____ ("Premises").

Your tenancy, if any, in the Premises is terminated **30 days** from service of this Notice, or on _____

(whichever is later).

If you fail to give up possession by the specified date, a legal action will be filed seeking possession and damages that

could result in a judgment being awarded against you.

Landlord (Owner or Agent) _____

Date _____

Address _____

City _____ **State** _____ **Zip** _____

Telephone _____

Fax _____

E-mail _____

(Keep a copy for your records)

SURE TRAC
The System for Success™

Published and Distributed by:
REAL ESTATE BUSINESS SERVICES, INC.
a subsidiary of the California Association of REALTORS®
525 South Virgil Avenue, Los Angeles, California 90020

NTT REVISED 1/06 (PAGE 1 OF 1)

| Reviewed by _____ Date_____ |

EQUAL HOUSING
OPPORTUNITY

NOTICE OF TERMINATION OF TENANCY (NTT PAGE 1 OF 1)

| Agent: | Phone: | Fax: | Prepared using WINForms® software |
| Broker: | | | |

Summary

In California, most real estate agents use the Residential Purchase Agreement and Joint Escrow Instructions (deposit receipt). This agreement is an offer to purchase property. Once the seller agrees to the offer and the buyer is informed of the seller's acceptance, the **deposit receipt** is a legally binding contract which all parties must sign.

Termination of offer occurs when the buyer withdraws the offer before the seller accepts it, the time limit for offer expires, the buyer dies before the seller accepts the offer, or the seller gives the buyer a **counteroffer.**

Generally, real estate agents use the California Association of REALTORS® Offer to Purchase (RPA-CA) to process an offer to purchase property in California. The Department of Real Estate does not recommend forms. Real estate agents also use the Area Edition Residential Purchase Agreement (AERPA11).

A **lease (rental agreement)** is a contract between an owner (**lessor** or **landlord**) and a **lessee** (tenant). A **tenant** takes possession and use of a property in return for rent payment. Leases over one year must be in writing.

There are three classifications of leases: types of real estate, length of term, or method of payment. There are two types of real estate: **ground lease** and **proprietary lease**. The length of time includes short-term and long-term leases. Method of rent payments include rent payments, such as gross, net, and percentage leases.

Rent is payment for the use of a property. If the rent is not paid when due, the tenant may be **evicted**. Most leases require a security deposit plus the first month's rent. A **security deposit** is money given to the landlord to prepay for damages whether accidental or intentional, failure to pay rent due or return keys, to clean the property to the original condition before the tenant took possession and to compensate the landlord for damages when the tenant quits the property. Security deposits on unfurnished property cannot exceed two months rent, and three months rent on furnished property.

The responsibilities of a landlord include a guarantee that health and safety codes are met, periodic inspection of the property with reasonable notice of intent to enter, 30-day advance notice when ordering the tenant to vacate and obeying fair housing rules and regulations.

A tenant's responsibilities include paying rent when due, giving proper notice before moving out, and not interfering with the rights of other tenants. Under certain conditions the tenant may also repair property (spending up to one month's rent) and subtract the amount from the rent twice a year. A tenant may transfer possession of a leased property to a new person (**sublessee**). A **sublease** is known as a **sandwich lease**.

Leases are commonly terminated by the expiration of the lease term or by mutual agreement between the landlord and tenant. Other methods to terminate a lease include destruction of property, breach of conditions by either lessor or lessee or eviction. When a tenant voluntarily gives up a lease before the expiration of its term, the tenant **surrenders** the property.

If a tenant fails to meet the terms of the rental agreement, or does not pay rent, the landlord is required to give a three-day notice in writing requesting the tenant to conform. The tenant must move out in three days or meet the landlord's requirements. The landlord can sue for damages, re-let the premises, or serve a three-day **notice to pay** or **quit** to the tenant.

The landlord can file an unlawful detainer action in municipal court if a tenant ignores or fails to respond to the notification. If the court grants a **writ of possession**, the sheriff physically removes the tenant from the premises after a five-day notice. A tenant can delay the eviction by filing an appeal.

The landlord must store any belongings left behind by the tenant for 30 days, charging a reasonable storage fee. After 30 days, the tenant's belongings are sold at a public sale; the proceeds are used to pay storage and sale costs. The balance remaining after payment to the landlord is returned to the tenant.

Chapter 6 Review Exercises

Matching Exercise

Instructions: Look up the meaning of the terms in the Glossary, then write the letter of the matching term on the blank line before its definition. Answers are in Appendix B.

Terms

a. assignee

b. assignment

c. counteroffer

d. CPI

e. deposit receipt

f. gross lease

g. ground lease

h. implied warranty of habitability

i. interim occupancy agreement

j. lease

k. leased-fee estate

l. lessee

m. lessor

n. liquidated damages clause

o. net lease

p. option

q. percentage lease

r. proprietary lease

s. rent

t. residential lease

u. retaliatory eviction

v. security deposit

w. sublease

x. "time is of the essence" clause

y. unlawful detainer action

Definitions

1. _____ A clause in a contract that emphasizes punctual performance as a requirement of the contract.

2. _____ A contract between an owner and tenant.

3. _____ A contract to keep open, for a set period of time, an offer to purchase real property.

4. _____ A lease for only the land.

5. _____ A lease is used for single family homes and duplexes.

6. _____ An eviction that occurs in revenge for some complaint made by the tenant.

7. _____ An index used for rent adjustments on commercial leases.

8. _____ Clause in a contract that allows parties to the contract to decide in advance the amount of damages to be paid, should either party breach the contract.

9. _____ Contract that acts as the receipt for earnest money given by the buyer to secure an offer, as well as being the basic agreement, between the buyer and seller.

10. _____ A lease used on co-op apartment buildings.

11. _____ An agreement used if a buyer takes possession of a property prior to close of escrow.

12. _____ Payment for the use of a property.

13. _____ The interest of the lessor.

14. _____ The transfer of the entire leasehold estate to a new person.

15. _____ The tenant pays an agreed-upon sum as rent, plus certain agreed-upon expenses per month (i.e., taxes, insurance, and repairs).

16. _____ The rejection of an original purchase offer and the submission of a new and different offer.

17. _____ The property will be maintained to meet bare living requirements.

18. _____ The person who owns the property and signs the lease to give possession and use to the tenant.

19. _____ The legal remedy to remove a tenant.

20. _____ Money given to a landlord to prepay for any damage that might occur to a property during a lease term that is more than just normal wear and tear.

Multiple Choice Questions

Instructions: Circle your response and go to Appendix B to read the complete explanation for each question.

1. The statute of frauds requires that contracts for the sale of real estate must:
   a. be recorded.
   b. be in writing.
   c. be bilateral contracts.
   d. have a cash deposit.

2. When purchasing property, the amount of the buyer's earnest money deposit is determined by:
   a. state law based on the purchase price of the property.
   b. local custom and location of the property.
   c. agreement between buyer and broker.
   d. agreement between buyer and seller.

3. What is the status of a contract during the period of time after a real estate sales contract is signed by both parties but before title actually passes? The contract is:
   a. unilateral.
   b. voidable.
   c. executory.
   d. interim.

4. A prospective buyer made an offer and gave the seller's broker a $500 check as a deposit for the sale of a residence. Before the offer was given to the seller, the buyer contacted the broker and withdrew the offer. What should the broker do with the $500 check?
   a. Deposit it in escrow
   b. Return it immediately
   c. Hold it until the seller is notified
   d. Keep it to be reimbursed for out-of-pocket expenses

5. Buyer Baker presented an offer to Seller Sam for the purchase of a 10 year-old home in a quiet neighborhood. Seller Sam made a counteroffer to buyer Baker. Under these circumstances, buyer Baker:
   a. is required to accept seller Sam's offer.
   b. does not have to accept the counteroffer, but is still obligated under his original offer.
   c. has no obligation under his original offer.
   d. is obligated to make a new offer to seller Sam, if the counteroffer is unacceptable.

6. Buyer Baker's agent presented an offer to purchase to seller Susan. Seller Susan was delighted because the offer met all of her terms. She had not expected her home to sell so quickly, so she accepted the offer, but changed the date for closing from 45 days to 90 days. In this situation, buyer Baker is:
   a. not bound by the original offer he sent to seller Susan.
   b. bound by seller Susan's acceptance because she only changed the closing date.
   c. bound by the original offer with the original closing date.
   d. is not bound by the original offer, but is bound by Susan's counteroffer.

7. Seller Chris listed a vacant lot with a broker at $111,400. Prospective buyer Jordan submitted an offer of $111,000 that was to expire in three days. The next day, Chris made a counteroffer of $111,200. When Jordan did not respond within the three-day period, Chris signed an acceptance of Jordan's $111,000 original offer and instructed the broker to deliver it to Jordan. Jordan told the broker that he had decided not to purchase the property, but Chris insisted they had a deal. Based on these circumstances, there is a(n) _____ contract.

    a. valid
    b. void
    c. invalid
    d. enforceable

8. An agreement not to close an offer is known as a(n):

    a. novation.
    b. option.
    c. rescission.
    d. subrogation.

9. Seller Pat gives an option to buyer Jordan to purchase Pat's ranch. This option most clearly constitutes a(n):

    a. voluntary lien on Pat's ranch.
    b. offer to enter into a contract.
    c. fiduciary agreement.
    d. contract to keep an offer open.

10. Which of the following statements is correct regarding an option contract to purchase real estate?

    a. The optionor is not obliged to sell the property.
    b. The option is a bilateral contract.
    c. The consideration must be money in excess of $100.
    d. The optionee is not obligated to purchase the property.

11. Which of the following statements is **incorrect?**

    a. A deposit receipt is a bilateral contract.
    b. An option is a unilateral contract.
    c. A net listing is a unilateral contract.
    d. An exclusive listing is a bilateral contract.

12. As used in real estate law, the term tenancy is best described as:
    a. the landlord-tenant relationship.
    b. retention of rights as a remainderman.
    c. a tenant in a lease agreement.
    d. a mode or method of holding title to real property by a lessee or owner.

13. Under a lease for an unfurnished apartment, the lessor may require a security deposit of no more than:
    a. $500.
    b. one month's rent.
    c. two months' rent.
    d. three months' rent.

14. If an owner grants possession of real property to another person for less than the owner's interest, it is known as a(n):
    a. subordinated lease.
    b. uninsured lease.
    c. lease.
    d. sale-leaseback.

15. The maximum amount of security deposit a landlord may demand from a prospective tenant depends upon:
    a. the total number of tenants who plan to occupy the premises.
    b. the number of children occupying the unit.
    c. the term of the lease and whether the unit is furnished or unfurnished.
    d. economic competition from nearby properties.

16. The right of quiet enjoyment most often means:
    a. freedom from annoyance from noisy neighbors.
    b. lack of interference from the paramount title holder.
    c. lack of interference from adjoining owners.
    d. none of the above

17. If real property is subleased, the interest held by the sublessor is commonly known as a(n):
    a. double lease.
    b. freehold lease.
    c. assignment.
    d. sandwich lease.

18. An unlawful detainer proceeding is most often taken by a:
    a. beneficiary.
    b. trustee.
    c. lessor.
    d. grantee.

19. A tenant may abandon a leased property and refuse to pay further rent if the landlord carries out a constructive eviction. Which of the following is considered to be a constructive eviction?
    a. The landlord has shown the property to another party and has entered into negotiations with that party to lease the premises.
    b. The landlord has failed to make needed major repairs and to maintain the property in the agreed-upon manner.
    c. The landlord has altered the property such that it no longer suits the original purpose for which it was leased.
    d. All of the above

20. If a tenant refuses to pay rent due according to terms of a written lease, the landlord may have the tenant evicted by:
    a. serving a 30-day notice.
    b. posting a three-day notice to quit or pay rent and allowing three days to pass.
    c. pursuing an action in court.
    d. filing a Notice of Default.

Disclosures in Real Estate

7

Chapter

Introduction

Caveat emptor, a Latin phrase meaning "let the buyer beware", is becoming a thing of the past. The buyer was put on notice to examine the property and buy it at his or her own risk. Now, several consumer protection laws place the responsibility of disclosing the condition of the property on the seller and the broker. As the buying and selling of real property becomes more complex, so do the required disclosures. As a real estate agent, you will be required to guide all parties through the disclosure minefield.

Learning Objectives

After reading this chapter, you will be able to:

- define disclosures.
- discuss the Real Estate Transfer Disclosure Statement (TDS).
- identify required disclosures in real estate.
- discuss how disclosure violations can be remedied.
- explain the legal consequences of not disclosing information and state two specific examples.

Disclosures Required in Agency Relationships

As we learned, brokers work within a legal relationship called agency. The agency relationship exists between the broker, as agent, and the principal. The essence of the agency relationship is that the agent has the authority to represent the principal in dealings with others. Agents and their sales associates are legally obligated to protect and promote the interests of their principals as they would their own.

Although home buyers and sellers use the services of real estate agents, most of them have limited understanding of the agency representation. Therefore, real estate agents are required to discuss and complete the Agency Relationship Disclosure form at the first personal meeting with potential sellers or buyers. The disclosure form gives your potential clients the opportunity to find out who will represent them and if there are conflicts of interest.

Disclosures Required in a Real Estate Transfer

One of the most critical responsibilities imposed on real estate licensees is the duty of full disclosure. It is your responsibility to make sure you comply with the law for each disclosure required. Many of the required disclosures are enumerated in the deposit receipt, and it is your job to explain each one to your clients and customers.

Real estate agents must be prepared to meet the duties and obligations required by law. If real estate agents do not comply with the law, they may be subject to civil, criminal and/or Department of Real Estate action and penalties. All over the country, courts and legislatures are continuing to hold real estate agents accountable for their activities. Increasingly, real estate agents must know what and how to disclose—as well as when, where, why, by, and to whom. The uninformed real estate agent is highly vulnerable to court action in our consumer-oriented society.

Easton v. Strassburger

The case of *Easton v. Strassburger*, 152 C.A. 3d 90, is about a home built on a land fill that had not been properly compacted, but was listed for sale. The owner did not tell the listing broker about the landslide problem that had developed as a result of the poor engineering on the slope. The property was sold and the buyer suffered a substantial loss as a result of land slippage.

In a court action, the buyer proved that one of the listing agents noticed the netting that had been placed on the slope to keep it in place, and another agent had noticed an uneven floor in the house that had occurred as a result of the undisclosed soil problem. The court stated that the "red flags" should have indicated to the real estate agents there was a problem, and the problem should have been investigated. A **red flag** is something that alerts a reasonably observant person of a potential problem. Typically a red flag could include cracks in walls, foundations and sidewalks; stains from leaks in the roof and similar items.

The court ruled that a broker has the duty to inspect a property and disclose any material facts affecting its value. A broker is required to uncover any "reasonably discoverable" problems and tell all interested parties. No property may be sold "**as is**" without a complete disclosure of the defect, even though a broker might possess a disclaimer of liability for the defect. An "as is" clause does not relieve a seller from the responsibility to disclose all known material facts to the buyer. However, an "as is" clause indicates that the seller will **not** be responsible for the cost of repairing any defect. Real estate licensees should continue to encourage sellers to disclose any known defects in the property.

Visual Inspection

The *Easton v. Strassburger* case findings stated real estate agents could be liable for defects in property that they know about as well as defects that they should know about as a result of a visual investigation. All listing brokers of a residential property and any cooperating brokers must conduct a reasonably competent and diligent visual inspection of the property. Additionally, they must disclose to a prospective buyer all material facts that may affect value, desirability and intended use of the property.

The real estate agent does not have to inspect areas of the property that are not reasonably accessible, nor public records and permits. If the property is a condominium, the real estate agent is responsible for inspecting the unit, not the common area.

The required certification of the visual inspection is contained in the Real Estate Transfer Disclosure Statement.

Transfer Disclosure Statement

The **Real Estate Transfer Disclosure Statement** (TDS) is a document that the seller must provide to any buyer of residential property (one-to-four units). It is a detailed statement telling what the seller knows about the condition of the property. The statement must list all known defects as well as any potential problems that might affect the property value. Usually a broker obtains this statement at the time the listing is taken and provides a copy to a buyer before an offer to purchase the property is presented. If the real estate agent gives a copy of the disclosure statement to the buyer after the offer to purchase the property is presented, the buyer may terminate the contract by written notice to the seller within three days after receiving the disclosure statement. A copy of this statement is included on the following pages.

The seller reveals any information that would be important to the buyer regarding the condition of the property in the TDS, and states that—to the seller's knowledge—everything important has been disclosed. Many facts about a residential property could materially affect its value and desirability. These include:

- age, condition and any defects or malfunctions of the structural components and/or plumbing, electrical, heating or other mechanical systems.

- easements, common driveways, or fences.

- room additions, structural alterations, repairs, replacements, or other changes, especially those made without required building permits.

- flooding, drainage, or soil problems on, near, or in any way affecting the property.

- zoning violations, such as nonconforming uses or insufficient setbacks.

- homeowners' association obligations and deed restrictions or common area problems.

- citations against the property, or lawsuits against the owner or affecting the property.

- location of the property within a known earthquake zone.

- major damage to the property from fire, earthquake, or landslide.

Under California law, a seller of a residential property (one-to-four units) must deliver a written disclosure statement about the condition of the property to the prospective buyer. This requirement extends to any transfer by: sale, exchange, installment land sale contract, lease with an option to purchase, any other option to purchase, or ground lease coupled with improvements.

CALIFORNIA ASSOCIATION OF REALTORS®

REAL ESTATE TRANSFER DISCLOSURE STATEMENT
(CALIFORNIA CIVIL CODE §1102, ET SEQ)
(C.A.R. Form TDS, Revised 10/03)

THIS DISCLOSURE STATEMENT CONCERNS THE REAL PROPERTY SITUATED IN THE CITY OF
_____ , COUNTY OF _____ , STATE OF CALIFORNIA,
DESCRIBED AS _____
THIS STATEMENT IS A DISCLOSURE OF THE CONDITION OF THE ABOVE DESCRIBED PROPERTY IN
COMPLIANCE WITH SECTION 1102 OF THE CIVIL CODE AS OF (date) _____ . IT IS NOT A
WARRANTY OF ANY KIND BY THE SELLER(S) OR ANY AGENT(S) REPRESENTING ANY PRINCIPAL(S) IN THIS
TRANSACTION, AND IS NOT A SUBSTITUTE FOR ANY INSPECTIONS OR WARRANTIES THE PRINCIPAL(S) MAY
WISH TO OBTAIN.

I. COORDINATION WITH OTHER DISCLOSURE FORMS

This Real Estate Transfer Disclosure Statement is made pursuant to Section 1102 of the Civil Code. Other statutes require disclosures, depending upon the details of the particular real estate transaction (for example: special study zone and purchase-money liens on residential property).

Substituted Disclosures: The following disclosures and other disclosures required by law, including the Natural Hazard Disclosure Report/Statement that may include airport annoyances, earthquake, fire, flood, or special assessment information, have or will be made in connection with this real estate transfer, and are intended to satisfy the disclosure obligations on this form, where the subject matter is the same:

☐ Inspection reports completed pursuant to the contract of sale or receipt for deposit.

☐ Additional inspection reports or disclosures: _____
_____

II. SELLER'S INFORMATION

The Seller discloses the following information with the knowledge that even though this is not a warranty, prospective Buyers may rely on this information in deciding whether and on what terms to purchase the subject property. Seller hereby authorizes any agent(s) representing any principal(s) in this transaction to provide a copy of this statement to any person or entity in connection with any actual or anticipated sale of the property.

THE FOLLOWING ARE REPRESENTATIONS MADE BY THE SELLER(S) AND ARE NOT THE REPRESENTATIONS OF THE AGENT(S), IF ANY. THIS INFORMATION IS A DISCLOSURE AND IS NOT INTENDED TO BE PART OF ANY CONTRACT BETWEEN THE BUYER AND SELLER.

Seller ☐ is ☐ is not occupying the property.

A. The subject property has the items checked below (read across)

☐ Range	☐ Oven	☐ Microwave
☐ Dishwasher	☐ Trash Compactor	☐ Garbage Disposal
☐ Washer/Dryer Hookups		☐ Rain Gutters
☐ Burglar Alarms	☐ Smoke Detector(s)	☐ Fire Alarm
☐ T.V. Antenna	☐ Satellite Dish	☐ Intercom
☐ Central Heating	☐ Central Air Conditioning	☐ Evaporator Cooler(s)
☐ Wall/Window Air Conditioning	☐ Sprinklers	☐ Public Sewer System
☐ Septic Tank	☐ Sump Pump	☐ Water Softener
☐ Patio/Decking	☐ Built-in Barbecue	☐ Gazebo
☐ Sauna		
☐ Hot Tub ☐ Locking Safety Cover*	☐ Pool ☐ Child Resistant Barrier*	☐ Spa ☐ Locking Safety Cover*
☐ Security Gate(s)	☐ Automatic Garage Door Opener(s)*	☐ Number Remote Controls _____
Garage: ☐ Attached	☐ Not Attached	☐ Carport
Pool/Spa Heater: ☐ Gas	☐ Solar	☐ Electric
Water Heater: ☐ Gas	☐ Water Heater Anchored, Braced, or Strapped*	☐ Private Utility or
Water Supply: ☐ City	☐ Well	Other _____
Gas Supply: ☐ Utility	☐ Bottled	
☐ Window Screens	☐ Window Security Bars ☐ Quick Release Mechanism on Bedroom Windows*	

Exhaust Fan(s) in _____ 220 Volt Wiring in _____ Fireplace(s) in _____
☐ Gas Starter _____ ☐ Roof(s): Type: _____ Age: _____ (approx.)
☐ Other: _____
Are there, to the best of your (Seller's) knowledge, any of the above that are not in operating condition? ☐ Yes ☐ No. If yes, then describe. (Attach additional sheets if necessary): _____
_____

(*see footnote on page 2)

Buyer's Initials (_____) (_____)
Seller's Initials (_____) (_____)

Reviewed by _____ Date _____

EQUAL HOUSING OPPORTUNITY

TDS REVISED 10/03 (PAGE 1 OF 3)

REAL ESTATE TRANSFER DISCLOSURE STATEMENT (TDS PAGE 1 OF 3)

Agent:	Phone:	Fax:	Prepared using WINForms® software
Broker:			

Property Address: _____ Date: _____

B. Are you (Seller) aware of any significant defects/malfunctions in any of the following? ☐ Yes ☐ No. If yes, check appropriate space(s) below.

☐ Interior Walls ☐ Ceilings ☐ Floors ☐ Exterior Walls ☐ Insulation ☐ Roof(s) ☐ Windows ☐ Doors ☐ Foundation ☐ Slab(s)
☐ Driveways ☐ Sidewalks ☐ Walls/Fences ☐ Electrical Systems ☐ Plumbing/Sewers/Septics ☐ Other Structural Components
(Describe: _____

_____

_____)

If any of the above is checked, explain. (Attach additional sheets if necessary): _____

_____

_____

_____

*This garage door opener or child resistant pool barrier may not be in compliance with the safety standards relating to automatic reversing devices as set forth in Chapter 12.5 (commencing with Section 19890) of Part 3 of Division 13 of, or with the pool safety standards of Article 2.5 (commencing with Section 115920) of Chapter 5 of Part 10 of Division 104 of, the Health and Safety Code. The water heater may not be anchored, braced, or strapped in accordance with Section 19211 of the Health and Safety Code. Window security bars may not have quick release mechanisms in compliance with the 1995 Edition of the California Building Standards Code.

C. Are you (Seller) aware of any the following:

1. Substances, materials, or products which may be an environmental hazard such as, but not limited to, asbestos, formaldehyde, radon gas, lead-based paint, mold, fuel or chemical storage tanks, and contaminated soil or water on the subject property . . . . ☐ Yes ☐ No
2. Features of the property shared in common with adjoining landowners, such as walls, fences, and driveways, whose use or responsibility for maintenance may have an effect on the subject property . . . . ☐ Yes ☐ No
3. Any encroachments, easements or similar matters that may affect your interest in the subject property . . . . ☐ Yes ☐ No
4. Room additions, structural modifications, or other alterations or repairs made without necessary permits. . . . . . . ☐ Yes ☐ No
5. Room additions, structural modifications, or other alterations or repairs not in compliance with building codes. . . . ☐ Yes ☐ No
6. Fill (compacted or otherwise) on the property or any portion thereof . . . . ☐ Yes ☐ No
7. Any settling from any cause, or slippage, sliding. or other soil problems . . . . ☐ Yes ☐ No
8. Flooding, drainage or grading problems . . . . ☐ Yes ☐ No
9. Major damage to the property or any of the structures from fire, earthquake, floods, or landslides . . . . ☐ Yes ☐ No
10. Any zoning violations, nonconforming uses, violations of "setback" requirements . . . . ☐ Yes ☐ No
11. Neighborhood noise problems or other nuisances . . . . ☐ Yes ☐ No
12. CC&R's or other deed restrictions or obligations . . . . ☐ Yes ☐ No
13. Homeowners' Association which has any authority over the subject property . . . . ☐ Yes ☐ No
14. Any "common area" (facilities such as pools, tennis courts, walkways, or other areas co-owned in undivided interest with others) . . . . ☐ Yes ☐ No
15. Any notices of abatement or citations against the property . . . . ☐ Yes ☐ No
16. Any lawsuits by or against the seller threatening to or affecting this real property, including any lawsuits alleging a defect or deficiency in this real property or "common areas" (facilities such as pools, tennis courts, walkways, or other areas, co-owned in undivided interest with others) . . . . ☐ Yes ☐ No

If the answer to any of these is yes, explain. (Attach additional sheets if necessary): _____

_____

_____

_____

_____

Seller certifies that the information herein is true and correct to the best of the Seller's knowledge as of the date signed by the Seller.

Seller _____ Date _____

Seller _____ Date _____

Buyer's Initials (_____)(_____)

TDS REVISED 10/03 (PAGE 2 OF 3)

| Reviewed by _____ Date _____ |

EQUAL HOUSING
OPPORTUNITY

REAL ESTATE TRANSFER DISCLOSURE STATEMENT (TDS PAGE 2 OF 3)

Property Address: _____ Date: _____

III. AGENT'S INSPECTION DISCLOSURE
(To be completed only if the Seller is represented by an agent in this transaction.)

THE UNDERSIGNED, BASED ON THE ABOVE INQUIRY OF THE SELLER(S) AS TO THE CONDITION OF THE PROPERTY AND BASED ON A REASONABLY COMPETENT AND DILIGENT VISUAL INSPECTION OF THE ACCESSIBLE AREAS OF THE PROPERTY IN CONJUNCTION WITH THAT INQUIRY, STATES THE FOLLOWING:

☐ Agent notes no items for disclosure.
☐ Agent notes the following items: _____
_____
_____
_____

Agent (Broker Representing Seller) _____ By _____ Date _____
                  (Please Print)   (Associate Licensee or Broker Signature)

IV. AGENT'S INSPECTION DISCLOSURE
(To be completed only if the agent who has obtained the offer is other than the agent above.)

THE UNDERSIGNED, BASED ON A REASONABLY COMPETENT AND DILIGENT VISUAL INSPECTION OF THE ACCESSIBLE AREAS OF THE PROPERTY, STATES THE FOLLOWING:

☐ Agent notes no items for disclosure.
☐ Agent notes the following items: _____
_____
_____
_____

Agent (Broker Obtaining the Offer) _____ By _____ Date _____
                 (Please Print)   (Associate Licensee or Broker Signature)

V. BUYER(S) AND SELLER(S) MAY WISH TO OBTAIN PROFESSIONAL ADVICE AND/OR INSPECTIONS OF THE PROPERTY AND TO PROVIDE FOR APPROPRIATE PROVISIONS IN A CONTRACT BETWEEN BUYER AND SELLER(S) WITH RESPECT TO ANY ADVICE/INSPECTIONS/DEFECTS.

I/WE ACKNOWLEDGE RECEIPT OF A COPY OF THIS STATEMENT.

Seller _____ Date _____ Buyer _____ Date _____

Seller _____ Date _____ Buyer _____ Date _____

Agent (Broker Representing Seller) _____ By _____ Date _____
                  (Please Print)   (Associate Licensee or Broker Signature)

Agent (Broker Obtaining the Offer) _____ By _____ Date _____
                 (Please Print)   (Associate Licensee or Broker Signature)

SECTION 1102.3 OF THE CIVIL CODE PROVIDES A BUYER WITH THE RIGHT TO RESCIND A PURCHASE CONTRACT FOR AT LEAST THREE DAYS AFTER THE DELIVERY OF THIS DISCLOSURE IF DELIVERY OCCURS AFTER THE SIGNING OF AN OFFER TO PURCHASE. IF YOU WISH TO RESCIND THE CONTRACT, YOU MUST ACT WITHIN THE PRESCRIBED PERIOD.

A REAL ESTATE BROKER IS QUALIFIED TO ADVISE ON REAL ESTATE. IF YOU DESIRE LEGAL ADVICE, CONSULT YOUR ATTORNEY.

SURE TRAC
The System for Success™

Published by the
California Association of REALTORS®

Reviewed by _____ Date _____

EQUAL HOUSING OPPORTUNITY

TDS REVISED 10/03 (PAGE 3 OF 3)

REAL ESTATE TRANSFER DISCLOSURE STATEMENT (TDS PAGE 3 OF 3)

T6429805.ZFX

Some exemptions from the disclosure requirement are transfers:

- pursuant to a court order.

- by a foreclosure sale.

- court-ordered by a fiduciary in the administration of a probate estate or a testamentary trust.

- to a spouse or another related person resulting from a judgment of dissolution of marriage or of legal separation or from a property settlement agreement incidental to such a judgment.

- from one co-owner to another.

- by the state controller for unclaimed property.

- as a result from the failure to pay taxes.

- from or to any governmental entity.

- where the first sale of a residential property within a subdivision and a copy of a public report is delivered to the purchaser or where such a report is not required.

The required disclosure must be made to the prospective buyer as soon as possible before transfer of title, or in the case of a lease option, sales contract, or ground lease coupled with improvements, before the execution of the contract. Should any disclosure or amended disclosure be delivered after the required date, the buyer/transferee has three days after delivery in person or five days after delivery by deposit in the U.S. mail to terminate the offer or agreement to purchase. A written notice of termination must reach the seller/transferor or the seller's agent.

The seller, listing broker, and cooperating broker have the obligation to prepare and deliver the disclosure. If more than one real estate agent is involved in the transaction (unless otherwise instructed by the seller), the agent obtaining the offer is required to deliver the disclosure to the prospective buyer.

If the prospective buyer receives a report or an opinion prepared by a licensed engineer, land surveyor, geologist, structural pest control operator, contractor, or other expert (with a specific professional license or expertise), the liability of the seller and the real estate agents may be limited when making required disclosures. The overall intention is to provide meaningful disclosures about the condition of the property being transferred. A violation of the law does not invalidate a transfer; however, the seller may be liable for any actual damages suffered by the buyer.

Disclosures Included with the Transfer Disclosure Statement

Environmental Hazard Disclosures

Numerous federal, state and local laws have been enacted to address the problems created by environmental hazards. Responsible parties, or persons considered responsible, for the improper disposal of hazardous waste and owners of contaminated property may be held liable for contamination cleanup.

Several disclosure laws relating to the transfer of land affected by hazardous waste contamination have been enacted. The California Real Estate Transfer Disclosure Statement requires sellers to disclose whether they are aware of the presence of hazardous substances, materials or products including—but not limited to—asbestos, form-aldehyde, radon gas, lead-based paint, fuel, or chemical storage tanks, contaminated soil, water, or mold.

Hazardous waste

Any owner of nonresidential property who knows or suspects that there has been a release of a hazardous substance or that it may occur on or beneath the property must notify a buyer, lessee or renter of that condition prior to the sale, lease, or rental of that property. Failure to give written notice may subject the owner to actual damages and/or civil penalties.

Under Proposition 65, certain businesses may not knowingly and intentionally expose any individual to a cancer-causing chemical or reproductive toxin without first giving clear, reasonable warning to such individuals. Proposition 65 has also imposed extensive asbestos disclosure requirements on owners of commercial buildings constructed prior to January 1, 1979.

Environmental Hazards Booklet

The Department of Real Estate and Office of Environmental Health Hazard Assessment have developed a booklet on environmental hazards to help educate and inform consumers about environmental hazards that may affect real property. The booklet identifies common environmental hazards, describes the risks involved with each, discusses mitigation techniques, and provides lists of publications and sources from which consumers can obtain more detailed information. The seller or seller's agent should give each buyer a copy of this booklet.

Hazards Discussed in the Environmental Hazard Booklet

- **Asbestos:** A mineral fiber used in construction materials which has been found to cause lung and stomach cancer.

- **Radon:** A colorless gas known to cause cancer. Radon can be detected with a spectrometer.

- **Lead:** A mineral that causes major health problems.

- **Formaldehyde:** A chemical organic compound found in building materials which may be a carcinogen.

- **Hazardous waste:** Materials—chemicals, explosives, radioactive, biological—whose disposal is regulated by the Environmental Protection Agency (EPA).

- **Household hazardous waste:** Consumer products such as paints, cleaners, stains, varnishes, car batteries, motor oil, and pesticides that contain hazardous components.

Once the booklet is provided to a prospective buyer of real property, neither the seller nor a real estate agent involved in the sale has a duty to provide further information on such hazards. Although not required to, the buyer should read through the booklet. However, if the seller or agent has actual knowledge of environmental hazards on or affecting the subject property, that information must be disclosed.

Window Security Bars

A seller must disclose if there are window security bars on the windows, and if present, any safety release mechanism on the bars.

Toxic Mold

There is always a little mold everywhere—in the air and on many surfaces. Mold is a fungus that reproduces by means of spores. Molds themselves are not toxic, or poisonous. However, certain molds are toxigenic because they can produce toxins (called mycotoxins). Currently, standards for judging what is an acceptable quantity of mold have not been established to determine toxicity. Therefore, no special disclosure requirements are in effect for toxic mold.

The California Department of Health Services is developing permissible exposure limits for toxic molds. The California Department of Health Sciences has prepared a consumer booklet on mold, which is available online. The Transfer Disclosure Statement has been modified to add the word "mold" in paragraph 11.C.1 and any transferor must disclose actual knowledge of mold on the property.

Toxic mold can generally be found in kitchens and bathrooms.

"Drug-Lab" Illegal Controlled Substance

The seller must inform the buyer in writing of toxic contamination by illegal controlled substance on the property, receipt of notice from the Department of Toxic Substance Control or another agency. The seller discloses this information by checking item 11.C.1 of the TDS form and attaching the DTSC notice, if there is one.

If the owner has actual knowledge of the presence of an illegal controlled substance release and knowingly and willfully fails to provide written notice to the buyer, the owner is liable for a civil penalty not to exceed five thousand dollars ($5,000) for each separate violation, in addition to any other damages provided by law.

Industrial Use Disclosure

The seller must disclose "actual knowledge" that the property is affected by or zoned for industrial use of the property. Examples of industrial use disclosure are manufacturing, commercial or airport use. This information may be disclosed on the TDS.

Military Ordnance Location

Federal and state agencies have identified certain areas once used for military training and which may contain live ammunition as part of the ordnance—or military supplies—from past activity. A seller of residential property (one-to-four dwelling units) located within one mile of such a hazard must give the buyer written notice as soon as possible before transfer of title. This obligation depends upon the seller having actual knowledge of the hazard. The location of military ordnance may be disclosed on the TDS.

Local Option Real Estate Transfer Disclosure Statement

If there is some local condition which may materially affect a buyer's use and enjoyment of residential property, an optional disclosure form may be required, called the Local Option Real Estate Transfer Disclosure Statement (LORETDS). Residential properties in cities and counties throughout California are typically subject to specific local ordinances on occupancy, zoning and use, building code compliance, fire, health and safety code regulations, and land subdivision descriptions. The various requirements for compliance as well as who and what is affected should be disclosed to the prospective buyer of the property by the seller or the seller's agent and any agent acting in cooperation with such agent. For example, based on the Farm Practices Protection Act of 1996, many jurisdictions in the Central Valley have enacted "Right to Farm" ordinances to protect existing agricultural uses adjacent to new residential uses.

Mello-Roos Disclosure

Currently, on purchase property taxes are limited by Proposition 13 to a maximum of 1% of the assessed value of the property. The city, through the sale of municipal bonds, can include the cost and maintenance of infrastructure items in the property tax bill as a special assessment, exempt from the limitations of Proposition 13.

The Mello-Roos Community Facilities Act of 1982 authorizes the formation of community facilities districts, the issuance of bonds and the levying of special taxes which will finance designated public facilities and services. A **Mello-Roos District** is an area where a special tax is imposed on those real property owners within a Community Facilities District. Public services such as roads, sewers, parks, schools, and fire stations in new developments may be financed under this law.

ANY CITY, CALIFORNIA

Mello Roos Disclosure Statement
Notice of Special Tax

Community Facilities District 20____-1
ABC Public Facilities Financing Agency
County of _____, State of California

To: The Prospective Purchaser of the Real Property Known as:

Address: Assessors Parcel Number:

_____

THIS IS A NOTIFICATION TO YOU PRIOR TO YOUR PURCHASING THIS
PROPERTY.

1. This property is subject to a special tax, which is in addition to the regular property
taxes and other charges and benefit assessments on the parcel. This special tax may not
be imposed on all parcels within the city or county where the property is located. If you
fail to pay this tax when due each year, the property may be foreclosed upon and sold.
The tax is used to provide public facilities or services that are likely to particularly
benefit the property. **You should take this tax and the benefits from the facilities and
services for which it pays into account in deciding to whether to buy this property.**

2. The maximum annual tax to which this property is subject is $_____ during the
20___ tax year and thereafter. The special tax will be levied each year until all of the
authorized facilities are built and all special tax bonds are repaid.

3. The authorized facilities which are being paid for by the special taxes, and by the
money received from the sale of bonds which are being repaid by the special taxes, are
set forth on Exhibit A attached hereto. These facilities may not yet have all been
constructed or acquired and it is possible that some may never be constructed or acquired.

4. The obligation to pay the special tax, attached to this property, was a condition
required in order to permit this property to be developed. The payment of tax is intended
to insure that there will be adequate capacity in the school district for the children that
may come from this property. However, the payment of the special tax does not
guarantee attendance at any particular school, nor does it guarantee attendance at a newly
constructed school. School attendance boundaries are set by the School Board and are
based on many criteria, only one of which is whether a property pays the special tax.

You may obtain a copy of the resolution of formation which authorized creation of the
community facilities district, and which specifies more precisely how the special tax is
apportioned and how the proceeds of the tax will be used, from the Comptroller of ABC
Public Facilities Financing Agency by telephoning (555) 123-4567. There may be a
charge for this document not to exceed the reasonable cost of providing this document.

I (we) acknowledge that I (we) have read this notice and received a copy of this
notice prior to entering into a contract to purchase or deposit receipt with respect
to the above-references property. I (we) understand that I (we) may terminate the
contract to purchase or deposit receipt within three days after receiving this notice
in person or within five days after it was deposited in the mail by giving written
notice of that termination to the owner, subdivider, or agent selling the property.

Date:

_____

A Mello-Roos lien is placed on each parcel in a new development by the developer to pay off municipal bonds issued to fund off-site improvements for the development. The developer must make the payments on the bond until the homes are sold, and then the new owners are responsible. Mello-Roos liens are a way a developer can make improvements and have each homeowner pay for them, without charging the improvements to property taxes.

Effective July 1, 1993, the seller of a property consisting of one-to-four dwelling units subject to the lien of a Mello-Roos community facilities district must make a good faith effort to obtain from the district a disclosure notice concerning the special tax and give the notice to a prospective buyer. Exempt from this requirement are the various transfers listed earlier for the Transfer Disclosure Statement. According to the California Tax Data website, Mello-Roos information should be on the property tax bill. Mello-Roos funds are used to finance subdivision costs. The transferor (seller) of residential property (one-to-four units) is responsible to disclose if a property is subject to a Mello-Roos assessment.

New buyers must be told by real estate agents that a project is subject to a Mello-Roos special assessment because their tax bill will be higher than if they only paid property taxes without the special assessment.

The listing agent does not have an affirmative duty to discover a special tax district or assessment not actually known to the agent. However, information about Mello-Roos assessments may be obtained from the county tax collector's office. The Real Estate Commissioner can discipline a real estate agent for failure to provide a Mello-Roos disclosure. Failure to give notice to a buyer or lessee (if more than five years) before signing a sales contract or lease allows the buyer or lessee a three-day right to cancel after receiving the disclosure.

Lead-Based Paint Hazards

The Residential Lead-Based Paint Hazard Reduction Act of 1992 (Title X) became effective on September 6, 1996 for owners of property with four or fewer units. A lead-hazard information brochure and disclosure form must be provided to a buyer or lessee by a seller or landlord. Also, the presence of any known lead-based paint must be disclosed.

This disclosure pertains to residential housing built before 1978 because the Act banned lead based paint for residential use in that year. Some pre-1978 properties, called **target housing**, are exempt from the disclosure.

CALIFORNIA ASSOCIATION OF REALTORS®

LEAD-BASED PAINT AND LEAD-BASED PAINT HAZARDS DISCLOSURE, ACKNOWLEDGMENT AND ADDENDUM
For Pre-1978 Housing Sales, Leases, or Rentals
(C.A.R. Form FLD, Revised 1/03)

The following terms and conditions are hereby incorporated in and made a part of the: ☐ California Residential Purchase Agreement, ☐ Residential Lease or Month-to-Month Rental Agreement, or ☐ other: _____ _____ , dated _____ , on property known as: _____ ("Property") in which _____ is referred to as Buyer or Tenant and _____ is referred to as Seller or Landlord.

LEAD WARNING STATEMENT (SALE OR PURCHASE) Every purchaser of any interest in residential real property on which a residential dwelling was built prior to 1978 is notified that such property may present exposure to lead from lead-based paint that may place young children at risk of developing lead poisoning. Lead poisoning in young children may produce permanent neurological damage, including learning disabilities, reduced intelligent quotient, behavioral problems and impaired memory. Lead poisoning also poses a particular risk to pregnant women. The seller of any interest in residential real property is required to provide the buyer with any information on lead-based paint hazards from risk assessments or inspections in the seller's possession and notify the buyer of any known lead-based paint hazards. A risk assessment or inspection for possible lead-based paint hazards is recommended prior to purchase.

LEAD WARNING STATEMENT (LEASE OR RENTAL) Housing built before 1978 may contain lead-based paint. Lead from paint, paint chips and dust can pose health hazards if not managed properly. Lead exposure is especially harmful to young children and pregnant women. Before renting pre-1978 housing, lessors must disclose the presence of lead-based paint and/or lead-based paint hazards in the dwelling. Lessees must also receive federally approved pamphlet on lead poisoning prevention.

1. SELLER'S OR LANDLORD'S DISCLOSURE

I (we) have no knowledge of lead-based paint and/or lead-based paint hazards in the housing other than the following:

_____
_____
_____
_____

I (we) have no reports or records pertaining to lead-based paint and/or lead-based paint hazards in the housing other than the following, which, previously or as an attachment to this addendum have been provided to Buyer or Tenant:

_____
_____
_____

I (we), previously or as an attachment to this addendum, have provided Buyer or Tenant with the pamphlet *"Protect Your Family From Lead In Your Home"* or an equivalent pamphlet approved for use in the State such as *"The Homeowner's Guide to Environmental Hazards and Earthquake Safety."*

<u>For Sales Transactions Only</u>: Buyer has 10 days, unless otherwise agreed in the real estate purchase contract, to conduct a risk assessment or inspection for the presence of lead-based paint and/or lead-based paint hazards.

I (we) have reviewed the information above and certify, to the best of my (our) knowledge, that the information provided is true and correct.

_____
Seller or Landlord   Date

_____
Seller or Landlord   Date

FLD REVISED 1/03 (PAGE 1 OF 2)

Buyer's Initials (_____) (_____)
Seller's Initials (_____) (_____)

| Reviewed by _____ Date _____ |

EQUAL HOUSING OPPORTUNITY

LEAD-BASED PAINT AND LEAD-BASED PAINT HAZARDS DISCLOSURE (FLD-11 PAGE 1 OF 2)

| Agent: | Phone: | Fax: | Prepared using WINForms® software |
| Broker: | | | |

Property Address:_____ Date: _____

2. LISTING AGENT'S ACKNOWLEDGMENT

Agent has informed Seller or Landlord of Seller's or Landlord's obligations under §42 U.S.C. 4852d and is aware of Agent's responsibility to ensure compliance.

I have reviewed the information above and certify, to the best of my knowledge, that the information provided is true and correct.

_____   By _____
Agent (Broker representing Seller) Please Print   Associate-Licensee or Broker Signature   Date

3. BUYER'S OR TENANT'S ACKNOWLEDGMENT

I (we) have received copies of all information listed, if any, in 1 above and the pamphlet *"Protect Your Family From Lead In Your Home"* or an equivalent pamphlet approved for use in the State such as *"The Homeowner's Guide to Environmental Hazards and Earthquake Safety."* **If delivery of any of the disclosures or pamphlet referenced in paragraph 1 above occurs after Acceptance of an offer to purchase, Buyer has a right to cancel pursuant to the purchase contract. If you wish to cancel, you must act within the prescribed period.**

<u>For Sales Transactions Only</u>: Buyer acknowledges the right for 10 days, unless otherwise agreed in the real estate purchase contract, to conduct a risk assessment or inspection for the presence of lead-based paint and/or lead-based paint hazards; OR, (if checked) ☐ Buyer waives the right to conduct a risk assessment or inspection for the presence of lead-based paint and/or lead-based paint hazards.

I (we) have reviewed the information above and certify, to the best of my (our) knowledge, that the information provided is true and correct.

_____   _____
Buyer or Tenant   Date   Buyer or Tenant   Date

4. COOPERATING AGENT'S ACKNOWLEDGMENT

Agent has informed Seller or Landlord, through the Listing Agent if the property is listed, of Seller's or Landlord's obligations under §42 USC 4852d and is aware of Agent's responsibility to ensure compliance.

I have reviewed the information above and certify, to the best of my knowledge, that the information provided is true and correct.

_____   By _____
Agent (Broker obtaining the Offer)   Associate-Licensee or Broker Signature   Date

SURE TRAC
The System for Success™

Published by the
California Association of REALTORS®

Reviewed by _____ Date _____

EQUAL HOUSING
OPPORTUNITY

FLD REVISED 1/03 (PAGE 2 OF 2)

LEAD-BASED PAINT AND LEAD-BASED PAINT HAZARDS DISCLOSURE (FLD-11 PAGE 2 OF 2)

They include housing for the elderly and vacation housing. The seller, landlord, and real estate agent involved in the sale or rental of pre-1978 housing each have certain obligations under the new law.

Seller/Landlord Obligations

Sellers or landlords must:

Sellers or landlords must give buyers/tenants a copy of *Protect Your Family From Lead in Your Home* pamphlet.

- give buyers/tenants *Protect Your Family From Lead in Your Home* pamphlet.

- disclose all known lead-based paint and lead-based paint hazards in the dwelling and provide buyer/tenants with any available reports.

- include standard warning language as an attachment to the contract or lease.

- complete and sign statements verifying completion of requirements.

- retain the signed acknowledgment for three years.

- give buyers a 10-day opportunity to test for lead (for sale transactions only).

Real Estate Agent Responsibilities

Real estate agents must ensure that:

- seller/landlords are aware of their obligations.

- seller/landlords disclose the proper information to buyers and tenants.

- leases and sales contracts include proper disclosure language and signatures.

- sellers give buyers the opportunity to conduct an inspection for 10 days or another mutually agreed-upon time.

Real estate agents must comply with the law if the seller or landlord fails to do so. However, the agent is not responsible if an owner conceals information or fails to disclose information.

Natural Hazard Disclosure Statement

California took an important step to standardize natural hazard disclosure requirements in real property transactions with the passage of the Natural Hazard Disclosure Law in 1998. In addition to the usual Transfer Disclosure

Statement the agent must give the prospective buyer a separate **Natural Hazard Disclosure Statement** (NHD) if the residential property lies within any of the following six statutorily specified areas:

1. a **special flood hazard** (Zone A or Zone V) area designated by the Federal Emergency Management Agency (FEMA).

2. an **area of potential flooding** in the event of a dam failure, designated by the California Office of Emergency Services.

3. a **very high fire hazard severity zone** designated by the California Department of Forestry and Fire Protection (CDF).

4. a **designated wild land fire area** that may contain substantial forest fire risks and hazards, designated by the State Board of Forestry.

5. an **earthquake fault zone** designated by the State Geologist.

6. a **seismic hazard zone** designated by the State Geologist.

All sellers and their real estate brokers must determine and disclose to prospective purchasers if a parcel is in certain officially mapped natural hazard zones (geologic, flood, and fire).

The law prescribes the contents of the Natural Hazard Disclosure Statement including a checklist. The statement warns prospective buyers: "these hazards may limit your ability to develop the real property; to obtain insurance; or to receive assistance after a disaster". It also advises buyers and sellers that they "may wish to obtain professional advice regarding those hazards". The disclosure must be made as soon as practicable before the transfer of title, unless the purchase contract provides for an earlier deadline. It is in the seller's and listing agent's best interest to disclose early because the buyer can annul the purchase contract during a certain period after getting the information. The rescission period is three days if the disclosures are hand-delivered or five days if the disclosures are mailed.

The new law requires six specific disclosures, but does not lessen the basic disclosure obligation a seller or agent has in telling prospective buyers of any other hazards of which they have actual knowledge.

Four of the six disclosures in the NHD statement are already required by law and deal with whether the property is located in an earthquake fault zone, a seismic hazard zone, a flood hazard area or a state-responsibility fire area. The two new disclosures inform the buyer whether the property is located in an area subject to flooding in a dam failure or a very high fire hazard severity zone.

NATURAL HAZARD DISCLOSURE STATEMENT
(C.A.R. Form NHD, Revised 10/04)

This statement applies to the following property: _____

The transferor and his or her agent(s) or a third-party consultant disclose the following information with the knowledge that even though this is not a warranty, prospective transferees may rely on this information in deciding whether and on what terms to purchase the subject property. Transferor hereby authorizes any agent(s) representing any principal(s) in this action to provide a copy of this statement to any person or entity in connection with any actual or anticipated sale of the property.

The following are representations made by the transferor and his or her agent(s) based on their knowledge and maps drawn by the state and federal governments. This information is a disclosure and is not intended to be part of any contract between the transferee and transferor.

THIS REAL PROPERTY LIES WITHIN THE FOLLOWING HAZARDOUS AREA(S):

A SPECIAL FLOOD HAZARD AREA (Any type Zone "A" or "V") designated by the Federal Emergency Management Agency.
Yes _____   No _____   Do not know and information not available from local jurisdiction _____

AN AREA OF POTENTIAL FLOODING shown on a dam failure inundation map pursuant to Section 8589.5 of the Government Code.
Yes _____   No _____   Do not know and information not available from local jurisdiction _____

A VERY HIGH FIRE HAZARD SEVERITY ZONE pursuant to Section 51178 or 51179 of the Government Code. The owner of this property is subject to the maintenance requirements of Section 51182 of the Government Code.
Yes _____   No _____

A WILDLAND AREA THAT MAY CONTAIN SUBSTANTIAL FOREST FIRE RISKS AND HAZARDS pursuant to Section 4125 of the Public Resources Code. The owner of this property is subject to the maintenance requirements of Section 4291 of the Public Resources Code. Additionally, it is not the state's responsibility to provide fire protection services to any building or structure located within the wildlands unless the Department of Forestry and Fire Protection has entered into a cooperative agreement with a local agency for those purposes pursuant to Section 4142 of the Public Resources Code.
Yes _____   No _____

AN EARTHQUAKE FAULT ZONE pursuant to Section 2622 of the Public Resources Code.
Yes _____   No _____

A SEISMIC HAZARD ZONE pursuant to Section 2696 of the Public Resources Code.
Yes (Landslide Zone) _____   Yes (Liquefaction Zone) _____
No _____   Map not yet released by state _____

Buyer's Initials (_____) (_____)
Seller's Initials (_____) (_____)
Reviewed by _____ Date _____

EQUAL HOUSING OPPORTUNITY

NATURAL HAZARD DISCLOSURE STATEMENT (NHD PAGE 1 OF 2)

Agent:	Phone:	Fax:	Prepared using WINForms® software
Broker:			

Property Address: _____ Date: _____

THESE HAZARDS MAY LIMIT YOUR ABILITY TO DEVELOP THE REAL PROPERTY, TO OBTAIN INSURANCE, OR TO RECEIVE ASSISTANCE AFTER A DISASTER.

THE MAPS ON WHICH THESE DISCLOSURES ARE BASED ESTIMATE WHERE NATURAL HAZARDS EXIST. THEY ARE NOT DEFINITIVE INDICATORS OF WHETHER OR NOT A PROPERTY WILL BE AFFECTED BY A NATURAL DISASTER. TRANSFEREE(S) AND TRANSFEROR(S) MAY WISH TO OBTAIN PROFESSIONAL ADVICE REGARDING THOSE HAZARDS AND OTHER HAZARDS THAT MAY AFFECT THE PROPERTY

Signature of Transferor(s) _____ Date _____

Signature of Transferor(s) _____ Date _____

Agent(s) _____ Date _____

Agent(s) _____ Date _____

Check only one of the following:

☐ Transferor(s) and their agent(s) represent that the information herein is true and correct to the best of their knowledge as of the date signed by the transferor(s) and agent(s).

☐ Transferor(s) and their agent(s) acknowledge that they have exercised good faith in the selection of a third-party report provider as required in Civil Code Section 1103.7, and that the representations made in this Natural Hazard Disclosure Statement are based upon information provided by the independent third-party disclosure provider as a substituted disclosure pursuant to Civil Code Section 1103.4. Neither transferor(s) nor their agent(s) (1) has independently verified the information contained in this statement and report or (2) is personally aware of any errors or inaccuracies in the information contained on the statement. This statement was prepared by the provider below:

Third-Party Disclosure Provider(s) _____ Date _____

Transferee represents that he or she has read and understands this document. Pursuant to Civil Code Section 1103.8, the representations made in this Natural Hazard Disclosure Statement do not constitute all of the transferor's or agent's disclosure obligations in this transaction.

Signature of Transferee(s) _____ Date _____

Signature of Transferee(s) _____ Date _____

Published and Distributed by:
REAL ESTATE BUSINESS SERVICES, INC.
a subsidiary of the California Association of REALTORS®
525 South Virgil Avenue, Los Angeles, California 90020

Reviewed by _____ Date _____

NHD REVISED 10/04 (PAGE 2 OF 2)

NATURAL HAZARD DISCLOSURE STATEMENT (NHD PAGE 2 OF 2)

xxx.zfx

Disclosures Included on the Natural Hazard Disclosure Statement

Special Flood Hazard Area (Any type Zone "A" or "V")

Flood hazard boundary maps identify the general flood hazards within a community. They are also used in flood plain management and for flood insurance purposes. These maps, developed by the **Federal Emergency Management Agency (FEMA)** in conjunction with communities participating in the National Flood Insurance Program (NFIP) show areas within a **100-year flood** boundary, termed "special flood zone areas". Also identified are areas between 100 and 500-year levels termed "areas of moderate flood hazards" and the remaining areas above the 500-year level termed "areas of minimal risk".

A seller of property located in a special flood hazard area, or the seller's agent and/or any agent cooperating in the deal, must disclose to the buyer that federal law requires flood insurance as a condition of obtaining financing on most structures located in a special flood hazard area. Since the cost and extent of flood insurance coverage may vary, the buyer should contact an insurance carrier or the intended lender for additional information.

The Local Option Real Estate Transfer Disclosure Statement (LORETDS) also lists disclosures, providing the local jurisdiction has mandated the use of this form.

Areas of Potential Flooding

Designated on an inundation map are areas that may flood as the result of a dam failure. If the property is on a list of properties posted at the County Public Works/Engineering Offices, Assessors Office, Water Agencies, or Planning Agency, the seller or listing broker must disclose this information to a prospective buyer. If the owner has received federal flood disaster assistance, the seller must tell the buyer to buy flood insurance. This is disclosed on the NHD.

Very High Fire Hazard Zone

The seller must disclose if the property is in this zone. Properties in this zone are subject to property maintenance requirements, such as clearing brush and maintaining firebreaks. Generally CDF requires a 30-foot clearance area around dwellings per the Public Resources Code. This disclosure is made on the NHD.

State Fire Responsibility Area

The Department of Forestry and Fire Protection has produced maps identifying rural lands classified as state responsibility areas. In such an area, the state, as opposed to a local or federal agency, has the primary financial responsibility for the prevention and extinguishing of fires. Maps of State Responsibility Areas and any changes, including new maps produced every five years, are to be provided to planning agencies in the affected counties.

Should the seller know his or her real property is located in a State Responsibility Area, or if the property is included on a map given by the department to the county assessor or planning agencies, the seller must disclose the possibility of substantial fire risk in such **wild land areas** and that the land is subject to certain preventative requirements.

With the department's agreement, and by ordinance, a county may assume responsibility for all fires, including those occurring in State Responsibility Areas. If there is such an ordinance, the seller of property located in the area must disclose to the buyer that the state is not obligated to provide fire protection services for any building or structure unless such protection is required by a cooperative agreement with a county, city, or district.

Disclosure of Earthquake Fault Zones

Geologists describe the surface of the earth as always changing. Some of these geological changes are relatively unimportant and do not require a disclosure. Other changes are apparent by casual inspection, i.e. they are of a nature that a potential buyer should be able to judge the impact of the existing geological condition on the intended property's use.

In some cases, disclosure of a geological condition must be made. This is true of potential hazards from earthquakes, flooding, landslides, erosion, and expansive soils. One condition requiring such disclosure is "**fault creep**", caused by stress and/or earthquake shaking.

Geology in the context of the required disclosures refers to the type of soil and how that soil will respond to earthquakes. Soft sediments tend to amplify shaking, whereas bedrock soils tend to lessen the shaking. Generally, the closer in location to the fault, the more intense the shaking will be. However, soil types and conditions may be more important than distance from the epicenter.

The state geologist is in the process of identifying areas of the state susceptible to "fault creep", to be shown on maps prepared by the State Division of Mines and Geology. These maps also identify known historic landslides. The seller or the seller's agent and any agent acting in cooperation with such agent may usually rely on the identification of the special studies zones by the state geologist for disclosure purposes.

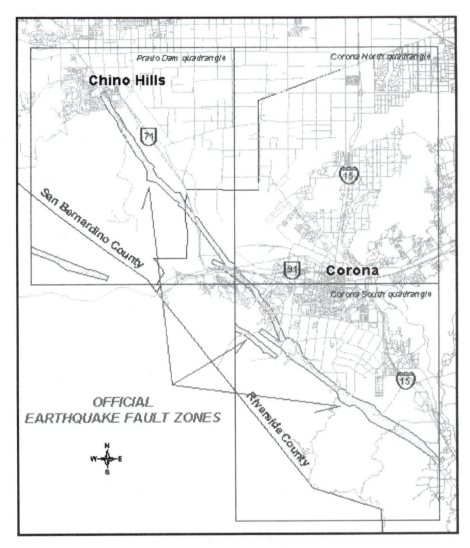

Official Earthquake Fault Zones

In some instances, additional investigation may be required. Construction on real property of any structure for human occupancy may be subject to the findings and recommendations of a geologic report prepared by a geologist or soils engineer registered in or licensed by the state of California.

A seller of real property situated in a special studies zone, or the agent of the seller and any agent acting in cooperation with such agent, must disclose to the buyer that the property is or may be situated in such a zone as designated under the Alquist-Priolo Special Studies Zones Act.

This disclosure must be made on either the Natural Hazard Disclosure Statement (NHDS) or the Local Option Real Estate Transfer Disclosure Statement (LORETDS).

Earthquake Hazards Booklet

The Seismic Safety Commission developed a **Homeowner's Guide to Earthquake Safety** for distribution to real estate licensees and the general public. The guide includes information on geologic and seismic hazards for all areas, explanations of related structural and nonstructural hazards, and recommendations for mitigating the hazards of an earthquake. The guide states that safety or damage prevention cannot be guaranteed with respect to a major earthquake and that only precautions such as retrofitting can be undertaken to reduce the risk of various types of damage.

If the buyer of real property receives a copy of the *Homeowner's Guide to Earthquake Safety,* neither the seller nor the agent is required to provide additional information regarding geologic and seismic hazards. Sellers and real estate agents must disclose that the property is in a special studies zone, however, and that there are known hazards affecting the real property being transferred.

It is required that the *Homeowner's Guide to Earthquake Safety* booklet be delivered in the following transactions:

- transfer of any real property with a residential dwelling built prior to January 1, 1960 and consisting of one-to-four units any of which are of conventional light-frame construction.

- transfer of any masonry building with wood-frame floors or roofs built before January 1, 1975.

Certain exemptions apply to the obligation to deliver the booklet when transferring either a dwelling of one-to-four units or a reinforced masonry building. These exemptions are essentially the same as those that apply to delivery of the Real Estate Transfer Disclosure Statement described earlier in this section.

The buyer and/or agent may be responsible for making further inquiries of appropriate governmental agencies. The obligation of the buyer and/or agent to make further inquiry does not eliminate the duty of the seller's agent to make a diligent inquiry to identify the location of the real property in relationship to a defined special studies zone—and to determine whether the property is subject to any local ordinance regarding geological and soils conditions. Full and complete disclosure is required of all material facts regarding a special studies zone, local ordinances or known structural deficiencies affecting the property.

The Seismic Safety Commission also has published the booklet *Commercial Property Owner's Guide to Earthquake Safety*. Each buyer receives a copy of DRE/OEHHA or the Seismic Safety Commission booklet from the seller or seller's agent.

Megan's Law (Data Base Disclosure)

Every lease and sales contract is required to include a statutorily defined notice regarding the existence of public access to data base information regarding sex offenders in the neighborhood.

Furnishing Controlling Documents

The owner (other than a subdivider) of a separate legal share in a common interest development (community apartment project, condominium project, planned development, or stock cooperative) must provide a prospective buyer with the following:

- a copy of the governing documents of the development.

- should there be an age restriction not consistent with the law, a statement that the age restriction is only enforceable to the extent permitted by law; and applicable provisions of the law.

- a copy of the homeowners association's most recent financial statement.

- a written statement from the association specifying the amount of current regular and special assessments as well as any unpaid assessment, late charges, interest and costs of collection which are or may become a lien against the property.

- any information on any approved change in the assessments or fees not yet due and payable as of the disclosure date.

- a preliminary list of construction defects if the association has commenced or plans to commence an action for damages against the developer.

- after resolution, by settlement agreement or otherwise, of a dispute between the association and developer regarding construction defects, a general description of the defects that will be corrected; the association's estimate of when the corrections will be completed; the status of any claims for other defects.

CALIFORNIA
ASSOCIATION
OF REALTORS®

HOMEOWNER ASSOCIATION INFORMATION REQUEST
FOR COMMON INTEREST DEVELOPMENTS
(C.A.R. Form HOA, Revised 4/05)

Property Address: _____

Owner of Property: _____ ("Seller")

Mailing Address: _____

To: Homeowner Association_____ ("HOA")

Pursuant to California Civil Code §1368 and the request of Seller, within 10 calendar days from the date of this request, please provide Seller the items or information listed on page 2 at the mailing address indicated above, or (if checked) to ☐ _____

_____

_____ .

On page 2, please indicate whether the item is attached or not available. In the Explanation column provide the information requested, indicate if the item is not applicable or otherwise explain.

Requested by Seller:

Seller or Seller's Agent _____ Date _____

The documents and information provided by the HOA referenced above were provided by:

_____ Its _____
(print name)   (title)

By signing below, the undersigned acknowledges that each has read, understands and has received a copy of this Homeowner Association Information Request.

Seller _____ Date _____

Seller _____ Date _____

| Reviewed by _____ Date _____ | EQUAL HOUSING OPPORTUNITY |

HOMEOWNER ASSOCIATION INFORMATION REQUEST (HOA PAGE 1 OF 2)

| Agent: | Phone: | Fax: | Prepared using WINForms® software |
| Broker: | | | |

Property Address: _____ Date: _____

HOMEOWNER ASSOCIATION INFORMATION REQUEST
FOR COMMON INTEREST DEVELOPMENTS

Item	HOA Response Attached	Not Available	Explanation *(or if checked not applicable)*
Statement that HOA is or is not incorporated			☐ N/A
CC&Rs			☐ N/A
Bylaws			☐ N/A
Rules and Regulations			☐ N/A
Age restrictions, if any			☐ N/A
Pro Forma Operating Budget, or summary including reserve study			☐ N/A
Assessment and Reserve Funding Disclosure Summary			☐ N/A
Financial Statement Review			☐ N/A
Assessment Enforcement Policy			☐ N/A
Insurance Summary			☐ N/A
Regular Assessment			☐ N/A
Special Assessment			☐ N/A
Emergency Assessment			☐ N/A
Other unpaid obligations of Seller			☐ N/A
Approved changes to assessments			☐ N/A
Preliminary list of defects			☐ N/A
Settlement Notice Regarding Common Area Defects			☐ N/A
Pending or anticipated claims or litigation by or against HOA			☐ N/A
Most recent 12 Months of HOA Minutes			☐ N/A
Number of designated parking spaces			☐ N/A
Location of parking spaces			☐ N/A
Number of designated storage spaces			☐ N/A
Location of storage spaces			☐ N/A
Any other document required by law			☐ N/A
Name of contact information of other HOAs governing property			☐ N/A
Other			☐ N/A

HOA _____ Date _____

By _____ Title _____

Seller _____ Date _____
Seller _____ Date _____

I acknowledge receipt of a copy of each item checked above. This document may be executed in counterparts.

Buyer _____ Date _____
Buyer _____ Date _____

Published and Distributed by:
REAL ESTATE BUSINESS SERVICES, INC.
a subsidiary of the California Association of REALTORS®
525 South Virgil Avenue, Los Angeles, California 90020

Reviewed by _____ Date _____

SURE TRAC
The System for Success™

EQUAL HOUSING OPPORTUNITY

HOA REVISED 4/05 (PAGE 2 OF 2)

HOMEOWNER ASSOCIATION INFORMATION REQUEST (HOA PAGE 2 OF 2)

xxx.zfx

Death and/or AIDS

Real estate agents must be very careful when making disclosures about stigmatized properties. A **stigmatized property**, as defined by the National Association of Realtors, is "a property that has been psychologically impacted by an event which occurred, or was suspected to have occurred, on the property, such event being one that has no physical impact of any kind". Although some might call a haunted house "stigmatized" the most common properties associated with stigmatized property are those in which there have been murders, suicides, or criminal activity.

Neither the transferor (seller/lessor) nor the agent has to disclose the fact of any death that occurred on the property to the transferee if the death was more than three years prior to the current date. However, if the transferee (buyer/lessee) asks a direct question about a death on the property, the seller or agent must answer their question honestly.

Neither the transferor (seller/lessor) nor the agent has to ever voluntarily disclose whether or not a person was afflicted with or died from AIDS. However, if the transferee (buyer/lessee) asks a direct question about a death on the property, the seller or agent must answer their question honestly.

Seller Instruction to Exclude Listing from MLS

A broker should discuss the benefits of submitting a listing to the multiple listing service (MLS) with the seller. When a seller does not want the listing submitted to the MLS, the broker should use this form to document the seller's request.

Market Conditions Advisory

Real estate market conditions are fluid; therefore, no one can guarantee that prices will continue to move in a particular direction. This form is used to document that a broker discussed market conditions with a buyer. In addition it also advises about the risks of making non-contingent offers or removing contingencies.

Disclosures in Financing

One of the purposes of financing disclosures is to help consumers become better shoppers for loan and settlement services. The required disclosures are given to borrowers at various times during the transaction. Some disclosures spell out the costs associated with the loan or the settlement, outline lender

**CALIFORNIA
ASSOCIATION
OF REALTORS®**

SUPPLEMENTAL STATUTORY
AND CONTRACTUAL DISCLOSURES
(C.A.R. Form SSD, Revised 10/04)

1. Seller makes the following disclosures with regard to the real property or manufactured home described as
_____ , Assessor's Parcel No. _____
situated in _____ , County of _____ , California, ("Property").

2. **THE FOLLOWING ARE REPRESENTATIONS MADE BY THE SELLER AND ARE NOT THE REPRESENTATIONS OF THE AGENT(S), IF ANY. THIS DISCLOSURE STATEMENT IS NOT A WARRANTY OF ANY KIND BY THE SELLER OR ANY AGENT(S) AND IS NOT A SUBSTITUTE FOR ANY INSPECTIONS OR WARRANTIES THE PRINCIPAL(S) MAY WISH TO OBTAIN. A REAL ESTATE BROKER IS QUALIFIED TO ADVISE ON REAL ESTATE TRANSACTIONS. IF SELLER OR BUYER DESIRE LEGAL ADVICE, CONSULT AN ATTORNEY.**

3. **Are you (Seller) aware of any of the following? (Explain any "yes" answers below.)**
   A. Within the last 3 years, the death of an occupant of the Property upon the Property. . . . . ☐ Yes ☐ No
   B. The release of an illegal controlled substance on or beneath the Property . . . . ☐ Yes ☐ No
   C. Whether the Property is located in or adjacent to an "industrial use" zone . . . . ☐ Yes ☐ No
       (In general, a zone or district allowing manufacturing, commercial or airport uses.)
   D. Whether the Property is affected by a nuisance created by an "industrial use" zone . . . . ☐ Yes ☐ No
   E. Whether the Property is located within 1 mile of a former federal or state ordnance location . . ☐ Yes ☐ No
       (In general, an area once used for military training purposes that may contain potentially explosive munitions.)
   F. Whether the Property is a condominium or located in a planned unit development or other
       common interest subdivision . . . . ☐ Yes ☐ No
   G. Insurance claims affecting the Property within the past 5 years . . . . ☐ Yes ☐ No
   H. Matters affecting title of the Property . . . . ☐ Yes ☐ No
   I. Material facts or defects affecting the Property not otherwise disclosed to Buyer . . . . ☐ Yes ☐ No
   Explanation, or☐ (if checked) see attached; _____
   _____
   _____
   _____
   _____
   _____

4. Seller represents that the information herein is true and correct to the best of Seller's knowledge as of the date signed by Seller. Seller hereby authorizes any agent(s) representing any principal(s) in this transaction to provide a Copy of this statement to any person or entity in connection with any actual or anticipated sale of the Property.
   Seller _____ Date _____
   Seller _____ Date _____

5. **By signing below, Buyer acknowledges Buyer has received, read, and understands this Supplemental Statutory and Contractual Disclosures form.**
   Buyer _____ Date _____
   Buyer _____ Date _____
   Agent (Broker Representing Seller) _____
   By _____ Date _____
   (Associate-Licensee or Broker Signature)
   Agent (Broker Obtaining the Offer) _____
   By _____ Date _____
   (Associate-Licensee or Broker Signature)

Published and Distributed by:
REAL ESTATE BUSINESS SERVICES, INC.
a subsidiary of the California Association of REALTORS®
525 South Virgil Avenue, Los Angeles, California 90020

Reviewed by _____ Date _____

SURE TRAC
The System for Success™

SSD REVISED 10/04 (PAGE 1 OF 1)

SUPPLEMENTAL STATUTORY AND CONTRACTUAL DISCLOSURES (SSD PAGE 1 OF 1)

Agent:	Phone:	Fax:	Prepared using WINForms® software
Broker:			

servicing and escrow account practices and describe business relationships between settlement service providers.

Disclosures discussed in Chapter 9 include: Seller Financing Disclosure Statement, Mortgage Loan Disclosure Statement, Adjustable-Rate Loan Disclosure, Lender Compensation Disclosure, Real Estate Settlement Procedures Act, Truth-in-Lending Act (Reg Z), and the Equal Credit Opportunity Act (ECOA).

Subdivision Disclosures

Subdividers and developers are subject to laws designed to protect buyers when purchasing or leasing lots or parcels in new subdivisions.

Public Report of the Subdivided Lands Law

The **Subdivided Lands Law** is designed to protect buyers from fraud, misrepresentation or deceit in the marketing of subdivided lots, parcels, units and **undivided interests** in new subdivisions. This even applies to lands outside the state, if they are being marketed in California. Before any subdivision can be offered for sale in California, the Real Estate Commissioner must determine that the offering meets certain standards and issue a public report. The **public report** is a document disclosing all important facts about the property, its marketing and the financing of the subdivision. These disclosures may alert a potential buyer to any negative aspects in the subdivision (e.g., natural or environmental hazards, unusual costs, restrictions, easements, or financing arrangements). The public report must show that the subdivider (owner) can complete and maintain all improvements and that the lots or parcels can be used for the purpose for which they are being sold.

Use of Public Report

Before a subdivider can sell each lot in the project, he or she must give a copy of the commissioner's final report to the prospective buyer for approval. The buyer signs a receipt for the report on a form approved by the Commissioner stating it has been read. The seller (subdivider) must keep a copy of the statement for three years. The subdivider must post a notice in the sales office that says that a copy of the public report must be given to any member of the public who asks for it. The public report is valid for five years, with any material changes in the development reported to the commissioner, who then can issue an amendment to the original report.

Violations - Penalties

Anyone who is found guilty of violating the Subdivided Lands Law is punishable by a maximum fine of $10,000; imprisonment for up to one year in the county jail or state prison; or by both fine and imprisonment. The district attorney of each county is responsible for prosecuting violators. In addition to possible fine and imprisonment, the Real Estate Commissioner may impose disciplinary actions for violations of the Subdivided Lands Law.

Preliminary Public Report

It can take many months for a developer to get project approval, once all the proper paperwork is submitted to the commissioner. During that time, the developer may want to begin marketing the project while waiting for the final report. By submitting a minimum application filing package, the developer can get a **preliminary public report**, which allows taking reservations for the project, but not accepting any non-refundable money or entering into any binding contracts until receiving the final report from the commissioner. Preliminary public reports have a one-year term and may be renewed.

Interstate Land Sales Full Disclosure Act

This federal law regulates land sales when there are two or more states involved. Subdividers must conform to this law if they have 50 or more lots in one state and want to sell them in another state. A public report from the U.S. Department of Housing and Urban Development (HUD) must be given to each prospective buyer as a protection from less- than-truthful advertising in far-away places.

Other Disclosures

Staying informed is probably the most important task left to the real estate agent. Those who make continuing efforts to learn and stay current on the real estate industry will be the ones to successfully compete in the future. Two excellent sources of current information are the California Department of Real Estate (www.dre.ca.gov) and for members, the California Association of REALTORS® (www.car.org).

Pest Control Inspection and Certification Reports

The law does not require that a structural pest control inspection be performed on real property prior to transfer. Should an inspection report and certification be required as a condition of transfer or obtaining financing, however, it must be done as soon as possible. Before transfer of title or before executing a real property sales contract, the selling agent must deliver to the buyer a copy of the report. There must also be written certification attesting to the presence or absence of wood-destroying termites in the visible and accessible areas of the property. Such an inspection report and written certification must be prepared and issued by a registered structural pest control company.

Upon request from the party ordering such a report, the company issuing the same must divide it into two categories: one to identify the portions of the property where existing damage, infection, or infestation are noted; and the other to point out areas that may have impending damage, infection, or infestation. Lenders usually require that any infestation or damage discovered in part one of the report be corrected prior to close of escrow. The cost of correction is usually paid for by the seller. Since part two of the inspection report does not show actual infestation—just a potential, the seller is not obligated to correct it.

Generally, there is more than one real estate agent in the transaction; the agent who obtained the offer is responsible for delivering the report unless the seller has given written directions regarding delivery to another agent involved in the transaction. Delivery of the required documents may be in person or by mail to the buyer. The real estate agent responsible for delivery must retain for three years a complete record of the actions taken to effect delivery. Anyone can get a copy of the pest control report by requesting it from the Structural Pest Control Board and paying a fee.

Smoke Detector Statement of Compliance

Whenever a sale or exchange of a single-family dwelling occurs, the seller must provide the buyer with a written statement representing that the property is in compliance with California law regarding smoke detectors. The state building code mandates that all existing dwelling units must have a smoke detector installed in a central location outside each sleeping area. In a two story home with bedrooms on both floors, at least two smoke detectors would be required.

New construction, or any additions, alterations or repairs exceeding $1,000 and for which a permit is required, must include a smoke detector installed in each bedroom and also at a point centrally located in a corridor or area outside the bedroom(s). This standard applies for the addition of one or more bedrooms, no matter what the cost. In new home construction, the smoke detector must be hard-wired, with a battery backup. In existing dwellings, the detector may be only battery operated.

CALIFORNIA
ASSOCIATION
OF REALTORS®

SMOKE DETECTOR STATEMENT OF COMPLIANCE
As required by California State Health and Safety Code §13113.8(b)
(C.A.R. Form SDS, Revised 4/05)

Property Address: _____

1. **STATE LAW:** California Law requires that every single-family dwelling and factory built housing unit sold on or after January 1, 1986, must have an operable smoke detector, approved and listed by the State Fire Marshal, installed in accordance with the State Fire Marshal's regulations. (Health and Safety Code §13113.8).

2. **LOCAL REQUIREMENTS:** Some local ordinances impose more stringent smoke detector requirements than does California Law. Therefore, it is important to check with local city or county building and safety departments regarding the applicable smoke detector requirements for your property.

3. **TRANSFEROR'S WRITTEN STATEMENT:** California Health and Safety Code §13113.8(b) requires every transferor of any real property containing a single-family dwelling, whether the transfer is made by sale, exchange, or real property sales contract (installment sales contract), to deliver to the transferee a written statement indicating that the transferor is in compliance with California State Law concerning smoke detectors.

4. **EXCEPTIONS: Exceptions to the State Law are generally the same as the exceptions to the Transfer Disclosure Statement Laws.**

5. **CERTIFICATION:** Seller represents that the Property, as of the Close Of Escrow, will be in compliance with Health and Safety Code §13113.8 by having operable smoke detector(s) approved and listed by the State Fire Marshal installed in accordance with the State Fire Marshal's regulations and in accordance with applicable local ordinance(s).

Seller _____ Date _____
         (Signature)   (Print Name)

Seller _____ Date _____
         (Signature)   (Print Name)

The undersigned hereby acknowledges receipt of a copy of this document.

Buyer _____ Date _____
         (Signature)   (Print Name)

Buyer _____ Date _____
         (Signature)   (Print Name)

SURE TRAC
The System for Success®

Published and Distributed by:
REAL ESTATE BUSINESS SERVICES, INC.
a subsidiary of the CALIFORNIA ASSOCIATION OF REALTORS®
525 South Virgil Avenue, Los Angeles, California 90020

Reviewed by _____ Date _____

EQUAL HOUSING
OPPORTUNITY

SDS REVISED 4/05 (PAGE 1 OF 1)

SMOKE DETECTOR STATEMENT OF COMPLIANCE (SDS PAGE 1 OF 1)

Phone: _____ Fax: _____   x.zfx

Produced with ZipForm™ by RE FormsNet, LLC 18025 Fifteen Mile Road, Clinton Township, Michigan 48035, (800) 383-9805 www.zipform.com

CALIFORNIA
ASSOCIATION
OF REALTORS®

WATER HEATER STATEMENT OF COMPLIANCE
Water Heater Bracing, Anchoring or Strapping
As required by California Health and Safety Code §19211
(Only required when there is a water heater on or in the property)
(C.A.R. Form WHS, Revised 4/05)

Property Address: _____

1. **STATE LAW:** California Law requires that all new and replacement water heaters and existing residential water heaters be braced, anchored or strapped to resist falling or horizontal displacement due to earthquake motion. "Water heater" means any standard water heater with a capacity of no more than 120 gallons for which a pre-engineered strapping kit is readily available. (Health and Safety Code §19211).

2. **LOCAL REQUIREMENTS:** Some local ordinances impose more stringent water heater bracing, anchoring or strapping requirements than does California Law. Therefore, it is important to check with local city or county building and safety departments regarding the applicable water heater bracing, anchoring or strapping requirements for your property.

3. **TRANSFEROR'S WRITTEN STATEMENT:** California Health and Safety Code §19211 requires the seller of any real property containing a water heater to certify, in writing, that the seller is in compliance with California State Law.

4. **EXCEPTIONS: There are no exceptions to the State Law.**

5. **CERTIFICATION:** Seller represents that the Property, as of the Close Of Escrow, will be in compliance with Health and Safety Code §19211 by having the water heater(s) braced, anchored or strapped in place, in accordance with those requirements.

Seller _____ Date _____
      (Signature)   (Print Name)

Seller _____ Date _____
      (Signature)   (Print Name)

The undersigned hereby acknowledges receipt of a copy of this document.

Buyer _____ Date _____
      (Signature)   (Print Name)

Buyer _____ Date _____
      (Signature)   (Print Name)

SURE TRAC
The System for Success®

Published and Distributed by:
REAL ESTATE BUSINESS SERVICES, INC.
a subsidiary of the CALIFORNIA ASSOCIATION OF REALTORS®
525 South Virgil Avenue, Los Angeles, California 90020

Reviewed by _____ Date _____

EQUAL HOUSING
OPPORTUNITY

WHS REVISED 4/05 (PAGE 1 OF 1)

WATER HEATER STATEMENT OF COMPLIANCE (WHS PAGE 1 OF 1)

Phone: Fax: x.zfx
Produced with ZipForm™ by RE FormsNet, LLC 18025 Fifteen Mile Road, Clinton Township, Michigan 48035, (800) 383-9805 www.zipform.com

Certification Regarding Water Heater's Security Against Earthquake

Water heaters are the cause of many common problems in an earthquake. If they are not secured, they can fall and break gas or electrical lines and cause a fire as well as cause extensive water damage.

The seller of any residential property must certify, in writing, to the buyer that all water heaters have been braced, anchored or strapped in accordance with local requirements to resist falling in an earthquake. The certification can be included in a transaction document, including, but not limited to, the *Homeowner's Guide to Earthquake Safety,* the real estate purchase contract or receipt for deposit, or the Real Estate Transfer Disclosure Statement.

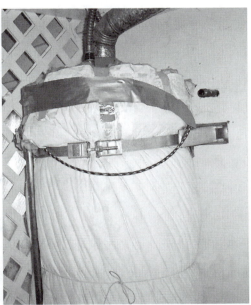

The seller of any residential property must certify, to the buyer, in writing, that all water heaters have been braced, anchored, or strapped in accordance with local requirements to resist falling in an earthquake. Water heaters may be wrapped in an insulation "blanket".

Energy Conservation Retrofit and Thermal Insulation Disclosures

State law prescribes minimum energy conservation standards for all new construction. Local governments also have ordinances that impose additional energy conservation measures on new and/or existing homes. Some local ordinances impose energy retrofitting as a condition of the sale of an existing home. The seller and/or agent should disclose to a prospective buyer the requirements of the various ordinances, as well as who is responsible for compliance. Federal law requires that a "new home" seller (including a subdivider) disclose in every sales contract the type, thickness, and **R-value** (resistance to heat loss) of the insulation which has been or will be installed.

Foreign Investment in Real Property Tax Act (FIRPTA)

Both federal and state tax laws are affected by the Foreign Investment in Real Property Tax Act (FIRPTA). In both cases the buyer is responsible for making sure either the proper disclosures have been made and/or the proper funds have been set aside. Generally, the broker and escrow agent make sure this is done. All documents must be kept by the broker and the buyer for five years.

Federal FIRPTA Disclosure

Federal law requires that a buyer of real property must withhold and send to the Internal Revenue Service (IRS) 10% of the gross sales price if the seller of the real property is a foreign person.

Exceptions

The following are exceptions from the FIRPTA withholding requirement:

- The buyer must sign a Buyer's Affidavit of Residency, stating whether he or she is a resident or citizen, that the sales price of the property does not exceed $300,000, and that the property will be used as a residence.

- The seller, under penalty of perjury, must sign a Seller's Affidavit of Non-foreign Status, stating that he or she is not a foreigner.

- The seller gives the buyer a qualifying statement obtained through the IRS saying arrangements have been made for the collection of or exemption from the tax.

Due to the number of exceptions and other requirements relating to this law, it is recommended that the IRS be consulted. Sellers and buyers and the real estate agents involved who desire further advice should consult an attorney, CPA, or other qualified tax advisor.

California FIRPTA Disclosure

California law requires that if property is sold by a non-citizen of the United States or a resident of another state, the buyer must withhold 3 $1/3$ % of the

CALIFORNIA ASSOCIATION OF REALTORS®

SELLER'S AFFIDAVIT OF NONFOREIGN STATUS AND/OR CALIFORNIA WITHHOLDING EXEMPTION
FOREIGN INVESTMENT IN REAL PROPERTY TAX ACT (FIRPTA) AND CALIFORNIA WITHHOLDING LAW
(Use a separate form for each Transferor)
(C.A.R. Form AS, Revised 10/05)

Internal Revenue Code ("IRC") Section 1445 provides that a transferee of a U.S. real property interest must withhold tax if the transferor is a "foreign person." California Revenue and Taxation Code Section 18662 provides that a transferee of a California real property interest must withhold tax unless an exemption applies.

I understand that this affidavit may be disclosed to the Internal Revenue Service and to the California Franchise Tax Board by the transferee, and that any false statement I have made herein may result in a fine, imprisonment or both.

1. **PROPERTY ADDRESS** (property being transferred): _____ ("Property")
2. **TRANSFEROR'S INFORMATION:**
   Full Name _____ ("Transferor")
   Telephone Number _____
   Address _____
   (Use HOME address for individual transferors. Use OFFICE address for "Entity" i.e.: corporations, partnerships, limited liability companies, trusts and estates.)
   Social Security No., Federal Employer Identification No. or California Corporation No. _____
   Note: In order to avoid withholding by providing this affidavit, IRC Section 1445 (b) (2) requires a Seller to provide the Buyer with the Seller's taxpayer identification number ("TIN").
3. **AUTHORITY TO SIGN:** If this document is signed on behalf of an Entity Transferor, THE UNDERSIGNED INDIVIDUAL DECLARES THAT HE/SHE HAS AUTHORITY TO SIGN THIS DOCUMENT ON BEHALF OF THE TRANSFEROR.
4. **FEDERAL LAW:** I, the undersigned, declare under penalty of perjury that, for the reason checked below, if any, I am exempt (or if signed on behalf of an Entity Transferor, the Entity is exempt) from the federal withholding law (FIRPTA):
   ☐ (For individual Transferors) I am not a nonresident alien for purposes of U.S. income taxation.
   ☐ (For corporation, partnership, limited liability company, trust, and estate Transferors) The Transferor is not a foreign corporation, foreign partnership, foreign limited liability company, foreign trust or foreign estate, as those terms are defined in the Internal Revenue Code and Income Tax Regulations.
5. **CALIFORNIA LAW:** I, the undersigned, declare under penalty of perjury that, for the reason checked below, if any, I am exempt (or if signed on behalf of an Entity Transferor, the Entity is exempt) from the California withholding law.
   Certifications which fully exempt the sale from withholding:
   ☐ The total sales price for the Property is $100,000 or less.
   ☐ The Property qualifies as my principal residence (or the decedent's, if being sold by the decedent's estate) within the meaning of IRC Section 121 (owned and occupied as such for two of the last five years).
   ☐ The Property was last used as my principal residence (or the decedent's, if being sold by the decedent's estate) within the meaning of IRC Section 121 without regard to the two-year time period.
   ☐ The transaction will result in a loss or zero gain for California income tax purposes. (Complete FTB Form 593-L.)
   ☐ The Property has been compulsorily or involuntarily converted (within the meaning of IRC Section 1033) and Transferor intends to acquire property similar or related in service or use to be eligible for non-recognition of gain for California income tax purposes under IRC Section 1033.
   ☐ Transferor is a corporation (or an LLC classified as a corporation) that is either qualified through the California Secretary of State or has a permanent place of business in California.
   ☐ Transferor is a partnership (or an LLC that is not a disregarded single member LLC, classified as a partnership) and recorded title to the Property is in the name of the partnership or LLC. If so, the partnership or LLC must withhold from nonresident partners or members as required.
   ☐ Transferor is exempt from tax under California or federal law.
   ☐ Transferor is an insurance company, qualified pension/profit sharing plan, IRA or charitable remainder trust.
   Certifications which may partially or fully exempt the sale from withholding:
   ☐ The Property is being, or will be, exchanged for property of like kind within the meaning of IRC Section 1031.
   ☐ The Property is subject to an installment sale, that Transferor will report as such, and Buyer has agreed to withhold on each principal payment instead of withholding the full amount at the time of transfer.

By _____ Date _____
(Transferor's Signature) (Indicate if you are signing as the grantor of a revocable/grantor trust.)

_____ _____
Typed or printed name   Title (If signed on behalf of Entity Transferor)

Buyer's unauthorized use or disclosure of Seller's TIN could result in civil or criminal liability.

Buyer _____ Date _____
(Buyer acknowledges receipt of a Copy of this Seller's Affidavit)

Buyer _____ Date _____
(Buyer acknowledges receipt of a Copy of this Seller's Affidavit)

SURE TRAC
The System for Success™

Published and Distributed by:
REAL ESTATE BUSINESS SERVICES, INC.
a subsidiary of the California Association of REALTORS®
525 South Virgil Avenue, Los Angeles, California 90020

Reviewed by _____ Date _____   EQUAL HOUSING OPPORTUNITY

AS REVISED 10/05 (PAGE 1 OF 1)

SELLER'S AFFIDAVIT OF NONFOREIGN STATUS AND/OR CALIFORNIA WITHOLDING EXEMPTION (AS PAGE 1 OF 1)

Agent:	Phone:	Fax:	Prepared using WINForms® software
Broker:			

total sales price as state income tax and deliver the sum withheld to the State Franchise Tax Board. The escrow holder, in applicable transactions, is required by law to notify the buyer of this responsibility.

A buyer's failure to withhold and deliver the required sum may result in penalties. Should the escrow holder fail to notify the buyer, penalties might be levied against the escrow holder.

The following transactions are subject to the law:

- seller shows an out-of-state address, or sale proceeds are to be disbursed to the seller's **financial intermediary**.

- sales price exceeds $100,000.

- seller does not certify that he or she is a California resident, or that the property being conveyed is his or her personal residence.

Remember, the buyer and the agent are responsible for making sure this law is observed. The paperwork is usually completed through escrow.

*For further information, contact the Franchise Tax Board. Their website is www.ftb.ca.gov.

The following transactions are exempt from the law:

- sales price is $100,000 or less.

- home is the seller's principal residence.

- seller signs the Seller's Affidavit of Nonforeign Status and the Buyer's Affidavit of Residency for California.

Home Inspection Notice

A borrower, who wants an FHA loan for any residential property of one-to-four units, must receive and sign the notice called "The Importance of a Home Inspection."

Notice Regarding the Advisability of Title Insurance

In an escrow for a sale (or exchange) of real property where no title insurance is to be issued, the buyer (or both parties to an exchange) must receive and sign the following notice as a separate document in the escrow:

Important: "In a purchase or exchange of real property, it may be advisable to obtain title insurance in connection with the close of escrow where there may be prior recorded liens and encumbrances which affect your interest in the property being acquired. A new policy of title insurance should be obtained in order to ensure your interest in the property that you are acquiring".

While the law does not expressly assign the duty, it is reasonable to assume that the escrow holder is obligated to deliver the notice. A real estate agent conducting an escrow also would be responsible for delivering the notice.

Disclosure of Sales Price Information

A broker must inform both buyer and seller, in writing, the sale price on a property within one month of close of escrow. The Escrow Closing Statement meets this requirement.

Commissions

A notice in 10-point type must be given to the person paying the Real Estate Commission that commissions are negotiable.

A broker can share his or her commission with an unlicensed buyer or seller if the broker discloses this to all parties.

Summary

One of the most important tasks that a real estate agent will perform is the duty of full disclosure. Full disclosure includes property defects, environmental hazards, ordinances, and special taxes. Real estate agents are legally required to explain disclosures to their clients and customers. If the real estate agent does not comply with California disclosure law, they become vulnerable to court action.

The **real estate agent** is responsible for documenting on the **Real Estate Transfer Disclosure Statement** (TDS) all visual and known defects found on the property. The buyer receives a copy of the TDS before the offer to purchase the property. If the buyer receives a copy of the TDS after the offer to purchase the property, the buyer has the option of terminating the contract within three days after receiving the statement.

The list of real estate disclosures is long and detailed. Included in the disclosure list are **Mello-Roos**, Megan's Law, association financial statements, pest control, smoke detectors, and water heater stabilization. Additional disclosure information includes real estate commissions, real estate taxes, and land sales.

The real estate agent also provides the buyer with written material to help educate and inform the consumer. Examples of written material are the *Natural Hazard Disclosure Statement*, *Protect Your Family From Lead in Your Home*, and *Homeowner's Guide to Earthquake Safety*. Once the buyer receives the printed material, the real estate agent is not obligated to provide additional information.

Local residential properties in cities and counties in California typically have ordinances on zoning, building codes, health, and safety codes. These ordinances have an effect on a potential buyer's use and enjoyment of residential property. The **seller** or real estate agent may need to complete an optional form for local disclosures (the Local Option Real Estate Transfer Disclosure Statement). The buyer also receives a copy of this form from the seller or real estate agent.

A real estate agent needs to remain current on all California disclosures or risk court action.

Chapter 7 Review Exercises

Matching Exercise

Instructions: Look up the meaning of the terms in the Glossary, then write the letter of the matching term on the blank line before its definition. Answers are in Appendix B.

Terms

a. 100-year flood
b. as is
c. asbestos
d. caveat emptor
e. *Easton v. Strassburger*
f. fault creep
g. FIRPTA
h. formaldehyde
i. hazardous household waste
j. hazardous waste

k. lead
l. Mello-Roos District
m. mold
n. public report
o. radon
p. red flag
q. stigmatized property
r. Subdivision Land Law
s. target housing
t. Transfer Disclosure Statement (TDS)

Definitions

1. _____ Term stating the seller will not be responsible for the cost of repairing any defect.

2. _____ Materials—chemicals, explosives, radioactive, biological—whose disposal is regulated by the EPA.

3. _____ Housing exempt from the lead based paint disclosure.

4. _____ Something that alerts a reasonably observant person of a potential problem.

5. _____ Boundary indicating areas of special flood zone areas.

6. _____ A fungus that reproduces by means of spores.

7. _____ State law designed to protect buyers when buying property in new subdivisions.

8. _____ A colorless, odorless, gas that is a carcinogen and can be detected by a spectrometer.

9. _____ A detailed statement telling what the seller knows about the condition of the property.

10. _____ Consumer products such as paints, cleaners, stains, varnishes, car batteries, motor oil, and pesticides that contain hazardous components.

11. _____ Special tax is imposed on real property owners within a Community Facilities District.

12. _____ A mineral fiber used in construction materials which has been found to cause lung and stomach cancer.

13. _____ Movement along an earthquake fault caused by stress and/or earthquake shaking.

14. _____ A chemical organic compound found in building materials which may be a carcinogen.

15. _____ Tax withholding requirement if the seller of the real property is a foreign person.

▌Multiple Choice Questions

Instructions: Circle your response and go to Appendix B to read the complete explanation for each question.

1. The phrase "as is" in real estate refers to _____ conditions.
   a. habitable
   b. observable
   c. concealed
   d. any and all

2. A private seller advertises a single-family home for sale "as is". Since the seller is not using the services of a real estate broker, the seller:
   a. has met the legal requirement of caveat emptor by putting the term "as is" in the newspaper advertisement.
   b. is not obliged to disclose any defects in the property because the property is being sold "as is".
   c. must give a Real Estate Transfer Disclosure Statement to prospective buyers.
   d. is not obliged to give a Real Estate Transfer Disclosure Statement to prospective buyers.

3. Broker Dana had a listing on a residential property and showed it to prospective Buyer Brown. Brown agreed to accept the property in an "as is" condition and submitted an offer which was accepted by the seller. Although Dana knew there was a major plumbing problem that was not apparent to an ordinary prudent person, Dana did not tell Brown. After escrow closed, Brown discovered the plumbing problem, and sued the seller for damages on grounds of fraud. In this instance, the lawsuit would probably:

    a. be unsuccessful because the "as is" provision in the deposit receipt shows there is a mutual understanding of possible defects.

    b. be unsuccessful because the deposit receipt prepared by the buyer specifically states that the buyer agreed to accept the property in an "as is" condition.

    c. be successful because the duty to disclose a material fact cannot be avoided by using an "as is" clause.

    d. be unsuccessful because an "as is" provision refers only to obvious structural defects.

4. Chris sells a house to Jordan using the services of broker Logan. Shortly after buying the house, Jordan discovers a serious leak in the roof. Chris stated that he had told broker Logan about the leaking roof when broker Logan came to the house for the listing appointment. What legal recourse is available to Jordan?

    a. Jordan should sue Chris and Logan; Chris in turn has a claim against Logan.

    b. Jordan should sue Chris, provided that there was no "as is" clause in the purchase agreement.

    c. Jordan should sue broker Logan for failure to disclose a material fact.

    d. Jordan has no recourse because the doctrine of caveat emptor applies.

5. During negotiations for the purchase of a house, the buyer was never informed that the house was served by a septic tank. Escrow closed and the buyer moved in. What recourse does the buyer have?

    a. Revoke the offer.

    b. Rescind the contract with the seller.

    c. Sue the broker.

    d. Sue the title company.

6. A Real Estate Transfer Disclosure Statement is required in the _____ of one-to-four residential units.

    a. sale

    b. lease

    c. foreclosure

    d. all of the above

7. Pat's home suffered damage to the foundation during an earthquake that caused the house to settle and created cracks down the walls. Pat didn't want to absorb the cost of repairing the damage so he just covered the cracked walls with new wallpaper and fresh paint and had new carpet and flooring installed to make the home "move-in ready". Then he listed the property with broker Jordan, not mentioning any of the damage. Broker Jordan made a visual inspection and didn't notice any obvious problems. Jordan marketed the home as "move-in ready" and in "pristine" condition. Buyer Davis bought the home and did not discover the damage until six months later. Under these circumstances:

    a. both Pat and Jordan are open to civil action, and Jordan has later recourse against Pat.

    b. only Jordan is liable because he had a duty to disclose material facts to the buyer.

    c. only Pat is liable because he withheld information from Jordan.

    d. nothing happens, according to the doctrine of caveat emptor.

8. Regarding environmental hazards, what should the listing broker and seller disclose to a prospective buyer?

    a. Give a copy of the *Environmental Hazards* booklet to the buyer.

    b. Disclose any known environmental hazards to the buyer.

    c. Complete the Transfer Disclosure Statement.

    d. All of the above

9. Seller Sam listed his newer ranch-style home built in 2002 with broker Bob. Regarding the lead based paint disclosure, Sam must:

    a. give the buyer the pamphlet, *Protect Your Family From Lead in Your Home*.

    b. complete statements verifying completion of the disclosure requirements.

    c. must give the buyers a 10-day opportunity to test for lead.

    d. do none of the above.

10. Broker Logan took a listing on a residential property and is filling out the Natural Hazard Disclosure Statement. Which of the following is not included in the NHDS?

    a. Flood hazard

    b. Seismic hazard

    c. Mold hazard

    d. Fire hazard

11. When a condominium is sold, the seller must, upon request, provide to the buyer:
    a. CC&Rs.
    b. bylaws.
    c. financial statements.
    d. all of the above

12. A broker took a listing on a property where a person died from AIDS. Does the broker have to disclose this information?
    a. Yes, the broker must disclose all material facts.
    b. No, the broker does not have to voluntarily disclose this information.
    c. Yes, but only if the death was within the previous three years.
    d. No, the law does not allow this disclosure to be made.

13. In the sale of real property, a copy of the structural pest control certification report, if requested, must be given to the:
    a. broker.
    b. escrow company.
    c. lender.
    d. buyer.

14. A pest-control company discovered no evidence of termite infestation or infection in a house offered for sale. But it did discover conditions that are likely to lead to infestation or infection. The cost of correcting such conditions is:
    a. always paid by the seller.
    b. always paid by the buyer.
    c. split 50/50 by the seller and the buyer.
    d. paid by the buyer only if he or she wishes to have these conditions corrected.

15. A copy of an inspection report filed by a licensed structural pest control operator may be obtained, for a fee, from the Structural Pest Control Board by:
    a. anyone.
    b. the seller only.
    c. the buyer only.
    d. only the seller or the buyer or their respective agent.

Escrow and Closing

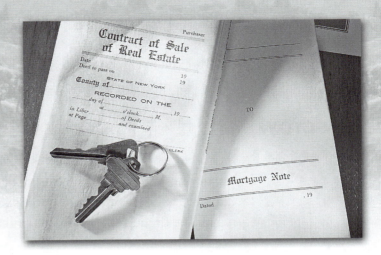

8
Chapter

Introduction

Escrow and title insurance are not required by law when transferring ownership to real property; however, they are extremely important. To determine if escrow and title insurance are needed, first decide how much your client can afford to lose. If the amount is relatively little, it may not be important to open an escrow. Obviously buying a home may be the most expensive purchase anyone will ever make; therefore, protections offered by escrow and title insurance are invaluable.

In the preceding chapters, you learned about ownership interests and real estate contracts which usually lead to a transfer of that interest.

The process for the transfer of ownership is the subject of this chapter. In this chapter, you will learn about escrow principles and rules, the relationship of the escrow holder and real estate agent, designating the escrow holder, and title insurance.

Learning Objectives

After reading this chapter, you will be able to:

- describe the escrow closing process.
- explain three ways to identify property.
- identify the system for locating land.

Escrow

For a large number of people, **escrow** is a mysterious, obscure process. They do not know what "going to escrow" means, nor how you "open an escrow". However, there is no real mystery about it. It is a period during which the paperwork required for the sale of real property is processed.

In California, when ownership transfers from one person to another there is usually a neutral third party, called an **escrow agent**, handling the details of the sale. After the principals of a sale make an agreement, an agent normally opens escrow on their behalf.

An **escrow holder**, otherwise known as an escrow company, or some other eligible person, acts as a neutral agent of both buyer and seller. The escrow holder follows the directions of the principals and collects and distributes documents and money as agreed upon in the purchase agreement.

If escrow instructions are drawn, they must reflect the understanding and agreement of the principals, who may not always be a buyer and seller, since transactions involving the sale of real estate are not the only kind that require the use of an escrow. Any time a neutral third party is needed to handle documents or money, such as leases, sales of personal property, sales of securities, loans, or mobile home sales, an escrow might be required. For the purpose of this chapter, we will discuss escrow as it relates to the sale of real estate.

No one is required by law to use an escrow for any of the above transactions, including the sale of real property. However, when a buyer and seller reach an agreement about the sale of property, including terms and price, it is usually advisable to invite a neutral third party to handle the details of completing the agreement. If the contract is not handled by an outside professional whose business it is to conduct escrows, misunderstanding, or even criminal or innocent negligence, on the part of the principals could be the cause of loss to one or both parties.

After escrow is opened, it is the **escrow holder's job to follow the buyer's and seller's instructions** and request all parties involved to observe the terms and conditions of the contract. The escrow holder coordinates communication between the principals, the agents involved and any other professionals—such as the lender, title company, or pest control company, whose services are called for in the escrow instructions.

An escrow is a small and short-lived trust arrangement. The principals trust that the escrow holder will carry out their wishes, and the escrow holder has a duty to be trustworthy, as the agent of both parties. As a neutral third party, the escrow holder does not make decisions for buyer or seller and may only operate at the direction of all parties to a transaction.

Designating the Escrow Holder

The escrow holder may be any disinterested third party and the choice of an escrow agent is always that of the buyer and seller. However, they probably do not have a relationship with an escrow agent and may rely on the advice of their real estate broker.

Basic Requirements for a Valid Escrow

Every sale escrow has two basic requirements to be valid: a binding contract between the buyer and seller and conditional delivery of transfer documents to a third party. The binding contract can be an offer to purchase (deposit receipt), agreement of sale, exchange agreement, option, or mutual escrow instructions of the buyer and seller.

Purchase Agreement as Escrow Instructions

A new approach to conducting escrow is to use the **purchase agreement** as escrow instructions. The California Association of REALTORS® provides a form, known as the Residential Purchase Agreement and Joint Escrow Instructions (purchase agreement), and seems to offer the best of all approaches to the escrow process. In an effort to make escrow all over the state more conforming and less redundant, the form combines the strength of the offer to purchase and escrow instructions into one contract. Because the purchase agreement is the original agreement between the buyer and seller, it will reflect the mutual and agreed-upon desires of the parties when it becomes the actual escrow instructions. Any mutual changes are made using an addendum to the original contract rather than amendments to escrow instructions.

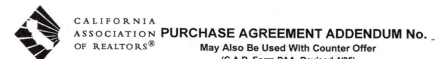

CALIFORNIA
ASSOCIATION **PURCHASE AGREEMENT ADDENDUM No.** _____
OF REALTORS®
May Also Be Used With Counter Offer
(C.A.R. Form PAA, Revised 4/05)

This is an addendum to the ☐ California Residential Purchase Agreement, ☐ Counter Offer No. _____ , ☐ Other _____
_____ , ("Agreement"), dated _____ ,
on property known as _____ ("Property"),
between _____ ("Buyer"),
and _____ ("Seller").
(The definitions in the California Residential Purchase Agreement are applicable to this Purchase Agreement Addendum.)

1. ☐ **CANCELLATION OF PRIOR SALE; BACK-UP OFFER** (If checked): This Agreement is in back-up position number _____ ,
   and is contingent upon written cancellation of any prior contracts and related escrows ("Prior Contracts") between Seller and other
   buyers. Seller and other buyers may mutually agree to modify or amend the terms of Prior Contracts. Buyer may cancel this
   Agreement in writing at any time before Seller provides Buyer Copies of written cancellations of Prior Contracts Signed by all parties
   to those contracts. If Seller is unable to provide such written Signed cancellations to Buyer by _____ (date),
   then either Buyer or Seller may cancel the Agreement in writing.
   A. BUYER'S DEPOSIT CHECK shall be: **(i)** held uncashed until Copies of the written cancellations Signed by all parties to the Prior
   Contracts are provided to Buyer; OR **(ii)** (if checked) ☐ immediately handled as provided in the Agreement.
   B. TIME PERIODS in the Agreement for Investigations, contingencies, covenants and other obligations **(i)** shall begin on the Day
   After Seller provides Buyer Copies of Signed cancellations of Prior Contracts; OR **(ii)** (if checked) ☐ all time periods shall begin
   as provided in this Agreement. However, if the date for Close Of Escrow is a specific calendar date, that date shall NOT be
   extended, unless agreed to in writing by Buyer and Seller.

2. ☐ **SELLER TO REMAIN IN POSSESSION AFTER CLOSE OF ESCROW** (If checked): This provision is intended for short-term
   occupancy (i.e. less than 30 Days). If occupancy is intended to be for 30 Days or longer, use Residential Lease After Sale (C.A.R.
   Form RLAS). **Note: Local rent control or other Law regarding tenant's rights may impact Buyer's and Seller's rights and
   obligations.**
   A. TERM: Seller to remain in possession of Property for _____ **Days** After Close Of Escrow (or ☐ _____).
   Seller has no right to remain in possession beyond this term and may be responsible for court awarded damages if seller does
   remain.
   B. COMPENSATION: Seller agrees to pay Buyer **(i)** $ _____ per Day (or ☐ _____),
   and **(ii)** a security deposit in the amount of $ _____ . Seller shall deposit such funds with escrow holder prior to
   Close Of Escrow or such funds shall be withheld from Seller's proceeds.
   C. LATE CHARGE/NSF CHECKS: If any payment from Seller to Buyer is required outside of escrow, and any such payment is not
   received by Buyer within **5 (or** ☐ _____ **) Days** After date due, Seller shall pay to Buyer an additional sum of
   $ _____ as a Late Charge. If a check is returned for non-sufficient fund ("NSF"), Seller shall pay to
   Buyer $25.00 as an NSF charge. Seller and Buyer agree that these charges represent a fair and reasonable estimate of the costs
   Buyer may incur by reason of Seller's late or NSF payment. Buyer's acceptance of any Late Charge or NSF fee shall not
   constitute a waiver as to any default by Seller.
   D. UTILITIES: Seller agrees to pay for all utilities and services, and the following charges: _____
   except _____ , which shall be paid for by Buyer.
   E. ENTRY: Seller shall make Property available to Buyer for the purpose of entering to make necessary or agreed repairs, or to
   supply necessary or agreed services, or to show Property to prospective or actual purchasers, tenants, mortgagees, lenders,
   appraisers or contractors. Buyer and Seller agree that 24 hours notice (oral or written) shall be reasonable and sufficient notice.
   In an emergency, Buyer may enter Property at any time without prior notice.
   F. MAINTENANCE: Seller shall maintain the Property, including pool, spa, landscaping and grounds, and all personal property
   included in the sale in substantially the same condition as on the date of Acceptance of the Agreement. Except as provided in the
   Agreement, Seller shall not make alterations to the Property without Buyer's written consent.
   G. ASSIGNMENT; SUBLETTING: Seller shall not assign or sublet all or any part of the Property, or assign or transfer the right to
   occupy the Property. Any assignment, subletting or transfer of the Property by voluntary act of Seller, by operation of Law or
   otherwise, without Buyer's prior written consent shall give Buyer the right to terminate Seller's right to possession.
   H. SELLER'S OBLIGATIONS UPON DELIVERY OF POSSESSION: Upon delivery of possession to Buyer, Seller shall deliver the
   Property in the condition and on the terms provided in the Agreement.
   I. INSURANCE: Seller's personal property (including vehicles) is not insured by Buyer, and, if applicable, owner's association,
   against loss or damage due to fire, theft, vandalism, rain, water, criminal or negligent acts of others, or any other cause. Seller is
   to carry Seller's own insurance to protect Seller from such loss.
   J. WAIVER: The waiver of any breach shall not be construed as a continuing waiver of the same or any subsequent breach.
   K. OTHER TERMS AND CONDITIONS/SUPPLEMENTS: _____
   _____

PAA REVISED 4/05 (PAGE 1 OF 2)

Buyer's Initials (_____) (_____)
Seller's Initials (_____) (_____)

| Reviewed by _____ Date_____ |

PURCHASE AGREEMENT ADDENDUM (PAA PAGE 1 OF 2)

| Agent: | Phone: | Fax: | Prepared using WINForms® software |
| Broker: | | | |

Property Address: _____   Date: _____

3. ☐ **TENANT TO REMAIN IN POSSESSION** (If checked): Buyer shall take Property subject to the rights of existing tenants. Seller shall, within **7** (or ☐ _____) **Days** After Acceptance, deliver to Buyer Copies of all: estoppel certificates sent to and received back from tenants; leases; rental agreements; and current income and expense statements ("Rental Documents"). Seller shall give Buyer written notice of any changes to existing leases or tenancies or new agreements to lease or rent ("Proposed Changes") at least **7** (or ☐ _____) **Days** prior to any Proposed Changes. Buyer's approval of the Rental Documents and Proposed Changes is a contingency of the Agreement. Buyer shall, within **5** (or ☐ _____) **Days** After receipt of Rental Documents or Proposed Changes remove the applicable contingency or cancel the Agreement. Seller shall transfer to Buyer, through escrow, all unused tenant deposits. No warranty is made concerning compliance with governmental restrictions, if any, limiting the amount of rent that can lawfully be charged, and/or the maximum number of persons who can lawfully occupy the Property, unless otherwise agreed in writing.

4. ☐ **SECONDARY OR ASSUMED LOAN** (If checked): Obtaining the secondary loan or assumption below and approval of such financing is a contingency of this Agreement. Buyer shall act diligently and in good faith to obtain the designated financing.

   A. ☐ **SECONDARY LOAN**

     (1) New second deed of trust in favor of LENDER encumbering the Property, securing a note payable at maximum interest of _____ % fixed rate or _____ % initial adjustable rate, with a maximum interest rate of _____ %, balance due in _____ years. Buyer shall pay loan fees/points not to exceed _____ .
(These terms apply whether the designated loan is conventional, FHA or VA.)

     (2) Within **17** (or ☐ _____ **Days)** After Acceptance, Buyer shall, as specified in the Agreement, remove this contingency or cancel this Agreement; OR (if checked) ☐ secondary loan contingency shall remain in effect until the loan is funded.

   B. ☐ **ASSUMPTION OF EXISTING LOAN:**

     (1) Assumption of existing deed of trust encumbering the Property, securing a note payable at maximum interest of _____ % fixed rate or _____ % initial adjustable rate, with a maximum interest rate of _____ %, balance due in _____ years. Buyer shall pay loan fees/points not to exceed _____ .
Seller shall, within **5** (or ☐ _____) **Days** After Acceptance, request from Lender, and upon receipt provide to Buyer, Copies of all applicable notes and deeds of trust, loan balances and current interest rates. Differences between estimated and actual loan balances shall be adjusted at Close Of Escrow by cash down payment. Impound accounts, if any, shall be assigned and charged to Buyer and credited to Seller. If this is an assumption of a VA Loan, the sale is contingent upon Seller being provided a release of liability and substitution of eligibility, unless otherwise agreed in writing.

     (2) Within **17** (or ☐ _____) **Days** After Acceptance, Buyer shall, as specified in the Agreement, remove this contingency or cancel this Agreement. However, if the assumed loan documents are not provided to Buyer within 7 Days After Acceptance, Buyer has **5** (or ☐ _____) **Days** after receipt of these documents, or the fixed time specified in 4B(2), whichever occurs last, to remove this contingency or cancel the Agreement; OR (if checked) ☐ assumed loan contingency shall remain in effect until the assumption is approved.

5. ☐ **SHORT PAY** (If checked): This Agreement is contingent upon Seller's receipt of written consent from all existing secured lenders and lienholders ("Short-Pay Lenders"), no later than 5:00 P.M. on _____ (date) ("Short-Pay Contingency Date"), to reduce their respective loan balances by an amount sufficient to permit the proceeds from the sale of the Property, without additional funds from Seller, to pay the existing balances on loans, real property taxes, brokerage commissions, closing costs, and other monetary obligations the Agreement requires Seller to pay at Close Of Escrow (including, but not limited to, escrow charges, title charges, documentary transfer taxes, prorations, retrofit costs and Repairs). If Seller fails to give Buyer written notice of all existing Short-Pay Lenders' consent by the Short-Pay Contingency Date, either Seller or Buyer may cancel the Agreement in writing. Seller shall reasonably cooperate with existing Short-Pay lenders in the short-pay off process. Buyer and Seller understand that Lenders are not obligated to accept a short-pay off and may accept other offers, and that Seller, Buyer and Brokers do not have control over whether Short-Pay Lenders will consent to a short-pay off, or any act, omission, or decision by any Short-Pay Lender in the short-pay off process. Seller is informed that a short-pay may create credit or legal problems, or may result in taxable income to Seller. Seller may present to Short-Pay Lender any additional offers that are received on the Property. **Seller is advised to seek advice from an attorney, certified public accountant or other expert regarding such potential consequences of a short-payoff.**

6. ☐ **COURT CONFIRMATION** (If checked): This Agreement is contingent upon court confirmation on or before _____ (date). If court confirmation is not obtained by that date, Buyer may cancel this Agreement in writing. Court confirmation may be required in probate, conservatorship, guardianship, receivership, bankruptcy, or other proceedings. The court may allow open, competitive bidding, resulting in Property being sold to the highest bidder. Broker recommends that Buyer appear at court confirmation hearing. Buyer understands that **(i)** Broker and others may continue to market the Property and **(ii)** Broker may represent other competitive bidders prior to and at the court confirmation.

Date _____   Date _____

Buyer _____   Seller _____

Buyer _____   Seller _____

SURE·TRAC The System for Success™

An escrow is opened when a real estate agent brings the signed purchase agreement to the escrow holder, who makes a copy and accepts it by signing off in the required box in the document. The escrow holder should be concerned that the contract is complete, fully signed and initialed before accepting it. The contract must be valid before becoming instructions for the escrow.

In addition to the purchase agreement as escrow instructions, an escrow holder will submit acceptance, or additional escrow instructions, for buyer and seller signature. These instructions include any other terms that need to be agreed upon by buyer and seller to complete the escrow.

Conditional Delivery

A conditional delivery of transfer documents and funds, the second requirement for a valid escrow, means the seller will deliver a signed grant deed which **conveys** the title to the buyer, and the buyer and/or the lender will deliver to escrow whatever funds are required for the sale.

In addition, the escrow agent will hold the security for any loan (trust deed) conditionally until directed by the terms of the escrow. The escrow agent will keep documents and funds until all other terms of the escrow are completed, and then distribute them according to the expressed conditions of the escrow.

Sometime before the escrow closes, the seller will be asked to sign a grant deed conveying title to the buyer. Because the seller will sign over the ownership to the buyer before getting the money, the escrow holder is instructed to hold the signed deed until funds from the buyer are deposited in escrow and all the other terms of the escrow have been met. Conditional delivery of the grant deed has been made.

Toward the end of the escrow period, the buyer will be asked to sign a note and trust deed for the loan. The buyer is promising to pay back the money, using the property as security for the loan. Escrow has not closed, and the buyer does not own the house yet. Nor has the seller been given the promised money, but the note and trust deed are signed and deposited into escrow, conditionally, until all other terms have been met. At that time the money will be released by the lender to escrow.

Complete Escrow

Properly drawn and executed escrow instructions become an enforceable contract. An escrow is termed "complete" when all terms of the instructions have been met.

After the escrow has been completed and recorded, the buyer gets a grant deed, and the seller gets the money. The escrow closes shortly thereafter.

General Escrow Principles and Rules

Once escrow instructions or the purchase agreement as escrow instructions have been signed by the buyer and seller and returned to the escrow holder, neither party may unilaterally change the escrow instructions. Any changes must be made by mutual agreement between the buyer and seller.

The escrow agent does not have the authority to make changes in the contract upon the direction of either the buyer or seller, unless both agree to the change in the form of an amendment or addendum to the purchase agreement.

Escrow instructions must be understood by the principals to the escrow and must be mutually binding.

Also, it should be noted, the broker has no authority whatsoever to amend or change any part of the escrow instructions without the knowledge of the principals. The written consent of both buyer and seller, in the form of an amendment to the original instructions or an addendum to the purchase agreement, must be given before any change may be made.

> Example: The Clarks and the Marshalls signed escrow instructions in June. The agreement reflected a sales price of $450,000, with $90,000 as a down payment. After signing the instructions, however, the buyers decided they only wanted to put $80,000 down, and told the escrow officer to change the instructions. An amendment was written for them to sign, and a copy sent to the sellers to sign.
>
> The buyers were disappointed when the Clarks did not want to change the contract and refused to sign the amendment. When the Marshalls wanted to back out, the escrow officer reminded them that they had a mutually binding legal agreement with the sellers. Neither side could change any part of the agreement, including terminating it, without the written agreement of the other.

As agent for both parties to an escrow, the escrow agent is placed in a position of trust. By operating as a dual agent, the escrow holder sits between the buyer and seller as a stakeholder with an obligation to both sides.

As a neutral third party, the escrow officer must observe the following rules:

1. Escrow instructions must be understood by the principals to the escrow and must be mutually binding. Carefully written instructions or the offer to purchase are very clear about the agreement between the buyer and seller. Each party must understand his or her obligation to carry out the terms of the contract without assuming the escrow holder has any power to force compliance. The escrow holder may not act unless directed by the principals.

2. The escrow holder does not get personally involved in disagreements between the buyer and seller, nor act as a negotiator for the principals. Escrow instructions make each party's obligations and agreements clear, and it is up to the buyer and seller to keep the promises they each made in their agreement with the other.

3. An escrow agent usually is not an attorney. The escrow agent must advise anyone seeking legal advice to get counsel from a lawyer.

4. An escrow agent has a limited capacity as agent for buyer and seller and may only perform acts described in the contents of escrow instructions. While acting as a dual agent, the escrow officer must operate in the best interests of both parties, without special preference to either. The escrow agent may serve each principal after escrow closes, in dealing with their separate interests.

5. All parties must sign escrow instructions or the offer to purchase as escrow instructions for the contract to be binding. An escrow is officially open when both buyer and seller have signed the instructions and delivered them to escrow.

6. If separate escrow instructions are written, they must be clear and certain in their language. When there is a conflict between the signed instructions and the original agreement of the principals, the signed instructions will prevail as long as they reflect the intent of the parties.

7. All documents to be recorded must be sent to the **title company** in a timely manner (as quickly as possible), and all interested parties should receive copies of recorded documents.

8. Escrow instructions should specify which documents or funds the escrow holder may accept.

9. Overdrawn escrow trust accounts (**debit balances**) are prohibited by law.

10. Information regarding any transaction is held **in trust** by the escrow officer and may not be released to anyone without written permission of the principals.

11. An escrow holder has a duty to disclose to the principals any previously **undisclosed information** that might affect them. An amendment would be drawn at the direction of the buyer and seller to reflect any change as a result of new disclosures.

12. A high degree of trust and good customer service must be provided by an escrow holder.

13. An escrow holder must remain strictly neutral regarding the buyer's and the seller's interests.

14. Escrow records and files must be maintained daily. A systematic review of open escrow files will make sure no procedure has been overlooked, or time limit ignored.

15. Before closing an escrow, all files must be audited carefully.

16. All checks or drafts must have cleared before any funds may be released to the seller.

17. Escrow must close in a timely manner, according to the agreement between buyer and seller. A prompt settlement must be made to all principals.

What Each Party Does During the Escrow Process

The Seller

As soon as possible following the opening of escrow, the seller should furnish escrow with the following items:

- escrow instructions signed by the seller(s).

- executed deed to the buyer with the escrow holder.

- evidence of pest inspection and any required repair work.

- latest available tax and assessment bills and any other statements or bills which are to be prorated through escrow.

- other required documents such as tax receipts, addresses of mortgage holders, insurance policies, equipment warranties or home warranty contracts, etc.

- fire insurance policies, if they are to be assigned to the buyer.

- certificates or releases showing satisfaction of mechanic's liens, security agreements (chattel mortgages), judgments, or mortgages which are to be paid off through escrow.

- executed bill of sale covering any personal property to be conveyed to the buyer, together with an inventory of the items for the buyer's approval.

- assignment to buyer of all leases affecting the property.

- subordination or other agreement required by the purchase contract, to be approved by the parties through escrow.

Sellers should always keep copies of any documents and instruments they sign, deliver to, or receive from any party in the real estate transaction.

The Buyer

As soon as possible after the opening of escrow, the buyer should furnish the escrow holder with certain documents and information, and should review or inspect personally all of the following items:

- escrow instructions signed by all purchasers.

- deposit the funds required, in addition to any borrowed funds, to pay the purchase price with the escrow holder.

- arrange for any borrowed funds to be delivered to the escrow holder.

- deposit funds sufficient for escrow and closing costs.

- review and approve the preliminary title report for the subject property to make sure that there are no items of record affecting the property which have not already been approved by the buyer.

- review and approve any Conditions, Covenants, and Restrictions affecting the property, whether of record or not.

- review and approve structural pest control and other reports to be delivered through escrow.

- confirm the terms of any mortgages or deeds of trust to be assumed by the buyer or which will remain an encumbrance on the property.

- carefully review all new loan documents prior to signing.

- compare the terms of the purchase contract, escrow instructions, title report, and deed to make sure there are no discrepancies in the transaction documents.

- fulfill any other conditions specified in the escrow instructions.

- review and approve any items to be prorated in escrow.

- reinspect the property to determine that it is in the same condition as it was when the buyer made the purchase offer. Recheck for any undisclosed items which might affect the use of the property, such as: party walls, access roads to other properties, irrigation canals or ditches, common drives, or persons in occupancy or possession of the property, which the county records would not disclose.

Buyers should always keep copies of any documents and instruments they sign, deliver to, or receive from any party in the real estate transaction.

The Lender

A lender involved in the transfer is responsible to:

- deposit proceeds of the loan to the purchaser.

- direct the escrow holder on the conditions under which the loan funds may be used.

The Escrow Holder

The escrow holder follows the directions of the principals in the transaction and:

- opens the order for title insurance.

- obtains approvals from the buyer on title insurance report, pest, and other inspections.

- receives funds from the buyer and/or any lender.

- prorates insurance, taxes, rents, etc.

- disburses funds for title insurance, recordation fees, real estate commissions, lien clearance, etc.

- prepares a final statement for each party indicating amount to be disbursed for services and any further amounts necessary to close escrow.

- records deed and loan documents, and delivers the deed to the buyer, loan documents to the lender and funds to the seller, thereby closing the escrow.

Escrow Procedures

Escrow procedures vary according to local custom. For example, in Northern California title companies handle closings through escrow, whereas in Southern California escrow companies or banks conduct escrows. It is typical in Southern California for sellers to pay the title insurance premium and transfer tax and to split the escrow costs with the buyer.

Not only do escrow procedures differ between Northern and Southern California, they also vary somewhat from county to county. Sellers also pay for the title insurance in Northern California except in the counties of Alameda, Calaveras, Colusa, Contra Costa, Lake, Marin, Mendocino, San Francisco, San Mateo, Solano, and Sonoma, where the buyers pay for it. Buyers and sellers equally share the costs of title insurance and escrow in the counties of

Amador, Merced, Plumas, San Joaquin, and Siskiyou. In Butte County, sellers pay 75%; buyers pay 25%.

In spite of the differences, there are certain procedures that are followed during the regular course of all escrows.

Open Escrow

The person who usually opens escrow, if there is a real estate agent involved, is the selling agent. That person usually has an earnest money check that must be deposited into escrow or some other trust account no more than three business days after buyer and seller have signed the deposit receipt.

At the first opportunity, the real estate agent must take the buyer's check to the escrow officer to put it in a trust account. The agent then gives the escrow officer all the information needed to draw escrow instructions, or may give the escrow holder the original signed purchase agreement which then becomes the escrow instructions. If instructions are being drawn, usually within a day or two, computer-generated instructions will be ready for the buyer and seller to sign. The instructions, as you recall, reflect the agreement between the buyer and seller as seen in the offer to purchase.

If there is no real estate agent involved, the principals may go to the escrow office and ask the escrow officer to prepare instructions according to their agreement.

Prepare Escrow Instructions

The escrow is officially opened when the escrow holder accepts the purchase agreement that has been signed by all parties to the escrow. When escrow instructions are drawn, the escrow holder prepares them on a computer generated form, with details of the particular transaction completed in the blank spaces on the form. All parties sign identical instructions, with the exception of the commission agreement that is prepared for the seller to sign— if the seller in fact is paying the commission.

Buyer and seller sign the instructions, which are then returned to the escrow holder who follows the directions in the agreement to complete the escrow.

Imagine you are involved in the sale of your home. The following would probably be included in your escrow instructions or purchase agreement. In California, the purchase agreement becomes the escrow instructions.

1. **Purchase Price:** The **purchase price** is the amount of consideration the buyer and seller have agreed upon for the sale of the property.

2. **Terms:** The buyer and seller agree on how the buyer will purchase the property: cash, new loan, loan assumption, VA or FHA loan, seller to carry a trust deed, trade, or any other special agreements provided in the contract between buyer and seller. This section describes the amount of the down payment and the terms of any loans for which the buyer will apply.

3. **Vesting:** The way title will be taken is called **vesting**. The buyer will take title in one of the following ways: sole ownership, joint tenancy, tenants in common, or tenancy in partnership. How the buyer will take title may be important for tax or inheritance purposes and the escrow holder must be directed how to draw the deed to reflect the wishes of the buyer.

4. **Matters of Record:** Buyer and seller may agree on some matter of record or, in other words, some matter that is recorded, affecting the property. It may be an easement, an existing street bond or a trust deed. An agreement may be made about who will be responsible for whatever exists as a recorded encumbrance on the title at the time of the sale.

5. **Closing:** Buyer and seller will agree on how long they want the escrow to last. They will mention a specific length of time for the escrow and instruct the escrow holder accordingly.

6. **Inspections:** Buyer and seller will agree on whether to have certain inspections of the property before the close of escrow, such as a pest control inspection, property inspection to identify any plumbing, electrical or structural problems, and a soil inspection to check for slippage or unstable compaction. The buyer's approval of the reports will be a contingency of the sale and must be mentioned in the escrow instructions.

7. **Prorations:** The division of expenses and income between the buyer and seller as of the date of closing is known as proration. Some items that are prorated are: taxes, rental deposits or income, and insurance premiums. The reason for prorations is that some payments may have been made by the seller for a time period beyond the agreed-upon date of closing of escrow, or the seller may be in arrears on taxes or insurance. The escrow holder debits or credits the seller or buyer, depending on the escrow closing date. Normally, prorations are based on a 30-day month and a 360-day year. Examples of calculating prorations are found in Appendix A.

8. **Possession:** The buyer and seller will have agreed on when the buyer can move into the house, and the escrow instructions must reflect their agreement on the date the buyer will take possession of the property. The close of escrow could be the date of possession, or sometimes the

seller will rent the property back from the buyer after the close of escrow. In that case, a lease agreement should be signed and deposited in escrow.

9. **Documents:** The escrow holder will need to know which documents to prepare, have signed by the proper party, and record at the close of escrow. Usually, these will be a grant deed and a trust deed.

10. **Disbursements:** The escrow holder must settle the accounts of the buyer and seller according to the escrow instructions. At the close of escrow, each party receives a closing statement of costs and charges along with a final distribution of funds.

Order Title Search

At the time the buyer and seller reached an agreement about the sale of the property, they also selected a title company. One of the jobs of the escrow officer, after escrow has been opened, is to order a search of the title of the subject property. The title company searches the records for any encumbrances or liens against the property, checks to make sure the seller is the owner of record, and inspects the history of ownership, or chain of title. The purpose is to ensure all transfers of ownership have been recorded correctly, that there are no unexplained gaps and that there are no liens or encumbrances which will not be released. After completing this search, the title company prepares a preliminary title report.

The buyer is allowed a certain number of days to approve this preliminary title report. Buyer approval is important to eliminate surprises regarding the title as the escrow progresses. The escrow holder should notify the buyer and seller if there is any difference in the preliminary report and the escrow instructions, by way of an addendum "for information only".

As you recall, the escrow agent is a neutral party and only has the authority to do what is described in the escrow instructions. The escrow officer must wait for instructions about what to do next. The preliminary title report is the foundation for the title insurance policy insuring the buyer's title as instructed by the buyer and seller in the escrow instructions.

> Example: The Clarks and the Marshalls instructed their escrow officer to order a preliminary title search. The Marshalls had three days to approve the report, as a contingency of the sale. When they examined it, however, they found there was a bond against the property for street repairs. They had not been aware of it.
>
> The bond was a lien in the amount of $3,500. The buyers could not approve the preliminary title report until the issue was cleared up. An agreement about who would pay the bond had to be reached by the buyers and sellers, then new

instructions given to the escrow officer, who would prepare an amendment for both parties' signatures, to indicate their agreement.

Request Demands and/or Beneficiary Statements

The escrow officer must also ensure that existing loans are paid off, or assumed, depending on the agreement of the buyer and seller. If the existing loan, or the seller's debt, is going to be paid off with proceeds from the sale, a demand from the lender holding the note and trust deed is needed, along with the unpaid principal balance and any other amounts that are due. The escrow officer requests a demand for payoff of a loan from the lender who holds a loan against the subject property. The exact amount of loans that are to be paid off must be known so the escrow officer's accounting will be correct at the close of escrow.

If an existing loan is going to be assumed, or taken "subject to", a beneficiary statement is requested by the escrow holder from the lender. A **beneficiary statement** is a statement of the unpaid condition of a loan and describes the condition of the debt.

The escrow agent follows instructions about financing the property, and prepares any documents necessary for completing the escrow at the close. These might be a note and trust deed or assumption papers.

> Example: The buyers are obtaining an adjustable loan in the amount of $360,000. The down payment will be $90,000, to make the purchase price of $450,000. The existing $250,000 loan on the property is held by Union Bank. The existing loan will be paid off when the buyer's new loan is funded, and the seller will get the remainder of $110,000 along with the down payment.
>
> Union Bank is notified of the expected payoff and asked by the escrow officer to send a statement of the unpaid balance and condition of the existing loan. This is known as a request for demand for payoff.

Accept Reports

The parties to an escrow may request any number of reports about the condition of the property. The escrow holder is asked in the instructions to accept any reports submitted into escrow. These may include a structural pest control report (termite report), property inspection report, soil condition report, or environmental report. Any approval from the buyer or seller about a report is held in escrow until needed or given to the appropriate party at the close of escrow.

New Loan Instructions and Documents

Escrow accepts loan documents or instructions about financing the subject property and completes them as directed. The escrow agent gets the buyer's approval of and signature on loan documents and receives and disburses loan funds as instructed.

Fire Insurance Policies

The parties to an escrow will have agreed on fire insurance policies and will instruct the escrow officer accordingly. The escrow holder will accept, hold, and deliver any policies and will follow instructions about transferring them. A lender will require fire insurance, and will expect the escrow holder and the buyer to be accountable for either a new policy or the transfer of an existing one.

Settlement

The escrow holder will be instructed by the buyer and seller about prorations and other accounting to be done at the close of escrow. **Proration** is the adjustment of interest, taxes, insurance, etc., on a pro-rata basis as of the closing or agreed-upon date. Hazard insurance policies that are terminated prior to the expiration date at the request of the insured are subject to a short rate cancellation fee. A **short rate cancellation fee** is a fee (or penalty) charged to the person who cancels the insurance policy before it expires. The money returned is the unused premium minus administrative expenses. However, if the insurance company cancels the policy early, there is no penalty.

The escrow holder will prepare a settlement (closing) statement for all parties to the escrow. A **settlement statement** is a complete breakdown of all cash received, all charges and credits made, and all costs involved in the transaction. The statement shows how all closing costs and prepaid expenses are allocated between the buyer and seller. In most transactions the seller pays for title insurance and any delinquent assessment liens which would show up as debits. If the seller prepaid the property taxes, he or she would expect to get the unused portion back, which would show up as a credit.

ABC - Assumption by the Buyer is a Credit

When a buyer assumes an existing loan, the assumption is shown on the closing statement as a debit to the seller and a credit to the buyer.

The buyer and seller will have agreed on impound accounts, and the escrow holder will be guided on how to handle the credits and debits. An **impound**

account is a trust account set up for funds set aside for future, recurring costs relating to a property. After the escrow agent completes the accounting, the agent tells the buyer to

> **Review - Prorations Normally Include**
> - Interest
> - Premiums on hazard (fire) insurance
> - Security deposits and rents (if the property is a rental)
> - Seller's current property taxes

deliver the down payment (usually a cashier's check is required), plus other escrow costs, to the escrow office.

At this time, the buyers sign the loan documents, and any other paperwork required for the financing is completed. If all is in order, the loan will be funded and the money sent to the escrow office along with the buyer's funds. Then the escrow may close.

Audit File

At the close of escrow, the escrow officer must examine each file to make sure all accounting has been accurate, and that escrow instructions have been followed. A cash **reconciliation** statement is completed by the escrow holder and closing statements are prepared for all principals.

Recording

The escrow holder records all transaction documents as instructed by the buyer and seller after a final check of the title company records to be sure nothing has changed since the preliminary title search was done. Then the title company will issue a policy of title insurance to insure the buyer's title. Documents that might require recording are the grant deed, trust deed, contract of sale, or option.

Closing the Escrow

Once all the terms and conditions of the instructions of both parties have been fulfilled, the last job of the escrow holder is to close the escrow. The escrow officer gives closing statements to buyer and seller, disburses all money, and delivers all documents to the proper parties after making sure all documents have been recorded by the title company. The seller gets a check for the proceeds of the sale minus escrow fees, real estate commissions, loan payoffs and all other costs of selling, and any pertinent documents; and the buyer gets a grant deed.

Termination of an Escrow

Full performance, by completion of the escrow, **terminates the escrow**. The authority to conduct an escrow is mutually given by the buyer and seller in the escrow instructions and may be terminated by mutual agreement. Neither party may end the escrow without the agreement of the other, in writing. Also, the escrow officer may not return any funds or documents to either party without agreement from all parties.

During escrow, the escrow officer is an agent for both buyer and seller, and must operate from the original escrow instructions. When they instruct the escrow agent to prepare an amendment canceling the escrow, a buyer and seller mutually end their agreement after they have both signed the amendment.

Rights and Obligations of the Parties to an Escrow

A buyer and a seller are known as principals in an escrow. The escrow holder is a neutral third party who is a dual agent for buyer and seller. A real estate agent is not a party to an escrow unless he or she is the buyer or the seller.

A buyer is the party purchasing the property and who will receive a deed conveying the title.

A seller is the owner of record who must deliver the title agreed upon in the contract.

An escrow agent is an impartial third party who collects all documents and money through the escrow and transfers them to the proper parties at the close of escrow.

An escrow agent may be a bank, savings and loan, title insurance company, attorney, real estate broker, or an escrow company. A real estate broker may act as an escrow agent in the course of a regular transaction for which a real estate license is necessary. The broker may conduct the escrow as a service only if he or she is the listing or selling broker to the subject sale.

Escrow Companies Must be Incorporated

The Commissioner of Corporations only licenses qualified corporations as escrow companies. An individual is not allowed to be an escrow company. A bond based upon predicted yearly average transactions and trust fund use must be furnished by an applicant for an escrow office license. A bond must be posted by all parties (officers, directors, trustees, and employees) having access to money or securities being held by the escrow company as safety against loss. Banks, savings and loans, title insurance companies, attorneys, and real estate brokers are exempt from Commissioner of Corporation licensing requirements.

Audit

An escrow company must keep accounts and records which can be examined by the Commissioner of Corporations. A yearly inspection prepared by an independent certified public accountant, describing operations, must be delivered to the Commissioner.

Prohibitions

- Referral fees may not be paid by an escrow company to anyone as a reward for sending business to them.

- Commissions may not be paid to a real estate broker until the closing of an escrow.

- Blank escrow instructions to be filled in after signing are not acceptable. Initials must be placed wherever there is a change or deletion.

- Information regarding an escrow may only be provided to parties of the escrow.

- Copies of escrow instructions must be provided to anyone signing them.

Agency

An escrow agent holds a limited agency, or authority. Any duties to be conducted must be mentioned specifically in escrow instructions or they are not authorized by the buyer and seller. The escrow holder must remain neutral, as the agent of both the buyer and seller, during the course of the escrow. After all conditions of the escrow have been met, the escrow officer is the agent of each of the parties in dealing with their individual needs.

Relationship of the Escrow Holder and the Real Estate Agent

No transaction can be completed without a good relationship between a broker and an escrow agent. The goodwill, positive guidance, and technical knowledge of an escrow officer has helped many brokers to get through an escrow, especially those new to the business.

After the real estate broker negotiates the sale, it is the job of the escrow agent to see that the agreements made by the parties are carried out. The broker and the escrow agent must check with each other regularly to make sure information is correct and to inform each other of how the escrow is progressing.

Assuring Marketability of Title

It is currently the general practice in California for buyers, sellers and lenders, as well as real estate brokers, to rely on title insurance companies for title information, title reports, and policies of title insurance. Title insurance that we use today grew from the need to protect real estate owners from challenges to their property titles. Under the old doctrine of caveat emptor, "let the buyer beware", the buyer had the final responsibility to verify title of a property prior to purchasing it. As a result, many buyers ultimately lost their properties. The goal of title insurance companies is to ensure the clear, marketable title of property. Marketable title is one that a reasonable person would accept as clear and free from likely challenge. Over the years, determining marketable title has gone through several phases: abstract of title, certificate of title, guarantee of title, and finally title insurance.

Abstract of Title

Before reliable histories of properties came into existence, abstractors investigated the status of title to property. They searched available records and pertinent documents, and prepared an abstract of title. An **abstract of title** is a written summary of all useful documents discovered in a title search. The abstract of title together with an attorney's opinion of the documents appearing in the abstractor's "chain of title" was the source of our earliest basis for establishing marketable title. The chain of title is the public record of prior transfers and encumbrances affecting the title of a parcel of land.

Certificate of Title

Over time, the abstracts were accumulated along with references to the recorded information. Information regarding the property was organized in "lot books" and information affecting titles was organized in "general indices." In time, these records became known as "title plants". The abstract company used these title plants to supply interested parties with a certificate of title. This stated that the property was found to be properly vested in the present owner, subject to noted encumbrances.

Guarantee of Title

The next step was the **guarantee of title** under which the title insurance company provided written assurances (not insurance) about the title to real property, insuring against loss.

Title Insurance

Title insurance was created in response to the need for reliable assurance of title combined with an insurance against loss caused by errors in searching records and reporting the status of title. The title insurance company uses the title plant to conduct the most accurate search of the public records (county recorder, county assessor, county clerk and the federal land office) as possible to make sure the chain of title is correct. If there is a missing connection in a property's history or ownership, if a deed was recorded in error or is incomplete, it clouds the title. Any problems that arise may be corrected during the escrow period so the new owner gets a clear title. The title company must determine insurability of the title as part of the search process which leads to issuance of a title policy. A marketable title is guaranteed because of title insurance, and a new owner is protected against recorded and unrecorded matters. If someone challenges the title, the title insurance company will defend the title and will pay losses that are covered under the policy.

Regulation of the Title Insurance Industry

Title insurance companies are controlled by the California Insurance Commissioner. Insurance rates are set by each company, not the state. Every title insurer must adopt a schedule of fees and charges for title policies and make it available to the public. In addition, each title insurance company must have a guarantee fund for the protection of title insurance policy holders on deposit with the Insurance Commissioner.

The title insurance premiums are a one-time fee and are not prorated in escrow. Title insurance remains in effect until the property is sold. If a property owner dies, the policy continues to protect the owner's heirs.

Rebate Law

Title insurance companies are prohibited from paying any commission, rebate or other consideration as an incentive for title insurance business, escrow, or other title business. The rebate law requires title insurance companies to charge for preliminary reports and to make sincere efforts to collect for them. However, title insurance companies can still furnish "the name of the owner of record and the record description of any parcel or real property" without charge.

ABC Title Company

PRELIMINARY REPORT

Order Number:

Title Officer: Phone:
Fax No.:   E-Mail:
Escrow Officer: Phone:
Fax No.:   E-Mail:
Borrower: Owner:
Property:

In response to the above referenced application for a policy of title insurance, this company hereby reports that it is prepared to issue, or cause to be issued, as of the date hereof, a Policy or Policies of Title Insurance describing the land and the estate or interest therein hereinafter set forth, insuring against loss which may be sustained by reason of any defect, lien, or encumbrance not shown or referred to as an Exception below or not excluded from coverage pursuant to the printed Schedules, Conditions, and Stipulations of said Policy forms.

The printed Exceptions and Exclusions from the coverage of said Policy or Policies are set forth in Exhibit A attached. Copies of the Policy forms should be read. They are available form the office which issued this report.

Please read the exceptions shown or referred to below and the exceptions and exclusions set forth in Exhibit A of this report carefully. The exceptions and exclusions are meant to provide you with notice of matters which are not covered under the terms of the title insurance policy and should be carefully considered.

It is important to note that this preliminary report is not a written representation as to the condition of title and may not list all liens, defects, and encumbrances affecting title to the land.

This report (and any supplements or amendments hereto) is issued solely for the purpose of facilitating the issuance of a policy title insurance and no liability is assumed hereby. If it is desired that liability be assumed prior to the issuance of a policy of title insurance, a Binder or Commitment should be requested.

Types of Title Insurance Policies

Policies of title insurance are commonly used throughout California, usually in the standardized forms prepared by the **California Land Title Association,** which is the trade organization of the title companies in the state.

The main benefit of title insurance is that it extends protection against matters of record and many non-recorded types of risks, depending on the type of policy purchased. Two types of title insurance are normally used: Standard Policy of Title Insurance and Extended Coverage Policy.

California Land Title Association (C.L.T.A.)

Standard Policy of Title Insurance, California Land Title Association (C.L.T.A.) This is the type of policy usually issued to home buyers. No physical inspection of the property is required and the buyer is protected against all recorded matters, and certain risks such as forgery and incompetence. When preparing a standard title insurance policy, the title company does not do a survey or check boundary lines

American Land Title Association (A.L.T.A.)

Extended Coverage Policy, American Land Title Association (A.L.T.A.) All risks covered by a standard policy are covered by this policy, as well as other unrecorded hazards such as outstanding mechanic's liens, unrecorded physical easements, facts a correct survey would show, certain water claims, and rights of parties in possession—including tenants and owners under unrecorded deeds.

Lenders may also purchase an A.L.T.A. policy, with the same extended coverage, to protect against loss of their investment in the property because of a defective title. Most title insurance companies now offer an owner's extended coverage policy that may be purchased at added cost called an extended policy. The American Land Title Association offers an owner extended coverage policy known as A.L.T.A. Owner's Policy. It includes the same coverage as a standard policy, with the following additions: (1) protection against claims of parties in physical possession of the property but no recorded interest, (2) reservations in patents, and (3) unmarketability of title.

Review - Standard Policy of Title Insurance
In addition to matters of record, protects against:

- off-record hazards such as forgery, impersonation, or failure of a party to be legally competent to make a contract.
- the possibility that a deed of record was not in fact delivered with intent to convey title.
- the loss which might arise from the lien of federal estate taxes, which is effective without notice upon death.
- the expense incurred in defending the title.

Does NOT Protect Against:

- defects in the title known to the holder to exist at the date of the policy, but not previously disclosed to the title insurance company.
- easements and liens which are not shown by the public records.
- rights or claims of persons in physical possession of the land, but whose claims are not shown by the public records.

- rights or claims not shown by public records, yet which could be discovered by physical inspection of the land.
- mining claims.
- reservations in patents or water rights.
- zoning ordinances.

Preliminary Title Report

A **preliminary title report** (prelim) is a title report that is made when escrow is opened. The prelim is not a policy of title insurance but is only an offer to issue a policy of title insurance in the future for a specific fee. It shows encumbrances, liens or any other items of record that might affect ownership and is used as the basis for the final title insurance policy. Since the prelim lists any liens affecting the property, it would show the existing seller's current loan or loans against the property. Therefore, the seller would appear as the trustor on the existing loan shown in the preliminary title report.

Since all title insurance policies require legal descriptions, the prelim is the best source for the legal description of the property.

Land Descriptions

Exploring new land captured the imagination of the hardy individuals and families who opened up the U.S. frontier. As they moved west and improved the land on which they settled, these pioneers created a need for systematic property description.

A street address was adequate for social contacts and for delivering mail, but it was not precise enough to identify a particular property.

Today, a legal description is required before a deed may be recorded to transfer title to a new owner. There are three common ways to describe property: lot, block, and tract system; rectangular survey system; and metes and bounds.

Review - Methods of Legal Descriptions
- Lot, Block, and Tract System
- Rectangular Survey System
- Metes and Bounds

Lot, Block, and Tract System

Other names for the **lot, block, and tract system** are **lot and block system, subdivision system,** or **recorded map system.** It is the most convenient and easily understood method of land description. When developers divide parcels of land into lots, they are required by the California Subdivision Map Act to prepare and record a subdivision map or plat map. The subdivision map shows the location and boundaries of each separate new lot in the subdivision, and must be recorded in the county recorder's office. After the **subdivision map** has been filed or recorded, it is public knowledge and is available to anyone. Each lot in a subdivision is identified by number, as is the block in which it is located; each lot and block is in a referenced tract. Recorded map descriptions of land are most likely to be found in cities where developers have planned communities and commercial growth areas.

```
        AVENUE                ONE
     100 Feet              100 Feet
                    THE                   NORTH BOULEVARD
85 Feet  Lot #3    THOROUGHFARE  85 Feet  Lot #4

        AVENUE                TWO
     100 Feet              100 Feet
85 Feet  Lot #5            85 Feet  Lot #6
```

Lot 5: block 8 of Clear Lake, recorded in Map Book 21, page 43 recorded in County Records.

U.S. Government Section and Township Survey

By the late 19th Century, the U.S. government had established a system of land description for new territories, states, and other public lands. The **rectangular survey system**, also known as the **U.S. Government Section and Township Survey,** uses imaginary lines to form a grid to locate land. North-south longitude lines, called **meridians,** and east-west latitude lines called **baselines,** intersect to form a starting point from which distances are measured.

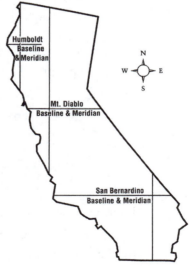

In California there are three such starting points: the Humboldt Baseline and Meridian (northwestern California), the Mt. Diablo Baseline and Meridian (northeastern and central California), and the San Bernardino Baseline and Meridian (southern California).

California has three starting points: the Humboldt Baseline and Meridian, the Mt. Diablo Baseline and Meridian, and the San Bernardino Baseline and Meridian.

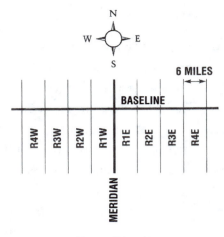

Range Lines

After establishing a starting point at the intersection of a chosen principal meridian and baseline, the government surveyors drew imaginary vertical lines called **range lines** every six miles east and west of the meridian to form columns called **ranges**. Each range was numbered either east or west of the principal meridian. For example, the first range east of the meridian was called Range 1 East (R1E), and the first range west of the meridian was called Range 1 West (R1W).

Imaginary **township lines** were drawn every six miles north and south of the baseline to form a horizontal row or **tier of townships**. These rows were numbered according to their distance from the baseline. For example, the first row of **townships** north of the baseline was called Township 1 North (T1N) and the first row of townships south of the baseline was called Township 1 South (T1S).

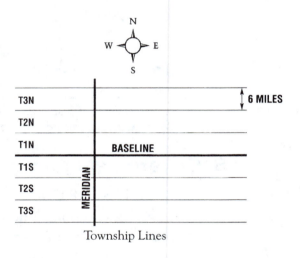

Township Lines

Thus, a grid of squares, called **townships**—each six miles by six miles (36 square miles)—appears. Townships run east-west in ranges and north-south in tiers.

> **Review - Township and Range**
> - Range Lines - every six miles east and west of meridian
> - Township Lines - every six miles north and south of baseline

Each township is described by its location, relative to the intersection of the baseline and meridian we have just discussed. A particular township in the fourth tier north of the baseline and in the third range west of the meridian—with "T" for township and "R" for range—would be described as follows: T4N, R3W, San Bernardino Baseline, and Meridian.

The way to locate T4N, R3W is to start at the intersection of the baseline and meridian and count up (or north) four rows and then count to the left (or west) three rows.

You have learned how to use the intersection of the baseline and meridian as a starting point to locate a particular township. Now look at a township, which is divided into 36 sections, each measuring one mile by one mile. The sections are numbered, starting with section 1 in the northeast corner, and continuing in a snake-like manner to section 36 in the southeast corner. Each section is one mile by one mile and contains 640 acres. A section may then be divided further into quarter sections containing 160 acres each, and then divided into smaller and smaller parcels. These parcels are identified by their compass direction (NE, SE, NW, and SW).

Armed with this knowledge, a student may locate any size parcel, no matter how large or small, by simply dividing the section. Another important number for you to know is 5,280—the number of feet in a mile. You may be asked to calculate an answer on the state exam regarding linear feet around a section. (**Linear feet** refers to length rather than area.)

Review - U.S. Government Section and Township Survey Baseline and Meridians in California
- Humboldt Baseline and Meridian
- Mt. Diablo Baseline and Meridian
- San Bernardino Baseline and Meridian

Facts About Townships and Sections
- Meridians run north and south
- Baselines run east and west
- Range Lines run north and south, parallel to the principal meridian, every six miles
- Township Lines run east and west, parallel to the baseline, every six miles
- Townships are six miles by six miles, 36 square miles
- Sections are one mile by one mile, 36 in each township and contain 640 acres
- 5,280 feet = one mile
- 43,560 square feet = one acre
- 640 acres = one square mile
- 16.5 feet = one rod
- Four miles = distance around a section/square mile

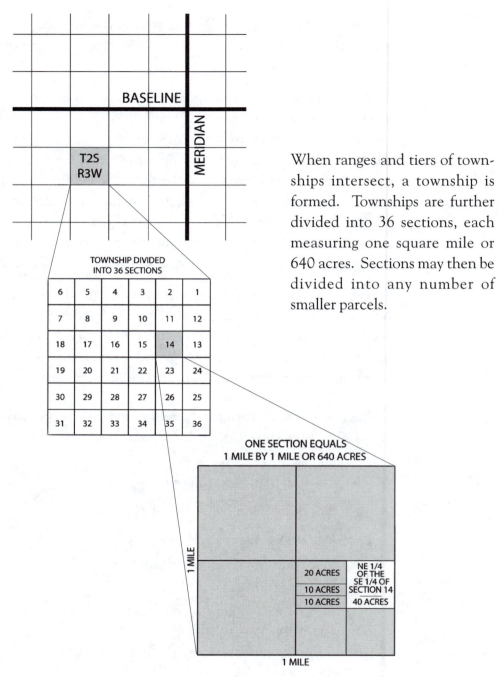

When ranges and tiers of townships intersect, a township is formed. Townships are further divided into 36 sections, each measuring one square mile or 640 acres. Sections may then be divided into any number of smaller parcels.

Government survey system

Using the government survey system, a particular piece of property could be described as the Northeast quarter of the Southeast quarter of section 22, Township 1 North, Range 1 East. It is normally expressed as a legal description in abbreviated form: NE 1/4 of the SE 1/4 of the section 22, T1N, R1E. The quickest way to calculate the acreage contained within this description is to multiply the fractions by 640 acres (acres within a section). 1/4 x 1/4 x 640 = 40 acres.

The government survey system is used for large rural tracts of land (farms).

Metes and Bounds

A **metes and bounds** description of land delineates boundaries and measures distances between landmarks to identify property. Landmarks (trees, boulders, creeks, fences, etc.) are called **monuments**. This is a method of land description in which the dimensions of the property are measured by distance and direction. Land that is irregular in shape or cannot be described using either of the two other methods may have a metes and bounds description.

Think of measuring when you think of metes, and boundaries when you think of bounds. Metes are measures of length: feet, yards, etc. Bounds are measures of boundaries, both natural and man-made: e.g., rivers and roads. Generally, you will only need to recognize this type of description when you see it. A surveyor will measure the distances and establish the legal description.

A metes and bounds description starts at a well-marked point of beginning (POB), and—following the boundaries of the land—measures the distances between landmarks, then returns to the beginning.

> Example: Here is a description of an uneven, hilly parcel of land with an avocado grove in Vista, California:
>
> Beginning at the intersection of the east line of Buena Creek Road and the south line of Cleveland Trail; thence east along the south line of Cleveland Trail 300 feet; thence south 657.5 feet to the center line of Buena Creek; thence northwesterly along the center line of Buena Creek to its intersection with the east line of Buena Creek Road; thence north 325 feet along the east line of Buena Creek road to the place of beginning.

As a real estate agent, you will not be required to be an expert in any of the three land description methods. You will find it helpful to be adequately informed, however, about which method is used for the type of property you most frequently sell.

Review - Methods of Land Description	
Method	**Use**
Section and Township Survey	Rural, undeveloped areas
Lot, Block, and Tract System	Urban areas, cities
Metes and Bounds	Irregular parcels of land

Tax Issues in Transferring Real Property

Most people have questions about taxes in a real estate transaction. It may not be apparent, but taxation is an indirect—yet important—factor in affecting the value of property. In this chapter, we will see how taxes impact buying and selling. As a student, use this chapter for general knowledge about real estate taxation; however, always refer your clients and customers to an expert for their own tax information as well as current tax laws.

Property Taxes

The idea of land taxation began in 1086 in England with the compilation of all land and resources into the Domesday Book commissioned by William the Conqueror. Taxation was based on the notion that taxes should be assessed according to an owner's ability to pay. At that time, such an ability was reliably determined by how much and how good the owner's agricultural holdings were—since most people's income came almost entirely from products of their land. Therefore, land became the basis for determining the amount of tax imposed.

Proposition 13

As of June 1978, Proposition 13 became the measure to use in assessing property in California. If there had been no change in ownership since March 1, 1975, the value of the property at that time was used as a starting point to assess the property (the initial full cash value). Under the new law, the maximum annual tax was limited to 1% of full cash value (market value). After that, a maximum increase of no more than 2% per year was allowed. Since June 1978, whenever property transfers to a new owner, it is re-assessed at 1% of fair market value, not necessarily the new sales price. Commonly, local taxes may be added to the 1% assessment.

Transfer of Ownership

Upon a change in ownership of real property unless the change is between spouses, a new assessment is made based on 1% of the new purchase price. For example, if the sale price is $350,000, the new property tax would be $3,500. Any person buying real property is required to file a change-in-ownership statement with the county recorder or assessor. The change-in-ownership statement must be filed within 45 days of the change date. Failure to report a change results in a $100 penalty. A supplementary tax bill will be sent to the new owner, reflecting the change in taxes as of the date of transfer.

Proposition 60

Homeowners who are at least 55 years of age may sell their homes and transfer their present base-year property tax value to another home of equal or lesser value. The new home must be in the same county, or in a county that allows Proposition 60 to be used. The base-year property value is whatever the value of the home was on March 1, 1975, or in the year they purchased the property after that time. Thus, they are allowed to continue with the original figure as their tax base, adding a maximum of 2% every year, to arrive at their tax bill, rather than be required to step up to 1% of the value of their new purchase.

> Example: Maggie and Marvin bought their home in 1976 for $80,000. Now that the kids are grown and the house is too big for them, they decided to sell and move to a smaller home in the same town. Over the years, their property had appreciated, and now sold for $250,000. The tax assessment on their original home was $102,400 at the time of the sale, and they were allowed to carry that to the new property because of Proposition 60. Instead of being taxed at 1% of the price of the new house ($250,000), their new tax bill was based on the assessed value of the one they sold.
>
> Comparison of Maggie and Marvin's Tax Bills
> * $250,000 x 1%= $2,500 tax bill
> * $102,400 x 1%= $1,024 tax bill

Assessment and Collection of Taxes

Real property is taxed at the local level through ad valorem property taxes, special assessments and transfer taxes. **Ad valorem** means according to value.

Taxes are imposed on real or personal property to raise money so the government can carry out its general duties. All property within the locality of the taxing authority, whether it is the state or local government, will be taxed unless specifically exempt.

Decisions are carried out by officials during the process of assessing and collecting taxes. The following is a list of officials responsible for the correct taxation of real property.

Implementing the Job of Taxation

*   County Board of Supervisors: determines the tax rate (limited to 1% of fair market value) plus any county bond debt or other assessments.

*   City or County Auditor: maintains tax rolls (public records identifying parcels of land to be taxed, the owner and the assessed value.)

- City or County Assessor: assesses the value of all taxable property in the county yearly to establish the tax base and then mails out the tax bills. The annual assessments appear in the **Assessment Roll or Tax Roll**, a public record. Real property is assessed at 100% of fair market value. The tax bill identifies a property by an assessor's parcel number, which is not a legal description but is used for taxation purposes only.

- City or County Tax Collector: decides how much tax is to be paid by each property owner, depending on individual assessments. Land and improvements are assessed separately, but taxed at one rate.

- City Councils: sets property tax rates for cities.

- Assessment Appeals Board: appeals board for taxpayers' complaints about unfair taxation.

Tax Calendar

A **fiscal year**, or tax year, is used for tax purposes as compared to a **calendar year**. The fiscal or tax year starts on July 1 and goes through June 30 of the following year.

Taxation Time Line						
Jan. 1	July 1	Nov. 1	Dec. 10	Feb.1	Apr. 10	June 30
taxes become a lien	tax year starts	1st installment due	1st installment delinquent	2nd installment due	2nd installment delinquent	tax year ends

On January 1, preceding the tax year, property taxes become a lien on real property. The first installment is due November 1, but no later than December 10. The second installment is due February 1, but no later than April 10.

Property Taxes are Due

Mnemonic - "NDFA"

N o	**N** ovember 1	(1st installment due)
D arn	**D** ecember 10	(delinquent after this date)
F ooling	**F** ebruary 1	(2nd installment due)
A round	**A** pril 10	(delinquent after this date)

Tax Sale

If a property owner does not pay the tax when it is due, the property is declared tax-defaulted and is then listed as a delinquent account by the tax collector. The property owner (or any interested party) may redeem the property from the tax collector by paying the total amount of all defaulted taxes. While the property is in a tax-defaulted status, the owner does not actually lose title and keeps possession for five years. If the taxes are not paid within that five-year period a tax sale takes place, and the property may be sold at public auction to the highest bidder for cash. At that time the owner loses possession and the buyer receives a **tax deed.**

> **Steps in a Tax Sale**
> 1. June 8 Delinquent Tax List Published
> 2. Tax-Delinquent Property Status
> 3. Five-Year Redemption Period (Owner has Possession)
> 4. Unredeemed Property Deeded to State
> 5. Tax Collector Publishes Notice of Intent to Sell
> 6. Public Auction Tax Sale
> 7. Tax Deed to Buyer

Tax Exemptions

Homeowners Exemption

A property owner may claim a **homeowners exemption** in California on a residence that is both owned and occupied at 12:01 a.m. on January 1. Claims must be filed by February 15 following the change of ownership. If the prior owner claimed the homeowners exemption, claim forms are mailed in the beginning of January for filing by February 15. The exemption reduces the assessed value by $7,000 and reduces the tax bill by at least $70.

It is the homeowner's responsibility to apply for the exemption. To receive the full exemption, the claim must be filed with the Assessor's office between January 1 and February 15, or within 30 days of a Notice of Supplemental Assessment. (A late filing is accepted from February 16 to December 10 for 80% of the exemption.) Your exemption automatically continues each year as long as you continue to own and occupy the property as your primary residence. It is the homeowner's responsibility to terminate the exemption when no longer eligible.

Example of a Homeowners Exemption	
Assessed Value	$350,000.00
Minus Homeowners Exemption	$ - 7,000.00
Taxable amount	$343,000.00

Veterans' Exemption

Another exemption available to some homeowners is the **veterans' exemption**. A resident of California who has been in the military during wartime is eligible to take a $4,000 tax exemption. If the resident takes the regular homeowners exemption, the veterans' exemption may not be taken on the same dwelling, but may be used for another property owned by the veteran.

Other Exemptions

Other tax exemptions are available for a variety of property owners. Certain senior citizens may qualify for tax relief. Churches, nonprofit organizations, and owners of timberlands, young orchards, or grapevines less than three years old may also qualify for tax exemptions.

Special Assessments

When specific improvements that benefit a certain area are needed—such as underground utilities, sewers or streets—special assessments are levied to pay for them. The difference between a special assessment and property taxes is that the latter are used to operate the government in general, whereas special assessments are used for specific local purposes. Special assessment liens are placed on the properties involved and usually paid at the same time as property taxes. The liens created by special assessments are equal in priority to general tax liens.

Street Improvement Act of 1911

One of the laws that empowers cities and counties to levy a special assessment to repair streets is the **Street Improvement Act of 1911**. This act is used more than any other for street improvements in this state. Each owner is assessed for the improvement based on the front footage of the property. The amount of the assessment appears on the tax bill as a lien against the property. The assessment may be paid off at any time or paid in equal installments during the term of the bonds.

Mello-Roos Community Facilities Act of 1982

Mello-Roos covers a wide variety of community improvements, other than bond acts, for special assessments such as streets and sewers. In some counties, Mello-Roos is on the tax bill, and in other counties it is collected separately. Refer to Chapter 7 for the Mello-Roos disclosures.

Documentary Transfer Tax

Documentary transfer tax is required whenever real property is transferred from one owner to another. In most cases, it is based on $.55 per $500 of purchase price, or $1.10 per $1,000 of purchase price. The money goes to local government, either city or county.

The full price of the property is taxed at the above rate if the sale is all cash, or if a new loan is involved, where the seller gets all cash. The tax is levied only on the **equity** transferred (or consideration) if the buyer assumes an existing loan. The tax is usually paid through escrow or at the time the deed is recorded. Appendix A includes documentary transfer tax calculations.

> Example: If a buyer purchased a home for $100,000 assuming an existing loan of $50,000, the tax would be based on the $50,000 the buyer paid as a down payment, or the new money put into the transaction. $50,000 divided by $1,000 equals 50, therefore 50 times $1.10 equals $55.00 for the tax.

The county recorder places stamps on the recorded grant deed to indicate the amount of the documentary transfer tax paid. These are sometimes called "doc stamps".

Tax Benefits of Home Ownership

The federal government taxes individuals based on their earnings by means of a progressive income tax. In a progressive tax, the more you earn the higher your tax rate. The important consideration of a progressive tax is that the tax rate on which the taxpayer's obligation increases rises with additional levels of income "brackets". One of the major reasons for buying real estate is to get relief from taxes.

The tax benefits of home ownership differ from those available to owners of investment property. The legal reduction of tax liability, otherwise known as tax shelter, is available to all owners of a primary residence as well as to a taxpayer owning investment property. Different rules apply to each type of property, however, and must be followed carefully to earn the desired tax shelter. Tax benefits of income property ownership will be discussed in Chapter 14.

Personal Residence

Tax Deductions

Tax deductions are another way a homeowner can limit tax liability. **Tax deductions** are expenses that a taxpayer is allowed to deduct from taxable income. Certain expenses are deductible to homeowners, such as interest and property taxes on first and second homes. Deducting maintenance expenses, depreciation, and capital improvements is not allowed. New tax laws may or may not allow a deduction for the loss on the sale of a personal residence.

Review - Tax Deductions on Personal Residence

Deductible

1. Interest
2. Property taxes

Non-Deductible

1. Maintenance
2. Depreciation
3. Capital improvements

Sale of the Property

Individuals are generally permitted to exclude from taxable income up to $250,000 ($500,000 for married couples) of gain on the sale of their principal residence. To qualify, the taxpayer must have owned and used the property as a principal residence for at least two years during the five years prior to the sale or exchange. The exclusion is generally not allowed more than once every two years. Taxpayers who fail to meet either of these two-year requirements because of an employment change, health problems, or other unforeseen circumstances may be eligible for a partial exclusion, scaled back to the amount of time they did occupy the residence compared to the two-year requirement.

This exclusion replaces the "rollover" rules that have allowed taxpayers to defer all or part of the gain on a sale or exchange of a principal residence that is replaced with a new principal residence within a four-year period. In addition, the once-in-a-lifetime $125,000 exclusion on a sale of a principal residence for taxpayers age 55 and over has been replaced. The new exclusion rules are effective for sales or exchanges of a principal residence occurring after May 6, 1997. However, in certain circumstances taxpayers may elect to apply the old rules (i.e., the rollover, or the $125,000 exclusion).

Capital Gain or Loss

The cost of **capital improvements**, or physical improvements made to the property, such as the cosmetic addition of a new roof, swimming pool, or driveway, may not be deducted yearly, but may be added to the cost basis of the property when it is sold. The **cost basis** is usually the original purchase price of the property. When capital improvements are added to the original cost basis, the **adjusted cost basis** is the result.

The **taxable gain** generally is the difference between the purchase price plus capital improvements and the price when sold. Closing costs on the sale also may be subtracted from the sales price. The gain, or profit, after the $250,000 ($500,000) exclusion from the sale of a personal residence is then taxed according to current capital gains tax law.

Calculate Capital Gain on Sale of Personal Property

1. **Calculate the Adjusted Cost Basis of the Property**
   Add the cost of improvements and subtract the depreciation from the property.

Purchase price (cost basis)	$250,000
Add cost of improvements	+ 50,000
Adjusted cost basis	$300,000

2. **Calculate the Adjusted Selling Price of the Property**

Selling price	$400,000
Subtract the expenses of sale	- 24,000
Adjusted selling price	$ 376,000

3. **Calculate the Capital Gain (or loss)**

Adjusted selling price	$376,000
Subtract adjusted cost basis	- $300,000
Capital gain (or loss)	$ 76,000

Hazard Insurance

Lenders require hazard insurance that covers the outstanding loan on the property. There are many casualty insurance companies that provide hazard insurance. In most cases, the lender is the loss payee on the policy and will receive the proceeds on a claim. The proceeds then will be used to pay for the repairs.

Summary

Escrow is the deposit of paperwork and funds with a third party to process the sale of real property. An escrow is a small and short-lived trust arrangement. The **escrow holder** coordinates communications between the principals, the agents involved and other professionals (lender, title company, pest control company). Every escrow has two requirements to be valid: a binding contract between the buyer and seller and conditional delivery of transfer documents to a third party. Escrow companies must comply with the Real Estate Settlement Procedures Act (RESPA).

The California Association of Realtors Residential Purchase Agreement and Joint Escrow Instructions, seems to offer the best approach in the escrow process. The sales contract should incorporate the addendum (mutual changes by the buyer and seller). Escrow starts when a real estate agent brings the signed purchase agreement to the escrow holder. The escrow holder keeps all documents and funds until the terms of the escrow are completed. The escrow process is a time-consuming detailed process. Included in the escrow process is the title search. **Title insurance** companies search, gather public title records, analyze records, and issue policies of title insurance. There are two major types of title insurance policies available: the C.L.T.A. standard and the A.L.T.A. extended coverage. Consumers are responsible for all items not included in the title insurance coverage.

Closing costs are either recurring and nonrecurring. The buyer prepays recurring closing costs to help offset expenses that will continue as long as the buyer owns the property. Nonrecurring closing costs are one-time charges paid upon escrow closing. The buyer and seller negotiate the payment of escrow fees, title insurance, and closing costs. Traditionally the buyer and seller are responsible for certain escrow closing costs. These traditions vary throughout California. Escrow and closing practices are also different between Northern and Southern California.

A **marketable title** is a title that a reasonable person would accept as clear and free from likely challenge. Title insurance is a contract that extends protection against risks depending on the type of policy purchased. An **American Land Title Association (A.L.T.A.)** owner's policy offers the same coverage as a standard policy with additional coverage.

Chapter 8 Review Exercises

▌Matching Exercise

Instructions: Look up the meaning of the terms in the Glossary, then write the letter of the matching term on the blank line before its definition. Answers are in Appendix B.

Terms

a. A.L.T.A. Owner's Policy
b. abstract of title
c. abstractors
d. ad valorem
e. assessment roll
f. baseline
g. beneficiary statement
h. C.L.T.A. standard policy
i. calendar year
j. complete escrow
k. documentary transfer tax
l. escrow
m. escrow holder
n. escrow instructions
o. fiscal year
p. guarantee of title
q. homeowner exemption

r. impound account
s. linear feet
t. marketable title
u. metes and bounds
v. monument
w. plat map
x. preliminary title report
y. property taxes
z. proration
aa. section
bb. special assessments
cc. Street Improvement Act of 1911
dd. tax deed
ee. title insurance
ff. title plant
gg. township
hh. vesting

Definitions

1. _____ Land description that delineates boundaries and measures distances between landmarks to identify property.

2. _____ Acts as a neutral agent of both buyer and seller.

3. _____ The way title will be taken.

4. _____ Begins on January 1 and continues through December 31 of the same year.

5. _____ Written summary of all useful documents discovered in a title search.

6. _____ A list of all taxable property showing the assessed value of each parcel; establishes the tax base.

7. _____ The storage facility of a title insurance company in which it has accumulated complete title records or properties in its area.

8. _____ A fixed landmark used in a metes-and-bounds land description.

9. _____ Taxes used to operate the government in general.

10. _____ An offer to issue a policy of title insurance in the future for a specific fee.

11. _____ An assurance of clear title.

12. _____ A small and short-lived trust arrangement.

13. _____ Refers to length rather than area.

14. _____ Good or clear saleable title reasonably free from risk of litigation over possible defects.

15. _____ A Latin prefix meaning "according to value".

16. _____ Starts on July 1 and runs through June 30 of the following year; used for real property tax purposes.

17. _____ A grid of squares—each six miles by six miles (36 square miles)

18. _____ All terms of the escrow instructions have been met.

19. _____ A policy of title insurance covering all matters of record.

20. _____ Historically, a person who searches out anything affecting the title to real property and summarizes the information in the findings.

21. _____ The division and distribution of expenses and/or income between the buyer and seller of property as of the date of closing or settlement.

22. _____ A survey line running east and west, used as a reference when mapping land.

23. _____ An area of land, one square mile, or 640 acres; 1/36 of a township.

24. _____ An owner's extended title insurance policy.

25. _____ A trust account set up for funds set aside for future costs relating to a property.

26. _____ Map of a subdivision indicating the location and boundaries of individual lots.

27. _____ Taxes used for specific local purposes.

28. _____ An insurance policy that protects the insured against loss or damage due to defects in the property's title.

29. _____ Law that empowers cities and counties to levy a special assessment to repair streets.

30. _____ A statement of the unpaid condition of a loan and describes the condition of the debt.

▌Multiple Choice Questions

Instructions: Circle your response and go to Appendix B to read the complete explanation for each question.

1. Escrow instructions must be:
   a. chartered.
   b. executed.
   c. notarized.
   d. recorded.

2. The reason for using an escrow when a deed of trust is conveyed is to:
   a. comply with the Civil Code.
   b. ensure that the conditions and instructions of the agreement are satisfied.
   c. allow for recordation of the deed.
   d. provide for third-party liability.

3. Which of the following best describes "complete" escrow?
   a. It is equivalent to a "perfect" escrow.
   b. The escrow holder has ceased being an agent for both parties.
   c. All escrow instructions have been carried out.
   d. All services of the escrow holder are involved.

4. Which of the following statements concerning escrow is correct?
   a. A "perfect" escrow exists when the buyer's closing statement and the seller's closing statement are exactly identical.
   b. In order for the escrow to be able to close, the buyer may be required to pay more than the amount stated in the escrow instructions.
   c. The amount in the final closing statement must be the same as the amount in the escrow instructions.
   d. None of the above

5. Which of the following statements regarding escrow procedures is correct?
   a. A broker may hold an escrow for compensation for other parties if the broker has no interest in the transaction.
   b. When the escrow requirements have been met, the escrow agency changes from being agent of both parties to an agent of each party.
   c. When the escrow holder is in possession of a binding contract between the buyer and seller, it is said to be a complete escrow.
   d. The escrow officer acts as an arbitrator of disputes between buyer and seller.

6. An escrow agent is authorized to:
   a. give the buyer advice about available financing.
   b. change the escrow instructions when asked to do so by the listing broker.
   c. call for funding of the buyer's loan.
   d. authorize a pest control company to make corrective repairs.

7. If an escrow holder receives pest control reports from two different companies the escrow officer should:
   a. submit the estimate requiring the most work.
   b. contact both inspectors and determine which of the two reports should be accepted.
   c. contact the broker to ask for instructions from the buyer and seller.
   d. contact the broker to ask for instructions from the seller.

8. Which of the following items would most likely appear as a credit in the seller's closing statement?
   a. Prepaid taxes
   b. Delinquent assessment lien
   c. An assumed loan
   d. Title insurance premium

9. If a buyer assumes an existing loan when purchasing a single-family residence, the settlement statement at close of escrow would show the assumption of the loan as:
   a. a debit to the buyer.
   b. a debit to the seller.
   c. a credit to the lender.
   d. neither a credit nor a debit.

10. How would the purchase price of a residence appear on the buyer's closing statement?
    a. Credit to buyer, debit to seller
    b. Debit to buyer, credit to seller
    c. Credit to buyer
    d. Debit to buyer

11. Which of the following is regarded as a recurring cost in a closing statement?
    a. Escrow fees
    b. Recording fees
    c. Impound accounts
    d. Premiums for title insurance

12. While conducting a title search, a title company might examine the documents in the _____ office.
    a. County Clerk's
    b. Federal Land
    c. County Recorder's
    d. All of the above

13. An abstract of title is a(n):
    a. brief description of the subject property.
    b. summary of all facts regarding evidence of title.
    c. guarantee of the validity of the title to property.
    d. informal description of the vesting.

14. A buyer who wishes to insure title to real property when it is purchased should secure a(n):
    a. guarantee of title.
    b. abstract of title.
    c. certificate of title.
    d. title insurance policy.

15. A.L.T.A. title insurance exceeds the protection afforded by a C.L.T.A. standard policy in guarding against:
    a. errors in the sequence of recording deeds of trust.
    b. deeds of reconveyance issued by a minor or a person not capable to make the transaction.
    c. relocation of property lines as a result of a formal survey.
    d. existing easements and liens shown in public records.

16. Which of the following title insurance policies protects against all risks?
    a. Standard policy
    b. Extended policy
    c. A.L.T.A. policy
    d. No policy insures against all risks.

17. Buyer Taylor purchased a parcel of real property and received a standard policy of title insurance. Taylor would be protected against all of the following except:
    a. the grantor's lack of mental capacity.
    b. forgery of the grantor's signature on the deed.
    c. easements and liens on the property not shown by public records.
    d. the delivery of a deed in the chain of title without actual intent to convey title.

18. When buying a home, a purchaser was given a grant deed and a standard policy of title insurance. Which of the following is warranted by the seller but is not covered by the standard policy of title insurance?
    a. The grantor is legally competent.
    b. The grantor actually signed the deed.
    c. The grantor has placed no undisclosed liens against the property.
    d. There are no forged deeds in the chain of title.

19. The standard policy of title insurance represents the final result of three successive processes. Which of the following would **not** be considered one of the processes?
    a. Examination and investigation of title
    b. Determination of the amount of insurance
    c. Protection of the insured against loss of title
    d. Determination of the correct boundary lines by a survey of the insured property

20. Which of the following is not covered by title insurance?
    a. A zoning ordinance, regulation, or plan
    b. Loss due to a missing signature of a spouse on a deed to community property
    c. Unpaid county property tax not shown in the policy
    d. Incompetence of a former seller

21. Which system of land description employs meridians and baselines?
    a. Metes and bounds
    b. Rectangular survey system
    c. Subdivision system
    d. Lot, block, and tract system

22. County governments levy taxes through:
    a. property taxes.
    b. special assessments.
    c. transfer taxes.
    d. all of the above.

23. An example of an ad valorem tax would be:
    a. income tax.
    b. estate tax.
    c. bridge toll.
    d. property tax.

24. How do special property tax assessments differ from annual property tax assessments?
    a. Annual assessments have priority over special assessments.
    b. Special assessments are imposed only by local authorities.
    c. Judicial foreclosure is required for unpaid special assessments.
    d. Special assessments provide for local improvements.

25. After a property is declared tax-defaulted for failure to pay property taxes, the occupant of the property:
    a. must vacate immediately.
    b. must pay rent to the State of California.
    c. may continue to reside on the property unhindered.
    d. is freed of tax obligations immediately.

Real Estate Finance: Loans

9
Chapter

Introduction

Imagine buying a house and being required to pay the total price in cash. With the average price of a single-family home being so high, buying a home would be unthinkable without the practical benefit of financing. By allowing a home buyer to obtain a loan for the difference between the sales price and the down payment, real estate lenders have provided the solution to the problem of how property can be bought and sold without the requirement of an all-cash sale.

What started out as a simple loan by a local bank—with an agreement that the borrower pay it all back in a timely manner—is now a complex subject. Buyers and sellers need to rely on experts to explain all the choices there are on financing the purchase or sale of property. You, as a real estate licensee, are one of the experts to whom they will turn.

Learning Objectives

After reading this chapter, you will be able to:

- describe the different types of promissory notes.
- explain trust deeds and mortgages.
- identify special clauses in financing instruments.
- discuss how to finance real estate property.
- name two types of loans secured by trust deeds.

Promissory Notes and Security Instruments

When a loan is made, the borrower signs a promissory note, or note—as it is called, which states that a certain amount of money has been borrowed. The **promissory note**, then, is the evidence of the debt.

When money is loaned for financing real property, some kind of **collateral**, or security, is usually required of the borrower, as well as the promise to repay the loan. That means the lender wants some concrete assurance of getting the money back beyond the borrower's written promise to pay. The property being bought or borrowed against is used as the security, or collateral, for the debt. The lender feels more secure about making the loan if assured of the property ownership in case of default, or nonpayment, of the loan. Then the lender can sell it to get the loan money back.

In California the most common **security instrument** for the note is a trust deed. After signing the promissory note, the borrower is required to **execute** (sign) a trust deed, which is the security guaranteeing loan repayment. The borrower (**trustor**) has possession of the property but transfers naked legal title of the property to a third party to hold as security for the lender in case of default on the loan. This process, known as **hypothecation**, allows a borrower to remain in possession of the property while using it to secure the loan. If the borrower does not make payments according to the terms of the agreement, he or she then loses the rights of possession and ownership. Hypothecation differs from a **pledge** because actual possession of pledged property is given to the lender. For example, in a pledge, personal property—such as stock certificates—are delivered to a lender, or jewelry is delivered to a pawn broker. Once the loan is repaid, the personal property is returned to the borrower.

The lender holds the original promissory note and the trust deed until the loan is repaid. The trust deed allows the lender, in case of loan default, to order the third party to sell the property described in the deed. Both promissory notes and security instruments will be explained in detail in later chapters.

Understanding Promissory Notes

A promissory note serves as evidence of the debt and is a written agreement between a lender and a borrower to document a loan. It is a promise to pay back a certain sum of money at specified terms at an agreed-upon time. Sometimes it is called "the note", "a debt repayment contract", or more informally, it could be called an "IOU".

A promissory note is a negotiable instrument. A **negotiable instrument** is a written unconditional promise or order to pay a certain amount of money at a definite time or on demand. A negotiable instrument is easily transferable from one person to another meaning it can be bought and sold. The most common type of negotiable instrument is an ordinary bank check. A check is an order to the bank to pay money to the person named. A promissory note is the same thing. It can be transferred by **endorsement** (signature), just like a check. If correctly prepared, it is considered the same as cash.

The **maker** is the person borrowing the money, or making the note. The note is a personal obligation of the borrower and a complete contract in itself, between the borrower and lender. The **holder** is the person loaning the money, or the one holding the note. A **holder in due course** is an innocent party who purchased a negotiable instrument without knowledge of any defects.

In order to be considered a negotiable instrument, however, the document must be consistent with statutory (legal) definition, and all of the following elements must be present.

Requirements for a Valid Promissory Note

A Promissory Note is:

- an unconditional written promise to pay a certain sum of money.

- made by one person to another, both able to legally enter into a contract.

- signed by the maker, or borrower.

- payable on demand or at a definite time.

- paid to bearer or to order.

- voluntarily delivered by the borrower and accepted by the lender.

In addition to showing the amount borrowed, a promissory note sets the terms of the loan, such as the interest rate, the repayment plan, and an acceleration clause in the event of default. With that information you can calculate the payments using a financial calculator, printed amortization schedule, or software.

Interest Rate

The interest charged on most real estate loans is **simple interest**—interest paid only on the principal owed. The interest rate stated in the note is called the **nominal** or "**named**" rate. The **effective interest rate** is the rate the borrower is actually paying, commonly called "the annual percentage rate" (APR). Lenders are compensated for their risk in the form of interest rates. If the lender thinks the borrower is a high risk, the lender will charge a higher interest rate for the privilege of borrowing their money. The lower the risk, the lower the rate.

Some promissory notes have a fixed interest rate, where the interest rate and term do not change over the life of the loan. Others may include a fluctuating interest rate as well as changes in the payment over the life of the loan. Based on this, some loans are called fixed-rate loans and others adjustable rate loans.

Limits on Interest Rates — Usury

The California Usury Law makes a distinction between loans that are exempt from the law and those that are covered under the Usury Law. Exempt loans include: loans made by banks, savings and loans, and credit unions; real estate loans made directly or arranged by a mortgage loan broker; and seller carry back loans. The Usury Law limits interest rates on hard money real estate loans made directly by private individuals without the services of a real estate broker. The limit is 10% on loans where the funds are used primarily for personal, family, or household purposes. All other loans made by a nonexempt lender are limited to the higher of 10% or 5% plus the discount rate charged by the San Francisco Federal Reserve Bank.

Types of Repayment Plans

A promissory note may stand alone as an unsecured loan or note, or may be secured by either a trust deed or mortgage. The promissory note, however, is the prime instrument; and if there are conflicts in the terms of the note and trust deed or mortgage, generally the terms of the note are controlling. The promissory note terms create the basis for the repayment plan. There are several types of repayment plans, each with a different kind of obligation made clear by the terms of the note. The terms of the note include interest, repayment plan, and default. Some repayment plans are: (1) a single payment of principal and interest at the end of the loan term, (2) interest-only payments, (3) partially amortized with a balloon payment, and (4) fully amortized payments.

Single Payment of Principal and Interest

Some loans have no regular payments of interest and/or principal. Instead, the loan is paid off all at once, at a specified future date. This payment includes the entire principal amount and the accrued interest.

Interest-Only Payments

An interest-only loan offers consumers greater purchasing power, increased cash flow and is a very popular alternative to traditional fixed-rate loans. The **interest-only loan** is also called a **straight loan** or **term loan**. It calls for regular interest payments during the term of the note. The interest rate is generally higher on a straight note and the principal does not decrease. A large payment is made at the end of the term to repay the principal and any remaining interest. This type of loan works well for people who only want to stay in a home for a just a few years. If the borrower plans to live in the house for only three to five years, an interest-only loan may be the right choice. With a conventional 30 year mortgage, most of the payment is applied directly to the interest of the loan with very little applied to the principal. With an interest-only loan the borrower will have a lower payment and have almost the same principal balance at the end of three-five years as if a conventional loan had been selected.

Partially Amortized (Installment) Payments

This type of repayment schedule is used to create lower payments. The **partially amortized installment note** calls for regular, level payments on the principal and interest during the term of the loan. Since the loan does not fully amortize over the original term, there is still a remaining principal loan balance. **Amortization** is described as the liquidation of a financial obligation. The last installment, called a **balloon payment**, is much larger than any of the other payments because it includes all of the remaining principal and interest. Balloon payments can have extra risks because the borrower may need to refinance the property—possibly at higher interest rates.

Amortized (Installment) Payments

With installment payments, the loan is repaid in equal payments, typically monthly, until the loan has been repaid in full. The principal and interest are calculated for the term of the loan, and payments are determined by dividing the total by the number of payments in the term of the loan. Regular, periodic payments to include both interest and principal are made, which pay off the debt completely by the end of the term. This type of loan is fully amortized because the loan and interest are fully paid when the last payment is made.

Escrow No. _____ Title Order No. _____

INSTALLMENT NOTE - INTEREST INCLUDED
(Balloon Payment)

$ _____ _____, California _____, 20____

FOR VALUE RECEIVED, we, or either of us, promise to pay in lawful money of the United States of America, to

_____

_____

or order, at place designated by payee, the principal sum of _____

_____ dollars,

with interest in like lawful money from _____, 20____ at _____ per cent

per annum on the amounts of principal sum remaining unpaid from time to time.

Principal and interest payable in _____ installments of _____

_____

or more each, on the _____ day of each and every _____ beginning on the

_____ day of _____, 20____ and continuing until _____

at which time the entire unpaid balance of principal and interest hereunder shall be due and payable.

Each payment shall be credited first on interest then due and the remainder of principal; and interest shall thereupon cease upon the principal so credited. Should default be made in payment of any installment of principal or interest when due the whole sum of principal and interest shall become immediately due at the option of the holder of this note. If action be instituted on this note I promise to pay such sum as the Court may fix as attorney's fees. This note is secured by a Deed of Trust in which the maker of this note is referred to as "Trustor".

THE FOLLOWING PARAGRAPH IS ONLY APPLICABLE ON ONE TO FOUR RESIDENTIAL UNITS:

This note is subject to Section 2966 of the Civil Code, which provides that the holder of this note shall give written notice to the Trustor, or his successor in interest, of prescribed information at least 90 and not more than 150 days before any balloon payment is due.

_____ _____

_____ _____

DO NOT DESTROY THIS NOTE
When paid, this note, with Deed of Trust securing same, must be surrendered to Trustee for cancellation before reconveyance will be made.

FD-30C INSTALLMENT NOTE - INTEREST INCLUDED (BALLOON PAYMENT)

There are loans that are not fully amortized. This occurs when the borrower makes lower payments than what should be made on a fully amortized loan. The difference between what should be paid and what is actually paid is added to the principal balance of the loan. This is called **negative amortization** and the principal increases instead of decreases.

Fixed-Rate Fully Amortized Note

A fully amortized fixed-rate note describes a loan with an interest rate that is fixed and payments that are level for the life of the loan. This type of note is the most common type with institutional lenders. It is characterized by regular, periodic payments of fixed amounts, to include both interest and principal, which pay off the debt completely by the end of the term.

> **Review - Two Features of Fixed-Rate Fully Amortized Loans**
> 1. Interest rate remains fixed for the life of the loan.
> 2. Payments remain level for the life of the loan and are structured to repay the loan at the end of the loan term.

During the early amortization period, a large percentage of the monthly payment is used for paying the interest. As the loan is paid down, more of the monthly payment is applied to principal. A typical 30-year fixed-rate mortgage takes 22.5 years of level payments to pay half of the original loan amount. Typically, the longer the term of the loan, the lower the monthly payment. However, the total financing costs over the life of the loan will be higher.

Although fixed-rate mortgages are available for 30 years, 20 years, 15 years and even 10 years, the most common fixed-rate loans are 15-year and 30-year mortgages. There are also biweekly mortgages, which shorten the loan by calling for half the monthly payment every two weeks. (Since there are 52 weeks in a year, the borrower makes 26 payments, or 13 months worth, every year.)

Adjustable Rate Mortgage (ARM)

Lenders have created alternative payment plans, such as the adjustable-rate mortgage, which allow borrowers to qualify for larger loans and at the same time help maintain the lender's investment return. An **adjustable-rate mortgage** (ARM) is one whose interest rate is tied to a movable economic index. The interest rate in the note varies upward or downward over the term of the loan, depending on the agreed-upon index. To protect the borrower from wild swings in interest rates there is usually a limit on how much the interest rate can change on an annual basis, as well as a lifetime cap, or limit, on changes in interest rate.

A lender may offer several choices of interest rates, terms, payments, or adjustment periods to a borrower with an ARM. The initial interest rate, or **qualifying rate**, is determined by the current rate of the chosen index. Then, a **margin**, which might be anywhere from one-to-three percentage points, is added to the initial interest rate to determine the actual beginning rate the borrower will pay. The margin is maintained for the life of the loan and does not change. The interest rate may change, however, as the chosen index changes, depending on the economic conditions that lead it.

The borrower's payment will stay the same for a specified time period, which might be six months or a year, depending on the agreement with the lender. At the agreed-upon time, the lender re-evaluates the loan to determine if the index has changed, either upward or downward, and calculates a new payment based on the changed interest rate plus the same margin. That will then be the borrower's payment until the next six months or year pass, and the loan will be reviewed again. The annual maximum increase is usually one to two percent while the lifetime cap is usually not allowed to go beyond five or six points above the starting rate.

Generally, adjustable-rate financing benefits the bankers because it allows for an inflow of extra cash during times of higher interest rates. In other words, the borrower's payments will increase because the interest rate will go up; therefore, more money will flow into the financial institution.

What is a Security Instrument?

The claim a creditor (lender) has in the property of a debtor (borrower) is called a security interest. The **security interest** allows certain assets of a borrower to be set aside so that a creditor can sell them if the borrower defaults on the loan. Proceeds from the sale of that property can be taken to pay off the debt. The rights and duties of lenders and borrowers are described in a document called a security instrument. **Security instruments** are used to secure promissory notes.

The security instruments used to secure the interest for the lender are the deed of trust, mortgage, and contract for sale. In California and other states, deeds of trust are the principal instruments used to secure loans on real property. Mortgages accomplish the same thing as deeds of trust and are used in other states as security for real property loans. As you will learn, trust deeds and mortgages differ in the number of parties involved, statute of limitations, and transfer of title. In fact, the only thing trust deeds and mortgages have in common is that the property is used as security for the debt. You will hear the term mortgage used loosely in California, as in mortgage company, mortgage broker, and mortgage payment—but the mortgage referenced here usually refers to a deed of trust.

Deed of Trust

In California, the deed of trust (or trust deed) is the most commonly used security instrument in real estate finance. A **trust deed** is a security instrument that conveys title of real property from a trustor to a trustee to hold as security for the beneficiary for payment of a debt. There are three parties to a trust deed: the borrower (**trustor**), lender (**beneficiary**), and a neutral third party called a **trustee**.

The trustor (borrower) signs the promissory note and the trust deed and gives them to the beneficiary (lender) who holds them for the term of the loan. Under the trust deed, the trustor has **equitable title** and the trustee has "bare" or "naked" legal title to the property.

Although bare legal title is conveyed using a trust deed it doesn't actually convey possession. Possession and equitable title remain with the borrower. **Equitable title** is the interest held by the trustor under a trust deed and gives the borrower the equitable right to obtain absolute ownership to the property when legal title is held by the trustee.

> ### Review - Interests Held under Equitable Title
> - Trustor under a trust deed
> - Vendee under a contract for deed
> - Buyer of real property from the time the sales contract is signed, and earnest money is paid until the closing

The trustee, who has bare legal title, acts as an agent for the beneficiary and has only two obligations. The first is to foreclose on the property if there is a default on the loan, and the second is to reconvey the title to the borrower when the debt is repaid in full. When the debt is repaid in full, the beneficiary signs a **Request for Full Reconveyance** and sends it to the trustee requesting the trustee to reconvey title to the borrower. The trustee signs and records a **Deed of Reconveyance** to show the debt has been repaid and to clear the lien from the property. The trust deed is recorded at the close of escrow. A

fictitious trust deed is a recorded trust deed containing details which apply to later loan documents.

Mortgage

Since its introduction in the early 1900s, the deed of trust virtually replaced the use of a note and mortgage when financing real estate. The promissory note shows the obligation of the debt, and the mortgage is a lien against the described property until the debt is repaid.

There are two parties in a mortgage: a **mortgagor** (borrower) and a **mortgagee** (lender). The mortgagor receives loan funds from a mortgagee and signs a promissory note and mortgage. Once signed by the borrower, both the note and mortgage are held by the lender until the loan is paid. Unlike a trust deed, under a mortgage both title and possession remain with the borrower.

Contract of Sale

The **contract of sale** is the financing instrument with many names. It may be called an installment sales contract, a contract of sale, an agreement of sale, a conditional sales contract, a contract for deed, or a land sales contract.

This is a contract within which the seller (**vendor**) becomes the lender to the buyer (**vendee**). The vendor pays off the original financing while receiving payments from the vendee on the contract of sale. The vendor and vendee's relationship is like that of a beneficiary and a trustor in a trust deed.

The buyer, (**vendee**) has possession and use of the property even though legal title is held by the seller (**vendor**). In a contract of sale, the vendor retains legal ownership of the property, and the vendee holds what is known as equitable title. When all the terms of the contract are met, the vendor will pass title to the vendee.

The vendor in a land contract may not use vendee's impound money for any other purpose without the consent of the payor (**vendee**). Land contracts are used in CalVet loans under the California Veterans Farm and Home Purchase Plan (discussed later in the chapter). The state of California is the vendor who has legal title, and the veteran is the vendee who has equitable title.

Terms Found in Finance Instruments

When a borrower signs a note promising to repay a sum, the lender usually will include some specific requirements in the note regarding repayment. In addition to the terms in the note, the trust deed lists several covenants (promises) regarding the relationship of the borrower and the lender. These special clauses are meant to protect the lender and the lender's interests.

Prepayment Clauses

Occasionally, a trust deed will include a **prepayment clause** in case a borrower pays off a loan early. When lenders make loans, they calculate their return, over the term of the loan. If a loan is paid off before that time, the lender gets less interest than planned, thus the return on investment is threatened. So the borrower has to make it up by paying a penalty. It may not make a lot of sense to us as consumers, but that is the banking business.

For residential property, the prepayment penalty cannot exceed six month's interest. A borrower may prepay up to 20% of the loan amount in any 12-month period without a penalty. A prepayment penalty can then be charged only on the amount in excess of 20% of the original loan amount. A prepayment penalty is not allowed on a loan against the borrower's residence after the loan is seven years old. Other rules apply for non-residential property.

"Or More" Clause

An **"or more" clause** allows a borrower to pay off a loan early, or make higher payments without penalty.

Lock-in Clause

A **lock-in clause** prohibits borrowers from paying off a loan in advance. It is not allowed on residential units of less than four units. In a land contract to purchase a home a lock-in clause may be ignored by the vendee (buyer).

Late Payments

Lenders may not impose a late charge on a payment until after the payment is ten days late.

Acceleration Clause

An **acceleration clause** allows a lender to call the entire note due, on occurrence of a specific event such as default in payment, taxes or insurance, or sale of the property. A lender may use the acceleration clause to call the entire note due if the borrower does not pay the loan payments, the real property taxes or insurance premiums, or if the borrower sells the property. In order to pay off the outstanding loan, a lender will foreclose on the loan.

Default and Foreclosure

Foreclosure is the legal procedure used by lenders to terminate all rights, title and interest of the trustor or mortgagor in real property by selling the property and using the sale proceeds to satisfy the liens of creditors.

There are two ways to foreclose: by trustee's sale and by judicial process. Any trust deed or mortgage with a **power-of-sale clause** may be foreclosed non-judicially by a trustee's sale or judicially by a court procedure. Without the power-of-sale clause, the only remedy a lender has is a judicial foreclosure by a court proceeding. Most trust deeds and mortgages in California include the power-of-sale clause, so the lender may choose either type of foreclosure method.

Foreclosure on Trust Deed by Trustee's Sale (Non-judicial)

Usually the lender will elect to foreclose on the loan using the trustee's sale because it is the quickest and easiest method-taking approximately four months. First the beneficiary (lender) notifies the trustor (borrower) of default and requests the trustee to record a **notice of default.** Anyone who has recorded a **Request for Notice** must be notified of the default. The trustee must wait at least three months after recording the notice of default before advertising the trustee sale. Then the trustee advertises a Notice of Sale once a week for three weeks (21 days) and posts a notice of sale on the property.

As you can see the minimum time between recording the notice of default and the trustee sale is three months and 21 days. During this time the trustor may **reinstate** (bring current) the loan up to five business days prior to the trustee's sale. The trustee holds the sale and issues a **trustee's deed** to the highest bidder. A trustor has no right of redemption after the trustee sale.

Proceeds from the sale of the property are paid out in the following order:

1. trustee's fees, costs, and expenses of the sale.

2. any tax and assessment liens that are due and owing.

3. trust deeds, mortgages, and mechanic's liens in their order of priority.

4. the defaulting borrower.

Sometimes the proceeds of the sale are not sufficient to satisfy the debt being foreclosed. If that happens, the lender may try to obtain a deficiency judgment against the borrower. A **deficiency judgment** is a personal judgment against a borrower for the balance of a debt owed when the security for the loan is not sufficient to pay the debt. However, the lender cannot obtain a deficiency judgment against the trustor under a trustee sale.

RECORDING REQUESTED BY

WHEN RECORDED MAIL TO

NAME

ADDRESS

CITY

STATE&ZIP

Title Order No.   Escrow No.

SPACE ABOVE THIS LINE FOR RECORDER'S USE

REQUEST FOR NOTICE OF DELINQUENCIES
UNDER SECTION 2924e CIVIL CODE

In accordance with Section 2924e. California Civil Code. request is hereby made that a written notice of any or all delinquencies of four months or more. in payments of principal or interest on any obligation secured under the Deed of Trust recorded as Instrument Number: on:
Official Records of   County, California, loan number
Wherein   is the trustor, and describing land therein as:

1. The ownership or security interest of the requester, is the beneficial interest under that certain deed of trust recorded as instrument Number: on   of the Official Records of:
County, California.
Wherein   is the trustor.
2.   is the date on which the interest of the requester will terminate as evidenced by the maturity date of the note of the trustor in favor of the requester.
3.   is the name of the current owner of the security property described above.
4. The street address of the security property as described above is:

5. Said notice of delinquency and the amount thereof shall be sent to:

(Requester Beneficiary)

at
          (Address)   (City)

          (State)   (Zip)

Dated

(Requester Beneficiary)

CONSENT BY TRUSTOR/OWNER

I _____ AUTHORIZE _____
          (Trustee)   (Senior Lienholder)
TO DISCLOSE IN WRITING TO _____
                              (Requesting Beneficiary)
NOTICE OF ANY AND ALL DELINQUENCIES OF FOUR MONTHS OR MORE, IN PAYMENT OF PRINCIPAL OR INTEREST ON ANY OBLIGATION SECURED BY THAT SENIOR LIEN MORE PARTICULARLY DESCRIBED AS INSTRUMENT NUMBER
_____ RECORDED ON _____
IN OFFICIAL RECORDS OF _____COUNTY. CALIFORNIA.
DATED _____

Foreclosure by Court Proceeding (Judicial)

Default on a mortgage, unless the mortgage includes a power-of-sale clause, requires a court foreclosure. The mortgagee (lender) goes to court to start the foreclosure. The court issues a decree of foreclosure and an order of sale. After publication and posting of the sale notice, the court-appointed commissioner sells the property to the highest bidder and gives the buyer a Certification of Sale. After a court foreclosure sale on a mortgage, the mortgagor (borrower) gets to keep possession of the property and has one year to redeem the property by satisfying the loan in full including court costs and any interest. This is called **equity of redemption**. If after one year, the mortgagor does not redeem the property, a **sheriff's deed** is issued to the new buyer.

If a trust deed is foreclosed in court, it is treated like a mortgage and the trustor (borrower) may keep possession during the redemption period. Sometimes a lender with a trust deed may elect to foreclose by a court foreclosure because it is the only way the beneficiary can obtain a deficiency judgment against the borrower.

Deficiency Judgments

As mentioned earlier, a deficiency judgment is a personal judgment against a borrower for the difference between the unpaid amount of the loan, plus interest, costs and fees of the sale, and the amount of the actual proceeds of the foreclosure sale. This means if the property sells for less than what is owed to the lender, the borrower will be personally responsible for repayment after the deficiency judgment is filed.

Deficiency Judgment Not Allowed

If a lender (beneficiary or mortgagee) chooses to foreclose a trust deed or mortgage with a power of sale using a trustee sale, no deficiency judgment is allowed if the proceeds do not satisfy the debt and all costs. Since trust deeds are used almost exclusively in California to secure loans, the only security for a beneficiary is the property itself. Any other personal assets of the borrower in default are protected from judgment under a trust deed.

Additionally a lender cannot get a deficiency judgment against a borrower if the loan is a purchase money loan secured by either a trust deed or a mortgage. Any loan made at the time of a sale, as part of that sale, is known as a **purchase-money loan**. This includes first trust deeds, junior loans used to purchase the property, and seller carry-back financing. A seller is said to **"carry back"** when the seller extends credit to a buyer by taking a promissory note executed by the buyer and secured by a trust deed on the property being purchased as a part of the purchase price.

Deficiency Judgment Permitted

A deficiency judgment is allowed on hard money loans. A **hard money loan** is one made in exchange for cash, as opposed to a loan made to finance the purchase of a home. Typically a hard money loan refers to junior loans used to take money out for consumer purchases, home equity loans, debt consolidation, and even a refinance.

Alienation Clause

The **alienation** or **due-on-sale clause** is a type of acceleration clause. A lender may call the entire note due if the original borrower transfers (alienates) ownership of the property to someone else. If the note contains an **acceleration clause** (due on sale), the trust deed must mention this clause in order to enforce the contract. This clause protects the lender from an unqualified, unapproved buyer taking over a loan. Justifiably, the lender fears possible default, with no control over who is making the payments.

Usually a lender will want the existing loan paid off if a property owner transfers the property to someone else. However, under certain circumstances, a property owner may transfer responsibility for the loan to the buyer when he or she sells the property to another party. A buyer may "assume" an existing loan, or may buy a property "subject to" an existing loan.

Loan Assumption

An **assumption clause** allows a buyer to assume responsibility for the full payment of the loan with the lender's knowledge and consent. When a property is sold, a buyer may assume the existing loan. Usually with the approval of the lender, the buyer takes over primary liability for the loan, with the original borrower secondarily liable if there is a default. What that means is that even though the original borrower is secondarily responsible, according to the loan assumption agreement, no actual repayment of the loan may be required of that person.

The original borrower (seller) can avoid any responsibility for the loan by asking the lender for a **substitution of liability (novation),** relieving the seller of all liability for repayment of the loan. In most cases, a buyer assumes an existing loan with the approval of the underlying lender. However, an **alienation clause** in the note would prevent a buyer from assuming the loan.

"Subject To"

A buyer may also purchase a property "subject to" the existing loan. A "subject to" clause allows a buyer to take over a loan, making the payments without the knowledge or approval of the lender. The original borrower remains responsible for the loan, even though the buyer takes title and makes

Escrow No. _____   Title Order No. _____

(DUE ON SALE CLAUSE)

$ _____, California _____, 20_____

_____ after date, for value received

I promise to pay to _____

_____ or order, at

_____

the sum of _____ DOLLARS

with interest from _____ until paid at the

rate of _____ per cent per annum, payable _____

_____

_____

Principal and interest payable in lawful money of the United States of America. should default be made in payment of interest when due the whole sum of principal and interest shall become immediately due at the option of the holder of this note and after said breach, said obligation shall continue to accrue interest at the rate of _____% per annum. If action be instituted on this note I promise to pay such sum as the Court may fix as Attorney's Fees. This note is secured by a Deed of Trust of even date herewith.

In the event the herein described property or any part thereof, or any interest therein which has been given as security for the payment of this obligation is sold, agreed to be sold, conveyed or alienated by the Trustor, or by the operation of the law or otherwise, all obligations secured by this instrument, irrespective of the maturity dates expressed therein, at the option of the holder hereof and without demand or notice shall immediately become due and payable.

_____   _____

_____   _____

_____   _____

DO NOT DESTROY THIS NOTE
When paid, this note, if secured by Deed of Trust, must be surrendered to Trustee for cancellation before reconveyance will be made.

FD-30G   STRAIGHT NOTE (DUE ON SALE CLAUSE)

the payments. In this case, also, the property remains the security for the loan. In the case of default, the property is sold and the proceeds go to the lender, with no recourse to the original buyer other than the foreclosure going against the borrower's credit.

When a buyer takes a property "subject to" the existing loan, the underlying lender may not always be informed. The buyer simply starts making the payments and the seller hopes he or she is diligent and does not default.

The occurrence of "subject to" sales is relative to economic and market conditions. In a real estate market where there are more buyers than sellers (a seller's market) a homeowner does not need to sell "subject to" his or her loan. When money is tight and interest rates high and sellers are wondering where all the buyers are, a "subject to" sale might be a seller's only option.

Review: Notes, Trust Deeds, and Mortgages

- A **note** is the evidence of a debt.
- A trust deed or mortgage, even though it is the security for the debt, is still only an incident of the debt.
- A trust deed or mortgage must have a note to secure, but a note does not need a trust deed or mortgage to stand alone.
- If there is a conflict in the terms of a note and the trust deed or mortgage used to secure it, the provisions of the note will control.
- If a note is unenforceable, the presence of a trust deed will not make it valid.

Conventional and Government-Backed Loans

All loans can be classified according to their loan terms and whether or not they have government backing. First, as we have already learned, all of the various loans are classified by their terms—fixed rate loans, adjustable-rate loans and their combinations. Second, loans are classified by whether or not they have government backing—conventional or government loans. Some lenders specialize in only conventional conforming loans, whereas full service lenders offer a wide selection of loan programs including conventional, government-sponsored FHA and VA loans, and non-conforming loans.

Conventional Loans

A **conventional loan** is any loan made by lenders without any governmental guarantees. The basic protection for a lender making conventional loans is the borrower's equity in the property. A low down payment will mean greater risk for the lender and a higher interest charged to the borrower. Conventional loans may be conforming or non-conforming.

Conforming Loans

Conforming loans have terms and conditions that follow the guidelines set forth by Fannie Mae and Freddie Mac. These loans are called "A" paper loans, or prime loans, and can be made to purchase or refinance homes (one-to-four residential units). Fannie Mae and Freddie Mac guidelines establish the maximum loan amount, borrower credit and income requirements, down payment, and suitable properties. Fannie Mae and Freddie Mac announce new loan limits every year. The 2006 conforming loan limit for a single family home is $417,000. This limit is reviewed annually and, if needed, modified to reflect changes in the national average price for single family homes. The current loan limit on second mortgages is $208,500. Both Fannie Mae and Freddie Mac will be discussed in the next chapter.

Private Mortgage Insurance (PMI)

Conventional lenders usually require private mortgage insurance (PMI) on low down payment loans for protection in the event that the homeowner fails to make his or her payments. **Private mortgage insurance** protects the lender against financial loss if a homeowner stops making mortgage payments. When the loan exceeds 80% of the value of the property, lenders usually require private mortgage insurance on conventional loans. Usually borrowers pay for this insurance as part of the monthly payment. There are a small number of companies that provide this insurance.

Non-Conforming Loans

Sometimes either the borrower's credit worthiness or the size of the loan does not meet conventional lending standards. These are called **non-conforming loans** and include jumbo loans and subprime loans.

Jumbo Loans

Loans which are above the maximum loan limit set by Fannie Mae and Freddie Mac are called **jumbo loans**. Because jumbo loans are not funded by these government sponsored entities, they usually carry a higher interest rate and some additional underwriting requirements.

Trust Deed	Mortgage Contract
1. Number of Parties (3) **Trustor**: Borrower who conveys title to trustee who holds as security for debt. **Beneficiary**: Lender who holds original note and trust deed during life of the debt. **Trustee**: Receiver of naked legal title who conveys it when debt is paid or will sell if foreclosure is necessary.	**1. Number of Parties (2)** **Mortgager**: Borrower retains title but gives lender a lien on the property as security. **Mortgagee**: Lender who holds the mortgage.
2. Title: Conveyed to trustee with trustor retaining equitable possession of the property.	**2. Title:** Held by mortgagor together with possession.
3. Statute of Limitations: The security for debt is held by trustee, rights of creditor are not ended when statute runs out on the note.	**3. Statute of Limitations**: Foreclosure is barred if no action is taken within four (4) years of delinquency on the note.
4. Remedy for Default: Foreclosure can be instituted through trustee's sale or court foreclosure. (Court foreclosure follows mortgage foreclosure procedure #7.)	**4. Remedy for Default**: Court foreclosure is usually the only remedy.
5. Right of Redemption: When title has been sold by trustee at trustee's sale no right or equity of redemption exists.	**5. Right of Redemption**: Mortgagor has up to one (1) year to redeem the property after court foreclosure called "equity of redemption."
6. Satisfaction: The beneficiary sends a request for full reconveyance to the trustee with the original note and trust deed. Upon payment of fees, the trustee issues a reconveyance deed which must be recorded.	**6. Satisfaction**: Upon final payment and on demand, the mortgagee signs the certificate that the debt is satisfied. Then the certificate or release is recorded.

Comparison Chart: Trust Deeds and Mortgage Contracts

7. Foreclosure by Trustee's Sale:	7. Foreclosure by Court:
Beneficiary notifies the trustee of default. The trustee notifies the trustor and records the notice. Anyone who has recorded the "Request for Notice for Default" must also be notified.	Court action is commenced by the mortgagee. The court issues a decree of foreclosure and an order of sale. A court appointed commissioner sells to the highest bidder after the publication and posting of the sale notice.
The trustee waits at least three (3) months. During the three (3) month period, the trustor can reinstate the loan. Then the trustee advertises a "notice of sale" once a week for three weeks (21 days) and posts a notice on the property.	The Certificate of Sale is issued. Mortgagor has one (1) year to redeem the property and remains in possession for that year. If sale proceeds satisfy the debt, court costs and interest then the mortgagor has only three (3) months to redeem the property.
Trustor can now invade the three (3) week advertising period and can reinstate the loan up to five (5) days prior to the trustee's sale.	If a trust deed is foreclosed in court, it is treated like a mortgage contract, and trustor remains in possession during the redemption period.
The trustee conducts the sale and issues a trustee's deed to the highest bidder.	A sheriff's deed is issued after one (1) year.
8. Deficiency Judgment: No deficiency judgment is available if the foreclosure is by trustee's sale.	**8. Deficiency Judgment** A deficiency judgment is available in a court foreclosure.
9. No deficiency judgment is available on a "purchase-money" trust deed or mortgage.	

Subprime Loans

Loans that do not meet the borrower credit requirements of Fannie Mae and Freddie Mac are called **subprime loans** or "B" and "C" paper loans as opposed to "A" paper conforming loans. Subprime loans are offered to borrowers that may have recently filed for bankruptcy or foreclosure, or have had late payments on their credit reports. Their purpose is to offer temporary financing to these applicants until they can qualify for conforming "A" financing. Due to the higher risk associated with lending to borrowers that have a poor credit history, subprime loans typically require a larger down payment and a higher interest rate.

Prior to 1990 it was very difficult for anyone to obtain a mortgage if they did not qualify for a conventional FHA or VA loan. Many borrowers with bad credit are good people who honestly intended to pay their bills on time. Catastrophic events such as the loss of a job or a family illness can lead to missed or late payments or even foreclosure and bankruptcy. Subprime loans were developed to help higher risk borrowers obtain a mortgage.

Government Participation in Real Estate Finance

There are two federal agencies and one state agency that help make it possible for people to buy homes they would never be able to purchase without government involvement. The two federal agencies that participate in real estate financing are the Federal Housing Administration (FHA) and the Veterans Administration (VA). The California Farm and Home Purchase Program, or CalVet loan, is a state program that helps eligible veterans.

Federal Housing Administration (FHA)

The FHA program, a part of HUD (U.S. Department of Housing and Urban Development) since 1934, has caused the greatest change in home mortgage lending in the history of real estate finance. The FHA was established to improve the construction and financing of housing. The main purpose of the FHA program has been to promote home ownership. Secondary results include setting minimum property requirements and systemizing appraisals. An appraiser would be reprimanded if he or she did not use FHA guidelines when preparing appraisals for FHA loans. Additionally, an appraiser who intention-ally misrepresents the value on FHA loan appraisals, which subsequently cause a loss, could be fined and face legal action.

The FHA does not make loans; rather, it insures lenders against loss. Loans are made by authorized lending institutions such as banks, savings banks, and independent mortgage companies. As long as FHA guidelines are used in funding the loan, the FHA, upon default by the borrower, insures the lender against loss. If the borrower does default, the lender may foreclose and the FHA will pay cash up to the established limit of the insurance.

The lender is protected, in case of foreclosure, by charging the borrower a fee for an insurance policy called Mutual Mortgage Insurance (MMI). The insurance requirement is how the FHA finances its program. The premium may be financed as part of the loan or paid in cash at the close of escrow.

The borrower applies directly to the FHA-approved lender (mortgagee), not the FHA, for a loan. FHA does not make loans, build homes or insure the property. A buyer who would like to purchase a home with FHA financing would apply to an FHA-approved mortgagee (lender) who would then request a **conditional commitment** from FHA. The conditional commitment is good for six (6) months. A firm commitment is requested when the FHA approves the borrower (mortgagor).

The FHA guidelines encourage home ownership by allowing 100% of the down payment to be a gift from family or friends and by allowing closing costs to be financed to reduce the up-front cost of buying a home. The down payment on FHA loans varies with the amount of the loan.

Interest rates are determined by mutual agreement between the borrower and the lender—they are not set by the Federal Reserve Board. Sometimes a borrower will pay points to the lender to increase the lender's yield and compensate the lender for the difference between FHA interest rates (which tend to be low) and conventional interest rates. **Points** are a percentage of the loan amount paid to the lender when negotiating a loan. The borrower must make monthly payments. The FHA does not allow a borrower to make semi-monthly or semi-annual payments.

The FHA maximum loan amounts vary from one county to another. It is important that the total loan amount, including financed closing costs, not exceed the maximum limit set by the FHA for the county in which the property is located. There are no income limits on FHA loans and an FHA loan will be based on the selling price when it is lower than the appraisal.

There are no alienation or prepayment penalty clauses allowed in FHA loans. Any qualified resident of the United States may obtain an FHA loan as long as the property will be the borrower's principal residence and is located in the United States.

The FHA insures a variety of types of loans. For example, borrowers can get qualified for an FHA loan before a builder starts construction, enabling both borrower and builder to count on the completion of the transaction.

Popular FHA Loan Programs

Section 203(b)

The FHA 203(b) loan offers financing on the purchase or construction of owner-occupied residences of one-to-four units. This program offers 30 year, fixed-rate, fully amortized, mortgages with a down payment requirement as low as 3%, allowing financing of up to 97% of the value of the home. FHA has mortgage limits which vary from county to county. Their website, https://entp.hud.gov/idapp/html/hicostlook.cfm, provides the current FHA mortgage limits for several areas.

Section 203(k)

A purchase rehabilitation loan (purchase rehab) is a great option for buyers who are looking to improve their property immediately upon purchase. This mortgage loan provides the funds to purchase your home and the funds to complete your improvement project all in one loan, one application, one set of fees, one closing, and one convenient monthly payment.

A purchase rehab loan could be used for a variety of improvements, such as: adding a family room or bedroom, remodeling a kitchen or bathroom, performing general upgrades to an older property, or even completing a total "tear-down" and rebuild.

Section 245 Graduated Payment Mortgage

A **graduated payment mortgage** (GPM) has a monthly payment that starts out at the lowest level and increases at a specific rate. Payments for the first five years are low, and cover only part of the interest due, with the unpaid amount added to the principal balance. After that time the loan is recalculated, with the new payments staying the same from that point on. In this loan the interest rate is not adjustable and does not change during the term of the loan. What actually changes is the amount of the monthly mortgage payment.

A GPM is offered by the FHA to borrowers who might have trouble qualifying for regular loan payments, but who expect their income to increase. This loan is for the buyer who expects to be earning more after a few years and can make a higher payment at that time. GPMs are available in 30-year and 15-year amortization and for both conforming and jumbo loans. The interest rate for a GPM is traditionally .5% to .75% higher than the interest rate for a straight fixed-rate mortgage. The higher note rate and scheduled negative amortization of the GPM makes the cost of the mortgage more expensive to the borrower in the long run.

Energy Efficient Mortgage

The Energy Efficient Mortgages Program (EEM) helps homebuyers or homeowners save money on utility bills by enabling them to finance the cost of adding energy-efficiency features to new or existing housing. The program provides mortgage insurance for the purchase or refinance of a principal residence that incorporates the cost of energy efficient improvements into the loan.

Section 255 Reverse Annuity Mortgages

Reverse Annuity Mortgages are also called Home Equity Conversion Mortgages (HECM). It is a program for homeowners who are 62 years and older who have paid off their mortgages or have only small mortgage balances remaining. The program has three options for homeowners: (1) borrow against the equity in their homes in a lump sum, (2) borrow on a monthly basis for a fixed term or for as long as they live in the home, or (3) borrow as a line of credit.

The borrower is not required to make payments as long as the borrower lives in the home. The loan is paid off when the property is sold. FHA collects an insurance premium from all borrowers to provide mortgage coverage which will cover any shortfall if the proceeds from the sale of the property are not sufficient to cover the loan amount. Senior citizens are charged 2% of the home's value as an up front payment plus ½% on the loan balance each year. These amounts are usually paid by the mortgage company and charged to the borrower's principal balance. FHA's reverse mortgage insurance makes this program less expensive to borrowers than the smaller reverse mortgage programs run by private companies without FHA insurance.

VA Loan

The Department of Veterans Affairs (DVA) does not make loans. It guarantees loans made by an approved institutional lender, much like the FHA. Both programs were created to assist people in buying homes when conventional loan programs did not fit their needs. There are two main differences between the two government programs: (1) only an eligible veteran may obtain a VA loan, and (2) the DVA does not require a down payment up to a certain loan amount which means qualified veterans could get 100% financing. As with FHA loans, alienation and prepayment penalty clauses are not allowed in VA loans.

VA loans are made by a lender, such as a mortgage company, savings and loan or bank. The DVA's guaranty on the loan protects the lender against loss if the payments are not made, and is intended to encourage lenders to offer veterans loans with more favorable terms. The amount of guaranty on the loan depends on the loan amount and whether the veteran used some entitlement previously.

VA Loan Process

A veteran must possess a **Certificate of Eligibility,** which is available from the Veteran's Administration, before applying for a VA loan. The certificate will show the veteran's entitlement or right to obtain the loan.

When a veteran finds a house he or she wants to purchase, a VA-approved conventional lender will take the loan application and the veteran's Certificate of Eligibility and process the loan according to VA guidelines. The lender will request the VA to assign a licensed appraiser to determine the reasonable value for the property. A **Certificate of Reasonable Value** (CRV) will be issued. A loan may not exceed the value established by the CRV appraisal. Once the loan has closed it is sent to the VA for guaranty. The Certificate of Eligibility is annotated to show how much of the entitlement has been used and will be returned to the veteran.

A veteran may get another VA loan, if the prior VA loan is paid off and the property sold. A VA loan may be assumed by a nonveteran buyer, upon approval by the VA. If a veteran sells his or her property and allows the buyer to assume the existing VA loan, he or she cannot get another VA loan until the buyer who assumed the VA loan has paid it off. If a VA loan is foreclosed and there is a loss, the veteran cannot have eligibility be restored until the loss has been repaid in full.

Fees and Closing Costs

Although a veteran can get 100% financing, he or she will be required to pay a 2.0% funding fee. The funding fee charged for loans to refinance an existing VA home loan with a new VA home loan is 0.5%. The funding fee can be paid in cash or included in the loan.

The lender may charge reasonable closing costs which may not be included in the loan. The closing costs may be paid by the buyer (veteran) or the seller. Typical closing costs include: Certificate of Reasonable Value, credit report, loan origination fee, discount points, title insurance, and recording fees. The VA allows the veteran to pay reasonable discount points on a refinance or a purchase. No commissions, brokerage fees, or buyer broker fees may be charged to the veteran.

California Veteran Loans (CalVet)

The California Department of Veterans Affairs administers the CalVet loan program to assist California veterans in buying a home or farm. Unlike other government financing, the CalVet program funds and services its own loans. Funds are obtained through the sale of State General Obligation Bonds. The CA DVA sells bonds to purchase homes and then sells the homes to qualified California veterans using a land sale contract.

An eligible California veteran (includes a 17-year old veteran) applies for the loan and makes loan payments directly to the Department of Veterans Affairs. Upon application for a CalVet loan and approval of the borrower and property, the Department of Veterans Affairs purchases the property from the seller, takes title to the property and sells to the veteran on a contract of sale. There are no discount points charged on a CalVet loan. The department holds legal title, with the veteran holding equitable title, until the loan is paid off. The veteran has an obligation to apply for life insurance, with the Department of Veterans Affairs as beneficiary, to pay off the debt in case of the veteran's death.

Priority of Recording

Priority is the order in which documents are recorded and is determined by the date stamped in the upper right-hand corner of the document by the county recorder. If there are several trust deeds recorded against a property, no mention will be made about which one is the first, second, third, or fourth trust deed. A person inquiring about the priority of the deeds should look at the time and date the deed was recorded.

First and Junior Trust Deeds

The trust deed recorded first against a property is called a **first trust deed.** All others are junior loans. A junior trust deed is any loan recorded after the first trust deed, secured by a second, third or subsequent trust deed. Secondary or junior financing is another way to finance a property, either at the time of a sale, or afterward. The interest rates are usually higher because there is a greater risk of default on a junior loan. The beneficiary of a junior loan should record a Request for Notice of Default in order to be notified if the borrower defaults on a prior loan.

VA Department of Veterans Affairs

VA LOAN SUMMARY SHEET

1. VA'S 12-DIGIT LOAN NUMBER

2. VETERAN'S NAME *(First, middle, last)*

3. VETERAN'S SOCIAL SECURITY NUMBER	**4. GENDER OF VETERAN** *(Check one)* ☐ MALE ☐ FEMALE	**5. VETERAN'S DATE OF BIRTH** *(mm/dd/yyyy)*

6A. ETHNICITY   **6B. RACE** (May select more than one)

☐ NOT HISPANIC OR LATINO   ☐ AMERICAN INDIAN OR ALASKAN NATIVE ☐ ASIAN   ☐ BLACK OR AFRICAN AMERICAN
☐ HISPANIC OR LATINO   ☐ NATIVE HAWAIIAN OR PACIFIC ISLANDER ☐ WHITE   ☐ UNKNOWN

7. ENTITLEMENT CODE *(01 to 11, from VA Certificate of Eligibility)*	**8. AMOUNT OF ENTITLEMENT AVAILABLE** *(from VA Certificate of Eligibility)*

9. BRANCH OF SERVICE *(Check one)*

☐ 1. ARMY   ☐ 2. NAVY   ☐ 3. AIR FORCE   ☐ 4. MARINE CORPS   ☐ 5. COAST GUARD   ☐ 6. OTHER

10. MILITARY STATUS *(Check one)*

☐ 1. SEPARATED FROM SERVICE   ☐ 2. IN SERVICE

11. FIRST TIME HOME BUYER *(Check one)*

☐ YES   ☐ NO

> This means a veteran who has not previously purchased a home, either by cash, assumption, or new financing.

12. LOAN PROCEDURE *(Check one)*

☐ AUTOMATIC   ☐ AUTO-IRRRL   ☐ VA PRIOR APPROVAL

13. PURPOSE OF LOAN *(Check one)*

☐ 1. HOME (INCLUDES MH ON PERMANENT FOUNDATION)   ☐ 2. MANUFACTURED HOME   ☐ 3. CONDOMINIUM
☐ 4. ALTERATIONS/IMPROVEMENTS   ☐ 5. REFINANCE

14. LOAN CODE *(Check one)*

☐ 1. PURCHASE   ☐ 2. IRRRL (STREAMLINE REFINANCE)   ☐ 3. CASH OUT REFINANCE (MAX 90% LTV)
☐ 4. MANUFACTURED HOME REFI   ☐ 5. REFINANCING OVER 90% OF RV

15. TYPE OF MORTGAGE *(Check one)*

☐ 0. REGULAR FIXED PAYMENT   ☐ 1. GPM-NEVER TO EXCEED CRV   ☐ 2. OTHER GPMs
☐ 3. GEM   ☐ 4. TEMPORARY BUYDOWN   ☐ 5. HYBRID ARM

16. TYPE OF HYBRID-ARM *(NOTE: Must be completed if Hybrid Arm selected in Item 15.)*

☐ 3/1   ☐ 5/1   ☐ 7/1   ☐ 10/1

17. TYPE OF OWNERSHIP *(Check one)* ☐ 1. SOLE OWNERSHIP (VETERAN & SPOUSE OR VETERAN ONLY) ☐ 2. JOINT - 2 OR MORE VETERANS ☐ 3. JOINT - VETERAN/NON-VETERAN	**18. CLOSING DATE** *(mm/dd/yyyy)*

19. PURCHASE PRICE *(N/A for Refinance Loans)*	$
20. REASONABLE VALUE *(For IRRRLs - If appraisal has not been done, loan amount of prior VA loan)*	$

21. ENERGY IMPROVEMENTS *(Check all applicable boxes)* $

☐ NONE   ☐ INSTALLATION OF SOLAR HEATING/COOLING
☐ REPLACEMENT OF A MAJOR SYSTEM   ☐ ADDITION OF A NEW FEATURE
☐ INSULATION, CAULKING, WEATHER-STRIPPING, ETC.   ☐ OTHER IMPROVEMENTS

22. LOAN AMOUNT (Purchase - Purchase Price or RV (lesser) + Funding Fee) (Refi - Max 90% LTV + Funding Fee) (IRRRL - Old Loan Payoff + All Closing Costs)	$

23. PROPERTY TYPE *(Check one)*

☐ NEITHER   ☐ PUD   ☐ CONDOMINIUM

24. APPRAISAL TYPE *(Check one)*

☐ IND - SINGLE PROPERTY-IND APPRAISAL   ☐ ONE - MASTER CRV CASE (MCRV)   ☐ LAPP - LENDER APPRAISAL
☐ MBL - MANUFACTURED HOME   ☐ HUD - CONVERSION   ☐ PMC - PROP. MGMT. CASE

VA FORM
OCT 2003   **26-0286**   SUPERSEDES VA FORM 26-0286, JUN 2003, WHICH WILL NOT BE USED.

25. TYPE OF STRUCTURE *(Check one)*
☐ 1. CONVENTIONAL CONSTRUCTION   ☐ 2. SINGLEWIDE M/H   ☐ 3. DOUBLEWIDE M/H
☐ 4. M/H LOT ONLY   ☐ 5. PREFABRICATED HOME   ☐ 6. CONDOMINIUM CONVERSION

26. PROPERTY DESIGNATION *(Check one)*
☐ 1. EXISTING OR USED HOME, CONDO, M/H   ☐ 2. APPRAISED AS PROPOSED CONSTRUCTION
☐ 3. NEW EXISTING - NEVER OCCUPIED   ☐ 4. ENERGY IMPROVEMENTS

27. NO. OF UNITS *(Check one)*	28. MCRV NO.
☐ SINGLE ☐ TWO UNITS ☐ THREE UNITS ☐ FOUR OR MORE	

29. MANUFACTURED HOME CATEGORY *(Check one)*
☐ 0. OTHER - NOT M/H   ☐ 1. M/H ONLY (RENTED SPACE)
☐ 2. M/H ONLY (VETERAN-OWNED LOT)   ☐ 7. M/H ON PERMANENT FOUNDATION

30. PROPERTY ADDRESS

31. CITY	32. STATE	33. ZIP CODE	34. COUNTY

35. LENDER VA ID NUMBER	36. AGENT VA ID NUMBER *(If applicable)*	37. LENDER LOAN NUMBER

FOR LAPP CASES ONLY

38. LENDER SAR ID NUMBER

39. GROSS LIVING AREA *(Square Feet)*	40. AGE OF PROPERTY *(Yrs.)*	41. DATE SAR ISSUED NOTIFICATION OF VALUE *(mm/dd/yyyy)*

42. TOTAL ROOM COUNT	43. BATHS *(No.)*	44. BEDROOMS *(No.)*

45. IF PROCESSED UNDER LAPP, WAS THE FEE APPRAISER'S ORIGINAL VALUE ESTIMATE CHANGED OR REPAIR RECOMMENDATIONS REVISED, OR DID THE SAR OTHERWISE MAKE SIGNIFICANT ADJUSTMENTS?
☐ YES *(If "Yes," there must be written justification by fee appraiser and/or SAR)*   ☐ NO

INCOME INFORMATION *(Not Applicable for IRRRLs)*

46A. LOAN PROCESSED UNDER VA RECOGNIZED AUTOMATED UNDERWRITING SYSTEM
☐ YES   ☐ NO   *(If "Yes," Complete Item 46B and 46C)*

46B. WHICH SYSTEM WAS USED? ☐ 01. LP	46C. RISK CLASSIFICATION
☐ 02. DU ☐ 03. PMI AURA ☐ 04. CLUES ☐ 05 ZIPPY	☐ 1. APPROVE ☐ 2. REFER

47. CREDIT SCORE *(Enter the median credit score for the veteran only)*	
48. LIQUID ASSETS	$
49. TOTAL MONTHLY GROSS INCOME *(Item 32 +Item 39 from VA Form 26-6393)*	$
50. RESIDUAL INCOME	$
51. RESIDUAL INCOME GUIDELINE	$

52. DEBT-INCOME RATIO *(If Income Ratio is over 41% and Residual Income is not 120% of guideline, statement of justification signed by underwriter's supervisor must be included on or with VA Form 26-6393)*   %

53. SPOUSE INCOME CONSIDERED	54. SPOUSE'S INCOME AMOUNT *(If considered)*
☐ YES ☐ NO *(If "Yes," Complete Item 54)*	$

DISCOUNT INFORMATION *(Applicable for All Loans)*

55. DISCOUNT POINTS CHARGED	% OR	$
56. DISCOUNT POINTS PAID BY VETERAN	% OR	$

57. TERM *(Months)*	58. INTEREST RATE	59. FUNDING FEE EXEMPT
	%	☐ Y - EXEMPT ☐ N - NOT EXEMPT

FOR IRRRLS ONLY

60. PAID IN FULL VA LOAN NUMBER

61. ORIGINAL LOAN AMOUNT	62. ORIGINAL INTEREST RATE
$	%

63. REMARKS

Subordination Clause

A **subordination clause** is used to change the priority of a financial instrument. A lender agrees to give up priority to later loans. Remember, the priority of a trust deed is fixed by the date it is recorded: the earlier the date, the greater the advantage. When a note and trust deed includes a subordination clause, a new, later loan may be recorded, and because of the subordination clause, assume a higher priority. This clause is used mainly when land is purchased for future purposes of construction that will require financing. The lender on the new financing would want to be in first position to secure his or her interest, so the trust deed on the land would become subordinate to a new loan on the structure when the new loan was funded and recorded. Typically the subordination clause benefits the trustor (borrower).

Loan Programs

Traditionally, fixed-rate loans were the only choice offered by commercial banks and savings and loans for a home buyer. Over the past few years lending institutions have been deregulated allowing them to offer consumers new solutions to credit demands.

Deregulation is a process where financial institutions that formerly had been restrained in their lending activities by the law, are allowed to compete freely for profits in the marketplace. Controls on lending practices still exist, but loans can now be marketed competitively by all lending institutions. As a result of deregulation the distinction between commercial and savings banks has practically been eliminated.

Because there are different kinds of lenders and different kinds of borrowers who are in need of credit to buy homes, there is no single type of financing that fits everyone. In an attempt to offer alternatives to consumers, and renew their faith in their ability to borrow money for homes, lenders found new ways to make loans consumer friendly.

Secondary Financing (Junior Loans)

Secondary financing or a **junior loan** is a loan secured by a trust deed or mortgage on a property, other than first-trust deed. One way to get the needed financing is for the buyer to obtain a secondary loan through an outside source, such as a mortgage lender, private investor or even the seller of the property. Junior loans take advantage of built-up equity in a property. **Equity** is defined as the difference between the value of the property and any outstanding loans or the initial down payment. Assuming there is enough equity, a homeowner can apply for a cash loan for any purpose. Being a homeowner can be advantageous, especially if there is built up equity in a house, townhouse, duplex or condominium. The equity can pay for home improvements, bill consolidation, or college tuition. Typical junior loans include: home equity loans, home equity lines of credit, and seller financing.

Home Equity Loan

In a **home equity loan** the borrower gets the entire loan balance at one time. It is a fixed-rate second mortgage with principal and interest payments remaining the same over the life of the loan.

A lender uses strict standards about the amount of equity required in a property before loaning money, and particularly for a junior loan. The reason is simple. All a lender wants is to get his or her money back in a timely manner, along with the calculated return on the investment. Care must be taken, in case of a decrease in the value of the subject property, to make sure there is enough of a margin between the total amount owed and the value of the property. If the lender has to sell the property at a foreclosure sale, he or she will be assured of getting the money back. By only loaning up to 75%-90% of the property value, the lender leaves some room for loss.

The priority of the loan will depend on what other instruments are recorded ahead of it, but it will be known as a hard money loan (subject to state laws) and will be secured by a deed of trust or mortgage against the property.

> Example: Michael's home was appraised at $400,000, with a $250,000 first trust deed recorded against it. Michael wants a $65,000 home equity loan. To determine whether or not to make the loan, the lender adds the amount owed to the amount desired in the loan to determine the percentage that would be encumbered by the existing first trust deed, and the desired second trust deed. If the lender would only loan up to 80% of the appraised value of the property, would Michael get his loan? (Of course Michael does get his loan because he has enough equity in the property to qualify).

Home Equity Line of Credit

With a **home equity line of credit** (HELOC), the borrower takes money as it is needed—up to the credit limit. It has a low starting interest rate, with a variable monthly rate based on outstanding balance. More and more lenders are offering home equity lines of credit. By using the equity in their home, borrowers may qualify for a sizable amount of credit, available for use when and how they please, at an interest rate that is relatively low. Furthermore, under the California tax law—depending on each borrower's specific situation—he or she may be allowed to deduct the interest because the debt is secured by their home.

What is a home equity line of credit?

A home equity line is a form of revolving credit in which a borrower's home serves as collateral. Because the home is likely to be a consumer's largest asset, many homeowners use their credit lines only for major items such as education, home improvements, or medical bills and not for day-to-day expenses.

With a home equity line, a borrower will be approved for a specific amount of credit—the credit limit—meaning the maximum amount he or she can borrow at any one time.

Many lenders set the credit limit on a home equity line by taking a percentage (75%-90%) of the appraised value of the home and subtracting the balance owed on the existing mortgage. In determining the borrower's actual credit line, the lender also will consider his or her ability to repay, by looking at income, debts, and other financial obligations, as well as a borrower's credit history.

Home equity plans often set a fixed time during which a homeowner can borrow money, such as 10 years. When this period is up, the plan may allow the borrower to renew the credit line. But in a plan that does not allow renewals, a borrower will not be able to borrow additional money once the time has expired. Some plans may call for payment in full of any outstanding balance. Others may permit a borrower to repay over a fixed time, for example 10 years.

Once approved for the home equity plan, usually a borrower will be able to borrow up to the credit limit whenever he or she wants. Typically, a borrower will be able to draw on the credit line by using special checks, or under some plans, borrowers can use a credit card.

Interest Rate Charges and Plan Features

Home equity plans typically involve variable interest rates rather than fixed rates. A variable rate must be based on a publicly available index (such as the prime rate published in some major daily newspapers or a U.S. Treasury bill rate); the interest rate will change, mirroring fluctuations in the index. To figure the interest rate that the borrower will pay, most lenders add a margin of one or two percentage points to the index value. Because the cost of borrowing is tied directly to the index rate, it is important to find out what index and margin each lender uses, how often the index changes, and how high it has risen in the past.

How will the borrower repay the home equity plan?

Before entering into a plan, a borrower should consider how he or she will pay back any money that is borrowed. Some plans set minimum payments that cover a portion of the principal (the amount borrowed) plus accrued interest. But, unlike the typical installment loan, the portion that goes toward principal may not be enough to repay the debt by the end of the term. Other plans may allow payments of interest alone during the life of the plan, which means that the borrower pays nothing toward the principal. If the homeowner borrows $10,000, he or she will owe that entire sum when the plan ends.

Whatever the payment arrangements during the life of the plan—whether the borrower pays some, a little, or none of the principal amount of the loan—when the plan ends the borrower may have to pay the entire balance owed, all at once. He or she must be prepared to make this balloon payment by refinancing it with the lender, by obtaining a loan from another lender, or by some other means.

If a homeowner is thinking about a home equity line of credit, he or she also might want to consider a more traditional second mortgage loan. This type of loan provides a fixed amount of money repayable over a fixed period. Usually the payment schedule calls for equal payments that will pay off the entire loan within that time.

Seller Financing - 2nd Trust Deed

Another common source for secondary financing of a sale is the seller. If the seller is going to be the lender, he or she agrees to carry back, or act as a banker, and make a loan to the buyer for the needed amount. That loan is secured by a trust deed, in favor of the seller, recorded after the first trust deed. In a seller carryback loan the seller acts as the beneficiary and the buyer is the trustor.

When a seller carries the paper on the sale of his or her home, it is also called a **purchase-money loan,** just like the loan made by an outside lender. If a seller receives a substantial amount from the proceeds of a first loan, plus the buyer's down payment, it may be in the seller's interest to carry a second trust deed—possibly for income or to reduce tax liability by accepting installment payments.

> Example: Dominick made an offer on a house owned by Bruno, who accepted an offer of $375,000 with $37,500 as the down payment. The buyer qualified for a new first loan in the amount of $318,750, and asked Bruno to carry a second loan in the amount of $18,750 to complete the purchase price.

When the seller extends credit in the form of a loan secured by a second deed of trust, the note may be written as a straight note, with interest-only payments, or even no payments. Or it could be an installment note with a balloon payment at the end, or fully amortized note with equal payments until it is paid off. The term of the loan is decided by the buyer and seller. The instructions of the buyer and seller regarding the seller financing are usually carried out through escrow.

If a trust deed held by the seller is sold to an outside party, usually a mortgage broker, the note and trust deed will be discounted. **Discounting a note** is selling a note for less than the face amount or the current balance. Even though the seller receives a reduction in value by the mortgage broker, it is one way a seller can get cash out of a trust deed that was carried back.

> Example: Bob and Todd owned a house together as investors. After several years, they put the house on the market for $550,000 and hoped to get a full-price offer so they could go their separate ways with the profit from the house.
>
> After a short time, they did get a full-price offer. The buyer offered to put $110,000 down, get a $385,000 new first loan and asked Bob and Todd to carry $55,000 for five years, as a second trust deed. Bob and Todd would have turned the offer down if their agent had not suggested they accept and sell the second trust deed after the close of escrow. Even though it would be discounted, it was one way they could get most of the cash out of their investment.
>
> If the second trust deed was sold at a discounted 20%, or $11,000, Bob and Todd would end up with $55,000, less $11,000, or $44,000. In that way they would get the cash out of the sale, though they would be netting less than they originally planned because of the discount. They followed their agent's suggestion, and were satisfied with the result.

Whenever there is seller financing in a real estate transaction, the law requires the buyer and seller to complete a **Seller Financing Disclosure Statement**. It gives both the seller and buyer all the information needed to make an informed decision about using seller financing to complete the sale.

The seller can see from the disclosure whether or not the buyer has the ability to pay off the loan by looking at the buyer's income, and whether or not the buyer has a good credit history. The buyer can see what the existing loans are, as well as such things as due date and payments on existing loans that would be senior to the loan in question.

Seller Financing - All-Inclusive Trust Deed (AITD)

The **all-inclusive trust deed (AITD)**, or **wrap-around mortgage**, is a type of seller financing. It is used in a transaction between buyer and seller to make the financing attractive to the buyer and beneficial to the seller as well. Instead of the buyer assuming an existing loan and the seller carrying back a second trust deed, the AITD can accomplish the same purpose with greater benefit to both parties. At the closing the buyer receives title to the property.

An AITD (wrap-around mortgage) wraps an existing loan with a new loan, and the borrower makes one payment for both. In other words, the new trust deed (the AITD) includes the present encumbrances, such as first, second, third, or more trust deeds, plus the amount to be financed by the seller.

Before trying to buy property using an AITD, it is important to be sure the existing loan can be legally combined with (or wrapped by) the new AITD. Many loans contain alienation (due on sale) clauses as part of the promissory note, which prohibit the transfer of the property to a new owner without the approval of the underlying lender.

The AITD is a junior loan and subordinate to existing encumbrances because the AITD is created at a later date. This means any existing encumbrances have priority over the AITD, even though they are included, or wrapped, by the new all inclusive trust deed.

The AITD does not disturb any existing loan(s). The seller, as the new lender, keeps making the payments while giving a new increased loan at a higher rate of interest to the borrower. The amount of the AITD includes the unpaid principal balance of the existing (underlying) loan, plus the amount of the new loan being made by the seller. The borrower makes payment on the new larger loan to the seller, who in turn makes payment to the holder of the existing underlying loan. The new loan "wraps around" the existing loan.

A seller usually will carry back a wrap-around trust deed at a higher rate of interest than the underlying trust deed, thereby increasing the yield. The seller continues to pay off the original trust deed from the payments on the wrap-around, while keeping the difference. This type of financing works best when the underlying interest rate is low and the seller can then charge a higher rate on the wrapped loan.

Example: Arthur wanted to sell his house, and listed it for $300,000. The existing first trust deed was for $90,000 at 6%, payable at $540 monthly. He thought about carrying a second trust deed at 7%, counting on the income from the note. However, Bonnie, his listing agent, explained he could get a greater return from carrying an all-inclusive trust deed (AITD) instead of just a note and second trust deed from a buyer. She also told him any offer that included an AITD should be referred to an attorney. Arthur, with his attorney's approval, accepted the following offer soon after listing the house:

Buyer's Offer

Sales price	$300,000
Less buyer's 20% cash down payment	- $60,000
AITD in favor of Arthur	$240,000

Buyer would make payments on new AITD of $240,000 at 7% to be $1,597 made monthly to Arthur. Arthur would continue to make payments on the underlying first trust deed of $90,000 at 6%, in the amount of $540 monthly.

Arthur's Cash Flow

AITD payment to Arthur	$1,597
Less payments on existing Trust Deed	- $540
Monthly difference to Arthur	$1,057

Other Types of Loans

Today, many "alphabet soup" loan programs are available to serve consumers. The right type of mortgage for a borrower depends on many different factors, such as:

- current financial picture.
- future financial expectations.
- length of time expected to own the home.
- comfort level of changing mortgage payments.
- ability to qualify for a conventional loan.
- amount of down payment.
- ability to qualify for a VA loan.
- desire to take advantage of FHA-insured loans.
- credit rating of the borrower.
- purpose of the loan: home purchase, refinance, equity loan.

As we've seen, various loan programs are determined by the terms in the promissory note—primarily interest rate and repayment schedule. The borrower's credit worthiness affects the interest rate quoted by the lender.

Unsecured Loan

Some consumers who need a small loan to fix the car, buy a new appliance or take a trip are choosing a closed-end, unsecured loan instead of using their credit cards or getting a home equity loan. An **unsecured loan** is one in which the lender receives a promissory note from the borrower, without any security for payment of the debt, such as a trust deed or mortgage. The only recourse is a lengthy court action to force payment. This is truly the traditional IOU.

Open-End Loan

An **open-end loan** is essentially a revolving line of credit. An additional amount of money may be loaned to a borrower in the future under the same trust deed. The effect is to preserve the original loan's priority claim against the property with this open-end loan.

Package Loan

A loan on real property secured by more than the land and structure is known as a **package loan**. It includes fixtures attached to the building (appliances, carpeting, drapes, air conditioning) and other personal property.

Blanket Loan

A trust deed or mortgage that covers more than one parcel of property may be secured by a **blanket loan**. It usually contains a **partial release clause** that provides for the release of any particular parcel upon the repayment of a specified part of the loan. Commonly, it is used in connection with housing tracts, or construction loans. When a house is sold in a subdivision, the partial release clause is signed releasing that parcel from the blanket construction loan. A **deed of partial reconveyance** is recorded to show that the obligation has been met.

Another use of a blanket loan is for a homeowner to buy or build a new home, even if the current home still needs to be sold. In this instance, a blanket loan would cover both homes, the current property, as well as the property being built or purchased. The result is making one monthly payment instead of two and eliminating the uncertainty of buying or building a home and selling a home at the same time. A blanket loan will save money and eliminate the inconvenience of obtaining a swing loan.

WRAP AROUND MORTGAGE RIDER

Rider and addendum to Security Instrument dated_____, _____

The attached security instrument is a "wrap-around" mortgage/deed of trust subordinate to a certain mortgage/deed of trust dated _____, _____, executed in favor of _____ and currently held by_____ in the original principal amount of $_____, which was recorded on the _____ day of _____, _____ in the county records of _____ County, State_____ as follows:

Book:_____
Page: _____
Libor: _____
Reception: _____
Date:_____

Borrower agrees to comply with all the terms and conditions of the above described mortgage including, but not limited to, those concerning taxes and insurance, other than with respect to the payment of principal or interest due under said mortgage. If Borrower herein shall fail to comply with all the terms, provisions and conditions of said mortgage so as to result in a default thereunder (other than with respect to payments of principal or interest due), that failure on the part of Borrower herein shall constitute a default under this security instrument and shall entitle the lender, at its options, to exercise any and all rights and remedies given this security instrument in the event of a default under this security instrument.

If the lender hereunder shall default in making any required payment of principal or interest under the above described mortgage or deed of trust, the Borrower shall have the right to advance funds necessary to cure that default and all funds so advanced by Borrower shall be credited against the next installment of principal and interest due under the Note secured by this security instrument.

_____   _____
Borrower   Borrower

Swing (Bridge) Loan

A **swing loan** (also called interim or bridge loan) is a temporary loan made on a borrower's equity in his or her home. It is usually a short term loan that is due in six (6) months or when the borrower's home sells, whichever occurs sooner. It is used when the borrower has purchased another property, with the present home unsold, and needs the cash to close the sale of the new home. The new loan is secured by a trust deed or mortgage against the borrower's home. Usually there are no payments, with interest accruing during the term of the loan. When the borrower's home sells, the swing loan plus interest is repaid, through escrow, from the proceeds of the sale.

Swing loans can be risky depending on the current real estate market. In a fast-paced real estate market, it's usually safe to assume that the home will sell within several months if it's priced right. However, if the market is stagnant, it could take longer than six (6) months to sell and the borrower would have to pay the carrying costs on two homes.

Pledged Account Mortgage

A **pledged account mortgage** (PAM) is a loan made against security, such as money held in a savings account or a certificate of deposit. When a borrower has a large amount of money in a savings or thrift account, one way he or she can use that to an advantage is to **pledge** the account as security for a lender. Another version enables the borrower to get 100% financing if a relative (or more than one relative) agrees to pledge a savings account or Certificate of Deposit as collateral for the loan. A benefit of this loan program is that the person who pledges the money continues to earn interest. When the borrower has sufficient equity in the property, the pledge money is returned.

The lender will require a certain ratio of the loan amount to the balance in the account, and the borrower must keep that amount in the account for a specified length of time. The lender may release the pledge account when the property has acquired enough equity to qualify under normal loan-to-value ratios.

Shared Appreciation Mortgage

A **shared appreciation mortgage** (SAM) is a loan in which the lender offers a below-market interest rate in return for a portion of the profits made by the home owner when the property is sold. The holding period (usually three to five years) and the percentage of shared equity are spelled out in the loan agreements.

Rollover Mortgage

The **rollover mortgage** (ROM) is a loan in which the unpaid balance is refinanced typically every five years at then current rates. This is good for the borrower and bad for the lender if interest rates are falling, and bad for the borrower and good for the lender if interest rates are rising.

Renegotiable Rate Mortgage

A **renegotiable rate mortgage** is a loan in which the interest rate is renegotiated periodically. The loan may be either a long-term loan with periodic interest rate adjustments, or a short-term loan that is renewed periodically at new interest rates, but based on a long-term mortgage. There is a maximum interest rate fluctuation of 5% over the term of the loan.

Construction Loans

Construction financing comprises two phases—the construction phase and completion. An interim loan is a short-term loan to finance construction costs, such as the building of a new home. The lender advances funds to the borrower as needed while construction progresses. Since it is a high-risk loan it has a higher interest rate. Upon completion of the construction, the borrower must obtain permanent financing or pay the construction loan in full. The permanent loan that pays off a construction loan is called a **takeout loan**. Interim construction loans are usually made by commercial banks, whereas standby commitments and takeout loans are arranged by mortgage companies for large investors such as insurance companies.

Do not confuse a takeout loan with a forward-takeout commitment (also called a standby commitment). A forward-takeout commitment is just a very expensive letter that promises to deliver a takeout loan in the future if the property is built according to plans and specifications and leased at the target rental rate. Typically forward-takeout commitment will cost a developer one-to-two points, plus at least one additional point if the loan eventually funds, however, the borrower does not have to take the loan.

Summary

Real estate financing in California is focused on promissory notes and deeds of trust. Promissory notes include interest only payments (straight notes or term loan) or payments of principal and interest (installment payments). The **promissory note** is a written agreement between a lender and a borrower to document a loan. This agreement also serves as evidence of the debt.

The most popular promissory notes are the fully amortized installment note, adjustable-rate loans, and fixed-interest rate loans.

In California, real estate loans are secured by a deed of trust. A **deed of trust** is a financial instrument consisting of a trustor (borrower), trustee (title holder), and a beneficiary (lender). The deed of trust is the security guaranteeing loan repayment. Upon repayment of a loan, the trustee transfers title back to the **trustor**. If the trustor neglects to pay on the loan, the **trustee** can **foreclose** on the property by a trustee's sale.

Promissory notes and deeds of trust may also include special clauses that give a general description of the duties and responsibilities of the trustor. The most common clauses are acceleration and alienation.

Loans can be classified as fixed-rate loans, adjustable-rate loans and/or combinations of the two. In addition, loans are classified as either conventional or government loans. A **conventional loan** is produced by lenders without any governmental guarantee. A **conforming loan** follows the regulations set by Fannie Mae and Freddie Mac. Loans that do not conform to standard conventional lending standards are called **non-conforming loans** (examples are **jumbo** and **subprime loans**). Popular government loans include Federal Housing Administration (FHA), Veterans Administration (VA) and CalVet.

Loan programs in general are varied and fit different kinds of borrowers who need credit to buy homes. Popular secondary financing loans are **junior loans**, **home equity loans** and **home equity line of credit.**

Chapter 9 Review Exercises

Matching Exercise

Instructions: Look up the meaning of the terms in the Glossary, then write the letter of the matching term on the blank line before its definition. Answers are in Appendix B.

Terms

a. acceleration clause

b. adjustable-rate mortgage

c. alienation clause

d. amortization

e. assumption clause

f. beneficiary

g. blanket loan

h. collateral

i. conforming loans

j. conventional loan

k. discounting a note

l. endorsement

m. equitable title

n. fictitious trust deed

o. mortgagee

p. mortgagor

q. nominal or "named" rate

r. promissory note

s. purchase-money loan

t. renegotiable rate mortgage

u. stand-by commitment

v. takeout loan

w. trust deed

x. vendee

y. vendor

Definitions

1. _____ Any loan made by lenders without any governmental guarantees.

2. _____ Selling a note for less than the face amount or the current balance.

3. _____ The lender under a mortgage.

4. _____ The interest held by the trustor under a trust deed.

5. _____ Any loan made at the time of a sale, as part of that sale.

6. _____ Recorded trust deed containing details which apply to later loan documents.

7. _____ Loan in which the interest rate is renegotiated periodically.

8. _____ The permanent loan that pays off a construction loan.

9. _____ The interest rate stated in the note.

10. _____   The seller under a contract of sale (land contract).

11. _____   A clause in a loan document describing certain events that would cause the entire loan to be due.

12. _____   The evidence of the debt.

13. _____   A clause in a loan document that would allow the lender to call the entire loan due upon the sale of the property.

14. _____   A note whose interest rate is tied to a movable economic index.

15. _____   A letter that promises to deliver a takeout loan in the future.

16. _____   The liquidation of a financial obligation.

17. _____   The borrower under a mortgage.

18. _____   The lender under a deed of trust.

19. _____   Something of value given as security for a debt.

20. _____   A security instrument that conveys naked legal title of real property.

Multiple Choice Questions

Instructions: Circle your response and go to Appendix B to read the complete explanation for each question.

1. A promissory note:
   a. is security for a trust deed.
   b. is evidence of a debt.
   c. must be recorded.
   d. is collateral for the loan.

2. All of the following are negotiable instruments **except** a(n):
   a. personal check.
   b. promissory note.
   c. installment note.
   d. trust deed securing a promissory note.

3. Which of the following statements is **correct** regarding effective interest rate and nominal interest rate?
    a. The effective interest rate is slightly above the average rate in the marketplace; the nominal interest rate is slightly below.
    b. The effective interest rate is the rate actually paid by the borrower; the nominal interest rate is the rate named in the note.
    c. The effective interest rate is the rate named in the contract; the nominal interest rate is the average rate in the marketplace.
    d. None of the above

4. The liquidation of financial obligation on an installment basis is known as:
    a. conversion.
    b. acceleration.
    c. conveyance.
    d. amortization.

5. If the payments on a loan financing a real estate purchase are insufficient to service the debt, the result will be:
    a. a smaller balloon payment.
    b. negative amortization.
    c. positive cash flow.
    d. default on the debt.

6. Which of the following will necessarily involve a balloon payment?
    a. Fully amortized loan
    b. Partially amortized loan
    c. Variable rate loan
    d. Fixed rate loan

7. When compared to a 25-year amortized loan, a 30-year amortized loan has:
    a. higher monthly payments of principal.
    b. higher monthly payments of principal and interest.
    c. lower monthly payments of principal.
    d. lower monthly payments of principal and interest.

8. A mortgage loan with an interest rate that changes along with money market rates is often referred to as a:
    a. growing equity.
    b. shared appreciation.
    c. adjustable rate.
    d. reverse annuity.

9. Which of the following statements best defines a "mortgage loan?"
    a. A loan secured by a mortgage on real estate
    b. Any means of creating a trusteeship
    c. An unsecured loan in which the mortgage itself serves as collateral
    d. None of the above

10. In a deed of trust, the power of sale in the event of default is given from the:
    a. beneficiary to the trustee.
    b. buyer to the seller.
    c. trustor to the trustee.
    d. trustee to the beneficiary.

11. A "power of sale" or "trustee's sale" foreclosure of a deed of trust:
    a. is similar to a court foreclosure.
    b. prohibits a deficiency judgment.
    c. allows for no reinstatement period.
    d. gives the trustor rights of redemption.

12. Mortgages and trust deeds are different in all of the following respects, **except**:
    a. parties.
    b. security.
    c. statute of limitations.
    d. title.

13. In the case of a contract of sale, the best analogy for the financial relationship of the parties is:
    a. landlord-tenant.
    b. beneficiary-trustor.
    c. optionor-optionee.
    d. grantor-grantee.

14. An "or more" clause of an installment note would:
    a. provide for an accelerated payoff.
    b. show that the note has several makers.
    c. provide for a moratorium on loans in case of a natural disaster.
    d. provide for borrowing more money on the same note.

15. According to law, a monthly mortgage payment is considered to be late when it is paid or tendered how many days after the due date?
    a. 3 days or more
    b. 5 days or more
    c. 10 days or more
    d. More than 10 days

16. Adding an acceleration clause to a note would:
    a. not make the note less negotiable.
    b. be of no benefit to the holder.
    c. make the note nonnegotiable.
    d. greatly limit the negotiability of the note.

17. Foreclosure of a deed of trust may be accomplished either by court action or by power of sale. Foreclosure by court action:
    a. is not a remedy available in California.
    b. prohibits a deficiency judgment.
    c. usually establishes a right-of-redemption period.
    d. is identical to foreclosure by trustee sale.

18. When real property subject to a mortgage is foreclosed judicially, the mortgagor may remain in possession of the property for what maximum amount of time after the foreclosure of the sale?
    a. 30 days
    b. 90 days
    c. 180 days
    d. one year

19. A broker sells a property and negotiates a first loan from a bank and a second loan from a seller. The broker would record a "Request for Notice of Default" for the protection of the _____ loan.
    a. beneficiary of the first
    b. beneficiary of the second
    c. trustor of the first
    d. trustee of the first

20. Buyer Taylor purchases a home from Seller Sanders and agrees to assume an existing conventional loan. The lender agrees to the assumption and signs a substitution of liability. Under these circumstances:
    a. Taylor becomes primarily responsible for the loan, and Sanders remains liable as a surety.
    b. Sanders remains primarily responsible for the loan, and Taylor becomes secondarily liable.
    c. Sanders is relieved from all liability.
    d. the loan may not be secured by a purchase-money deed of trust.

21. The main purpose of the FHA was to:
    a. help stabilize the housing market.
    b. promote home ownership by insuring home loans.
    c. raise building standards on a national basis.
    d. provide a source of home-loan funds at low rates.

22. For an FHA insured loan, the interest rate is:
    a. set by market conditions.
    b. set by the FHA.
    c. determined by agreement between the borrower and lender.
    d. set by the borrower only.

23. Rose, a prospective home buyer, asked Steve at ABC Real Estate Brokerage Company to help her get FHA financing. The broker would most likely contact:
    a. a mutual mortgage insurer.
    b. the Federal Reserve Bank
    c. the Federal Housing Administration.
    d. an approved mortgagee.

24. One of the special features of VA financing is that:
    a. the down payment cannot exceed 3% of the assessed value.
    b. the down payment varies with the property value.
    c. the down payment is determined by the CRV.
    d. there is no down payment if the selling price does not exceed the CRV.

25. Which of the following statements is not correct regarding land contracts?
    a. The buyer has equitable ownership of the property.
    b. The buyer has possession of the property.
    c. The seller has legal title of the property.
    d. The seller is known as the vendee.

26. Excluding the down payment, a home buyer would be most likely to pay the lowest closing costs if the buyer were to secure a _____ loan.
    a. CalVet
    b. FHA
    c. VA
    d. conventional

27. A deed of trust and note are given to a seller to finance the purchase of vacant land. The buyer intends to place a short term construction loan on the land. Such a deed of trust is most likely to include a(n) _____ clause.
    a. subrogation
    b. "or more"
    c. subordination
    d. prepayment

28. Which of the following is true regarding a hard-money second deed of trust?
    a. It is a real property purchase loan.
    b. It has the highest possible lien priority.
    c. Through this type of deed, equity in real property is the collateral for a cash loan.
    d. It cannot be used to purchase personal property.

29. Harper borrowed money from Roberts. As security for the loan, Harper gave Roberts a trust deed covering six separate parcels of previously unencumbered real property that Harper owned. Such a trust deed would be regarded as a(n) _____ trust deed.
    a. blanket
    b. subordinated
    c. all-inclusive
    d. purchase-money

30. Which of the following terms are most nearly identical?
    a. Takeout loan/deficit financing
    b. Takeout loan/interim loan
    c. Construction loan/take-out loan
    d. Construction loan/interim loan

Real Estate Finance: Lending Institutions

10 Chapter

Introduction

In the previous chapter we discussed promissory notes, security instruments and types of loans. Now we will direct our attention to the banking system, the primary and secondary mortgage markets and the intricacies of obtaining a loan.

Learning Objectives

After reading this chapter, you will be able to:

- discuss the different types of real estate loans.
- describe the types of FHA-insured loans.
- identify loan documents.
- explain loan underwriting.
- interpret real estate financial terminology.

The Importance of Real Estate Finance

At the center of nearly all real estate transactions is some kind of financing. Without an understanding of how real property is financed, the developer, the contractor, the real estate professional, and the property manager would find themselves out of a job. Most sellers would not be able to sell, because most buyers would be financially unable to pay cash, or unwilling to purchase unless a large part of the purchase price could be borrowed.

The purchase of a home is generally the largest acquisition consumers make in their lifetime. Most consumers do not have the financial wherewithal to purchase a home outright and must obtain a real estate loan to finance the transaction.

We learned in Chapter 1 about the circular nature of the national economy; financial markets are circular in nature as well. The circle starts with the Federal Reserve System and ends with a consumer obtaining a loan from a regulated institution.

The Federal Reserve System

The **Federal Reserve Bank System** (the Fed) is the nation's central bank and acts as the banker's bank. The Fed's primary purpose is to regulate the flow of money and credit, and to promote economic growth with stability. The Fed develops national monetary policy and shares responsibility with the 12 Federal Reserve banks for applying that policy and setting money supply goals.

In addition to serving as the banker's bank, the Federal Reserve System acts as banker for the U.S. Government. Federal Reserve Banks maintain accounts for the U.S. Treasury, process government checks, postal money orders and U.S. Savings bonds, and collect federal tax deposits.

Structure of the Federal Reserve System

The Federal Reserve System consists of a seven-member **Board of Governors** (BOG) headquartered in Washington, D.C., and a network of 12 Federal Reserve Banks (FRBs) located in major cities throughout the United States. For the purpose of carrying out these day-to-day operations of the Federal Reserve System, the nation has been divided into 12 Federal Reserve Districts. California is part of District 12, with the Federal Reserve Bank in San Francisco and four Federal Reserve Branches located in Los Angeles, Portland, Salt Lake City, and Seattle.

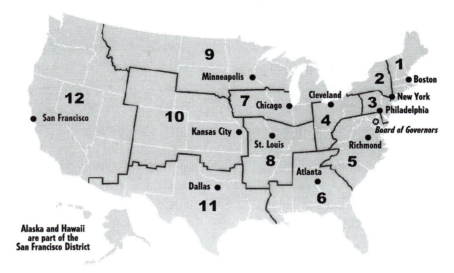

The 12 Federal Reserve Districts

Board of Governors

The primary responsibility of the Board of Governors of the Federal Reserve System is to formulate monetary policy. Monetary policy refers to the actions taken by the Fed to influence the availability and cost of money and credit as a means of promoting national economic goals. Additionally they have the responsibility to supervise the Federal Reserve Banks. Supervising banks generally means one of three duties: establishing safe and sound banking practices, protecting consumers in financial transactions, and ensuring the stability of U.S. financial markets by acting as lender of last resort. The common goal of all three duties is to minimize risk in the banking system.

Federal Reserve Banks

Federal Reserve Banks are the operating arms of the central bank. They serve other lending institutions, the U.S. Treasury and, indirectly, the public. A **Federal Reserve Bank** (FRB) is often called the banker's bank, storing currency and coin, and processing checks and electronic payments. The 12 Federal Reserve Banks supervise state-chartered commercial banks, the companies that own banks (bank holding companies) and international organizations that do banking business in the United States.

The Federal Reserve is charged with the critical task of providing a safe and efficient method of transferring funds throughout the banking system. Reserve banks and their branches carry out this mission, offering payment services to all financial institutions in the United States, regardless of size or location. Hand in hand with that mission is the obligation to improve the payment system by encouraging efficiency and technological advances.

Essentially, a Federal Reserve Bank serves as a bankers' bank, offering a wide variety of payment services. It distributes currency and coin, processes checks and offers electronic forms of payment. The Fed competes with the private sector in its financial services to foster competition in the marketplace, and to promote innovation and efficiency in the payment system. It does not seek to make a profit from its participation; it sets prices only to recover costs.

Regional FRBs are responsible for meeting public demand for currency and coin within their districts. In addition, FRBs also process commercial checks. Every day billions of dollars are transferred electronically among U.S. financial institutions. The FRBs provide two electronic payment services: funds transfer and the automated clearing house, or ACH. The funds transfer service provides a communications link among financial institutions and government agencies. The ACH provides a nationwide network to exchange paperless payments among financial institutions and government agencies. The ACH accommodates a wide range of recurring corporate and consumer transactions, such as payroll deposit, electronic bill payment, insurance payments, and Social Security disbursements.

Federal Open Market Committee

The Federal Open Market Committee (FOMC) is the most important monetary policy-making body of the Federal Reserve System. It is responsible for developing policies to promote economic growth, full employment, and stable prices. The FOMC makes key decisions regarding the conduct of open market operations-purchases and sales of U.S. government and federal agency securities.

How Does the Fed Implement Monetary Policy?

In an effort to avoid the peaks and valleys of the business cycle that cause liquidity and credit crises, the Fed monitors changing economic conditions and applies appropriate controls. The Fed influences the supply of money and credit available, thus controlling the behavior of lenders and borrowers. These controls are far reaching, often affecting interest rates, jobs and economies worldwide. To accomplish its goals, the Fed uses three basic tools: (1) reserve requirements, (2) setting the discount rates, and (3) open market operations.

Reserve Requirements

All member banks must set aside a certain percentage of their deposits as a reserve. The reserve is money that the banks cannot lend. The Board of Governors sets the reserve requirements. The Board increases or decreases the amount of money in circulation by raising or lowering reserve requirements for member banks. When the Board requires a larger reserve, the banks have less to lend, thus interest rates increase while borrowing and spending decrease. When the board lowers the reserve requirement, the banks have more money to lend, so interest rates may decrease, and borrowing and spending increase. Through its discount window, the Fed lends money to banks so that a shortage of funds at one institution does not disrupt the flow of money and credit in the entire banking system. Typically, the Fed makes loans to satisfy a bank's unanticipated needs for short-term funds. But the Fed also makes longer-term loans to help banks manage seasonal fluctuations in their customers' deposit or credit demands.

Discount Rate

A bank that needs to increase its reserve requirements would borrow money directly from the Federal Reserve Bank at the discount rate. A decrease in the interest rate allows more bank borrowing from the Fed. Bank borrowing increases money available for lending. Raising the discount rate produces less money available for lending to the consumer.

Open Market Operations

The Federal Open Market Committee (FOMC) of the Fed also buys and sells government securities, typically existing bonds, to influence the amount of available credit. The open market operations process is the most flexible and widely used technique for expanding or slowing the economy.

To stimulate or expand the economy, the Fed buys government securities from the public. This increases the bank's cash which increases the money supply and lowers interest. This causes more money to be available in the banks to lend. To slow down the economy, the Fed sells government securities to the public. This reduces the banks' cash, tightens up the money supply, and increases interest rates.

Deregulation and Reform

Before deregulation in the early 1980s, lending institutions were restricted on their activities, such as what interest rates they could pay on their deposits, and where branches could be set up. Additionally, the federally chartered Savings and Loans (S&Ls) were required by federal regulation to hold at least 80% of their assets in residential loans to encourage lending on residential real estate. Many people felt that the government should remove the strict banking regulations and let them compete on the open market. In fact, this was the belief during both the Carter and Reagan administration. The result of this rather laissez faire approach was deregulation. **Deregulation** is a process whereby regulatory restraints are gradually relaxed. Limits were applied on the interest rate that could be paid on savings accounts, giving the savings and loan associations a dependable source of funds, at a fixed interest rate, which made possible long-term loans at reasonable rates.

The first indication of a problem came in the late 1970s, when savers began to take their money out of S&Ls and put it into investments that paid a higher rate of interest. This process, called **disintermediation**, began as a result of uncontrolled inflation, causing interest rates to soar to heights unseen in any market at any time. The regulated S&Ls were restricted by law from offering competitive interest rates; so depositors moved their money out of the S&Ls and put it into government securities, corporate bonds, and money market funds. The reason was that customers could get a higher interest rate on their savings from the unregulated institutions than the regulated lenders were allowed to pay under the law. The S&Ls had to pay a higher interest rate to their depositors than they were getting on their long-term loans. Since S&Ls could not compete with the higher returns from other sources, depositors began to drift away along with their money.

It became difficult to find affordable real estate loans because money was scarce and demand was high creating a **"tight" money market** which led to high interest rates. The higher interest rates translated into higher monthly payments. Potential home buyers could not qualify for the high monthly payments required on the new loans. Home ownership often was postponed by the crisis in the banking industry, which caused a crisis in the real estate industry. If no one could buy, no one could sell. Builders and developers stopped operations and the economy was immobilized.

Depository Institution's Deregulation and Monetary Control Act

The Depository Institutions Deregulation and Monetary Control Act of 1980 had sweeping changes, one of which was to raise deposit insurance from $40,000 to $100,000. It also permitted Savings and Loans to offer a much wider range of services than ever before. The deregulatory measures allowed savings and loan associations to enter the business of commercial lending, trust services, and non-mortgage consumer lending.

The S&Ls moved away from their traditional low-risk residential lending practices and began making higher-risk loans on undeveloped land, real estate development, and joint ventures. Some S&Ls engaged in large-scale real estate speculation leading to the financial failure of over 500 institutions during the 1980s. Finally in 1989, the Federal Savings and Insurance Corporation (FSLIC), the insurer who provided a recovery fund for depositors in the event of an S&L failure, did not have enough funds to bail out the failing S&Ls, became insolvent and also failed.

Financial Institutions Reform, Recovery and Enforcement Act

The "inevitable legislative backlash" to the behavior of the savings and loan industry was the enactment by Congress of the Financial Institutions Reform, Recovery and Enforcement Act (FIRREA) in 1989.

This was an attempt to rebuild an industry that had disgraced itself by disregarding the welfare of consumers and nurturing greed and profiteering within the banking business.

Under FIRREA, the Office of Thrift Supervision (OTS) and the Housing Finance Board were authorized to oversee the savings and loan regulation responsibilities. The **Federal Deposit Insurance Corporation** (FDIC) now insures deposits in all federally chartered banks and savings institutions up to $100,000 per account for commercial and savings banks. The FDIC also supervises the Savings Association Insurance Fund (SAIF) and the Resolution Trust Corporation (RTC).

The Mortgage Market

The real estate lending industry has grown substantially over the past years and is approaching $4 trillion in outstanding loan balances. The total real estate debt in the country is the largest in the world, second only to the debt of the United States government. Consumers use money and credit for the purpose of developing and acquiring real property. The environment of real estate mortgage financing is made up of the institutions that create and purchase instruments of finance, and the markets where they are transferred. Those institutions and markets facilitate the flow of funds in the financial system.

The residential real estate lending industry is comprised of two distinct markets: the primary mortgage market and the secondary mortgage market.

Primary Mortgage Market

The **primary mortgage market** is where lenders make mortgage loans by lending directly to borrowers. Participants in the primary mortgage market sell loans in the secondary mortgage market to replenish their funds.

Lenders

Lenders that make real estate loans are known as financial intermediaries. As the word "intermediary" indicates, these financial institutions stand between the suppliers and users of credit. As a liaison, the **financial intermediary** combines funds from many sources (individual savers, short-term or long-term investors) and adapts them into loans for the consumer. This process is called **intermediation**.

All mortgage lenders are financial intermediaries, even though they are not all depository institutions. A **depository institution** is one that accepts deposits in the form of savings accounts, and makes loans using their depositors' monies. These loans are carefully regulated by law because they consist of other peoples' money. Mortgage bankers do not accept deposits from savers so they are non-depository institutions. They make mortgage loans by using their own funds or by borrowing from lenders, and then selling the loans they originate.

Lenders are also classified as institutional lenders and non-institutional lenders. Institutional lenders are depository institutions. Non-institutional lenders are non-depository institutions.

Institutional Lenders

An institutional lender, as a depository, such as a commercial bank, accepts deposits which are then pooled to be invested in various ways, including trust deeds and mortgages. Institutional lenders receive most of their deposits from "household savings" (savings of individual investors). The main job of institutional lenders is to transfer money from the people who invest money to those who want to borrow it.

They make their money by lending money at a higher interest rate than what they pay their depositors or pay to borrow from the Fed. On mortgages, the lender receives the interest as well as the origination fees and points expressed as a percentage, called mortgage yield. **Mortgage yield** is the amount received or returned from an investment expressed as a percentage.

Institutional lenders include: commercial banks, thrifts, credit unions, and life insurance companies. Although most people do their personal banking at commercial banks, thrifts or credit unions, few know that they are different kinds of financial institutions, with similar banking services but operating under different regulations.

Commercial Banks

Commercial banks are the all-purpose lenders whose real estate loans represent only a portion of their overall activity. They make the widest range of loans, including loans for buying real estate, home equity loans, business loans, and other short-term loans. The major type of lending activity funded by commercial banks is for short-term (6-to-36 months) construction loans, even though they do make other types of loans as well. Typically, though, a commercial bank will make short-term, or interim, loans to finance construction. Long-term, take-out loans may be available after a construction loan is paid off. Commercial banks rely on the creditworthiness of and past experience with the borrower to assure repayment of the loan. When dealing with commercial loans, a borrower deposits funds with the bank in order to induce the lender into making a loan. This is known as a **"compensating balance."**

Thrifts

Thrifts are the largest single resource for residential mortgage credit. A thrift institution can be any one of the following major depositories of consumer savings: savings and loan associations (S&Ls), savings banks, and mutual savings banks. Any thrift can be owned either as a mutual organization or as a stock institution. Deposits for both institutions are insured by the Federal Deposit Insurance Corporation (FDIC).

Mutual ownership means that all the depositors share ownership in the savings and loan or bank, which is managed by a board of trustees. The depositors (investors) in S&Ls, savings banks or mutual savings banks are paid dividends on their share of the earnings of the organization. Mutual organizations issue no stock. On the other hand, if the institution is organized as a stock institution, investors can purchase stock through their stock broker. A stock institution is managed by a board of directors who represent the stockholders of the bank.

Savings & Loan Associations

Traditionally, savings and loan institutions (S&Ls) have played a major role in the economy by pooling the savings of individuals to fund residential mortgages. The first customers of S&Ls were depositors as well as borrowers, and as their customer base grew, the S&L associations became a primary source of loans to finance homebuilding. Deregulation in the early 1980s allowed the S&Ls to participate in a wide range of investment opportunities. Within less than 10 years, 20% of S&Ls were insolvent, 20% were marginal, and only 60% were financially sound. This led to many S&L failures and for others to change their charters to savings banks.

Savings Banks

Savings banks have been described as distinctive types of thrift institutions, behaving sometimes like commercial banks and sometimes like S&Ls. While savings banks are authorized to make mortgage loans, most specialize in consumer and commercial loans.

Banks are authorized to make mortgage loans.

As mentioned previously, many financially troubled savings and loan associations were issued federal savings bank charters in an attempt to keep the S&Ls out of bankruptcy. By switching to the federal charters the new savings banks could offer their depositors the safety of deposit insurance under Federal Deposit Insurance Corporation—the same as commercial banks.

Currently savings and loan associations and savings banks are the largest single resource for residential mortgage credit.

Mutual Savings Banks

When lending institutions were being established in the first part of the 19th Century, the average income worker was ignored mostly due to their lack of extra funds to invest or save. Mutual savings banks were established to encourage savings by people who did not have a large amount of disposable income left after their living expenses, but who did want to invest in their future.

Initially, mutual savings banks were state-chartered, mutual organizations relying on their customers' savings to provide all the capital they needed to be successful. They did not sell stock in the company to shareholders. Recently, mutual savings banks were permitted to change their charter from mutual ownership to become federally chartered stock institutions that issue stock to raise capital. These institutions operate similarly to savings and loan associations and are located primarily in the northeastern section of the United States.

Credit Unions

A credit union is an association whose members usually have the same type of occupation. The members join together for mutual benefit by saving money in their own bank and receiving better interest rates. Both secured and unsecured loans are made at rates lower than other lenders can offer. Because of the low overhead and other costs of doing business, credit unions are a growing source of funds for consumers. They are supervised by the National Credit Union Association Board (NCUAB) and deposits are insured by the federally insured National Credit Union Share Insurance Fund. Credit unions are limited by their charters to providing services for members of a particular organization, such as employees of fire departments, utilities, corporations or other specific group.

Insurance Companies

Insurance companies are major suppliers of money for large commercial loans to developers and builders. Commercial real estate is a good, long-term investment for insurance companies because of the long time-line of their investment goals. They usually don't make construction loans, but make take out loans on large properties. For example, a developer who wants a long-term $3,000,000 loan to purchase and rehabilitate an existing shopping center would borrow the money from an insurance company.

Loans made by insurance companies have low interest rates and the lowest loan-to-value ratio. Usually loans are made through loan correspondents (mortgage companies) who negotiate and service the loans.

They don't usually get involved with the single home residential market, but can buy loans from mortgage companies and invest in GNMA government insured or guaranteed loans. Life insurance companies, in particular, receive regular periodic payments from customers in return for assurance that any loss would be covered if certain described events occur for which the customer is insured.

Non-Institutional Lenders

In addition to institutional lenders, there is another group of lenders referred to as non-institutional lenders. Non-institutional lenders are non-depository institutions and do not take deposits. They are private lenders that invest their own funds or borrowed funds. This group includes private individuals, mortgage companies, and investment companies, as well as others—like pension funds and title companies.

Private Individuals

Private individuals (sellers) are the major source of junior loans. The most common way to create a junior loan is by sellers carrying back a trust deed on the sale of their own homes. Usually, private loans are short term, with the main focus of the lender being the safety of the loan, and a high return on the investment.

Mortgage Companies

Mortgage companies (mortgage bankers) are the originators of a majority of all residential loans. Since they are not depository institutions, they lend their own or borrowed money to make mortgage loans. They act as financial intermediaries by connecting borrowers with lenders. Mortgage companies (bankers) make mortgage loans to consumers and sell them to institutional investors and then continue to service the loan after the sale.

Mortgage Banker

The mortgage banker often acts as a mover of funds from an area of the country with an abundance of money to be loaned, to another area that is capital deficient. The biggest role of mortgage companies, however, is to originate and service loans which they package. The process of assembling a number of mortgage loans into one package, prior to selling them to an investor, is called **warehousing**. The sale of these loan packages provides added capital with which to make more loans, which can then be packaged and sold, thus repeating the cycle.

A mortgage company prefers loans that are most readily sold in the secondary market, such as FHA, VA, or conventional mortgages. Therefore, the mortgage banker is careful to follow guidelines established by those who will be buying the loans. The name, "mortgage banker", sounds like a bank but in fact, a mortgage banker uses borrowed money in the course of originating loans.

Mortgage Broker

A mortgage broker is similar to a mortgage banker, but with a major difference. A mortgage broker originates a loan by taking the application from a borrower and sells that unclosed loan to another mortgage lender. The mortgage broker does not service the loan and has no other concern with that loan once he or she has sold it and been paid.

Investment Companies

Pooling the funds of many investors, these companies invest in a portfolio of assets. The investment companies might specialize in investing in certain types of investments or industries, such as income stocks or growth stocks or **Real Estate Investment Trusts** (REITs).

A REIT is another way private individuals can operate in the real estate market as investors, by joining together—each with a small amount of capital—to pool their resources to buy real estate, with the risk of loss spread out among the investors. REITs invest in an assorted mix of real estate and mortgage investments as a group, with a minimum of 100 investors required. There are serious legal requirements to qualify as a trust and for the special tax treatment given a REIT: 75% of assets must be in real estate and the REIT must distribute 95% or more of its annual real estate ordinary income to the investors.

Essentially a creation of the Internal Revenue Code, a REIT may be a real estate company or a group of individuals that has chosen to qualify under certain tax provisions. It then becomes an entity that distributes to its share-holders the greater part of its profits generated from the sale of its properties. The REIT itself does not pay taxes on its profits, but individual members of the trust are taxed, at their own tax rates, on the dividends distributed to them.

Non-Financial Institutions

Non-financial institutions, as you have read, are non-depository institutions. Universities, pension funds, trust departments of banks and title companies are all non-financial institutions and all hold real estate loans as investments.

Secondary Mortgage Market

In contrast to the primary mortgage market, where lending institutions make mortgage loans directly to borrowers, the secondary mortgage market is for buying and selling existing mortgages from the primary mortgage market or from each other. Participants in the secondary mortgage market do not originate loans.

The mortgage market consists of the loan originator sellers (primary market) and the loan buyers (secondary market). As we have seen, the primary market lenders (banks, thrifts or mortgage bankers) make real estate loans and then package them into mortgage pools to be sold to the participants in the **secondary mortgage market**.

The secondary mortgage market can be seen as a resale marketplace for loans—where existing loans are bought and sold. The secondary mortgage market exists because of the need, by thrifts and other financial institutions, to have the ability to sell their assets quickly when they need more money, particularly in a market where consumers are demanding more home loans. This important market is the foundation of the lending process and an essential part of our national economy's health. The secondary market's main function is to get the money to primary lenders by buying their existing mortgages. The primary lenders then have more cash with which to make new loans. These loans are then sold in the secondary market, continuing the cycle of putting money back into the primary market.

America's secondary mortgage market attracts capital from around the world to finance a wide range of mortgage products designed specifically to make homeownership affordable and accessible. No other country has a comparable secondary market.

Participants in the secondary market who purchase existing mortgages buy them with funds they have acquired by issuing bonds or other types of debt instruments. The mortgages they buy are used as security for those debt instruments. The **debt instruments**, known as mortgage-backed securities, are collateralized by the mortgages that have been bought in the secondary market. These mortgage backed securities also are bought and sold in the secondary market.

The original source of the funds used to buy the mortgage-backed securities is investors who purchase the securities from the secondary market agency or company. That agency then uses the funds from the investor to buy more mortgages—for example, from a thrift or mortgage banker. The originator of the loan uses the funds they receive from the sale of the loan to originate more mortgage loans. Consumers and the entire economy benefit by the investors supplying the funds that end up, eventually, as home loans to consumers.

There are three major participants in the secondary mortgage market: (1) the Federal National Mortgage Association, (2) the Government National Mortgage Association, and (3) the Federal Home Loan Mortgage Corporation. They do not make direct loans to the public.

Federal National Mortgage Association

The **Federal National Mortgage Association** (FNMA or Fannie Mae) was originally created for the purpose of increasing the amount of housing credit available in the economy by purchasing FHA-insured and VA-guaranteed loans. As the largest investor in the secondary market, FNMA now purchases conventional loans as well.

Fannie Mae supports the secondary mortgage market by issuing mortgage-related securities and purchasing mortgages. Fannie Mae buys loans from lenders who conform to FNMA guidelines, and by doing so, puts mortgage money back into the system so lenders can make more loans. FNMA is the largest investor in the secondary market.

Today, Fannie Mae is a private, shareholder-owned company that works to make sure mortgage money is available for people in communities all across America. FNMA is not a demand source of money—it is a supply source. **Demand sources** include borrowers securing loans for construction or purchasing and refinancing a property. Fannie Mae does not lend money directly to home buyers. Instead, it works with lenders to make sure they don't run out of mortgage funds, so more people can achieve homeownership.

Fannie Mae is the country's second largest corporation in terms of assets, and the nation's largest source of financing for home mortgages. Fannie Mae stock (FNM) is actively traded on the New York Stock Exchange and other exchanges and is part of the Standard & Poors' 500 Composite Stock Price Index.

In 1968, the Federal National Mortgage Association was divided into two separate systems: Fannie Mae and Ginnie Mae. FNMA became a privately owned corporation operating with private capital on a self-sustaining basis, while GNMA remained government owned.

At that time FNMA's role was expanded to buy conventional mortgages meeting the FNMA guidelines not just the FHA and VA loans. Today, Fannie Mae operates under a congressional charter that directs it to channel its efforts into increasing the availability and affordability of home ownership for low, moderate, and middle-income Americans.

Government National Mortgage Association

The **Government National Mortgage Association** (GNMA or Ginnie Mae) was created in 1968 as a government owned corporation within the Department of Housing and Urban Development (HUD). Its purpose was—and is—to serve low-to moderate-income homebuyers. Ginnie Mae does not buy or sell loans or issue mortgage-backed securities (MBS). What Ginnie Mae does is guarantee investors the timely payment of principal and interest on MBS backed by federally insured or guaranteed loans—mainly loans insured by FHA or guaranteed by the VA.

Mortgage-backed securities (MBS) are pools of mortgages used as collateral for the issuance of securities in the secondary market. MBS are commonly referred to as **pass-through securities** because the principal and interest of the underlying loans are passed through to investors. Ginnie Mae MBS are fully modified pass-through securities guaranteed by the full faith and credit of the United States government. Regardless of whether or not the mortgage payment is made, investors in Ginnie Mae MBS will receive full and timely payment of principal as well as interest.

Ginnie Mae does not buy mortgages or issue securities but acts in a support role to other participants in the secondary market.

Federal Home Loan Mortgage Corporation

The **Federal Home Loan Mortgage Corporation** (FHLMC or Freddie Mac) is a stockholder-owned corporation charted by Congress in 1970 to stabilize the mortgage markets and support homeownership and affordable rental housing. This mission is accomplished by linking Main Street to Wall Street—purchasing, securitizing and investing in home mortgages, and ultimately providing homeowners and renters with lower housing costs and better access to home financing. Since its inception, Freddie Mac has financed one out-of-every-six homes in America.

Freddie Mac conducts its business by buying mortgages that meet the company's underwriting and product standards from lenders, packaging the mortgages into securities and selling the securities—guaranteed by Freddie Mac to investors, such as insurance companies and pension funds. About half of all new single-family mortgages originated today are sold to secondary market conduits.

Freddie Mac was created to increase the availability of mortgage credit by developing and maintaining a nationwide secondary market for residential conventional mortgage loans. Approved existing mortgage loans are bought and resold to individual investors or financial institutions. By bringing efficiency to the securities markets, Freddie Mac lowers funding costs, making housing more affordable for the nation's families and increasing shareholder value.

Mortgage lenders use the proceeds secured from selling loans to Freddie Mac to fund new mortgages, constantly replenishing the global pool of funds available for lending to homebuyers and apartment owners. Just as the stock market has put investor capital to work for corporations, the secondary mortgage market puts private investor capital to work for home buyers and apartment owners, providing a continuous flow of affordable funds for home financing.

For the most part, the process is invisible to borrowers and renters. But because Freddie Mac exists, millions of people have benefited from lower monthly mortgage payments and better access to home financing.

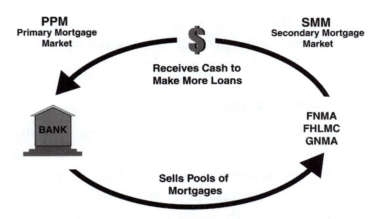

The Mortgage Market Cycle

Getting a Loan (Underwriting)

Getting a loan is an integral part of the real estate transaction since very few people have the amount of ready cash to buy a home with no financing. The first step in getting a loan is for the borrower to fill out a loan application. Once the lender has the borrower's completed application the underwriting process can begin. Simply put, **underwriting** is the process of evaluating a borrower's risk factors before the lender will make a loan.

The lender will determine the ability of a borrower to pay the loan and determine if the value of the property is sufficient to repay the loan in the event of a default by the borrower. The purpose of underwriting is to determine if the borrower and the property meet the minimum standards established by the primary lender and the secondary market investor. Once both the borrower and the property qualify, the loan process continues until it closes.

Loan Application

The underwriting process begins with the borrower filling out a loan application and gathering the documents needed by the lender. Usually the lender will ask for three monthly bank statements, the two most recent pay stubs, two year's previous tax returns, and proof of any investments. Once received the lender will verify the information and order an appraisal in order to qualify the property.

Qualifying the Borrower

Several risk factors are taken into consideration when evaluating a borrower for a loan, such as the borrower's debt-to-income level, employment history, type of property, and assets. The lender will order a credit report which will show the borrower's payment history, balance of outstanding debt, credit history, number of credit inquiries, and types of credit held. The most important being the payment and credit history.

Credit Report

The lender requests a credit report from one of the credit reporting agencies: Experian, Equifax, or Transunion. These companies research the credit records of consumers and memorialize the findings in a factual credit report. They have access to databases that store credit information on most consumers in the country. Additionally, they search the public records for derogatory items that may have been filed against a consumer, such as judgments, bankruptcies, and liens. The credit report indicates a credit score for the loan applicant. Credit scores only consider the information contained in the credit profile. They do not consider income, savings, down payment amount, or demographic factors—like gender, nationality, or marital status.

Credit scoring is an objective, statistical method that lenders use to quickly assess the borrower's credit risk. The score is a number that rates the likelihood that a borrower will repay a loan.

Past delinquencies, derogatory payment behavior, current debt level, length of credit history, types of credit, and number of inquiries are all considered in credit scores. Establishing a good track record of making payments on time will raise the credit score, but late payments will lower the score.

Scores range from 350 (high risk) to 950 (low risk). There are a few types of credit scores; the most widely used are **FICO** scores, which were developed by Fair Isaac & Company, Inc. The FICO scores run from 40 to 620 for the applicants who are late in paying bills and between 700 to above 800 for those applicants who always pay bills on time.

Under the Fair Credit Reporting Act, a person who has been denied credit, housing, or employment may receive a free copy of his or her credit report by contacting one of the credit reporting agencies directly.

Qualifying the Property

The lender's first line of defense in getting repaid on the loan is the borrower's creditworthiness. However, the underlying security for the loan is the property; therefore, an accurate valuation of the property is important. The lender will require an appraisal to determine fair market value of the property prior to making a loan. Once the appraised value is determined, the lender will calculate the loan amount. Most lenders want an 80% loan-to-value ratio. **Loan-to-value** is the percentage of appraised value to the loan. An 80% loan would require the borrower to make a 20% down payment. Loans made with less than a 20% down payment will require mortgage insurance.

The difference between the appraised value and the loan is called **equity**. Therefore, property is purchased with **equity funds** (down payment) and loan funds.

Electronic Underwriting Credit Report and Evaluation

The mortgage industry uses electronic underwriting systems that predict multiple-risk factors in a loan application. Approximately 98% of mortgage companies use some form of automated underwriting with about 60 % using either Fannie Mae's Desktop Underwriter or Freddie Mac's Loan Prospector. Fannie Mae offers its lenders electronic loan processing with its Desktop Underwriter system. Users receive an analysis of the borrower's credit, estimate of the property's value, and an opinion of the risk involved. This information is prepared from the data submitted on the loan application and is available in a matter of minutes. The use of a common automated underwriting standard will simplify the electronic mortgage application process and reduce its cost.

Disclosures in Financing

Since 1968, credit protections have multiplied rapidly. The concepts of "fair" and "equal" credit have been written into laws that prohibit unfair discrimination in credit transactions, require that consumers be told the reason when credit is denied, let borrowers find out about their credit records, and set up a way for consumers to settle billing disputes.

Each law was meant to reduce the problems and confusion about consumer credit, which—as it became more widely used in our economy—also grew more complex. Together, these laws set a standard for how individuals are to be treated in their financial dealings.

Uniform Residential Loan Application

This application is designed to be completed by the applicant(s) with the Lender's assistance. Applicants should complete this form as "Borrower" or "Co-Borrower," as applicable. Co-Borrower information must also be provided (and the appropriate box checked) when ☐ the income or assets of a person other than the "Borrower" (including the Borrower's spouse) will be used as a basis for loan qualification or ☐ the income or assets of the Borrower's spouse will not be used as a basis for loan qualification, but his or her liabilities must be considered because the Borrower resides in a community property state, the security property is located in a community property state, or the Borrower is relying on other property located in a community property state as a basis for repayment of the loan.

I. TYPE OF MORTGAGE AND TERMS OF LOAN

Mortgage Applied for:	☐ VA ☐ FHA	☐ Conventional ☐ USDA/Rural Housing Service	☐ Other (explain):	Agency Case Number	Lender Case Number

Amount $	Interest Rate %	No. of Months	Amortization Type:	☐ Fixed Rate ☐ GPM	☐ Other (explain): ☐ ARM (type):

II. PROPERTY INFORMATION AND PURPOSE OF LOAN

Subject Property Address (street, city, state, & ZIP)	No. of Units

Legal Description of Subject Property (attach description if necessary)	Year Built

Purpose of Loan ☐ Purchase ☐ Construction ☐ Other (explain): ☐ Refinance ☐ Construction-Permanent	Property will be: ☐ Primary Residence ☐ Secondary Residence ☐ Investment

Complete this line if construction or construction-permanent loan.

Year Lot Acquired	Original Cost $	Amount Existing Liens $	(a) Present Value of Lot $	(b) Cost of Improvements $	Total (a + b) $

Complete this line if this is a refinance loan.

Year Acquired	Original Cost $	Amount Existing Liens $	Purpose of Refinance	Describe Improvements ☐ made ☐ to be made Cost: $

Title will be held in what Name(s)	Manner in which Title will be held	Estate will be held in: ☐ Fee Simple ☐ Leasehold (show expiration date)

Source of Down Payment, Settlement Charges and/or Subordinate Financing (explain)

III. BORROWER INFORMATION

Borrower	Co-Borrower
Borrower's Name (include Jr. or Sr. if applicable)	Co-Borrower's Name (include Jr. or Sr. if applicable)

Social Security Number	Home Phone (incl. area code)	DOB (MM/DD/YYYY)	Yrs. School	Social Security Number	Home Phone (incl. area code)	DOB (MM/DD/YYYY)	Yrs. School

☐ Married ☐ Separated	☐ Unmarried (include single, divorced, widowed)	Dependents (not listed by Co-Borrower) no. ages	☐ Married ☐ Separated	☐ Unmarried (include single, divorced, widowed)	Dependents (not listed by Borrower) no. ages

Present Address (street, city, state, ZIP) ☐ Own ☐ Rent _____ No. Yrs.	Present Address (street, city, state, ZIP) ☐ Own ☐ Rent _____ No. Yrs.

Mailing Address, if different from Present Address	Mailing Address, if different from Present Address

If residing at present address for less than two years, complete the following:

Former Address (street, city, state, ZIP) ☐ Own ☐ Rent _____ No. Yrs.	Former Address (street, city, state, ZIP) ☐ Own ☐ Rent _____ No. Yrs.

IV. EMPLOYMENT INFORMATION

Borrower	Co-Borrower

Name & Address of Employer ☐ Self Employed	Yrs. on this job	Name & Address of Employer ☐ Self Employed	Yrs. on this job
	Yrs. employed in this line of work/profession		Yrs. employed in this line of work/profession

Position/Title/Type of Business	Business Phone (incl. area code)	Position/Title/Type of Business	Business Phone (incl. area code)

If employed in current position for less than two years or if currently employed in more than one position, complete the following:

Name & Address of Employer ☐ Self Employed	Dates (from – to)	Name & Address of Employer ☐ Self Employed	Dates (from – to)
	Monthly Income $		Monthly Income $

Position/Title/Type of Business	Business Phone (incl. area code)	Position/Title/Type of Business	Business Phone (incl. area code)

Name & Address of Employer ☐ Self Employed	Dates (from – to)	Name & Address of Employer ☐ Self Employed	Dates (from – to)
	Monthly Income $		Monthly Income $

Position/Title/Type of Business	Business Phone (incl. area code)	Position/Title/Type of Business	Business Phone (incl. area code)

V. MONTHLY INCOME AND COMBINED HOUSING EXPENSE INFORMATION

Gross Monthly Income	Borrower	Co-Borrower	Total	Combined Monthly Housing Expense	Present	Proposed
Base Empl. Income*	$	$	$	Rent	$	
Overtime				First Mortgage (P&I)		$
Bonuses				Other Financing (P&I)		
Commissions				Hazard Insurance		
Dividends/Interest				Real Estate Taxes		
Net Rental Income				Mortgage Insurance		
Other (before completing, see the notice in "describe other income," below)				Homeowner Assn. Dues		
				Other:		
Total	$	$	$	Total	$	$

* Self Employed Borrower(s) may be required to provide additional documentation such as tax returns and financial statements.

Describe Other Income *Notice:* **Alimony, child support, or separate maintenance income need not be revealed if the Borrower (B) or Co-Borrower (C) does not choose to have it considered for repaying this loan.**

B/C		Monthly Amount
		$

VI. ASSETS AND LIABILITIES

This Statement and any applicable supporting schedules may be completed jointly by both married and unmarried Co-Borrowers if their assets and liabilities are sufficiently joined so that the Statement can be meaningfully and fairly presented on a combined basis; otherwise, separate Statements and Schedules are required. If the Co-Borrower section was completed about a spouse, this Statement and supporting schedules must be completed about that spouse also.

Completed ☐ Jointly ☐ Not Jointly

ASSETS Description	Cash or Market Value	Liabilities and Pledged Assets. List the creditor's name, address and account number for all outstanding debts, including automobile loans, revolving charge accounts, real estate loans, alimony, child support, stock pledges, etc. Use continuation sheet, if necessary. Indicate by (*) those liabilities which will be satisfied upon sale of real estate owned or upon refinancing of the subject property.	Monthly Payment & Months Left to Pay	Unpaid Balance
Cash deposit toward purchase held by:	$			
		LIABILITIES		
List checking and savings accounts below		Name and address of Company	$ Payment/Months	$
Name and address of Bank, S&L, or Credit Union				
		Acct. no.		
Acct. no.	$	Name and address of Company	$ Payment/Months	$
Name and address of Bank, S&L, or Credit Union				
		Acct. no.		
Acct. no.	$	Name and address of Company	$ Payment/Months	$
Name and address of Bank, S&L, or Credit Union				
		Acct. no.		
Acct. no.	$	Name and address of Company	$ Payment/Months	$
Name and address of Bank, S&L, or Credit Union				
		Acct. no.		
Acct. no.	$	Name and address of Company	$ Payment/Months	$
Stocks & Bonds (Company name/number & description)	$			
		Acct. no.		
		Name and address of Company	$ Payment/Months	$
Life insurance net cash value	$			
Face amount: $				
Subtotal Liquid Assets	$			
Real estate owned (enter market value from schedule of real estate owned)	$	Acct. no.		
		Name and address of Company	$ Payment/Months	$
Vested interest in retirement fund	$			
Net worth of business(es) owned (attach financial statement)	$			
Automobiles owned (make and year)	$	Acct. no.		
		Alimony/Child Support/Separate Maintenance Payments Owed to:	$	
Other Assets (itemize)	$			
		Job-Related Expense (child care, union dues, etc.)	$	
		Total Monthly Payments	$	
Total Assets a. $		Net Worth (a minus b) ▶ $	**Total Liabilities b.** $	

VI. ASSETS AND LIABILITIES (cont.)

Schedule of Real Estate Owned (If additional properties are owned, use continuation sheet.)

Property Address (enter S if sold, PS if pending sale or R if rental being held for income) ➥	Type of Property	Present Market Value	Amount of Mortgages & Liens	Gross Rental Income	Mortgage Payments	Insurance, Maintenance, Taxes & Misc.	Net Rental Income
		$	$	$	$	$	$
Totals		$	$	$	$	$	$

List any additional names under which credit has previously been received and indicate appropriate creditor name(s) and account number(s):

Alternate Name	Creditor Name	Account Number

VII. DETAILS OF TRANSACTION

a.	Purchase price	$
b.	Alterations, improvements, repairs	
c.	Land (if acquired separately)	
d.	Refinance (incl. debts to be paid off)	
e.	Estimated prepaid items	
f.	Estimated closing costs	
g.	PMI, MIP, Funding Fee	
h.	Discount (if Borrower will pay)	
i.	Total costs (add items a through h)	
j.	Subordinate financing	
k.	Borrower's closing costs paid by Seller	
l.	Other Credits (explain)	
m.	Loan amount (exclude PMI, MIP, Funding Fee financed)	
n.	PMI, MIP, Funding Fee financed	
o.	Loan amount (add m & n)	
p.	Cash from/to Borrower (subtract j, k, l & o from i)	

VIII. DECLARATIONS

If you answer "Yes" to any questions a through i, please use continuation sheet for explanation.

		Borrower Yes	Borrower No	Co-Borrower Yes	Co-Borrower No
a.	Are there any outstanding judgments against you?	☐	☐	☐	☐
b.	Have you been declared bankrupt within the past 7 years?	☐	☐	☐	☐
c.	Have you had property foreclosed upon or given title or deed in lieu thereof in the last 7 years?	☐	☐	☐	☐
d.	Are you a party to a lawsuit?	☐	☐	☐	☐
e.	Have you directly or indirectly been obligated on any loan which resulted in foreclosure, transfer of title in lieu of foreclosure, or judgment? (This would include such loans as home mortgage loans, SBA loans, home improvement loans, educational loans, manufactured (mobile) home loans, any mortgage, financial obligation, bond, or loan guarantee. If "Yes," provide details, including date, name and address of Lender, FHA or VA case number, if any, and reasons for the action.)	☐	☐	☐	☐
f.	Are you presently delinquent or in default on any Federal debt or any other loan, mortgage, financial obligation, bond, or loan guarantee? If "Yes," give details as described in the preceding question.	☐	☐	☐	☐
g.	Are you obligated to pay alimony, child support, or separate maintenance?	☐	☐	☐	☐
h.	Is any part of the down payment borrowed?	☐	☐	☐	☐
i.	Are you a co-maker or endorser on a note?	☐	☐	☐	☐
j.	Are you a U.S. citizen?	☐	☐	☐	☐
k.	Are you a permanent resident alien?	☐	☐	☐	☐
l.	Do you intend to occupy the property as your primary residence? If "Yes," complete question m below.	☐	☐	☐	☐
m.	Have you had an ownership interest in a property in the last three years?	☐	☐	☐	☐
	(1) What type of property did you own—principal residence (PR), second home (SH), or investment property (IP)?				
	(2) How did you hold title to the home—solely by yourself (S), jointly with your spouse (SP), or jointly with another person (O)?				

IX. ACKNOWLEDGMENT AND AGREEMENT

Each of the undersigned specifically represents to Lender and to Lender's actual or potential agents, brokers, processors, attorneys, insurers, servicers, successors and assigns and agrees and acknowledges that: (1) the information provided in this application is true and correct as of the date set forth opposite my signature and that any intentional or negligent misrepresentation of this information contained in this application may result in civil liability, including monetary damages, to any person who may suffer any loss due to reliance upon any misrepresentation that I have made on this application, and/or in criminal penalties including, but not limited to, fine or imprisonment or both under the provisions of Title 18, United States Code, Sec. 1001, et seq.; (2) the loan requested pursuant to this application (the "Loan") will be secured by a mortgage or deed of trust on the property described herein; (3) the property will not be used for any illegal or prohibited purpose or use; (4) all statements made in this application are made for the purpose of obtaining a residential mortgage loan; (5) the property will be occupied as indicated herein; (6) any owner or servicer of the Loan may verify or reverify any information contained in the application from any source named in this application, and Lender, its successors or assigns may retain the original and/or an electronic record of this application, even if the Loan is not approved; (7) the Lender and its agents, brokers, insurers, servicers, successors and assigns may continuously rely on the information contained in the application, and I am obligated to amend and/or supplement the information provided in this application if any of the material facts that I have represented herein should change prior to closing of the Loan; (8) in the event that my payments on the Loan become delinquent, the owner or servicer of the Loan may, in addition to any other rights and remedies that it may have relating to such delinquency, report my name and account information to one or more consumer credit reporting agencies; (9) ownership of the Loan and/or administration of the Loan account may be transferred with such notice as may be required by law; (10) neither Lender nor its agents, brokers, insurers, servicers, successors or assigns has made any representation or warranty, express or implied, to me regarding the property or the condition or value of the property; and (11) my transmission of this application as an "electronic record" containing my "electronic signature," as those terms are defined in applicable federal and/or state laws (excluding audio and video recordings), or my facsimile transmission of this application containing a facsimile of my signature, shall be as effective, enforceable and valid as if a paper version of this application were delivered containing my original written signature.

Borrower's Signature	Date	Co-Borrower's Signature	Date
X		X	

X. INFORMATION FOR GOVERNMENT MONITORING PURPOSES

The following information is requested by the Federal Government for certain types of loans related to a dwelling in order to monitor the lender's compliance with equal credit opportunity, fair housing and home mortgage disclosure laws. You are not required to furnish this information, but are encouraged to do so. The law provides that a lender may discriminate neither on the basis of this information, nor on whether you choose to furnish it. If you furnish the information, please provide both ethnicity and race. For race, you may check more than one designation. If you do not furnish ethnicity, race, or sex, under Federal regulations, this lender is required to note the information on the basis of visual observation or surname. If you do not wish to furnish the information, please check the box below. (Lender must review the above material to assure that the disclosures satisfy all requirements to which the lender is subject under applicable state law for the particular type of loan applied for.)

BORROWER ☐ I do not wish to furnish this information.	CO-BORROWER ☐ I do not wish to furnish this information.
Ethnicity: ☐ Hispanic or Latino ☐ Not Hispanic or Latino	**Ethnicity:** ☐ Hispanic or Latino ☐ Not Hispanic or Latino
Race: ☐ American Indian or Alaska Native ☐ Asian ☐ Black or African American ☐ Native Hawaiian or Other Pacific Islander ☐ White	**Race:** ☐ American Indian or Alaska Native ☐ Asian ☐ Black or African American ☐ Native Hawaiian or Other Pacific Islander ☐ White
Sex: ☐ Female ☐ Male	**Sex:** ☐ Female ☐ Male

To be Completed by Interviewer This application was taken by: ☐ Face-to-face interview ☐ Mail ☐ Telephone ☐ Internet	Interviewer's Name (print or type)	Name and Address of Interviewer's Employer
	Interviewer's Signature Date	
	Interviewer's Phone Number (incl. area code)	

Continuation Sheet/Residential Loan Application

Use this continuation sheet if you need more space to complete the Residential Loan Application. Mark **B** for Borrower or **C** for Co-Borrower.	Borrower:	Agency Case Number:
	Co-Borrower:	Lender Case Number:

I/We fully understand that it is a Federal crime punishable by fine or imprisonment, or both, to knowingly make any false statements concerning any of the above facts as applicable under the provisions of Title 18, United States Code, Section 1001, et seq.

Borrower's Signature	Date	Co-Borrower's Signature	Date
X		X	

Consumer Credit Protection Act

The Consumer Credit Protection Act of 1968—which launched Truth in Lending disclosures—was landmark legislation. For the first time, creditors had to state the cost of borrowing in a common language so that the consumer could figure out what the charges are, compare the costs of loans, and shop for the best credit deal.

Truth-in-Lending Act (Regulation Z)

The Truth in Lending Act (TILA), Title I of the Consumer Credit Protection Act, is aimed at promoting the informed use of consumer credit by requiring disclosures about its terms and costs. The TILA is intended to enable the customer to compare the cost of a cash transaction with the cost of a credit transaction and to see the difference in the cost of credit among different lenders. Its purpose is to assure a meaningful disclosure of credit terms. In general, the law applies to all real estate loans for personal, family, or household purposes; to lenders who offer credit or help arrange credit; and to the advertising of most credit offerings. Real estate loans that are exempt from the TILA include credit extended primarily for business, commercial, or agricultural purposes, or credit extended to other than a natural person. Additionally, loans over $25,000 that are not real estate loans are exempt.

Regulation Z

To accomplish the objectives of TILA, the Board of Governors of the Federal Reserve System issued a directive known as **Regulation Z** (Reg. Z). A creditor must furnish certain disclosures to the consumer before a contract for a loan is made. A **creditor** includes a lender (person or company) who regularly makes real estate loans; who extends credit for loans secured by a dwelling; and the credit extended is subject to a finance charge or is payable in more than four installments, excluding the down payment.

Disclosure Statement

TILA requires lenders to disclose the important terms and costs of their loans, including the annual percentage rate, finance charge, the payment terms, and information about any variable-rate feature. The **finance charge** is the dollar amount the credit will cost and is composed of any direct or indirect charge as a condition of obtaining credit. That would include interest, loan fees, finder fees, credit report fees, insurance fees, and mortgage insurance fees (PMI or MMI). In real estate, the finance charge does not include appraisal fees or credit report fees. The **annual percentage rate**

(APR) is the relative cost of credit expressed as a yearly rate. It is the relationship of the total finance charge to the total amount financed, expressed as a percentage.

In general, neither the lender nor anyone else may charge a fee until after the borrower has received this information. The borrower usually gets these disclosures when he or she receives an application form and will get additional disclosures before the plan is opened. If any term has changed before the plan is opened (other than a variable-rate feature), and if the borrower decides not to enter into the plan because of a changed term, the lender must return all fees.

Regulation Z requires that creditors disclose the following items for real property secured loans. The first four disclosures must include simple descriptive phrases of explanation similar to those shown in *italics*:

1. **Amount financed** - *The amount of credit (principal amount borrowed less prepaid finance charges includable) provided to you or on your behalf.*

2. **Finance charge** - *The dollar amount the credit will cost you.*

3. **Annual Percentage Rate** - *The cost of your credit expressed as a yearly rate.*

4. **Total of payments** - *The amount you will have paid when you have made all the scheduled payments.*

5. **Payment schedule** - The number, amount, and timing of payments.

6. **Name of the lender**/creditor making the disclosure.

7. Written itemization of the amount financed, or a statement that the consumer has a right to receive a written itemization, and a space in the statement for the consumer to indicate whether the itemization is requested.

8. Variable interest rate and discounted variable rate disclosures, including limitations and effects of a rate increase and an example of payment terms resulting from the increase. This may be accomplished by giving the consumer the "Consumer Handbook on Adjustable Rate Mortgages" or a suitable substitute.

9. In addition to the above-mentioned disclosure, the regulation also requires disclosures regarding due-on-sale clauses, prepayment penalties, late payment charges, description of the property, insurance requirements, and loan assumptions.

Advertising

The Truth-in-Lending Act also establishes disclosure standards for advertisements that refer to certain credit terms. If the annual percentage rate (APR) is disclosed, no more disclosures are required. If the APR is not stated, then all the specifics of all credit terms must be disclosed. An advertisement that discloses the number of payments must also disclose the amount or percentage of down payment, number of payments, amount of any payments, the finance charge, interest rate, property description, etc. In fact, if the interest rate is stated, it must also disclose the APR. Ads that would require complete disclosure would include "No money down" or "100% financing".

Right of Rescission

The right to rescind (cancel) a real estate loan applies to most consumer credit loans (hard money loans) or refinance loans. Loans used for the purchase or construction of the borrower's personal residence (purchase money loans) have no right of rescission. The lender must provide a written rescission disclosure to every borrower who is entitled to rescind. When the right of rescission applies, the borrower has a right to rescind the agreement until midnight of the third business day after the promissory note is signed.

Adjustable Rate Loan Disclosure

A lender offering adjustable rate residential mortgage loans must provide prospective borrowers with a copy of the most recent Federal Reserve Board publication which provides information about adjustable rate loans. The title is "Consumer Handbook on Adjustable Rate Mortgages". The publication must be given to the borrower upon request of the prospective borrower, or when the lender first provides information concerning adjustable rate mortgages.

Lenders who have adopted or are subject to federal rules may provide the disclosures at the same time and under the same circumstances as when the lender makes the federally required disclosures pursuant to the Truth-in-Lending Act.

Real Estate Settlement Procedures Act

The Real Estate Settlement Procedures Act (RESPA), first passed in 1974, is a federal loan disclosure law which helps protect buyers or borrowers who obtain federally related loans—FHA, VA or conventional loans that are sold to FNMA, GNMA, or FHLMC. These include most first and junior loans, such as home purchase loans, refinance loans, improvement loans, lender-approved assumptions, and equity lines of credit.

RESPA applies to all federally related, 1-4 unit residential mortgage loans. The act requires lenders to give special disclosures and to use special procedures and forms for closing costs on most home loans.

The lender must furnish a copy of a **Special Information Booklet,** together with a **Good Faith Estimate (GFE)** of the amount or **range** of closing costs to every person from whom the lender receives a written application for any federally related loan. The Good Faith Estimate provides detailed information on escrow costs so that the borrower can shop around for escrow services. Additionally buyers and borrowers will be able to make informed decisions during the loan/sale transaction and the settlement/escrow process. A lender may not charge anyone in connection with the preparation of the Good Faith Estimate (Uniform Settlement Statement) or distribution of the Special Information Booklet.

Almost all lenders fall under RESPA, except for loans made by private parties. The disclosure requirements are primarily the responsibility of the lender. RESPA regulates specified disclosures at the time of the loan application and at or before the time of settlement or closing of escrow. Violators of this law can be penalized by up to one year in jail and/or a $10,000 fine.

Real estate brokers acting as mortgage brokers do not have to give borrowers a separate California-mandated **mortgage loan disclosure statement** in federally related loan transactions when the borrower receives a good faith estimate (GFE) of settlement costs as required under RESPA and all disclosures required by the Truth-in-Lending Act. In all non-federally related brokered loans and in all "Article 7" loans under California law (with first trust deeds of less than $30,000 and junior loans of less than $20,000, whether they are federally related or not); mortgage brokers are still required to provide the California Mortgage Loan Disclosure Statement to the borrower.

Equal Credit Opportunity Act

Credit is used by millions of consumers to finance an education or a house, remodel a home, or get a small business loan. The **Equal Credit Opportunity Act** (ECOA) ensures that all consumers are given an equal chance to obtain credit. This doesn't mean all consumers who apply for credit get it because factors such as income, expenses, debt, and credit history are considerations for credit-worthiness. The law protects a borrower when dealing with any creditor who regularly extends credit, including banks, small loan and finance companies, retail and department stores, credit card companies, and credit unions. Anyone involved in granting credit, such as real estate brokers who arrange financing, is covered by the law. Businesses applying for credit also are protected by the law.

Financial Disclosures Required by California Law

It is federal policy to ensure fair housing by prohibiting discrimination based on race, color, religion, sex, national origin, marital status, age, or physical disabilities in connection with the sale, rental, construction, or financing of housing. Many state laws are passed to supplement federal legislation.

Housing Financial Discrimination Act of 1977 (Holden Act)

The Holden Act prohibits the discriminatory practice known as "redlining". **Redlining** is an illegal lending policy of denying real estate loans on properties in older, changing urban areas, usually with large minority populations, because of alleged higher lending risks, without due consideration being given by the lending institution to the credit-worthiness of the individual loan applicant.

The **Holden Act** encourages increased lending in neighborhoods where, in the past, financing has been unavailable. The major goal of the Holden Act is to ensure and increase the supply of safe and decent

The Holden Act prohibits redlining and helps to promote regeneration of older, decaying urban neighborhoods.

housing for credit-worthy borrowers and to prevent neighborhood decay. To ensure that prospective borrowers are aware of their rights under this law, lenders must notify all applicants of the provisions of the Holden Act at the time of their loan application.

Lender Compensation Disclosure

Commissioner's Regulation 2904 requires that all real estate licensees must disclose to their principals all **compensation**, or expected compensation, regardless of the form, time, or source of payment. The disclosure is required even if the broker does not handle the financing aspect of the transaction and it must be given to each party to the transaction before the transaction closes escrow.

Additionally, a real estate licensee may not receive compensation for referring customers to an escrow company, pest control firm, home inspection company, or title insurance company. Any compensation received would be considered commercial bribery.

Real Property Loan Law - Article 7

In the area of mortgage loans, the Department monitors certain activities of real estate licensees doing business as mortgage lenders and mortgage brokers. The real estate law requires anyone negotiating a loan to have a real estate license. In the past, abuses have occurred in the form of excessive commissions, inflated costs and expenses, the negotiating of short-term loans with large balloon payments, and misrepresentation or concealment of material facts by licensees negotiating these loans.

As a result of this mistreatment of consumers by some corrupt agents, legislation was passed to correct the situation. The Real Property Loan Law now applies to loans secured by first trust deeds under $30,000 and by junior trust deeds under $20,000. No balloon payment is allowed for loans on owner-occupied homes, where a broker has been involved in the negotiation, if the term is six years or less. This requirement does not apply when a seller carries back a trust deed as part of the purchase price.

A real estate broker negotiating or making loans subject to the Real Property Loan Law is limited by law in the amount that may be charged as a commission. For example, the maximum commission that the broker could charge for a $7,500 second trust deed with a five-year term would be 15%. However, on loans $30,000 and over for first trust deeds, and $20,000 or more for junior trust deeds, the broker may charge as much as the borrower will agree to pay.

The law requires anyone negotiating a loan to provide a Mortgage Loan Broker's Statement (sometimes called a Mortgage Loan Disclosure Statement) to a prospective borrower, with information concerning all important features of a loan to be negotiated for the borrower.

Mortgage Loan Disclosure Statement

A real estate broker who negotiates loans, on behalf of borrowers or lenders, to be secured by liens on real property must deliver a written disclosure statement to the borrower. It must be delivered within three business days of receipt of the borrower's written loan application, or before the borrower becomes obligated to complete the loan, whichever is earlier.

The required statement, known as the Mortgage Loan Disclosure Statement (MLDS), must be in a form approved by the Real Estate Commissioner. The MLDS needs to disclose expected maximum costs and expenses of making the loan which are to be paid by the borrower, including fees for appraisal, escrow, credit report, title insurance, recording, and notary services. In addition, the total amount of real estate commissions to be received by the broker for services performed in arranging the loan must be disclosed. These fees include: points, loan origination fees, bonuses, rebates, premiums, discounts as well as other charges received by the real estate broker in lieu of interest in transactions where the broker acts as the lender.

The MLDS must be signed by the borrower and the agent negotiating the loan. The broker negotiating the loan must keep a signed copy of the statement on file for three years.

If the loan is a federally related loan controlled by RESPA, real estate mortgage brokers do not have to deliver the MLDS as long as the borrower receives a good faith estimate of settlement costs as required under RESPA and all disclosures required by the Truth-in-Lending Act (Regulation Z).

Seller Financing Disclosure Statement

Some sellers help sell their homes by extending credit to the buyer in the form of seller "carryback" financing. This is usually in the form of a promissory note secured by a deed of trust. To prevent abuses involving some of these seller assisted financing plans the state requires the arranger of credit to give the borrower a written disclosure. An arranger of credit is a person who is

not a party to the transaction, but will be compensated for arranging the credit, negotiating the credit terms, completing the credit documents, and facilitating the transaction.

The arranger of credit must deliver a disclosure statement as soon as possible before the execution of any note or security document. The statement must be signed by the arranger of credit, the buyer and the seller, who are each to receive a copy.

Some sellers will offer carryback financing.

The disclosure statement must include: comprehensive information about the financing; cautions applicable to certain types of financing; and suggestions of procedures which will protect the parties during the terms of the financing.

The arranger of credit does not have to deliver a disclosure statement to a buyer or seller who is entitled to receive a disclosure under the regulations of the Federal Truth-in-Lending Act, Real Estate Settlement Procedures Act (RESPA) or a mortgage loan disclosure statement.

STATE OF CALIFORNIA

DEPARTMENT OF REAL ESTATE
MORTGAGE LENDING

MORTGAGE LOAN DISCLOSURE STATEMENT/GOOD FAITH ESTIMATE

RE 883 (New 12/93)

Borrower's Name(s): _____

Real Property Collateral: The intended security for this proposed loan will be a Deed of Trust on (street address or legal description) _____

This joint Mortgage Loan Disclosure Statement/Good Faith Estimate is being provided by _____ , a real estate broker acting as a mortgage broker, pursuant to the Federal Real Estate Settlement Procedures Act (RESPA) and similar California law. In a transaction subject to RESPA, a lender will provide you with an additional Good Faith Estimate within three business days of the receipt of your loan application. You will also be informed of material changes before settlement/close of escrow. The name of the intended lender to whom your loan application will be delivered is:

☐ Unknown   ☐ _____ (Name of lender, if known)

GOOD FAITH ESTIMATE OF CLOSING COSTS

The information provided below reflects estimates of the charges you are likely to incur at the settlement of your loan. The fees, commissions, costs and expenses listed are estimates; the actual charges may be more or less. Your transaction may not involve a charge for every item listed and any additional items charged will be listed. The numbers listed beside the estimate generally correspond to the numbered lines contained in the HUD-1 Settlement Statement which you will receive at settlement if this transaction is subject to RESPA. The HUD-1 Settlement Statement contains the actual costs for the items paid at settlement. When this transaction is subject to RESPA, by signing page two of this form you are also acknowledging receipt of the HUD Guide to Settlement Costs.

HUD-1	Item	Paid to Others	Paid to Broker
800	*Items Payable in Connection with Loan*		
801	Lender's Loan Origination Fee	$ _____	$ _____
802	Lender's Loan Discount Fee	$ _____	$ _____
803	Appraisal Fee	$ _____	$ _____
804	Credit Report	$ _____	$ _____
805	Lender's Inspection Fee	$ _____	$ _____
808	Mortgage Broker Commission/Fee	$ _____	$ _____
809	Tax Service Fee	$ _____	$ _____
810	Processing Fee	$ _____	$ _____
811	Underwriting Fee	$ _____	$ _____
812	Wire Transfer Fee	$ _____	$ _____
		$ _____	$ _____
900	*Items Required by Lender to be Paid in Advance*		
901	Interest for ____ days at $_____ per day	$ _____	$ _____
902	Mortgage Insurance Premiums	$ _____	$ _____
903	Hazard Insurance Premiums	$ _____	$ _____
904	County Property Taxes	$ _____	$ _____
905	VA Funding Fee	$ _____	$ _____
		$ _____	$ _____
1000	*Reserves Deposited with Lender*		
1001	Hazard Insurance: ____ months at $_____ /mo.	$ _____	$ _____
1002	Mortgage Insurance: ____ months at $_____ /mo.	$ _____	$ _____
1004	Co. Property Taxes: ____ months at $_____ /mo.	$ _____	$ _____
		$ _____	$ _____
1100	*Title Charges*		
1101	Settlement or Closing/Escrow Fee	$ _____	$ _____
1105	Document Preparation Fee	$ _____	$ _____
1106	Notary Fee	$ _____	$ _____
1108	Title Insurance	$ _____	$ _____
		$ _____	$ _____
1200	*Government Recording and Transfer Charges*		
1201	Recording Fees	$ _____	$ _____
1202	City/County Tax/Stamps	$ _____	$ _____
		$ _____	$ _____
1300	*Additional Settlement Charges*		
1302	Pest Inspection	$ _____	$ _____
		$ _____	$ _____
	Subtotals of Initial Fees, Commissions, Costs and Expenses	$ _____	$ _____
	Total of Initial Fees, Commissions, Costs and Expenses	$ _____	

Compensation to Broker (Not Paid Out of Loan Proceeds):

Mortgage Broker Commission/Fee $ _____

Any Additional Compensation from Lender   ☐ No   ☐ Yes $ _____ (if known)

ADDITIONAL REQUIRED CALIFORNIA DISCLOSURES

I. Proposed Loan Amount: $ _____

    Initial Commissions, Fees, Costs and
        Expenses Summarized on Page 1: $ _____

    Payment of Other Obligations (List):
        Credit Life and/or Disability Insurance (see VI below) $ _____

        _____ $ _____

        _____ $ _____

    Subtotal of All Deductions: $ _____

    Estimated Cash at Closing ☐ **To You** ☐ **That you must pay** $ _____

II. Proposed Interest Rate: _____%   ☐ Fixed Rate   ☐ Initial Variable Rate

III. Proposed Loan Term: _____   ☐ Years   ☐ Months

IV. Proposed Loan Payments: Payments of $_____ will be made ☐ Monthly ☐ Quarterly ☐ Annually for _____ (number of months, quarters or years). If proposed loan is a variable interest rate loan, this payment will vary (see loan documents for details).

    The loan is subject to a balloon payment: ☐ No ☐ Yes. If Yes, the following paragraph applies and a final balloon payment of $_____ will be due on ___/___/___ [estimated date (day/month/year)].

    NOTICE TO BORROWER: IF YOU DO NOT HAVE THE FUNDS TO PAY THE BALLOON PAYMENT WHEN IT COMES DUE, YOU MAY HAVE TO OBTAIN A NEW LOAN AGAINST YOUR PROPERTY TO MAKE THE BALLOON PAYMENT. IN THAT CASE, YOU MAY AGAIN HAVE TO PAY COMMISSIONS, FEES, AND EXPENSES FOR THE ARRANGING OF THE NEW LOAN. IN ADDITION, IF YOU ARE UNABLE TO MAKE THE MONTHLY PAYMENTS OR THE BALLOON PAYMENT, YOU MAY LOSE THE PROPERTY AND ALL OF YOUR EQUITY THROUGH FORECLOSURE. KEEP THIS IN MIND IN DECIDING UPON THE AMOUNT AND TERMS OF THIS LOAN.

V. Prepayments: The proposed loan has the following prepayment provisions.

    ☐ No prepayment penalty.

    ☐ Other (see loan documents for details).

    ☐ Any payment of principal in any calendar year in excess of 20% of the ☐ original balance ☐ unpaid balance will include a penalty not to exceed _____ months advance interest at the note rate, but not more than the interest that would be charged if the loan were paid to maturity (see loan documents for details).

VI. Credit Life and/or Disability Insurance: The purchase of credit life and/or disability insurance by a borrower is NOT required as a condition of making this proposed loan.

VII. Other Liens: Are there liens currently on this property for which the borrower is obligated?   ☐ No ☐ Yes
    If Yes, describe below:

Lienholder's Name	*Amount Owing*	*Priority*
_____	_____	_____
_____	_____	_____
_____	_____	_____

    Liens that will remain or are anticipated on this property after the proposed loan for which you are applying is made or arranged (including the proposed loan for which you are applying):

Lienholder's Name	*Amount Owing*	*Priority*
_____	_____	_____
_____	_____	_____
_____	_____	_____

    NOTICE TO BORROWER: Be sure that you state the amount of all liens as accurately as possible. If you contract with the broker to arrange this loan, but it cannot be arranged because you did not state these liens correctly, you may be liable to pay commissions, costs, fees, and expenses even though you do not obtain the loan.

VIII. Article 7 Compliance: If this proposed loan is secured by a first deed of trust in a principal amount of less than $30,000 or secured by a junior lien in a principal amount of less than $20,000, the undersigned licensee certifies that the loan will be made in compliance with Article 7 of Chapter 3 of the Real Estate Law.

    A. This loan ☐ may ☐ will ☐ will not be made wholly or in part from broker controlled funds as defined in Section 10241(j) of the Business and Professions Code.

    B. If the broker indicates in the above statement that the loan "may" be made out of broker-controlled funds, the broker must inform the borrower prior to the close of escrow if the funds to be received by the borrower are in fact broker-controlled funds.

Name of Broker	*License #*	*Broker's Representative*	*License #*
_____	_____	_____	_____

Broker's Address
_____

Signature of Broker	*Date*	OR	*Signature of Representative*	*Date*
_____	_____		_____	_____

IX. NOTICE TO BORROWER: THIS IS NOT A LOAN COMMITMENT. Do not sign this statement until you have read and understood all of the information in it. All parts of this form must be completed before you sign. Borrower hereby acknowledges the receipt of a copy of this statement.

Borrower	*Date*	*Borrower*	*Date*
_____	_____	_____	_____

Review completed on _____ by _____

Date	*Broker or Designated Representative*	*Dept. of Real Estate License #*

RE 883 — Page 2 of 2

Summary

Most customers do not have the financial resources to purchase a home, and must borrow to finance the transaction. Today many loan packages are available to meet the customer's financial needs. However, finding the right financial package to fit these needs can be confusing and intimidating.

The **mortgage market** consists of primary markets (loan-originator sellers) and the secondary market (loan buyers). There are two divisions in the primary mortgage market—the institutional lenders and the non-institutional lenders. The **institutional lender** is a depository such as a commercial bank. They receive most of their deposits from household savings or individual investors. The major type of lending activity funded by commercial banks is for short term (six to thirty-six months) construction loans, even though they do make other types of loans as well. **Non-institutional lenders** are non-depositories and include private individuals, mortgage companies, and investment companies as well as pension funds and title companies. The primary market lenders make real estate loans and package them into mortgage pools to be sold to the customers in the secondary mortgage market. The **secondary mortgage market** is comparable to a resale marketplace for loans (where existing loans are bought and sold).

Mortgage lenders are concerned about a customer's ability to repay a loan. Lenders use qualifying ratios with a review of the customer's credit report and net worth to screen potential borrowers. Security for the loan is the property. An appraisal of the property is made to obtain an accurate valuation.

Real estate laws require anyone negotiating a loan to provide a mortgage loan broker's statement to a prospective borrower, with information disclosing all important features of a loan to be negotiated for the borrower. Among these laws are: the Consumer Credit Protection Act, Truth-in-Lending Act, **Regulation Z**, Adjustable-Rate Loan Disclosure, **Equal Credit Opportunity Act**, Lender Compensation Disclosure, and Seller Financing Disclosure Statement.

Any borrower who is denied credit must be told the reason why credit was denied, be given access to the credit report, and told how to challenge any disputed entries.

Chapter 10 Review Exercises

Matching Exercise

Instructions: Look up the meaning of the terms in the Glossary, then write the letter of the matching term on the blank line before its definition. Answers are in Appendix B.

Terms

a. APR
b. commercial banks
c. compensating balance
d. credit scoring
e. credit union
f. deregulation
g. disintermediation
h. Equal Credit Opportunity Act
i. FDIC
j. finance charge
k. good faith estimate
l. loan to value
m. monetary policy
n. mortgage broker
o. mortgage companies

p. mortgage loan disclosure statement
q. mortgage yield
r. mortgage-backed securities
s. pass-through securities
t. pledge
u. primary mortgage market
v. real estate investment trust
w. reconveyance deed
x. redlining
y. secondary mortgage market
z. security agreement
aa. tight money
bb. Truth-in-Lending Act
cc. underwriting
dd. warehousing

Definitions

1. _____ An objective, statistical method that lenders use to quickly assess the borrower's credit risk.

2. _____ Originators of a majority of all residential loans, and are not depository institutions.

3. _____ Consumer-protection law passed to promote the informed use of consumer credit by requiring disclosures about its terms and costs.

4. _____ Private individuals, each with a small amount of capital, who pool their resources to buy real estate.

5. _____ The relative cost of credit expressed as a yearly percentage rate.

6. _____ The process of assembling a number of mortgage loans into one package, prior to selling them to an investor.

7. _____ Lending institutions that make mortgage loans directly to borrowers.

8. _____ Real estate licensee who originates a loan by taking the application from a borrower and then selling that unclosed loan to a mortgage lender.

9. _____ An economic situation in which the supply of money is limited, and the demand for money is high, as evidenced by high interest rates.

10. _____ A resale marketplace for loans.

11. _____ The percentage of appraised value to the loan.

12. _____ The process of evaluating a borrower's risk factors before the lender will make a loan.

13. _____ Corporation that insures deposits in all federally chartered banks and savings institutions up to $100,000 per account for commercial and savings banks.

14. _____ A borrower deposits funds with the bank in order to induce the lender into making a loan.

15. _____ Mortgage backed securities that pass through the principal and interest of the underlying loans to investors.

16. _____ Actions taken by the Fed to influence the availability and cost of money and credit as a means of promoting national economic goals.

17. _____ An illegal lending policy of denying real estate loans on properties in older, changing urban areas.

18. _____ Federal act to ensure that all consumers are given an equal chance to obtain credit.

19. _____ A process whereby regulatory restraints are gradually relaxed.

20. _____ An association whose members usually have the same type of occupation.

21. _____ The amount received or returned from an investment expressed as a percentage.

22. _____ The dollar amount the credit will cost and is composed of any direct or indirect charge as a condition of obtaining credit.

23. _____ Pools of mortgages used as collateral for the issuance of securities in the secondary market.

24. _____ Document that provides detailed information on escrow costs so that the borrower can shop around for escrow services.

25. _____ A statement, which must be in a form approved by the Real Estate Commissioner, that informs the buyer of all charges and expenses related to a particular loan.

▎Multiple Choice Questions

Instructions: Circle your response and go to Appendix B to read the complete explanation for each question.

1. The most effective method for the Federal Reserve to create a "tight" money market is to:
   a. buy government bonds and increase the reserve requirement.
   b. sell government bonds and decrease the reserve requirement.
   c. buy government bonds and raise the discount rate.
   d. sell government bonds and raise the discount rate.

2. If economic conditions create a tight money market, which of the following would arise concerning offers to purchase real property?
   a. There will be more cash offers.
   b. Land contracts of sale will see a greater use.
   c. There will be more offers to assume the seller's loan.
   d. Any of the above

3. Which of the following is the best description of the term "mortgage yield?"
   a. The total amount of balloon payments
   b. A net increase in the equity value of a mortgaged property
   c. The effective return of interest to the investor
   d. Subrogation of the original mortgage

4. The process of gradually relaxing regulatory restraints is called:
   a. disintermediation.
   b. deregulation.
   c. depreciation.
   d. none of the above

5. The type of lenders having the greatest percentage of its assets invested in residential real estate mortgages are:
   a. commercial banks.
   b. credit unions.
   c. life insurance companies.
   d. thrifts.

6. Which of the following lenders would be most likely to loan funds for construction costs for a single-family residence?
   a. Commercial bank
   b. Pension fund
   c. Savings and loan association
   d. Life insurance company

7. Which real estate lender has lending policies characterized by long-term financing, few construction loans, larger loans preferred, loans that usually are not serviced?
   a. Commercial banks
   b. Mortgage companies
   c. Insurance companies
   d. Savings and loan associations

8. Life insurance companies that do not deal directly with mortgagors or trustors usually make real estate mortgage loans to purchase indirectly through _____, for which they pay a loan preparation and service fee.
   a. the FHA or VA
   b. mortgage companies
   c. savings and loan associations
   d. all of the above

9. In the context of financing real property, the term "ware housing" most closely refers to:
   a. a large loan on a storage facility.
   b. a mortgage banker collecting loans before selling them.
   c. loans regulated by Article 7 of the California Real Estate Law.
   d. underwriting stock issues with loans secured by industrial property.

10. Which of the following are not considered to be institutional lenders?
    a. Mortgage companies
    b. Commercial banks
    c. Insurance companies
    d. Savings and loan associations

11. Most junior loans negotiated in today's market are secured from the following source:
    a. private lenders.
    b. commercial banks.
    c. private mortgage insurance companies.
    d. savings and loan associations.

12. In the field of real estate financing, the term "secondary mortgage market" usually refers to:
    a. junior liens.
    b. secondary financing.
    c. unsecured financial instruments.
    d. the resale or transfer of existing trust deed loans.

13. The original purpose of the Federal National Mortgage Association (FNMA) was:
    a. buying and selling FHA-insured and VA-guaranteed loans in the secondary market.
    b. buying and selling conventional loans in the secondary market.
    c. buying FHA and VA loans in the primary market.
    d. selling FHA and VA loans in the primary market.

14. Which of the following does not participate in the secondary market for mortgage loans?
    a. GNMA
    b. FHA
    c. FNMA
    d. FHLMC

15. Regulation Z requires that consumers be informed of credit terms by the:
    a. broker.
    b. trustee.
    c. creditor.
    d. escrow officer.

16. The main purpose of the federal Truth-in-Lending Act is to:
    a. eliminate or minimize usury.
    b. establish the maximum annual percentage rate.
    c. limit the cost of credit available to consumers.
    d. require disclosure of credit terms so consumers can compare loans.

17. Which of the following would be exempt from Regulation Z?
    a. A loan for agricultural purposes made by a federally chartered bank.
    b. A loan for household purposes obtained from a credit union.
    c. A $90,000 mortgage from a savings and loan institution secured by a single family residence.
    d. A $15,000 loan used to purchase an owner occupied mobile home.

18. If only the annual percentage rate (APR) is disclosed in an advertisement for property, which additional disclosures must be made?
    a. The amount or percentage of the down payment
    b. The terms of repayment
    c. The amount of any finance charge
    d. No other disclosures are required

19. Which of the following fees may **not** be included in the finance charge according to the federal Truth-in-Lending Act?
    a. Interest
    b. Finder's fees
    c. Buyer's points
    d. Appraisal fees

20. In advertising the availability of real estate loans, using any of the following phrases by itself would be a violation of the federal Truth-in-Lending Act's Regulation Z except:
    a. 5% down payment.
    b. 360 payments.
    c. easy terms available.
    d. 30-year loans.

21. When advertising a property for sale, which of the following statements would place the broker in violation of the federal Truth-in-Lending Act?
    a. 3-bedroom, 2 bath, excellent FHA or VA financing available; total price $225,000
    b. 4-bedroom, 2 bath, easy terms; total price $225,000
    c. 3-bedroom, 2 bath, large lot, with 10% down; total price $225,000
    d. 3-bedroom, 3 bath, owner will help finance; total price $225,000

22. Which of the following is the main purpose of RESPA?
    a. To regulate all real estate loans
    b. To choose a lender that can process applications for loans
    c. To regulate home improvement loans
    d. To require that disclosures be made by lenders that make loans on 1-to-4 unit dwellings.

23. The Federal Real Estate Settlement Procedure Act of 1974 (RESPA) pertains to:
    a. all residential property.
    b. residential properties with 1-to-4 units.
    c. commercial properties only.
    d. agricultural property.

24. On loans governed by RESPA, a buyer or seller may legally be charged for all of the following except:
    a. preparation of the loan documents.
    b. conducting an appraisal prior to the loan.
    c. preparation of the Uniform Settlement Statement.
    d. preparation of credit reports.

25. The maximum commission that can be charged by a licensee for negotiating a second trust deed of $7,500 for a period of five (5) years is:
    a. 5%.
    b. 10%.
    c. 15%.
    d. unlimited because this loan is not regulated by Article 7.

Valuation and Appraisal

Introduction

Probably the most asked question in real estate is, "How much do you think it is worth?" Every day a client or customer will ask about the fair price or fair rental for a property and an agent must be prepared to answer knowledgeably. Some of the most important services a listing agent can provide are to be familiar with how the worth of property is determined and to be able to explain it to the client.

Most homeowners know, within a range, the value of their homes. They probably are not aware they have used some of the same techniques the listing agent and the professional appraiser will use in determining the value of their home. For example, they may know the selling price of their neighbors' house, and the selling price of the house down the street. They have added to—or subtracted from—the value of their own house, depending on amenities, location and condition to come up with a pretty accurate value, if they are being honest with themselves. This chapter will examine the appraisal process and the methods used to determine property values so that you as an agent can answer when a client or customer asks the question, "How much do you think it is worth?"

In this chapter, you will learn how real estate appraisal influences real estate value; forces that influence value; principles of valuation; the appraisal process; methods of appraising property; appraisal licensing standards; and professional appraisal organizations.

Learning Objectives

After reading this chapter, you will be able to:

- discuss the appraisal process.
- name the elements and forces that influence real estate value.
- explain how depreciation influences real estate value and how to calculate depreciation.
- describe the methods used in determining real estate value and the steps used in each method.

Definition of Appraisal

An **appraisal** is an unbiased estimate or opinion of the property value on a given date. **Value** is the present worth of rights to future benefits that come from property ownership. An appraiser gives his or her opinion of value in a written statement called an **appraisal report**. It is the conclusion of the appraiser's research and analysis of all relevant data regarding the subject property.

Most of the time, an objective and third party opinion are needed to determine the value of real property. The professional appraiser because of training, experience, and ethics, is responsible for giving clients an objective opinion of value, reached without bias. An appraiser has a serious responsibility to be correct in evaluating data and not allow other factors to influence evaluation of a property. The appraiser must remember to be a neutral party, responding only to the forces affecting value and not to any other special interests who might want to influence his or her judgment.

Purpose of an Appraisal
• Taxation
• Insurance
• Condemnation
• Financing and credit
• Transfer of property ownership

An appraisal can be made for many different purposes. There are several reasons for determining the value of a particular property. The estimate of value may be different depending on the reason for ordering the appraisal. The condemnation value is going to be different from the taxation value, the insurance value, or the market value. An appraiser must know what those differences are and how to estimate the value of a property based on the purpose for which it is being used.

The purpose of the appraisal is distinct from the intended use of the appraisal report. The **purpose of the appraisal** helps define how the appraisal process will be laid out. The **intended use** helps decide which report type is most appropriate for communicating the results of the process.

Definition of Value

Value or worth is the present and future anticipated enjoyment or profit from the ownership of property. It is the relationship between the thing desired and the purchaser. It is also the power of one commodity to attract other commodities in exchange.

Cost represents expenses in money, labor, material or sacrifices in acquiring or producing something. Price is what a property actually sold for. The value of a parcel can be defined in many ways, typically market value and utility value.

Market Value

Real estate includes both land and anything belonging to the land, as well as rights or interests in that land. The price a property would bring if freely offered on the open market, with both a **willing buyer** and a **willing seller,** is known as **fair market value**—or market value. Market value is sometimes called the **objective value**, since it may be determined by actual data.

A property that is offered for sale as a result of default, foreclosure, bankruptcy, divorce, death or any other unusual circumstances cannot be said to be freely and willingly offered on the open market, and the sale price of such properties would not represent fair market value. An appraiser would take into account that there were special circumstances in those sales and would not use the price paid as a comparable measure of value. The following can be assumed of all fair market value sales.

> **Review - Fair Market Value**
> - Buyer and seller are operating in their own interest.
> - Buyer and seller are knowledgeable about the transaction and make careful decisions.
> - The property is available for a reasonable time on the open market.
> - The sale is for cash or trade or is specifically financed.
> - Normal financing, available to qualified borrowers, is used.

Price, Cost, and Value

Sometimes market price, cost and market value are the same, but this is misleading. Remember, market price is what a property *actually* sold for, whereas market value, or fair market value as it is sometimes called, is the price that it *should* have sold for. The conditions of the sale affect the price, such as good financing or a forced sale.

The circumstances of one buyer and one seller may affect the sale of a specific property, giving it its own value, apart from some other similar parcel. The job of an appraiser is to determine the special factors of a sale and assign a value based on each individual transaction.

> Example: Pamela and John wanted to buy their first house. They looked at several with their real estate agent and finally decided on one that was beyond their means. They made a hopeful, low offer. Unknown to them, the seller had lost his job and was desperate to sell. He accepted their offer, which was well below market value.

In the above case, the seller did not sell freely for market value, and the sales price only reflected his desperate situation, not the real value of the house.

Market value has very little to do with the original cost. Neither cost nor appreciation is considered an essential element of value.

Utility Value

Utility value is the usefulness of the property to its owner. This is **subjective value** or the value given for personal reasons. For example, a swimming pool might be important to one family but of little value to another. Other **amenities** (features that add value to a property) fall into this category as well. Six bedrooms would not be useful or have utility value to a couple with no children nor would a home deep in the woods to a city worker.

Four Elements to Create Value

There are four elements of value, all of which must be present for a property to have market value. They are demand, utility, scarcity, and transferability. **Demand** is the desire to buy or obtain a commodity. **Effective demand** is desire coupled with purchasing power. Demand and purchasing power available will affect the value of a property. **Utility** is the ability of a property to satisfy a need or desire, such as shelter, income, or amenities. **Functional utility** is the combined factors of usefulness with desirability. **Scarcity** refers to the availability of a commodity in the marketplace. An oversupply diminishes value whereas an undersupply (or increased demand) increases value.

Each by itself cannot create value. For example, something may be scarce, but if it has no utility there is no demand for it. Air has utility and may be in great demand, but is so abundant that it has no commercial value. Real estate has value because it may represent the maximum utility of limited resources.

> **Mnemonic - "DUST"**
> **D** emand
> **U** tility
> **S** carcity
> **T** ransferability

The appraiser must decide if there is a demand for a property, such as a high-rise residential building, or a low-cost housing project. Can it be used for the purpose it was intended, such as a family home or residential complex? How many projects like this one are there in the area? The fewer there are, the more value the subject property has. Is the title clear, and can the seller easily give ownership to a buyer? As you can see, all of these factors are important in assigning a value to a property. An appraiser must hold each one up to the property in question to arrive at a correct estimate of value.

Forces Influencing Value

The essence of life is change, and real estate is not excluded from that force. Value is created, maintained, modified, and destroyed by the relationship of the following four forces: **physical** characteristics, **economic** influences, **political** or governmental regulations, and **social** ideals.

Physical Characteristics including Environmental Forces

Physical characteristics are also called external characteristics. This includes: quality of conveniences; availability of schools, shopping, public transportation, churches; and similarity of land use. **Environmental** forces may be climate, soil, topography, oceans, and mountains.

Location: This may be the most important factor influencing value, as far as highest and best use.

Size: The use of a property may be determined by the width and depth of the land. A **depth table** is used to estimate the value of commercial properties.

Corner influence: Commercial properties benefit from more exposure, while residential parcels may lose privacy and incur higher maintenance costs from increased **frontage**.

Thoroughfare condition: Width of streets, traffic congestion, and condition of pavement affect the value of properties fronting on those streets. The term front foot defines the width of a property along a street.

Exposure: The south and west sides of business streets are usually preferred by shopkeepers because customers will seek the shady side of the street and window displays will not be damaged by the sun. The north and east sides are less desirable.

Orientation: Orientation is the placement of a building on its lot in relation to exposure to sun, prevailing wind, traffic, and privacy from the street.

Plottage increment: By putting several smaller, less-valuable parcels together under one ownership through the process of **assemblage**, the value of the parcels will be increased.

Shape: Irregular-shaped lots are more difficult and expensive to develop.

Topography and soil: Construction costs will be affected by the terrain and soil condition. Limited irregularity in the contour is best for residential property.

Economic Influences

Some economic forces that influence value are: natural resources, industrial and commercial trends, employment trends, wage levels, availability of money and credit, interest rates, price levels, tax loads, regional and community economic base, new development, and rental and price patterns.

A blighted section of a city.

Blighted area: A section of a city, generally the inner city, where a majority of the buildings are run-down and the property values are extremely low.

Inflation: This is an **unearned increment** that affects property values.

Business climate: The presence of shopping areas, offices and medical suites as well as financial, wholesale, industrial and other consumer-friendly businesses is important to establishing value.

Obsolescence: This may be caused by external or economic changes and decreases the usefulness of property or causes deterioration.

Political or Government Regulations

Some political forces that can affect value are: building codes, zoning laws, public health measures, fire regulations, rent controls, environmental legislation and the community economic base.

Political or government regulations can affect value.

Directional growth: This is determined by how the area or city expands. Property in a growth area tends to increase in value.

Utility: The property's ability to be used for the purpose it was intended fulfills its utility. Building restrictions and zoning ordinances affect utility.

Building restrictions and zones: These may increase or depress values.

Social Ideals and Standards

Population growth and decline, age, marriage, birth, divorce, and death rates all combine to cause changes in social patterns.

Demography: This refers to the study of the population.

> **Four Main Forces Influencing Value**
> **Mnemonic - "PEPS"**
>   **P**   hysical forces
>   **E**   conomic forces
>   **P**   olitical forces
>   **S**   ocial forces

Principles of Valuation

Valuation is the process of estimating market value for real property as of a specific time. There are many valuation principles that interact to determine the final value of a piece of real estate. Not every property exhibits each principle; however, a real estate agent or professional appraiser must know the following basic principles of valuation before assigning value to any property.

Principle of Change

Cities and neighborhoods are always changing, and individual homes within those neighborhoods reflect that change. An appraiser must be aware of trends that affect the value of real estate. Economic, social, environmental, and governmental forces are always dynamic, causing changing values in real property.

Neighborhoods are dynamic and are always changing.

Principle of Conformity

When land uses are compatible and homes are similar in design and size, the maximum value is realized. Conformity (similarity) upholds neighborhood values. Where there are mixed homes, unstable real estate values may occur.

Principle of Supply and Demand

Increasing supply or decreasing demand will reduce the price in the market. Reducing supply or increasing demand will raise the price in the market. The less there is of something, the higher the cost; the more there is, the lower the cost.

If home prices decrease, the result will be an increase in the value of money because a given amount of money has more purchasing power. Basically, the home buyer gets more for his or her money.

Principle of Substitution

The principle of substitution is the basis of the appraisal process. Explained simply, value is set by the cost of getting an equally desirable substitute. An owner cannot expect to sell for more than someone would ordinarily pay for a similar property, under similar conditions.

Value is set by the cost of getting an equally desirable substitute.

Principle of Highest and Best Use

The principle **of highest and best use** is based on the reasonable use of real property at the time of the appraisal, which is most likely to produce the greatest net return to the land and/or the building over a given period of time. Evaluating the highest and best use includes: assessing buyers' reasons for buying, the existing use of the property, benefits of ownership, the market's behavior, and community or environmental factors.

Interim use is a short-term and temporary use of a property until it is ready for a more productive highest and best use.

Multiple factors are involved in evaluating the highest and best use.

Principle of Progression

A lesser-valued property will be worth more because of the presence of greater-valued properties nearby.

Principle of Regression

A greater-valued property will be worth less because of the presence of lower-valued properties nearby.

Principle of Contribution

The **principle of contribution** is the worth of an improvement and what it adds to the entire property's market value, regardless of the actual cost of the improvement. A remodeled attic may not contribute its entire cost to the value of the property; but a new family room will increase the value of the house by more than the cost to build. This principle must be kept in mind by homeowners who want to change the character of their house in such a way that it no longer fits in the neighborhood. The cost of the improvement may not add to the value if the house is overbuilt for the area.

Principle of Anticipation

Probable future benefits to be derived from a property will increase the value. An appraiser estimates the present worth of future benefits when he or she assigns a value based on anticipated returns.

Principle of Competition

When considerable profits are being made, competition is created. When there is a profitable demand for homes, there will be competition among builders. The supply would then increase in relation to the demand, bringing lower selling prices and unprofitable competition, leading to more declines in supply.

Principle of Balance

When contrasting, opposing, or interacting elements are in balance in a neighborhood or area, value is created. A careful mix of varying land use creates value also. Over-improvement or under-improvement will cause imbalance.

Principle of Three-Stage Life Cycle

All neighborhoods change. They start out as young dynamic areas, and eventually disintegrate in the process of passing years. All property goes through three distinct stages.

Three Stages of Property Change

Property goes through three distinct changes in its life cycle: (1) development, (2) maturity, and (3) old age.

Growth and decline is normal in all areas, and many times it can be reversed just as it reaches the last stages. For example, when a lovely neighborhood grows to be old and worn-out, young families may choose to move in and completely restore the process of change by starting the life cycle of the neighborhood all over again with development.

The Appraisal Process

At the end of an appraisal, an appraiser must be prepared to answer the following two questions:

"What is the highest and best use of the property?"
"What is this use worth?"

Professional appraisers have developed an orderly systematic method—known as the **appraisal process**—to arrive at an estimate of value.

The appraisal process is made up of four main steps: (1) state the problem, (2) gather data (general and specific), (3) decide on the appraisal method to be used, and (4) reconcile or correlate the data for final value estimate.

> **Review - Steps in the Appraisal Process**
> 1. State the problem.
> 2. Gather the data.
> 3. Decide on the appraisal method to be used.
> 4. Reconcile or correlate the data for final value estimate.

State the Problem

The appraiser must know why the appraisal is necessary. He or she must identify and describe the property to be evaluated and indicate the purpose of the appraisal. Then the extent of ownership to be appraised must be identified. Rights affect value because they set the limits within which the property may be used, and the appraiser must know how the property is owned in order to determine the value of those rights. Is it a fee simple? Are there restrictions on use or possibly a life estate or co-ownership? The purpose of the appraisal will determine the types of information that will be gathered.

Purposes of an Appraisal

- Market value for a sale
- Value for mortgage loan purposes
- Value for insurance purposes
- Value for condemnation proceedings
- Value for inheritance purposes
- Value for Internal Revenue Service purposes
- Value for property tax purposes
- Value for liquidation purposes

Once the appraiser knows the purpose for the property evaluation, it is possible to move on to the next step.

Gather the Data

To determine the property's value, data can be obtained from government publications, newspapers, magazines, the Internet, and personal observation. There are two types of data: general and site specific.

General Data	Specific Data
Region	Location
Community	Lot type
Neighborhood	Legal
Market	Improvements (buildings)

Data should be gathered on population trends, income levels, and employment opportunities.

General Data

General data is information about the area where the property is located that affects the value of the property.

Regional Data

A region is a metropolitan area such as San Francisco Bay, Southern California, or the Central Coast. **Regional data** is information about the region's economic health and amenities. Regional data can be gathered from monthly bank summaries, regional planning commissions, and government agencies. Governmental agencies such as the Association of Bay Area Governments (ABAG) in the San Francisco Bay area, the San Diego Association of Governments (SANDAG), or the Southern California Association of Governments (SCAG) are also excellent sources for regional information.

Community Data

A community is the town or city where the property is located. **Community data** can be obtained from the Chamber of Commerce, City Planning Commission, city government agencies, banks, and real estate boards. As with the regional data, community data should be searched for information about the community's economic health and amenities.

Neighborhood Data

Neighborhood data concerning the neighborhood's condition and amenities can be obtained from personal inspections, real estate agents, or area builders. The appraiser notices the age and appearance of the neighborhood; any negative influences such as physical or social hazards (rundown buildings, evidence of criminal activity); evidence of future development; and proximity to schools, businesses, recreation, and transportation.

The sales and listing prices of property in the neighborhood is the neighborhood's **market data**. It must be collected and analyzed. Sources for sales information are assessor's records and county recorder's office, title insurance companies, other property owners in the area, and the appraiser's own database.

Another factor that can affect value is the age of the buildings in the neighborhood. Information on structure age and other information regarding improvements can be gathered from the tax assessor's office, city building department, or personal inspection of the improvements.

Site Specific Data

Site specific data is information that has to do with the specific location being appraised. Appraisers rely on available market information such as listings, offers, leases, and sales reports as the foundation of their appraisal methods.

Location

Even though the location of the neighborhood and city must be considered in any analysis of a specific site or plot of ground, the exact spot of the site itself is the most important factor in determining value. Since most sites are different sizes and in different locations, some are more desirable than others and should be evaluated separately from improvements for the highest and best use.

Types of Lots

The type of lot on which a property is located can affect its value.

A **cul-de-sac** is sometimes known as dead-end street. It is a street that has only one way in and out. This may be desirable because of the privacy and quietness, but the lot may be undesirable if oddly pie-shaped on the turn-around section of the street.

A **corner lot** is found at the intersection of two streets. It may be desirable because of its accessibility, but may also be noisy and expensive to maintain because of the increased frontage.

A **T-intersection lot** is one that is fronted head-on by a street. The noise and glare from headlights may detract from this type of lot.

An **interior lot** is one that is surrounded by other lots, with frontage on the street. It is the most common type lot and may be desirable or not, depending on other factors.

A **flag lot** looks like a flag on a pole. The pole represents the access to the site, which is usually located to the rear of another lot fronting a main street.

A **key lot**, so named because it resembles a key fitting into a lock, is surrounded by the backyards of other lots. It is the least desirable because of the lack of privacy.

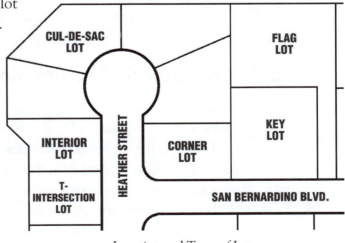

Location and Types of Lots

374 California Real Estate Principles

> **Review - Physical Factors of Site for Appraiser to Consider**
> - Shape of lot
> - Topography and soil conditions
> - Corner influence
> - Relation to surroundings
> - Availability of public utilities
> - Encroachments
> - Landscaping and subsurface land improvements
> - **Front foot** of a commercial property is usually the most valuable

Legal Data

An appraiser must evaluate all legal data connected with the site, including the legal description, any taxes, the zoning, general plan, and any restrictions or easements. Additionally, the appraiser needs to determine if there are any other interests in the property.

Improvements

When an appraiser considers **improvements**, it means looking at any buildings or other permanent structures, such as a fence, a swimming pool, a sauna, or a built-in whirlpool. Real property is divided into land and improvements, and each adds its own value to a site. Improvements can be either on-site or off-site:

- On-site improvements are structures permanently attached to the land, such as buildings, swimming pools, and fences.

- Off-site improvements are items in areas that border the site and add to its value, such as street lights, sidewalks, greenbelts, and curbs.

Decide on Method of Appraising Property

There are three main approaches to appraising property to arrive at a market value estimate: (1) sales comparison approach, (2) cost approach, and (3) income approach. The sales approach depends on recent sales and listings of similar properties in the area and are evaluated to form an opinion of value. The cost approach estimates the value of the land as if vacant and adds that to the depreciated cost of new improvements to determine an estimate of value for the entire property. The income or capitalization approach calculates the potential net income of the property considered and then capitalized into value.

> **Review - Which Appraisal Approach to Use**
> - Single family homes   Sales comparison approach
> - New or unusual buildings Cost approach
> - Rental properties   Income approach

Sales (or Market) Comparison Approach

The **sales comparison approach** is the one most easily and commonly used by real estate agents. It is best for single family homes or condominiums and vacant lots because sales information is readily available and easily compared. The market comparison approach uses the principle of substitution to compare similar properties.

As you recall, the principle of substitution states that a buyer will not pay more for a property than the cost of a similar one. The market comparison approach takes the current selling price of a similar property and adjusts it for any differences to arrive at the market value for the subject property.

The appraiser will collect data on comparable (called **comps**) properties that are as "like-kind" to the property in question as possible, in certain categories. Typical categories include: neighborhood location, size (comparable number of bedrooms/bathrooms as well as square footage), age, architectural style, financing terms, and the general price range.

The market comparison approach is based on the idea that property is worth what it will sell for when there is no extra stress, if reasonable time is given to find a buyer. Because of this, the appraiser will research comparable sales to discover any special circumstances influencing those sales. Only those similar properties—sold on the open market, with approval of the seller, offered for a reasonable length of time—will be used for comparables. Also, if possible, only those properties that have sold within the past six months are selected. If the comparables are older than that, they are considered less reliable.

Features in either the property or the transaction itself are elements that can cause appraisals to vary. Estimates of value vary due to differences in the financing terms, time of the sale, sale conditions (**arm's length transaction**), location, physical features, and in any income that is derived from the property.

Thus, a price is found for each comparable property that should reflect its present value in the current market where the subject property is being sold. Those properties not as comparable are excluded, and greater weight is given to the comparable sales most like the property being appraised. By using judgment to reconcile the comparables, the appraiser arrives at the final estimate of value for the subject property, using the compatible comparables to show the value and price to be asked for the subject property.

Advantages of Sales Comparison Approach

- Most easily understood method of valuation and most commonly used by real estate agents.

- Easily applied for the sale of single family homes.

- The sales comparison approach is best for single family homes or condominiums and vacant lots.

Disadvantages of Sales Comparison Approach

- Finding enough recently sold similar properties to get comparable values.

- Correctly adjusting amenities to make them comparable to the subject property.

- Older sales unreliable with changing economic conditions.

- Difficulty in confirming transaction details.

> **Review - The Sales Comparison Approach Procedure**
> 1. Find similar properties, select and verify data.
> 2. Select appropriate elements of comparison, adjust sales price of each comparable. (Adjustment is always made to the comparable, not the subject property.)
> 3. Adjust sales prices of comparables by subtracting the adjustment if the subject property is inferior to the comparable and by adding the adjustment if the subject property is superior.

Cost Approach

The **cost approach** looks at the value of the appraised parcel as the combination of two elements: the value of the land as if vacant and the cost to rebuild the appraised building as new on the date of valuation, less the accrued depreciation.

To determine value of a property using the cost approach, first obtain the value of the land, add the cost to build structure new, and then subtract any accrued depreciation.

The cost approach tends to set the upper limit of value for a property. In other words, the most something would cost if it were built new. Using the principle of substitution, a person will not pay more for a substitute if he or she can get the subject property for less. In the cost approach, the substitute is the cost of reconstructing the present building new on vacant land.

> **Review - The Cost Approach Procedure**
> 1. Estimate the value of the land as if it were vacant, using comparable land sales. (Principle of Substitution)
> 2. Estimate the replacement or reproduction cost of the existing building as of the appraisal date. **Replacement cost** is the cost of restoring a property to its previous condition or replacing it with something of like-kind and quality. **Reproduction cost** is the cost of replacing the improvement with one that is the exact replica, having the same quality of workmanship, design and layout.
> 3. Estimate the amount of accrued depreciation to the improvements.
> 4. Deduct the amount of the accrued depreciation from the **replacement cost** (new) to find the estimate of the depreciated value of the improvements.
> 5. Add the estimated present-depreciated value for the improvements to the value of the land. The result is an estimate of value for the subject property.

The cost approach is used most often for appraising new buildings and special-purpose or unique structures. Depreciation on a new building is relatively easy to determine, whereas the cost approach is impractical with older buildings because of the difficulty in estimating depreciation. The cost approach is also used with buildings where it is difficult to find comparables because they are unique or one-of-a-kind, such as a church, fire station, or hospital.

Occasionally, the cost approach is the only one an appraiser can use. If there have been no recent sales (such as during recession or when interest rates are too high), there will be no comparables for the market comparison approach. If the subject is not an income-producing property, the income method (to be discussed next) cannot be used. So the cost method is a reliable way for an appraiser or real estate agent to determine the value of a property when all else fails.

Methods to Estimate the Cost of a New Building

To estimate the cost of building the structure new, an appraiser can use one of several methods.

Square-foot method

An appraiser can use various methods to estimate the cost of a new building

The square-foot method is the most common, used by appraisers and real estate agents to estimate the cost of construction. The size of the building in question is compared, by square foot, to other buildings with the same area. The building being appraised is compared with the most comparable standard building, and its cost per square foot is used for the subject property. This is the fastest way to estimate value using the cost method.

Cubic-foot method

This is a lot like the square-foot method, except that it takes height as well as area into consideration. The cubic contents of buildings are compared instead of just the square footage.

Quantity-survey method

This method is a detailed estimate of all labor and materials used in the components of a building. Items such as overhead, insurance, and contractor's profit are added to direct costs of building. This method is time-consuming but very accurate.

Unit-in-place cost method

Cost of units in the building as installed is computed and applied to the structure cost. The total costs of walls in place, heating units, and roof are figured on a square-foot basis, including labor, overhead and profit. This is the most detailed method of estimating value.

Depreciation

Depreciation means loss in value from any cause. It is usually measured by estimating the difference between the current cost to replace new and the estimated value of the property as of the date of appraisal.

The opposite of depreciation is **appreciation**, or an increase in value, usually as a result of inflation or some special supply and demand force relating to that specific property. Appreciation may balance the normal decrease of value due to depreciation.

All of the influences that reduce the value of a property below its cost new are included in the definition of depreciation.

Physical Deterioration

This type of depreciation can come from wear and tear, negligent care (sometimes called deferred maintenance), damage by dry rot or termites, or severe changes in temperature. This may or may not be curable.

Economic Obsolescence

This type of depreciation occurs because of forces outside the property. Changes in the social or economic make up of the neighborhood, zoning changes, over-supply of homes, under-supply of buyers, recession, or legislative restrictions can cause economic obsolescence. It is almost always incurable.

Many things cause physical deterioration.

Functional Obsolescence

Poor architectural design and style can contribute to functional obsolescence, as can lack of modern facilities, out-of-date equipment, changes in styles of construction, or changes in utility demand. It may or may not be curable.

Many older homes have features that contribute to functional obsolescence.

> ### Review - Three Types of Depreciation
> 1. Physical Deterioration
> 2. Functional Obsolescence
> 3. Economic Obsolescence

Depreciation for Appraisal Purposes

The book depreciation calculated by an accountant is not the depreciation considered by the appraiser, as we have seen. The appraiser does not look at the owner's original cost to purchase but uses the cost to build new on the date of the appraisal as the basis for evaluation, using the cost method. An appraiser subtracts the estimate of accrued actual (not book) depreciation on the building from the cost to build new.

As you recall, in using the cost method, the value of the land and the value of the building (improvements) are determined separately, then added together to calculate the value of the entire property. So, the appraiser figures the actual depreciation on the building and subtracts it from the cost to construct the building new. The next step is to add that amount to the value given the land (using the principle of substitution from other land sales) to estimate the value of the whole parcel.

There are several ways to calculate accrued depreciation; however, for our purposes we will only discuss the straight-line (or age-life) method. It is the one most commonly used by real estate agents and appraisers because it is easy to calculate, is used by the Internal Revenue Service, and is easily understood by the consumer.

Using the straight-line method to determine accrued depreciation, the appraiser assumes a building will decline in value the same amount each year, until nothing is left. For example, a property with an estimated effective age of 50 years would be said to depreciate at an equal rate of 2% per year (2% x 50 years equals 100% depreciation). In using this method of calculating accrued depreciation, the appraiser probably will not use the actual age of the building, rather the effective age, which is determined by its condition, not the number of years since it was built.

Actual age is the real age of a building. **Effective age** is not determined by the actual age of a building but by its condition and usefulness. **Economic life** is the estimated period over which a building may be profitably used. Economic life is usually shorter than physical (actual) life. For example, if the subject property was really 25 years old, but was as well-maintained and would sell for as much as nearby 20-year-old properties, it would be said to have an effective age of 20 years.

Depreciation for Tax Purposes

Depreciation for income tax purposes is book depreciation, or a mathematical calculation of steady depreciation or loss, from the owner's original purchase price (**cost basis**). This allows the owner to recover the cost of investment over the **useful life** of the building. It is mathematically accrued annually and taken as an income tax deduction from the owner's gross income.

Many times, this deduction makes gross income a negative amount on paper. The building seems to be losing value, giving the owner a "paper loss" that can be offset against other income. This "paper loss," or tax shelter, is why many people invest in income property.

Book value is the current value (for accounting purposes) of a property, calculated as the original cost plus **capital improvements** and minus accumulated or accrued depreciation. Remember, this is used as an accounting method, not to be confused with actual depreciation of a building. Depreciation is allowed on buildings only, not on land. The depreciation, for accounting—or tax—purposes, is only a mathematical wasting away of the improvements. Property buyers have the least interest in an owner's book value.

The book value of a property may be calculated by adding the depreciated value of the improvement (the building) to the assigned value of the land. It is important to remember that book value and book depreciation are used only to figure income tax and are not particularly relevant to an appraiser.

> Book value equals the original cost of the property plus the cost of any improvements minus accrued depreciation.

Income Approach

The **income approach** estimates the present worth of future benefits from ownership of a property. The value of the property is based on its capacity to continue producing an income. This method is used to estimate the value of income-producing property (rentals), usually in combination with one or both of the other methods. This approach is based mainly on the appraisal principles of comparison, substitution and anticipation.

> The value of the property is based on its capacity to continue producing an income.

Contract rent, or the amount actually paid by a renter for use of the premises, may or may not be the same as **economic rent**, or the amount the rental could bring in an open market. An appraiser valuating a property looks at the economic rent, rather than the contract rent, in order to discover the fair income of the property. Properties are valued using both the income capitalization approach and gross rent multiplier approach.

Using Capitalization of Income

The process of calculating a property's present worth on the basis of its capacity to continue producing an income stream is called capitalization. Capitalization converts the future income stream into an indication of the property's present worth. Risk determines the capitalization rate to be used. The higher the perceived risk, the higher the capitalization rate. The appraiser evaluates the expected future income and expenses of a property using the income approach to determine its present value.

Formulas Used to Estimate the Value of an Income Property
NOI divided by the Cap Rate equals the Value of the Property.
NOI divided by Value of Property equals Cap Rate.

The appraiser must determine the amount, reliability, and durability of the income stream. There are five basic steps to do this.

Step 1. Calculate the Effective Gross Income

The effective gross income is the total annual income from the property minus any vacancy or rental losses. That includes rental income plus any other income generated by the property such as laundry room income or parking fees. Loss of income because of a vacant unit is known as the **vacancy factor**. Current market rents are used to determine the loss from the vacancy factor. **Market rent** is the rent the property should bring in the open market, while contract rent is the actual, or contracted, rent paid by the tenants. The appraiser uses the market rent in his or her calculations.

Calculation:

Gross scheduled annual income	$36,000
Subtract vacancy factor / rental loss	-3,600
Effective gross income	$32,400

Step 2. Determine Operating Expenses

Expenses are generally classified as being either fixed or variable. Fixed expenses include property taxes, insurance, and utilities. Variable expenses include management and maintenance.

> **Review - Operating Expenses**
> **Mnemonic - "TIMMUR"**
>   **T** axes
>   **I** nsurance
>   **M** anagement
>   **M** aintenance
>   **U** tilities
>   **R** eserves

Step 3. Calculate Net Operating Income

The net operating income (NOI) is the income after paying all expenses including a maintenance reserve. It does not include the principal and interest paid on a loan.

Calculation:

Taxes	$1,920
Insurance	480
Management	2,400
Maintenance	1,000
Utilities	800
Reserves (roof, water heaters, etc.)	800
Total expenses	$7,400
Effective gross income	$32,400
Subtract expenses	-7,400
Net operating income	$25,000

4. Select a Capitalization Rate

The capitalization rate (more accurately called the **internal rate of return (IRR)** in the financial community) provides for the return of invested capital plus a return on the investment. The rate is dependent upon the return a buyer will demand before investing money in the property. The greater the risk of recapturing the investment price (making a profit), the higher the cap rate and the lower the price. The lower the risk, the lower the cap rate and the higher the price of the property.

> - The greater the risk, the higher the cap rate and the lower the price.
> - The lower the risk, the lower the cap rate and the higher the price.

Choosing a capitalization rate is the hardest part for appraisers using the income approach. Generally, a real estate agent will need further study and practice to use this approach to valuation. One way a capitalization rate can be determined is by a market analysis of similar income properties and using the same capitalization rate as have those recent sales. The net operating income is divided by the sales price to determine the cap rate used in each sale. There are other methods of calculating a capitalization rate which may be learned through more study of appraisal.

Step 5. Calculate the Market Value

Calculate the market value by dividing the net operating income by the chosen cap rate.

Calculation:

Net Operating Income is $25,000 and the Cap Rate is 8%
$25,000 divided by .08 equals $312,500
Market value = $312,500

Using the Gross Rent Multiplier

Real estate agents and appraisers use the gross rent multiplier to quickly convert gross rent into market value. It is used for income-producing properties and is an easy way to get a rough estimate of the value of rental units.

Gross rent is income (calculated annually or monthly) received before any expenses are deducted. A gross rent multiplier, when multiplied by the total annual rents, will give a rough estimate of a property value that can then be compared with other like properties. Generally, gross multipliers will be somewhere between x5 and x10, depending on the market, the condition, and the location of the property.

In other words, a property with a gross annual income of $36,000, when multiplied by the current gross multiplier of 10, will be valued roughly at $360,000. So when you hear property values described as ten times gross, five times gross, or seven times gross, it means the value is shown by whatever multiplier is used, times the gross income. This is only a quick estimate of value, and does not take the place of a professional appraisal.

The reverse process can be used to calculate the gross multiplier, rather than the market value. The reason you might want to do that is to compare properties to see if they are priced right or are above or below market value. If you know that most rental properties are selling for around eight times the gross annual multiplier (eight times gross), simply divide the listed price by the gross income to arrive at the multiplier.

Calculation to find Gross Rent Multiplier:
Listed price is $360,000 and the gross annual income is $ 36,000
Divide the list price by the gross annual income
$360,000 divided by $36,000 equals 10
Gross Rent Multiplier is 10

The gross rent multipliers of several income properties may be compared using the market comparison method to estimate their value. A gross rent multiplier can be stated on either an annual or monthly basis.

Reconcile or Correlate

The final step in an appraisal is to examine the values derived by the various approaches. **Reconciliation,** or correlation, of value occurs when the appraiser decides which of the values is the most appropriate for the subject property, and uses that figure to determine the final estimate for the property in question.

Many times an appraiser will use all three methods to arrive at the market value of a property. In most appraisals, all three approaches will have something to add. Each method is used independently to reach an estimated value. Finally, by giving to each separate value a weight that is most compatible to the subject property, the appraiser will arrive at a value for the property. This process is called reconciliation or correlation.

The Appraisal Report

Each written appraisal report must be prepared according to the following Uniform Standards of Professional Appraisal Practice (USPAP) standards: Self-Contained Appraisal Report, Summary Appraisal Report, or Restricted Use Appraisal Report.

When the intended users of the report include parties other than the client, the report must be either a Self-Contained Appraisal Report or a Summary Appraisal Report. When the intended users do not include parties other than the client, the report can be a Restricted Use Appraisal Report. The difference among the options is in the content and level of information provided.

An appraiser must be careful in deciding which type of report to use. Appraisal standards set minimum requirements for the content and level of information in each type of report. The final report is presented in either a short-form or narrative style. Appraisals are valid on the date that the appraiser signs and dates the report.

Self-Contained Appraisal Report

The Self-Contained Appraisal Report includes the identity of the client and any intended users (by name or type), the intended use of the appraisal, the real estate involved, the real property interest appraised, the purpose of the appraisal, and dates of the appraisal and of the report. It also describes work used to develop the appraisal, the assumptions and limiting conditions, the information that was analyzed, the procedures followed, and the reasoning that supports the conclusions. The report states the current use of the real estate and the use reflected in the appraisal, the support for the appraiser's opinion of the highest and best use, and any departures from the standards. It includes a signed certification.

Summary Appraisal Report

The Summary Appraisal Report covers the same categories as the Self-Contained Appraisal Report, but where the Self-Contained Appraisal Report includes descriptions, the Summary Appraisal Report contains summaries.

Restricted Use Appraisal Report

The Restricted Use Appraisal Report covers the same categories as the other two reports with several differences: only the client is named because there are no other users; the use of the report is limited to the client; and the report refers to the appraiser's work file as the source of necessary additional information about the appraisal.

Steps in the Appraisal Process

1. State the problem.
↓
2. Gather the data needed and the sources.
↓
3. Gather, record, and verify the necessary data.
↓

General Data	**Specific Data**	**Data for Each Approach**
Region	Location	Sales data
City	Lot	Cost data
Neighborhood	Improvements	Income and expense data
		Population trends
		Income level
		Employment opportunities

4. Determine the highest and best use.
↓
5. Estimate the land value.
↓
6. Estimate value by one of several methods.
↓
7. Reconcile or correlate the estimated values for the final value estimate.
↓
8. The Appraisal Report.

Appraisal Licensing Standards

The Appraisal Foundation, a non-profit educational organization, was established in 1987 in response to the crisis in the savings and loan industry in the early 1980s. This crisis confirmed the importance of basing appraisals on established recognized standards, free from outside pressures.

The Appraiser Qualifications Board (AQB) was included in the foundation structure to develop these standards. It created the Uniform Standards of

Professional Appraisal Practice (USPAP) and established educational and experience requirements for the licensing of appraisers in all states. USPAP is recognized nationwide as the standard of professional appraisal practice, and all appraisers are required to abide by these standards.

In California, the Office of Real Estate Appraisers (OREA) was established in 1990 to license appraisers. OREA has licensed over 18,000 real estate appraisers.

Types of Appraisal Licenses

There are four levels of real estate appraiser licensing in California:

1. Trainee License
2. Residential License
3. Certified Residential License
4. Certified General License

Each level requires a specific amount of education and experience, and each licensee must pass a state exam. Trainees must work under the supervision of a licensed appraiser. The types of structures that can be appraised are specified for each level. An appraisal on commercial property is conducted by a Certified General Appraiser. Continuing education is required to maintain the license.

Professional Appraisal Organizations

The major objective of these organizations is to make sure the members of the appraisal profession are knowledgeable and conform to a code of ethics and standards of professional appraisal practice.

The main professional organization is the Appraisal Institute (AI). Members may hold the title of Member Appraisal Institute (MAI) or Senior Residential Appraiser (SRA).

Appraisal Institute Designations
- Member Appraisal Institute (MAI)
- Senior Residential Appraiser (SRA)
- Senior Real Property Appraiser (SRPA)
- Senior Real Estate Analyst (SREA)
- Residential Member (RM)

FannieMae. **Uniform Residential Appraisal Report** File No. ____

Property Address	Unit No. ___ City ___ State ___ Zip Code ___
Legal Description	County ___
Assessor's Parcel No.	Tax Year ___ R.E. Taxes $ ___ Special Assessments $ ___
Property Rights Appraised ☐ Fee Simple ☐ Leasehold ☐	Map Reference ___ Census Tract ___
Borrower	Current Owner of Record ___ Occupant ☐ Owner ☐ Tenant ☐ Vacant
Neighborhood Name	Project Type ☐ PUD ☐ Condominium ☐ HOA $ ___ /Mth.
Purpose ☐ Purchase ☐ Refinance ☐	Sale Price $ ___ Date of Sale ___ Sale Concessions ☐ Yes ☐ No
$ ___ loan charges and/or sale concessions to be paid by any party on behalf of the borrower (describe).	
Lender/Client	Appraiser ___

Note: Race and the racial composition of the neighborhood are not appraisal factors.

			Single-Family Housing		Condominium Housing	
			PRICE	AGE	PRICE	AGE
Location ☐ Urban ☐ Suburban ☐ Rural	Property Values ☐ Increasing ☐ Stable ☐ Declining		$ (000)	(yrs)	$ (000)	(yrs)
Built-Up ☐ Over 75% ☐ 25–75% ☐ Under 25%	Demand/Supply ☐ Shortage ☐ In Balance ☐ Over Supply		Low		Low	
Growth ☐ Rapid ☐ Stable ☐ Slow	Marketing Time ☐ Under 3 mths ☐ 3–6 mths ☐ Over 6 mths		High		High	
Neighborhood Boundaries and Description:			Pred.		Pred.	

Dimensions	Area	Shape	View	
Specific Zoning Classification	Zoning Description			
Zoning Compliance ☐ Legal ☐ Legal Nonconforming (Grandfathered Use) ☐ No Zoning ☐ Illegal (describe)				
Is the highest and best use of subject property as improved (or as proposed per plans and specifications) the present use? ☐ Yes ☐ No If No, describe.				

Utilities	Public	Other (describe)		Public	Other (describe)	Off-site Improvements—Type	Public	Private
Electricity	☐	☐	Water	☐	☐	Street	☐	☐
Gas	☐	☐	Sanitary Sewer	☐	☐	Alley	☐	☐

Are the utilities and/or off-site improvements typical for the market area? ☐ Yes ☐ No If No, describe.
Are there any adverse site conditions (easements, encroachments, drainage, flood areas, etc.)? ☐ Yes ☐ No If Yes, describe.
Factory Built Housing: ☐ Manufactured Housing (Fannie Mae Form 1004C Required) ☐ Modular Housing ☐ Other (panelized, sectional, etc.)

Units ☐ One ☐ Accessory/In-law	Roof Surface	Foundation ☐ Poured Concrete ☐ Block ☐ Other	
No. of Stories	Exterior Walls	Basement Area ☐ Full ☐ Partial ☐ Crawl Space ☐ Slab	
Type ☐ Detached ☐ Attached	Interior Walls	Finished ☐ Yes ☐ No % Finished ☐ Sump Pump ☐ Dampness ☐ Other	
☐ Existing ☐ Proposed	Year Built	Attic ☐ None ☐ Stairs ☐ Drop Stair ☐ Floor ☐ Insulation ☐ Finished/Heated	
Car Storage # of Cars ☐ Garage ☐ Carport ☐ Driveway		Evidence of Repairs, Remodeling, or Renovation? ☐ Yes ☐ No If Yes, describe.	

Are there any physical deficiencies or conditions (including needed repairs, deferred maintenance, etc.)? ☐ Yes ☐ No If Yes, describe.
Do the physical deficiencies or conditions affect the livability or soundness or structural integrity of the property? ☐ Yes ☐ No If Yes, describe.
Are there any adverse external factors or environmental conditions that impact the property? ☐ Yes ☐ No If Yes, describe.
Does the property generally conform to the neighborhood (functional utility, style, condition, use, construction, etc.)? ☐ Yes ☐ No If No, describe.
Describe Property Condition:

FEATURE	SUBJECT	COMPARABLE SALE NO. 1		COMPARABLE SALE NO. 2		COMPARABLE SALE NO. 3	
Address							
Proximity to Subject							
Sale Price	$		$		$		$
Sale Price/Gross Liv. Area	$ sq. ft.	$ sq. ft.		$ sq. ft.		$ sq. ft.	
Data & Verification Sources							
VALUE ADJUSTMENTS	DESCRIPTION	DESCRIPTION	+(-) $ Adjustment	DESCRIPTION	+(-) $ Adjustment	DESCRIPTION	+(-) $ Adjustment
Sale or Financing Concessions							
Date of Sale/Time							
Location							
Leasehold/Fee Simple							
Site/View							
Design (Style)							
Actual Age/Effective Age							
Condition							
Above Grade Room Count	Total Bdrms. Baths	Total Bdrms. Baths		Total Bdrms. Baths		Total Bdrms. Baths	
Gross Living Area	sq. ft.	sq. ft.		sq. ft.		sq. ft.	
Basement & Finished Rooms Below Grade							
Heating/Cooling							
Garage/Carport							
Net Adjustment (Total)		☐ + ☐ -	$	☐ + ☐ -	$	☐ + ☐ -	$
Adjusted Sale Price of Comparables		Net Adj. % Gross Adj. %	$	Net Adj. % Gross Adj. %	$	Net Adj. % Gross Adj. %	$

Indicated Value by: Sales Comparison Approach $ ___ Cost Approach (optional) $ ___ Income Approach (optional) $ ___
Reconciliation and Final Value Conclusion:

This appraisal is made ☐ "as is," ☐ subject to completion per plans and specifications on the basis of a hypothetical condition that the improvements have been completed, or ☐ subject to the following repairs, alterations, inspections, or conditions:

Based on an interior and exterior property inspection, my (our) opinion of the market value, as defined, of the real property that is the subject of this report is $ ___ as of ___, which is the date of inspection and the effective date of this appraisal.

FannieMae.   **Uniform Residential Appraisal Report**   File No.

There are _____ comparable listings in the subject neighborhood ranging in list price from $ _____ to $ _____

There are _____ comparable sales in the subject neighborhood ranging in sale price from $ _____ to $ _____

Have there been any sales or transfers of the subject property or comparable sales for the three years prior to the effective date of the appraisal? ☐ Yes ☐ No If Yes, provide the sale or transfer history. If the history is not available for the subject property or the comparable sales describe the research performed.

ITEM	SUBJECT	COMPARABLE SALE NO. 1	COMPARABLE SALE NO. 2	COMPARABLE SALE NO. 3
Date of Prior Sale or Transfer				
Price of Prior Sale or Transfer				
Seller				
Buyer				
Data Source(s)				
Effective Date of Data Source(s)				
Date of Prior Sale or Transfer				
Price of Prior Sale or Transfer				
Seller				
Buyer				
Data Source(s)				
Effective Date of Data Source(s)				

SALE HISTORY

Are the prior sales or transfers of the subject property and/or the comparable sales arm's length transactions? ☐ Yes ☐ No If No, describe and explain the conditions of sale.

Is the current agreement of sale for the subject property an arm's length transaction? ☐ Yes ☐ No If No, describe and explain the conditions of sale.

Has the subject property been listed for sale in the 12 months prior to the effective date of this appraisal? ☐ Yes ☐ No If Yes, report each listing price and the name and telephone number of the listing broker.

Provide an analysis of the listing history of the subject property and the sale or transfer history for subject property and each of the comparable sales.

For a purchase money transaction, is the seller the current owner of record? ☐ Yes ☐ No If No, identify the seller and explain below why he/she is not the same.

PUD

Project information for PUD's (if applicable)—Project's legal name:

Is the developer/builder in control of the Homeowners' Association (HOA)? ☐ Yes ☐ No

Provide the following information for PUD's ONLY if the developer/builder is in control of the HOA and the subject property is an attached dwelling unit:

Project description ☐ Detached ☐ Row or Townhouse ☐ Other

Total number of phases _____ Total number of units _____ Total number of units sold _____

Total number of units rented _____ Total number of units for sale _____ Data source _____

Was the project created by the conversion of existing building(s) into a PUD? ☐ Yes ☐ No If Yes, date of conversion: _____

Does the project contain any multi-dwelling units? ☐ Yes ☐ No Data source: _____

Are the units, common elements, and recreation facilities complete? ☐ Yes ☐ No If No, describe the status of completion.

Are the common elements leased to or by the Homeowners' Association? ☐ Yes ☐ No If Yes, describe the rental terms and options.

Describe common elements and recreational facilities.

CONDOMINIUM

Project information for condominium projects (if applicable)—Project's legal name:

Is the developer/builder in control of the Homeowners' Association (HOA)? ☐ Yes ☐ No

Project description ☐ Detached ☐ Row or Townhouse ☐ Garden ☐ Mid-rise ☐ High-rise ☐ Other

Project primary occupancy ☐ Principal Residence ☐ Second Home or Recreational ☐ Tenant

Total number of units in the project _____ Total number of units for sale _____ Total number of units rented _____

Total number of phases _____ Are all of the phases complete? ☐ Yes ☐ No If No, describe. Data Source _____

What is the percent of the total units that have been conveyed (or under contract) to purchasers who are occupying (or will occupy) the property as their principal residence and/or second home? _____ %.

Does any single entity (the same individual, investor group, corporation, etc.) own more than 10% of the total units in the project? ☐ Yes ☐ No

Describe common elements and recreational facilities.

Are the units, common elements, and recreation facilities complete? ☐ Yes ☐ No If No, describe the status of completion.

Are any common elements leased to or by the Homeowners' Association? ☐ Yes ☐ No If Yes, describe the rental terms and options.

Was the project created by the conversion of existing building(s) into a condominium? ☐ Yes ☐ No If Yes, date of conversion: _____

Has all rehabilitation work involved in the condominium conversion been completed? ☐ Yes ☐ No If No, describe the work to be completed.

Is the zoning a legal, non-conforming use? ☐ Yes ☐ No If Yes, do the zoning regulations prohibit rebuilding to current density? ☐ Yes ☐ No

Are the parking facilities adequate for the project size and type? ☐ Yes ☐ No If No, describe and comment on the effect on market value.

Management group ☐ Homeowners' Association ☐ Developer ☐ Management agent

Page 2 of 2   Fannie Mae Test Form 1004   May 2004

Summary

There are several types of real estate appraisal licenses in California. The appraisal license or certificate is specific and independent from a real estate license.

An **appraisal** is an unbiased estimate or opinion of the property value on a given date. Most appraisals are based on market value. **Market value** is the price a property would bring if freely offered on the open market, with both a willing buyer and a willing seller. Properties excluded from market value result from default, foreclosure, bankruptcy, divorce, and death.

The appraisal process is a series of four steps leading to a final value estimate: (1) stating the problem, (2) gathering data (general and specific), (3) deciding on the appraisal method, and (4) reconciling the data for final value estimate. Appraisal techniques include the cost approach, income approach, and market approach. The gross multiplier technique also determines estimated value.

Appraisal theory focuses on principles of value, which include change, substitution, supply and demand, highest and best use, progression, and competition.

Included in the appraisal process are the four elements for estimating value: demand, utility, scarcity, and transferability. After the value of the property is established, the appraiser reviews other forces such as physical, economic, political, and social changes.

Another factor in the appraisal process is depreciation. **Depreciation** is a loss of value, and results from physical deterioration, functional obsolescence and economic obsolescence. Classifications of depreciation are curable or incurable or as accrued or accrual for depreciation.

The final step in the appraisal process is the examination of the different values (reconciling). The appraiser decides which of the values is the most appropriate for the property. The final value conclusions are documented in a restricted summary or self-contained appraisal report.

Chapter 11 Review Exercises

Matching Exercise

Instructions: Look up the meaning of the terms in the Glossary, then write the letter of the matching term on the blank line before its definition. Answers are in Appendix B.

Terms

a. actual age
b. amenities
c. appraisal process
d. appraisal report
e. appraisal
f. assemblage
g. capitalization
h. conformity
i. contract rent
j. corner influence
k. cost
l. cul-de-sac lot
m. depreciation
n. economic life
o. economic rent
p. effective age
q. effective demand
r. fair market value
s. flag lot
t. front foot

u. functional utility
v. improvements
w. interim use
x. key lot
y. location
z. market price
aa. market rent
bb. market value
cc. orientation
dd. plottage increment
ee. price
ff. reconciliation
gg. replacement cost
hh. scarcity
ii. T-lot
jj. transferability
kk. utility value
ll. utility
mm. vacancy factor
nn. value

Definitions

1. _____ An unbiased estimate or opinion of the property

2. _____ A lot that looks like a flag on a pole, which represents the access to the site; usually located to the rear of another lot fronting a main street.

3. _____ The increase in the value when several smaller parcels are combined together into one larger parcel.

4. _____ The power of goods or services to command other goods in exchange for the present worth of future benefits arising from property ownership.

5. _____ Desire coupled with purchasing power.

6. _____ When land uses are compatible and homes are similar in design and size, the maximum value is realized.

7. _____ Real age of a building.

8. _____ Features that add value to a property.

9. _____ The price the property would bring if freely offered on the open market with both a willing buyer and a willing seller.

10. _____ The rent a property should bring in the open market.

11. _____ The cost of replacing improvements with modern materials and techniques.

12. _____ Commercial properties benefit from more exposure on a corner lot.

13. _____ The ability of a property to satisfy a need or desire, such as shelter, income or amenities.

14. _____ The placement of a building on its lot in relation to exposure to sun, prevailing wind, traffic, and privacy from the street.

15. _____ Age of a building determined by its condition and usefulness.

16. _____ The expenses in money, labor, material or sacrifices in acquiring or producing something.

17. _____ An orderly systematic method to arrive at an estimate of value.

18. _____ Sometimes called the objective value.

19. _____ The process that can be employed to convert income to value.

20. _____ The availability or lack of availability of a commodity in the marketplace.

21. _____ The usefulness of the property to its owner. This is subjective value or the value given for personal reasons.

22. _____ Title to property must be marketable with an unclouded title.

23. _____ The estimated period over which a building may be profitably used.

24. _____ What a property actually sold for.

25. _____ Lot that is the least desirable due to the lack of privacy because it is surrounded by the back yards of other lots.

26. _____ A lot that is fronted head-on by a street; noise and glare from headlights may be detractors from this type of lot.

27. _____ This may be the most important factor influencing value.

28. _____ The combined factors of usefulness with desirability.

29. _____ A lot found on a dead-end street with same way for ingress and egress.

30. _____ The final step in an appraisal is to examine the values derived by the various approaches.

31. _____ The process of putting several smaller less valuable lots together under one ownership.

32. _____ Any buildings or structures on a lot.

33. _____ Loss in value from any cause.

34. _____ Short-term and temporary use of a property until it is ready for a more productive highest and best use.

35. _____ The width of a property along a street.

▌Multiple Choice Questions

Instructions: Circle your response and go to Appendix B to read the complete explanation for each question.

1. "The relationship between a thing desired and a potential purchaser" is one definition of:
   a. economic function.
   b. economic necessity.
   c. effective public demand.
   d. value.

2. The market value of real property is most nearly its _____ price.
   a. asking
   b. listing
   c. market
   d. offered

3. Market value of improved real property is least affected by:
    a. an open market.
    b. its exchange value.
    c. its objective value.
    d. the original cost of materials.

4. The value of real property is best measured by which of the following characteristics?
    a. Demand, depreciation, scarcity, and utility
    b. Cost, demand, transferability, and utility
    c. Cost, feasibility, scarcity, and utility
    d. Demand, scarcity, transferability, and utility

5. The ultimate test of functional utility is:
    a. design.
    b. marketability.
    c. utility.
    d. maintenance costs.

6. In the appraisal of real property, the term "unearned increment" most nearly means:
    a. an increase in value due to population increase.
    b. a decrease in value due to social forces rather than personal effort.
    c. a decrease of property taxes.
    d. depreciation.

7. Which of the following appraisal approaches is based on the principle of substitution?
    a. Replacement cost
    b. Reproduction cost
    c. Market comparison
    d. Capitalization

8. In determining the value on an unimproved parcel of land, the first thing to establish is its:
    a. listing price.
    b. purchase price.
    c. highest and best use.
    d. closest comparable properties.

9. In a well-planned residential community, which of the following contributes most to the maintenance of value?
   a. Conformity to proper land-use objectives
   b. Deed restrictions
   c. Variances to permit the highest and best use of every parcel of land
   d. Prevention of major thoroughfare construction through the community

10. Land is generally valued at its highest and best use. If someone buys land with a building on it that must be torn down, the appraiser should:
    a. add the salvage value.
    b. add nothing to the value of the land.
    c. deduct the cost of demolition.
    d. appraise the building using the income approach.

11. In the market approach to appraisal, what is the most important as well as the most difficult step?
    a. Collection of data on comparable properties
    b. Analysis of data on comparable properties
    c. Adjustment of data to reflect differences between subject and comparable properties
    d. Establishing the correct unit of comparison

12. The comparison approach to appraisal would be least reliable:
    a. in an inactive market.
    b. in a neighborhood where the land uses are rapidly changing.
    c. when the comparables are in the same price range.
    d. when the comparables are located in another neighborhood.

13. An appraiser is using the market approach. A comparable property has an amenity that is not present in the subject property. The appraiser would therefore:
    a. add the value of the amenity to the subject property's value.
    b. subtract the value of the amenity from the comparable property's value.
    c. realize it doesn't matter because no two properties are exactly alike.
    d. list the value of the amenity separately.

14. In appraising the value of a building using the replacement-cost approach, an appraiser would consider all of the following except:
    a. the cost of improvements to the land.
    b. a separate estimate for the value of the land.
    c. allowances for depreciation.
    d. the appropriate capitalization rate.

15. The replacement-cost approach is more difficult to apply to older properties than to newer properties because:
    a. historic costs are difficult to obtain.
    b. land prices are difficult to estimate on older properties.
    c. depreciation schedules are difficult to determine on older properties.
    d. zoning and building codes are subject to change.

16. Functional obsolescence would not include which of the following?
    a. Eccentric design
    b. Items of surplus utility
    c. Lack of air conditioning
    d. Proximity to nuisances

17. The major cause of loss of value of real property is usually due to:
    a. deterioration.
    b. passage of physical life.
    c. obsolescence.
    d. lack of maintenance.

18. A building that constitutes an improper improvement to its site is an example of:
    a. curable physical.
    b. incurable physical.
    c. curable functional.
    d. incurable functional.

19. Economic rent is best defined as the rent:
    a. required to produce a suitable return for the owner.
    b. generated by the property in a theoretically perfectly informed market.
    c. agreed to by a lessor and lessee under the terms of a written lease.
    d. received for comparable space in the competitive open market.

20. To calculate accurately a gross rent multiplier, the appraiser needs _____ from comparable properties.
    a. net income and selling price
    b. original cost and the annual income
    c. annual rent and the selling price
    d. net income and the capitalization rate

21. The capitalization approach is based primarily on the appraisal concepts of:
    a. change.
    b. competition.
    c. anticipation.
    d. retribution.

22. The effective annual gross income of a property is the difference between the annual gross income and:
    a. vacancy factor and rent collection losses.
    b. allowable expenses and depreciation.
    c. capitalization rate.
    d. administrative expenses and capital improvements.

23. The estimated period of time over which a property will yield a return on investment over and above the economic rent attributable to the land itself is known as its:
    a. earning period.
    b. economic life.
    c. investment period.
    d. productive life.

24. Which of the following would be used by an appraiser who has chosen the income approach to establish the value of an apartment building?
    a. Excess rent
    b. Percentage rent
    c. Economic rent
    d. Contract rent

25. A 12-year-old building that has been maintained in excellent condition is given an age of 6 years by an appraiser. This would be known as its:
    a. actual age.
    b. economic life.
    c. effective age.
    d. physical life.

26. When comparing the economic and physical life of a building, the economic life is usually:
    a. equal.
    b. longer.
    c. shorter.
    d. shorter or longer depending on the maintenance.

27. When calculating the net income, which of the following is not deducted?
    a. Maintenance expenses
    b. Management fees
    c. Mortgage interest
    d. Vacancy losses

28. In the capitalization approach to appraisal, the most difficult step is to determine:
    a. gross income.
    b. effective net income.
    c. net income.
    d. the capitalization rate.

29. The gross rent multiplier is defined as:
    a. sales value/gross rent.
    b. gross rent/sales value.
    c. assessed value/gross rent.
    d. gross rent/market value.

30. Usually an appraiser estimates the value of a property by using all three major approaches. To obtain a final estimate of value, the appraiser _____ the three indications of value.
    a. amortizes
    b. averages
    c. finalizes
    d. reconciles

Land Use, Subdivision, and Housing

12
Chapter

Introduction

Due to the rapid and continuing growth of cities and the movement of people into once quiet rural areas, the government has found itself in the real estate business. Such population changes have created problems which have led to an increase in regulation.

The range of problems is wide and varied: ensuring adequate public facilities such as schools and parks; preventing fraud and misrepresentation in the selling of subdivided real property; regulating lot design and physical improvements for the orderly and proper development of communities; constructing streets, highways, and parking areas; regulating airways over the land; providing a water supply; protecting life and property by means of police and firemen; maintaining clean air; mandating noise abatement; providing sewage and waste disposal and utility services.

When cities grow rapidly without design or control, problems are made worse, and the need for regulation and planning is greater. Communities try to ensure quality places to work and live by using the tools at hand: subdivision regulations, county and city master plans, zoning laws, and building codes.

In this chapter, you will examine the principles of land-use planning, development, and building.

Learning Objectives

After reading this chapter, you will be able to:

- explain the difference between eminent domain and police power.
- explain the goals of community planning.
- recognize the difference between the Subdivision Map Act and the Subdivided Lands Law.
- identify the types of government controls in real estate.

Government Regulation of Land Use

Continued urban growth and population increases overwhelm the existing infrastructure and place the burden of expanding public services in the hands of local, state, and federal agencies. As the demand for more schools, roads, hospitals, and public services increases, these agencies need to plan for and manage growth. Accommodating and managing this growth is accomplished through the legal powers of eminent domain and police power.

Eminent Domain

The Takings Clause of the Fifth Amendment to the Federal Constitution seems clear about the "public use" restrictions on the power of eminent domain. Recently, cities, counties, and states have been extending the power of eminent domain to take private property, not for public use, but to benefit private groups. Instead of building a highway or school, they take the private property and sell it to private developers to build shopping centers, luxury residences, and factories.

The Michigan Supreme Court overturned the Poletown eminent domain ruling.

In 1981, Detroit used the power of eminent domain to take homes in the Poletown neighborhood, a well-kept, working-class neighborhood with more than 1,000 homes, 600 businesses, several churches, and a hospital. The only thing wrong with the neighborhood was that General Motors (GM) wanted the land to build a new assembly plant. GM threatened to take the plant out of Detroit if the city did not take the property by force. Using the excuse that the economic well-being of Detroit was dependent on the plant expansion, the city condemned and took the property under eminent domain and then sold it to General Motors. The Supreme Court of Michigan upheld this decision. However, in 2004, the Michigan Supreme Court was asked to "restore the constitutional protections which ensure that private property cannot be taken to benefit powerful interest groups at the expense of the less powerful". The Supreme Court voted unanimously to overturn the Poletown eminent domain ruling, 20 years after the neighborhood was razed.

In June 2005, the United States Supreme Court decided on the case of *Kelo v. City of New London*. The courts heard from a group of New London, Connecticut homeowners who did not want their homes razed in order to allow the building of a hotel, health club, and offices. The city wanted to build these new structures to complement a multi-million dollar research facility, recently built by Pfizer, the corporation. The court decided 5–4 to allow the neighborhood to be razed for the new structures. The majority opinion stated that the city had carefully planned for the economic development which is not limited to new jobs and increased tax revenue. The minority opinion stated that the decision effectively deleted the words "for public use" from the Takings Clause of the Fifth Amendment.

Police Power

Police power is the power of the state to enact laws within constitutional limits to promote the order, safety, health, morals and general welfare of our society. The power to pass such laws is given to the states by the United States Constitution and to each county and city in California by the State Constitution. Thus, all citizens of California benefit from this empowerment of government to regulate the law.

> The following excerpt from a United States Supreme Court case describes police power:
>
> *"The possession and enjoyment of all rights are subject to this power. Under it the state may prescribe regulations promoting the health, peace, morals, education and good order of the people, and legislate so as to increase the industries of the state, develop its resources and add to its welfare and prosperity."*

> *Police power does not give the state legislature authority to issue arbitrary laws that force unreasonable or unnecessary burdens on people or their property.*

Any laws made as a result of the exercise of police power must be necessary and proper for the protection of the public interest. Currently, the business of real estate is regulated and controlled by licensing real estate professionals; monitoring subdivisions; enforcing the numerous building, health, and safety codes; and determining growth with master plans and zoning. Almost every aspect of the real estate industry, from land use and development to sales and leasing of property, is controlled in some way under police power.

The following examples of regulation by police power are reasonable uses of legislation to promote general well-being in communities: zoning in cities so that neighborhoods may be kept free of objectionable businesses; limitation of districts in which cemeteries, slaughterhouses, factories and the like may be located; controls for speeding and other careless driving on the highways; prohibiting adulteration or selling of impure goods; garbage disposal; vaccination of school children; regulation or prohibition of liquor, prostitution and gambling; and requiring safety devices at places of employment. Even though some laws may seem to be restrictive on the conduct of private persons, their measure is in their worth to the common good.

Review - Government Control of Land Use
- Eminent Domain
- Police Power
  - General Plans
    - Zoning
    - Specific Plans
    - Subdivision Regulations
    - Building Codes
    - Health Codes

Planning and Development

In California, every city and county must adopt a comprehensive or **master plan**, known as a "**General Plan**", for long-term physical development. Every General Plan must cover the development issues in the following seven major categories: land use, circulation, housing, conservation, open space, noise, and safety. Cities or counties located on the coast must also address coastal development and protection of natural resources and wetlands.

A General Plan is the basis of and sets the direction for a community's future development. All community development decisions such as re-zoning, subdivision map approvals, and public works projects are required to be consistent with the General Plan. The land use proposals outlined in a General Plan are implemented in many ways—zoning being the best known and most frequently used tool. Additionally, General Plan land uses are carried out through specific plans, subdivision regulations, property tax incentives, land banking, and public finance measures, to name a few.

Coastal communities must address the effects of development on natural resources.

Zoning

The regulation of structures and uses of property within selected districts is known as **zoning**. Zoning ordinances are exercises of a city's or county's **police power**, and are upheld as long as they reasonably protect the public health, safety and general welfare of an area. When the state uses police power, it is not required to compensate a property owner for any loss in property values as a result of the regulation, as it must do under the power of eminent domain.

Most cities and counties have ordinances that create land use districts or zones. A zoning ordinance does not duplicate the General Plan, even though both deal with land use. A zoning ordinance primarily implements the General Plan by regulating land use for individual projects, whereas the General Plan is more far-reaching and future-oriented. Each zone has a specific set of regulations that control the use of land, lot sizes, types of structures permitted, building heights, building setbacks, and density. There are zones for single-family residences, multi-family dwellings, commercial uses, industrial uses, and open space or agriculture land.

Symbols Used to Show Different Zoning Areas

- **A** - Agricultural
- **C** - Commercial
- **M** - Manufacturing
- **P** - Public Uses
  (like parking lots and parks)
- **R** - Residential

- **R1** - Single family home
- **R2** - Duplex
- **R3** - Multiple residential units
- **R4** - Four units or higher
  density dwellings
- **PUD** - Planned Unit Development

A - Agricultural

C - Commercial

M - Manufacturing

P - Public Uses

R - Homes, other residences

R1 - Single family home

Each zone has a specific set of regulations.

R2 - Duplex

R3 - Multiple residential units

R4 - Four units or higher density dwellings

PUD - Planned Unit Development

Usually every district is zoned for different types of uses, known as permitted uses and conditional uses. **Permitted uses** meet the current use requirements within the district. **Conditional uses** do not meet the current use requirements but may be allowed by obtaining a special permit known as a conditional use permit. When an area is rezoned to another use, existing properties may retain the previous zoning under a grandfather clause. Such uses or structures are termed to be non-conforming. An owner who wants to use his or her property in a way that does not meet the current use requirements may be able to obtain a conditional use permit or a variance.

Conditional Use Permits

A **conditional use permit** allows a land use that may be incompatible with other uses existing in the zone. The use is allowed as long as the project owner complies with the conditions specified in the permit. If the owner does not comply with the conditions, the permit may be revoked. A conditional use permit runs with the land, and its provisions still apply even if there is a change in ownership.

Zoning and Use Variances

A city or county may allow a **variance**, or an exception to existing zoning regulations for special reasons. For example, if a lot has an irregular shape and does not meet the standard zoning for a side-yard setback, the owner is at a disadvantage when trying to develop the property. The owner may ask the city or county for a waiver or zoning variance, which would allow the property to be developed. In summary, a variance is simply a deviation from a development standard.

Specific Plans

After a General Plan is adopted, some cities and counties carry out the proposed land uses through a specific plan. A specific plan pertains to a particular development site or area of the General Plan. Since they pertain to just one specific project, they are able to consolidate many of the factors needed to develop a project and monitor the development costs.

Environmentally Sensitive Lands

Land and water areas containing natural features or ecological functions of such significance as to warrant their protection are considered **environmentally sensitive lands**. The public's desire to protect the natural environment is reinforced by federal and state laws, which require cities and counties to take into account environmental issues in arriving at planning decisions.

Local Coastal Programs

Under the **California Coastal Act**, 15 coastal counties and 58 cities, along with the state of California, have stewardship of the 1,100 miles of coast that stretches from Oregon to the border with Mexico. The coastal

The coastal zone contains over 1.5 million acres of land.

zone contains over 1.5 million acres of land and reaches from three miles at sea to an inland boundary that varies from a few blocks in urban areas to about five miles in less-developed areas.

Each city and county in the coastal zone must prepare Local Coastal Programs (LCPs) which adhere to the California Coastal Commission's strict standards for coastal development and protection. The LCPs are the basic planning tools used to review and decide permits for new development in coastal areas. Additionally, they protect the shoreline and environmentally sensitive habitats, determine ways to improve and expand existing ports, improve public access to the shoreline, and establish urban-rural boundaries to direct new development into areas with existing services to avoid wasteful urban sprawl and leapfrog development.

If property is located in the coastal zone, the owner or developer must apply for a coastal development permit (CDP) before any new construction can begin. Permits are routinely approved provided the projects comply with the Coastal Act policies and standards. In many areas, the California Coastal Commission retains permit authority over the coastal zone, and many local actions can be appealed up to the Coastal Commission.

Clean Water Act of 1977

The Clean Water Act (CWA) of 1977 regulates the discharge of pollutants into waters of the United States, including wetlands. **Wetlands** are areas where water covers the soil, or is present either at or near the surface of the soil all year or for varying periods during the year, including during the growing season. Wetlands can vary widely because of regional differences and are found from the tundra to the tropics and on every continent except Antarctica. There are two types of wetlands: coastal wetlands and inland wetlands.

Wetlands are areas where water covers the soil all year for varying periods of time during the year.

Coastal or tidal wetlands are found along California's Pacific shoreline and estuaries. A shoreline is the intersection of the land with the water (mean high water line). An estuary is an area where sea water and fresh water mix. Inland wetlands are found in deltas, swamps, marshes, low-lying areas of lakes and ponds, and in floodplains along rivers and streams. A **floodplain** is the low land adjacent to a river, lake, or ocean.

Rangeland, Grazing Land, and Grassland Protection Act

In 2002 the Rangeland, Grazing Land and Grassland Protection Act was passed to protect California's rangeland, grazing land, and grasslands. Its threefold program includes: (1) prevent the conversion of rangeland, grazing land, and grassland to nonagricultural uses; (2) protect livestock grazing areas; and (3) ensure continued wildlife, water quality, watershed, and open-space benefits to the State of California from livestock grazing.

Oak Woodlands Conservation Act

In 2001, the **California Oak Woodlands Conservation Program** was enacted to protect the oak woodlands from residential, commercial and industrial development or conversion of the oak woodlands to intensive agricultural development. Since over 80% of the remaining oak trees are found on private property, this program offers landowners an opportunity to obtain funding to maintain and restore the oak woodlands. Additionally, the program is designed to help local governments implement oak conservation elements in local General Plans to achieve oak woodland protection.

Subdivision

A subdivision is the division of land into five or more lots for the purpose of sale, lease, or financing. Practically every place where people live has been subdivided at some time. All developments started as a large parcel of land that was divided up and sold to separate individuals. Sometimes the parcels were large enough to be subdivided repeatedly, creating a need for some control to make sure a desirable quality of life was protected.

Commonly, we think of a subdivision as a partition of a large piece of property into units designed for sale or lease for specific purposes. Usually, this is the case. The majority of subdivisions might be designated as lot and residential subdivisions. The parcels are meant to be sold to private individuals who plan to build homes on them or to speculators who will build houses "on spec" because they expect to sell them later. In most cases, the parcels are sold to a developer who will build multiple houses and sell the dwelling and lot as one package in a project that the developer will supervise. Some subdivisions are also developed for commercial purposes. A commercial acre is the area remaining from an acre of newly subdivided land after deducting the area devoted to streets, sidewalks, alleys, curbs, etc. It is also referred to as a buildable acre.

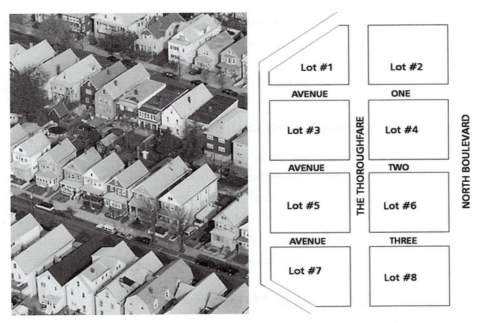

A parcel of land is subdivided into lots for the purpose of
sale, lease, or finance.

Basic Subdivision Laws

There are two basic laws under which subdivisions are controlled in
California—the **Subdivision Map Act** and the **Subdivided Lands Law**. To
understand these two laws, it is important to know they were enacted for
separate purposes. Different meanings of a subdivision were adopted in each
law to achieve each of their objectives. However, both were created for the
protection of the consumer.

> **Review - Two Laws Control Subdivisions in California**
> 1. Subdivision Map Act
> 2. Subdivided Lands Law

Complete compliance with all provisions of both subdivision laws is required
in any subdivided development. Developers and their professional consult-
ants must be thoroughly familiar not only with the provisions of state laws
but also with specific provisions in local subdivision control ordinance in
the community where the subdivision is being developed. In various local
subdivision ordinances, there are many differences because of the great
diversity in types of communities and conditions throughout California.

Land developers and subdividers should always consult the Department of Real Estate at an early planning stage in any subdivision development. A developer should be fully aware of the Real Estate Commissioner's current requirements for the subdivision qualification under consideration.

Laws Regulating Subdivisions Differ

Under the **Subdivision Map Act**, the city or county is authorized to control the orderly and proper development of the community. Under the **Subdivided Lands Law**, the Real Estate Commissioner regulates conditions surrounding the sale or lease of subdivided real property while the city or county regulates the lot design and physical improvements. The commissioner is concerned with preventing fraud and misrepresentation in selling.

Subdivision Map Act

The main objective of the Subdivision Map Act is to define the rules and procedures for filing maps to create subdivisions. It is directly controlled by local authorities (city and county) and is concerned with the physical aspects of a subdivision—such as building design, streets, and any adverse effects to the environment.

California has adopted the guidelines set forth by the **California Environmental Quality Act** (CEQA) to ensure that government agencies consider the environment prior to approving building projects. As a result, an environmental impact report may be required by authorities before issuing a building permit to private parties or prior to approving a subdivision tract map. An **environmental impact report** (EIR) is a study of how a development will affect the ecology of its surroundings. If it is determined that a proposed subdivision will have no adverse effect on the environment, the city or county prepares a **negative declaration** prior to making a decision on the project. A negative declaration is a written statement by the lead agency briefly describing the reasons that a proposed project, not exempt from the CEQA,

A subdivision is controlled by local authorities. They are concerned with building design, streets, and any adverse affects to the environment.

will not have a significant effect on the environment and, therefore, does not require the preparation of an EIR.

Because of the Subdivision Map Act, the direct control of the kind and type of subdivisions to be allowed in each community and the physical improvements to be installed are left to local jurisdictions (city and county) within certain general limits specified in the act.

Subdivision Map Act has Two Major Objectives

The first is to coordinate the subdivision plans and planning, including lot design, water supply, street patterns, right-of-way for drainage and sewers, etc., with the community pattern and plan as laid out by the local planning authorities.

Every city and county is required by the Subdivision Map Act to regulate subdivisions for a final tract map (five or more lots) or parcel map (two to four lots).

The second objective is to ensure initial proper improvement of areas dedicated for public purposes by having the subdivider file subdivision maps, including public streets and other public areas, so that these necessities will not become an undue burden in the future for taxpayers in the community.

The Subdivision Map Act requires every city and county to regulate subdivisions for which a tentative and final tract map (for five-or-more lots), or a parcel map (for two-to-four lots), is required. A **tentative tract map** is a map of the proposed subdivision that is submitted to a planning commission for approval or disapproval. It is used to make sure that the improvements, such as lot layouts, sizes, and configurations; grading plans; traffic access and street alignments; storm drainage, sewers, and water facilities; and other project features have been designed to conform to city or county General Plans. A **final tract map** indicates any changes required by the planning commission and is recorded in the county where the property is located. A **parcel map** pertains to a parcel of land that will be subdivided into less than five parcels or units and shows land boundaries, streets, and parcel numbers.

In addition, the Act allows cities and counties to adopt laws for subdivisions for which no map is required. The diagram on the next page shows typical steps in subdivision procedure under the Act.

Basic Outline of Final Map Preparation and Approval

Preparation	*Approval*

Economic analysis of feasibility
Locational analysis
Physical survey of site

↓

Preliminary discussion with agencies having jurisdiction over subdivision, including question of environmental impact report. → On basis of preliminary conference subdivider obtains requirements from local authorities, state agencies, title company, and financial source (lenders).

↓

Subdivider prepares tentative tract map

↓

Tentative map submitted for approval to:
1. local government
2. governmental loan insuring agency, e.g., F.H.A. → Planning commission accepts map from subdivider and obtains approval from other city or county offices. Copies forwarded to Department of Real Estate by applicant for Public Report.

↓

Subdivider prepares final map and secures all necessary signatures (record owners, public utilities, public entities).

↓

Final map submitted for local approval to:
1. local government approval
2. governmental loan insuring → Officer designated in local ordinance accepts map from subdivider and obtains approval from other city or county offices.

↓

Approved map is recorded. Copy sent to Department of Real Estate by applicant for public report.

↓

Development is started.

Health and Sanitation

Every tentative tract map submitted must comply with health and sanitation regulations. The local health officer enforces state and local health laws to ensure the sanitary condition of all housing. Proper drainage, sewage disposal, and water supply are crucial health and sanitation considerations. The local health officers may determine if water is **potable** (safe to drink) or requires a percolation test. A **percolation test** is used to determine the ability of the land to absorb and drain water and is frequently used when installing septic systems. A **septic tank** is a sewage settling tank which must be at least five feet away from the improvements. The sewage is converted into gas and liquids before the remaining waste is discharged by gravity into a leaching bed underground.

A septic tank is a sewage settling tank which is at least five feet from the improvement. Septic tanks are underground and covered.

To insure proper drainage the water table must be determined. The **water table** is the natural level at which water will be found, either above or below the surface of the ground. **Percolating water** is underground water not flowing in a defined channel. A **defined channel** is any natural watercourse, even though dry during a good portion of the year. Local health officers have the authority to stop any development with problems in these areas.

> **Review - Subdivision Map Act**
> - Enforced by city or county authorities
> - Concerned with physical aspects of a subdivision

Subdivided Lands Law

The **Subdivided Lands Law** is directly administered by the Real Estate Commissioner. Its objective is to protect buyers of property in new subdivisions from fraud, misrepresentation, or deceit in the marketing of subdivided lots, parcels, units, and undivided interests.

The Real Estate Commissioner must issue a subdivision public report before any subdivision can be offered for sale in California. This even applies to lands outside the state, if they are being marketed in California.

The public report is a document disclosing all important facts about the marketing and financing of the subdivision. The public report must show that the subdivider (developer) can complete and maintain all improvements and that the lots or parcels can be used for the purpose for which they are being sold.

Before a developer can sell each lot in the project, he or she must give a copy of the commissioner's final report to the buyer for approval. The buyer signs a receipt for the report stating it has been read. The seller (developer) must keep a copy of the statement for three years.

The public report is valid for five years, with any material changes in the development reported to the commissioner, who then can issue an amendment to the original report.

RECEIPT FOR PUBLIC REPORT

The Laws and Regulations of the Real Estate Commissioner require that you as a prospective purchaser or lessee be afforded an opportunity to read the public report for this subdivision before you make any written offer to purchase or lease a subdivision interest or before any money or other consideration toward purchase or lease of a subdivision interest is accepted from you.

In the case of a preliminary subdivision public report you must be afforded an opportunity to read the report before a written reservation or any deposit in connection therewith is accepted from you.

In the case of a conditional subdivision public report, delivery of legal title or other interest contracted for will not take place until issuance of a final subdivision public report. Provision is made in the sales agreement and escrow instructions for the return to you of the entire sum of money paid or advanced by you if you are dissatisfied with the final public report because of a material change. (See Business and Professions Code §11012.)

DO NOT SIGN THIS RECEIPT UNTIL YOU HAVE RECEIVED A COPY OF THE REPORT AND HAVE READ IT.

I read the Commissioner's public report on _____
[File Number]

_____
[Tract Number or Name]

I understand the report is not a recommendation or endorsement of the subdivision, but is for information only.

The issue date of the public report which I received and read is: _____

_____   _____
Signature   *Date*

_____
Address

It can take many months for a developer to get project approval once all the proper paperwork is submitted to the commissioner. During that time, the developer may want to begin marketing the project while waiting for the final report. By submitting a minimum application filing package the developer can get a preliminary public report which allows taking reservations for the project but not accepting any non-refundable money or entering into any binding contracts until receiving the final report from the commissioner.

> **Review - Subdivided Lands Law**
> - Administered by Real Estate Commissioner
> - Concerned with protecting the public from fraud

As a student of real estate, sometimes it is difficult to sort out the differences between two very like-sounding laws. The following list comparing the Subdivision Map Act and the Subdivided Lands Law will help you compare the two laws.

> **Review - Comparison of Subdivision Laws**
> - Subdivision Map Act
> - Two or more lots or parcels
> - Lots must be adjacent to each other
> - No exemption for 160 acres and larger parcels
> - Administered by local authorities
> - No public report needed
>
> **Subdivided Lands Law**
> - Five or more lots or parcels
> - Parcels need not be adjacent
> - 160 acres and selected larger parcels are exempt
> - Administered by Real Estate Commissioner
> - Requires a final public report

Types of Subdivisions

Due to the scarcity of land suitable for subdividing, the subdivision process has become more sophisticated, often resulting in higher land prices and new types of subdivisions. The legislature recognized this trend and has enacted laws to regulate such developments, including planned neighborhoods, community apartment houses, condominiums, limited-equity housing cooperatives, and undivided interest subdivisions. These projects do not follow the traditional subdivision model as being the simple division of a large piece of land into smaller parcels for the construction of individual homes. Typically there are three types of subdivisions: standard subdivisions, common interest developments, and undivided interest development.

Standard Subdivision

A **standard subdivision** is a land division with no common or mutual rights of either ownership or use among the owners of the parcels created by the division. This type of subdivision is a typical tract of single family homes on individual lots.

Land Project

Subdivisions located in sparsely populated areas (fewer than 1,500 registered voters within the subdivision or within two miles of its boundaries), made up of 50 parcels or more, are known as **land projects.** In the past, it appeared that these projects had been sold more on the intense promotion of alleged benefits than on the actual value of the project. There was a need for legislation to regulate these sales.

The Real Estate Commissioner was given the authority to oversee sales in land projects to make sure the consumer was protected. The law now allows a buyer 14 days after signing a contract to purchase property in a land project to rescind the offer, with a full refund of any money paid. This gives the buyer time to investigate the project and decide, unpressured, whether he or she still wants to go through with the purchase, and whether it was represented accurately or not.

> **Review - Land Project Subdivisions**
> * 50 parcels or more
> * In a sparsely populated area

Common Interest Developments

A **common interest development** (CID) combines the individual owner-ship of private dwellings with the shared ownership of common facilities of the entire project. The common facilities can range from roads and water systems to clubhouses, swimming pools, golf courses and even stables and private airport facilities. The CID provides a system of self-governance through a community association, sometimes called a **homeowners' association**. The association has the authority to enforce special rules called CC&Rs (Covenants, Conditions, and Restrictions) and to raise money through regular and special assessments. Restrictions on lots in a new subdivision would be found in a recorded declaration of restrictions. Common interest developments vary both in physical design and legal form. The following CIDs are all considered subdivisions and under the control of the subdivision laws: condominiums, planned developments, stock cooperatives, community apartment projects, and time-share projects.

Upon sale of an existing common-interest development, a buyer must be provided:

1. a copy of the Conditions, Covenants and Restrictions (CC&Rs), articles of incorporation, association by-laws, governing documents, and a current financial statement on the homeowners association.

2. written notification of any known pending special assessments, claims, or lawsuits against the seller or the homeowners association.

3. a statement showing whether the seller's account with the homeowners association is paid up-to-date.

Condominiums

A **condominium** consists of a separate fee interest in a particular specific space (the unit), plus an undivided interest in all common or public areas of the development. All owners are allowed to use any of the facilities in the common area. Each unit owner has a deed, separate financing, and pays the property taxes for their unit.

Review - Condominiums
- Fee simple ownership to living unit
- Undivided interest in land and common areas
- Separate property tax bill, deed, deed of trust
- Operations controlled by elected governing board

Planned Developments

A **planned development** (previously called planned unit development) is a planning and zoning term describing land not subject to conventional zoning requirements. It allows clustering of residences or other characteristics of the project which differ from normal zoning. In a planned development subdivision the owner has title to the unit and land under it, together with membership in an association which owns common area. Sometimes the owners of separate interests also have an undivided interest in the common area. The planned development is popular in suburban and rural areas. Owners have private ownership of their individual homes and lots but share the ownership of the common features. Shared facilities can include private roadways, water systems, septic systems, parks and open space, ponds and lakes, airport landing strips, trails, and ocean access. Some planned developments even share the ownership of forests and agricultural lands which produce income for the community.

Stock Cooperatives

A corporation formed for the purpose of owning property is known as a **stock cooperative.** Each stockholder is given the use of a living unit and any amenities and community recreational facilities, with the building being owned by the corporation.

In a community apartment project, a buyer receives an undivided interest in the land coupled with the right of exclusive occupancy of one of the apartments in the project.

Time-share Ownership

Time-sharing is a favorite way to have an interest in a building, with the right to occupy limited to a specific time period. This type of ownership is popular in resorts and other desirable areas where people like to vacation once or twice a year but do not need the right of possession the rest of the time.

Undivided Interest

In an **undivided interest,** the land itself is not divided—just the ownership. The buyer receives an undivided interest in a parcel of land as a tenant in common with all the other owners. All owners have the nonexclusive right to the use and occupancy of the property. A recreational vehicle park with campground and other leisure-time amenities is an example.

Regulation of Housing and Construction

The housing and construction industries in California are regulated by three laws: the State Housing Law, local building codes, and the Contractors' State License Law.

In addition, through the role of federal home building financing programs, both FHA and VA financing impose housing and construction regulations. It is critical in a subdivision where there is FHA or VA participation that the developer consults with those and any other appropriate agencies. These programs require, as a prerequisite to participation, that the house involved meet Minimum Property Requirements (MPRs). In some instances, MPRs are more demanding than either the State Housing Law or local building codes. An example of MPRs is the FHA 7-feet-6 inch minimum requirement for residential ceiling height.

State Housing Law

The **State Housing Law** (Health and Safety Code Section 17910, et seq.) outlines the minimum construction and occupancy requirements for dwellings. Local building inspectors enforce the construction regulations while local health officers enforce the occupancy and sanitation regulations. One way of enforcing the construction regulations is by the issuance of a building permit. In order to issue a building permit, the building inspector reviews and approves plans, specifications, plot plan, and accompanying exhibits for a proposed project. All new construction rehabilitation or remodeling projects must have a building permit issued by the local building inspector prior to beginning any work. **Rehabilitation** is the restoration of a property to its former or improved condition without changing the basic design or plan. **Remodeling** changes the basic design or plan of the building to correct deficiencies.

All new construction or remodeling projects must have a building permit.

Local Building Codes

Prior to 1970, local governments could use their own building codes. However, in 1970 the California Legislature made the Uniform Housing Code, **Uniform Building Code** (UBC), Uniform Plumbing Code, Uniform Mechanical Code, and National Electric Code the applicable building codes for the entire state. Local government still has the power to set requirements for local zoning, local fire zones, building setbacks, side and rear yards, and property lines.

Currently, factory-built housing must be built to the standards of the most recent editions of the uniform building codes. Local government has the power to supervise and regulate on-site installation of factory-built housing.

Contractors' State License Law

In order to protect California consumers, contractors are licensed in California under the **Contractors' State License Law**. Contractors must meet certain experience and knowledge qualifications and must post a bond or cash deposit to the state of California for the benefit of anyone damaged by the contractor. Except for minor work not exceeding $500, a valid California Contractor's License is required for the license category in which the contractor is to work. Currently there are 42-different types of contractor licenses, including general and specialty contractors. General building contractors usually oversee projects and coordinate the specific subcontractors for a job. Specialty contractors or subcontractors usually are hired to perform a single job.

A contractor may have his or her license suspended or revoked if the contractor abandons a project, diverts funds, departs from plans and specifications, violates work safety provisions, violates building codes and regulations, or breaches the contract.

Construction and Building Styles

Unless a real estate licensee works for a builder/developer or specializes in new home sales, it is not usually necessary to know the details of home construction, installation methods, or the price and quality of building materials. However, a licensee should be familiar with architectural styles, types of roofs, styles of windows, parts of a building, typical exterior materials, and different types of heating/cooling systems (HVAC). Additionally, a licensee should be able to answer questions about current insulation standards for roofs and walls and window systems that prevent excess sun infiltration for homes in the area.

Terms Relevant to Energy Efficiency

Insulation
> Material inserted into walls and ceilings to help keep the heat inside the home in the winter and outside the home in the summer. Insulation's resistance to heat is measured by the R-value.

R-Value
> The R-value is a rating that measures how well insulation resists heat loss. When the R-value is higher, the insulation is better. New homes have minimum insulation requirements and the R-value rating of the insulation used in the homes must be disclosed.

Energy Efficient Ratio (EER)
> A measurement of the efficiency of energy; used to determine the effectiveness of appliances

British Thermal Unit (BTU)
> A measurement that calculates heat; the amount of heat needed to raise one pound of water one degree Fahrenheit

---

Many home buyers express common concerns about the condition of the soil on which the house is built because it can affect the stability of the foundation. Filled or compacted ground and expansive soil frequently cause foundation damage. **Compaction** refers to extra soil that is added and compressed to fill in the low areas or raise the level of the parcel. Clay soils are generally classified as **expansive soil**. This means that a given amount of clay will tend to expand (increase in volume) as it absorbs water and it will shrink (lessen in volume) as water is drawn away. **Adobe** is one of the most expansive of the clay soils. **Backfill** is soil that is used to fill in holes or support a foundation. It is also used to fill in trenches and around excavations.

Parts of a Building

Common terms used in building:

1. **Anchor Bolt**
   Attaches mud sill to foundation; embedded in concrete foundation

2. **Bracing**
   Diagonal board nailed across wall framing to prevent sway

3. **Building paper**
   Waterproof paper used between sheathing and roof covering

4. **Closed sheathing**
   Foundation for exterior siding; boards nailed to studding

5. **Crawlspace**
   A crawlspace is the area or space between the ground and floor joists used to access plumbing and electrical connections beneath the house. For FHA loans the minimum crawlspace is 18 inches.

6. **Cripple**
   Stud above or below a window opening or above a doorway

7. **Eaves**
   Part of roof that hangs over the exterior walls

8. **Fire stop**
   Boards nailed between studs to block the spread of fire in the walls

9. **Flashing**
   Sheet metal or other material that keeps water from seeping into a building.

10. **Footing**
    A footing is an extended part of foundation at the base or bottom of a foundation wall, pier or column.

11. **Foundation**
    Base of house; usually concrete

12. **Header**
    The horizontal, load-bearing board over a doorway or window opening

13. **Joists**
    Parallel boards supporting floors or ceilings (The boards supporting them are girders, beams or bearing walls.)

14. **Mud sill**

The lowest part of the frame of a house. It is fastened with bolts to the foundation and supports the upright studs of the frame. **Redwood** is frequently used because of its high resistance to termites. **Subterranean termites**, ant-like insects that eat wood, are the most destructive.

15. **Open sheathing**

Boards nailed to rafters to form foundation for roof

16. **Rafters**

Slanted boards of a roof that are designed to support the roof boards and shingles. To strengthen the load-bearing factor of a roof, the rafters should be placed closer together.

17. **Ridge board**

Highest structural part of a frame building

18. **Sill**

The lower edge of a window

19. **Sole plate**

A board, usually 2" x 4", on which wall and partition studs rest. Support for studs

20. **Studs**

Vertical, supporting 2"x 4" boards in the walls spaced 16" on center

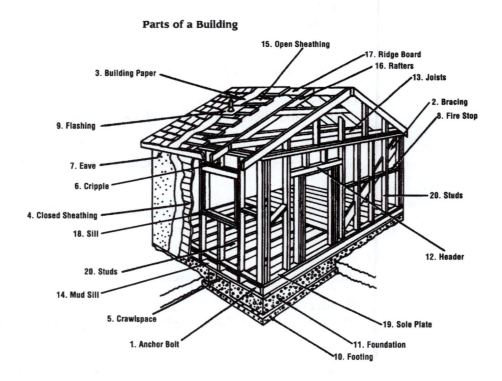

Parts of a Building

Other Building - Development Terms

Bearing wall: A wall that supports a vertical load as well as its own weight.

Board foot (144 cubic inches): A measurement of lumber equal to the volume of a board 12"x12"x1".

Conduit: A flexible pipe in which electrical wiring is installed.

Deciduous: Plants and trees that lose their leaves seasonally in the fall.

Drywall: Gypsum panels used in place of wet plaster to finish the inside of buildings.

Elevation sheet: A drawing that shows front and side exterior views of a building as it will be when finished.

Foundation plan: A drawing that shows foundation, sub-floors, footing, and pier placement.

Kiosk: A free-standing small booth, such as a jewelry store in a mall.

Linear foot: A measurement of length, rather than area (square foot) or volume (cubic foot).

Party Wall: A wall erected on the line between two adjoining properties, which are under different ownership, for the use of both parties.

Residential ceiling height measurements: Minimum = 7.5 feet; Normal = 8 feet

Schematics: Preliminary drawings and sketches by an architect, such as site plans and elevations.

Setback: The distance a building must be set back from the street, property line, or curb; usually determined by local building code. A **side-yard setback** is the distance a building must be set back for the lot line at the side of the property.

Shopping centers' population requirements:

*Neighborhood shopping center (5,000-10,000 population required)

*Major shopping center or mall (50,000-100,000 population required)

Wainscoting: The bottom portion of a wall that is covered with wood siding; the top part is treated with another material.

Walk-up: An apartment of more than one story with no elevator.

Water-pressure test: Water pressure can be tested by turning on all faucets and flushing all toilets at the same time.

Roof Types

A licensee should know the most desirable roof pitches and be able to distinguish a hip roof from a gable roof. The **pitch** of a roof is its incline or rise. The steeper the pitch of a roof, the longer its life expectancy. A **gable roof** has a pitched roof with two sloping sides. A **gambrel roof**, typically seen in Dutch colonial architecture, is a curbed roof, with a steep lower slope with a flatter one above. A **hip roof** is a pitched roof with sloping sides and ends (all four sides).

Additionally a licensee should know the types of roofing materials that are permitted or required (in fire hazard areas, for example) in the community. Roof types are determined by the direction, steepness, and number of roof planes.

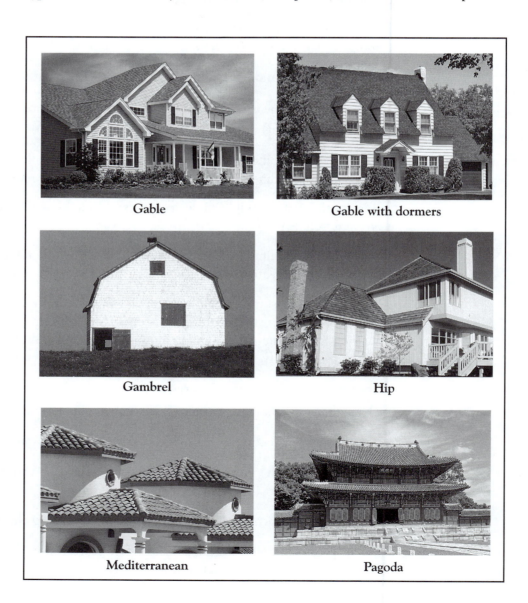

Gable

Gable with dormers

Gambrel

Hip

Mediterranean

Pagoda

Shed

Flat

A-frame

Pyramid

Thatched

Dome

Mansard

Cone

House Styles

Traditional house styles used in building are interesting for their variety and important for a real estate agent to know.

Mediterranean

California Bungalow

Contemporary

Ranch

Contemporary with traditional
Tudor influence

Cape Cod

Georgian Colonial

Tudor Revival

| Pueblo | Victorian | Townhouse |

Summary

Land use is regulated and controlled through government agencies, private regulations, and direct public ownership of land. The government can acquire property by the power of **eminent domain** through condemnation proceedings from a private owner for public use. This power can extend beyond the federal government down to public agencies. When the government acquires property by eminent domain, the property owner is reimbursed for fair market value. Property owners displaced by federal condemnation are assisted in relocation.

Police power is the right of the state to create laws that regulate property use for the protection of the public interest. The state is not required to compensate the owner for any resulting loss in property due to police power.

A **master plan** is used to develop cities. The primary form of land-use regulation is zoning. Property owners who want to use property for nonconforming use must seek a conditional use permit or zoning variance. Each city and county in the coastal zone must prepare Local Coastal Programs to comply with the California Coastal Commission's strict standards for coastal development and protection.

A subdivision is the division of land into lots for the purpose of sale, lease, or financing. There are two basic laws that control subdivisions in California—the **Subdivision Map Act** and the **Subdivided Lands Law**. Local authorities administer the Subdivision Map Act. The objectives of the Subdivision Map Act are: (1) to coordinate the subdivision plans and planning and (2) to ensure initial proper improvement of areas dedicated for public purposes by filing detailed subdivision maps to avoid problems for future taxpayers. Included in the Subdivision Map Act are lot design, water supply, street patterns, and right-of-way for drainage and sewers. The Real Estate Commissioner directly administers the Subdivided Lands Law. The objective of this law is to protect property buyers in new subdivisions from fraud, misrepresentation, or deceit in the marketing of subdivided lots, parcels, units, and undivided interests. The Real Estate Commissioner must issue a subdivision public report before the subdivision can be offered for sale in California. A copy of this report is given to the buyer upon request.

Regulation of housing and construction in California consists of three laws: (1) the State Housing Law, (2) local building codes, and (3) the Contractor's State License Law. Federal laws also regulate housing and construction through the FHA and VA building financing programs. These programs require that housing meet minimum property requirements.

Chapter 12 Review Exercises

▌ Matching Exercise

Instructions: Look up the meaning of the terms in the Glossary, then write the letter of the matching term on the blank line before its definition. Answers are in Appendix B.

Terms

a. backfill
b. bearing wall
c. board foot
d. BTU
e. CID
f. condemnation
g. conduit
h. deciduous
i. drywall
j. EER
k. EIR
l. eminent domain
m. final tract map
n. General Plan
o. linear foot
p. parcel map
q. party wall
r. percolating water

s. percolation test
t. planned development
u. police power
v. potable
w. R-value
x. schematics
y. setback
z. Subdivided Lands Law
aa. subdivision
bb. Subdivision Map Act
cc. tentative tract map
dd. variance
ee. wainscoting
ff. water pressure test
gg. water table
hh. wetlands
ii. zoning

Definitions

1. _____ The division of land into five or more lots for the purpose of sale, lease or financing.

2. _____ A measurement of length, rather than area (square foot) or volume (cubic foot).

3. _____ A wall that supports a vertical load as well as its own weight.

4. _____ Underground water not flowing in a defined channel.

5. _____ The regulation of structures and uses of property within selected districts.

6. _____ Plants and trees that lose their leaves seasonally in the fall.

7. _____ Map showing a parcel of land that will be subdivided into less than five parcels or units and shows land boundaries, streets, and parcel numbers.

8. _____ The right of the government to take private property from an owner, for public use, paying fair market value.

9. _____ The natural level at which water will be found, either above or below the surface of the ground.

10. _____ Fresh water that is safe and agreeable for drinking.

11. _____ Water pressure can be tested by turning on all faucets and flushing all toilets at the same time.

12. _____ A measurement of lumber equal to the volume of a board 12"x12"x1" (144 cubic inches).

13. _____ Gypsum panels used in place of wet plaster to finish the inside of buildings.

14. _____ A measurement of the efficiency of energy; used to determine the effectiveness of appliances (Energy Efficient Ratio).

15. _____ Test used to determine the ability of the land to absorb and drain water and is frequently used when installing septic systems.

16. _____ Areas where water covers the soil, or is present either at or near the surface of the soil all year or for varying periods of time during the year, including during the growing season.

17. _____ A measurement that calculates heat; the amount of heat needed to raise one pound of water one degree Fahrenheit (British Thermal Unit).

18. _____ A common-interest development combining the individual ownership of private dwellings with the shared ownership of common facilities of the entire project.

19. _____ A state law protecting purchasers of property in new subdivisions from fraud, misrepresentation or deceit in the marketing of subdivided property.

20. _____ A flexible pipe in which electrical wiring is installed.

21. _____ An exception granted to existing zoning regulations for special reasons.

22. _____ Soil that is used to fill in holes or support a foundation bearing wall.

23. _____ Preliminary drawings and sketches by an architect, such as site plans and elevations.

24. _____ Map of the proposed subdivision that is submitted to a planning commission for approval or disapproval.

25. _____ A study of how a development will affect the ecology of its surroundings (Environmental Impact Report).

26. _____ A rating that measures how well insulation resists heat.

27. _____ The law that authorizes a city or county to control the orderly and proper development of the community.

28. _____ A wall erected on the line between two adjoining properties, which are under different ownership, for the use of both parties.

29. _____ The distance a building must be set back from the street; usually determined by local building code.

30. _____ The proceeding to exercise the power of eminent domain.

Multiple Choice Questions

Instructions: Circle your response and go to Appendix B to read the complete explanation for each question.

1. Which of the following rights cannot be vested in an individual?
    a. Littoral
    b. Severance
    c. Riparian
    d. Eminent domain

2. A grandfather clause:
    a. is a change in zoning.
    b. is an example of downzoning.
    c. permits continuation of a nonconforming use.
    d. is an inheritance right to property.

3. A builder is allowed to make a change in construction that does not conform to the local building code. This is an example of:
    a. rezoning.
    b. a variance.
    c. a conditional-use permit.
    d. a restriction.

4. The intersection of the land with the water at the mean high-water line describes:
    a. wetlands.
    b. a shoreline.
    c. a floodplain.
    d. an estuary.

5. The division of land into five or more lots for the purpose of sale, lease or financing is called a:
    a. land project.
    b. time-share.
    c. tentative map.
    d. subdivision.

6. The law giving the city or county authority to control the orderly and proper development of the community is called the:
    a. Subdivided Lands Law.
    b. State Housing Law.
    c. Subdivision Map Act.
    d. Contractors' State License Law.

7. Under the Subdivided Lands Law, property can be subdivided into a minimum of _____ interest(s).
    a. one
    b. two
    c. four
    d. five

8. Waters that seep from the ground, arising from an indeterminable source, are known as _____ water.
    a. riparian
    b. percolating
    c. littoral
    d. appropriated

9. The purpose of a percolation test is to determine the:
   a. quality and potability of the water.
   b. acidity of the water.
   c. capacity of the soil to absorb water.
   d. location of any abandoned wells.

10. Which of the following statements is incorrect?
    a. State Housing Law outlines the minimum construction requirements for dwellings.
    b. State building inspectors enforce the construction regulations.
    c. Local building inspectors enforce the construction regulations.
    d. Local health officers enforce the occupancy and sanitation regulations.

11. The main purpose of the Uniform Building Code is to:
    a. provide for the health, safety, public welfare, and property rights of the general public.
    b. provide construction data useful for scheduling.
    c. indicate styles of architecture and prevailing sizes for use in calculating construction estimates.
    d. none of the above

12. The restrictions for a subdivision state that the maximum lot size is 10,000 square feet. Local zoning ordinances state that the maximum is 13,000 square feet. In this case, which would prevail?
    a. Restrictions
    b. Zoning
    c. Whichever recorded first
    d. The county planning commission will decide the matter.

13. If a local building code is more stringent than a state code or the UBC:
    a. the stricter code prevails.
    b. contractors may choose between them.
    c. state or federal codes always take precedence over local codes.
    d. the local codes take precedence because they are more responsive to local situations.

14. The R-value is a rating that measures:
    a. how well insulation resists heat.
    b. the efficiency of energy; used to determine the effectiveness of appliances.
    c. the amount of heat needed to raise one pound of water one degree Fahrenheit.
    d. insulation.

15. The soil that is used to fill in holes or support a foundation is called:
    a. expansive soil.
    b. compaction.
    c. backfill.
    d. adobe.

16. Crawlspace is the area or space between the ground and floor joists used to access plumbing and electrical connections beneath the house. For FHA loans the minimum crawlspace is _____ inches.
    a. 12
    b. 18
    c. 24
    d. 36

17. Which of the following is not part of the foundation?
    a. Anchor bolts
    b. Footing
    c. Mud sill
    d. Ridge board

18. A free-standing small booth, such as a jewelry stand or a newsstand is known as a:
    a. joist.
    b. joint.
    c. kiosk.
    d. walk-up.

19. Drawing that shows front and side exterior views of a building as it will be when finished is called:
    a. a foundation plan.
    b. an elevation sheet.
    c. plot plan.
    d. none of the above

20. The words, "gambrel", "hip", "gable", and "flat" refer to:
    a. styles of houses.
    b. types of conduit.
    c. types of insulation.
    d. types of roofs.

Real Estate Brokerage

13
Chapter

Introduction

As you have journeyed through this book, you have studied the regulation of real estate and the legal, financial, economic, and political aspects of real estate practice. Now you have reached the chapter where you will see how a real estate brokerage works. This section examines the business and practical aspects of a brokerage and the real estate business in general.

We also will discuss how licensees must ethically conduct themselves. Know this well, for it could mean the difference between a successful real estate career and none at all.

Learning Objectives

After reading this chapter, you will be able to:

- define brokerage.
- explain why ethical business practices are important.
- describe how advertising guidelines, name and license status, court cases, and penalties affect real estate marketing and advertising.
- name three "For Sale" sign regulations.
- explain how to handle trust funds.
- discuss the purpose of real estate associations and identify three major associations.
- list five U.S. and California Fair Housing laws.

Definition of Brokerage

People commonly refer to a firm where real estate agents work as a real estate agency, but the firm is actually a real estate brokerage. The term **brokerage** generally means an activity involving the sale of something through an intermediary who negotiates the transaction for payment. In the case of a real estate brokerage, the product is real property, with the broker as negotiator and agent of the principal, expecting a commission at the end of the negotiation.

A licensed broker creates this business for the purpose of bringing together (brokering) parties who want to make transactions in real estate. The broker who creates the firm is the broker-owner of the real estate brokerage and sets all the policies of the firm. But a broker does not have to own a brokerage firm to be in business—a broker can even work from home.

A broker who creates a firm is the broker-owner of the real estate brokerage.

Let's review the definition of an agent, a broker, a salesperson, and a broker-associate. An **agent** is someone who represents a principal in negotiating with a third party. Many times the term agent will be used loosely by the public, or even by a licensee, to mean a real estate salesperson. Legally, it is the broker who is the agent—the person who represents the principal in dealing with the third party. The **broker** is the agent of the principal and the salesperson is the agent of his or her employing broker. A **salesperson** must be in the employ of—and supervised by—a broker who is ultimately responsible for the actions of those operating under his or her broker license. That's why the salesperson is the agent of the broker, not of the principal. A broker who puts his or her license under an employing broker is called a broker-associate. The employing broker would supervise and be ultimately responsible for the actions of this second broker, and all those operating under his or her broker license. The important thing to remember is that a real estate brokerage company is operated by a licensed broker who employs licensed salespersons and licensed broker-associates who help conduct the business, and who all earn commissions for selling real estate.

A licensed salesperson is the agent of his or her employing broker (principal) and must deal fairly with third parties (broker's clients). The real estate salesperson employed by the broker is an agent for the broker, who bears the final responsibility for any agency relationships created by a salesperson in the broker's employ.

> Example: Dan is a sales associate in the employ of broker Rosa. Dan listed a property owned by Kim. Under the law, the agency relationship has been created between Kim and Rosa, the broker. Dan is bound by the agency because, as Rosa's employee, he represents Rosa with every action he makes as a real estate sales associate.

Business Ownership

A real estate broker may open a real estate brokerage in his or her name, or a fictitious business name. The broker may have multiple locations and take ownership in a variety of ways, such as: sole proprietorship, partnership, corporation, or limited liability company (LLC).

Fictitious Business Name

A **fictitious business name** is a name that does not include the last name of the owner in the name of the business. A fictitious business name, frequently referred to as a "**DBA**" (for "doing business as") or "trade name," is used when a business uses a name that is different from its owner's legal name. For instance, if Jane Smith names her business Jane's Best Real Estate Brokerage, the name "Jane's Best Real Estate Brokerage" is a fictitious business name because it does not contain Jane's last name, "Smith".

Before a broker can use a fictitious business name for a real estate company, the name must be filed, published, and approved by the Department of Real Estate. The Real Estate Commissioner may refuse to issue a license to a company with a fictitious business name if the fictitious name is misleading, creates false advertising, or includes the name of a real estate salesperson.

Multiple-Business Locations

A broker may conduct business only at the address listed on his or her license. However, a broker may open more than one location but must apply for and receive an additional branch office license for each location.

Sole Proprietorship

A **sole proprietorship** is one of the easiest ways to own a business. Since it is owned and operated by one person, it is used frequently to set up a real estate brokerage office. The owner is personally and fully liable for all business debts. This means that personal property could be taken to pay business debts. The broker reports all debts and reports any income or loss directly on his or her personal income tax return.

Partnership

A **partnership** is a form of business in which two or more persons join their money and skills in conducting the business. The Department of Real Estate

A partnership is made up of two or more people.

does not issue partnership licenses. However, a partnership may perform acts for which a real estate broker license is required, as long as every partner has a real estate broker license. Just like a sole proprietorship, the broker-owners of a partnership are jointly and severally liable for all business debts. **Joint and several liability** is a legal term used in reference to a debt, in which each debtor is responsible for the entire amount of the debt. Partnerships do not file tax returns; instead, all partnership income, expenses, gains, and losses pass through to the individual partners and are reported on their personal income tax returns.

Corporation

A **corporation** is a legal entity whose rights in business are similar to that of an individual: it exists indefinitely; it has centralized management in a board of directors; its shareholder liability is limited to the amount of their individual investment; and its corporate stocks are freely transferred. If permitted by its articles of incorporation, a corporation may take title to real estate. Due to its indefinite duration, a corporation may not hold title as a joint tenant.

S-Corporation

The **S corporation** (formerly called subchapter S corporation) is a corporation that operates like a corporation but is treated like a partnership for tax purposes. It avoids the double tax feature of a corporation because any gains and losses pass directly to the shareholders.

Limited Liability Company

A **limited liability company** (LLC) is an alternative business entity that has characteristics of both corporations and limited partnerships. The LLC offers its owners the advantage of limited personal liability (like a corporation) and a choice of how the business will be taxed. Partners can choose for the LLC to be taxed as a separate entity (like a corporation) or as a partnership-like entity in which profits are passed through to partners and taxed on their personal income tax returns.

Measuring Profitability

Real estate brokerage firms are in business to provide a service and to be profitable. The owner of the firm needs to know how much money is available to operate the business. Additionally, the broker needs to know how much each sales associate must produce to cover office expenses. Two quick ways the broker can determine profitability are the company dollar and the desk cost.

The company dollar and desk cost can help determine profitability.

The **company dollar** is the amount a broker has left after all commissions have been paid. The **desk cost** shows how much each sales associate must earn to cover expenses. It is calculated by dividing the total operating expenses of the firm by the number of licensed sales associates. A profit margin for the broker is not included as an operating expense.

Employment Relationships

An ordinary **employee** is defined as someone who is under the control and direction of an employer. An **independent contractor** is a person who is hired to do work for another person but who is not an employee of that person. Independent contractors are responsible for the results of their labor, unlike employees who must follow employers' directions in completing the work.

The independent contractor decides on the method to use in accomplishing the work under contract, and is held accountable for the results—not how they are accomplished, as long as all is within the law. Even though brokers are employed by principals (buyers or sellers) to represent them, real estate brokers almost always act as independent contractors.

As we have seen, a listing contract is the most common way an agency is created, and only gives the agent the right to be paid after doing the job, or producing results. Think of it as simply an employment contract between the seller and the broker.

Under the law of agency, the listing broker is a special agent who deals in the name of the principal to negotiate the sale of property. The broker does not have control over the property itself, while acting within the course of a special agency but only has the right to represent that principal. A listing contract does not give the listing broker the right to convey any property belonging to the principal unless the agent has a power of attorney to do so.

Legal Status of a Licensed Salesperson

The real estate license law considers a licensed salesperson an employee of the broker for purposes of supervision. For all other purposes he or she is an independent contractor. The broker-associate relationship is viewed in this manner only by the license law, not by other agencies. A salesperson's status under one law does not establish what that status is under different circumstances, such as federal and state income tax, workers' compensation, unemployment insurance, or other matters not covered by the real estate law. Except for purposes of supervision under the license law, a salesperson is employed as an independent contractor.

Real Estate Broker: Person holding a broker license and permitted by law to employ those holding either a salesperson or a broker license, who may negotiate sales for other people.

Real Estate Salesperson and Real Estate Broker-Associate:

- Person holding a broker license or a salesperson license and employed by a real estate broker, for pay, to perform real estate activities

- Person holding a salesperson license and employed by a real estate broker, for pay, to perform real estate activities

- Agent of the broker—not the buyer or the seller

- Employed and supervised by the broker, under real estate license law

- Acts as an independent contractor for income tax, workers' compensation, and unemployment insurance purposes

Determining Independent Contractor Status

There are three basic tests used to determine independent contractor status and they must comply with both federal and state laws. The first requirement is that the salesperson must have a valid real estate license. In California the license must be issued by the California Department of Real Estate. Next, the salesperson must be compensated on the basis of the number of sales closed and commissions earned—not on the basis of the number of hours worked. And finally, there must be a written contract between the employing broker and the salesperson. The contract must specify that the salesperson would be considered an independent contractor for both federal and California tax purposes.

Fortunately the same contract can cover both federal and California requirements. A broker can create and use his or her own employment contract; however, be advised that the C.A.R. Broker Associate Licensee Contract contains the required language. When the employment agreement has the correct language, a real estate salesperson is an independent contractor for income tax purposes; and therefore, withholding tax is generally not taken out of any commissions paid.

Employment Agreement

The real estate law requires that every broker must have a written agreement with each of his or her salespersons, whether they are licensed as a salesperson or as a broker under a broker-associate arrangement. Although the employment agreement does not have to be on a form approved by the Commissioner, it must cover the important aspects of the employment relationship, including supervision of licensed activities, licensee's duties, and the compensation arrangement. In addition, in order to protect the independent contractor status of the sales associates, it must also include the required language as previously discussed.

The agreement shall be dated and signed by both parties and both the salesperson and the broker must keep copies of it for three years after termination of employment. A salesperson can only be paid by his or her employing broker and cannot receive compensation or referral fees from a lender, developer, or seller.

CALIFORNIA
ASSOCIATION
OF REALTORS®

INDEPENDENT CONTRACTOR AGREEMENT
(Between Broker and Associate-Licensee)
(C.A.R. Form ICA, Revised 10/04)

This Agreement, dated _____ is made between _____
_____ ("Broker") and
_____ ("Associate-Licensee").
In consideration of the covenants and representations contained in this Agreement, Broker and Associate-Licensee agree as follows:

1. **BROKER:** Broker represents that Broker is duly licensed as a real estate broker by the State of California, ☐ doing business as _____
_____ (firm name), ☐ a sole proprietorship, ☐ a partnership, or ☐ a corporation.
Broker is a member of the _____
Association(s) of REALTORS®, and a subscriber to the _____ Multiple
Listing Service(s). Broker shall keep Broker's license current during the term of this Agreement.

2. **ASSOCIATE-LICENSEE:** Associate-Licensee represents that: (i) he/she is duly licensed by the State of California as a ☐ real estate broker,
☐ real estate salesperson, and (ii) he/she has not used any other names within the past five years, except _____
_____ . Associate-Licensee shall keep his/her license current during
the term of this Agreement, including satisfying all applicable continuing education and provisional license requirements.

3. **INDEPENDENT CONTRACTOR RELATIONSHIP:**
   A. Broker and Associate-Licensee intend that, to the maximum extent permissible by law: **(i)** This Agreement does not constitute an employment agreement by either party; **(ii)** Broker and Associate-Licensee are independent contracting parties with respect to all services rendered under this Agreement; and **(iii)** This Agreement shall not be construed as a partnership.
   B. Broker shall not: **(i)** restrict Associate-Licensee's activities to particular geographical areas or, **(ii)** dictate Associate-Licensee's activities with regard to hours, leads, open houses, opportunity or floor production, prospects, sales meetings, schedule, inventory, time off, vacation, or similar activities, except to the extent required by law.
   C. Associate-Licensee shall not be required to accept an assignment by Broker to service any particular current or prospective listing or parties.
   D. Except as required by law: **(i)** Associate-Licensee retains sole and absolute discretion and judgment in the methods, techniques, and procedures to be used in soliciting and obtaining listings, sales, exchanges, leases, rentals, or other transactions, and in carrying out Associate-Licensee's selling and soliciting activities, **(ii)** Associate-Licensee is under the control of Broker as to the results of Associate-Licensee's work only, and not as to the means by which those results are accomplished, **(iii)** Associate-Licensee has no authority to bind Broker by any promise or representation and **(iv)** Broker shall not be liable for any obligation or liability incurred by Associate-Licensee.
   E. Associate-Licensee's only remuneration shall be the compensation specified in paragraph 8.
   F. Associate-Licensee shall not be treated as an employee with respect to services performed as a real estate agent, for state and federal tax purposes.
   G. The fact the Broker may carry worker compensation insurance for Broker's own benefit and for the mutual benefit of Broker and licensees associated with Broker, including Associate-Licensee, shall not create an inference of employment.
   (Workers' Compensation Advisory: Even though Associate-Licensees may be treated as independent contractors for tax and other purposes, the California Labor and Workforce Development Agency considers them to be employees for workers' compensation purposes. According to this agency, **(i)** Broker must obtain workers' compensation insurance for Associate-Licensees and **(ii)** Broker, not Associate-Licensees, must bear the cost of workers' compensation insurance. Penalties for failure to carry workers' compensation include, among others, the issuance of stop-work orders and fines of up to $1,000 per agent, not to exceed $100,000 per company.)

4. **LICENSED ACTIVITY:** All listings of property, and all agreements, acts or actions for performance of licensed acts, which are taken or performed in connection with this Agreement, shall be taken and performed in the name of Broker. Associate-Licensee agrees to and does hereby contribute all right and title to such listings to Broker for the benefit and use of Broker, Associate-Licensee, and other licensees associated with Broker. Broker shall make available to Associate-Licensee, equally with other licensees associated with Broker, all current listings in Broker's office, except any listing which Broker may choose to place in the exclusive servicing of Associate-Licensee or one or more other specific licensees associated with Broker. Associate-Licensee shall provide and pay for all professional licenses, supplies, services, and other items required in connection with Associate-Licensee's activities under this Agreement, or any listing or transaction, without reimbursement from Broker except as required by law. Associate-Licensee shall work diligently and with his/her best efforts: **(i)** sell, exchange, lease, or rent properties listed with Broker or other cooperating Brokers; **(ii)** solicit additional listings, clients, and customers; and **(iii)** otherwise promote the business of serving the public in real estate transactions to the end that Broker and Associate-Licensee may derive the greatest benefit possible, in accordance with law. Associate-Licensee shall not commit any unlawful act under federal, state or local law or regulation while conducting licensed activity. Associate-Licensee shall at all times be familiar, and comply, with all applicable federal, state and local laws, including, but not limited to, anti-discrimination laws and restrictions against the giving or accepting a fee, or other thing of value, for the referral of business to title companies, escrow companies, home inspection companies, pest control companies and other settlement service providers pursuant to the California Business and Professions Code and the Real Estate Settlement Procedures Acts (RESPA). Broker shall make available for Associate-Licensee's use, along with other licensees associated with Broker, the facilities of the real estate office operated by Broker at _____
_____ and the facilities of any other office locations made available by Broker pursuant to this Agreement.

ICA REVISED 10/04 (PAGE 1 OF 3)

Broker's Initials (_____) (_____)
Associate-Licensee's Initials (_____) (_____)
Reviewed by _____ Date _____

EQUAL HOUSING
OPPORTUNITY

INDEPENDENT CONTRACTOR AGREEMENT (ICA PAGE 1 OF 3)

Agent: _____ Phone: _____ Fax: _____ Prepared using WINForms® software
Broker: _____

5. **PROPRIETARY INFORMATION AND FILES: (A)** All files and documents pertaining to listings, leads and transactions are the property of Broker and shall be delivered to Broker by Associate-Licensee immediately upon request or termination of this Agreement. **(B)** Associate-Licensee acknowledges that Broker's method of conducting business is a protected trade secret. **(C)** Associate-Licensee shall not use to his/her own advantage, or the advantage of any other person, business, or entity, except as specifically agreed in writing, either during Associate-Licensee's association with Broker, or thereafter, any information gained for or from the business, or files of Broker.

6. **SUPERVISION:** Associate-Licensee, within 24 hours (or ☐ _____) after preparing, signing, or receiving same, shall submit to Broker, or Broker's designated licensee: **(i)** All documents which may have a material effect upon the rights and duties of principals in a transaction, **(ii)** Any documents or other items connected with a transaction pursuant to this Agreement in the possession of or available to; Associate-Licensee and, **(iii)** All documents associated with any real estate transaction in which Associate-Licensee is a principal.

7. **TRUST FUNDS:** All trust funds shall be handled in compliance with the Business and Professions Code, and other applicable laws.

8. **COMPENSATION:**

    A. **TO BROKER:** Compensation shall be charged to parties who enter into a listing or other agreements for services requiring a real estate license:

    ☐ as shown in "Exhibit A" attached, which is incorporated as a part of this Agreement by reference, or
    ☐ as follows: _____
    _____

    Any deviation which is not approved in writing in advance by Broker, shall be: **(1)** deducted from Associate-Licensee's compensation, if lower than the amount or rate approved above; and, **(2)** subject to Broker approval, if higher than the amount approved above. Any permanent change in commission schedule shall be disseminated by Broker to Associate-Licensee.

    B. **TO ASSOCIATE-LICENSEE:** Associate-Licensee shall receive a share of compensation actually collected by Broker, on listings or other agreements for services requiring a real estate license, which are solicited and obtained by Associate-Licensee, and on transactions of which Associate-Licensee's activities are the procuring cause, as follows:

    ☐ as shown in "Exhibit B" attached, which is incorporated as a part of this Agreement by reference, or
    ☐ other: _____
    _____

    C. **PARTNERS, TEAMS, AND AGREEMENTS WITH OTHER ASSOCIATE-LICENSEES IN OFFICE:** If Associate-Licensee and one or more other Associate-Licensees affiliated with Broker participate on the same side (either listing or selling) of a transaction, the commission allocated to their combined activities shall be divided by Broker and paid to them according to their written agreement. Broker shall have the right to withhold total compensation if there is a dispute between associate-licensees, or if there is no written agreement, or if no written agreement has been provided to Broker.

    D. **EXPENSES AND OFFSETS:** If Broker elects to advance funds to pay expenses or liabilities of Associate-Licensee, or for an advance payment of, or draw upon, future compensation, Broker may deduct the full amount advanced from compensation payable to Associate-Licensee on any transaction without notice. If Associate-Licensee's compensation is subject to a lien, garnishment or other restriction on payment, Broker shall charge Associate-Licensee a fee for complying with such restriction.

    E. **PAYMENT: (i)** All compensation collected by Broker and due to Associate-Licensee shall be paid to Associate-Licensee, after deduction of expenses and offsets, immediately or as soon thereafter as practicable, except as otherwise provided in this Agreement, or a separate written agreement between Broker and Associate-Licensee. **(ii)** Compensation shall not to be paid to Associate-Licensee until both the transaction and file are complete. **(iii)** Broker is under no obligation to pursue collection of compensation from any person or entity responsible for payment. Associate-Licensee does not have the independent right to pursue collection of compensation for activities which require a real estate license which were done in the name of Broker. **(iv)** Expenses which are incurred in the attempt to collect compensation shall be paid by Broker and Associate-Licensee in the same proportion as set forth for the division of compensation (paragraph 8(B)). **(v)** If there is a known or pending claim against Broker or Associate-Licensee on transactions for which Associate-Licensee has not yet been paid, Broker may withhold from compensation due Associate-Licensee on that transaction amounts for which Associate-Licensee could be responsible under paragraph 14, until such claim is resolved. **(vi)** Associate-Licensee shall not be entitled to any advance payment from Broker upon future compensation.

    F. **UPON OR AFTER TERMINATION:** If this Agreement is terminated while Associate-Licensee has listings or pending transactions that require further work normally rendered by Associate-Licensee, Broker shall make arrangements with another associate-licensee to perform the required work, or Broker shall perform the work him/herself. The licensee performing the work shall be reasonably compensated for completing work on those listings or transactions, and such reasonable compensation shall be deducted from Associate-Licensee's share of compensation. Except for such offset, Associate-Licensee shall receive the compensation due as specified above.

9. **TERMINATION OF RELATIONSHIP:** Broker or Associate-Licensee may terminate their relationship under this Agreement at any time, with or without cause. After termination, Associate-Licensee shall not solicit: **(i)** prospective or existing clients or customers based upon company-generated leads obtained during the time Associate-Licensee was affiliated with Broker; **(ii)** any principal with existing contractual obligations to Broker; or **(iii)** any principal with a contractual transactional obligation for which Broker is entitled to be compensated. Even after termination, this Agreement shall govern all disputes and claims between Broker and Associate-Licensee connected with their relationship under this Agreement, including obligations and liabilities arising from existing and completed listings, transactions, and services.

Broker's Initials (_____)(_____)
Associate-Licensee's Initials (_____)(_____)

Reviewed by _____ Date _____

EQUAL HOUSING OPPORTUNITY

ICA REVISED 10/04 (PAGE 2 OF 3)

INDEPENDENT CONTRACTOR AGREEMENT (ICA PAGE 2 OF 3)

xxx.zfx

10. **DISPUTE RESOLUTION:**
   A. **Mediation:** Mediation is recommended as a method of resolving disputes arising out of this Agreement between Broker and Associate-Licensee.
   B. **Arbitration:** All disputes or claims between Associate-Licensee and other licensee(s) associated with Broker, or between Associate-Licensee and Broker, arising from or connected in any way with this Agreement, which cannot be adjusted between the parties involved, shall be submitted to the Association of REALTORS® of which all such disputing parties are members for arbitration pursuant to the provisions of its Bylaws, as may be amended from time to time, which are incorporated as a part of this Agreement by reference. If the Bylaws of the Association do not cover arbitration of the dispute, or if the Association declines jurisdiction over the dispute, then arbitration shall be pursuant to the rules of California law. The Federal Arbitration Act, Title 9, U.S. Code, Section 1, et seq., shall govern this Agreement.

11. **AUTOMOBILE:** Associate-Licensee shall maintain automobile insurance coverage for liability and property damage in the following amounts $ _____ /$ _____ . Broker shall be named as an additional insured party on Associate-Licensee's policies. A copy of the endorsement showing Broker as an additional insured shall be provided to Broker.

12. **PERSONAL ASSISTANTS:** Associate-Licensee may make use of a personal assistant, provided the following requirements are satisfied. Associate-Licensee shall have a written agreement with the personal assistant which establishes the terms and responsibilities of the parties to the employment agreement, including, but not limited to, compensation, supervision and compliance with applicable law. The agreement shall be subject to Broker's review and approval. Unless otherwise agreed, if the personal assistant has a real estate license, that license must be provided to the Broker. Both Associate-Licensee and personal assistant must sign any agreement that Broker has established for such purposes.

13. **OFFICE POLICY MANUAL:** If Broker's office policy manual, now or as modified in the future, conflicts with or differs from the terms of this Agreement, the terms of the office policy manual shall govern the relationship between Broker and Associate-Licensee.

14. **INDEMNITY AND HOLD HARMLESS:** Associate-Licensee agrees to indemnify, defend and hold Broker harmless from all claims, disputes, litigation, judgments, awards, costs and attorney's fees, arising from any action taken or omitted by Associate-Licensee, or others working through, or on behalf of Associate-Licensee in connection with services rendered or to be rendered pursuant to this Agreement. Any such claims or costs payable pursuant to this Agreement, are due as follows:
   ☐ Paid in full by Associate-Licensee, who hereby agrees to indemnify and hold harmless Broker for all such sums, or
   ☐ In the same ratio as the compensation split as it existed at the time the compensation was earned by Associate-Licensee
   ☐ Other: _____
   _____
   _____

   Payment from Associate-Licensee is due at the time Broker makes such payment and can be offset from any compensation due Associate-Licensee as above. Broker retains the authority to settle claims or disputes, whether or not Associate-Licensee consents to such settlement.

15. **ADDITIONAL PROVISIONS:** _____
   _____
   _____

16. **DEFINITIONS:** As used in this Agreement, the following terms have the meanings indicated:
   (A) "Listing" means an agreement with a property owner or other party to locate a buyer, exchange party, lessee, or other party to a transaction involving real property, a mobile home, or other property or transaction which may be brokered by a real estate licensee, or an agreement with a party to locate or negotiate for any such property or transaction.
   (B) "Compensation" means compensation for acts requiring a real estate license, regardless of whether calculated as a percentage of transaction price, flat fee, hourly rate, or in any other manner.
   (C) "Transaction" means a sale, exchange, lease, or rental of real property, a business opportunity, or a manufactured home, which may lawfully be brokered by a real estate licensee.

17. **ATTORNEY FEES:** In any action, proceeding, or arbitration between Broker and Associate-Licensee arising from or related to this Agreement, the prevailing Broker or Associate-Licensee shall be entitled to reasonable attorney fees and costs.

18. **ENTIRE AGREEMENT:** All prior agreements between the parties concerning their relationship as Broker and Associate-Licensee are incorporated in this Agreement, which constitutes the entire contract. Its terms are intended by the parties as a final and complete expression of their agreement with respect to its subject matter, and may not be contradicted by evidence of any prior agreement or contemporaneous oral agreement. This Agreement may not be amended, modified, altered, or changed except by a further agreement in writing executed by Broker and Associate-Licensee.

Broker:

_____
(Brokerage firm name)
By _____
Its ☐ Broker ☐ Office manager (check one)

_____
(Print name)

_____
(Address)

_____
(City, State, Zip)

_____
(Telephone)   (Fax)

Associate-Licensee:

_____
(Signature)

_____
(Print name)

_____
(Address)

_____
(City, State, Zip)

_____
(Telephone)   (Fax)

Published and Distrubuted by:
REAL ESTATE BUSINESS SERVICES, INC.
a subsidiary of the California Association of REALTORS®
525 South Virgil Avenue, Los Angeles, California 90020

Reviewed by _____ Date _____

ICA REVISED 10/04 (PAGE 3 OF 3)

INDEPENDENT CONTRACTOR AGREEMENT (ICA PAGE 3 OF 3)

xxx.zfx

Workers' Compensation Insurance

For federal and state income tax purposes, sales associates are considered independent contractors. However, due to their employee status, a broker must provide workers' compensation coverage to all sales associates as well as any non-licensee employees of the firm. Compliance with workers' compensation insurance requirements is enforced by the Employment Development Department (EDD). Failure to provide workers' compensation coverage for their real estate sales agents could result in fines up to $100,000.

Choosing a Brokerage

Hopefully you have selected your brokerage with great care and for the right reasons. The new broker should be available to give guidance and problem-solving advice and should be trained, confident, informed, and up-to-date on developments in the real estate industry. The broker's professional advice should come from knowledge and experience. Also, the sales associates in the office should be full-time professionals. They too should be trained, confident, informed, and up-to-date. Most importantly, they should be honest and straightforward with clients, co-brokers, business contacts, and each other.

If you have selected your new office carefully, the brokerage will have a big inventory of in-house listings in all price ranges and a great deal of referral business. The main points you're looking for are ethical business practices, training, and of course, the commission split.

A brokerage should have a large inventory of in-house listings.

Ethical Business Practices

You should look for a company that adheres to legal and ethical business practices. Since your livelihood will depend on the integrity of your employing broker's license, it is imperative to choose a brokerage firm that follows all legal and ethical business practices. If the Department of Real Estate suspends or revokes your employing broker's license, you will have to immediately transfer your license to another broker or stop working.

Your prospective broker will ask you many questions during your employment interview. Before accepting an offer to join a brokerage firm, you should be prepared to ask a few of your own. Of course you'll ask the usual questions about the working environment, benefits, items provided by the brokerage, and items you will have to pay for. Additionally, you should ask questions regarding the trust fund account, handling the transaction paperwork, availability of errors and omissions insurance, advertising policies, and adherence to fair housing practices.

Training

Training is something else to look for when selecting a brokerage. A new salesperson may get good, indifferent, or no training, depending on the company. Firms who are more selective of their salespersons tend to judge their potential and think of them as valuable additions to their staff, to be trained and treated with respect.

Most real estate companies do provide extensive sales training, as well as on-the-job training, with the broker accompanying new agents to their first appointments. Remember, the broker is responsible for everything a salesperson does, and does not want anyone making costly mistakes—in money and/or reputation.

Most real estate companies provide extensive training.

Commission Split

More than likely, you will be paid on a commission basis. A **commission** is a fee for services rendered usually based on a certain percentage of the sales price of a property. The amount is not set by law and must be decided between the employing broker and each employed sales associate. You, as a sales associate, will receive your share of the commission from your broker when a transaction for which you are responsible closes. It will be based on the **commission split** agreement you have with your broker. Your split will be a certain percentage of the commission that comes to the brokerage from your sales.

Usually, a new agent can count on a 50-50 split at first. That means the broker gets 50% and you get 50% of the commission on any sale you make. For example, if the agreed-upon commission split is 50-50, and the commission paid to the brokerage on one of your sales was $6,000, the broker gets $3,000, and you get $3,000. Usually commissions will be cash, but they can be anything agreed upon by the listing broker and the principal.

The escrow agent disburses the commissions to the broker(s) at the close of escrow. The commission paid to your brokerage is probably one-half the total commission paid if there is an agent from another brokerage involved. That is the normal split between a selling broker and listing broker.

How Commissions are Paid

A home sold for $425,000, with a 6% commission paid by the seller: ABC Real Estate Company was the listing broker, and EFG Real Estate Company was the selling broker. Individual agents for each company were on a 50-50 split with their brokers.

1. Commission equals $425,000 x 6% or $25,500

2. $25,500 divided by 2 brokerage firms equals $12,750 to each broker

3. $12,750 split 50/50 between broker and agent equals $6,375 to broker and $6,375 to salesperson

Operations of a Real Estate Brokerage

The operations of a brokerage are varied and can be divided into five separate areas: securing listings, finding buyers, negotiating transactions, arranging financing, and closing transactions.

> **Review - Brokerage Activities**
> - Prospecting for listings
> - Selling and marketing the properties
> - Negotiating transactions between buyers and sellers
> - Arranging financing
> - Closing transactions

All of these activities are conducted in a competitive and mostly cooperative way. Agents in a single real estate office and agents from different offices all compete to get listings and to find buyers yet usually cooperate to sell each other's listings. Generally, a spirit of friendly competition prevails.

Prospecting for listings and selling properties are the main activities of a real estate brokerage. There is also a major amount of paperwork such as: filling out forms, keeping track of listings, open escrows and closings, completing loan applications, ordering special reports, and keeping records of prospects. The agent who does not keep adequate records or who does not complete paperwork will not be in the business long.

A real estate transaction usually starts at the time a broker obtains a listing from a property owner. The most common type of listing is an Exclusive Authorization and Right to Sell. As you recall, with this type of listing, the seller must pay a commission no matter who sells the property—even if the owner makes the sale. The agent promises to use due diligence to find a "ready, willing, and able" buyer under the exact terms of the listing contract, and the seller promises to pay a commission when the agent fulfills the contract. At some point, either the listing agent or an agent from another brokerage will find a buyer and write an offer.

Listings Remain with Broker

Also, as you recall, since a salesperson represents his or her broker in all operations, listings belong to the broker and not to the salesperson. When a salesperson leaves the employ of a particular broker, any listings he or she has will remain with that broker. The reason is that the seller's listing contract is with the broker, not the sales associate who took the listing (unless the broker happens to be the listing agent). This is a common source of confusion and sometimes disagreement between brokers and their associate licensees who want to take their listings with them to a new broker. However, the law says the listings stay with the original broker.

What is the Sales Associate's Function?

The people you call will rely on your expertise to help them buy or sell property. Real estate agents are licensed and are expected to have a certain degree of product knowledge about the business. Become an expert in your area and your community. Keep up with current real estate trends.

> Example: In October 2004, the California Association of REALTORS® released a new disclosure form called, the "Statewide Buyer and Seller Advisory", or the "I-5 Disclosure". This 8-page document is not a disclosure in the true sense of the word. Instead, it advises buyers and sellers about matters regarding the transaction that may be relevant. Since it is not a mandatory form, some companies may choose not to use it, while others may include it as a supplement to their existing forms and disclosures.

You should understand the basics of the real estate business. In fact, you should know more than your clients and customers about your chosen area.

Every salesperson performs the five functions listed earlier in the course of pursuing a career in real estate. However, a newly licensed salesperson will spend the majority of his or her time prospecting. Prospecting is an excellent way to market yourself to the community and let them know you're in the real estate business.

Topics an Agent Needs to Know

Agency relationships	Mortgage market
Appraisal	Ownership
Business brokerage	Planning
Contracts	Probate
Deeds	Promissory notes
Development	Property management
Disclosures	Property taxes
Easements	Real property
Encroachments	Personal property
Eminent domain	Restrictions
Encumbrances	Solving real estate math
Escrow	Technology
Estates	The real estate law
Fair housing	Title insurance
Investments	Transferring ownership
Leases	Trust accounts
Lenders	Trust deeds
Liens	Trust funds
Loans	Water rights
Mobile homes	Zoning/land usage

Prospecting

As with any business, success in real estate depends upon your effectiveness in prospecting for new clients. **Prospecting** is the process of identifying potential customers. The majority of sales associates prospect by cold calling or sending text through mailings, faxes, or e-mails. **Cold calling** is the practice of making unsolicited calls to people you do not know in order to get new business.

Anytime real estate solicitation involves the use of the telephone, cell phone, fax, or e-mail, the sales associate must comply with applicable federal and state "do not call" and "CAN-SPAM" laws. You may still call, fax, and e-mail potential clients, but you must follow certain procedures.

Do-Not-Call and Do-Not-Fax Rules

The federal "do-not-call" rules are forcing real estate agents to try new methods of prospecting. We will discuss prospecting using the telephone, cell phone, fax, and e-mails.

Telephone and Cell Phone Calls

In general, both real estate licensees and unlicensed assistants may make cold calls providing the calls are made only between 8:00 a.m. and 9:00 p.m. Additionally, callers must introduce themselves, state the purpose of the call, and give the company's name, address, and phone number. If a person asks to be put on a "do-not-call" list, include his or her name on the company list. These calling restrictions do not apply if the person is already your customer, if you have written permission to call them, or if you have a personal relationship with them.

How would a newly licensed real estate salesperson develop a clientele and get referrals if he or she is prevented from making cold calls? To build your business, mail flyers or postcards offering a free Comparative Market Analysis (CMA). Include a response card asking for telephone and cell phone numbers and permission to call them. The written permission exempts you from the "do-not-call" requirements. Another example would be to obtain permission from potential buyers by using an open house registry list. Tell them that by signing the registry and including phone numbers or an e-mail address, they are giving permission for you to call them with market updates and relevant property information.

Autodialers and Prerecorded Messages

Autodialers (automatic telephone dialing systems) are generally used for placing computerized or prerecorded messages. An autodialer refers to equipment that can generate and dial telephone or cell phone numbers randomly or sequentially. Using an autodialer is an acceptable business practice provided you follow a few simple rules. First, the autodialer

If a salesperson uses an autodialer, the call must be connected to a live sales associate within two seconds after the recorded greeting has finished.

cannot place calls after 9:00 p.m. and before 9:00 a.m. Secondly, if a salesperson or broker uses an autodialer, the call must be connected to a live sales associate within two seconds after the recorded greeting has finished.

Violating the "do-not-call" rules can be very expensive. The broker of a salesperson who violates the FCC rules could be fined up to $11,000 for each violation or each day of a continuing violation, not to exceed a total of $87,500 for each violation.

Faxing Advertisements

Along with the "do not call" rules, the FCC adopted "do-not-fax" rules as well. Real estate agents are not exempt from these rules. In fact, as of January 1, 2005, real estate agents are no longer allowed to fax flyers advertising the availability of real estate services or property data sheets offering a real property for sale without prior written permission from the person receiving the fax. Bottom line, the advertisements may be mailed, downloaded from your website, or hand-delivered, but they generally cannot be faxed.

Once you have written permission to fax advertising material to a person, the fax must include: the date and time it is sent; the name of person or company sending the message; and telephone number of the sending fax machine. Violating the "do-not-fax" rules carries the same penalties as violations of the "do-not-call" rules.

CAN-SPAM Act of 2003

The CAN-SPAM Act of 2003 became effective on January 1, 2004 and regulates commercial e-mail messages. The CAN-SPAM Act defines a commercial e-mail message as: "any electronic mail message the primary purpose of which is the commercial advertisement or promotion of a commercial product or service." E-mails sent as part of an ongoing commercial transaction, called "transactional e-mail messages," are excluded from the Act.

A transactional e-mail message is an e-mail message sent to:
* facilitate or confirm an existing commercial transaction.
* give notice about product updates or upgrades.
* provide notice about certain changes in a subscription, membership, account, or loan.
* provide warranty information, product recall information, or safety or security information with respect to a commercial product or service used or purchased by the recipient.
* to provide information directly related to an employment relationship in which the recipient is currently involved.

Unsolicited e-mail messages sent by a real estate agent to people on a mailing list for the purpose of offering that agent's services is a "commercial e-mail message." However, an e-mail sent to a client concerning an existing listing or sales transaction is a "transactional e-mail" message and is exempt from the rules.

Commercial E-mail Requirements

A commercial e-mail message must contain all of the following items:

1. Clear and conspicuous identification that the message is an advertisement or solicitation

2. Valid and conspicuous physical postal address of the sender

3. Clear and conspicuous notice that the recipient may opt out of further commercial e-mail messages from the sender

4. Clear and conspicuous return e-mail address for the recipient to opt out

The penalties for violating the CAN-SPAM Act e-mail rules vary. They depend on the nature and severity of the violation and include monetary fines and imprisonment up to a maximum of five years. However, unlike the "do-not-call" and "do-not-fax" rules, there is no specific private right of action for consumers to pursue e-mail violations.

Marketing and Advertising

Successful real estate businesses pay careful attention to advertising and marketing the firm. Typically the marketing and advertising effort is done through use of television, radio, Internet websites, and printed pieces such as company brochures, property flyers, newspapers, and real estate magazines.

Real estate companies need to be careful when advertising their services and the property they are selling. They need to be aware of both the legal and ethical restrictions on advertising to avoid liability. Real estate advertising is regulated in any medium, including, but not limited to, newspapers, flyers, business cards, e-mails, faxes, radio, and television.

Advertising Guidelines

Real estate advertising is regulated by state and federal agencies that expect real estate companies to be truthful when advertising property or services. Legally, licensees may be held liable for fraud, intentional misrepresentation, or negligent misrepresentation if they make material false statements or material omissions in any medium of advertising.

Advertising guidelines help real estate agents avoid penalties and possible suspension or loss of license. Avoid any advertising in which the advertisement can be interpreted a number of different ways. Avoid "half truths," inflated claims, and ambiguous or superlative terms. Example: Both the phrases "Fast Loans" and "Low Rates" are ambiguous because they do not explain how fast is "fast" and how low is "low."

Name and License Status

A real estate broker or firm must disclose its license status in all advertising. Anytime a broker advertises real estate services, a term such as broker, agent, or licensee (or the abbreviations bro. or agt.) must be included in the advertisement. This requirement applies to all real estate licensees, both brokers and salespersons.

The real estate broker does not have to use the actual name of the real estate firm. However, a company name that does not make it clear that it is a real estate company must include identifying designations. For example, if the name of the real estate company is "The Jane Doe Real Estate Brokerage Company," the name alone would be sufficient to identify the company as a real estate firm. On the other hand, the name, "The Jane Doe Company," does not clearly show that the firm is a real estate brokerage. In this instance, Jane Doe would have to add the term "broker" (bro. or bkr.) to the ad.

A salesperson may not use his or her name and telephone number in an advertisement without including the broker's name. Real estate agents may use the term "free" and similar terms in their advertising—provided that all terms governing availability of the offered product or service are clearly disclosed at the same time. It is not unethical or illegal for real estate agents to offer premiums or prizes to induce seller and buyer to do business with them. A real estate licensee may not advertise an illegal real estate lottery.

When mortgage loan brokers advertise on the radio or television or in printed ads, they must include the license under which the loan would be made or arranged. In addition, every licensed real estate broker must display his or her own eight-digit DRE license number on all advertisements soliciting borrowers. The following statements show the correct way to advertise.

> **Correct Advertising**
> "Real estate broker, California Department of Real Estate, License #"
> "California Department of Real Estate, Real Estate Broker, License #"

Use of Words

Real estate ads should not have words that state or imply a preference or limitation with regard to race, color, religion, handicap, sex, or familial status. Some words are clearly objectionable while other words and phrases are marginally objectionable because they convey a wrong signal, particularly to those who have been victims of discrimination in the past.

Advertisers should avoid offensive and marginal expressions. The following words and phrases typify those most often used in real estate ads to convey discriminatory preferences or limitations.

Offensive, Marginal, and Acceptable Phrases
Clearly Offensive

Adult Building	Racially Integrated Neighborhood
Hispanic Area	Near Synagogue
Ideal for Physically Fit	Prefer Bright, Healthy Person
Restrictive	Catholic Church Nearby
Chinese Businesses in Area	Male or Female Only
Singles Only	No Children

Marginally Offensive

Exclusive
Private Community
For Mature Adults
For Active Adults

Acceptable Words

Gated
Parks Nearby
Houses of Worship
Quiet Residential Area

Court Cases Regarding Advertising Practices

There have not been a large number of court cases that illustrate advertisements using offensive phrases.

Saunders vs. General Services Corporation: This large real estate company located in Richmond, Virginia was fined $12,800 for using white models almost exclusively in the company's advertising materials.

Housing Rights Center vs. Donald Sterling Corporation: In Los Angeles, California, several tenants sued their landlord, the Donald Sterling Corporation, because the landlord preferred Korean tenants over non-Korean tenants. The landlord actively discouraged other ethnic groups from moving into the apartment buildings. The lawsuit was based on the name of the apartment buildings. For example, the "Mark Wilshire Towers" was renamed the "Korean

World Towers" and another building was renamed to include the word "Korean". A Federal District Court told the Donald Sterling Corporation that they could not use the word "Korean" in the names of the buildings and had to stop demanding information about national origin in rental applications.

Penalties

A licensed real estate salesperson or broker who engages in false or misleading advertising is subject to imprisonment in the county jail for up to six months and penalties as high as $2,500 per violation, or both. A licensee may also face suspension or revocation of his or her license.

Real Estate Signs

The ability to display real estate signs has some protection under the United States and California Constitutions as a form of free speech. Even so, a city, county, or private entity, such as a homeowners' association, may regulate the size of signs and how they are displayed.

Sign Regulations

- A city, county, or state may ban all signs on publicly owned property.

- A city, county, or state cannot completely ban signs on privately owned property.

- A city, county, or state may impose reasonable restrictions on the time, place, and manner of displaying signs regardless of whether it is on privately or publicly owned property.

In fact, private real estate signs may be banned completely from public property. However, a homeowners' association or CC&Rs cannot prohibit private owners from displaying real estate signs on their own property. The signs must be reasonably located, in plain view of the public, of reasonable dimensions and design, and used to advertise the property for sale or lease or to advertise directions to the property. The real estate sign may include the owner's name or the agent's name, along with address and telephone number.

Real estate signs must be reasonably located, in plain view of the public, of reasonable dimensions and design.

Handling Trust Funds

Real estate brokers and salespersons, in their capacity as agents, receive money from people, usually in the form of a check to be used in a real estate transaction. The law is very clear about how these funds, called trust funds, should be handled. When an agent receives funds on behalf of someone else, a fiduciary duty is created to the owner of the funds. Agents must handle, control, and account for these trust funds according to specific legal guidelines. Noncompliance with the law can result in unfavorable business consequences. A license can be suspended or revoked for improper handling of trust funds, and an agent can be held financially responsible for damages occurring because of inept, negligent, or criminal actions regarding trust funds.

First of all, a licensee must be able to identify trust funds and distinguish them from non-trust funds. Trust funds are money, or anything of value, received from the buyer by an agent on behalf of a seller. Examples of trust funds are: cash, a check used as a deposit for a purchase, or a personal note made payable to the seller. Do not confuse other monies such as commissions, general operating funds, and rents and deposits from broker-owned real estate with trust funds. The licensee has a fiduciary responsibility to the owners of the funds entrusted to his or her care. The funds can only be used for purposes authorized by the funds' owners and the licensee must maintain accurate, complete, lawful, and up-to-date records.

When a broker or salesperson receives trust funds from a principal in connection with the purchase or lease of real property, the transaction begins. Trust funds must be placed into the hands of the owner of the funds, into a neutral escrow depository or into a lawful trust account no later than three business days following receipt of the funds by the broker or the broker's salesperson.

The only exception is when a check is received from an offeror in connection with an offer to purchase or lease real property. A deposit check may be held uncashed by the broker until acceptance of the offer under certain conditions. A broker may hold a deposit check uncashed if the check is not made out to the broker, or if the offeror (buyer) has given written instructions that the check may not be deposited or cashed until acceptance of the offer. Additionally, the offeree (seller) must be informed before or at the time the offer is presented for acceptance that the check is being held uncashed.

It is very important to remember that after acceptance of the offer, unless otherwise directed, the check must be placed no later than three business days into a neutral escrow depository, into the broker's trust fund bank account or into the hands of the offeree if expressly authorized in writing by both the offeror and offeree. A neutral depository is an escrow business conducted by someone who is a licensed escrow holder.

Before the seller accepts an offer, the buyer owns the funds, and they must be handled according to the buyer's instructions. After the seller accepts the offer, the funds must be handled according to instructions from both the buyer and seller.

Examples of Trust Funds Handled as Instructed

- An offeror's check held uncashed by the broker before an offer is accepted may be held uncashed after acceptance only upon written authorization from the offeree.

- The offeror's check may be given to the offeree only if both expressly authorize it in writing.

- All or part of an offeror's deposit may not be refunded by an agent or subagent of the seller without the express written permission of the offeree to make the refund.

Commingling

Trust funds may not be commingled (mixed) with funds belonging to the broker. Commingling is strictly prohibited by real estate law and may be punished by revocation or suspension of a real estate license.

Examples of Commingling

- Personal or company funds are deposited into the trust fund bank account. This violates the law even if separate records are kept.

- Trust funds are deposited into the licensee's general or personal bank account rather than into the trust fund account.

- Commissions, fees, or other income earned by the broker and collected from the trust account are left in the trust account for more than 25 days from the date they were earned.

A broker may keep up to $200 of personal funds in the trust fund account to pay for bank charges or service fees related to the trust account. When receiving commissions or other earned payment from the trust fund account, the broker may not use those moneys to pay bills or other expenses directly from the trust account. Rather, a check to the broker must be written first and deposited in a personal account for personal use.

Review - Trust Fund Bank Account Check List
A Broker's Trust Fund Account Must Meet These Requirements:

- It must be designated as a trust account in the name of the broker as trustee.

- It must be maintained with a bank or recognized depository located in California.

- It may not be an interest-bearing account for which prior written notice can be required for withdrawal of funds, except for certain instances.

- Withdrawals from a trust account may be made upon the signature of one or more specified persons.

Who Can Withdraw Funds from a Trust Account?

- The broker in whose name the account is maintained.

- The designated broker-officer if the account is in the name of a corporate broker.

- An individual specifically authorized in writing by the broker or a salesperson licensed to the broker.

- An unlicensed employee of the broker, if specifically authorized in writing by the broker, and if the employee is covered by a fidelity bond at least equal to the maximum amount of the trust fund to which the employee has access at any time.

A broker's trust fund account must be maintained with a bank or recognized depository located in California.

CALIFORNIA
ASSOCIATION
OF REALTORS®

**TRUST BANK ACCOUNT RECORD FOR ALL
TRUST FUNDS DEPOSITED AND
WITHDRAWN**

Broker: _____

Address: _____

DATE	DEPOSIT (Received From)	OR	WITHDRAWAL (Paid To)	AMOUNT	BALANCE
	Name: _____ ☐ check ☐ cash ☐ _____ For: _____		Name: _____ Check # _____ For: _____	$	$
	Name: _____ ☐ check ☐ cash ☐ _____ For: _____		Name: _____ Check # _____ For: _____	$	$
	Name: _____ ☐ check ☐ cash ☐ _____ For: _____		Name: _____ Check # _____ For: _____	$	$
	Name: _____ ☐ check ☐ cash ☐ _____ For: _____		Name: _____ Check # _____ For: _____	$	$
	Name: _____ ☐ check ☐ cash ☐ _____ For: _____		Name: _____ Check # _____ For: _____	$	$
	Name: _____ ☐ check ☐ cash ☐ _____ For: _____		Name: _____ Check # _____ For: _____	$	$
	Name: _____ ☐ check ☐ cash ☐ _____ For: _____		Name: _____ Check # _____ For: _____	$	$
	Name: _____ ☐ check ☐ cash ☐ _____ For: _____		Name: _____ Check # _____ For: _____	$	$
	Name: _____ ☐ check ☐ cash ☐ _____ For: _____		Name: _____ Check # _____ For: _____	$	$
	Name: _____ ☐ check ☐ cash ☐ _____ For: _____		Name: _____ Check # _____ For: _____	$	$

R E B S INC

Published and Distributed by:
REAL ESTATE BUSINESS SERVICES, INC.
a subsidiary of the CALIFORNIA ASSOCIATION OF REALTORS®
525 South Virgil Avenue, Los Angeles, California 90020

┌─ OFFICE USE ONLY ─┐
Reviewed by Broker
or Designee _____
Date _____

EQUAL HOUSING
OPPORTUNITY

FORM TAA-11 REVISED 10/99

STATE OF CALIFORNIA

DEPARTMENT OF REAL ESTATE
MORTGAGE LENDING

TRUST ACCOUNT REPORT *(Multi-Lender Transactions)*

RE 852 (Rev. 1/04)

GENERAL INFORMATION

- A broker must file CPA prepared quarterly reports with DRE only if they are, or become the servicing agent for multi-lender notes and their servicing volume on multi-lender loans exceeds $125,000 in collections in a three month period or if the number of investors entitled to the payments exceeds 120. See Business and Professions Code Sections 10238(k)(3) and 10238(j)4).

- This form to be completed by an independent accountant as part of a trust account inspection for multi-lender transactions.

- Read instructions on pages 3 and 4 before completing this report.

BROKER INFORMATION

NAME OF BROKER/SERVICING AGENT

TELEPHONE NUMBER

BUSINESS ADDRESS

BROKER LICENSE ID#

CITY, STATE, ZIP CODE

REPORT PERIOD

REPORT PERIOD (CHECK ONE)

☐ 1ST QUAR. ☐ 2ND QUAR. ☐ 3RD QUAR.

☐ 4TH QUARTER – NON-THRESHOLD BROKER ONLY

(See instructions under "Who must file.")

DATE QUARTER ENDED (M/D/Y)

START OF FISCAL YEAR (M/D/Y)

END OF FISCAL YEAR (M/D/Y)

DEPOSITORIES FOR TRUST FUNDS

List the banks or other financial institutions in which the broker's trust accounts are maintained for transactions subject to B&P Code 10238. If the account is not in the broker's name as trustee, give the account name.

LEVEL OF BUSINESS

To be provided by broker/servicing agent. If the information requested below is not available, so indicate and note the reason under Comments area.

Number of notes being serviced ....

Aggregate principal amount of such notes .... $

Aggregate payments due during report period .... $

Number of persons entitled to such payments ....

Number of sales during report period ....

NUMBER OF ITEMS INSPECTED BY ACCOUNTANT	
Number of multi-lender sales transactions inspected	_____
Aggregate principal amount of notes sold in above transactions ..	$ _____
Number of payments inspected	_____
Dollar amount of payments inspected...	$ _____
Number of notes on which payment inspected	_____
Number of persons receiving payments inspected	_____

COMMENTS

List deficiencies noted (including trust account shortages or overages), corrective action taken, etc. Attach additional pages if needed.

_____

_____

_____

_____

_____

_____

_____

_____

_____

_____

_____

_____

_____

_____

_____

_____

Certification

The above report is made pursuant to Business & Professions Code (B&P) Section 10238 for the trust account(s) of the above-named broker/servicing agent. Unless otherwise noted herein, this report is made in compliance with Section 10238 and with the instructions for the inspection contained in this form.

The undersigned is a Certified Public Accountant and independent of the above-named broker/servicing agent (see instructions for definition of "independent.")

SIGNATURE OF CERTIFIED PUBLIC ACCOUNTANT	DATE
»	
PRINTED/TYPED NAME OF CPA	

NAME OF FIRM	TELEPHONE NUMBER
BUSINESS ADDRESS	

Detach and retain instructions for your use.

INSTRUCTIONS

These instructions have been prepared as a guide to the independent certified public accountant for the inspection and review report (RE 852) required of certain brokers who conduct transactions pursuant to Business & Professions (B&P) Code Section 10238. Set forth below are the requirements which must be included in the accountant's comments and certain auditing procedures to be performed in the conduct of the inspection. These instructions set forth the minimum audit procedures and do not restrict the judgment of the independent accountant when circumstances warrant the employment of additional procedures.

PART I — GENERAL INSTRUCTIONS

A. Who Must File

Pursuant to Sections 10238(k)(3) and 10238(j)(4), if the broker, is or becomes the servicing agent for notes or interests sold, upon which the payments due during any period of three consecutive months in the aggregate exceed one hundred twenty-five thousand dollars ($125,000) or the number of persons entitled to the payments exceeds 120, the trust account or accounts of that broker or affiliate shall be inspected at no less than three-month intervals during which the volume is maintained, by an independent certified public accountant. If the broker is required to file an annual report pursuant to B&P Code Sections 10238(o) or 10232.2, the quarterly report need not be filed for the last quarter of the broker's fiscal year.

B. Independence of Accountant

The review report includes a representation by the accountant that he or she is independent of the broker. An accountant is not "independent" if the accountant is: employed by the broker; responsible directly or indirectly for the maintenance of the records of the broker; has a financial interest in the business of the broker or an affiliate of the broker; or is an "affiliate" of the broker. (An "affiliate" of a person is a person controlling, controlled by, or under common control with, such person.)

C. Trust Account Liability

The review should determine the trust fund liability, trust account balance, and any overage or shortage, as of the close of the period (generally the end of broker's fiscal quarter) for which the report is made. Any deficiency should be noted under the Comments area of RE 852, with such comment as the accountant considers relevant.

D. Currency of Records

The trust account records will be considered current if they, and the subsidiary ledgers and control account, are posted on a daily basis and the subsidiary ledgers balanced to the control account at least once each week or in accordance with B&P Code Section 10145 and Regulations 2831, 2831.1 & 2831.2 The trust account(s) should be reconciled to the adjusted control account's balance and the subsidiary ledger balance(s) as of each month's end by the 15th day of the following month. If the trust account records are not current in accordance with the above, this should be noted with the reason in Comments area of the report and the actual currency of the account indicated.

E. Examination of Sales Transactions

1. A "sales transaction" is defined in B&P Code Section 10238(j)(5) as "... the series of transactions by which a series of notes of a maker, or the interests in the note of a maker, are sold or issued to their various purchasers under this section, including all receipts and disbursements in that process of funds received from the purchasers or lenders."

2. B&P Code Section 10238(j)(4) specifies that the sample of sales transactions shall be selected at random by the accountant from all such transactions and shall consist of three sales transactions or 5% of the sales transactions, whichever is greater. The independent accountant may restrict the inspection only if the condition of the records or the accounts is so deficient that the accountant under the inspection procedure can not make an adequate review. This action and the basis for it are to be noted in the Comments area of the report.

3. The inspection of sales transactions should emphasize the proper handling of trust funds in accordance with the instructions of the parties to the sale and in accordance with B&P Code Section 10238. All funds received by the broker from the purchasers or lenders shall be handled in accordance with B&P Code Section 10145 for disbursement to the persons entitled thereto. The broker shall not accept any purchase or loan funds or other consideration from a prospective lender or purchaser, or directly or indirectly cause the funds or other consideration to be deposited in an escrow or trust account, except as to a specific loan or note secured by deed of trust that the broker owns, is authorized to negotiate, or is unconditionally obligated to buy. The books and records of the broker or servicing agent, or both, shall be maintained in a manner that readily identifies transactions under B&P Code Section 10237 and the receipt and disbursement of funds in connection with these transactions. The authorization and documentation for all disbursements for the sales inspected shall be verified.

F. Examination of Payments Processed

1. B&P Code Section 10238(j)(5) defines a "payment," as the receipt of a payment from the person obligated on the note (or from some other person on behalf of the person so obligated, including the broker or servicing agent) and the distribution of the payment to the persons entitled thereto.

2. Section 10238(j)(5) specifies that the sample inspected by the accountant shall consist of 10 payments processed or 2% of payments processed under this section during the

period for which the examination is conducted, whichever is greater. The independent accountant may restrict the inspection only if the condition of the records or the accounts is so deficient that the accountant under the inspection procedure can not make an adequate review. This action and the basis for it are to be noted in the Comments area of the report.

3. Payments received should be traced to the bank to determine that they are being immediately deposited to the trust account. Any commingling of trust funds with those of the broker, except as provided for under Regulation 2835, and any use of such funds for any other transaction or purpose other than that for which they are received is prohibited by Section 10238. In addition, payments received are required to be disbursed within 25 days after receipt by the broker or servicing agent. The broker or servicing agent is also required to notify the lenders or purchasers if the source for any payment is not the maker of the note. The books and records of the broker or servicing agent, or both, shall be maintained in a manner that readily identifies transactions under B&P Code Section 10237 and the receipt and disbursement of funds in connection with these transactions

PART II. COMPLETION OF REPORT (RE 852).

Broker Information
Broker's name and address should appear as it appears in the notice filed by the broker under B&P Code 10238 along with the broker license identification number. If there has been a subsequent change, the new name should also be indicated.

Report Quarter
If the report is for a quarterly period, indicate the closing date of the quarter for which the report is prepared. If for a longer or shorter period than a quarter, indicate the opening and closing dates of the period.

Depositories for Trust Funds
List the name and address of each depository in which a trust account is maintained. If the account is not in the broker's name as trustee, give the account name.

Level of Business
This information should be provided by the broker. Information should relate solely to transactions conducted pursuant to B&P Code 10238 and should not include those conducted pursuant to some other exemption from qualification or pursuant to a qualification under the Corporate Securities Law. If the broker has a qualification, the broker's attorney will be able to assist the broker and accountant as to the foregoing.

Any specified items not available from the records of the broker should be noted in the report along with reason the items were not available.

1. "Number of notes being serviced" is the number being serviced at the end of the period.

2. "Payments due" means those payments, whether or not received, of principal and/or interest on outstanding notes which became due and payable during the report period, including

balloon payments (but excluding any prepayment, late or other penalties).

3. The term "sales" means "sales transactions" and is defined in Part I item D above.

Number of Items Inspected by Accountant
The accountant should indicate in this item the number of items inspected (sales and payments) and provide, with respect to those items, the information specified.

Comments
Deficiencies noted should be briefly described and their location indicated (account number or other identifier employed by the broker).

If corrective action has been taken by the broker with respect to any deficiency, that should also be noted.

If more space is needed, use an attachment labeled "Comments continued."

PART III — EXECUTION AND FILING

1. The accountant should sign the report and furnish the information specified in the Certification area.

2. A copy of the report should be mailed or delivered to the broker.

3. The report should be filed with the Commissioner at the address below within 30 days after the close of the period for which it is filed.

4. Mail to:

   Department of Real Estate
   Mortgage Lending Activity Section
   P.O. Box 187000
   Sacramento, CA 95818-7000

5. If you have any questions, please call: (916) 227-0770.

Trade and Professional Organizations

A **trade association** is a voluntary nonprofit organization of independent and competing business units engaged in the same industry or trade, formed to help solve industry problems, promote progress, and enhance service.

A **real estate board** or association is made up of members who share an interest in the business of real estate. Usually, members who join a local association of realtors automatically become members of the California Association of REALTORS® (C.A.R.) and the National Association of REALTORS® (NAR). The purpose of a real estate association is to: bring together people in the real estate business; encourage professional conduct; protect the public from irresponsible licensees; and do anything in its power to upgrade the reputation and dignity of the real estate business.

A member of NAR is known as a **REALTOR**® and must follow NAR's rules and the Code of Ethics. C.A.R. performs the same function as NAR, but on the state level.

Major Real Estate-related Trade Associations

- **California Association of REALTORS®**
  525 South Virgil Avenue
  Los Angeles, CA 90020
  Phone: (213) 739-8200

- **California Association of Real Estate Brokers**
  1301 85th Avenue
  Oakland, CA 94621
  Phone: (510) 568-4577

- **California Mortgage Association**
  2520 Venture Oaks Way, Suite 150
  Sacramento, CA 95833
  Phone: (916) 239-4080, Fax: (916) 924-7323

- **California Association of Mortgage Brokers**
  785 Orchard Drive, Suite 225
  Folsom, CA 95630
  Phone: (916) 448-8236, Fax: (916) 448-8237

- **California Association of Business Brokers**
  50 Airport Parkway
  San Jose, CA 95110
  Phone: (877) 470-2222, Fax: (408) 516-9445

- **California Mortgage Bankers Association**
  980 Ninth Street, Suite 2120
  Sacramento, CA 95814
  Phone: (916) 446-7100, Fax: (916) 446-7105

- **California Building Industry Association**
  1215 K Street, Suite 1200
  Sacramento, CA 95814
  Phone: (916) 443-7933

- **Association of Community Managers**
  23461 South Pointe Drive, Suite 200
  Laguna Hills, CA 92653
  Phone: (949) 916-2226, Fax: (949) 916-5557

Code of Ethics

Ethics is a set of principles or values by which an individual guides his or her own behavior and judges that of others. The professional behavior set forth in real estate law is a course which a licensee must follow. By observing the code of ethics, members of local, state, and national trade associations promote **good will** and harmony, and further the interests of the real estate industry as well as the public.

You can review a copy of the NAR Code of Ethics at www.realtor.com.

Diversity

As the most populous state in the nation, it is not surprising that California is also the most culturally diverse. In fact, it has been multicultural since its beginning. California's continual attraction has brought an ever-increasing population growth of immigrants including minorities. Home ownership has always represented prosperity and the American way of life. Minorities account for over 40% of first-time home buyers; therefore, it is good business for real estate agents to help everyone obtain the goal of home ownership.

Fair Housing Laws

Decent, safe, affordable housing is the goal of fair housing laws. Although much progress has been made, housing discrimination still affects people of all races, ethnicities, national origins, and religions. Women, people with disabilities, and families with children may also face barriers to their fair housing rights.

Real estate licensees must not only be aware of federal and state fair housing laws and issues but must also apply this knowledge daily. By learning the fair housing laws, including advertising guidelines, your job will be made easier.

Federal Laws

1866 Civil Rights Act

This federal law prohibits discrimination based on race in all property transactions. However, it was basically ignored until 1968.

1968 U.S. Supreme Court Case of *Jones vs. Mayer*

Jones vs. Mayer prohibits discrimination based on race by upholding the 1866 Civil Rights Act and the 13th Amendment to the U.S. Constitution prohibiting slavery.

Fair Housing Act

Title VIII of the Civil Rights Act of 1968 and the Fair Housing Amendments Act of 1988, taken together, constitute the Fair Housing Act. In leasing or selling residential property, the Civil Rights Act of 1968 expanded the definition of discrimination to include not only race, but national origin, color, and religion. The Fair Housing Amendments Act of 1988 further broadened the definition to include age, sex, and handicap status. Under these laws, real estate offices are required to display Fair Housing posters. Any complaints must be filed with HUD.

Specifically, the Fair Housing Act provides protection against the following discriminatory housing practices if they are based on race, sex, religion, color, handicap, familial status, or national origin.

Actions Prohibited by the Fair Housing Act

- Refusing to rent housing
- Refusing to sell housing
- Treating applicants differently from one another for housing
- Treating residents differently from one another in connection with terms and conditions
- Advertising a discriminatory housing preference or limitation
- Providing false information about the availability of housing
- Harassing, coercing, or intimidating people from enjoying or exercising their rights under the act
- Blockbusting: persuading an owner to sell or rent housing by saying that people of a particular race, religion etc., are moving into the neighborhood
- Imposing different loan terms for purchasing, constructing, improving, repairing, or maintaining a residence
- Denying use of, or participation in, real estate services such as brokers' organizations or multiple-listing services

Protection for People with Disabilities

The **Americans with Disabilities Act** (ADA) protects anyone with a handicap and includes mental illness, AIDS, blindness, hearing impairment, mental retardation, and mobility impairment. A handicap is defined as any physical or mental impairment which substantially limits one or more major life activities; having a record of such an impairment; or being regarded as having such an impairment.

Housing for Older Persons

In response to the concerns of senior citizens residing in retirement communities, Congress provided exemptions for housing for older persons which meets certain criteria.

Senior Citizen Housing Exemptions

- The housing is provided under a state or federal program specifically designed and operated to assist the elderly.
- The housing is intended for and solely occupied by people 62 years or older.
- The housing is intended and operated for occupancy by at least one person 55 years or older in each unit.
- 80% of the units are occupied by at least one person 55 years or older.

U.S. Department of Housing and Urban Development

**EQUAL HOUSING
OPPORTUNITY**

We Do Business in Accordance With the Federal Fair Housing Law

(The Fair Housing Amendments Act of 1988)

It is Illegal to Discriminate Against Any Person Because of Race, Color, Religion, Sex, Handicap, Familial Status, or National Origin

---

■ In the sale or rental of housing or residential lots

■ In advertising the sale or rental of housing

■ In the financing of housing

■ In the provision of real estate brokerage services

■ In the appraisal of housing

■ Blockbusting is also illegal

Anyone who feels he or she has been discriminated against may file a complaint of housing discrimination:
   1-800-669-9777 (Toll Free)
   1-800-927-9275 (TDD)

**U.S. Department of Housing and
Urban Development
Assistant Secretary for Fair Housing and
Equal Opportunity
Washington, D.C. 20410**

Previous editions are obsolete

form HUD-928.1A(8-93)

- The housing has significant facilities and services to meet the physical or social needs of older persons.
- The policies and procedures demonstrate the intent to provide housing for persons 55 years or older.

Enforcement of the Fair Housing Act

The Fair Housing Act gives HUD the authority to hold administrative hearings unless one of the parties elects to have the case heard in U.S. District Court and to issue subpoenas. The Administrative Law Judge in these proceedings can issue an order for relief, including actual damages, injunctions, or other equitable relief and penalties.

The penalties range from up to $10,000 for a first violation, to up to $50,000 for the third violation and those thereafter. The penalties are paid to the federal government. The damage payments go to the proven victims.

The act adds criminal penalties of a $100,000 maximum fine and imprisonment as sanctions against people who willfully fail to give information and evidence or willfully give false information in a fair-housing investigation or proceeding.

California Laws

California has enacted several laws and regulations to complement the Federal Fair Housing laws.

Unruh Civil Rights Act

The Unruh Civil Rights Act covers discrimination in business. It is against the law for anyone to deny a person the right to business products and services. The Unruh Act applies to a real estate brokerage because it is a business and may not discriminate against clients or customers. It is particularly important for the real estate licensee to be aware of **steering** (the illegal practice of only showing clients property in certain areas) and **redlining** (the illegal use of a property's location to deny financing). **Blockbusting**, or causing **panic selling** by telling people that property values in a neighborhood will decline because of a specific event, such as the purchase of homes by minorities, is also prohibited by this law.

California Civil Code (Section 54-55.1)

This section of the Civil Code prohibits discrimination in the rental, leasing, or sale of housing accommodations to the blind, visually handicapped, deaf, or otherwise physically disabled. It also precludes restrictions on seeing-eye dogs and signal dogs from "no pet" clauses.

Commissioner's Regulation 2780

The California Real Estate Commissioner has made it very clear that a person's real estate license will be restricted, suspended, or revoked for any violation of the fair housing laws. The Commissioner regulates all aspects of the real estate transaction from prospecting for listings through the closing of the transaction. In fact, every conceivable activity is regulated. It covers refusing to list and show property to selected people, processing some applications more slowly than others, stating to some people that property is not available when it is, using "special" codes on applications, actively discouraging other licensees from working with minorities, charging more for the cleaning or security deposit to some applicants, or assisting other licensees to discriminate—just to name a few.

California Fair Employment and Housing Act

The **California Fair Employment and Housing Act** (formerly the Rumford Act) prohibits discrimination in the sale, rental, or financing of practically all types of housing. Violations are reported to the state Department of Fair Employment and Housing.

Housing Financial Discrimination Act

The Housing Financial Discrimination Act (Holden Act) prohibits all financial institutions from discriminating in real estate loan approvals based on the geographic location, the neighborhood, or any other characteristic of the property. In particular, redlining—the practice of disapproving real estate loans in economically or physically blighted areas—is forbidden unless it can be proved to be based on sound business practice. Violations may be reported to the state Secretary for Business and Transportation, who must act on the complaint within 30 days.

Federal Policy on Real Estate Advertising

The Federal Fair Housing Law states in part "... it shall be unlawful to make, print, or publish, or cause to be made, printed, or published any notice, statement, or advertisement, with respect to the sale or rental of a dwelling that indicates any preference, limitation, or discrimination based on race, color, religion, sex, handicap, familial status, or national origin, or any intention to make any such preference, limitation or discrimination."

All advertising media, advertising agencies, and other persons who use advertising with respect to the sale, rental, or financing of dwellings are required to take care that their words, phrases, symbols, and visual aids do not signal a prohibited preference or limitation.

All residential real estate advertising should contain the equal housing opportunity logotype and slogan. The logotype should be sufficiently large or visible to be noticed and understood. When the size of the logotype is so small that the facial features (ethnicities) of the people are not clearly distinguishable, then it is too small. The logotype should be a clear sign or symbol of welcome to all potentially qualified buyers or renters regardless of race, color, etc.

Human models in photographs, drawings, or other graphic techniques may not be used to indicate exclusiveness because of race, color, religion, sex, handicap, familial status, or national origin. If models are used in display advertising campaigns, they should be clearly definable as reasonable representation of majority and minority groups in the metropolitan area, both sexes and—when appropriate—families with children. Models, if used, should portray persons in an equal social setting and indicate to the general public that the housing is open to all without regard to race, color, religion, sex, handicap, familial status, or national origin, and is not for the exclusive use of one such group.

Use of the HUD advertising criteria will be considered by the HUD General Counsel in deciding if there is reasonable cause to believe that the Fair Housing Act has been violated.

Summary

A real estate brokerage business consists of a broker who may employ one or more salespersons or other brokers. The salespersons (or brokers) are considered employees of the broker. However, for tax purposes, they are considered independent contractors. The broker-officer relationship enables a brokerage to be incorporated. A brokerage may be a **sole proprietorship**, a **partnership**, a **corporation**, or a **limited liability company** (LLC).

The modern real estate brokerage office is constantly changing as a result of the advances in technology. Modern technology includes laptop computers, the Internet, e-mail, cell phones, and PDAs. Real estate salespeople and brokers are no longer restricted to working in the office. With the advances of technology, new laws are created to protect consumers. Some of these laws involve CAN-SPAM and "do-not-call" lists.

Professional conduct is important in maintaining a brokerage's reputation. There are real estate license laws and regulations that govern the professional conduct of brokers and salespersons. Many real estate brokerages are members of professional real estate organizations and follow their ethical standards.

Trust fund handling is regulated by real estate law. Trust funds cannot be commingled with funds belonging to the broker. However, a broker may keep up to $200 of personal funds in the trust fund account to pay for bank charges or service fees related to the trust account.

Real estate is also regulated by the fair housing laws. Federal and state laws prohibit discrimination in housing and business establishments. The Civil Rights Act of 1968 and 1988 amendments are federal laws that prohibit housing discrimination. California has two antidiscrimination laws: the Unruh Civil Rights Act and the **California Fair Housing Act** (Rumford Act).

Chapter 13 Review Exercises

Matching Exercise

Instructions: Look up the meaning of the terms in the Glossary, then write the letter of the matching term on the blank line before its definition. Answers are in Appendix B.

Terms

a. Americans with Disabilities Act

b. blockbusting

c. brokerage

d. California Fair Employment and Housing Act

e. "CAN-SPAM" laws

f. cold calling

g. commercial e-mail message

h. commission

i. commingle

j. company dollar

k. corporation

l. "DBA"

m. desk cost

n. "do-not-call"

o. employee

p. ethics

q. fictitious business name

r. Housing Financial Discrimination Act

s. independent contractor

t. joint and several liability

u. *Jones v. Mayer*

v. limited liability company

w. partnership

x. prospecting

y. redlining

z. S corporation

aa. sole proprietorship

bb. steering

cc. trust funds

dd. Unruh Civil Rights Act

Definitions

1. _____ Money or other things of value received from people by a broker to be used in a real estate transaction.

2. _____ Any electronic mail message whose primary purpose is the commercial advertisement or promotion of a commercial product or service.

3. _____ The practice of making unsolicited calls to people you don't know in order to get new business.

4. _____ A legal term used in reference to a debt or a judgment for negligence, in which each debtor or each judgment defendant is responsible for the entire amount of the debt or judgment.

5. _____ A legal entity whose rights in business are similar to that of an individual.

6. _____ A name that does not include the last name of the owner in the name of the business.

7. _____ A case that prohibits discrimination based on race by upholding the 1866 Civil Rights Act and the 13th Amendment to the U.S. Constitution prohibiting slavery.

8. _____ A set of principles or values by which an individual guides his or her own behavior and judges that of others.

9. _____ The process of identifying potential customers.

10. _____ An alternative business entity that has characteristics of both corporations and limited partnerships.

11. _____ Federal and state regulations regarding unsolicited phone calls.

12. _____ State law that prohibits discrimination by businesses.

13. _____ A person who is hired to do work for another person but who is not an employee of that person.

14. _____ The illegal use of a property's location to deny financing.

15. _____ A fee for services rendered usually based on a certain percentage of the sales price of a property.

16. _____ The amount a broker has left after all commissions have been paid.

17. _____ A business that is owned and operated by one person.

18. _____ State law that prohibits discrimination in the sale, rental or financing of practically all types of housing.

19. _____ Profitability measure calculated by dividing the total operating expenses of the firm by the number of licensed sales associates.

20. _____ Someone who is under the control and direction of a broker.

21. _____ The illegal practice of telling people that property values in a neighborhood will decline because of a specific event, such as the purchase of homes by minorities.

22. _____ A corporation that operates like a corporation but is treated like a partnership for tax purposes.

23. _____ Federal and state law regulating commercial e-mail messages.

24. _____ Federal law passed in 1990 that prohibits discrimination against individuals with disabilities.

25. _____ Another name for a "fictitious business" or "trade name."

Multiple Choice Questions

Instructions: Circle your response and go to Appendix B to read the complete explanation for each question.

1. Which of the following statements is **correct** regarding a real estate brokerage business?
   a. A real estate broker may open a real estate brokerage in his or her name.
   b. The Real Estate Commissioner does not allow a fictitious business name to be used for a real estate brokerage.
   c. The broker may have only one office.
   d. The ownership of the brokerage must be as a corporation.

2. All of the following businesses can get a California real estate broker license, **except** a(n):
   a. sole proprietorship.
   b. partnership.
   c. corporation.
   d. S corporation.

3. Which of the following business entities would be subject to double taxation?
   a. S corporation
   b. Limited liability company
   c. Partnership
   d. Corporation

4. The amount a broker has left after all commissions have been paid is called the:
   a. desk cost.
   b. profit.
   c. company dollar.
   d. brokerage cost.

5. Which of the following statements is **incorrect**?
   a. The real estate license law considers a licensed salesperson an employee of the broker.
   b. For federal income tax purposes, the salesperson is considered an employee.
   c. Except for purposes of supervision under the license law, a salesperson is employed as an independent contractor.
   d. The broker must pay workers' compensation for both clerical workers and sales associates.

6. Which of the following statements is **correct** regarding the basic tests used to determine independent contractor status?
   a. The salesperson must have a valid California real estate license.
   b. The salesperson must be compensated on the basis of the number of sales closed and commissions earned—not on the basis of the number of hours worked.
   c. There must be a written contract between the employing broker and the salesperson specifying that the salesperson would be considered an independent contractor for both federal and California tax purposes.
   d. All of the statements are correct.

7. Which statement is incorrect regarding the broker/salesperson employment agreement?
   a. The real estate law requires that every broker must have a written agreement with each of his or her salespersons.
   b. The employment agreement must be on a form approved by the Commissioner.
   c. Both parties must sign the employment agreement.
   d. After termination of employment, both broker and salesperson must keep copies of it for three years.

8. Even though sales associates are considered independent contractors for federal and state income tax purposes, a broker must provide Workers' Compensation insurance for:
   a. all clerical workers.
   b. all sales associates.
   c. both (a) and (b).
   d. neither (a) nor (b).

9. When a salesperson transfers his or her license to another broker, the listings obtained by the salesperson:
   a. may be taken to the new broker.
   b. will be divided evenly between the old and new broker.
   c. will remain with the original broker.
   d. belong to the salesperson who may decide how to divide them.

10. Ben just took a listing on a three-bedroom fixer-upper home located in an area with very good schools. Although it is a mixed neighborhood, it is primarily Hispanic. He's eager to sell the home and wrote the following ads. Which of the ads best follows acceptable advertising guidelines?
    a. "This is the best home in the neighborhood in a good school district."
    b. "Nice fixer, located by parks and good schools with three-bedrooms for the family."
    c. "Clean, bright, and move-in ready for the right family."
    d. "Beautiful home near parks, looking for Hispanic family."

11. Which of the following e-mail messages is a commercial e-mail message? An e-mail sent to:
    a. facilitate or confirm an existing commercial transaction.
    b. give notice about product updates or upgrades.
    c. provide notice about certain changes in a subscription, membership, account or loan.
    d. none of the above

12. Which of the following items must be included in a commercial e-mail message?
    a. Clear and conspicuous identification that the message is an advertisement or solicitation
    b. Valid and conspicuous physical postal address of the sender
    c. Clear and conspicuous notice that the recipient may opt out of further commercial e-mail messages from the sender
    d. All of the above

13. Under the "do-not-call" rules, when may a real estate licensee make cold calls?
    a. Only between 8:00 a.m. and 9:00 p.m.
    b. Never
    c. Anytime
    d. Only between 9:00 a.m. and 6:00 p.m.

14. Which of the following statements regarding advertising is correct?
    a. A real estate broker or firm must disclose its licensed status in all advertising.
    b. Anytime a broker advertises real estate services, a term such as broker, agent, licensee (or the abbreviations bro. or agt.) must be included in the advertisement.
    c. A salesperson may not use his or her name and telephone number in an advertisement without including the broker's name.
    d. All of the statements are correct.

15. Real estate ads should not have words that state or imply a preference with regard to race, color, religion, handicap, sex, or familial status. Of the following words, which would be clearly offensive?
    a. Gated
    b. Parks nearby
    c. Catholic church nearby
    d. Houses of worship nearby

16. Which of the following statements is **incorrect** regarding real estate signs?
    a. A homeowners' association can prohibit private owners from displaying real estate signs on their own property.
    b. A city, county or state may ban all signs on publicly owned property.
    c. A city, county, or state cannot completely ban signs on privately owned property.
    d. A city, county or state may impose reasonable restrictions on the time, place, and manner of displaying signs regardless of whether it is on privately or publicly owned property.

17. Which of the following would not be considered trust funds?
    a. Cash
    b. Check
    c. Commission
    d. Personal note made payable to the seller

18. A broker may keep up to _____ of personal funds in the trust fund account to pay for bank charges or service fees related to the trust account.
    a. $100
    b. $200
    c. $300
    d. $400

19. The illegal practice of telling people that property values in a neighborhood will decline because of a specific event, such as the purchase of homes by minorities is called:
    a. blockbusting.
    b. steering.
    c. redlining.
    d. panicking.

20. The California law that prohibits discrimination in the sale, rental or financing of practically all types of housing is called the:

    a. Holden Act.

    b. Housing Financial Discrimination Act.

    c. California Fair Employment and Housing Act.

    d. Unruh Civil Rights Act.

Real Estate Specialization

14 Chapter

Introduction

Usually the majority of real estate transactions take place in the residential market. Most licensees start out in real estate offices that specialize in selling homes, spending most of their time prospecting for listings on homes and buyers to buy them. After a time, the licensee may decide to specialize and become an expert in only one particular area of real estate, such as appraisal, property management, mortgage brokerage, commercial real estate, mobile-home brokerage, or business opportunities.

We have discussed lending, appraisal, development, and residential sales in other parts of this book. This chapter examines the detailed special knowledge and capability required in mobile home sales, business opportunity brokerage, investment, property management, probate sales, and revitalization.

Learning Objectives

After reading this chapter, you will be able to:

- explain the legal definitions of a mobile home and a manufactured home.
- outline the normal course of a business opportunity sale.
- list three advantages and disadvantages in real estate investing.
- summarize the functions of property management.
- identify probate court procedures.
- discuss three areas of real estate development that contribute to smart growth.

Mobile Home Brokerage

Due to the increased need for affordable housing and the relative low cost to build, manufactured housing has become a major source of the residential housing supply. The Census reports that mobile homes make up 7% of the total housing stock.

What is the difference between a mobile home and a manufactured home? A **mobile home** is a factory-built home manufactured prior to June 15, 1976, constructed on a chassis and wheels, and designed for permanent or semi-attachment to land. In the past, mobile homes were known as trailers and were used mainly as a second, traveling home. **Manufactured homes** are homes built in a factory after June 15, 1976 and must conform to the U.S. government's Manufactured Home Construction and Safety Standards (HUD code). The federal standards regulate manufactured housing design and construction, strength and durability, transportability, fire resistance, energy efficiency, and quality. The HUD Code also sets performance standards for the heating, plumbing, air conditioning, thermal, and electrical systems of the home. It is the only federally regulated national building code. Each home or segment

A mobile home is a factory-built home manufactured prior to June 15, 1976, constructed on a chassis and wheels, and designed for permanent or semi-attachment to land.

of a home is labeled with a red tag that is the manufacturer's guarantee the home was built to conform to the HUD code. Manufactured homes are built on a non-removable steel chassis and transported to the building site on their own wheels.

Today many manufactured homes are attached to a permanent foundation, and are considered real property. Once transported from the factory to a permanent lot, very few are ever moved again. They are built in 8-,10- and 12-foot widths, and up to 60 feet in length, making them expensive and difficult to move once they are put in place. When two or more sections are put together side by side, the result is an extra-large residence. Onsite additions, such as garages, decks and porches, often add to the attractiveness of manufactured homes and must be built to local building codes.

Today many manufactured homes are attached to a permanent foundation, and are considered real property.

For the purpose of our discussion we will refer to both mobile homes and manufactured homes as mobile homes.

Mobile Homes as Personal or Real Property

As we have seen, mobile homes have become part of the residential home supply, providing a source of employment for real estate agents involved in their purchase and sale. The status of the mobile home (whether it is considered personal property or real property) determines whether or not a real estate licensee may sell mobile homes. Real estate agents may list and sell real property mobile homes because they are treated just like other real property. However, real estate agents may only sell a personal property mobile home under certain circumstances.

A mobile home is personal property unless it has been converted into real property. (Real property, you remember, is immovable.) A mobile home is considered real property when it is attached to a permanent foundation. For a mobile home to be real property:

1. a building permit must be acquired.

2. the mobile home must be set on a permanent foundation.

3. a certificate of occupancy must be obtained.

4. a recorded document must be filed stating that the mobile home has been placed on a foundation. This typically is done by the local building department.

After meeting the requirements, the mobile homes are registered with the county recorder and taxed as real property. They do not have to be registered with the Department of Motor Vehicles (DMV).

If an owner wants to move a mobile home after it has become real property, anyone who has an interest in it must approve. Thirty days before moving it the owner must notify the Department of Housing and Community Development (HCD) as well as the local tax assessor. The mobile home becomes personal property once again and returns to the unsecured property tax rolls after the owner obtains a new registration or transportation permit from the HCD or DMV.

Mobile Home Parks

A **mobile home park** is any area or tract of land where two or more mobile-home lots are rented or leased or held out for rent or lease to accommodate manufactured homes or mobile homes used for human habitation.

The rental of lots in a mobile-home park is regulated by the state Department of Housing and Community Development (HCD). The HCD registers and licenses mobile homes, and must be notified by anyone acquiring or releasing an interest in mobile homes within 10 days after a sale. A copy of the registration will then be provided to all lien holders. Both the buyer and seller must sign a certificate of title. A **certificate of title** transfers ownership of a mobile home owned as personal property. If the mobile home is real property, a **clearance of tax liability** must be signed by the county tax collector.

Failure on the part of a real estate agent to become familiar with the rules and regulations of a mobile home park could result in a cancelled sale, bad feelings, or even a lawsuit. The mobile home's desirability to a buyer may be affected by the rules of the park. The real estate agent must disclose all known facts.

For example, many parks have a minimum age requirement that at least one of the buyers must be age 55 or over. There may be strict rules about animals, where they may be kept and how they must be supervised when outside. Most mobile home parks require buyers to sign a copy of the rules and agree to comply with them. At the time the licensee accepts the mobile home listing, a copy of the park's rules and regulations should be obtained.

Whenever a buyer takes title to a mobile home, a new rental agreement must be negotiated with the owner of the mobile home park. The new tenant (mobile home owner) of the park must be approved by the owner and must agree to all terms of the park's rules and regulations.

Mobile Home Sales by Real Estate Agents

There are many laws and regulations involved in the practice of mobile home brokerage. It is a relatively new specialty area for real estate licensees, with limitations on the actions of agents. Real estate agents can only sell mobile homes which are considered real property and are located in established mobile home parks. All sales must be reported within 10 calendar days to the Department of Housing and Community Development (HCD). Only licensed mobile home dealers can sell new or used dwellings which are still on chassis and movable. Licensed real estate agents who also have a mobile home dealer's license issued by the HCD may sell new or used personal property mobile homes.

The following is a summary of approved activities for licensees involved in the sale of mobile homes.

> **Review - Approved Activities for Licensees**
> - A real estate agent may sell any mobile home that has been classified as real property. It may be listed and sold in the same manner as any other residence.
> - Sales of new mobile homes are restricted to specially licensed dealers.
> - All sales must be reported by the licensee to the Department of Housing and Community Development (HCD) within 10 days.

Financing of mobile homes is available from the same sources as for fixed-foundation residences. Loans are available through government participation programs such as the FHA, VA, and CalVet.

Marketing Mobile Homes

The mobile home park cannot prohibit "For Sale" signs within the mobile home park. Mobile home owners, or their agents, have the right to display "For Sale" signs and "For Rent" signs if the mobile home park management permits renting in the park.

The signs can be displayed in the window of the mobile home, on the side or front of the mobile home facing the street. Signs can be at least 24" wide and 36" high and can state the name, address, and telephone number of the mobile home owners or their agents. Additionally, folders containing leaflets which provide information on the mobile home for sale or rent may be included on the sign.

CALIFORNIA
ASSOCIATION
OF REALTORS®

MANUFACTURED HOME LISTING AGREEMENT
FOR REAL AND PERSONAL PROPERTY

1. **EXCLUSIVE RIGHT TO SELL:** _____ ("Seller")
hereby employs and grants _____ ("Broker") the exclusive and irrevocable right, commencing on
(date) _____ and expiring at 11:59 P.M. on (date) _____ ("Listing Period"), to sell or
exchange the Manufactured Home Situated In _____ , County Of _____ ,
California, described as _____ , and as further described below, ("Property").

2. **TYPE OF MANUFACTURED HOME:** (Check box below which applies: A(1), A(2), or B. Check ONLY one.):
   A. **PERSONAL PROPERTY MANUFACTURED HOME**
      (1) ☐ **A Manufactured Home On Leased Or Rented Land** (complete paragraph 2A(3)).
      Space Number _____ Park Name _____
   OR (2) ☐ **A Manufactured Home To Be Sold With Real Property** (complete paragraph 2A(3)) described as _____
      _____ ,
      PURCHASE PRICE ALLOCATED AS FOLLOWS: Manufactured Home $_____ Land $_____
      (3) **ADDITIONAL DESCRIPTION:** (For personal property manufactured home only)
      Manufacturer's Name _____ Model _____ Date of Manufacture _____ Date Of First Sale _____
      Property is: ☐ On Local Property Tax Roll, ☐ Department of Housing and Community Development ("HCD") registered (Use
      Tax Applies).
      Approximate Width _____ Approximate Length _____ (Without Hitch) Expando Size _____
      HCD/HUD License/Decal Number _____
      SERIAL NUMBERS: 1. _____ 2. _____ 3. _____
      HCD/HUD Label/Insignia: 1. _____ 2. _____ 3. _____
   OR B. ☐ **A REAL PROPERTY MANUFACTURED HOME** (A real property manufactured mobile home is one that meets the following
      requirements: **(1)** a building permit is obtained from local authorities pursuant to Health and Safety Code §18551, **(2)** the
      manufactured home is affixed to a foundation pursuant to Health & Safety Code §18551, **(3)** a certificate of occupancy is
      issued by local authorities, and **(4)** there is recordation with the local authorities of a form pursuant to Health and Safety Code
      §18551.)

3. **TERMS OF SALE:**
   A. **LIST PRICE:** The listing price shall be _____ ($_____).
   B. **PERSONAL PROPERTY:** The following items of personal property (exclusive of the Property) are included in the above price:
      _____
   C. **ADDITIONAL TERMS:** _____
      _____
      _____

4. **MULTIPLE LISTING SERVICE:** Information about this listing ☐ will, ☐ will not, be provided to a multiple listing service ("MLS") of
   Broker's s election and a ll t erms o f t he t ransaction, i ncluding, i f a pplicable, f inancing w ill b e p rovided t o t he M LS f or p ublication,
   dissemination and use by persons and entities on terms approved by the MLS. Seller authorizes Broker to comply with all applicable
   MLS rules.

5. **TITLE AND COMPLIANCE WITH MANUFACTURED HOME LAWS:**
   A. Seller warrants that Seller and no other persons have title to the Property, except as follows: _____
      _____ .
   B. Seller agrees Property shall be free of liens and encumbrances, recorded, filed, registered or known to Seller.
   C. Seller agrees that **(1)** evidence of title to the manufactured home, if personal property, shall be in the form of a duly endorsed,
      dated and delivered Certificate of Ownership; and **(2)** Seller shall deliver the current Registration Certificate of Title as required by
      law.
   D. Seller represents that Property, if personal property, is either: **(1)** Located within an established mobilehome park as defined in
      California Health and S afety C ode §18214, and t hat advertising or o ffering it for s ale i s n ot contrary to any provision of any
      contract between Seller and mobilehome park ownership; OR **(2)** That Property is located pursuant to a local zoning ordinance or
      permit on a lot where its presence has been authorized or its continued presence and such use would be authorized for a total
      and uninterrupted period of at least one year.
   E. If applicable, Seller agrees to deliver as soon as possible to Broker, for submission to buyer, a copy of Seller's lease or rental
      agreement and all current park and/or Homeowners' Association rules and regulations, and to inform Broker of any changes to
      either during the Listing Period.

   Seller and Broker acknowledge receipt of copy of this page, which constitutes Page 1 of _____ Pages.
   Seller's Initials (_____) (_____)   Broker's Initials (_____) (_____)

Published and Distributed by:
REAL ESTATE BUSINESS SERVICES, INC.
a subsidiary of the CALIFORNIA ASSOCIATION OF REALTORS®
525 South Virgil Avenue, Los Angeles, California 90020

REVISED 10/99

OFFICE USE ONLY
Reviewed by Broker
or Designee _____
Date _____

EQUAL HOUSING
OPPORTUNITY

MANUFACTURED HOME LISTING AGREEMENT (MHL-11 PAGE 1 OF 3)

Property Address: _____   Date: _____

6. **COMPENSATION TO BROKER:**

   Notice: The amount or rate of real estate commissions is not fixed by law. They are set by each Broker individually and may be negotiable between Seller and Broker.

   A. Seller agrees to pay to Broker as compensation for services irrespective of agency relationship(s), either ☐ _____ percent of the listing price (or if a sales contract is entered into, of the sales price), or ☐ $_____, AND _____ as follows:

   (1) If Broker, Seller, cooperating broker, or any other person, produces a buyer(s) who offers to purchase the Property on the above price and terms, or on any price and terms acceptable to Seller during the Listing Period, or any extension;

   (2) If within _____ calendar days after expiration of the Listing Period or any extension, the Property is sold, conveyed, leased, or otherwise transferred to anyone with whom Broker or a cooperating broker has had negotiations, provided that Broker gives Seller, prior to or within **5 calendar days** after expiration of the Listing Period or any extension, a written notice with the name(s) of the prospective purchaser(s);

   (3) If, without Broker's prior written consent, the Property is withdrawn from sale, conveyed, leased, rented, otherwise transferred, or made unmarketable by a voluntary act of Seller during the Listing Period, or any extension.

   B. If completion of the sale is prevented by a party to the transaction other than Seller, then compensation due under paragraph 6A shall be payable only if and when Seller collects damages by suit, settlement, or otherwise, and then in an amount equal to the lesser of one-half of the damages recovered or the above compensation, after first deducting title and escrow expenses and the expenses of collection, if any.

   C. In addition, Seller agrees to pay: _____

   D. Broker is authorized to cooperate with other brokers and, provided the Property is or includes a personal property manufactured home, with HCD licensed dealers, and divide with other brokers and dealers the above compensation in any manner acceptable to Broker.

   E. Seller hereby irrevocably assigns to Broker the above compensation from Seller's funds and proceeds in escrow.

   F. Seller warrants that Seller has no obligation to pay compensation to any other broker or dealer regarding the transfer of the Property, except: _____

   If the Property is sold to anyone listed above during the time Seller is obligated to compensate another broker or dealer; (a) Broker is not entitled to compensation under this Agreement; and (b) Broker is not obligated to represent Seller with respect to such transaction.

7. **BROKER'S AND SELLER'S DUTIES:** Broker agrees to exercise reasonable effort and due diligence to achieve the purposes of this Agreement, and is authorized to advertise and market the Property in any medium selected by Broker. Seller agrees to consider offers presented by Broker, and to act in good faith toward accomplishing the sale of the Property. Seller further agrees, regardless of responsibility, to indemnify, defend and hold Broker harmless from all claims, disputes, litigation, judgments and attorney's fees arising from any incorrect information supplied by Seller, whether contained in any document, omitted therefrom, or otherwise, or from any material facts which Seller knows but fails to disclose.

8. **AGENCY RELATIONSHIPS:** Broker shall act as the agent for Seller in any resulting transaction. Depending upon the circumstances, it may be necessary or appropriate for Broker to act as an agent for both Seller and buyer, exchange party, or one or more additional parties ("Buyer"). Broker shall, as soon as practicable, disclose to Seller any election to act as a dual agent representing both Seller and Buyer. If a Buyer is procured directly by Broker or an associate licensee in Broker's firm, Seller hereby consents to Broker acting as a dual agent for Seller and such Buyer. In the event of an exchange, Seller hereby consents to Broker collecting compensation from additional parties for services rendered, provided there is disclosure to all parties of such agency and compensation.

   Seller understands that Broker may have or obtain listings on other properties, and that potential buyers may consider, make offers on, or purchase through Broker, property the same as or similar to Seller's Property. Seller consents to Broker's representation of sellers and buyers of other properties before, during, and after the expiration of this Agreement.

9. **DEPOSIT:** Broker is authorized to accept and hold on Seller's behalf a deposit to be applied toward the sales price.

10. **LOCKBOX:**

    A. A lockbox is designed to hold a key to the Property to permit access to the Property by Broker, cooperating brokers, MLS participants, their authorized licensees and representatives, and accompanied prospective buyers.

    B. Broker, cooperating brokers, MLS and Associations/Boards of REALTORS® are **not** insurers against theft, loss, vandalism, or damage attributed to the use of a lockbox. Seller is advised to verify the existence of, or obtain, appropriate insurance through Seller's own insurance broker.

    C. ☐ (If checked:) Seller authorizes Broker to install a lockbox. If Seller does not occupy the Property, Seller shall be responsible for obtaining occupant(s)' written permission for use of a lockbox.

11. **SIGN:** ☐ (If checked:) Seller authorizes Broker to install a FOR SALE/SOLD sign on the Property.

Seller and Broker acknowledge receipt of copy of this page, which constitutes Page 2 of _____ Pages.
Seller's Initials (_____) (_____)   Broker's Initials (_____) (_____)

┌─ OFFICE USE ONLY ─┐
Reviewed by Broker
or Designee _____
Date _____

REVISED 10/99

MANUFACTURED HOME LISTING AGREEMENT (MHL-11 PAGE 2 OF 3)

Property Address: _____ Date: _____

12.DISPUTE RESOLUTION:

A. MEDIATION: Seller and Broker agree to mediate any dispute or claim arising between them out of this Agreement, or any resulting transaction, before resorting to arbitration or court action, subject to paragraph 12C below. Mediation fees, if any, shall be divided equally among the parties involved. If any party commences an action based on a dispute or claim to which this paragraph applies, without first attempting to resolve the matter through mediation, then that party shall not be entitled to recover attorney's fees, even if they would otherwise be available to that party in any such action. THIS MEDIATION PROVISION APPLIES WHETHER OR NOT THE ARBITRATION PROVISION IS INITIALED.

B. ARBITRATION OF DISPUTES: Seller and Broker agree that any dispute or claim in Law or equity arising between them regarding the obligation to pay compensation under this Agreement, which is not settled through mediation, shall be decided by neutral, binding arbitration, subject to paragraph 12C below. The arbitrator shall be a retired judge or justice, or an attorney with at least five years of residential real estate experience, unless the parties mutually agree to a different arbitrator, who shall render an award in accordance with substantive California law. In all other respects, the arbitration shall be conducted in accordance with Part III, Title 9 of the California Code of Civil Procedure. Judgment upon the award of the arbitrator(s) may be entered in any court having jurisdiction. The parties shall have the right to discovery in accordance with Code of Civil Procedure §1283.05.

   "NOTICE: BY INITIALING IN THE SPACE BELOW YOU ARE AGREEING TO HAVE ANY DISPUTE ARISING OUT OF THE MATTERS INCLUDED IN THE 'ARBITRATION OF DISPUTES' PROVISION DECIDED BY NEUTRAL ARBITRATION AS PROVIDED BY CALIFORNIA LAW AND YOU ARE GIVING UP ANY RIGHTS YOU MIGHT POSSESS TO HAVE THE DISPUTE LITIGATED IN A COURT OR JURY TRAIL. BY INITIALING IN THE SPACE BELOW YOU ARE GIVING UP YOUR JUDICIAL RIGHTS TO DISCOVERY AND APPEAL, UNLESS THOSE RIGHTS ARE SPECIFICALLY INCLUDED IN THE `ARBITRATION OF DISPUTES' PROVISION. IF YOU REFUSE TO SUBMIT TO ARBITRATION AFTER AGREEING TO THIS PROVISION, YOU MAY BE COMPELLED TO ARBITRATE UNDER THE AUTHORITY OF THE CALIFORNIA CODE OF CIVIL PROCEDURE. YOUR AGREEMENT TO THIS ARBITRATION PROVISION IS VOLUNTARY."

   "WE HAVE READ AND UNDERSTAND THE FOREGOING AND AGREE TO SUBMIT DISPUTES ARISING OUT OF THE MATTERS INCLUDED IN THE 'ARBITRATION OF DISPUTES' PROVISION TO NEUTRAL ARBITRATION." Seller's Initials _____ **Broker's Initials** _____

C. EXCLUSIONS FROM MEDIATION AND ARBITRATION: The following matters are excluded from Mediation and Arbitration hereunder: (a) A judicial or non-judicial foreclosure or other action or proceeding to enforce a deed of trust, mortgage, or installment land sale contract as defined in Civil Code §2985; (b) An unlawful detainer action; (c) The filing or enforcement of a mechanic's lien; (d) Any matter which is within the jurisdiction of a probate, small claims, or bankruptcy court; and (e) An action for bodily injury or wrongful death, or for latent or patent defects to which Code of Civil Procedure §337.1 or §337.15 applies. The filing of a court action to enable the recording of a notice of pending action, for order of attachment, receivership, injunction, or other provisional remedies, shall not constitute a violation of the mediation and arbitration provisions.

13.EQUAL HOUSING OPPORTUNITY: The Property is sold in compliance with federal, state, and local anti-discrimination Laws.

14.ATTORNEY'S FEES: In any action, proceeding, or arbitration between Seller and Broker regarding the obligation to pay compensation under this Agreement, the prevailing Seller or Broker shall be entitled to reasonable attorney's fees and costs, except as provided in paragraph 12A.

15. ADDITIONAL TERMS: _____
_____

16.ENTIRE CONTRACT: All prior discussions, negotiations, and agreements between the parties concerning the subject matter of this Agreement are superseded by this Agreement, which constitutes the entire contract and a complete and exclusive expression of their agreement, and may not be contradicted by evidence of any prior agreement or contemporaneous oral agreement. This Agreement and any supplement, addendum, or modification, including any photocopy or facsimile, may be executed in counterparts.

Seller warrants that Seller is the owner of the Property or has the authority to execute this contract. Seller acknowledges that Seller has read and understands this Agreement, and has received a copy.

Seller _____ Date _____

Address/City/State/Zip _____

Phone _____ Fax _____ E-mail _____

Seller _____ Date _____

Address/City/State/Zip _____

Phone _____ Fax _____ E-mail _____

Real Estate Broker (Firm Name) _____

By (Agent) _____ Date _____

Address/City/State/Zip _____

Phone _____ Fax _____ E-mail _____

REVISED 10/99

Page 3 of _____ Pages.

┌─ OFFICE USE ONLY ─┐
Reviewed by Broker
or Designee _____
Date _____
└────────────────────┘

EQUAL HOUSING
OPPORTUNITY

MANUFACTURED HOME LISTING AGREEMENT (MHL-11 PAGE 3 OF 3)

Houseboat Living

Houseboats are a common sight in Richardson Bay in Sausalito—and have been since the late 1900s. A **houseboat** is basically a barge that is designed and equipped for use as a dwelling. Initially they were used as summer retreats for wealthy San Francisco and Marin families. During the sixties they became lawless floating neighborhoods running along the west shore north from Sausalito. Regulation of the houseboats increased to solve the problems of pollution and

Houseboats are a common sight in Richardson Bay in Sausalito.

safety and now they are a colorful addition to the Tiburon shoreline. Those that are permanently attached to city utilities are considered real houses.

Houseboats range from 15-years to 100-years old, and from one-to-three bedrooms. Most have just one bathroom, but a few of the more expensive homes have two or three.

Time-share Properties

A **time-share** is a real estate development in which a buyer can purchase the exclusive right to occupy a unit for a specified period of time each year. The

Time-shares are frequently purchased as a vacation investment.

time is usually in one-week intervals and can be a fixed week or a floating week. In addition to the one-time purchase price, time-share owners pay an annual fee for property management and maintenance. Time-shares are usually resort-type subdivisions created with the intention of selling them to people who want a retirement home or second vacation home.

Time-shares are frequently purchased as a vacation investment because the cost of owning a good time-share is less than renting comparable hotel accommodations year after year. Another advantage is the ability to trade vacations with other time-share owners through exchange programs and travel to destinations all over the world.

The most common type of time-share is a resort condominium (which can range from a studio with a partial kitchen, all the way up to a five-bedroom unit with a full kitchen and luxury amenities). Other less-common time-share accommodations include hotel rooms, houseboats, and even motor homes.

In order to sell time-shares in California, a person must have a California real estate license.

Agricultural Properties

Agriculture plays an important role in the economy of California. It is ranked as the third-largest industry in the state providing an estimated 105,000 jobs. Farms and ranches generate about $15- billion gross income.

Agricultural property is defined as property zoned for use in farming, including the raising of crops and livestock. A farm produces plant and animal products like grains, milk, eggs, and meat. A ranch is land that is used for grazing livestock. Livestock includes domestic animals (cattle, horses, sheep, etc.) that are used for food, breeding, or draft purposes.

Agriculture plays an important role in the economy of California.

Farms and ranches include improvements, such as structures, buildings, fixtures, fences, and water rights attached to the land.

There is a tendency for many individuals to invest in small farms, ranches, and vineyards as hobbies as is seen in the wine grape growing regions. Sometimes this is referred to as the "gentleman farmer" syndrome. Some buyers are looking for working farms, recreational ranches, or horse properties, while others are developers looking to buy land for subdivisions.

Regardless of the purpose, real estate licensees who specialize in agricultural and rural properties need to become familiar with the carrying capacity of the land and soils when dealing with farms and ranches. The carrying capacity refers to the number of animal units or tonnage of crops per acre that the land can support. In addition, a general knowledge of local farming practices, climate, hydrology, and soils would be useful when marketing agricultural properties.

Some buyers are looking for working farms, others for recreational ranches or horse property.

Business Opportunity Brokerage

A business opportunity is any type of business that is for lease or sale. It also includes the intangible but salable asset of goodwill which is the expectation of the continued patronage of an existing business. The sale of a business is considered to be the sale of personal property; and the rules about the transfer of chattels are applied. A real estate broker, as well as both buyer and seller, should be aware of the application of the bulk transfer laws on the sale of a business.

A licensee, in the course of the usual business opportunity sale, may become involved in the sale of shoe stores, bars, hotels, and book stores. Stock, fixtures and goodwill almost always will be included in the sale of a business. A licensee must be aware of certain legal demands, however, that might not be required in the sale of other types of non-business properties. The sale of a business opportunity may be negotiated by anyone holding a real estate license.

In dealing with the sale of a business, a real estate agent usually will be dealing with three elements: the real property or a lease, the personal property or the inventory and equipment, and the goodwill or the reputation enjoyed by the business. Each of the three elements in the sale is worth value and must be considered when listing a business opportunity.

> **Review - Elements of the Sale of a Business**
> - Lease or Real Property
> - Inventory
> - Goodwill

The sale of a business requires special knowledge and experience by a real estate agent, and the steps involved in the sale can be complicated. All sales do not include the same order of events, but the following is a general outline of the normal course of a business opportunity sale.

Steps in a Business Opportunity Sale

- The business is listed.

- A special business opportunity deposit receipt is completed when a buyer is found.

- The offer is presented to the seller by the broker for approval.

- Escrow is opened if offer is acceptable.

- Creditors are notified of the sale and a notice of intended bulk sale is published, according to the requirements of the Bulk Sales Act.

- A financing statement (a written notice of a creditor's interest in personal property) is filed with the secretary of state and/or the recorder's office, according to the requirements of the Uniform Commercial Code (UCC).

- If a liquor license is part of the sale, the required forms are filed with the Department of Alcoholic Beverage Control (ABC).

- Arrangements for the assignment or transfer of the lease are made with the landlord.

- Copies of the seller's permit and a clearance receipt are obtained from the Board of Equalization, according to the Sales and Use Tax Law. The buyer then is protected from liability from any unpaid sales tax that the seller might owe.

- Information about employee's salaries, benefits, and unemployment insurance tax is noted.

- An inventory is taken of stock, fixtures and any other personal property that will be transferred by the sale and the seller executes a bill of sale which transfers ownership of all personal property belonging to the business.

- At the close of escrow, buyer and seller receive closing statements.

Regulating the Sale of a Business Opportunity

There are certain legal requirements that must be met in the sale of a business. In order to complete the transaction, a real estate agent must understand the requirements of the Uniform Commercial Code, the Bulk Transfer Act, California Sales and Use Tax Regulations, and the Alcoholic Beverage Control Act.

Uniform Commercial Code

Whenever money has been borrowed for the sale of a business opportunity, it follows that someone has a security interest in the personal property belonging to the business. These transactions are regulated by the Uniform Commercial Code (UCC) Divisions 6 and 9.

Bulk Sales

Bulk sales, or the sale of a substantial part of the inventory of a business, are regulated by Division 6 of the UCC. The purpose of the Bulk Transfer Act is to protect the creditors of a person who sells a business. When a business is sold and most or all of the inventory, supplies, and other materials are transferred with the sale, public notice must be given.

Twelve business days before the transfer, notice of the sale must be filed with the county recorder, published in a local newspaper in the county where the business is located, and delivered to the county tax collector.

The above requirements give fair warning of the business inventory's sale to possible creditors. Any bulk sale that takes place without complying with the requirements of the **bulk transfer law** are considered valid between the buyer and seller but fraudulent and void against creditors. This means creditors have recourse against the debtor (the seller) because he or she sold the security for the debt without notifying them.

Security Transactions in Personal Property and Fixtures

Division 9 of the Uniform Commercial Code (UCC) sets out the requirements for regulating security transactions in personal property and fixtures. The documents used are the promissory note, the security agreement, and the financing statement.

When money is borrowed, a **promissory note** is signed, just as in the financing of non-business property. The note is the evidence of the debt. At the same time, the borrower executes a security agreement that gives the lender an interest in the personal property. A **security agreement** is the document commonly used to secure a loan on personal property, much as a trust deed secures a loan on real property. The security agreement creates a lien on personal property, including fixtures. As you recall, personal property is something that is movable, and is not real property. Jewelry and bulk items—such as retail inventory, autos and boats—are examples of personal property that might be used to secure a debt. The security agreement contains all the details of the agreement, and is the document that describes the obligation.

To protect, or "perfect" as it is called, the interest created by the security agreement, or prevent the security from being sold by someone else, a financing statement must be filed. The **financing statement** is merely the document used to record the debt; it is not actual evidence of the debt. By recording the financing statement, public notice of the security interest is given, and all parties are made aware of any interests in the property, much as a recorded trust deed gives public notice of a debt against a non-business property.

Once the interest created by the security agreement is perfected, the secured party's interest is protected against the debtor's other creditors. A financing statement must be filed with the secretary of state or in the county recorder's office giving public notice of the security interest created by the debt.

California Sales and Use Tax

The **Sales and Use Tax Law** protects a buyer from liability for unpaid sales tax owed by the seller. **Sales tax** is collected as a percentage of the retail sale of a product, by a retailer. The owner of a retail business may obtain a **seller's permit**, which allows him or her to buy products at wholesale prices without paying sales tax. The retailer must then collect the proper sales tax from customers and pay it to the State Board of Equalization, usually quarterly. Before assuming the ownership of a business, a copy of the seller's permit and a clearance receipt stating that the business is current on sales taxes from the State Board of Equalization should be requested by a buyer.

Use tax is a tax imposed on the buyer who purchases goods from an out-of-state supplier for use in-state. Sales and use tax are "mutually exclusive", which means that a person will either pay sales tax or use tax, but not both.

Alcohol Beverage Control Act

Whenever transfer of a liquor license is involved in a business opportunity sale, a buyer must not assume an automatic transfer of the liquor license. The **Department of Alcoholic Beverage Control** (ABC) issues liquor licenses and must approve a buyer who requests transfer of a liquor license. A buyer must apply for the license and may be turned down for various reasons (e.g., criminal record). The maximum price for a new general liquor license is $12,000, but after two years from the issue date of the original license the price is negotiable between buyer and seller.

> **Review - Codes and Laws Involved in the Sale of a Business**
> * Uniform Commercial Code
> * Bulk Transfer Act
> * California Sales and Use Tax Law
> * Alcoholic Beverage Control Act

<u>California Gazette Classifieds</u>
Public Notices
To place your ad, call 1-123-4567, ext. 8910 or Fax 1-111-2345

NOTICE OF PUBLIC SALE

NOTICE TO CREDITORS OF BULK SALE (SECS. 6104, 6105 U.C.C.) Notice is hereby given to creditors of the within named seller that a bulk sale is about to be made of the assets described below. The names and business addresses of the Seller are ABC INC. 1234 YERBA AVE., FULLERTON, CA 92800. The location in California of the chief executive office of the seller is: (If "same as above", so state) SAME AS ABOVE As listed by the seller, all other business names and addresses used by the seller within three years before the date such list was sent or delivered to the buyer are: (If "none", so state.) NONE. The names and business addresses of the buyer are TOM BANKS 12354 POPE STREET, LOS ANGELES, CA 90020. The assets to be sold are described in general as A BUSINESS INCLUDING FURNITURE, FIXTURE AND EQUIPMENT, GOODWILL, CORPORATION, AND TRADE NAME, LEASE, AND LEASEHOLD IMPROVEMENTS and are located at: 1234 YERBA AVE., FULLERTON, CA 92800. The business name used by the seller at that location is GOOD BUYS. The anticipated date of the sale/transfer is 12/28/2004 at the office of ABC Escrow, 12345 Brook Street, Westminster, CA 92600. This bulk sale IS subject to California Uniform Commercial Code Section 6106.2. If so subject, the name and address of the person with who claims may be filed is Tony Apellido. ABC Escrow, 12345 Brook Street, Westminster, CA 92600 and the last date for filing claims shall be 12/27/04, which is the business day before the sale date specified above. Dated: 10/27/04 /s/ TOM BANKS Published: Fullerton News October 29, 2004.

NOTICE TO CREDITORS OF BULK SALE AND OF INTENTION TO TRANSFER ALCOHOLIC BEVERAGE LICENSE (U.C.C. 6105 et seq. and B & P 24073 et seq.) Notice is hereby given that a bulk sale of assets and a transfer of alcoholic beverage license is about to be made. The names, Social Security or Federal Tax Numbers, and addresses of the Seller/Licensee are DEC INC.,18922 SAND AVENUE, HUNTINGTON BEACH, CA 92000. The business is known as OUR PLACE. The names, Social Security or Federal Tax Numbers, and addresses of the Buyer/Transferee are MICHAEL APELLIDO, 110 ASH BLVD., LOS OSOS, CA 94500, SS#123-00-1960. As listed by the Seller/Licensee, all other business names and addresses used by the Seller/Licensee within three years before the date such list was sent or delivered to the Buyer/Transferee are: (if none, so state.) NONE The Assets to be sold are described in general as: A BUSINESS INCLUDING FURNITURE, FIXTURES AND EQUIPMENT, GOODWILL, TRADE-NAME, LEASE AND LEASEHOLD IMPROVEMENTS and are located at: 18922 SAND AVENUE, HUNTINGTON BEACH, CA 92000. The kind of license to be transferred is: ON-SALE GENERAL EATING PLACE #11-112345 now issued for the premises located at: 18922 SAND AVENUE, HUNTINGTON BEACH, CA 92000. The anticipated date of the sale/transfer is 12/15/2004 at the office of ABC Escrow, 12345 Brook Street, Westminster, CA 92600. It has been agreed between the Seller/Licensee and the intended Buyer/Transferee, as required by Sec. 24073 of the Business and Professions Code, that the consideration for the transfer of the business and license is to be paid only after the transfer has been approved by the Department of Alcoholic Beverage Control. Dated: 10/15/04 DEC, INC. BY: PAT SMITH, Published: Beach Wave, November 4, 2004

Examples of bulk sales published in a newspaper.

Investing in Real Estate

The main benefits of commercial real estate are appreciation, equity buildup, income, and tax benefits.

Why invest in Real Estate? With so many investment opportunities available, it is a valid question. Historically real property has shown a consistent growth in value and remains the best **hedge against inflation.** By owning assets that rise in value with inflation, e.g. real estate, you can beat inflation. Over the years, the value of real estate has appreciated considerably. If your objective is capital appreciation then buying a promising piece of property in a promising neighborhood will help you achieve this. On the other hand, if you are looking for income, then buying a rental building can help provide regular income. Some investors purchase projects that are ready for occupancy, called **turnkey projects**.

The four main benefits of commercial real estate are: (1) appreciation, (2) equity buildup, (3) income, and (4) tax benefits.

Appreciation and Equity Buildup

The benefits of appreciation and equity buildup are available to the patient investor. **Appreciation** is an increase in property value with the passage of time. The increase in value of a mortgaged property generally accrues to the benefit of the trustor. The trustor is the owner and would benefit from this appreciation. This is called an **unearned increment**. In addition, payments made on a mortgage loan are like a monthly savings plan and build up equity. **Equity buildup** is the gradual increase of the borrower's equity in a property caused by amortization of loan principal.

Income

Most investors look for a return on their investment. Over the years many ask, "Which performs better, the stock market or real estate?" If we compare the Dow in 1980 at 830, to 2004 at 10,000 +/-, that's about a 1,100% gain. Home prices across the nation have increased by about 400% during the same time frame. This makes the stock market look pretty good. However, the comparison should be made on the basis of the cash actually invested and not just sale prices.

When a buyer invests a small down payment and obtains a loan to purchase property, he or she is using the lender's money to finance the sale. This is known as **leverage**—the use of borrowed capital to buy real estate, and is a process that permits the buyer to use little of one's own money and large amounts of someone else's. Now, let's go back to our comparison of the real estate investment to the stock market. Let's assume you made a 10% down payment on a $100,000 home in 1980. By 2004, if the home increased 400% it is now valued at $400,000. Your gain on the sale would be $310,000. This means your initial $10,000 investment grew to $310,000 which is a gain of about 3,000%, which is far better than the stock market. If you had invested the $10,000 in stocks, it would have grown to $110,000 in the same 24-year period.

As you can see, the use of leverage is appealing to both home buyers and real estate investors. The investor can use leverage to control several investments rather than just one, each purchased with a small amount of personal funds and a large amount of a lender's money. The investor can then earn a return on each property, therefore increasing the amount of yield on investment dollars.

Tax Benefits of Income Property Ownership

Another benefit of investing in real estate is the tax benefits. People considering the purchase of real property must examine the tax benefits and burdens of their purchase. Many times, the tax implications will seriously affect a sale and cause a buyer or seller to realize that—because of the taxes—full value of ownership may not be possible. What might look like a good deal could turn into a losing proposition after tax considerations.

The tax laws reward an investor for the financial risk taken and benefit the economy from the investment by allowing the taxpayer to reduce tax liability in numerous ways. As long as an investment is income producing, such as with an apartment building or commercial property, certain reductions in tax liability are allowed.

Depreciation

An investor may claim depreciation and other deductions, such as, mortgage interest, property taxes, insurance, management, maintenance, and utilities to reduce the tax bill. One of the most important tax benefits of income property ownership is the depreciation allowance. **Depreciation** is a tax advantage of ownership of income property.

Depreciation for tax purposes is not based on actual deterioration but on the calculated useful life of the property. The theory is that improvements, not land, deteriorate and lose their value. A building is thought to have a certain number of years in which it can generate an income, and after that it is no longer considered a practical investment. The investor is compensated for the loss by being allowed to deduct a certain dollar amount each year based on the useful life of the property until, on paper at least, the property no longer has any value as an investment.

However, tax laws regarding depreciation change so often that it is advisable for the reader to check current Internal Revenue Service (IRS) rules for calculating depreciation.

A common method that one can use to determine the dollar amount per year that may be deducted is the straight line method, where the same amount is deducted every year over the depreciable life of a property. When using the **straight-line method** to calculate depreciation, the value of the improvements is divided by the depreciable life of the property, to arrive at the annual depreciation that can be taken. Here is how it works:

Steps to Calculate Depreciation

1. Determine what the IRS allowance for the depreciable life of a residential income property is by checking current tax law. For our purposes let's assume it is 27 1/2 years.

2. Subtract the value of the land from the value of the property to determine the value of the building.

Value of property	$400,000
Subtract the value of land	-160,000
Value of building	$240,000

3. $240,000 divided by 27 1/2 years = $8,727 annual depreciation allowance.

Example: Jaime and Chris bought a four-plex at the beach and paid $600,000 for the property. The land was valued at 40% of the total investment, leaving 60% for the value of the improvements. How much depreciation could they claim each year when filing their income tax if they were allowed to depreciate the property over 27 1/2 years?

Step #1: Calculate the value of the improvements.
$600,000 x 60% (.60) = $360,000

Step #2: Divide the value of the improvements by the years.
$360,000 divided by 27 1/2 years = $13,091 allowable annual depreciation.

When Jaime and Chris sell the property, the amount depreciated over the years will be subtracted from their cost basis to determine their capital gain. Also, when the property is sold, the new owner is allowed to begin depreciating the building as if the building were new, based on the new sales price.

Capital Gains

The gain on an income-producing property is calculated much like that for a personal residence, except any depreciation that has been claimed over the years must be subtracted from the adjusted cost basis. This means the dollar amount that has been deducted for depreciation over the time of property ownership must be subtracted from the cost basis to arrive at the adjusted cost basis. The amount of taxable gain is then calculated by subtracting the adjusted cost basis from the selling price.

Unlike a primary residence where a certain amount of gain may be excluded from being taxed, taxes are owed on any profit made whenever income producing property is sold. However, there are ways an investor may legally defer the gain to a later time. If an income property is sold at a loss, the loss may be deducted.

Taxes are owed on any profit made whenever income producing property is sold.

Calculate Capital Gain on the Sale of Income Property

1. Calculate the Adjusted Cost Basis of the Property

Add the cost of improvements and subtract the depreciation from the property.

Purchase price (cost basis)	$600,000
Add cost of improvements	100,000
	$700,000
Subtract depreciation	- 75,000
Adjusted cost basis	$625,000

2. Calculate the Adjusted Selling Price of the Property

Selling price	$700,000
Subtract the expenses of sale	- 42,000
Adjusted selling price	$ 658,000

3. Calculate the Capital Gain (or Loss)

Adjusted selling price	$658,000
Subtract adjusted cost basis	- 625,000
Capital gain (or loss)	$ 33,000

Installment Sale

An installment sale is one where payments are made by the buyer to the seller, over a period of more than one year. This is one way capital gain and the tax payments owed can be spread out over a period of time. Part of the tax liability can be deferred by the seller taking back a note and trust deed, or an All Inclusive Trust Deed (AITD) or contract of sale, with monthly payments. Only the amount of the gain that is collected in the tax year is taxable income, and the tax due on the rest can be deferred until collected. Once again, the reader should check current tax laws about installment sales.

1031 Tax-Deferred Exchange

The **1031 Exchange**, sometimes called a "tax-free" exchange, is a method of deferring tax liability. It allows an investor to exchange a property for a "like" property, and defer the gain until the property is sold. It is not really a tax-free exchange. The taxes are simply put off until a later date. The exchange can be simultaneous or non-simultaneous (deferred). The deferred exchange is often called a **"Starker" exchange**. In a Starker exchange, the investor must identify a replacement property within 45 days from the date the relinquished property is sold, and must go to settlement on the replacement property within 180 days from the previous sale. A two-party, simultaneous exchange seldom occurs because it is difficult to find two parties with properties of equal value who are willing to trade. Therefore, the Starker delayed-exchange which allows the investor 45 days to locate and identify a replacement property is used.

Most real property qualifies as "like" property, as long as it is held as an investment. It may be investment property (raw land), property held for the production of income (apartment or commercial building) or property used in a trade or business (an operating business). However, a personal residence would not qualify as a "like" property in an exchange with investment property.

If equities are not equal in two properties being exchanged, money or anything of value (cars, boats, stocks, furniture), other than like-kind property, may be put in by the investor who is "trading up" to balance the equities. This extra cash or non like-kind property put into an exchange is known as **boot**. The person who receives boot will be taxed on the net amount received up to any gain recognized from the exchange.

Example:

	Property A	Property B
Value	$400,000	$600,000
Less: Loans	- 50,000	- 200,000
Equity	$350,00	$400,000

To qualify for a tax-deferred exchange, Investor A needs to add $50,000 (boot) to the sale to make the equities match. Investor A would have no tax liability on the sale and Investor B would be taxed on the amount of the boot received in the year of the sale (if he or she realized a gain from the sale). If the amount of the boot exceeds the amount of the gain, tax liability is limited to the amount of the gain.

In calculating the gain on each property, the cost basis of the property being exchanged becomes the cost basis of the property being acquired, if no boot is given or received, and the cost basis follows the taxpayer through subsequent exchanges or sales. The profit or taxable gain is determined by subtracting the adjusted cost basis from the fair market value of the property. Tax-deferred exchanges can become very complicated. An accountant should be consulted before entering into the sale of a tax-deferred property. In this text, our discussion is mainly an overview of the subject. We recommend that you study the topic further if you find it of interest. As a real estate agent, never give tax advice. Always recommend that your clients and customers see a tax specialist for their special needs before making any decisions to purchase or sell property.

> **A personal residence does not qualify for a tax-deferred exchange.**

Probate Sales

A probate sale is a court-approved sale of the property of a person who is deceased. Ownership of property that is inherited may be subject to the approval of the probate court. In California, any estate over $60,000 must be approved by the probate court.

The purpose of a probate court is to discover any creditors of the deceased and pay them out of the estate of the person who died. After all debts are paid, anything of value that remains is distributed to the proper heirs, either according to a will or to the law of succession. The probate court sets the amount of commission when there is a real estate agent involved in the sale.

Even though it is called the probate court, the section where probate action occurs is not a separate court but a department of the Superior Court. When there is a probate sale of real property, certain procedures must be followed.

Summary of Probate Court Procedures

1. An offer to purchase must be for at least 90% of the appraised value.
2. The buyer, or a representative, must petition the court to approve the sale. When the court has set a hearing, others may bid at that time.
3. To open the bidding, there must be an increase of at least 10% of the first $10,000 of the original bid, and 5% of anything over that amount.
4. The court decides which bid is the best obtainable and confirms the sale.
5. At the time the sale is confirmed, the court will set the amount of commission to be paid if there is a real estate agent involved.

After court confirmation of a sale, usually normal escrow procedures are used to complete the transaction on the terms and conditions approved by the court.

Estate, Inheritance, and Gift Taxes

An **estate tax** is a federal tax on the transfer of assets owned by the estate of a person who has died. Depending on how much you own when you die, your estate may have to pay estate taxes before your assets can be fully distributed.

Estate taxes are different from, and in addition to, probate expenses and final income taxes owed on income you receive in the year you die. They also are separate from inheritance taxes that are collected by some states. Federal estate taxes may be due on estates greater than $1,000,000. However, there is no limitation on the amount of property left to a spouse.

There are no inheritance taxes in California. An **inheritance tax** is a tax levied by states on inherited property and paid by the person receiving the property.

A **gift tax** is a tax that can be due when you give property or other assets to someone. Federal tax laws allow a donor to give $11,000 per year to any number of donees with no gift tax due. There are no gift taxes in California.

Developers Revitalize Urban America

California communities are expressing a growing concern that the current development pattern of "urban sprawl" is not in the best interests of our cities, small towns, rural communities, and wilderness areas. **Urban sprawl** describes the unplanned and often haphazard growth of an urban area into adjoining areas. They are finding it economically unfeasible to abandon the existing infrastructure in the city, only to rebuild it further out. Developing further out from the commercial centers pollutes the air for entire regions as people drive further to their destinations. They question the wisdom of using up the open space and prime agricultural lands at the suburban fringe instead of filling in areas within the city and reusing the abandoned "brownfields", (contaminated property-explained below). As an alternative to sprawl, planners encourage and implement smart growth development practices that better serve the economic, environmental, and social needs of communities.

Smart Growth

Smart growth planning tries to reconcile the needs of development with the quality of life. Smart growth focuses on revitalizing older suburbs and older city centers. It usually has a greater mix of housing with commercial and retail uses. Where possible, it preserves open space and many other natural areas.

Principles of Smart Growth Planning

- Create a range of prices and types of housing using compact building designs to make the best use of the available land.

- Create walkable communities where people want to live, work, and play.

- Create communities that integrate mixed land uses into the planning.

- Preserve open space, farmland, and natural beauty.

- Encourage development in communities.

Types of Smart Growth

Typical smart growth plans the best ways to absorb growth without destructive traffic and pollution increases. It calls for mixed-use, higher-density, pedestrian-friendly, transit-oriented development. Some types of smart growth planning are: mansionization, in-fill development, and brownfield development.

Mansionization

A new trend of home remodeling and construction is emerging in older neighborhoods with small-to-medium-sized homes. In many of these neighborhoods developers and homeowners are tearing down the existing homes and building larger, more extravagant ones. The process, called **mansionization**, is a response to incredible land costs. In many of the older, built-out communities in California, land is valued as high as $1 million per acre or more.

In many older neighborhoods, developers and homeowners are tearing down the existing homes and building larger, more extravagant ones.

This process has become popular with developers who want to balance the cost of construction with the cost of land. It is also popular with homeowners who cannot afford to buy the larger homes in expensive neighborhoods, but who can afford to purchase smaller homes and add on at a later time. However, in some communities residents claim that the houses are eyesores, out of character, and that they can depress property values.

Some local planning commissions are trying to control mansionization by adopting a variety of restrictions on the design of homes, such as the size of side yards and the height and total square footage of a house. Many communities in California have adopted floor area ratios (FAR) in order to maintain the character of neighborhoods and to minimize the large, out-of-proportion "monster" homes. A **floor area ratio** (FAR) is a planning tool used to regulate a building's mass in relation to the size of its lot. The FAR is the ratio of the total building floor area to the total lot area and is determined by dividing the total floor area of a building by the area of the lot.

Infill Development

An **infill development** is simply the development of vacant parcels in existing urban and suburban areas. Development of this type typically brings the density of the area closer to that allowed by the existing zoning regulations. Industrial, commercial, and residential development projects can take advantage of land availability closer to urban centers. Infill developments not only keep green fields green; they are able to take advantage of proximity to a larger pool of potential employees, transportation, and utility infrastructures.

More cities and counties regulate development and restrict growth to preserve greenbelts and avoid suburban sprawl. This causes developers to consider infill development within existing neighborhoods and communities. In many areas it is easier to get the necessary building permits for infill development because these projects are considered more environmentally and urban friendly.

However, with more infill development taking place, there also has been a greater backlash toward such developments from neighboring residents, known as NIMBY, or the "Not In My Back Yard" syndrome.

Brownfield Properties

A **brownfield** is an abandoned commercial or industrial site or under-utilized neighborhood where redevelopment is complicated by actual or perceived contamination. Traditionally, state governments have tried to cleanup and revitalize these sites under their "State Superfund" programs. The EPA's 2002 Brownfields

Example of a brownfield.

Revitalization Act is a program designed to empower states to change the way contaminated property is perceived, addressed, and managed. It is estimated that there are more than 450,000 brownfield sites in the country. Cleaning up and reinvesting in these properties increases local tax base; facilitates job growth; utilizes existing infrastructure; takes development pressures off undeveloped, open land; and both improves and protects the environment.

Successful Land Revitalization in Hawthorne

A new retail and industrial complex is under construction at a site in Hawthorne previously owned by Northrop. Since 1939, Northrop has manufactured military and commercial aircraft parts. A by-product of the manufacturing operations was hazardous wastes which contaminated soils and groundwater on and off the site. As of March 2004, cleanup of soil in some areas is complete, while groundwater cleanup is underway and will continue for several years.

The newly cleaned up site is being redeveloped with a new 260,000-square foot retail center including a Lowe's Home Improvement Warehouse store. Existing buildings will be redeveloped to create 375,000 square feet of office space and 260,000 square feet of space for industrial research and development. New construction will include approximately 600,000 square feet of industrial warehouse space. The project's first tenant AT&T, will occupy a 300,000-square foot data center. Of the two remaining parcels of the original facility, one was sold to Vought Aircraft to manufacture aircraft fuselages and the other parcel was leased to an international mail courier.

Once the project is completed, it will generate approximately $3 million in annual revenue and create over 2,000 new jobs. These reuses for the old Northrop facility are economically revitalizing the Hawthorne community.

Property Management

The management of a property on behalf of the owner is called **property management**. The main goal of property management is to protect the owner's investment as well as maximize the owner's return on that investment. The property manager takes over the mundane, day-to-day management of a property. Depending on the scope of the management contract, he or she will attract new tenants, retain existing tenants, collect rents, pay expenses, hire and supervise repairs, and maintain the property.

Any type of property may be managed—homes, duplexes, and apartment buildings, as well as large projects such as office and industrial complexes and shopping centers.

Property managers are usually classified as: individual property managers, building managers, and resident managers. The **individual property manager** is usually a real estate broker who owns his or her own company and manages properties for various owners. Some property managers work for a property management firm or for a corporation as an asset manager.

Example of a managed property.

The **building manager** may be employed by a property manager or directly by an owner, and he or she usually manages a single, large building or office complex.

Resident managers are employed to manage an apartment building on either a part-time or full-time basis.

The Management Contract

The **management contract** shows the terms of the agreement between the owner and the property manager. The owner employs and authorizes the broker to perform the duties listed in the contract. The agreement should be a written contract which clearly sets forth the responsibilities of both parties. The contract should include the terms and period of the contract, the policies pertaining to the management of the premises, management fees, and the authority and powers that are given by the owner to the agent.

Property managers need a basic understanding of the laws concerning real estate licensing, contracts, agency, fair housing, employment, property protection, and tenant/landlord relationships. However, the preparation of leases, tax reports, and other matters may involve legal and accounting expertise that should be sent to a legal or tax expert.

Management Fees

Management fees are negotiated between the owner and the property manager. They can be either a flat amount per month, a percentage of the gross rents collected, or a combination of the two. Property managers usually base their fees on a percentage of the gross rents collected. This may vary from 3% on large structures to as high as 20% on individual houses or small buildings. Property managers who also act as leasing agents will often receive additional compensation for the renewal of leases and for supervising major repairs or alterations.

CALIFORNIA
ASSOCIATION
OF REALTORS®

MOVE IN / MOVE OUT INSPECTION
(C.A.R. Form MIMO, Revised 4/03)

Property Address _____

Unit No. _____

Inspection: Move In _____ (Date) Move Out _____ (Date)

Tenant(s) _____

> When completing this form, check the Premises carefully and be specific in all items notes. Check the appropriate box:
> **N - NEW   S - SATISFACTORY/CLEAN   O - OTHER   D - DEPOSIT DEDUCTION**

	MOVE IN N S O	Comments	MOVE OUT S O D	Comments
Front Yard/Exterior				
Landscaping	☐ ☐ ☐	_____	☐ ☐ ☐	_____
Fences/Gates	☐ ☐ ☐	_____	☐ ☐ ☐	_____
Sprinklers/Timers	☐ ☐ ☐	_____	☐ ☐ ☐	_____
Walks/Driveway	☐ ☐ ☐	_____	☐ ☐ ☐	_____
Porches/Stairs	☐ ☐ ☐	_____	☐ ☐ ☐	_____
Mailbox	☐ ☐ ☐	_____	☐ ☐ ☐	_____
Light Fixtures	☐ ☐ ☐	_____	☐ ☐ ☐	_____
Building Exterior	☐ ☐ ☐	_____	☐ ☐ ☐	_____
Entry				
Security/Screen Doors	☐ ☐ ☐	_____	☐ ☐ ☐	_____
Doors/Knobs/Locks	☐ ☐ ☐	_____	☐ ☐ ☐	_____
Flooring/Baseboards	☐ ☐ ☐	_____	☐ ☐ ☐	_____
Walls/Ceilings	☐ ☐ ☐	_____	☐ ☐ ☐	_____
Light Fixtures/Fans	☐ ☐ ☐	_____	☐ ☐ ☐	_____
Switches/Outlets	☐ ☐ ☐	_____	☐ ☐ ☐	_____
Living Room				
Doors/Knobs/Locks	☐ ☐ ☐	_____	☐ ☐ ☐	_____
Flooring/Baseboards	☐ ☐ ☐	_____	☐ ☐ ☐	_____
Walls/Ceilings	☐ ☐ ☐	_____	☐ ☐ ☐	_____
Window Coverings	☐ ☐ ☐	_____	☐ ☐ ☐	_____
Windows/Locks/Screens	☐ ☐ ☐	_____	☐ ☐ ☐	_____
Light Fixtures/Fans	☐ ☐ ☐	_____	☐ ☐ ☐	_____
Switches/Outlets	☐ ☐ ☐	_____	☐ ☐ ☐	_____
Fireplace Equipment	☐ ☐ ☐	_____	☐ ☐ ☐	_____
Dining Room				
Flooring/Baseboards	☐ ☐ ☐	_____	☐ ☐ ☐	_____
Walls/Ceilings	☐ ☐ ☐	_____	☐ ☐ ☐	_____
Window Coverings	☐ ☐ ☐	_____	☐ ☐ ☐	_____
Windows/Locks/Screens	☐ ☐ ☐	_____	☐ ☐ ☐	_____
Light Fixtures/Fans	☐ ☐ ☐	_____	☐ ☐ ☐	_____
Switches/Outlets	☐ ☐ ☐	_____	☐ ☐ ☐	_____

Tenant's Initials (_____)(_____)   Tenant's Initials (_____)(_____)

MIMO REVISED 4/03 (PAGE 1 OF 5)

Reviewed by _____ Date _____

EQUAL HOUSING OPPORTUNITY

MOVE IN / MOVE OUT INSPECTION (MIMO PAGE 1 OF 5)

Agent:	Phone:	Fax:	Prepared using WINForms® software
Broker:			

Property Address _____ Date: _____

	MOVE IN			**Comments**	**MOVE OUT**			**Comments**
	N	**S**	**O**		**S**	**O**	**D**	

Other Room _____
Doors/Knobs/Locks
Flooring/Baseboards
Walls/Ceilings
Window Coverings
Windows/Locks/Screens
Light Fixtures/Fans
Switches/Outlets

Bedroom # _____
Doors/Knobs/Locks
Flooring/Baseboards
Walls/Ceilings
Window Coverings
Windows/Locks/Screens
Light Fixtures/Fans
Switches/Outlets
Closets/Doors/Tracks

Bedroom # _____
Doors/Knobs/Locks
Flooring/Baseboards
Walls/Ceilings
Window Coverings
Windows/Locks/Screens
Light Fixtures/Fans
Switches/Outlets
Closets/Doors/Tracks

Bedroom # _____
Doors/Knobs/Locks
Flooring/Baseboards
Walls/Ceilings
Window Coverings
Windows/Locks/Screens
Light Fixtures/Fans
Switches/Outlets
Closets/Doors/Tracks

Bedroom # _____
Doors/Knobs/Locks
Flooring/Baseboards
Walls/Ceilings
Window Coverings
Windows/Locks/Screens
Light Fixtures/Fans
Switches/Outlets
Closets/Doors/Tracks

Tenant's Initials (_____)(_____)   Tenant's Initials (_____)(_____)

MIMO REVISED 4/03 (PAGE 2 OF 5)

Reviewed by _____ Date _____

EQUAL HOUSING OPPORTUNITY

MOVE IN / MOVE OUT INSPECTION (MIMO PAGE 2 OF 5)

Property Address _____

_____ Date: _____

	MOVE IN				**MOVE OUT**			
	N	S	O	Comments	S	O	D	Comments
Bath #_____								
Doors/Knobs/Locks	☐	☐	☐	_____	☐	☐	☐	_____
Flooring/Baseboards	☐	☐	☐	_____	☐	☐	☐	_____
Walls/Ceilings	☐	☐	☐	_____	☐	☐	☐	_____
Window Coverings	☐	☐	☐	_____	☐	☐	☐	_____
Windows/Locks/Screens	☐	☐	☐	_____	☐	☐	☐	_____
Light Fixtures	☐	☐	☐	_____	☐	☐	☐	_____
Switches/Outlets	☐	☐	☐	_____	☐	☐	☐	_____
Toilet	☐	☐	☐	_____	☐	☐	☐	_____
Tub/Shower	☐	☐	☐	_____	☐	☐	☐	_____
Shower Door/Rail/Curtain	☐	☐	☐	_____	☐	☐	☐	_____
Sink/Faucets	☐	☐	☐	_____	☐	☐	☐	_____
Plumbing/Drains	☐	☐	☐	_____	☐	☐	☐	_____
Exhaust Fan	☐	☐	☐	_____	☐	☐	☐	_____
Towel Rack(s)	☐	☐	☐	_____	☐	☐	☐	_____
Toilet Paper Holder	☐	☐	☐	_____	☐	☐	☐	_____
Cabinets/Counters	☐	☐	☐	_____	☐	☐	☐	_____
Bath #_____								
Doors/Knobs/Locks	☐	☐	☐	_____	☐	☐	☐	_____
Flooring/Baseboards	☐	☐	☐	_____	☐	☐	☐	_____
Walls/Ceilings	☐	☐	☐	_____	☐	☐	☐	_____
Window Coverings	☐	☐	☐	_____	☐	☐	☐	_____
Windows/Locks/Screens	☐	☐	☐	_____	☐	☐	☐	_____
Light Fixtures	☐	☐	☐	_____	☐	☐	☐	_____
Switches/Outlets	☐	☐	☐	_____	☐	☐	☐	_____
Toilet	☐	☐	☐	_____	☐	☐	☐	_____
Tub/Shower	☐	☐	☐	_____	☐	☐	☐	_____
Shower Door/Rail/Curtain	☐	☐	☐	_____	☐	☐	☐	_____
Sink/Faucets	☐	☐	☐	_____	☐	☐	☐	_____
Plumbing/Drains	☐	☐	☐	_____	☐	☐	☐	_____
Exhaust Fan	☐	☐	☐	_____	☐	☐	☐	_____
Towel Rack(s)	☐	☐	☐	_____	☐	☐	☐	_____
Toilet Paper Holder	☐	☐	☐	_____	☐	☐	☐	_____
Cabinets/Counters	☐	☐	☐	_____	☐	☐	☐	_____
Bath #_____								
Doors/Knobs/Locks	☐	☐	☐	_____	☐	☐	☐	_____
Flooring/Baseboards	☐	☐	☐	_____	☐	☐	☐	_____
Walls/Ceilings	☐	☐	☐	_____	☐	☐	☐	_____
Window Coverings	☐	☐	☐	_____	☐	☐	☐	_____
Windows/Locks/Screens	☐	☐	☐	_____	☐	☐	☐	_____
Light Fixtures	☐	☐	☐	_____	☐	☐	☐	_____
Switches/Outlets	☐	☐	☐	_____	☐	☐	☐	_____
Toilet	☐	☐	☐	_____	☐	☐	☐	_____
Tub/Shower	☐	☐	☐	_____	☐	☐	☐	_____
Shower Door/Rail/Curtain	☐	☐	☐	_____	☐	☐	☐	_____
Sink/Faucets	☐	☐	☐	_____	☐	☐	☐	_____
Plumbing/Drains	☐	☐	☐	_____	☐	☐	☐	_____
Exhaust Fan	☐	☐	☐	_____	☐	☐	☐	_____
Towel Rack(s)	☐	☐	☐	_____	☐	☐	☐	_____
Toilet Paper Holder	☐	☐	☐	_____	☐	☐	☐	_____
Cabinets/Counters	☐	☐	☐	_____	☐	☐	☐	_____

Tenant's Initials (_____)(_____)   Tenant's Initials (_____)(_____)

MIMO REVISED 4/03 (PAGE 3 OF 5)

Reviewed by _____ Date _____

MOVE IN / MOVE OUT INSPECTION (MIMO PAGE 3 OF 5)

Property Address _____ Date: _____

| | MOVE IN | | | | | | MOVE OUT | | | | |
| | N | S | O | Comments | | | S | O | D | Comments | |

Kitchen
Flooring/Baseboards ☐ ☐ ☐ _____ ☐ ☐ ☐ _____
Walls/Ceilings ☐ ☐ ☐ _____ ☐ ☐ ☐ _____
Window Coverings ☐ ☐ ☐ _____ ☐ ☐ ☐ _____
Windows/Locks/Screens ☐ ☐ ☐ _____ ☐ ☐ ☐ _____
Light Fixtures ☐ ☐ ☐ _____ ☐ ☐ ☐ _____
Switches/Outlets ☐ ☐ ☐ _____ ☐ ☐ ☐ _____
Range/Fan/Hood ☐ ☐ ☐ _____ ☐ ☐ ☐ _____
Oven(s)/Microwave ☐ ☐ ☐ _____ ☐ ☐ ☐ _____
Refrigerator ☐ ☐ ☐ _____ ☐ ☐ ☐ _____
Dishwasher ☐ ☐ ☐ _____ ☐ ☐ ☐ _____
Sink/Disposal ☐ ☐ ☐ _____ ☐ ☐ ☐ _____
Faucet(s)/Plumbing ☐ ☐ ☐ _____ ☐ ☐ ☐ _____
Cabinets ☐ ☐ ☐ _____ ☐ ☐ ☐ _____
Counters ☐ ☐ ☐ _____ ☐ ☐ ☐ _____

Hall/Stairs
Flooring/Baseboards ☐ ☐ ☐ _____ ☐ ☐ ☐ _____
Walls/Ceilings ☐ ☐ ☐ _____ ☐ ☐ ☐ _____
Light Fixtures ☐ ☐ ☐ _____ ☐ ☐ ☐ _____
Switches/Outlets ☐ ☐ ☐ _____ ☐ ☐ ☐ _____
Closets/Cabinets ☐ ☐ ☐ _____ ☐ ☐ ☐ _____
Railings/Banisters ☐ ☐ ☐ _____ ☐ ☐ ☐ _____

Laundry
Faucets/Valves ☐ ☐ ☐ _____ ☐ ☐ ☐ _____
Plumbing/Drains ☐ ☐ ☐ _____ ☐ ☐ ☐ _____
Cabinets/Counters ☐ ☐ ☐ _____ ☐ ☐ ☐ _____

Systems
Furnace/Thermostat ☐ ☐ ☐ _____ ☐ ☐ ☐ _____
Air Conditioning ☐ ☐ ☐ _____ ☐ ☐ ☐ _____
Water Heater ☐ ☐ ☐ _____ ☐ ☐ ☐ _____
Water Softener ☐ ☐ ☐ _____ ☐ ☐ ☐ _____

Other _____

Tenant's Initials (_____)(_____)   Tenant's Initials (_____)(_____)

Reviewed by_____ Date_____

EQUAL HOUSING OPPORTUNITY

MOVE IN / MOVE OUT INSPECTION (MIMO PAGE 4 OF 5)

Property Address _____

_____ Date: _____

	MOVE IN				MOVE OUT			
	N	S	O	Comments	S	O	D	Comments

Garage/Parking
Garage Door
Other Door(s)
Driveway/Floor
Cabinets/Counters
Light Fixtures
Switches/Outlets
Electrical/Exposed Wiring
Window(s)
Other Storage/Shelving

Back/Side/Yard
Patio/Deck/Balcony
Patio Cover(s)
Landscaping
Sprinklers/Timers
Pool/Heater/Equipment
Spa/Cover/Equipment
Fences/Gates

Safety/Security
Smoke/CO Detector(s)
Security System
Security Window Bars

Personal Property

Keys/Remotes/Devices
Keys
Remotes/Devices

☐ Attached Supplement(s) _____

THIS SECTION TO BE COMPLETED AT MOVE IN: Receipt of a copy of this form is acknowledged by:
Tenant _____ Date _____
Tenant _____ Date _____
New Phone Service Established? ☐ Yes ☐ No   New Phone Number _____
Landlord (Owner or Agent) _____ Date _____
Landlord _____
        (Print Name)

THIS SECTION TO BE COMPLETED AT MOVE OUT: Receipt of a copy of this form is acknowledged by:
Tenant _____ Date _____
Tenant _____ Date _____
Tenant Forwarding Address _____

Landlord (Owner or Agent) _____ Date _____
Landlord _____
        (Print Name)

THIS FORM HAS BEEN APPROVED BY THE CALIFORNIA ASSOCIATION OF REALTORS® (C.A.R.). NO REPRESENTATION IS MADE AS TO THE LEGAL VALIDITY OR ADEQUACY OF ANY PROVISION IN ANY SPECIFIC TRANSACTION. A REAL ESTATE BROKER IS THE PERSON QUALIFIED TO ADVISED ON REAL ESTATE TRANSACTIONS. IF YOU DESIRE LEGAL OR TAX ADVICE, CONSULT AN APPROPRIATE PROFESSIONAL.
This form is available for use by members of the NATIONAL ASSOCIATION OF REALTORS® who subscribe to its Code of Ethics.

SURE TRAC
The System for Success™

Published by the
California Association of REALTORS®

Reviewed by _____ Date _____

EQUAL HOUSING
OPPORTUNITY

MIMO REVISED 4/03 (PAGE 5 OF 5)   **MOVE IN / MOVE OUT INSPECTION (MIMO PAGE 5 OF 5)**

Functions of a Property Manager

In addition to the basic real estate knowledge of agency, contracts, fair housing, rentals, and leases, a property manager needs to know about business administration, marketing, insurance, repairs and maintenance, and taxes.

The property manager must be a "jack-of-all trades" because the duties are many and varied. Property managers have a dual responsibility to both the owner and the tenants. The owner wants the highest possible return from the property, and the tenants want the best value for their money. With this in mind, property managers must: keep the properties rented the highest market rent possible, implement reasonable safety measures, keep operational and other costs within budget, and preserve and enhance the physical value and prestige of the property. In addition, he or she must do all of this along with the legal requirements of managing his or her own business.

Reports to Owner

The owner relies on the information provided by the property manager about the profitability of his or her property. Therefore, the property manager must set up and maintain accurate records and send regular reports to the owner. In addition to the monthly accounting statement, a detailed annual statement should be prepared. Through the monthly and annual reports, both owner and property manager can assess the fluctuations of income and expense and formulate future rental and maintenance policies.

Managing Properties Subject to Rent Control

Rent control, or **rent stabilization**, is a collection of laws in some communities that limit or prohibit rent increases. They also limit the reasons for eviction. Typical provisions of rent stabilization regulations include: (1) control the amount that may be charged for a rental unit, (2) determine the amenities and services that are included as part of the rent, and (3) provide for only "good cause" evictions. These regulations work together so that the landlord cannot circumvent a rent limit by just evicting the tenant.

Rent control has been in effect in a number of major cities for many years. The best-known example is New York City, which still uses the same rent controls from the 1940s. In 1979, two California cities, Berkeley and Santa Monica,

Rent control stabilizes rents and helps prevent unfair evictions.

imposed strict rent control ordinances. Shortly thereafter, more cities followed suit—including San Francisco, Los Angeles, San Jose, West Hollywood, East Palo Alto, Beverly Hills, Hayward, Los Gatos, Oakland, Palm Springs, San Jose, and San Leandro. San Diego is the only major California city to go against the trend by rejecting rent control by a 2-to-1 vote in a 1985 referendum.

Review - California Cities with Rent Control

Berkeley	Los Gatos	San Leandro
Beverly Hills	Oakland	Santa Monica
East Palo Alto	Palm Springs	West Hollywood
Hayward	San Francisco	
Los Angeles	San Jose	

Stabilization of Rent

Although regulations differ from city to city, rents usually can only be raised once a year. The amount of the increase is decided by the Rent Stabilization Board of the city. The **Maximum Allowable Rent** (MAR) is the maximum legal rent that a landlord may charge for a controlled rental unit. Many of the rent control laws allow tenants to request rent decreases when landlords do not maintain their rental property or do not continue to provide housing services or amenities.

Lawful Evictions

Rent control laws are specific on tenant evictions. A **good cause eviction** includes failing to pay the rent, violating an important condition of the rental agreement or causing a substantial nuisance.

A **no-fault eviction** is a type of lawful eviction in which the tenant is not at fault. This would include things like the owner wanting to occupy the apartment or get out of the rental housing business. Most no-fault evictions require the landlord to pay substantial relocation benefits to the displaced tenants.

A property manager or an owner of a rent-controlled property should consult an attorney whenever an eviction is necessary because there are specific legal requirements that must be followed.

Property Manager's Duties

Some of the specific duties a property manager must perform are:

- create rental schedule.
- merchandise the space.
- advertise vacancies through selected media.
- develop a tenant/resident relations policy.
- qualify and investigate a prospective tenant's credit.
- prepare and execute leases.
- collect the rent.
- review and pay bills.
- obtain and pay insurance premiums and taxes.
- create and supervise maintenance schedules and repairs.
- maintain proper records and make regular reports to the owner.
- comply with Fair Housing Laws.

Duties of a Property Manager with Employees

- Hire and keep personnel to staff the building(s).
- Instruct and supervise employees.
- Develop employee policies, including an Injury Prevention Plan.
- Set up payroll system for all employees.
- Comply with applicable federal, state, and local laws.
- Keep abreast of the times and competitive market conditions.

Summary

Most people obtain a real estate license to sell homes; however, many other opportunities in real estate can be pursued. Licensees can specialize in mobile home brokerage, business opportunity brokerage, **property management**, probate sales, real estate investment, and new areas of expertise such as smart growth.

New fields of specialization or expertise are also emerging in real estate. One of these fields, **smart growth**, utilizes the city's existing infrastructure and redevelops rather than abandons property. An example of smart growth is the clean up and redevelopment of brownfields. Developers are now revitalizing urban America by redeveloping the industrial, commercial, and residential areas close to the urban center rather than focusing on **urban sprawl**.

Chapter 14 Review Exercises

Matching Exercise

Instructions: Look up the meaning of the terms in the Glossary, then write the letter of the matching term on the blank line before its definition. Answers are in Appendix B.

Terms

a. 1031 Exchange

b. agricultural property

c. appreciation

d. boot

e. brownfield

f. building manager

g. bulk sales

h. business opportunity

i. certificate of title

j. clearance of tax liability

k. Department of Alcoholic Beverage Control

l. depreciation

m. equity buildup

n. estate tax

o. financing statement

p. gift tax

q. goodwill

r. hedge against inflation

s. houseboat

t. infill development

u. installment sale

v. leverage

w. management contract

x. mansionization

y. manufactured home

z. mobile home park

aa. mobile home

bb. probate sale

cc. promissory note

dd. resident manager

ee. sales tax

ff. security agreement

gg. seller's permit

hh. straight-line method

ii. time-share

jj. turnkey project

kk. unearned increment

ll. Uniform Commercial Code

mm. urban sprawl

nn. use tax

Definitions

1. _____ A factory-built home manufactured prior to June 15, 1976, constructed on a chassis and wheels, and designed for permanent or semi-attachment to land.

2. _____ Home built in a factory after June 15, 1976, and must conform to the U.S. government's Manufactured Home Construction and Safety Standards.

3. _____ Any area or tract of land where two or more mobile-home lots are rented or leased or held out for rent or lease to accommodate manufactured homes or mobile homes used for human habitation.

4. _____ Certificate signed by the county tax collector in mobile home sales.

5. _____ A barge that is designed and equipped for use as a dwelling.

6. _____ A real estate development in which a buyer can purchase the exclusive right to occupy a unit for a specified period of time each year.

7. _____ Property zoned for use in farming, including the raising of crops and livestock.

8. _____ Any type of business that is for lease or sale.

9. _____ The expectation of the continued patronage of an existing business.

10. _____ Code that regulates any security interest in the personal property belonging to the business.

11. _____ The sale of a substantial part of the inventory of a business.

12. _____ The document commonly used to secure a loan on personal property.

13. _____ The document used to record the debt; it is not actual evidence of the debt.

14. _____ Tax collected as a percentage of the retail sales of a product, by a retailer.

15. _____ Permit which allows a person or business to buy products at wholesale prices without paying sales tax.

16. _____ Real property appreciation keeps pace or exceeds inflation rates.

17. _____ Projects that are ready for occupancy.

18. _____ An increase in property value with the passage of time.

19. _____ The increase in value of a mortgaged property generally accrues to the benefit of the trustor.

20. _____ The gradual increase of a borrower's equity in a property caused by amortization of loan principal.

21. _____ The use of borrowed capital to buy real estate is a process that permits the buyer to use little of one's own money and large amounts of someone else's.

22. _____ Tax advantage of ownership of income property.

23. _____ Depreciation method where the same amount is deducted every year over the depreciable life of a property.

24. _____ Sale in which payments are made, by the buyer, to the seller, over a period of more than one year.

25. _____ Sometimes called a "tax-free" exchange is a method of deferring tax liability.

26. _____ Extra cash or non like-kind property put into an exchange.

27. _____ A court-approved sale of the property of a person who is deceased.

28. _____ Federal tax on the transfer of assets owned by the estate of a person who has died.

29. _____ The unplanned and often haphazard growth of an urban area into adjoining areas.

30. _____ A new trend of home remodeling and construction is emerging in older neighborhoods with small to medium-sized homes.

31. _____ The development of vacant parcels in existing urban and suburban areas.

32. _____ An abandoned commercial or industrial site or under-utilized neighborhood where redevelopment is complicated by actual or perceived contamination.

33. _____ Person employed by a property manager or directly by an owner, and usually manages a single, large building or office complex.

34. _____ Person employed to manage an apartment building on either a part-time or full-time basis.

35. _____ Contract that shows the terms of the agreement between the owner and the property manager.

Multiple Choice Questions

Instructions: Circle your response and go to Appendix B to read the complete explanation for each question.

1. A real estate licensee can sell:
    a. a new mobile home.
    b. a one-year-old mobile home.
    c. a mobile home over 31 feet in length.
    d. any mobile home with a deed.

2. Which of the following documents is used to transfer ownership of a mobile home?
   a. Certificate of Title
   b. Deed
   c. DMV vehicle registration certificate
   d. Bill of sale

3. Time-share properties are primarily designed for buyers looking for:
   a. income-producing real property.
   b. vacation property.
   c. a primary residence.
   d. agricultural property.

4. In a security transaction in personal property, the document used to "perfect" the security interest is called the:
   a. promissory note.
   b. security agreement.
   c. mortgage.
   d. financing statement.

5. In the sale of business opportunity, the Notice to Creditors of Bulk Transfer must be recorded at least how many days before the auction is to commence?
   a. 12 business days
   b. 14 business days
   c. 18 calendar days
   d. 21 calendar days

6. Which of the following would provide an investor with the best hedge against inflation?
   a. United States government bonds
   b. A savings account in a bank
   c. Ownership of real property
   d. A note secured by a first deed of trust

7. Which of the following would provide an investor with the best hedge against inflation?
   a. An investment with high liquidity
   b. A high-risk, high-income deed of trust
   c. An income property that will maintain its value
   d. An investment with the characteristics of an annuity

8. When considering investment opportunities in real estate, a real estate investor would probably devote least attention to:
   a. protection against inflation.
   b. quantity and safety of annual income.
   c. quantity and safety of the initial capital outlay.
   d. liquidity of any capital invested.

9. Value that increases with the passage of time is called:
   a. cash flow.
   b. leverage.
   c. depreciation.
   d. appreciation.

10. Which of the following is the best example of leverage?
    a. Investing primarily personal funds
    b. Investing personal and borrowed funds equally
    c. Investing primarily borrowed funds
    d. Investing in properties with diminishing values

11. An appreciation in value of a mortgaged home generally accrues to the benefit of the:
    a. trustor.
    b. beneficiary.
    c. trustee.
    d. none of the above

12. All of the following would be considered "boot" except:
    a. cash.
    b. antique furniture.
    c. vacant land in the outskirts of a large city.
    d. a commercial fishing boat.

13. In a probate sale, the amount of a commission to be paid a real estate agent is set by the:
    a. owner.
    b. executor.
    c. administrator.
    d. court.

14. As more cities and counties regulate development and restrict growth to preserve greenbelts and avoid suburban sprawl, developers are encouraged to develop vacant parcels in existing urban and suburban areas. This is called:

    a. greenbelt development.

    b. brownfield development.

    c. infill development.

    d. reurbanization.

15. A property manager should:

    a. protect the owner's investment.

    b. maximize the owner's return on the property.

    c. maintain accurate records and send regular reports to the owner.

    d. all of the above

Getting and Keeping Your Real Estate License

15 Chapter

Introduction

Early real estate transactions were very simple. People transferred property ownership by exchanging symbolic lumps of dirt for something of value. As life became more complicated, however, there was a need for a more sophisticated way to transfer real property.

At the same time, the need emerged for some kind of regulation of the practice and the practitioners. Unethical people were taking advantage of the average citizen's lack of knowledge about real estate and the law.

Today, the California Department of Real Estate (DRE) protects consumers and regulates real estate agents. Real estate agents are now licensed and accountable for their actions.

As a licensee, you are regulated by the DRE. The following discussion of the DRE and its related activities serves as the foundation for your career as a real estate agent.

Learning Objectives

Upon completion of this chapter, you will be able to:

- name the license requirements for real estate salespersons and brokers.
- list license renewal requirements for real estate sales associates and brokers.
- explain the importance of government regulations in brokerage transactions.
- discuss the operations of the Department of Real Estate (DRE).
- describe two license requirements.
- identify common violations and DRE enforcement policies.
- evaluate the importance of real estate continuing education.

The Real Estate Law

California has long been a leader in real estate trends. As a matter of fact, the nation's first real estate licensing law was passed in California in 1917. In an attempt to create and maintain higher professional standards, and develop greater trust from the public in general, the real estate industry has supported legislation that protects consumer interests. As time went by the law was codified and organized into two parts of the Business and Professions Code. Part 1 is titled "Licensing of Persons" and is called the **Real Estate Law**, which we will discuss in this chapter. Part 2 is titled "Regulation of Transactions" and is called the Subdivided Lands Law, which was discussed in Chapter Twelve.

The real estate law, sometimes referred to as the license law, is designed mainly for the protection of the public in real estate transactions where a licensee is involved. When you hear the term "real estate law" it means the law that affects the licensing and conduct of real estate brokers and salespersons. It must be seen separately from what is known as real property law, law of agency, contract law, or other legal aspects of real estate ownership and transfer.

Review - The Real Estate Law
- **The two main purposes are to protect:**
  1. consumers from loss because of dishonest and incompetent agents.
  2. the good standing of ethical agents from the adverse publicity caused by unprincipled licensees.
- **It pertains to the:**
  1. licensing of Real Estate Brokers and Salespersons.
  2. conduct of Real Estate Brokers and Salespersons.

The Real Estate Commissioner

The **Real Estate Commissioner** (Commissioner), appointed by the governor, determines administrative policy and enforces the provisions of the real estate law and the Subdivided Lands Law to ensure that the public is protected when dealing with licensees and when purchasing subdivided real property. To be appointed, the designee must have been a real estate broker for five years and actively engaged in the real estate business in California.

The real estate law is not upheld in a court of law but is enforced by the Real Estate Commissioner at special hearings, which will be discussed later in the chapter. One of the jobs not assigned to the Commissioner is settling commission disputes. That issue falls under the power of a court of law, and must be handled through an attorney if the parties involved cannot settle the matter agreeably.

Responsibilities of the Real Estate Commissioner

- Screen and qualify applicants for license

- Issue, restrict, suspend or revoke real estate licenses

- Examine complaints against licensees

- Pursue formal action against licensees, where appropriate

- Monitor real property securities transactions

- Regulate prepaid rental listing services

- Regulate specific aspects of the sale of subdivisions

The Real Estate Advisory Commission

The Commissioner appoints a Real Estate Advisory Commission for consultation and advice on matters pertinent to the DRE. The Advisory Commission is made up of 10 members: six licensed real estate brokers and four public members. None but the Commissioner receives payment for tenure on the Commission, which meets at least four times yearly.

Real Estate Licensing

Real estate brokers and salespersons are entrusted with people's hopes, dreams, and money. Consumers must have a great deal of confidence in the real estate industry to place their trust in a broker or salesperson. With that in mind, the state places strict requirements on those who wish to practice real estate in the form of real estate licensing.

As we have seen, the purpose of a real estate license is to protect both the consumer and the licensee. It is important for both to understand the obligations and restrictions of the different licenses that may be held. Any person who wants to engage in the real estate business and act as a real estate broker or real estate salesperson within the state of California must obtain a license from the Department of Real Estate (DRE).

The two main types of real estate licenses are the broker's license and the salesperson's license.

Real estate brokers and salespersons are entrusted with people's hopes, dreams, and money.

Terminology

Real Estate Broker

A **real estate broker** is someone who holds a broker license issued by the Department of Real Estate. The license legally permits the broker to perform any acts for which a real estate license is required. A real estate broker is also an independent businessperson who can employ someone who holds a salesperson or a broker license. Brokers are legally responsible for all the business actions of their employees.

Real Estate Salesperson

A **real estate salesperson** is someone who holds a salesperson license issued by the Department of Real Estate. The salesperson must be employed by a real estate broker in order to perform any of the activities that require a license.

Real Estate Sales Associate

Real estate sales associate is a term used to refer to employees of a broker. They may hold either a salesperson or a broker license. A sales associate who has a salesperson license must be employed by a broker. A person who has a broker license may operate independently or put his or her license under an employing broker and is then called a sales associate or broker associate.

Real Estate Agent

Both brokers and salespersons can be agents. A licensed broker is legally an agent of the principal. A licensed salesperson is legally an agent of his or her employing broker.

When is a License Required?

Under section 10131 of the Business and Professionals Code, a real estate broker is someone who, for compensation, does perform or negotiates to perform one or more of the acts requiring a real estate license. A salesperson, if employed by a real estate broker, may also do any of the following activities.

Acts Requiring a Real Estate License

- Soliciting sellers
- Soliciting buyers
- Negotiating sales
- Negotiating leases
- Soliciting for tenants or rentals
- Negotiating sales contracts
- Negotiating loans
- Negotiating a promissory note secured by real property
- Negotiating exchanges

Unlicensed Person Penalties

No unlicensed person may receive payment for any act requiring a real estate license. The fine for paying a fee to an unqualified person is $100 for each offense. Prior to paying a commission, an escrow holder should require a broker to present evidence he or she is a regularly licensed real estate broker at the time such compensation is earned.

The fine for paying a fee to an unqualified person is $100 for each offense.

It is unlawful for any unlicensed person to pose as a real estate broker or salesperson or to advertise that he or she is a real estate broker. The punishment for an individual falsely claiming to be a broker or salesperson is a fine of up to $10,000 or imprisonment up to six months, or both. A corporation is subject to a criminal fine not to exceed $50,000. The maximum fine against a broker paying an unlicensed person for soliciting borrowers or negotiating real estate loans is $10,000.

Exemptions to the License

Certain exemptions from licensing requirements are allowed. The following list shows many but not all of the people who are exempt from obtaining a real estate license.

Real Estate License Exemptions

- A person who deals only with his or her own property

- A corporation that performs any of the specified activities through one of its regular officers, who must receive no special compensation for doing so

- Anyone holding a duly executed power of attorney from the owner of property

- An attorney-at-law performing services in the regular course of business as an attorney

- Resident managers of apartment buildings and complexes or their employees

- Short-term (vacation) rental agents

- Employees of certain lending institutions

- Clerical employees of real estate brokers for specific, limited functions

- Licensed personal property brokers

- Any film location representative employed to arrange for the use of real property for photographic purposes

- Cemetery authorities

- Certain collectors of payments for lenders or on notes for owners in connection with loans secured directly or collaterally by liens on real property, provided such collectors annually meet exemption criteria

- Any receiver, trustee in bankruptcy or person acting under order of any court

- Any trustee selling under a deed of trust

- Lenders making loans guaranteed or insured by an agency of the federal government

- An employee of lending institutions, pension trusts, credit unions, or insurance companies, in connection with loans secured by liens on real property or a business opportunity

- Escrow agents collecting funds in connection with loans secured by liens on real property when the funds are deposited in the escrow agent's trust account

Steps in Getting a Real Estate License

Before an applicant for a real estate salesperson or broker license may obtain a license, he or she must fulfill certain real estate education requirements and then apply for and pass a real estate examination.

Basic Requirements for both Salesperson and Broker

- Be at least 18 years old

- Be honest and truthful

- Complete real estate course(s) as required by law

- Apply for the state examination on a form prescribed by the Commissioner

- Pass the qualifying examination

Additional Requirements: Salesperson License

A salesperson must submit proof of completion of an approved Real Estate Principles course prior to or along with the real estate license application. Within 18 months of the issuance of a salesperson license, the licensee must submit proof of the successful completion of an approved course in Real Estate Practice and one additional course selected from the chart below. A salesperson must be employed by a licensed broker to perform acts regulated by a salesperson license.

Additional Requirements: Broker License

An applicant for an original real estate broker license must meet specific education and experience standards. A broker candidate must complete eight approved real estate courses: five mandatory real estate courses (Real Estate Appraisal, Real Estate Practice, Real Estate Finance, Legal Aspects of Real Estate, and Real Estate Economics or General Accounting) and three electives selected from the chart that follows.

In addition, a broker candidate must also have two years of full-time licensed real estate experience within the past five years or the equivalent. Acceptable equivalents include a four-year degree from an accredited college or one year of full-time experience combined with a two-year degree from an accredited college.

Required Education

You must submit evidence, in the form of transcripts or certificates, that you have completed the statutory license courses. Courses may be taken from a

DRE-approved private vocational real estate school or from a college that is accredited by the Western Association of Schools and Colleges or a comparable regional accrediting entity. Unless the California Real Estate Commissioner has granted prior approval, no private vocational real estate school outside California may grant credit for the required prelicense courses. The required number of hours for a statutory course is 45 hours if taken from a real estate school. If taken at an accredited college, a course for three-semester units or four quarter units is acceptable.

Real Estate Courses	Salesperson	Broker
Real Estate Principles	Required	Elective
Real Estate Practice	Required -18 Month	Required
Legal Aspects of Real Estate	Elective	Required
Real Estate Appraisal	Elective	Required
Real Estate Finance	Elective	Required
Real Estate Economics	Elective	Required
General Accounting	May waive RE Economics	May waive RE Economics
Business Law	Elective	Elective
Common Interest Developments	Elective	Elective
Computer Applications in RE	Elective	Elective
Escrows	Elective	Elective
Mortgage Loan Brokering/Lending	Elective	Elective
Property Management	Elective	Elective
Real Estate Office Administration	Elective	Elective
Adv. Legal Aspects of Real Estate	Not allowed	Elective
Adv. Real Estate Appraisal	Not allowed	Elective
Adv. Real Estate Finance	Not allowed	Elective

Real Estate Education and Research Fund

The real estate industry depends on the public's trust to perform its job. In order to better serve the consumer, the Real Estate Education and Research Fund was created for the advancement of real estate education. Like the Real Estate Recovery Fund, money is collected from license fees for the Education and Research Fund.

Real Estate Examination

The purpose of the real estate license examination is to make sure consumers are protected in all transactions where they are to be represented by an agent. License applicants must have knowledge of the English language, including reading, writing, and spelling; and of arithmetical computations common to real estate and business opportunity practices.

The salesperson exam has 150 multiple-choice questions and a maximum time limit of 3 hours and 15 minutes. Examinees must correctly answer 70% of the questions on the test to pass the salesperson examination and become eligible for a license.

The broker examination has two 100-question multiple-choice tests administered in two sessions—2 ½ hours in the morning and 2 ½ hours in the afternoon. Examinees must correctly answer 75% of the questions on the test to pass the broker examination and become eligible for a license.

The exam tests an applicant's general knowledge of real estate, appraisal, finance, forms, and other fundamentals of the industry. The subject matter covered in the examination is based on laws and procedures appropriate within California. The following lists of examination topics are for informational purposes and should not be considered totally comprehensive.

Subjects Tested on the Real Estate License Examinations

Area of Knowledge	Salesperson Exam	Broker Exam
Property Ownership and Land Use Controls	18%	15%
Laws of Agency	12%	12%
Valuation and Market Analysis	12%	11%
Financing	13%	13%
Transfer of Property	9%	10%
Practice of Real Estate and Mandated Disclosures	24%	27%
Contracts	12%	12%

Examination Rules and Grading		
	Salesperson	**Broker**
Time	3 ¼ hours	5 hours
Number of multiple-choice questions	150	200
Passing score	70%	75%

Applying for the Examination

The applications and fee schedule for both the sales and broker license examination can be obtained from the DRE website at http://www.dre.ca.gov. A person has two years from the date the application is received to complete all qualifications and take the examination. After the two-year period, the application will expire and the applicant will have to resubmit everything again and pay another fee.

A person applying for the salesperson examination fills out the salesperson examination application and mails it to the DRE along with the appropriate fee and proof of completion of the Real Estate Principles course or proof of enrollment in the Real Estate Principles course. Once the application is processed, the DRE will send notification of the examination date, time, and location. You can also check online at the DRE website http://www.dre.ca.gov/ examinees_sub.htm to see if your examination has been scheduled.

An applicant who fails to pass the state exam may apply for reexamination any number of times by filing an application and paying the fee. The person must take the exam within two years or file a new application and pay a new fee.

Upon passing the state exam, the applicant may apply for the salesperson or broker license within one year of the examination date.

Applying for the License

After passing the real estate examination, the DRE sends either a broker or a salesperson license application. Within one year after passing the examination, you must complete and return the form along with the appropriate fee.

Unless you are currently licensed as a salesperson or hold a real estate license which expired less than two years ago, there are other documents you will need to include with your license application. You will need to submit one set of classifiable fingerprints, proof of legal presence in the United States, and, if you are an out-of-state applicant, you must include an irrevocable Consent to Service of Process.

Fingerprint Requirements

An applicant for an original real estate license must submit one set of classifiable fingerprints. The fingerprints must be submitted electronically to the state Department of Justice (DOJ) using the Live Scan Program, which takes and transmits fingerprints to the DOJ and the Federal Bureau of Investigation (FBI). Social Security numbers are now required on examination applications so fingerprint results can be processed. An original license will not be issued until a report from the DOJ and the FBI is received either stating that there is no criminal history, or disclosing criminal history information, which then must be reviewed and evaluated. More information can be found on the DRE website at http://www.dre.ca.gov/fees.htm.

An applicant for an original real estate license must submit one set of classifiable fingerprints.

Proof of Legal Presence

On August 1, 1998, the DRE began enforcing a federal law which requires all applicants applying for an original, or renewal real estate license to submit proof that they are either a United States citizen or a legal resident alien who is entitled to receive a public benefit.

Although the most common document used to establish proof of U.S. citizenship is a birth certificate, there are other acceptable documents. For a list of the most common documents which can be used to establish U.S. citizenship or legal alien status, go to the DRE website at http://www.dre.ca.gov/proof.htm. Since it can take a while to get a certified copy of a birth certificate, and possibly longer for other kinds of documents, be sure to obtain the appropriate documentation as early as possible to avoid processing delays. The document that is submitted to establish legal presence must be accompanied by a completed state Public Benefits Statement. A license certificate cannot be issued until the appropriate documentation showing legal presence is received and approved by the DRE.

Out-of-State Applicants

A person does not have to live in California in order to become licensed in this state, but you must take the appropriate written examination in California and meet all other requirements. California has no reciprocity with any other state to allow a waiver of any of the requirements to obtain a license.

Out-of-state residents must file an irrevocable Consent to Service of Process with the California Department of Real Estate. Brokers must maintain a California business address if engaging in business in California, and salespersons must be licensed with a California broker if engaging in business in California.

Types of Licenses

Currently the DRE issues real estate broker and salesperson licenses for a four-year period as well as the 18-month conditional salesperson license. If a license is obtained by fraud, misrepresentation, or deceit, the Commissioner may suspend the license, without a hearing, within 90 days after its issuance.

Salesperson License

A person who applies for the salesperson license with proof of completion of Real Estate Principles, as well as Real Estate Practice and one more college level real estate course, will be issued a four-year license. However, most people apply for their license after having completed Real Estate Principles and will be issued an 18-month conditional license. A salesperson with a conditional license must submit evidence of coursework completion to the DRE showing completion of Real Estate Practice and one more real estate licensing course. If the DRE does not receive the proof of completion, the conditional license will be suspended. The suspension can be lifted by submitting the required course information within four years from the date the license was issued. If not, the license may not be renewed.

Broker License

A real estate broker is a person who may run a brokerage business under his or her own name, or under a fictitious business name. Any broker who places his or her license with an employing broker is called a broker associate and must have a written employment agreement.

Fictitious Business Name

A licensed real estate broker, corporation, or partnership may use a **fictitious name** (DBA) or any name other than their own. They must submit a copy of a Fictitious Business Name Statement that is filed with the county clerk's office in the county where the principal place of business is located. Each fictitious business name is an addition to the existing license, and it will expire at the same time as the license. The broker's main office license certificate will show the multiple fictitious business names. All other business locations will be designated as branch offices. For each additional business location, the broker must obtain a branch office license permit. A broker and his or her sales associates may work under any fictitious business name at any business location maintained by the broker. Filing a Fictitious Business Name Statement is good for five years from December 31st of the year filed.

Corporate Real Estate License

A **corporation** may be licensed as a real estate broker as long as one officer of the corporation is a qualified real estate broker and acts as the corporation's responsible designated broker-officer. Salespersons may be employed by a corporate real estate broker as long as they are supervised by the designated broker-officer.

Partnership

The DRE does not issue partnership licenses. A real estate business may be run as a partnership as long as every partner through whom the partnership acts is a licensed real estate broker. A salesperson may be employed by a broker who is a member of a partnership formed by written agreement and may work in any branch office managed by any one of the partners.

Broker's Responsibilities

An active broker must maintain an office (home office is acceptable), and if associate licensees are employed, the licenses must be available for inspection. A broker must have written agreements with his or her sales associates, whether licensed as a salesperson or as a broker associate. Licenses must be available for inspection in the broker's main office, not a branch office. A broker must supervise his or her associate licensees (both sales associates and broker associates). All contracts generated by the associate licensees must be reviewed, initialed, and dated within five working days by the broker. A broker can designate a salesperson with two years of experience within the last five years to manage an office and review contracts as long as the broker supervises the salesperson.

The broker must notify the Commissioner if a salesperson or associate broker transfers his or her license to another broker. The broker must return the license certificate to the salesperson or broker associate within three business days following the transfer. The old broker must notify the Commissioner immediately of the associate licensee's departure; and the new employing broker must notify the Commissioner within five days of arrival. If an associate licensee is fired for cause, the broker must immediately send the Commissioner a certified written statement of facts of the termination.

The broker must obtain workers' compensation coverage either through the state-recognized self-insurance program or through a carrier recognized by the California Department of Insurance for all employees.

Restricted License

The Commissioner will sometimes issue a restricted license. A **restricted license** is a type of probationary license issued when a license has been suspended, revoked, or denied after a hearing. Typically, restrictions are placed by: term (one month, three months, etc.), employment by a particular broker (for a salesperson), limitation to a certain type of activity, requiring detailed reports of each transaction, requiring the filing of a surety bond, or any combination.

If a real estate broker license is revoked or suspended by the DRE, any salesperson licenses held by that broker are cancelled until the license is transferred to a new employing broker.

> **Review - License Facts:**
> - Brokers and salespersons are both licensees.
> - Brokers are agents of the principal.
> - Salespersons are agents of their broker (not the principal).
> - A salesperson must be employed by a broker to be paid.
> - A salesperson can only be paid by his or her employing broker.

Renewing a Real Estate License

In general, both types of licenses may be renewed by submitting the appropriate fee and application, along with evidence of completion of 45 hours of DRE-approved continuing education courses. Both broker and salesperson licenses are valid for four years and may be renewed at that time upon payment of a fee and evidence that the requirements for continuing education have been met.

If there are delinquent child support payments, a four-year license will not be renewed or issued. The California Department of Child Support Services prepares a list of people, called "obligors", who owe child support payments. A child support obligor may be issued a 150-day temporary license. During the 150 days, a person must show the DRE proof that the delinquency is cleared and that he or she has been removed from the list, so that a permanent license can be issued. In addition, a license may be suspended if a licensee's child support remains unpaid.

eLicensing Transactions

The DRE now offers eLicensing, an interactive online system that lets you complete license renewal and change transactions via the Internet. The following list includes many of the available transactions.

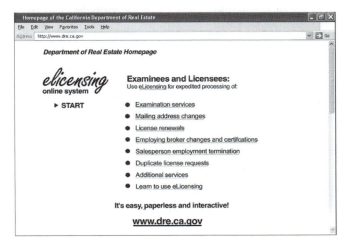

The DRE home page

eLicensing Transactions

- License renewals

- Searches for approved CE courses

- Searches for approved pre-license education courses

- Examination services

- License status checks

- Licensee mailing address changes

- Broker main office address changes

- Salesperson requests to change employing broker

- Broker certification of salesperson employment

- Duplicate license requests

- Requests to receive the Real Estate Bulletin electronically

User-friendly features include customized menus, e-mail confirmations, status tracking of online transactions, and clear instructions. eLicensing is available on the DRE website at http://www.dre.ca.gov/

Late Renewal

A real estate license that has expired may be renewed within two years of the expiration date. A **two-year grace period** for renewal is allowed as long as all real estate activity has ceased during that time and a late fee is paid at the time of renewal. There is no provision for an inactive license status. Two years after a license expires, all license rights lapse, and the person will have to go through the state examination process again to get another real estate license.

However, if a broker's license expires, all licensed activities of the broker must stop and all of the broker's salespersons (if any) are immediately placed in a non-working status. Any branch office licenses are cancelled. That means no listing, selling, showing, leasing or any licensed activity between the date of license expiration, and the date of late renewal. A commission may not be claimed without a valid license. Once the broker has renewed his or her license, all the salesperson licenses and branch office licenses must be reactivated.

When a salesperson is discharged for a violation of any of the provisions of the Real Estate Law, the employing broker must immediately file a certified written statement of the facts with the Commissioner.

Continuing Education

Each time brokers and salespersons renew their licenses—every four years—they must present evidence of completing the required continuing education (CE) courses.

Initial Renewal - Salesperson

There is a 12-hour CE requirement for the first renewal of a salesperson license. The required courses are three hours of agency, three hours of ethics, three hours of fair housing, and three hours of trust fund accounting.

Initial Renewal - Broker

There is a 45-hour CE requirement for the first renewal of a broker license. The required courses are three hours of agency, three hours of ethics, three hours of fair housing, three hours of trust fund accounting, and 33 more CE hours of which 18 hours must be in the consumer protection category.

Subsequent Renewals - Broker and Salesperson

There is a 45-hour CE requirement for subsequent renewal of a broker or salesperson license. Everyone must take the mandatory courses and may choose from either the four three-hour courses or the six-hour survey course. The balance of the required hours must include at least 18 hours of consumer protection topics.

Initial Renewals

Initial Salesperson Renewal - 12 hrs		Initial Broker Renewal - 45 hrs	
Renewal Course	Hours	Renewal Course	Hours
Agency	3	Agency	3
Ethics	3	Ethics	3
Fair Housing	3	Fair Housing	3
Trust Funds	3	Trust Funds	3
Consumer Protection	0	Consumer Protection	33
Total Hours	12	*Total Hours*	45

Subsequent Renewals - Broker and Salesperson

Choice A - 45 Hours		Choice B - 45 Hours	
Renewal Course	Hours	Renewal Course	Hours
Agency	3	Agency	0
Ethics	3	Ethics	0
Fair Housing	3	Fair Housing	0
Trust Funds	3	Trust Funds	0
Consumer Protection	33	Consumer Protection	0
Survey Course	0	Survey Course	6
Consumer Protection	0	Consumer Protection	39
Total Hours	45	*Total Hours*	45

Enforcing the Real Estate Law

The license law is only effective if it can be enforced. The Commissioner can only investigate non-licensed persons but can discipline licensed persons.

Non-Licensed Activities

Representatives of the Commissioner also investigate persons or firms who appear to be operating improperly, without benefit of a license, or who subdivide land without complying with the subdivision laws enforced by the Commissioner. If sufficient evidence of a violation is obtained, an **Order to Desist and Refrain** is issued, or a complaint is brought, and the parties are prosecuted in a court of competent jurisdiction.

Licensed Activities

The Commissioner enforces the provisions of the real estate law and has the power to restrict, suspend, or revoke the real estate license. Some violations may result in civil injunctions, criminal prosecutions, or substantial fines. When the Commissioner investigates a complaint, which may involve criminal activities, it is the duty of the local district attorneys to prosecute all criminals in their respective counties.

The Commissioner must follow the established legal procedures found in the Administrative Procedure Act to discipline licensees.

> **Only the Commissioner—not the courts—can restrict, suspend or revoke a real estate license.**

Investigation and Accusation

Usually an investigation of the actions of a licensee is based upon receipt of a verified written complaint from someone who believes a licensee, while acting as an agent, has wronged them. Investigations are made by the DRE's Enforcement and Audit Sections and include taking statements from witnesses and the licensee and obtaining and verifying documents, if needed. An informal conference may be called to determine the validity and seriousness of the complaint. If it appears that the complaint is of a serious nature and that a violation of law has occurred, an accusation is filed, and there may be a formal hearing, which could result in suspension or revocation of the license.

Investigations are made by the DRE and include taking statements and obtaining documents if needed.

Formal Hearings

A formal hearing is held according to the Administrative Procedures Act. The accusation or statement of issues is served upon the affected licensee. In the hearing, the Commissioner is the complainant and brings the charges against the licensee. The licensee, known as the respondent, may appear with or without an attorney. The Commissioner's counsel presents the case to an administrative law judge who issues a proposed decision based upon the findings.

The Commissioner may accept, reject, or reduce the proposed penalty from the administrative law judge and makes an official decision. Sometimes the charges against the respondent (licensee) are dismissed, but if the charges are

A formal hearing is held according to the Administrative Procedure Act.

sufficiently serious, the license of the respondent is suspended or revoked. A person whose license has been revoked or suspended must wait one year until he or she can apply for reinstatement.

Recovery Account

A **Real Estate Recovery Fund** is a separate account funded through collection of a fixed amount from each license fee. It assures the payment of otherwise non-collectable court judgments against licensees who have committed fraud, misrepresentation, deceit, or conversion of trust funds in a transaction. Under specific conditions of law, the person with a qualifying judgment may seek reimbursement from the Recovery Account for actual and direct loss to a statutory maximum. Currently the amount paid will be $20,000 per transaction, with a possible total aggregate maximum of $100,000 per licensee.

If the Commissioner pays a judgment on behalf of a broker or salesperson, the license is automatically suspended. A suspended license will only be reinstated after full reimbursement, plus interest, is repaid to the DRE.

Violations of the Real Estate Law

Staying informed is probably the most important task left to the real estate agent. Real estate agents who make continuing efforts to learn and stay current on issues concerning the real estate industry will have successful careers.

Real estate agents must be prepared to meet the duties and obligations required by law. If they do not comply, they may be subject to civil, criminal and/or Department of Real Estate action and penalties. All around the country, courts, and legislatures are continuing to hold real estate agents accountable for their activities. Increasingly, agents must know what and how to disclose—as well as when, where, why, by, and to whom. The uninformed real estate agent is highly vulnerable to court action in our consumer-oriented society.

The Real Estate Commissioner is empowered to adopt regulations to enforce the real estate law. Duly adopted regulations become part of the California Code of Regulations and, in effect, have the force and authority of the law itself. Real estate law is found in the Business and Professions Code.

Therefore, all licensees and prospective licensees should be thoroughly familiar with the Real Estate Commissioner's Regulations. They should be considered in conjunction with the law, as they specifically outline procedures directed and authorized by the statutes. The following is a partial listing of the Business and Professions Code sections that are of utmost importance to those who practice real estate.

The Business and Professions Code, Article 3, Section 10175 authorizes the Real Estate Commissioner to enforce the real estate law. Upon grounds provided in this article and the other articles of this chapter, the license of any real estate licensee may be revoked or suspended in accordance with the provisions of this part relating to hearings.

Although most violations of real estate law occur under sections 10176 and 10177 of the Business and Professions Code, we are including some of the other sections that need discussion and mention. Section 10176 refers to actions committed while conducting business under a real estate license. Section 10177 refers to circumstances when a licensee is not necessarily acting as an agent.

Section 10176:   Violations When Acting as an Agent in a Real Estate Transaction

The Commissioner may upon his or her own motion, and shall upon the verified complaint in writing of any person, investigate the actions of any person engaged in the business or acting in the capacity of a real estate licensee within this state. He also may temporarily suspend or permanently revoke a real estate license at any time where the real estate licensee, in performing or attempting to perform any of the acts within the scope of this chapter has been guilty of any of the following:

Section 10176(a)   Misrepresentation

A great majority of the complaints received are about misrepresentation on the part of the broker or salesperson. The failure of a broker or salesperson to disclose to his or her principal material facts of which the principal should be made aware is included as a cause for discipline under this section.

Section 10176(b)   False Promise

A false promise and a misrepresentation are not the same thing. A misrepresentation is a false statement of fact. A false promise is a false statement about what someone is going to do in the future.

Section 10176(c)   Continued Misrepresentation

The Commissioner has the right to discipline a licensee for a continued and flagrant course of misrepresentation or making of false promises.

Section 10176(d)   Dual Agency

A licensee must inform all principals if the licensee is acting as agent for more than one party in a transaction.

Section 10176(e)   Commingling

Commingling is the mixing of the principal's funds with the broker's own money. Commingling is not the same thing as conversion. Conversion is misappropriating and using principal's funds.

Section 10176(f)   Definite Termination Date

A specified termination date is required on all exclusive listings relating to transactions for which a real estate license is required.

Section 10176(g)   Secret Profit

Secret profit cases usually arise when the broker already has a higher offer from another buyer, but the seller is not aware of it yet. The broker makes a low offer, usually through a "dummy" purchaser. The broker then sells the property to the interested buyer for the higher price. The difference is the secret profit.

Section 10176(h)   Listing-Option

A licensee who has both a listing and an option to buy on a property must inform the principal of the amount of profit the licensee will make and obtain the written consent of the principal approving the amount of such profit, before the licensee may exercise the option.

Section 10176(i)   Dishonest Dealing

"Dishonest dealing" is a catch-all section similar to Section 10177(f). The difference is that under Section 10176(i) the acts must have been those requiring a license, while there is no such need under Section 10177(f).

Section 10176(j)   Signatures of Prospective Purchasers

Brokers must obtain a written authorization to sell from a business owner before securing the signature of a prospective purchaser to any such agreement.

10176.5(a)   Real Estate Transfer Disclosure Statement Violations

The commissioner may suspend or revoke a licensee's license if the licensee has willfully or repeatedly violated any of the provisions of the Transfer Disclosure Statement provisions.

Section 10177: Violations When Not Acting as an Agent in a Real Estate Transaction

The Commissioner may suspend or revoke the license of a real estate licensee or may deny the issuance of a license to an applicant, who has done any of the following, or may suspend or revoke the license of a corporation, or deny the issuance of a license to a corporation, if an officer, director, or person owning or controlling 10 percent or more of the corporation's stock has done any of the following:

Section 10177(a)   Obtaining a License by Fraud

The Commissioner may proceed against a licensee for misstatements of fact in an application for a license and in those instances where licenses have been procured by fraud, misrepresentation, or deceit.

Section 10177(b)   Convictions

This section permits proceeding against a licensee after a criminal conviction for either a felony or a misdemeanor which involves moral turpitude and is substantially related to the qualifications, functions, or duties of a real estate licensee. Moral turpitude would be perjury, embezzlement, robbery, and the like.

Section 10177(c)   False Advertising

Licensees who are parties to "bait and switch" and false advertising are subject to disciplinary action.

Section 10177(d)   Violations of Other Sections

This section is the Department's authority to proceed against the licensee for violation of any of the other sections of the Real Estate Law, the Regulations of the Commissioner, and the subdivision laws.

Section 10177(e)   Misuse of Trade Name

Only active members of the National Association of REALTORS® may use the term REALTOR®. It is unlawful and unethical to misuse the terms "REALTOR®" and/or "Realtist" or any trade name or insignia of which the licensee is not a member.

Section 10177(f) Conduct Warranting Denial

This is a general section of the Real Estate Law. Almost any act involving a crime or dishonesty will fall within this section including the denial or suspension of a license issued by another government agency.

Section 10177(g)   Negligence or Incompetence

Demonstrated negligence or incompetence, while acting as a licensee, is cause for disciplinary action.

Section 10177(h)   Supervision of Salespersons

A broker is subject to disciplinary action if the broker, or the officer designated by a corporate broker licensee, fails to exercise reasonable supervision over the activities of the broker's salespersons.

Section 10177(i)   Violating Government Trust

A licensee may not use government employment to violate the confidential nature of records thereby made available.

Section 10177(j)   Other Dishonest Conduct

Any other conduct which constitutes fraud or dishonest dealing may subject the one so involved to license suspension or revocation.

Section 10177(k)   Restricted License Violation

Violations of the terms, conditions, restrictions, and limitations contained in any order granting a restricted license are grounds for disciplinary action.

Section 10177(l)   Inducement of Panic Selling

This is also called blockbusting or panic peddling. A licensee may not solicit or induce the sale, lease, or the listing for sale or lease of residential property on the grounds of loss of value, increase in crime, or decline in the quality of schools due to the present or prospective entry into the neighborhood of a person or persons of another race, color, religion, ancestry, or national origin.

Section 10177(m)   Franchise Investment Law

A licensee may not violate any of the provisions of the Franchise Investment Law or any regulations of the Corporations Commissioner Franchise Investment Law.

Section 10177(n)   Corporations Code

A licensee may not violate any of the provisions of the Corporations Code or of the regulations of the Commissioner of Corporations relating to securities as specified by the Corporations Code.

Section 10177(o)   Conflict of Interest

A licensee must disclose to the buyer of real property, in a transaction in which the licensee is an agent for the buyer, the nature and extent of a licensee's direct or indirect ownership interest in that real property.

Section 10177.1.   Obtaining a License by Fraud

Within 90 days of issuing a license, the Commissioner may without a hearing suspend the license of any person who procured the issuance of the license to himself by fraud, misrepresentation, deceit, or by the making of any material misstatement of fact in his application for such license.

Section 10177.2.   Mobile Home Sales Violations

When dealing with mobile homes/manufactured homes a licensee could have his or her license suspended or revoked if he or she is found guilty of any of the following acts: committed fraud on an application for the registration of a mobile home; did not deliver a properly endorsed certificate of ownership from the seller to the buyer; knowingly purchased or sold a stolen mobile home; or gave the Department of Housing and Community Development a bad check, draft, or money order.

Section 10177.4.   Referral of Customers for Compensation

A real estate licensee must not receive a commission, fee, or other consideration as compensation or inducement for referral of customers to any escrow agent, structural pest control firm, home protection company, title insurer, or controlled escrow company.

Section 10177.5.   Fraud in a Civil Action

If a final judgment is obtained in a civil action against any real estate licensee upon grounds of fraud, misrepresentation, or deceit with reference to any transaction for which a license is required, the commissioner may, after hearing, suspend or revoke the license of such real estate licensee.

ABC Real Estate Company
REAL ESTATE HALL OF SHAME
VIOLATIONS

FALSE PROMISE
Section 10176b

COMMINGLING
Section 10176e

MISREPRESENTATION
Section 10176a

Real estate agents must be prepared to meet the duties and obligations required by law.

Other Violations

Section 10137. and 10138. Employing or Paying an Unlicensed Person.

A broker may not pay a commission to an unlicensed person, except to a broker of another state. A licensed salesperson may not accept compensation from anyone except his or her employing broker. The broker may be fined $100.

Section 10140. False Advertising

Every broker, associate licensee, officer, or employee of any company who knowingly authorizes or directs the publication, distribution, or circulation of any written statement that is false or fraudulent is guilty of a public offense. Punishment includes a $1,000 fine, imprisonment up to one year, or both. In addition a real estate licensee may have his or her license revoked by the Commissioner. The district attorney of each county prosecutes all violations in the counties in which the violations occur.

Section 10140.5. License Name and Designation

An advertisement must include the name of the broker and that he or she is a licensed California real estate broker.

Section 10140.6. Blind Advertising

Failing to disclose that the party is a licensee acting as an agent and the use of the terms "broker", "agent", "REALTOR®", "loan correspondent" or the abbreviations "bro.", "agt.", or other similar terms or abbreviations is deemed sufficient identification to fulfill the designation requirements of Section 10140.6 of the Business and Professions Code. (Commissioner's Regulation 2770.1).

Section 10141. Selling Price Disclosure

A broker must notify the buyer and the seller of the selling price within one month after completion of the sale. It is usually done by the escrow company.

Section 10141.5. Recording Trust Deed

A broker (or escrow company) must record a trust deed created on the sale of a property within one week of closing.

Section 10142. Delivery of Agreement

A broker must give a copy of any contract to the party signing it at the time that it is signed.

Section 10148. Document Retention

A broker must retain the following documents for three years from the date of the closing or, if the transaction is not closed, from the date of the listing: listings, deposit receipts, cancelled checks, trust records, disclosure documents and other related documents. A Mortgage Loan Disclosure Statement needs to be kept for only three years.

10175.2(a) Monetary Penalty in Lieu of Suspension

The Real Estate Commissioner may permit a real estate licensee to pay a monetary penalty to the department in lieu of an actual license suspension.

Section 10178. Broker Must Report Discharge of Salesperson for Violation

When any real estate salesperson is discharged by his or her employer for a violation of any of the provisions of the Real Estate Law, a certified written statement of the facts with reference thereto shall be filed forthwith with the Commissioner by the employer. If the employer fails to notify the Commissioner as required by this section, the Commissioner may temporarily suspend or permanently revoke the real estate license of the employer, in accordance with the provisions of this part relating to hearings.

Section 10182. Reinstatement Examination

As a condition to the reinstatement of a revoked or suspended license, the Commissioner may require the applicant to take and pass a qualifying examination.

Section 10185. Violations Are Misdemeanors

Any person, including officers, directors, agents, or employees of corporations, who willfully violates or knowingly participates in the violation of this division shall be guilty of a misdemeanor punishable by a fine not exceeding $10,000, imprisonment in the county jail not exceeding six months, or a fine and imprisonment.

Summary

Real estate licensees have many responsibilities. Initially, they must complete qualifying courses and pass a real estate license examination. Later on they have to complete continuing education courses to renew their licenses. Licensees are also responsible to their broker, the real estate law, and the Department of Real Estate (DRE).

Each real estate brokerage office must have one responsible broker who may have salespersons or brokers working out of the office. A brokerage may be incorporated or a partnership.

The cornerstone of real estate transactions is ethics and fair dealing. Real estate licensees must obey the real estate law and the Regulations of the Real Estate Commissioner. The **Real Estate Commissioner** and the Department of Real Estate (DRE) supervise the education, licensing, and conduct of real estate professionals. Real estate licensees involved in business opportunities need to be familiar with the Uniform Commercial Code.

Real estate regulations uphold the federal and state fair housing laws which prohibit discrimination in housing and business establishments. Examples of prohibited practices are block-busting (causing panic selling by telling people that values in a neighborhood will decline because of a specific event), steering (the practice of only showing clients property in certain areas), and redlining (the use of the location of the property to deny financing).

Real estate regulations uphold fair housing laws which prohibit discrimination based on factors such as age, race, sex, or religion.

Chapter 15 Review Exercises

Matching Exercise

Instructions: Look up the meaning of the terms in the Glossary, then write the letter of the matching term on the blank line before its definition. Answers are in Appendix B.

Terms

a. 18-month conditional license

b. accusation

c. blind advertising

d. branch offices

e. conversion

f. false promise

g. fictitious business name

h. license law

i. misrepresentation

j. obligors

k. panic peddling

l. Real Estate Advisory Commission

m. real estate broker

n. Real Estate Commissioner

o. real estate law

p. Real Estate Recovery Fund

q. real estate salesperson

r. restricted license

s. secret profit

t. two-year grace period

Definitions

1. _____ Another name for the Business and Professions Code, Part 1 entitled "Licensing of Persons."

2. _____ Another term for the real estate law.

3. _____ Person appointed by the governor to determine administrative policy and enforce the provisions of the real estate law and the Subdivided Lands Law.

4. _____ A 10-member commission that offers advice to the Commissioner on matters pertinent to the DRE.

5. _____ Someone with real estate license who must be employed by a real estate broker in order to perform any of the activities that require a license.

6. _____ Initial license issued to real estate salesperson who has only completed the Real Estate Principles course.

7. _____ Type of probationary license issued when a license has been suspended, revoked or denied after a hearing.

8. _____ A person listed by Child Support Services as delinquent in paying child support.

9. _____ The period of time after a license that renewal is allowed, as long as all real estate activity has ceased during that time and a late fee is paid at the time of renewal.

10. _____ A separate account funded through collection of a fixed amount from each license fee.

11. _____ A false statement of fact.

12. _____ A false statement about what someone is going to do in the future.

13. _____ Misappropriating and using principal's funds.

14. _____ Undisclosed profit made by a broker at his or her principal's expense.

15. _____ Advertising that fails to disclose that the party is a licensee acting as an agent.

Multiple Choice Questions

Instructions: Circle your response and go to Appendix B to read the complete explanation for each question.

1. Broker Larwin held an open listing to sell a house that provided for Larwin to receive a 6% commission. Larwin orally agreed to split the commission with Broker Porter if Porter found the buyer. Porter did so, but at close of escrow Larwin kept the entire commission. Under these circumstances, Porter:
    a. has recourse by means of a civil suit.
    b. has recourse under the real estate law.
    c. has recourse under the Statute of Frauds.
    d. does not have a legal claim for a commission because Larwin had an open listing.

2. The Department of Real Estate regards a salesperson's relationship with a broker as a(n):
    a. employee.
    b. independent contractor.
    c. general partner.
    d. limited partner.

3. Someone places an advertisement for real estate services without listing a real estate license number. In fact, the person does not have a real estate license. Such an individual could be liable for prosecution by the:
   a. Department of Real Estate.
   b. local district attorney.
   c. office of the Attorney General.
   d. local law enforcement agencies.

4. Which of the following is required to hold a current and valid California real estate license?
   a. A mortgage loan broker
   b. A resident manager of an apartment building
   c. A trustee conducting a trust deed foreclosure sale
   d. A short-term (vacation) rental agent

5. A broker must have a written contract with which of the following employees?
   a. Secretaries
   b. Janitorial service
   c. Brokers acting as salespersons who do not have their own office
   d. All of the above

6. If a real estate licensee is listed as an "obligor" by the California Department of Child Support Services, can he or she renew his or her real estate license?
   a. No, the DRE revokes the license of anyone who owes child support.
   b. Yes, the DRE is not concerned with the "obligor" list.
   c. No, whenever a person is listed as an "obligor" for delinquent child support, all licenses, including the driver license, are canceled.
   d. Yes, the licensee may be issued a 150-day temporary license.

7. A licensed salesperson gave notice of leaving the real estate brokerage office to the salesperson's employing broker. What, if anything, must the broker do with the salesperson's license?
   a. The broker leaves the license unmarked and gives it to the next broker who employs the salesperson.
   b. The broker returns the license to the salesperson and notifies the Real Estate Commissioner.
   c. The broker marks the license "inactivated," returns it to the salesperson, and notifies the Real Estate Commissioner.
   d. The broker marks the license "cancelled" and mails it to the Real Estate Commissioner.

8. In the course of his or her duties, a real estate salesperson might prepare or sign documents or legal instruments that may have a material effect on the rights or obligations of those entering the transaction. The supervising broker must review, initial, and date these documents or instruments within five days or before the close of escrow. However, the broker may delegate these duties to a salesperson to review items prepared by other salespeople provided that the delegated salesperson has:
    a. been employed by that same broker for at least two years full time.
    b. been employed by that same broker for at least two years full time and has completed at least 18 units of college-level courses related to real estate.
    c. at least two years full-time experience as a real estate salesperson within the past five years.
    d. at least two years full-time experience as a real estate salesperson within the past five years and has completed at least 18 units of college-level courses related to real estate.

9. A broker holding an unrestricted license negotiated the sale of real estate. The broker defrauded the buyer during the sales transaction. The defrauded buyer brought a civil suit against the broker on grounds of fraud and was awarded a final judgment. The Real Estate Commissioner:
    a. may suspend the broker's license when the Commissioner receives a copy of the final judgment of the court.
    b. must wait to take action until the buyer files a formal complaint with the Commissioner.
    c. may suspend the broker's license until a formal hearing is convened.
    d. may hold a hearing but may not suspend or revoke the license until the hearing is concluded.

10. A broker assured a client that a loan could be found at 5% even though there were no such loans available. When it came time to sign the agreement, the rate offered was 7%. The buyer felt he had to accept the loan because he had already given notice at his apartment complex.
    a. The broker acted unethically.
    b. The broker acted illegally.
    c. The broker acted legally.
    d. The doctrine of caveat emptor applies.

11. By law, a broker must keep a copy of the deposit receipt for at least three years from:
    a. the first date on the deposit receipt.
    b. the closing of the transaction.
    c. the recording of the deed.
    d. whichever of the above is earliest.

12. Davis did not have a real estate license but negotiated a contract with Taylor to buy Taylor's 20-acre lot for $5,000/acre. Taylor accepted Davis' offer. During negotiations, Davis himself was offered $20,000/acre by a third party for the same 20 acres. Davis did not disclose this fact to Taylor and went ahead with the purchase. Davis later sold the 20 acres to the third party for $20,000/acre. Taylor subsequently learned that Davis resold the lot. Under these circumstances, an attorney will probably advise that:

    a. Taylor may rescind the contract if Taylor reimburses the third party for expenses incurred in the transaction.

    b. Taylor has no recourse against Davis.

    c. Taylor has a cause of action against Davis because Davis had special knowledge of the property that was not disclosed during the transaction.

    d. Taylor must show that the third party had knowledge of the realistic property value.

13. A licensed real estate salesperson regularly accepted a fee for every client she referred to a lender who signed up for a new mortgage loan. When her employing broker discovered this arrangement, the broker took two steps: (1) The broker fired the salesperson. (2) The broker explicitly warned the rest of the office not to engage in such practices. Who, if anyone, is liable for disciplinary action?

    a. No one. The Real Estate Law was not violated.

    b. Only the broker can be disciplined.

    c. Only the salesperson can be disciplined because the broker had no "guilty knowledge" of the offense.

    d. Both the salesperson and broker can be disciplined.

14. If an employing broker discharges a salesperson for violating a provision of the Real Estate Law, the broker:

    a. must notify the Real Estate Commissioner within three days of the termination of the salesperson.

    b. must telephone the Commissioner immediately.

    c. must notify the Commissioner immediately by mailing a certified written statement of the facts.

    d. is under no duty to inform the Commissioner.

15. Broker Kim, who is not a member of any trade organization, has been trying out a new advertising slogan: "A new breed of Realtor." This practice is:

    a. grounds for revocation or suspension of her real estate license.

    b. permissible, providing the word "realtor" is not capitalized.

    c. acceptable as long as she is not licensed in more than one state.

    d. a violation of the Fair Housing Laws.

16. An advertisement for a listing placed by a real estate salesperson must include the:
    a. name of the employing broker.
    b. employing broker's name and address.
    c. salesperson's name.
    d. both (b) and (c).

17. Broker Pat has a property listed for nine months without success. He believes the property is 10% overpriced, and he knows that major structural repairs are required. Pat writes and pays for the following advertisement to run in a local newspaper: "Charming 2 BDRM Victorian. Move in right away! Wait `til you see the price! Ready for you! Call Pat at 555-1212." What, if anything, is wrong with the advertisement?
    a. There is no asking price: Regulation Z was violated.
    b. It was unlawful because Pat knew structural work was required and the ad did not state this.
    c. It was unethical to advertise for overpriced property.
    d. The newspaper publisher would be liable for damages if anyone purchased the property as a result of the advertisement.

18. A "blind" ad does not disclose the:
    a. price of the property.
    b. name of the broker.
    c. name of the seller.
    d. address of the property.

19. A broker who holds a valid listing on a property places the following classified advertisement in the local newspaper: "FOR SALE: 3 bedroom, 2 bath home, swimming pool. $129,000. Telephone 555-1234." The advertisement is an example of a _____ ad.
    a. silent
    b. display
    c. qualified
    d. blind

20. After close of escrow, the actual selling price of the property must be disclosed to both buyer and seller within:
    a. 5 business days.
    b. 10 business days.
    c. 15 days.
    d. 1 month.

Real Estate Math

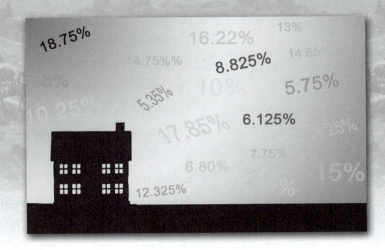

Appendix

Introduction

This chapter will explain the basic mathematical procedures you will need to be successful in your new real estate career. Many people are intimidated by the word "math", but in this case the concepts presented for your understanding are mainly a review of information you already possess—and probably use in your daily life. An understanding of the principles and formulas explained in this chapter will help you as a licensee in solving math problems you will meet everyday.

Learning Objectives

After reading this appendix, you will be able to:

- calculate the selling price of a property.
- calculate the broker (any sales associate) split of a commission.
- calculate the original amount of a note.
- calculate the yield on a discounted trust deed purchase.
- prorate insurance in escrow.
- calculate documentary tax.
- calculate net operating income and property value.
- calculate a percentage of profit.
- calculate acreage in multiple parcels.

Basic Math Principles

It is important to review math basics including terminology, decimals, percentages, measurements, conversions, and formulas before starting our study of how to solve various real estate problems.

Terminology

Decimal point	The period that sets apart a whole number from a fractional part of that number.
Divisor	A number by which another number is divided.
Dividend	A number to be divided by another number.
Interest	The charge for the use of money.
Principal	The amount of money borrowed.
Proration	The process of making a fair distribution of expenses, through escrow, at the close of the sale.
Rate	The percentage of interest charged on the principal.
Time	The duration of a loan.
Annual	Once per year
Semiannual	Twice per year at 6-month intervals
Biannual	Twice per year
Monthly	Every month
Bimonthly	Every 2 months
Semimonthly	Twice a month
1 year	For escrow and proration purposes, 360 days, 12 months, 52 weeks
1 month	For escrow purposes, 30 days

Decimals and Percentages

It will be beneficial to review the concept of decimals here before starting our study of how to solve various real estate problems. The period that sets apart a whole number from a fractional part of that number is called a **decimal point**. The value of the number is determined by the position of the decimal point.

Any numerals to the right of the decimal point are less than one. The "10th" position is the first position to the right of the decimal point, the "100th" position is the second to the right of the decimal point, the "1,000th" position is the third to the right of the decimal point, and so forth.

The whole numerals are to the left of the decimal point. The "units" are in the first position to the left of the decimal point, the "10s" in the second position to the left of the decimal point, the "100s" in the third position to the left of the decimal point, the "1,000s" in the fourth position to the left of the decimal point, and so forth.

Equivalent Amounts

Percentage	Decimal	Fraction
4 1/2%	0.045	45/1000
6 2/3%	0.0667	1/15
10%	0.10	1/10
12 1/2%	0.125	1/8
16 2/3%	0.1667	1/6
25%	0.25	1/4
33 1/3%	0.33	1/3
50%	0.50	1/2
66 2/3%	0.667	2/3
75%	0.75	3/4
100%	1.00	1/1

Converting Percentages to Decimals

Looking at a number expressed as a percentage, such as 10% or 20%, the decimal point is assumed to be on the right side of the number. Move the decimal point two places to the left to remove the percentage sign and add a zero if necessary.

Example:

6.0%	becomes	0.06
30.0%	becomes	0.30
2.3%	becomes	0.023
210.0%	becomes	2.10

Converting Decimals to Percentages

Reverse the above process to convert a number expressed as a decimal to a percentage; in other words, move the decimal point two places to the right.

Example:	0.02	becomes	2.0%
	0.57	becomes	57.0%
	0.058	becomes	5.8%
	9.02	becomes	902.0%

Addition of Decimal Numbers

All numbers must be in a vertical column when adding numbers with decimals. Always be sure to line up the decimals vertically.

Example:

$$\begin{array}{r} 902.360 \\ 2.053 \\ \text{Add} \quad \underline{387.100} \\ 1{,}291.513 \end{array}$$

Subtraction of Decimal Numbers

In subtracting numbers with decimals, the same process is used, making sure to line up the decimals vertically.

Example:

$$\begin{array}{r} 43{,}267.23 \\ \text{Subtract} \quad \underline{235.10} \\ 43{,}032.13 \end{array}$$

Multiplication of Decimal Numbers

After multiplying the numbers just as you would in a non-decimal problem, count the total number of decimal places in the numbers being multiplied and place the decimal point in the answer that many places from the right.

Example:

$$\begin{array}{r} 4.327 \\ \text{Multiply} \quad \underline{82.2000} \\ 355.6794 \end{array}$$

Division of Decimal Numbers

The decimal point must be removed before solving the problem when there is a decimal in the **divisor**. Move the decimal point in the divisor to the right, then move the decimal point in the **dividend** the same number of places to the right. Add zeros to the dividend if it has fewer numerals than are needed to carry out this procedure. Put the decimal point in the answer directly above the new decimal point in the dividend.

Example: $840 \div .021 = 40.000$

$840,000 \div 21 = 40,000$

Quotient

$$\begin{array}{r} 40,000 \\ 02. \overline{\smash{\big)}\,840,000.} \end{array}$$

Dividend

Measurements

1 foot	12 inches
1 square foot	A unit of area equal to 1 foot by 1 foot square (144 square inches)
1 board foot	144 cubic inches (1 foot x 1 foot x 1 inch =144 cu. inches)
Square footage	The number of square feet of livable space in a home
Perimeter	The distance measured around the outside of a geometric shape
1 yard	36 inches or 3 feet
1 square yard	9 square feet
1 mile	5,280 feet or 320 rods
1 rod	16 ½ feet
1 acre	43,560 square feet

Conversions

Convert feet to inches:	multiply the number of feet by 12
Convert inches to feet:	divide the number of inches by 12
Convert yards to feet:	multiply the number of yards by 3
Convert feet to yards:	divide the number of feet by 3
Convert sq. feet to sq. inches:	multiple the number of sq. feet by 144
Convert sq. inches to sq. feet:	divide the number of square inches by 144
Convert sq. yards to sq. feet:	multiply the number of sq. yards by 9
Convert sq. feet to sq. yards:	divide the number of sq. feet by 9

Basic Real Estate Formulas

There are usually only three variables in any real estate problem—two things that are known and one that is unknown. One way to solve these types of problems is to imagine a circle divided into three sections. One third is labeled Made, one third is labeled Paid, and the last third is labeled Rate or Percentage.

Here are the 3 variations of the "Made-Paid" formula.
"Made" equals "Paid" times "Rate"
"Paid" equals "Made" divided by "Rate"
"Rate" equals "Made" divided by "Paid"

Stop and think about this simple way to solve most real estate math problems and look carefully at the circle until you grasp this easy concept.

- Made = Paid x Rate
- Paid = Made ÷ Rate
- Rate = Made ÷ Paid

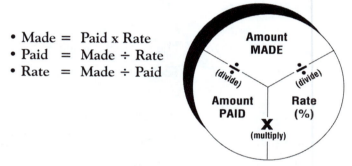

The circle concept for basic real estate formulas.

Whenever you have a math problem, one of these formulas probably can be used. You will always know two of the quantities and will be asked to find the third. From the information given in the problem, you must decide whether to multiply or divide the two numbers that you know in order to find the unknown third number.

When you are asked to find an amount resulting from an interest rate, it usually will be an annual number. Make sure you annualize, or convert any monthly figures to annual or yearly figures by multiplying the monthly figures by 12.

Some math problems will have a two-step solution. In other words, some process (add, subtract, multiply) will have to be performed either before or after the above formula can be applied. Use the circle concept as an easy way to solve the math problems included here. Once you know into which section of the circle your information fits, simply perform the math function indicated.

Solving Real Estate Problems

The following problem-solving techniques are explained for the beginning math student or someone who has not used math techniques for quite some time and just needs a little practice to become proficient.

There are several ways any of the following examples may be solved, and we have attempted to be consistent in our explanations for the beginner. Some students will recognize the algebraic solutions presented, and will use their own techniques for solving the problems.

The math problems presented are similar to those you will experience in real life. Learn to recognize the type of problem, and the math solution it requires, and you will be proficient in your real estate career.

Here are several guidelines for you to follow to answer some of the most basic math questions you will need to solve.

The amount MADE, or earned income, is shown as "**I**" in the formulas. It stands for different types of **income**. For example: commission Income earned by a real estate agent, interest Income earned by the lender or investor and paid by the borrower, net operating Income from an income property, and earned Income from an investment. There are two dollar amounts in a problem: a small amount and a large amount. The amount MADE is the smaller of the two amounts. For example, the broker's commission on a property that sold for $200,000 is never going to be $300,000—that is larger than the sales price! On the following chart, the small "$" sign represents the smaller amount of money.

The amount PAID is also shown as "**P**" in the formulas. It stands for different types of amounts **paid**. For example, sales Price for a property, Principal amount of a loan, the Property value, or the amount Paid for an investment. The amount PAID is the larger of the two amounts because it represents the large amount that is paid or invested. On the following chart, the large "$" sign represents the larger amount of money.

The RATE is also shown as "**R**" in the formulas. The "R" stands for different percentage rates. Whenever you see a "%", it is referring to a **rate**. For example, commission Rate, interest Rate, capitalization Rate, and Rate of return.

Review – Solving Real Estate Problems			
	$	$	%
	MADE	PAID	RATE
	I	P	R
Commissions	Commission Income	Sales Price	Commission **R**ate
Loans	Interest	Principal	Interest **R**ate
Appraisal	Net operating Income	Property value	Cap **R**ate
Investment	Earned Income	Amount Paid	Rate of Return
Selling Price	Increase	Purchase Price	Rate of Profit
Seller's Net	Net Income	Sales Price	Commission **R**ate

Commission Problems

- Paid = Selling Price of Property
- Made = Amount of Commission
- Rate = Commission Rate

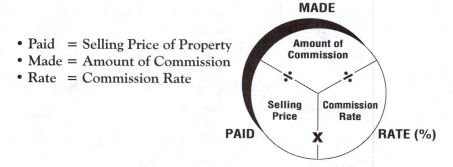

The circle concept for commission problems.

Commission problems involve these three variables:

$$\text{Made} = \mathbf{I} = \$ = \text{Amount of commission Income}$$
$$\text{Paid} = \mathbf{P} = \$ = \text{Selling Price of the property}$$
$$\text{Rate} = \mathbf{R} = \% = \text{Commission Rate}$$

Formulas:

1. When the amount of selling price and the commission rate (%) are given and you are solving for the commission paid (smaller $), use:

$$I = P \times R \quad \text{(Commission Income = Sales Price x \% Rate)}$$

2. When the commission income and commission rate are given and you are solving for sales price (larger $), use:

$$P = I \div R \quad \text{(Sales Price = Commission Income} \div \% \text{ Rate)}$$

3. When the commission income and the sales price are given and you are solving for % (commission rate) use:

$$R = I \div P \quad \text{(\% Rate = Commission Income} \div \text{ Sales Price)}$$

Practice Problem #1

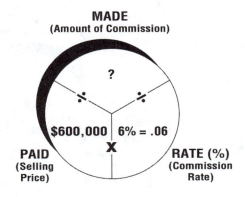

The circle concept for Practice Problem #1.

Effie, a real estate salesperson, found a buyer for a $600,000 house. The seller agreed to pay a 6% commission on the sale to Effie's broker. Effie is on a 50-50 split with her broker. **What is the amount of her commission?**

Known: P (Sales Price, $) and R (Commission Rate %)

> P = $600,000
> R = 6% or 0.06

Unknown: I (Commission Income, $) What we do not know is the dollar amount of the commission paid to the salesperson Effie. First, the total commission paid to the broker must be calculated, then calculate the amount due Effie.

Formula: I = P x R, or Commission Income = Sales Price x Rate

> I = P x R
> I = $600,000 x 0.06
> I = $36,000 (Total commission income earned by the broker.)

Effie's commission = ½ of the total commission earned
Effie's commission = $36,000 ÷ 2
Effie's commission = $18,000

MATH

Practice Problem #2

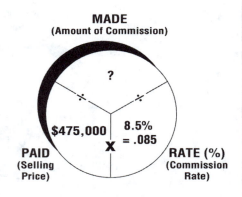

MADE
(Amount of Commission)

?

$475,000

8.5%
= .085

X

PAID
(Selling
Price)

RATE (%)
(Commission
Rate)

The circle concept for Practice Problem #2.

Paul, a real estate broker, listed a parcel of land for $500,000, with a commission of 10%. A few days later he presented an offer which was 5% less than the listed price. The seller agreed to accept the price if the broker would reduce his commission by 15%. If Paul agrees to the seller's proposal, **how much will his commission be?**

Known: P (Sales Price, larger $) and R (Commission Rate, %)

P = $500,000 less 5% ($25,000) = $475,000

R = 10% less 15%

[First calculate 15% of 10% (0.15 x 0.10 = .0150), then subtract it from 10% (.10 - 0.015 = 0.085, or 8.5%]

Unknown: I (Commission Income, smaller $)

What we do not know is the amount of the commission income.

Formula: I = P x R, or Commission Income = Sales Price x Rate

I = P x R

I = $475,000 x 0.085

I = $40,375

Interest and Loan Problems

The charge for the use of money is called **interest**. The rate of interest that is charged will determine the total dollar amount of the payments. When money is borrowed, both the principal and interest must be repaid according to the agreement between the borrower and lender.

> **Review – Interest Terms**
> (P) Principal: dollar amount of money borrowed, loan amount
> (I) Interest: charge for the use of money
> (R) Rate: percentage of interest charged
> (T) Time: duration of loan

When using the Circle Formula to solve interest and loan problems, MADE is the dollar amount of interest, PAID is the principal amount of the loan, and RATE refers to the annual interest rate of the loan.

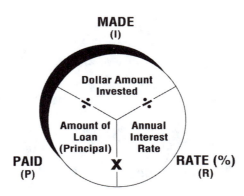

The circle concept for solving interest and loan problems.

Interest and loan problems involve these three variables:

$$\text{Paid} \; = \; \mathbf{P} \; = \; \$ \; = \; \textbf{P}\text{rincipal}$$
$$\text{Made} \; = \; \mathbf{I} \; = \; \$ \; = \; \textbf{I}\text{nterest}$$
$$\text{Rate} \; = \; \mathbf{R} \; = \; \% \; = \; \text{Interest } \textbf{R}\text{ate}$$

Formulas:

1. When the amount of principal and interest rate (%) are given and you are solving for amount of interest earned (smaller $), use:

$$\mathbf{I} = \mathbf{P} \times \mathbf{R} \times \mathbf{T} \quad (\text{Interest} = \textbf{P}\text{rincipal} \times \textbf{R}\text{ate} \times \textbf{T}\text{ime})$$

2. When the interest income and interest rate are given and you are solving for the principal (larger $), use:

$$P = I \div (R \times T) \text{ [Principal = Interest} \div (\% \text{ Rate} \times \text{Time)]}$$

3. When the interest income and the principal are given and you are solving for % (interest rate), use:

$$R = I \div (P \times T) \text{ [Rate = Interest} \div (\text{Principal} \times \text{Time)]}$$

Practice Problem #3

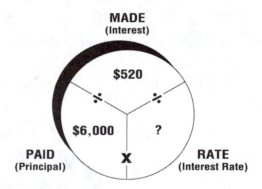

The circle concept for Practice Problem #3.

Andrea borrowed $6,000 for one year and paid $520 interest.

What was the interest rate she paid?

Known: I (Interest Income), P (Principal), and T (Time)

     P = $6,000 (Principal amount of loan)

     I = $520 (Interest income bank made on the loan)

     T = 1 year

Unknown: I (Interest Rate)

     What we do not know is the interest rate Andrea paid.

Formula: R = I ÷ (P x T), or Rate = Income ÷ Principal x Time

     R = I ÷ (P x T)

     R = $520 ÷ ($6,000 x 1)

     R = $520 ÷ $6,000

     R = 0.0867 or 8.67%

Practice Problem #4

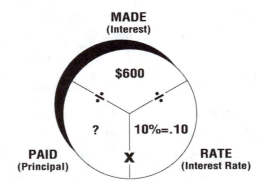

The circle concept for Practice Problem #4.

If one month's interest is $50 on a five-year, straight interest-only note, and the interest rate on the note is 10% per year, **what is the amount of the loan?**

Known: I (Interest Income), P (Principal), and T (Time)

I = $600 (**I**nterest income bank made on the loan)
($50 per month x 12 months = $600)

R = 10% or 0.10

T = 1 year

Unknown: P (Principal)
What we do not know is the larger $ amount of the loan.

Formula: P = I ÷ (R x T), or Principal = Interest ÷ (Rate x Time)

P = $I ÷ (R x T)$

P = $600 ÷ (0.10 x 1)$

P = $600 ÷ 0.10$

P = $6,000

> **Review – Monthly Loan Payment Mnemonic – "PITI"**
>
> **P** Principal
> **I** Interest
> **T** Taxes
> **I** Insurance

As we discussed in Chapter 9, the majority of real estate loans are fully amortized, fixed rate loans. By using a calculator or mortgage tables, you can **calculate the monthly payment of principal (P) and interest (I).** If a lender has requested an impound account to collect taxes and insurance, the borrower will make monthly payments of principal (P), interest (I), property taxes (T), and hazard insurance (I).

Discounting Notes

As you recall, when someone buys a note at a discount, it means the buyer pays less than the dollar amount shown on the note, and the profit is the difference between what the buyer paid and the amount paid when the note is due. In other words, a certain amount is paid for the note, but a greater amount is received when the note is paid off.

When using the Made/Paid formula for discounting notes remember: (1) Made is the total interest payment plus the discount amount, (2) Paid is the original note amount less the discount amount, and (3) Rate is the rate of return on the investment. Before the rate of return can be determined, the dollar amount of profit made by the investor must be known.

Discounting note problems involve these three variables:

- Made = **I** = $ = **I**ncome (Interest + discount)
- Paid = **P** = $ = Amount **P**aid (Note amount less discount)
- Rate = **R** = % = **R**ate of return on investment

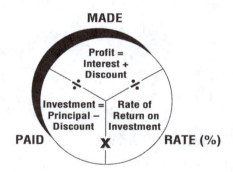

The circle formula for discounting notes.

Formulas:

1. When the amount of money paid and the rate of return (%) are given and you are solving for income or profit (smaller $), use:

   I = P x R (**I**ncome = Amount **P**aid x **R**ate)

2. When the income and rate of return are given (%) and you are solving for the amount paid (larger $), use:

   P = I ÷ R   (Amount **P**aid = **I**ncome ÷ **R**ate)

3. When the income and the dollar amount invested are given and you are solving for % (rate of profit) use:

   R = I ÷ P   (**R**ate = **I**ncome ÷ Amount **P**aid)

Practice Problem #5

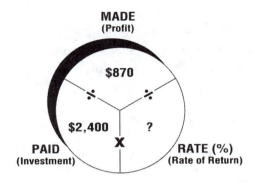

The circle formula for Practice Problem #5.

Tex signed a note for $3,000, in favor of (or owed to) a private lender, which is to be paid off in 12 months. He owes the $3,000 plus 9% interest when the note is due. An investor buys the note at a 20% discount. **What is the rate of return on the amount invested by the investor?**

Known: I (Income) and P (Amount Paid)

    I = Income (Calculate the interest and the discount)
           Interest = $3,000 x 0.09 = $270 (interest owed on due date).

           Discount = $3,000 x 0.20 = $600 (20% discount allowed investor)

    I = $870 ($270 + $600).

    P = Amount Paid (Calculate the discount and subtract from the amount of the note.)
           Discount = $3,000 x 0.20 = $600

    P = $2,400 ($3,000 - $600)

Unknown: Rate (Rate of Return on amount invested)
    What we do not know is the rate (%).

Formula: R = I ÷ P or Rate = profit) ÷ Paid (invested):

    Rate = Profit ÷ Amount Invested
    Rate = $870 ÷ $2,400
    Rate = 36.25%

Capitalization Problems

- Paid = Value of Property
- Made = Annual Net Income or Loss
- Rate = Capitalization Rate

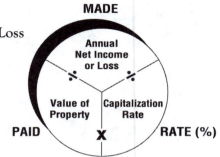

The circle concept for capitalization problems.

Capitalization problems involve these three variables:

$$\text{Made} = \mathbf{I} = \$ = \text{Net Operating } \mathbf{I}\text{ncome (NOI)}$$
$$\text{Paid} = \mathbf{P} = \$ = \text{Value of } \mathbf{P}\text{roperty}$$
$$\text{Rate} = \mathbf{R} = \% = \text{Capitalization } \mathbf{R}\text{ate (Cap } \mathbf{R}\text{ate)}$$

Formulas:

1. When the amount of value of the property and the cap rate (%) are given and you are solving for the NOI (smaller $), use:

$$\mathbf{I} = \mathbf{P} \times \mathbf{R} \ (\text{NOI} = \mathbf{P}\text{roperty Value x Cap } \mathbf{R}\text{ate})$$

2. When the NOI and capitalization rate are given and you are solving for the value of the property (larger $), use:

$$\mathbf{P} = \mathbf{I} \div \mathbf{R} \ (\mathbf{P}\text{roperty Value} = \text{NOI} \div \text{Cap } \mathbf{R}\text{ate})$$

3. When the NOI and the property value are given and you are solving for % (capitalization rate), use:

$$\mathbf{R} = \mathbf{I} \div \mathbf{P} \ (\text{Cap } \mathbf{R}\text{ate} = \text{NOI} \div \mathbf{P}\text{roperty Value})$$

Practice Problem #6

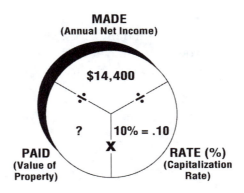

MADE
(Annual Net Income)

$14,400

?

10% = .10

X

PAID
(Value of
Property)

RATE (%)
(Capitalization
Rate)

The circle concept for Practice Problem #6.

A duplex brings in $600 per month per unit. Gail and Kevin are interested in buying the property as an investment, and need an investment rate (capitalization rate, or cap rate) of a 10% return. **What should Gail and Kevin pay for the duplex?**

Known: I (NOI) and Rate (Cap Rate)

> I = $600 per unit x 2 units = $1,200 net income per month
> $1,200 x 12 months = $14,400 annual net income

R = 10% or 0.10

Unknown: P (Value of the Property)

What we do not know is what they should pay for the duplex.

Formula: P = I ÷ R, or Property value = NOI ÷ Cap Rate

> P = I ÷ R
> P = $14,400 ÷ 0.10
> P = $144,000

MATH

Practice Problem #7

- Paid = Amount Invested or Investment
- Made = Income or Profit Earned
- Rate = Rate of Return or Profit

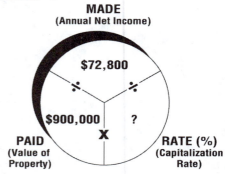

The circle concept for Practice Problem #7.

Shirley paid $900,000 for an eight-unit apartment building. The gross income is $800 per month per unit, with expenses of $4,000 annually. **What capitalization rate (%) will Shirley make on her investment?**

As you recall, net operating income, rather than gross income is used to calculate a capitalization rate. Therefore, the first step is to calculate the gross income and then subtract the annual expenses to arrive at the net operating income.

Gross Income = $800 per month x 8 units = $6,400 per /month x 12 months = $76,800 annual gross income.

Annual Expenses = $4,000

Net Operating Income = $76,800 - $4,000 = $72,800

Known: I (NOI) and P (Property value)

$$I = \$72,800$$
$$P = \$900,000$$

Unknown: R (Cap Rate)

What we do not know is the capitalization rate.

Formula: R = I ÷ P, or Cap Rate = NOI ÷ Property value

$$R = I \div P$$
$$R = \$72,800 \div \$900,000$$
$$\mathbf{R = .081 \text{ or } 8.1\%}$$

Investments

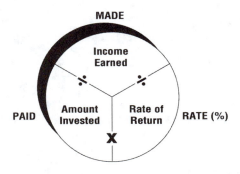

The circle concept for investments.

Investment problems involve these three variables:

Made $=$ **I** $=$ \$ $=$ **I**ncome or profit earned
Paid $=$ **P** $=$ \$ $=$ Amount **P**aid or invested in the **P**roperty
Rate $=$ **R** $=$ % $=$ **R**ate of Return or Profit

Formulas:

1. When the amount of money invested and the rate (%) are given and you are solving for \$ (smaller dollar amount) use:

$$I = P \times R \quad (\text{Income} = \text{Amount Paid} \times \text{Rate of Return})$$

2. When the income and rate of return are given and you are solving for \$ (larger dollar amount) use:

$$P = I \div R \quad (\text{Amount Paid} = \text{Income} \div \text{Rate of Return})$$

3. When the income and the dollar amount invested are given and you are solving for % (percentage of rate of profit) use:

$$R = I \div P \quad (\text{Rate of Return} = \text{Income} \div \text{Amount Paid})$$

MATH

Practice Problem #8

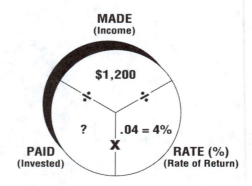

The circle concept for Practice Problem #8.

Steve has a savings account and wants to earn $100 per month in interest. If the account pays 4% interest, **how much should Steve keep in the account?**

Known: I (Income) and R (Cap Rate)

I = $1,200 per year ($100 x 12 months)
R = 4% or 0.04

Unknown: P (Amount Paid)

The amount of the investment is what we do not know.

Formula: P = I ÷ R, or Amount Paid = Income ÷ Rate

P = $1,200 ÷ 0.04
P = $30,000

Practice Problem #9

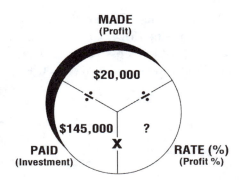

The circle concept for Practice Problem #9.

Mitch bought a house for $145,000. The house was later sold for $165,000. **What is the rate (%) of profit Mitch made on this sale?**

Known: P (Amount Paid) and I (Income)

P = $145,000
I = $20,000 ($165,000 – $145,000)

Unknown: R (Rate)
The rate of profit is not known.

Formula: R = I ÷ P, Rate = Income ÷ Amount Paid

R = $20,000 ÷ $145,000
R = 13.8 or 13.8%

Cost and Selling Price Problems

- Paid = Purchase Price or Cost
- Made = Selling Price
- Rate = Profit or Loss Rate

If a profit is made add the % to 100%

The circle concept for cost and selling price problems.

Profit or Loss on Sales involves these three variables:

Made = I = $ = Increase in value

Paid = P = $ = Purchase price or original cost of **P**roperty

Rate = **R** = % = **R**ate of Return (profit or loss)

Formulas:

1. When the purchase price and the rate of return (%) are given and you are solving for the sales price (increase in value), use:

    I = P x R (**I**ncrease = **P**urchase Price x **R**ate)

2. When the sales price (increase in value) and rate of return are given and you are solving for the original purchase price, use:

    P = I ÷ R (**P**urchase Price = **I**ncrease ÷ **R**ate)

3. When the sales price (increase in value) and the original purchase price are given and you are solving for % (rate of return), use:

    R = I ÷ P (**R**ate = **I**ncrease ÷ **P**urchase Price)

This type of problem is easy to identify because you will be given a selling price and be asked to calculate the amount of profit or the cost before a profit. Sometimes determining the percentage to use can be confusing. Just remember that if a profit is made, add the % to 100%, and if a loss occurs, subtract the % from 100%.

Review – Calculating the Rate of Profit or Loss
When a profit is made add the % to 100%
(15% profit: 100% + 15% = 115% rate or 1.15)

When a loss occurs subtract the % from 100%
(20% loss: 100% - 20% = 80% or 0.80)

Practice Problem #10

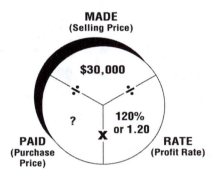

The circle concept for Practice Problem #10.

Maureen sold a rural cabin for $30,000, which allowed her to make a 20% profit. **What did she pay for the property?**

Known: I (Increase) and R (% Rate of profit)

I = $30,000 (Increase earned on the sale of the property. The amount actually earned is the smaller $ because it is the difference between the selling price and the original pur chase price.)

R = 100% + 20% = 120% = 1.20

Unknown: P (Purchase Price)

What we do not know is the larger $ amount that she paid for the property.

Formula: P = I ÷ R, or Purchase price = Increase ÷ Rate

P = $30,000 ÷ 1.20

P = $25,000

We have determined that she paid $25,000 for the property and sold it for $30,000, which is an increase in value of $5,000 (the smaller $ amount). Is $5,000 a 20% profit? We can determine this by using the formula: R = I ÷ P. We know the increase in value is $5,000 and that she paid $25,000 for the property, so we divide $5,000 by $25,000 to get the rate of profit, which is 0.20 or 20%.

You may be asked to find the selling price or amount of a loan when the seller receives a net amount.

Practice Problem #11

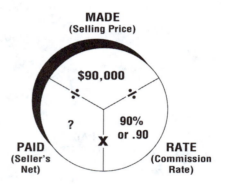

The circle concept for Practice Problem #11.

A farmer put his land on the market, wanting to net a certain amount. The real estate agent who found a buyer gave the farmer a check for $90,000, after deducting a 10% commission. **What was the selling price of the farm?**

Known – I (net Income) and R (Commission Rate)

    I = $90,000 (Income made from sale)

    R = 100% – 10% = 90% or 0.90 (commission rate)

Unknown – P (Selling Price)
What we do not know is the selling price of the farm.

Formula: P = I ÷ R, or Selling Price = Income ÷ Rate

    P = I ÷ R

    P = $ 90,000 ÷ 0.90

    P = $100,000 (Selling Price)

Proration

When property is bought and sold, there are certain expenses that are charged to each party. It is one of the jobs of escrow to credit and debit the buyer and seller correctly as of the closing date of escrow. **Proration** is the process of making a fair distribution of expenses, through escrow, at the close of the sale. For prorating purposes, use 30 days for a month and 360 days in a year.

Review - Proration

The Proration Process:

1. Determine the number of days to be prorated

2. Calculate the cost per day

3. Multiply the number of days by the cost per day

4. Decide whether the item should be a credit or a debit to the seller or to the buyer

5. Expenses that have been paid to some time after escrow closes, credit the seller and debit the buyer.

6. Expenses that will be due after the close of escrow, debit the seller and credit the buyer.

Common Expenses that usually are prorated:

- Property taxes
- Interest on assumed loans
- Fire and hazard insurance
- Rents

MATH

Practice Problem #12

Lynn sold her home on September 1, 2005. She has an existing loan of $200,000 on the house. The interest on the loan is 8%. Terry took over Lynn's loan with interest paid to August 15, 2005. Terry also assumed an existing three-year fire insurance policy for $360 per year, paid by Lynn until November 15, 2006. Lynn also owes property taxes of $1,900 for the year.

Calculate the following:

- Prorate interest, and who is credited or debited
- Prorate insurance, and who is credited or debited
- Prorate tax, and who is credited or debited

1. Prorate the interest:

August 15 to September 1 = 15 days

$200,000 x 8% = $16,000 annual interest

$ 16,000 ÷ 360 days in year = $44.44 per day

15 days x $44.44 per day = $666.60 interest

Credit the buyer and debit the seller.

2. Prorate the insurance:

September 1, 2005, through November 15, 2006 = 435 days

$360 ÷ 360 = $1.00 per day

435 days x $1.00 = $435

Credit the seller and debit the buyer.

3. Prorate the property taxes:

July 1 to September 1 = 60 days

$1,900 ÷ 360 = $5.27 per day

60 days x $5.27 = $316.66

Debit the seller and credit the buyer.

Documentary Transfer Tax

Each county, upon the transfer of property, may charge a documentary transfer tax. As you recall, the amount of the transfer tax is stamped in the upper right-hand corner of a recorded deed. The amount of the tax is based on $1.10 per $1,000 or $.55 per $500 of transferred value. When a sale is all cash, or a new loan is obtained by the buyer, the tax is calculated on the entire sales price. When an existing loan is assumed by a buyer, the tax is calculated on the difference between the assumed loan and the sales price.

Practice Problem #13

Denise sold her home for $250,000, with the buyer obtaining a new loan. **What is the amount of the documentary tax?**

Known – Sales Price and Tax Rate

> Sales price = $250,000
>
> The sale involves a new loan so the tax is based on entire sales price
>
> Tax rate = $1.10 per $1,000

Unknown – Amount of Tax Due
What we do not know is the amount of the tax due.

Calculation – Tax Due = Sales Price ÷ $1,000 x $1.10

> Tax due = $250,000 ÷ $1,000 = $250.00
>
> Tax due = $250.00 x $1.10
>
> **Tax due = $275.00**

MATH

Square Footage and Area Calculations

Occasionally you may be asked to solve problems about square footage. Square footage problems are fairly simple and can be solved easily using these simple formulas.

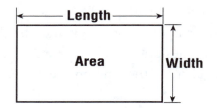

Area = Length x Width
Length = Area ÷ Width
Width = Area ÷ Length

The concept for square footage and area calculations.

As you recall, the way to determine the value of a building using the cost method is to measure the square footage (buildings are measured on the outside). Then check with a contractor to determine the standard cost to build per square foot. Multiply that cost by the square footage of the building to derive the cost to build new, or the upper limit of value.

Review - Basic Area Formulas

The Area of a Square = Length x Width
The Area of a Rectangle = Length x Width
The Area of a Right Triangle = Altitude x Base ÷ 2

Practice Problem #14

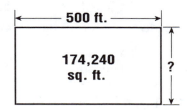

The concept for Practice Problem #14.

Felix owned four acres of land with a front footage of 500 feet along the street. **What is the depth of the land?**

Known – Area and Width

Area = 4 acres or 174,240 sq. ft. (43,560 sq. ft. per acre x 4 acres)
Width = 500 feet

Unknown - Length

What we do not know is the length (depth) of the parcel.

Formula – Length = Area ÷ Width

Length = 174,240 sq. ft. ÷ 500 feet
Length = 348.48 feet

All buildings are not square or rectangular and therefore may be irregular in shape. Always reduce the building to squares, rectangles and triangles, for which you know the formula to determine the square footage.

Practice Problem #15

Lydia and Cliff bought a lot, with the intention of building a house on it. They needed to determine how much it would cost them to build the house. They were told by contractors the cost to build was $40 per square foot for a garage and $80 per square foot for a home.

Lydia and Cliff had plans drawn for the house. They used the total square footage of the house and garage to figure the cost to build.

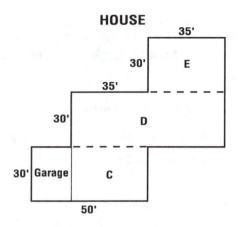

The concept for Practice Problem #15.

Known – Measurements of structure and cost per square foot.

Unknown – The cost to build the house and garage
To find the square footage of the house, divide the diagram into imaginary rectangles and use the formula: Area = Width x Length

1. Calculate the area of the house

   Rectangle A = 35' x 30' = 1,050 square feet

   Rectangle B = 70' x 30' = 2,100 square feet

   Rectangle C = 30' x 35' = 1,050 square feet

   Area of house = 4,200 square feet

2. Calculate the area of the garage

   Garage = 15 x 30 = 450 square feet

3. Calculate the cost to build the house and garage

Building: 4,200 square feet x $80 per square foot = $336,000
Garage: 450 square feet x $40 per square foot   = $18,000
Total cost to build house and garage   = $354,000

Appendix B
Answer Key

Chapter 1 - California's Diversity

Answers - Matching

1. E	3. B	5. K	7. H	9. D
2. M	4. J	6. F	8. I	10. O

Answers - Multiple Choice

1. (b) California has the 5th largest economy in the world—after the United States, Japan, Germany, and United Kingdom. **Page 2**

2. (d) At over 37 million people, California is the most culturally diverse and the most populous state in the country, and has been since 1962. In fact, one out of every eight United States residents lives in California. **Page 2**

3. (a) More than 2.6 million small businesses account for 98% of all employers in California. **Page 8**

4. (a) Capitalism is an economic system in which most of the economy's resources are privately owned and managed. **Page 7**

5. (d) Appreciation is the increase in market value of real estate. **Page 11**

6. (a) Inflation is an increase in the general price level of goods and services, or as a decrease in purchasing power of the dollar. **Page 11**

7. (d) The housing market is shaped mainly by the inventory of available housing, housing affordability, and mortgage interest rates. **Page 11**

8. (b) The best housing market would be created with adequate housing inventory, a high affordability index, and low interest rates. **Page 11**

9. (c) The median home price is the price that is midway between the least expensive and the most expensive home sold in an area during a given period. It is used by economists to compare home sale prices, and measure increases and decreases. **Page 11**

10. (b) In California, if you want to work in a real estate brokerage business, you must have a real estate license. There are two types of real estate licenses: salesperson license and broker license. **Page 13**

Chapter 2 - Property, Estates, and Ownership

Answers - Matching

1. A	5. H	9. G	13. U	17. O
2. B	6. Y	10. R	14. W	18. X
3. C	7. V	11. P	15. D	19. E
4. F	8. M	12. L	16. N	20. T

Answers - Multiple Choice

1. (a)   "Property" refers to the bundle (collection) of rights a person has in the thing owned. **Page 28**

2. (d)   Personal property becomes real property if it is permanently affixed to land or improvements. "Pledge" means to give up possession of property as security for a loan (pawnshop). "Alienate" means to transfer property from one person to another. "Hypothecate" means to pledge something as security without giving up possession (car loan). **Page 29**

3. (b)   Land includes the surface, the space above, and the space beneath for an indefinite distance. Timber, crops, and landfill soil are movable personal property. **Page 29**

4. (b)   The less-than-freehold estate, also known as a leasehold estate, is a personal property estate of a tenant. **Pages 34-35**

5. (b)   Water on the surface, flowing in a stream or underground (percolating) is real property. If it is taken and bottled, then it becomes personal. **Page 30**

6. (c)   The owner of property bordering a stream or river has riparian rights (a riparian owner). Riparian property owners have reasonable use of flowing water, providing it does not injure other riparian landowners. Riparian rights have been ruled in court to be real property. Such rights, like most others, are not immune from actions such as prescription and condemnation. **Page 30**

7. (d)   Easements, mineral rights, and trees are all real property. **Pages 29-31, 34**

8. (d)   "Appurtenant" means "belongs to". An appurtenance is anything used with the land for its benefit. Easements and stock in a mutual water company are the two most common appurtenances to real property. **Page 34**

9. (b)   In addition to (a), (c), and (d), the other two general tests are the relationship between the parties and an agreement between the parties. **Page 31**

10. (a)   Crops that are intended to be harvested and trade fixtures are personal property. A mobile home not attached to a foundation, including its contents, is considered personal property. **Pages 29, 33-34**

11. (c)   Freehold estates are real property estates of ownership. This type of estate continues for an indefinite period and is sometimes called an estate of inheritance. **Pages 34-35**

12. (b)   The rights of possession and use would return to Jones, so Jones has a reversionary interest. A remainder interest would be one that goes to a third party. **Page 37**

13. (c) An estate for years is one of the four types of less-than-freehold estates. They are: (1) estate for years, (2) estate from period to period, (3) estate at will, and (4) estate at sufferance. Choices (a), (b), and (d) are freehold estates. **Page 39**

14. (c) It cannot be community property. Joint tenancy is impossible due to the unequal interest and lack of survivorship. The interests are unequal so there is no partnership interest, therefore, a tenancy in common would be created. **Page 41**

15. (d) Property owned by one person or entity is known as sole and separate, or ownership in severalty. "Severalty" means you are "severed" from other owners. **Page 40**

16. (d) Tenants in common are free to sell, convey, or mortgage their own interest, but not the other co-tenants' interest. There is unity of possession but also separate and distinct titles. **Page 41**

17. (b) There are four unities of a joint tenancy. If formed properly, a joint tenancy creates a right of survivorship. **Page 43**

18. (a) A joint tenancy requires equal interests. Community property ownership is also an equal 50/50 interest. Anyone may form a joint tenancy, so answer (b) is false. Answer (c) is true of community property, but one member of a joint tenancy may convey interest (and thereby dissolve the joint tenancy). Answer (d) is false because a spouse may convey his or her interest by means of a will to someone other than the surviving spouse. **Pages 43-44**

19. (a) A person may sell a joint tenancy interest, but may not will it. When Chris sold her interest to Payton, Payton became a tenant in common. Jordan and Logan remained as joint tenants. When Jordan died, Jordan's third was automatically conveyed to Logan, who then became a tenant in common. So Logan ends up owning 2/3 and Payton 1/3 both as tenants in common. **Page 43**

20. (d) A contract to sell real community property must be signed by both spouses. If it is signed by only one, the contract cannot be enforced. The general idea here is that each spouse has an equal interest in property acquired after marriage. An attempt to sell community property, mortgage it, give it away, or lease it for one year or longer requires the written consent of both spouses by law. **Page 44**

Chapter 3 - Encumbrances and Transfer of Ownership

Answers - Matching

1. H	4. M	7. B	10. D	13. N
2. P	5. F	8. C	11. K	14. R
3. I	6. O	9. S	12. L	15. Q

Answers - Multiple Choice

1. (b) This is the DRE's definition of an encumbrance. Choice (a) defines equity; choice (c) defines a lien that is a type of encumbrance. **Page 58**

2. (c) A lien creates an obligation on a specific property. **Page 59**

3. (b) A recorded abstract of judgment creates an involuntary general lien on all real property of the debtor that is located in the county where the judgment was recorded. **Pages 59-63**

4. (c) Recording a lis pendens creates a cloud on title and prevents the owner from transferring marketable title. Marketable title is title that a fully informed and reasonable purchaser would be willing to accept. The property may still be conveyed, but most buyers would be concerned due to the lis pendens. **Page 62**

5. (b) Income tax liens, court judgments, and California Franchise Tax liens are general liens and affect all of the property of the owner in the county where recorded. **Page 62**

6. (a) The statement of the question is a good definition of a license. **Page 64**

7. (a) An easement in gross is a personal easement that is not attached to the land, and cannot be revoked. Sam does not have a license because the right is irrevocable. It is not an easement appurtenant because Sam owns no land and it is not an easement by prescription because Roger gave the easement in gross to Sam. **Page 64**

8. (b) Zoning ordinances are public, not private restrictions. Private restrictions can be created by CC&Rs, deeds, leases, and other written agreements. **Pages 66-67**

9. (d) The terms alienation, convey, and transfer are used interchangeably when transferring ownership of property from one person to another. **Page 73**

10. (b) Delivery and acceptance are required elements of a valid deed. The deed does not have to be acknowledged or recorded. **Page 75**

11. (b) One of the requirements for a valid deed is that the deed must be executed (signed) by the grantor. **Page 75**

12. (a) The grantor must have the intention, during his or her lifetime, that the deed is delivered and title is transferred. **Page 75**

13. (b) Possession is considered constructive notice, just like recording. If a deed is not recorded, but the buyer moves in, that sale has priority over any later recorded deeds. **Page 77**

14. (a) Ingress and egress mean to enter and to exit. An easement may be created by deed or written agreement which is an express grant. An unlocated easement is valid. **Page 64**

15. (d) A lawsuit to establish or settle title to real property is called a quiet title action or an action to quiet title. **Page 80**

Chapter 4 - Contracts: The Basics

Answers - Matching

1. F	4. S	7. D	10. O	13. M
2. K	5. Q	8. P	11. C	14. J
3. E	6. T	9. G	12. N	15. H

Answers - Multiple Choice

1. (a) A contract is a legally enforceable agreement, made by competent parties, to perform or not perform a certain act. **Page 88**

2. (b) A bilateral contract is an agreement in which each person promises to perform an act in exchange for another person's promise to perform. **Page 88**

3. (b) A listing agreement is an employment contract, so all four elements to create a valid contract must be present to be valid. A minor cannot enter into a valid and binding contract because of incapacity. If capacity is lacking, the contract is void from the start. **Page 89**

4. (a) A valid contract does not require a sufficient writing. However, according to the Statute of Frauds, sufficient writing is required for an enforceable real estate contract. The question is asking the valid requirements for a contract not a valid real estate contract. **Page 89**

5. (a) Choice (a) is correct because consideration is required—not necessarily as money. The following items are essential for a valid contract: capacity, mutual consent, lawful object, and consideration. Choices (b), (c), and (d) are required. **Page 92**

6. (d) Performance is not essential to create a valid contract. Choices (a), (b), and (c) are required to create a valid contract. **Page 89**

7. (b) Mutual consent or mutual assent is sometimes called a "meeting of the minds". It is an offer by one party and acceptance by the other party. **Page 89**

8. (b) Duress is unlawful and makes the contract voidable. A voidable contract is valid and enforceable on its face, but may be rejected by the person who signed it under duress, menace, or undue influence. **Page 91**

9. (d) All of the choices are examples of consideration. **Page 92**

10. (a) The Statute of Frauds does not cover the sale of a business; therefore, the sale of a business does not require a written contract to be valid. **Page 93**

11. (a) According to the Statute of Frauds, the employment agreement must be in writing to be enforceable. **Page 94**

12. (c) Under the parol evidence rule, when two parties make oral promises to each other, and then write and sign a contract promising something different, the written contract will be considered the valid one. **Page 94**

13. (b) A waiver is the relinquishment or refusal to accept a right. A tender of performance is an offer by one of the parties to carry out his or her part of the contract. Novation is the substitution, by agreement, of a new obligation for an existing one, with the intent to extinguish the original contract. Forbearance is forgiving a debt or obligation, or giving up an interest or a right. **Page 95**

14. (b) Rescind means to annul or cancel. Rescission is a legal remedy to terminate or annul a contract and restore the parties to their original positions. Abate means to decrease

or lessen. Abolish means to revoke formally or get rid of. Abrogate means to abolish or get rid of. **Page 95**

15. (c) Novation substitutes one contract for another, by mutual agreement. The intent is to extinguish the former contract and create a new one. **Pages 95-96**

Chapter 5 - Agency Relationships

Answers - Matching

1. Q	5. I	9. M	13. N	17. U
2. V	6. C	10. P	14. B	18. T
3. W	7. H	11. F	15. G	19. Y
4. R	8. E	12. S	16. K	20. O

Answers - Multiple Choice

1. (b) Although not actually a test of agency, the Agency Relationship Disclosure form discusses disclosure, election of representation, and confirmation (DEC) as necessary parts of the disclosure process. Compensation does not create an agency relationship. In fact, a person can be a **gratuitous agent** meaning the agent will receive no pay. A gratuitous agent still owes full fiduciary duty to the principal. **Pages 112 & 116**

2. (b) Under an exclusive agency or an open listing Weiss could sell the property himself and owe no commission. Weiss cancelled Horning's listing prior to accepting the offer from another broker, so Horning is not entitled to a commission. However, if another agent sold the property during Horning's listing agreement, Weiss could be liable for two full commissions. **Pages 121 & 122**

3. (c) The agent must act in the best interests of the seller and must present all offers, unless patently frivolous. It is best to present them at the same time. **Page 126**

4. (d) A listing agreement is a written contract by which a principal, or seller, employs a broker to sell real estate. When the seller signs a listing agreement promising payment for service by the listing broker, and the broker promises to "use due diligence" in finding a buyer, it is a bilateral contract—in that a promise is given in exchange for a promise. **Page 117**

5. (a) A fiduciary relationship implies a position of trust or confidence. The agent has the fiduciary duty of loyalty, integrity, and utmost care to the principal. This means that the agent bound by agency law acts in the best interest of the principal. **Pages 106 & 122**

6. (c) Usually a commission is paid to an agent, but payment of consideration is not necessary to create an agency. **Page 116**

7. (d) An agency is created by agreement, ratification, or by estoppel. The agreement must be in writing to be enforceable. **Page 116**

8. (b) At any time during the agency, the principal or agent may terminate the agency, except

in an agency coupled with an interest. An agency is also terminated by the destruction of the property or by the parties to terminate the agency. In choice (b) the seller's refusal to accept an offer does not terminate the agency. **Page 120**

9. (a)   Under an exclusive agency listing, if the owner finds a buyer, no commission is due the broker. **Page 121**

10. (a)   The Statute of Frauds requires that an agreement for the sale of property must be in writing; however, listing agreements are not recorded, and therefore not acknowledged. **Page 117 & 121**

11. (d)   An agency relationship is created by mutual agreement between the principal and the agent. It cannot be established by someone simply offering to be an agent. **Page 116**

12. (d)   In an exclusive right-to-sell listing agreement, the broker is entitled to a commission if the property is sold by any broker or the owner within the specified time limit. **Page 121**

13. (a)   Every exclusive agency agreement must have a definite termination date. It may be whatever is agreeable to both parties, but it must be specified in the listing agreement. **Page 121**

14. (c)   An exclusive right-to-sell listing agreement stipulates the broker will be paid a commission regardless of who sells the property—the broker, the seller, or another cooperating broker. **Page 121**

15. (a)   In an open listing, the seller may sell the property without paying the broker a commission. **Page 122**

16. (d)   As we learned in Chapter 4, valid grant deed does not require a legal description. It only needs to be adequately described. The same is true for the listing agreement. The best source to find the legal description of a property is the title insurance policy or a preliminary title report, which will be discussed in Chapter 8. **Page 74**

17. (d)   The types of listing agreements in choices (a), (b), and (c) require the broker to prove he or she was the procuring cause. In the exclusive right-to-sell listing agreement, the broker is entitled to a commission regardless of who sells the property. **Pages 121 & 129**

18. (b)   The broker's fiduciary duty requires full disclosure of material facts. If the buyer instructs the listing broker to hold the check uncashed until the offer is accepted, this material fact must be disclosed to the seller when the offer is presented. **Page 126**

19. (c)   A listing agent must present all written offers to the owner before closing unless expressly instructed otherwise or unless the offer is patently frivolous (not a serious offer). **Page 126**

20. (b)   As a fiduciary, the agent is bound by law to show good faith, loyalty, and honesty to the principal. If the building looks as if it has settled, the agent needs to tell the principal to get the opinion of a licensed soils engineer. **Page 122**

21. (b)   Almost all listing agreements give the broker express authority to accept a deposit as an agent of the owner. It does not authorize the broker to convey property on behalf of a principal or legally bind the seller to make a deal. **Pages 121 & 126**

22. (b) If a broker passes along a misrepresentation made by the seller, the broker is not liable for the consequences. **Page 128**

23. (b) A listing broker has the duty of fair and honest dealings with third parties—the buyer. This duty includes full disclosure of all material facts. **Page 127**

24. (b) The seller has no agency relationship with the buyer's agent and is not responsible for his or her actions. **Page 106**

25. (d) Communication of the seller's acceptance to the buyer shows that the broker is the procuring cause of the sale and that the broker has found a "ready, willing, and able buyer". **Page 129**

Chapter 6 - Real Estate Contracts

Answers - Matching

1. X	5. T	9. E	13. K	17. H
2. J	6. U	10. R	14. B	18. M
3. P	7. D	11. I	15. O	19. Y
4. G	8. N	12. S	16. C	20. V

Answers - Multiple Choice

1. (b) According to the Statute of Frauds, to be enforceable, real estate contracts must be in writing. **Page 141**

2. (d) The buyer indicates the amount of the deposit in the offer. Then it is always negotiated by buyer and seller until the seller accepts the offer. There is no state law specifying the amount of the deposit. **Page 142**

3. (c) Usually there are terms in the contract that must be met during the escrow period; therefore, the contract is considered executory until all the terms are completed and escrow closes. **Page 143**

4. (b) Until an offer is accepted by the seller, the buyer owns the funds, and the broker must obey the buyer's instructions. If the seller refuses the offer, the check is returned to the buyer. **Pages 142 & 154**

5. (c) If a seller rejects the offer and submits a counteroffer, the original offer automatically terminates. **Page 154**

6. (a) By changing the number of days for the closing, seller Susan has created a counteroffer; therefore, the original offer automatically terminates. **Page 154**

7. (b) Chris' counteroffer terminated the buyer's original offer. **Page 154**

8. (b) An option is an agreement to keep an offer open. **Page 154**

9. (d) An option is a form of contract to keep an offer open. **Page 154**

10. (d) The optionee (buyer) is not required to buy the property. If the optionee decides to

exercise the option and buy the property, the optionor (seller) must sell. An option is a unilateral contract, and the option must have actual monetary consideration to be valid, but no specific amount is required. **Page 156**

11. (c)   Listings (even a net listing) and deposit receipts are bilateral contracts. Options are unilateral contracts. **Page 154**

12. (d)   Tenancy is the interest of a person holding property by any right or title. **Page 156**

13. (c)   The maximum security deposit may be no more than two months rent for unfurnished residential property or three months rent for a furnished residential property. **Page 166**

14. (c)   A lease is a contract for exclusive possession of property in consideration for rent. The owner is giving his "bundle of right of possession" to a tenant for a period of time. **Page 156**

15. (c)   The maximum deposit allowed for an unfurnished property is not more than the amount of two month's rent. The maximum deposit allowed for a furnished property is not more than the amount of three months rent. **Page 166**

16. (b)   Quiet enjoyment is an implied warranty that the tenant may enjoy the premises in peace and without disturbance from the landlord. This warranty protects the tenant from serious interference with his or her tenancy. The term "**paramount title holder**" refers to the owner. **Page 167**

17. (d)   The original tenant has a lease. He or she becomes a sublessor upon subletting the lease to another tenant, called the sublessee. The original tenant/sublessor still owes rent to the owner and collects rent from the sublessee, therefore the tenant is "sandwiched" between the owner and the sublessor (current tenant). **Page 169**

18. (c)   The lessor is the landlord. An unlawful detainer action is the legal remedy to remove a defaulting tenant. **Pages 170-171**

19. (d)   In all the choices the tenant still has possession, but the landlord has made the premises unsuitable for occupancy, resulting in a **constructive eviction**. **Page 168**

20. (c)   A three-day notice is a request by the landlord that the tenant pay the rent or quit the premises. To actually evict the tenant, the landlord must file an unlawful detainer action in court and request an order of eviction. **Page 170**

Chapter 7 - Disclosures in Real Estate

Answers - Matching

1. B	4. P	7. R	10. I	13. F
2. J	5. A	8. O	11. L	14. H
3. S	6. M	9. T	12. C	15. G

Answers - Multiple Choice

1. (b)   The intent of an "as is" clause is to alert prospective buyers that visible conditions should be taken into account when offering to purchase property. An "as is" clause

does not relieve a seller from the responsibility to disclose all known material facts to the buyer. However, an "as is" clause indicates that the seller will not be responsible for the cost of repairing any defect. **Page 183**

2. (c)   The seller of a 1-4 unit residential property must give a Transfer Disclosure Statement to a prospective buyer. A seller can sell a home "as is" but must still disclose any defects. The "as is" clause lets the buyer know that the seller does not plan to repair any defects. **Page 183**

3. (c)   A broker has the duty to visually inspect a property and disclose any material facts affecting its value and the "as is" clause does not relieve the agent of the disclosure duty. Even if a defect is not apparent during a reasonable inspection, the agent and the seller must inform the buyer of the defect. **Page 183**

4. (a)   The seller and broker may both have liability for the leak, but the seller also has recourse against the broker because he had, in fact, revealed the leak to the broker. **Page 190**

5. (b)   This is a material fact that should have been disclosed. If the offer had not been accepted, the buyer could revoke his offer. Once escrow closed, the buyer could rescind the sales contract based on fraud. As we learned in Chapter 4, fraud is an act meant to deceive—such as a lack of disclosure. **Page 184**

6. (a)   The Transfer Disclosure Statement is required on a sale of 1-4 residential units whether sold through a broker or by the owner directly. Choice (b) is not correct, because it must be a lease with an option of purchase. **Page 184**

7. (a)   A broker has a responsibility to conduct a reasonably competent and visual inspection of the property. Since the seller withheld known facts, the broker can sue Pat for damages. **Page 188**

8. (d)   Once the booklet is provided to a prospective buyer of real property, neither the seller nor a real estate agent involved in the sale has a duty to provide further information on such hazards. However, a seller or agent who knows about any environmental hazards on or affecting the property must disclose that material fact. **Pages 189 & 190**

9. (d)   The home was built in 2002, so there is no disclosure requirement. This disclosure pertains to residential housing built before 1978 because the Act banned lead based paint for residential use in that year. **Pages 194 & 197**

10. (c)   Choices (a), (b), and (d) are included on the statement; mold is discussed on the Transfer Disclosure Statement. **Pages 197-198**

11. (d)   The owner must furnish CC&Rs, bylaws, and the most recent financial statements. **Page 205**

12. (b)   Neither the transferor (seller/lessor) nor the agent has to ever voluntarily disclose whether or not a person was afflicted with or died from AIDS. However, if the transferee (buyer/lessee) asks a direct question about a death on the property, the seller or agent must answer their question honestly. **Page 208**

13. (d)   The report is given to the buyer. Sometimes the question will have **transferee** (buyer) as the choice. **Page 212**

14. (d) The seller usually pays to have problems discovered in Part One of the report corrected. Any potential problems discovered in Part Two are usually paid for by the buyer, if he or she wants to correct the condition. This is usually specified in the Deposit Receipt. **Page 212**

15. (a) Anyone can get a copy of the pest control report by requesting it from the Structural Pest Control Board and paying a fee. The reports are available for the preceding two years. **Page 212**

Chapter 8 - Escrow and Closing

Answers - Matching

1. U	6. E	11. P	16. O	21. Z	26. W
2. M	7. FF	12. L	17. GG	22. F	27. BB
3. HH	8. V	13. S	18. J	23. AA	28. EE
4. I	9. Y	14. T	19. H	24. A	29. CC
5. B	10. X	15. D	20. C	25. R	30. G

Answers - Multiple Choice

1. (b) One of the meanings of the term "execute" is "to sign". All parties to the transaction sign the escrow instructions. All parties must sign escrow instructions or the offer to purchase as escrow instructions for the contract to be binding. An escrow is officially open when both buyer and seller have signed the instructions and delivered them to escrow. **Pages 232-234 & 238**

2. (b) Escrow is not required. However, escrow, acting as a neutral third party helps to guarantee that all terms and conditions of the agreement are met. **Page 228**

3. (c) A perfect escrow is one for which all documents, funds, and instructions required to close escrow are completed and are in the hands of the escrow agent. A complete escrow is one in which all of the instructions have been satisfied. When an escrow is both perfect and complete, it is ready to close. Escrow is considered closed when the agent presents settlement statements to the buyer and seller, disburses escrow funds, and delivers all necessary documents. **Page 232**

4. (b) Closing costs are generally not included in escrow instructions. They are calculated just prior to closing and are included in the closing statement. **Pages 237-243**

5. (b) During escrow, the escrow officer is a neutral third party who acts as an agent for both parties. At the close of escrow, the escrow officer becomes a single agent for each party. A broker may only act as an escrow in transactions in which he or she has an interest. The escrow officer delivers the deed to the buyer and the funds to the seller. **Page 245**

6. (c) Escrow agents may not offer legal advice, and may only act on written instructions from the parties to the escrow. Escrow agents write lenders of record for payoff amounts

and funding. They accept pest control and similar reports, but cannot authorize any work. **Pages 241-242**

7. (c)   The escrow officer does not give advice; he or she waits for proper instructions from both parties' broker(s). **Page 233**

8. (a)   A seller who prepays the taxes would expect to get the unused portion back, which would show up as a credit. In most transactions, sellers pay for title insurance and any delinquent assessment liens which would show up as debits. The assumed loan is a debit to the seller and a credit to the buyer. **Page 242**

9. (b)   Since the loan shifts from the seller to the buyer, the loan amount is debited against the seller and credited to the buyer. An assumed loan is shown as a credit to the buyer and a charge or debit to the seller. [Hint: **ABC - A**ssumption by the **B**uyer is a **C**redit] If it were a NEW loan, only the buyer would be credited. **Page 242**

10. (c)   Whenever a buyer has a loan (new or assumed) it is shown as a credit on the settlement statement. **Page 242**

11. (c)   An impound account is a trust account set up for funds set aside for future, recurring costs relating to a property. It is used as needed. **Pages 242-243**

12. (d)   The title insurance company uses the title plant to conduct as accurate a search of the public records (county recorder, county assessor, county clerk and the federal land office) as soon as possible to make sure the chain of title is correct. **Page 247**

13. (b)   An abstract of title is a summary of the public record pertaining to property. **Page 246**

14. (d)   Title insurance insures and protects title to property. **Page 247**

15. (c)   An American Land Title Association (ALTA) policy extends the standard (CLTA) policy coverage to rights or claims that an accurate survey would show. **Page 249**

16. (d)   For example, no form of title insurance will insure against changes in zoning regulations. **Pages 249-250**

17. (c)   There is also no protection against rights or claims not shown by public records if they could be determined by physical inspection, appropriate inquiry, or correct survey. **Pages 248-249**

18. (c)   As we learned in Chapter 3, a grant deed offers an implied warranty that there are no undisclosed liens made by the grantor. A standard title insurance policy does not protect against undisclosed liens, although an extended policy would. **Page 249**

19. (d)   The property is not inspected or surveyed for a standard coverage policy, but is for an extended coverage policy. **Page 249**

20. (a)   Generally, title insurance does not cover legislative regulations like zoning laws. **Page 248**

21. (b)   The rectangular survey system also called the U.S. Government Section and Township Survey uses imaginary lines to form a grid to locate land. North-south longitude lines (meridians) and east-west latitude lines (baselines) intersect to form a starting point from which distances are measured. **Page 251**

22. (d) Real property is taxed at the local level through ad valorem property taxes, special assessments, and transfer taxes. **Pages 257-258**

23. (d) Ad valorem means according to value. **Page 258**

24. (d) Special assessments are spent on specific local improvements such as streets, sidewalks, parks, water supply, and sewage treatment facilities. Only owners who are affected by the improvements pay the assessment. **Page 261**

25. (c) While the property is in a tax-defaulted status, the owner does not actually lose title and keeps possession for five years. **Pages 259-260**

Chapter 9 - Real Estate Finance: Loans

Answers - Matching

1. J	5. S	9. Q	13. C	17. P
2. K	6. N	10. Y	14. B	18. F
3. O	7. T	11. A	15. U	19. H
4. M	8. V	12. R	16. D	20. W

Answers - Multiple Choice

1. (b) A promissory note is evidence of the debt. **Page 274**

2. (d) A negotiable instrument is a written unconditional order to pay a certain amount of money at a definite time or on demand. The most common type of negotiable instrument is an ordinary bank check. Negotiable instruments are freely transferable. The trust deed is not a negotiable instrument. **Page 275**

3. (b) The interest rate stated in the note is called the nominal or "named" or "face" rate. The effective interest rate is the rate the borrower is actually paying, commonly called "the annual percentage rate" (APR). **Page 276**

4. (d)   Amortization is described as the liquidation of a financial obligation. **Page 277**

5. (b) Negative amortization means that a portion of the interest is not paid each month. This portion is added to the unpaid principal. **Page 279**

6. (b) If it were fully amortized, it would be paid off at the end of the term. Partial amortization means that a large (balloon) payment will be due at the end of the loan term. **Page 277**

7. (d) The longer the term of the loan, the lower the monthly payments. Since interest will be paid for a longer period, the total financing costs over the life of the loan would be higher. **Page 279**

8. (c) The interest rate of an ARM changes with an agreed-upon index, so the monthly payments vary accordingly. This loan is also called a variable-rate mortgage (VRM). **Page 279**

9. (a) The mortgage or trust deed on the real property acts as security for the repayment of the loan. The borrower becomes the mortgagor and the lender the mortgagee. **Page 282**

10. (c) The buyer is the trustor and gives the power of sale to the trustee. If the buyer defaults, the trustee is authorized by the lender (beneficiary) to sell the property and give the proceeds to the lender. **Page 281**

11. (b) A trustee's sale is a non-judicial sale. In a trustee's sale, no deficiency judgments are permitted. The borrower has reinstatement rights prior to the trustee sale, but does not have redemption rights after the sale. **Page 284**

12. (b) The only thing they have in common is that they are both security for the promissory note. **Page 281**

13. (b) The vendor (seller) is financing the buyer (vendee) just as the lender (beneficiary) finances the buyer (trustor). **Page 282**

14. (a) An "or more" clause allows a borrower to pay off a loan early, or make higher payments without penalty. **Page 283**

15. (d) Lenders may not impose a late charge on a payment until the payment is more than ten days late. **Page 283**

16. (a) Most promissory notes have acceleration clauses, which have no affect on the negotiability of the note. **Page 283**

17. (c) A judicial foreclosure has a redemption period in which the borrower may buy back the property. Under a trustee's sale, there is no right of redemption. **Page 286**

18. (d) The mortgagor may remain in possession for up to one year after the foreclosure sale, but must pay rent. **Page 286**

19. (b) The beneficiary of the second loan is a junior lien holder who could be wiped out by a senior lien foreclosure. A Notice of Default gives the junior beneficiary time to protect his or her interest. **Page 298**

20. (c) If a loan is assumed with the lender's approval, the buyer becomes the principal debtor. **Page 287**

21. (b) The FHA's purpose is to promote affordable housing for low and moderate income families. **Page 293**

22. (c) Even though interest rates are market driven, the borrower and lender agree to the interest rate. At one time, FHA and VA interest rates were set by the government. **Page 294**

23. (d) FHA insures loans made by FHA approved mortgagees (lenders). **Page 294**

24. (d) A veteran may purchase a home with no down payment provided the selling price is less than the Certificate of Reasonable Value (CRV) (appraisal) and the veteran is eligible to borrow under the VA program. The VA does not usually require a down payment, but the lender may. **Pages 296-297**

25. (d) Choices (a), (b), and (c) are correct. The seller is called the vendor. **Page 282**

26. (a) For a Cal-Vet loan, the State never charges the buyer discount points. FHA allows a 1% initial service charge. VA loans often involve a 1% funding fee. **Page 298**

27. (c) A mortgage or deed of trust may contain a subordination clause stating that the lien created will have a lesser priority to a specified existing or future lien. It is frequently used by developers to allow the placement of construction loans after the execution of purchase—money trust deeds with the original landowner. Construction lenders will require that their loan is secured by a lien first in priority, so a subordination clause is essential for prior liens. The term "subrogation" means the substitution of one person (creditor) for another. **Page 301**

28. (c) A "hard-money" mortgage is one given to a borrower in exchange for cash as opposed to one given to finance a specific real estate purchase. **Page 287**

29. (a) A blanket mortgage is a voluntary lien placed over more than one parcel. A blanket deed of trust is one secured by several distinct properties or lots. **Page 308**

30. (d) A construction loan (interim loan) is eventually replaced by a long-term loan called a take-out loan. **Page 311**

Chapter 10 - Real Estate Finance: Lending Institutions

Answers - Matching

1. D	6. DD	11. L	16. M	21. Q
2. O	7. U	12. CC	17. X	22. J
3. BB	8. N	13. I	18. H	23. R
4. V	9. AA	14. C	19. F	24. K
5. A	10. Y	15. S	20. E	25. P

Answers - Multiple Choice

1. (d) A "tight" money market means the supply of money is relatively limited and the demand is high. Therefore, interest rates would generally increase. Selling government bonds takes money out of circulation as bonds are purchased. Raising the discount rate will mean less money will be borrowed and circulated. The reserve requirement is the amount of money that Fed member banks are required to keep in reserve. As the reserve requirement is raised, the amount of money available for making loans by banks is limited. **Page 325**

2. (d) Since money will be more expensive to borrow in a tight money market, a buyer must find other ways to purchase a home or postpone home ownership. **Page 326**

3. (c) In general, "yield" is the amount received or returned from an investment (expressed as a percentage). **Page 328**

4. (b) Deregulation is a process whereby regulatory restraints are gradually relaxed. Disintermediation occurs when savers take money out of S&Ls and put it into investments that pay a higher rate of interest. Depreciation is a loss in value from any cause. **Page 326**

5. (d) Among institutional lenders, thrifts (savings and loan associations) provide the majority of home loans. **Page 329**

6. (a)   Commercial banks make interim, short-term (6 to 36 months) construction loans. **Page 329**

7. (c)   Insurance companies prefer to make loans on properties where larger and longer-term loans are required. **Page 331**

8. (b)   Mortgage companies also known as "loan correspondents", make mortgage loans in their areas, and then deliver these loans to the life insurance companies. The mortgage companies act as service agencies for these loans for a fee. **Pages 331-332**

9. (b)   "Warehousing" is the practice of extending a line of credit by a commercial bank to a mortgage banker. The banker borrows money to fund loans, and the loans are then offered as collateral. The collateral loans are "warehoused" or collected at the bank and later sold to secondary market investors. **Page 332**

10. (a)   Other non-institutional lenders include private individuals, pension funds, and trust departments of banks. **Page 331**

11. (a)   Junior loans refer to secondary financing. A seller will take back a second trust deed to help finance the purchase of the property. **Page 332**

12. (d)   The secondary mortgage market is for buying and selling existing mortgages from the primary mortgage market or from each other. Participants in the secondary mortgage market do not originate loans. **Page 333**

13. (a)   FNMA (Fannie Mae) was originally created to purchase FHA and VA loans in the secondary market. However in recent years, Fannie Mae has also purchased conventional mortgages from approved lenders. **Pages 334-335**

14. (b)   FHA neither builds homes nor lends money directly. Instead, it insures loans on real property made by approved lending institutions. FHA insured loans are sold to the secondary mortgage market. **Page 334**

15. (c)   The creditor (lender) is responsible for providing Truth-in-Lending disclosures to the consumer. A creditor is defined as someone who extends credit more than 25 times a year or more than five times a year for transactions secured by a dwelling. Real estate brokers or others who merely arrange credit are not considered creditors under Regulation Z. **Page 344**

16. (d)   The main purpose of the Act is to promote the informed use of consumer credit by requiring creditors to disclose credit terms so consumers can make comparisons between different sources of credit. The Act is implemented by Regulation Z. **Page 344**

17. (a)   Agricultural and other business loans are exempt from Regulation Z. Even though a mobile home may be considered personal property, if it is intended as the consumer's principal dwelling, it is governed by Regulation Z. **Page 344**

18. (d)   It is correct to disclose just the APR and does not trigger the requirement for additional disclosures. **Pages 345-346**

19. (d)   Regulation Z specifies the items included in the finance charge: interest, loan fees, assumption fees, finder's fees, buyer's points, investigation and credit report fees, and

premiums for mortgage guarantee or similar insurance. Regulation Z also specifies the items that are not to be included in the finance charge: seller's points, title fees, fees for preparing documents, notary charges, appraisal fees, and credit-report fees. **Page 344**

20. (c) An ad that contains any one of the four "triggering" terms: (1) the down payment, (2) the number or term of payments, (3) the amount of any payment, or (4) the finance charge must disclose additional credit terms. If only the annual percentage rate (APR) is disclosed, the additional disclosures are not required. **Page 346**

21. (c) An ad must disclose all credit terms if it contains any one of the following four "triggering" terms: (1) the down payment, (2) the number, or term of payments, (3) the amount of any payment, or (4) the finance charge. In this case, the 10% down payment triggers the other disclosures. **Page 346**

22. (d) RESPA's main purpose is to provide purchasers of real property with information to take the mystery out of settlement (closing) process. **Page 346**

23. (b) RESPA applies to all federally related mortgage loans made by lenders for the sale or transfer of 1-4 unit residential dwellings. **Page 346**

24. (c) As provided by RESPA, a lender may not assess a fee or charge anyone in connection with or on account of the preparation or distribution of the Uniform Settlement Statement. **Page 347**

25. (c) Article 7 of the Business & Professions Code, Section 10242 limits a licensee's commission to 15% where the loan term is three years or longer. **Page 349**

Chapter 11 - Valuation and Appraisal

Answers - Matching

1. E	7. A	13. LL	19. G	25. X	31. F
2. S	8. B	14. CC	20. HH	26. II	32. V
3. DD	9. R	15. P	21. KK	27. Y	33. M
4. NN	10. AA	16. K	22. JJ	28. U	34. W
5. Q	11. GG	17. C	23. N	29. L	35. T
6. H	12. J	18. BB	24. Z	30. FF	

Answers - Multiple Choice

1. (d) Value or worth is the present and future anticipated enjoyment or profit from the ownership of property. It is the relationship between the thing desired and the purchaser. It is also the power of one commodity to attract other commodities in exchange. **Page 363**

2. (c) Market value is the amount of money (cash or its equivalent) for which a property can be sold or exchanged under prevailing, open, and competitive market conditions. Asking and listing prices are usually higher than the market price, whereas the offered price is usually lower. **Page 364**

3. (d) The original cost of materials on improvement has little to do with current value. **Page 364**

4. (d)   The four elements of value can be remembered by the mnemonic "DUST"—demand, utility, scarcity, and transferability. Cost is not one of the 4 elements to create value. **Page 364**

5. (b)   Functional utility is concerned with the desirability and usefulness of a property which affect its marketability. An owner may love a feature in his or her home but it may not be desirable to the general buying public so that the home isn't easily sold on the market. **Page 364**

6. (a)   An unearned increment is appreciation of a property through no effort of the property owner. **Page 366**

7. (c)   Using the principle of substitution, value is set by the cost of acquiring an equally desirable substitute property. The sales (market) comparison approach uses the principle of substitution to compare similar properties. **Pages 368 & 375**

8. (c)   In order to determine the value, the first step is to determine its highest and best use. **Page 368**

9. (a)   Conformity upholds values in a neighborhood. **Page 368**

10. (c)   Land is always valued as if it were vacant and able to be developed to its highest and best use. Review the steps in Cost Approach . Whenever an existing structure needs to be removed, the appraiser would deduct the demolition costs that must be expended to make the property vacant. This is part of Step 1 in the cost approach procedure. **Pages 373 & 376-377**

11. (c)   One of the disadvantages of the sales comparison approach is correctly adjusting amenities to make them comparable to the subject property. **Page 376**

12. (a)   An inactive market would make it difficult to find enough similar comparable properties to obtain comparable values. Comparable properties can be included in the data from the same or similar neighborhoods. **Pages 375-376**

13. (b)   An amenity is a feature that adds to the value of a property. Adjustments are always made to the comparable, not the subject property. In this case, the value of the amenity is subtracted from the value of the comparable to arrive at the value of a subject property that lacks the amenity. **Pages 376-377**

14. (d)   The replacement-cost method is used to calculate the cost new. Choice (d) is not used in the cost approach. The capitalization rate is used in the income approach. **Page 377**

15. (c)   Depreciation on a new building is relatively easy to determine. The cost approach is impractical with older buildings because of the difficulty in estimating depreciation. **Page 377**

16. (d)   Functional obsolescence describes a factor arising from the property itself, as shown in choices (a), (b), and (c). The proximity to nuisances in choice (d) describes external or economic obsolescence. **Page 379**

17. (c)   Obsolescence includes both functional and economic (external) factors. Functional

obsolescence may or may not be curable. Economic obsolescence is usually incurable. **Page 379**

18. (d) An improper improvement or an improperly placed (oriented) structure are examples of functional obsolescence. This would be considered incurable if the cost to correct the problems is not economically feasible. **Page 379**

19. (d) Economic rent is the "reasonable rental expectancy if the property were available for renting at the time of its valuation". **Page 381**

20. (c) To calculate a gross rent multiplier, simply divide the sales price by the gross income (either annual or monthly). **Page 384**

21. (c) The principle of anticipation means that value is created by benefits anticipated from the property in the future. **Page 381**

22. (a) Effective gross income is calculated by subtracting the vacancy factor and rent collection losses from the annual gross income. **Page 382**

23. (b) Economic life is the estimated period over which a building may be profitably used. Economic life is usually shorter than physical (actual) life. Land is not considered to have an economic life because it is thought to be impossible to determine its useful lifetime. **Page 380**

24. (c) An appraiser valuating a property looks at the economic rent, rather than the contract rent, in order to discover the fair income of the property. Contract rent is the actual income received for the property. Market rent is the basis for rent, vacancy, and collection factors. **Page 381**

25. (c) Actual age is the real age of a building. Effective age is not determined by the actual age of a building, but by its condition and usefulness. The effective age could be longer, shorter, or identical to the actual age. **Page 380**

26. (c) Economic life is usually shorter than physical (actual) life. In many cases, the building may still be standing but is not producing any income. **Page 380**

27. (c) The net operating income (NOI) is the income after paying all expenses including a maintenance reserve. It does not include the principal and interest (debt service) paid on a loan. **Page 383**

28. (d) Choosing a capitalization rate is the hardest part for appraisers using the income approach. **Page 384**

29. (a) The gross rent multiplier is calculated by dividing the sales price by the gross rent. It relies on comparable sales figures to derive a quick estimate of market value. **Pages 384-385**

30. (d) The final step in the appraisal process is reconciliation (correlation) of the various estimates. An appraiser does not average the final estimates. **Page 385**

Chapter 12 - Land Use, Subdivision, and Housing

Answers - Matching

1. AA	6. H	11. FF	16. HH	21. DD	26. W
2. O	7. P	12. C	17. D	22. A	27. BB
3. B	8. L	13. I	18. E	23. X	28. Q
4. R	9. GG	14. J	19. Z	24. CC	29. Y
5. II	10. V	15. S	20. G	25. K	30. F

Answers - Multiple Choice

1. (d) Eminent domain is the government's right to acquire property for the public good and for an urgent public purpose. An individual may have littoral rights (water rights by a lake), riparian rights (water rights along a river or stream), or severance rights (right to remove something attached to land). **Page 402**

2. (c) A grandfather clause allows a prior use to continue despite subsequent changes in zoning. **Page 407**

3. (b) A variance is a special exception to the building code. **Page 408**

4. (b) A shoreline is the intersection of the land with the water (mean high water line). Wetlands are areas where water covers the soil, or is present either at or near the surface of the soil all year or for varying periods during the year, including during the growing season. A floodplain is the low land adjacent to a river, lake, or ocean. An estuary is where sea water and fresh water mix together. **Page 409**

5. (d) The division of land into five or more lots for the purpose of sale, lease, or financing is a subdivision. Subdivisions located in sparsely populated areas of California, made up of 50 parcels or more is a land project. A time-share is a type of subdivision. A tentative map is a map of the proposed subdivision that is submitted to a planning commission for approval or disapproval. **Page 410**

6. (c) The Subdivision Map Act authorizes cities and counties to control the orderly and proper development of the community. The Real Estate Commissioner regulates the sale or lease of subdivided real property under the Subdivided Lands Law. Contractors are licensed in California under the Contractors' State License Law. The State Housing Law outlines the minimum construction and occupancy requirements for dwellings. **Page 412**

7. (d) The Subdivided Lands Law applies to a subdivision of five or more parcels. **Page 417**

8. (b) Percolating water is underground water not flowing in a defined channel. A defined channel is any natural watercourse, even though dry during a good portion of the year. **Page 415**

9. (c) A percolation test is used to determine the ability of the land to absorb and drain water, and is frequently used when installing septic systems. **Page 415**

10. (b) The State Housing Law outlines the minimum construction and occupancy requirements for dwellings. Local building inspectors enforce the construction regulations while local health officers enforce the occupancy and sanitation regulations. **Pages 420-421**

11. (a)   Government regulations' purpose is always to protect the public. **Page 421**

12. (a)   As we learned in Chapter 3, the more restrictive use prevails. In this instance, it is the CC&Rs. **Page 421**

13. (a)   A stricter local code will take precedence over state or federal building codes. (UBC = Uniform Building Code) **Pages 420-421**

14. (a)   The R-value is a rating that measures how well insulation resists heat. The BTU (British Thermal Unit) measures the efficiency of energy; used to determine the effectiveness of appliances. The Energy Efficient Ratio (EER) measures the amount of heat needed to raise one pound of water one degree Fahrenheit. Insulation is a material inserted into walls and ceilings to help keep the heat inside the home in the winter and outside the home in the summer. **Page 422**

15. (c)   Backfill is soil that is used to fill in holes or support a foundation. Compaction refers to extra soil that is added and compressed to fill in the low areas or raise the level of the parcel. Expansive soil is soil that expands and shrinks. Adobe is one of the most expansive of the clay soils. **Page 423**

16. (b)   Crawlspace is the area or space between the ground and floor joists. For FHA loans, the minimum crawlspace is 18 inches. **Page 423**

17. (d)   Anchor bolts attach the mud sill to the foundation. A footing is an extended part of the foundation at the base or bottom of a foundation wall, pier, or column. A mud sill is a redwood board that is fastened with bolts to the foundation. The ridge board is the highest part of a frame building. **Page 424**

18. (c)   A kiosk is a freestanding small booth, such as a jewelry stand or a newsstand in a mall. Joists are boards supporting floors or ceilings. A walk-up is an apartment of more than one story with no elevator. **Page 425**

19. (b)   An elevation sheet is a drawing that shows front and side exterior views of a building as it will be when finished. A foundation plan is drawn to scale showing foundation, sub-floors, footing, and pier placement. A plot plan (map) shows the location of improvements on the lot. **Page 425**

20. (d)   These are all types of roofs. Roof types are determined by the direction, steepness, and number of roof planes. **Page 426**

Chapter 13 - Real Estate Brokerage

Answers - Matching

1. CC	6. Q	11. N	16. J	21. B
2. G	7. U	12. DD	17. AA	22. Z
3. F	8. P	13. S	18. D	23. E
4. T	9. X	14. Y	19. M	24. A
5. K	10. V	15. H	20. O	25. L

Answers - Multiple Choice

1. (a) A real estate broker may open a real estate brokerage in his or her name or a fictitious business name. The broker may have multiple locations and take ownership in a variety of ways, such as: sole proprietorship, partnership, corporation, or limited liability company (LLC). **Page 441**

2. (b) The Department of Real Estate does not issue real estate partnership licenses. **Page 442**

3. (d) Corporations are subject to double taxation. S-corporations avoid the double tax feature of a corporation because any gains and losses pass directly to the shareholders. LLC partners can choose to be taxed as a separate entity (like a corporation) or as a partnership-like entity in which profits are passed through to partners and taxed on their personal income tax returns. Partnerships do not file tax returns. All partnership income, expenses, gains, and losses pass through to the individual partners and are reported on their personal income tax returns. **Page 442**

4. (c) The company dollar is the amount a broker has left after all commissions have been paid. The desk cost shows how much each sales associate must earn to cover expenses. It is calculated by dividing the total operating expenses of the firm by the number of licensed sales associates. **Page 443**

5. (b) The license law considers a salesperson as employed by a broker. For tax purposes, a salesperson is an independent contractor. **Pages 444 & 449**

6. (d) The three answers correctly list the three requirements. **Page 445**

7. (b) The employment agreement does not have to be on a form approved by the Real Estate Commissioner. It must cover the important aspects of the employment relationship, including supervision of licensed activities, licensee's duties, and the compensation arrangement. **Page 445**

8. (c) Due to their employee status, a broker must provide workers compensation coverage to all sales associates as well as any non-licensee employees of the firm. **Page 449**

9. (c) The sales associates are employees of the broker, and as we have learned, all listing contracts are between the seller and the broker, not the sales associate who took the listing. When a salesperson leaves the employ of a particular broker, any listings he or she has will remain with that broker. **Page 441**

10. (b) Choices (a), (c), and (d) used half-truths, offensive terms, inflated claims, and ambiguous or superlative terms. **Page 457**

11. (d) A commercial e-mail message is "any electronic mail message the primary purpose of which is the commercial advertisement or promotion of a commercial product or service." E-mails sent as part of an ongoing commercial transaction, called "transactional e-mail messages", are excluded from the Act. **Page 455**

12. (d) All must be included in a commercial e-mail. **Page 456**

13. (a) Under the "do-not-call" rules, real estate licensees or unlicensed assistants may make cold calls provided that the calls are only made between 8:00 a.m. and 9:00 p.m. **Page 454**

14. (d) All statements are correct: Choice (a) - B&P Code Section 10140.5, Choice (b) - B&P 10140.6 & Reg 2770.1, Choice (c) - Reg 2770. **Page 457**

15. (c) It is discriminatory to single out one faith to the exclusion of others. **Page 458**

16. (a) A homeowners' association or CC&Rs **cannot** prohibit private owners from displaying real estate signs on their own property. The signs must be reasonably located, in plain view of the public, of reasonable dimensions and design, used to advertise the property for sale or lease, or to advertise directions to the property. **Page 459**

17. (c) Trust funds are money or anything of value received from the buyer by an agent on behalf of a seller. They include cash, a check used as a deposit for a purchase, or a personal note made payable to the seller. Do not confuse other monies such as commissions, general operating funds, rents, and deposits from broker-owned real estate with trust funds. **Page 460**

18. (b) Only $200 of personal funds may be in the trust fund account. **Page 461**

19. (a) Blockbusting or panic selling is illegal. Steering is the illegal practice of only showing clients property in certain areas. Redlining is the illegal use of a property's location to deny financing. **Page 473**

20. (c) The California Fair Employment and Housing Act (Rumford Act) prohibits discrimination in the sale, rental or financing of housing. The Housing Financial Discrimination Act (Holden Act) prohibits discrimination in real estate lending. The Unruh Civil Rights Act covers discrimination in business. **Page 474**

Chapter 14 - Real Estate Specialization

Answers - Matching

1. AA	7. B	13. O	19. KK	25. A	31. T
2. Y	8. H	14. EE	20. M	26. D	32. E
3. Z	9. Q	15. GG	21. V	27. BB	33. F
4. J	10. LL	16. R	22. L	28. N	34. DD
5. S	11. G	17. JJ	23. HH	29. MM	35. W
6. II	12. FF	18. C	24. U	30. X	

Answers - Multiple Choice

1. (d) A real estate licensee can sell a mobile home classified as real property. **Pages 487 & 489**

2. (a) In general, a certificate of title is used to transfer ownership of a mobile home. Ownership of a mobile home classified as real property is transferred by a grant deed. **Page 488**

3. (b) Time-shares are frequently purchased as a vacation investment because the cost of owning a good time-share is less than renting comparable hotel accommodations year after year. **Page 493**

4. (d) To protect, or "perfect", the interest created by the security agreement, or prevent the security from being sold by someone else, a financing statement must be filed. The financing statement is merely the document used to record the debt. **Pages 497-498**

5. (a) This is one of many requirements of the Uniform Commercial Code, Division 6, relating to bulk sales. **Page 497**

6. (c) Stocks, bonds, savings, and notes usually remain constant during an inflationary period. The value of real estate typically rises along with inflation. **Page 500**

7. (c) An income-generating property will create income as inflation rises. **Page 500**

8. (d) The four main benefits of commercial real estate are: (1) appreciation, (2) equity buildup, (3) income, and (4) tax benefits. Real estate is not a liquid investment such as savings, stocks, or bonds. Therefore, liquidity would be less of a concern than the other variables. **Page 500**

9. (d) Appreciation is an increase in the market value of an asset (e.g., real property), over, and above its value at the date when purchased. **Page 500**

10. (c) Leverage, means using primarily borrowed funds to increase buying power and, ideally, profits from investments. A large investment is controlled with a small amount of the investor's or borrower's own equity capital. **Page 501**

11. (a) The trustor is the borrower (owner), beneficiary is the lender, and the trustee is the third party in a trust deed. Therefore, the trustor (owner) would benefit from an appreciation in the home's value. **Page 500**

12. (c) Boot is money or anything of value (cars, boats, stocks, furniture) other than like-kind property that is put in by the investor who is "trading up" to balance the equities. **Page 505**

13. (d) At the time the sale is confirmed, the court will set the amount of commission to be paid if there is a real estate agent involved. **Page 506**

14. (c) An infill-development is simply the development of vacant parcels in existing urban and suburban areas. **Page 509**

15. (d) The main goal of property management is to protect the owner's investment as well as maximize the owner's return on that investment. The property manager must maintain accurate records and send regular reports to the owner. **Pages 510 & 517**

Chapter 15 - Getting and Keeping Your Real Estate License

Answers - Matching

1. O	4. L	7. R	10. P	13. E
2. H	5. Q	8. J	11. I	14. S
3. N	6. A	9 T	12. F	15. C

Answers - Multiple Choice

1. (a) The Real Estate Commissioner has the power to regulate and control the issuance and revocation of all licenses and regulate licensed activities, B&P Code Section 10071. Commission disputes are generally civil, not criminal matters. **Page 529**

2. (a) According to B&P Code Section 10137, salespersons are always employees of their brokers and can only be paid by their brokers. **Page 530**

3. (b) B&P Code Section 10139 covers penalties for unlicensed persons. The violation could be turned over to the local district attorney to determine whether or not to prosecute the case. **Page 531**

4. (a) B&P Code Section 10131 lists activities for which a California real estate license is required—mortgage loan brokers being one of them. B&P Code Section 10133 lists those who are not required to have a license including: resident managers (and their employees) of apartment buildings and complexes, employees of certain lending institutions, lenders making loans guaranteed or insured by the federal government, clerical employees, trustees conducting a trust deed sale, and vacation rental agents. **Pages 531-532**

5. (c) Choices (a) and (b) do not refer to licensees or licensed activities. Commissioner's Regulation 1726 states, "Every real estate broker shall have a written agreement with each of his sales associates, whether licensed as a salesperson or as a broker under a broker-salesperson arrangement. The agreement shall be dated and signed by the parties and shall cover material aspects of the relationship between the parties, including supervision of licensed activities, duties, and compensation." **Page 539**

6. (d) A child support obligor may be issued a 150-day temporary license. During the 150 days, a person must show the DRE proof that the delinquency is cleared and that he or she has been removed from the list, so that a permanent license can be issued. **Page 540**

7. (b) The broker must immediately notify the Commissioner in writing and return the license certificate to the salesperson. The form used is the Salesperson Change Application (Form RE214). Whenever real estate salespeople enter the employ of a new real estate broker, they shall mark out the name of their former broker on the face of the license and type or write the name of the new employing broker in ink on the reverse side, and date and initial same. The new broker and the salesperson must complete and mail RE214 to the Department of Real Estate within 5 days. The new broker retains the certificate in the main office. B&P Code Section 10161.8d **Page 539**

8. (c) Commissioner's Regulation 2724 gives the experience requirements for delegation of a broker's responsibility and authority to a salesperson. A salesperson must have at least two years full-time experience as a salesperson licensee within the past five years (plus a written agreement with the broker regarding delegation). **Page 539**

9. (d) A hearing is required before an unrestricted (standard) license can be suspended or revoked; no such protection is afforded a restricted license. B&P Code Section10156.7(a). **Pages 544-545**

10. (b) The broker is guilty of misrepresentation and fraud. B&P Code Sections 10776(a), (b), and (i). **Page 547**

11. (b) B&P Code Section 10148a requires the broker to keep records for three years. The obligatory retention period runs from the date the transaction is closed or from the date a listing is made if the transaction is not completed. **Page 552**

12. (b) Since Davis is not a real estate licensee, he has no duty to disclose his profit. However, if Davis were licensed, the prohibition against secret (undisclosed) profit would apply. B&P Code Section 10176g. **Page 547**

13. (d) The salesperson violated B&P Code Section 10176g by benefiting from a "secret profit". The employing broker violated B&P Code Section 10177h by not exercising supervision over the activities of his or her salespersons. Additionally the broker violated B&P Code 10178 because he or she should have immediately notified the Commissioner of the firing. **Page 547**

14. (c) B&P Code 10178 "When any real estate salesperson is discharged by his or her employer for a violation of any of the provisions of the Real Estate Law, a certified written statement of the facts with reference thereto shall be filed forthwith with the Commissioner by the employer and if the employer fails to notify the Commissioner as required by this section, the Commissioner may temporarily suspend or permanently revoke the real estate license of the employer, in accordance with the provisions of this part relating to hearings." The code's term "forthwith," means without delay, within a reasonable time under the circumstances, or at the first opportunity that arises. **Page 552**

15. (a) Broker Kim violated B&P Code Section 10177e by misusing the REALTOR® trade name. This misrepresentation is grounds for disciplinary action by the Commissioner. **Pages 547 & 549**

16. (a) Advertising of any licensed service "shall not be under the name of a salesman unless the name of the employing broker is set forth". Commissioner Regulation 2770. **Page 551**

17. (b) The ad is misleading. The broker knows that major structural repairs are needed, so the property can hardly be described as being ready to move into. False advertising regarding any real estate is unlawful. B&P Code Section 10140. **Page 551**

18. (b) B&P Code Section 10140.5 requires that the name of the broker must be disclosed in an ad. In addition, B&P Code Section 10140.6 requires that the ad must also reveal that the broker is licensed by the State of California. **Page 551**

19. (d) B&P Code Section 10140.6 requires that the broker disclose his or her involvement in the sale. A "blind" ad does not reveal the name of the broker responsible for placing the ad, and/or it fails to indicate that the advertiser is an agent or broker and not a principal (owner). **Page 551**

20. (d) B&P Code Section 10141 requires that the broker notify the buyer and the seller of the selling price within one month after completion of the sale. It is usually done by the escrow company. **Page 551**

Appendix C
Websites Used in this Book

Entity	Website
California Apartment Association	http://ca-apartment.org
California Association of REALTORS®	http://www.car.org
California Coastal Commission	http://www.coastal.ca.gov
California Dept. of Alcoholic Beverage Control	http://www.abc.ca.gov
California Dept. of Forestry and Fire Protection	http://www.fire.ca.gov/php/
California Dept. of Insurance	http://www.insurance.ca.gov/
California Dept. of Real Estate	http://www.dre.ca.gov
California Dept. of Veterans Affairs	http://www.cdva.ca.gov
California Franchise Tax Board	http://www.ftb.ca.gov/
California Housing & Community Development	http://www.hcd.ca.gov/
California Office of Real Estate Appraisers	http://www.orea.ca.gov
California Property Tax Resources	http://calproptax.com
Dept. of Housing and Urban Development	https://www.hud.gov
Federal Emergency Management Agency	http://www.fema.gov/
Federal Home Loan Mortgage Corporation	http://www.freddiemac.com/
Federal National Home Mortgage Association	http://www.fanniemae.com/
Government National Mortgage Association	http://www.ginniemae.gov/
Manufactured Housing Communities Association	http://www.wma.org
Mello-Roos Property Tax Information	http://www.mello-roos.com
myFICO, a division of FairIsaac	http://www.myfico.com/
National Association of Real Estate Brokers	http://www.nareb.com
National Association of REALTORS®	http://www.realtor.org
The Appraisal Foundation	http://www.appraisalfoundation.org
The Appraisal Institute	http://www.appraisalinstitute.org
The Federal Reserve System	http://www.federalreserve.gov/
U. S. Internal Revenue Service	http://www.irs.ustreas.gov
U. S. Small Business Administration	http://www.sba.gov
Veterans Home Loan Guaranty Services	http://www.homeloans.va.gov/

WEBSITES

WEBSITES

Appendix D
Spanish-English Key Terms

A

abogado-en-hecho .... attorney-in-fact
acceptación .... acceptance
aceramiento del coste .... cost approach
accessión .... accession
acciónen el ejectment .... action in ejectment
acreedor hipotecario .... mortgagee
adelanto .... earnest money
adjusted base del coste .... adjusted cost basis
administración de
 propiedad .... property management
agencia .... agency
agente .... agent
agua potable .... potable water
alquiler .... rent
amenidades .... amenities
amortización .... amortization
análisis del mercado comparative
 o competitivo .... analysis of the market
aprecio .... appreciation
arrendador .... landlord
arrendamiento ....lease
arrendamiento neto .... net lease
arrendatorio .... tenant
asignación .... assignment
asociación de los dueños ....homeowner's association
asunción de la hipoteca ...... assumption of mortgage
aumento .... accretion
autoridad real .... actual authority
avalúo .... appraisal
avulsión .... avulsion

B

bancarrota .... bankruptcy
beneficiario .... beneficiary
bienes inmuebles .... real property
bienes raíces .... real estate

C

cadena de título .... chain of title
capital ....capital
capitalización .... capitalization
casa abierta .... open house
caveat emptor .... caveat emptor
CC&Rs ....CC&Rs
certificado de título .... certificate of title
certificado de
 valor razonable .... certificate of reasonable value
cesionario .... assignee
cierre .... closing
cláusula de aceleración .... acceleration clause
cláusula de enajención .... alienation clause
cliente .... client
coerción .... duress
código de éticas .... code of ethics
condominio .... condominium
contrato .... contract
contrato bilateral .... bilateral contract
contrato de asociación
 en participación ....joint venture
contrato de compraventa .... contract of sale
contrato de garantía .... security agreement
contrato unilateral .... unilateral contract
contraoferta ....counteroffer
corporación .... corporation
corredor.. broker
costo de reposición .... replacement cost
costo de reproducción .... reproduction cost
credito .... credit

D

débito .... debit
declaración del beneficiario .... beneficiary statement
Declaración de Impacto
 Ambiental .... Environmental Impact Report

demanda .... demand
demografía .... demography
depreciación .... depreciation
depreciación acumulada .... accrued depreciation
derechos aéreos .... air rights
deudor .... debtor
deudor hipotecario .... mortgagor
documento .... document

E

edad real .... actual age
el anuncio valoren .... ad valorem
embargo .... attachment
en custodia de tercera persona .... escrow
energía del abogao .... power of attorney
ensambladura .... assemblage
escritura de propiedad .... deed
escritura de traspaso .... conveyance
estudio de costas .... quantity survey
evaluación .... assessment
evicción .... eviction
exclusivo .... exclusive listing
extracto del juicio .... abstract of judgment

F

fideicomisario .... trustee
fideicomiso de Inversiones en Bienes
    Inmuebles .. .. Real Estate Investment Trust (REIT)
franquicia .... franchise

G

gravamen .... lien
gravamen de tributación .... tax lien
gravamen de una constructora
    o de un constructor... ....mechanic's lien

H

hacer reformas .... improvements
heredero .... heir
hipoteca .... mortgage
hipoteca de tarifa
    ajustable .... adjustable rate mortgage (ARM)

I

informe de impacto
    ambiental .... environmental impact statement
información de la evaluación .... appraisal report
ingreso neto
    de operación .... net operating income (NOI)
instrumento .... instrument
interés .... interest
intestado .... intestate

J

jurisdicción .... jurisdiction

K

L

Ley de Prescripción .... Statute of Limitations
Ley de Veracidad en
    los Préstamos .... Truth-in-Lending Act
licencia .... license
limitaciones en la escritura .... deed restrictions

M

marca de fija .... bench mark
mediación .... brokerage
menor de edad .... minor
mercado de hipotecario
    primario .... primary mortgage market
mercado de hipotecario
    secundario .... secondary mortgage market

N

negligencia .... negligence
nota promisoria .... promissory note
novación .... novation

O

obsolescencia .... obsolescence
oferente .... offeror
opción .... option

orientación .... orientation

P

pago de globo .... balloon payment

pie de tablero .... board foot

préstamo amortizado .... amortized loan

préstamo combinado .... blanket loan

prorratear .... prorate

Q

R

rebaja .... discount/rebate

reconocimiento .... acknowledgment

rédito .... yield

redlining .... "redlining"

reformas menor .... underimprovement

relación de la agencia .... agency relationship

relleno .... backfill

requerimiento judicial .... injunction

rompe cuadras .... blockbusting

S

subarrendamiento .... sublease

subdivisión .... subdivision

subrogación .... subrogation

seguro hipotecario

    privado .... private mortgage insurance

seguro de título .... title insurance

T

tasa de capitalización .... capitalization rate

tasador .... appraiser

tercero .... third party

testador/testatrix .... testator, testatrix

testamento .... will

título .... title

transferidor .... assignor

U

uso no conforme .... nonconforming use

usura .... usury

utilidad .... utility

V

valor de mercado .... market value

valor económica .... economic life

variación .... variance

vida económica .... economic life

W

X

Y

Z

SPANISH - ENGLISH TERMS

SPANISH - ENGLISH TERMS

Glossary

A

A.L.T.A. owner's policy
An owner's extended title insurance policy.

A.L.T.A. title policy
A type of title insurance policy issued by title insurance companies that expands the risks normally insured against under the standard type policy to include unrecorded mechanic's liens; unrecorded physical easements; facts a physical survey would not show; water and mineral rights; and rights of parties in possession, such as tenants and buyers under unrecorded instruments.

abandonment *(abandono)*
The obvious and intentional surrender of the easement.

abandonment of homestead *(abandono de casa)*
A legal document that proves a homestead was abandoned. An owner must file an abandonment of homestead on the old property in order to obtain a homestead on a new property.

abatement of nuisance
Extinction or termination of conduct or activity that interferes with use or enjoyment of property.

abrogation *(abrogación)*
(1)The rescission or annulling of a contract. (2) The revocation or repealing of a contract by mutual consent of parties to the contract, or for cause by either party to the contract. (Pronounced "ab-ro-ga-tion")

abstract of judgment *(extracto del juicio)*
A summary of a court decision.

abstract of title *(titulo de sumario)*
Written summary of all useful documents discovered in a title search.

abstractor *(abstractor)*
A person who, historically, searches out anything affecting the title to real property and summarizes the information in the findings.

acceleration clause *(cláusula de aceleración)*
A clause in a loan document describing certain events that would cause the entire loan to be due.

acceptance *(aceptación)*
An unqualified agreement to the terms of an offer.

accession *(accesión)*
(1) The acquisition of title to additional land or to improvements as a result of annexing fixtures or as a result of natural causes such as alluvial deposits along the banks of streams by accretion. (2) A process by which there is an addition to property by the efforts of man or natural forces.

accretion *(aumento)*
A buildup of soil by natural causes on property bordering a river, lake, or ocean.

accrued
Accumulated over a period of time.

accrued depreciation *(depreciación acumulada)*
The difference between the cost to replace the property and the property's current appraised value.

acknowledgment *(reconocimiento)*
(1) A signed statement, made before a notary public, by a named person confirming the signature on a document and that it was made of free will. (2) A formal declaration to a public official (notary) by a person who has signed an instrument which states that the signing was voluntary.

acquisition *(adquisición)*
The act or process by which a person procures property.

acre
(1) A measure of land equaling 160 square rods, or 4,840 square yards, or 43,560 square feet. (2) A tract about 208. 71 feet square.

action
A lawsuit brought to court.

action in ejectment *(acción en el ejectment)*
(1) The legal remedy to remove a tenant. (2) Also known as unlawful detainer action.

actual age *(edad real)*
(1) The chronological age of a building. (2) Real age of a building.

actual authority *(autoridad real)*
Authority expressly given by the principal or given by the law and not denied by the principal.

actual notice *(aviso real)*
A fact, such as seeing the grand deed or knowing a person inherited a property by will.

"ADAM E. LEE"
The mnemonic for the eight ways to terminate an easement: Abandonment, Destruction, Adverse possession, Merger, Express agreement, Lawsuit, Estoppel, and Excessive use.

ad valorem *(el anuncio valoren)*
A Latin prefix meaning "according to value". (Pronounced "adva-lo-rem")

addendum
Additional documents attached to and made part of a contract.

adjustable rate mortgage *(hipoteca de tarifa adjustable)*
A note whose interest rate is tied to a movable economic index.

adjusted cost basis *(adjused base del coste)*
Original basis plus capital improvements and costs of the sale, less depreciation if income producing.

administrator *(administrador)*
A person appointed by the probate court to administer the estate of a deceased person. His or her duties include making an inventory of the assets, managing the property, paying the debts and expenses, filing necessary reports and tax returns, and distributing the assets as ordered by the probate court.

advance fees *(honorarios anticipados)*
A fee paid in advance of any services rendered. Sometimes unlawfully charged in connection with an illegal practice of obtaining a fee in advance for the advertising of property or businesses for sale, with no intent to obtain a buyer, by persons representing themselves as real estate licensees, or representatives of licensed real estate firms.

adverse possession *(posesión adversa)*
Acquiring title to property owned by someone else by continued possession and payment of taxes.

affirm *(afirme)*
(1) To conform, to aver, to ratify, to verify. (2) To make a declaration.

after-acquired title *(titulo despues-adquirido)*
Any benefits that come to a property after a sale must follow the sale and accrue to the new owner.

agency *(agencia)*
A legal relationship in which a principal authorizes an agent to act as the principal's representative when dealing with third parties.

agency coupled with an interest *(agencia juntada con un interés)*
An agent acquires an interest in the subject of the agency (the property).

agency relationship *(relación de la agencia)*
A special relationship of trust by which one person (agent) is authorized to conduct business, sign papers, or otherwise act on behalf of another person (principal). This relationship may be created by expressed agreement, ratification, or estoppel.

agent *(agente)*
A person who acts for and in the place of another, called a principal, for the purpose of affecting the principal's legal relationship with third persons.

agreement
A mutual exchange of promises (either written or oral). Although often used as synonymous with contract, technically it denotes mutual promises that fail as a contract for lack of consideration.

agreement of sale
(1) A contract for the sale of real property where the seller gives up possession, but retains the title until the purchase price is paid in full. (2) Also called contract for sale or land contract.

agricultural property
Property zoned for use in farming, including the raising of crops and livestock.

air rights *(derechos aéros)*
The rights in real property to the reasonable use of the air space above the surface of the land.

airspace *(espacio aéreo)*
The interior area which an apartment, office or condominium occupies. Airspace is considered real property to a reasonable height. For example, an owner or developer of condominiums may sell the airspace as real property.

alienate
(1) To transfer, convey, or sell property to another. (2) The act of transferring ownership, title, or interest.

alienation clause *(cláusula de enajenación)*
(1) A clause in a loan document that would allow the lender to call the balance of the loan due upon the sale of the property. (2) Also called the due-on-sale clause.

all-inclusive trust deed
A purchase money deed of trust subordinate to but still including the original loan.

alluvial deposit *(depósito alluvial)*
Sand or mud, carried by water and deposited on land.

alluvium *(alluvium)*
The gradual build-up of soil.

amenities *(amenidades)*
Features that add value to a property.

Americans with Disabilities Act
Federal law passed in 1990 that prohibits discrimination against individuals with disabilities.

amortization *(amortización)*
The liquidation of a financial obligation on an installment basis.

amortized loan *(préstamo amortizado)*
(1) A loan to be repaid, interest and principal, by a series of regular payments that are equal or nearly equal, without any special balloon payment prior to maturity. (2) Also called a level payments loan.

anchor bolt
(1) Attaches mud sill to foundation. (2) Embedded in concrete foundation.

annual
Once per year.

annual percentage rate
The relationship of the total finance charge to the total amount to be financed as required under the Truth-in-Lending Act.

anticipation, principle of
Affirms that value is created by anticipated benefits to be derived in the future.

appraisal *(avalúo)*
An unbiased estimate or opinion of the property value on a given date.

appraisal process
An orderly systematic method to arrive at an estimate of value.

appraisal report *(información de la evaluación)*
A written statement where an appraiser gives his or her opinion of value.

appraiser *(tasador)*
A person qualified by education, training and experience who is hired to estimate the value of real and personal property based on experience, judgment, facts, and use of formal appraisal processes.

appreciation *(aprecio)*
(1) An increase in the worth or value of property. (2) The increase in market value of real estate. (3) An increase in property value with the passage of time.

appropriation
The right to use water for a beneficial use by diverting surface water.

appurtenance
Anything used with the land for its benefit. (Pronounced "ap-pur-te-nance").

appurtenant
Belonging, appended or annexed to. Appurtenant items transfer with the land when property is sold.

architectural style
Generally the appearance and character of a building's design and construction.

arm's-length transaction
A transaction, such as a sale of property, in which all parties involved are acting in their own self-interest and are under no undue influence or pressure from other parties.

arranger of credit
A person who is not party to the real estate transaction, but will be compensated for arranging the credit, negotiating the credit terms, completing the credit documents, and facilitating the transaction.

articles of incorporation
An instrument setting forth the purposes, power and basic rules under which a private corporation is formed.

as is
Term stating the seller will not be responsible for the cost of repairing any defect.

asbestos
A mineral fiber used in construction which has been found to cause lung and stomach cancer.

assemblage *(ensambladura)*
The process of putting several smaller less valuable lots together under one ownership.

assessed value
Value placed on property by a public tax assessor as a basis for taxation.

assessment *(tasación)*
The valuation of property for the purpose of levying a tax or the amount of the tax levied.

assessment roll *(rodillo del gravamen)*
A list of all taxable property showing the assessed value of each parcel; establishes the tax base.

assessor
The official who has the responsibility of determining assessed values.

assignee *(cesionario)*
Party to whom a lease is assigned or transferred.

assignment *(asignación)*
The transfer of entire leasehold estate to a new person.

assignor *(transferidor)*
The person transferring a claim, benefit or right in property to another.

associate licensee
Another term used for a licensed real estate salesperson employed by a licensed real estate broker.

assumption clause *(cláusula de la asunción)*
A clause in a document that allows a buyer to take over the existing loan and agree to be liable for the repayment of the loan.

assumption fee *(honorarios de la asunción)*
A lender's charge for changing over and processing new records for a new owner who is assuming an existing loan.

assumption of mortgage *(asunción de la hipoteca)*
The taking of a title to property by a grantee wherein grantee assumes liability for payment of an existing note secured by a mortgage or deed of trust against the property, becoming a co-guarantor for the payment of a mortgage or deed of trust note.

GLOSSARY

attachment *(embargo)*
The process by which the court holds the property of a defendant pending outcome of a lawsuit.

attachment lien *(embargo preventivo del accesorio)*
(1) The process by which the court holds the real or personal property of a defendant as security for a possible judgment pending the outcome of a lawsuit. (2) Also known as writ of attachment.

attorney-in-fact *(abogado en hecho)*
(1) The person holding the power of attorney. (2) A competent and disinterested person who is authorized by another person to act in his or her place in legal matters.

avulsion *(avulsion)*
The sudden washing or tearing away of land by the action of water.

 B

backfill *(relleno)*
Soil that is used to fill in holes or support a foundation.

balloon payment *(pago de globo)*
Under an installment loan, a final payment that is substantially larger than any other payment and repays the debt in full.

bankruptcy *(bancarrota)*
A court proceeding to relieve a person's or company's financial insolvency.

base and meridian
Imaginary lines used by surveyors to find and describe the location of public or private lands.

baseline *(linea de fondo)*
A survey line running east and west, used as a reference when mapping land.

beam
A long thick piece of wood, metal or concrete, used to support weight in a building.

bearing wall
A wall that supports a vertical load as well as its own weight.

bench mark *(marca de fija)*
Location indicated on a permanent marker by surveyors.

beneficiary *(beneficiario)*
The lender under a deed of trust.

beneficiary statement *(declaración del beneficiario)*
A statement of the unpaid balance of a loan and describes the condition of the debt.

bequeath *(legar)*
To convey real or personal property by will.

bequest
A gift of personal property by will. (See *legacy*)

bilateral contract *(contrato bilateral)*
An agreement in which each person promises to perform an act in exchange for another person's promise to perform.

bill of sale
A written agreement used to transfer ownership in personal property.

blanket loan *(préstamo cubre)*
A loan secured by several properties. The security instrument used can be a blanket deed of trust or a blanket mortgage.

blighted area *(area marchitada)*
A section of a city, generally the inner city, where a majority of the buildings are run-down, and the property values are extremely low.

blind advertising
Advertising that fails to disclose that the party is a licensee acting as an agent.

blind pool
A type of syndication where money is raised for unspecified properties that meet specific investment criteria.

blockbusting *(rompe cuadras)*
The illegal practice of telling people that property values in a neighborhood will decline because of a specific event, such as the purchase of homes by minorities.

board foot *(pie de tablero)*
A unit of measurement for lumber equal to the volume of the board: one foot wide, one foot long, one inch thick (144 cubic inches).

bona fide purchaser
Bona fide means good faith (auténtico), so a bona fide purchaser is one who pays fair value for property in good faith, and without notice of adverse claims.

book value *(valor de la libro)*
The current value (for accounting purposes) of a property, calculated as the original cost, plus capital improvements, minus accumulated or accrued depreciation.

boot
Extra cash or non like-kind property put into an exchange.

bracing
Diagonal board nailed across wall framing to prevent sway.

breach of contract *(abertura del contrato)*
A failure to perform on part or all of the terms and conditions of a contract.

bridge loan
(1) A loan to "bridge" the gap between the termination of one mortgage and the beginning of another, such as when a

borrower purchases a new home before receiving cash proceeds from the sale of a prior home. (2) Also known as a swing loan.

British Thermal Unit
(1) A measurement that calculates heat; the amount of heat needed to raise one pound of water one degree Fahrenheit. (2) Also known as BTU.

broker *(corredor)*
An agent who earns income by arranging sales and other contracts. A real estate broker is an individual licensed by the state of California to arrange the sale or transfer of interests in real property for compensation.

broker's trust fund account
An account set up by a broker; withdrawals from this account may be made only by the broker.

brokerage *(corretaje)*
An activity involving the sale of something through an intermediary who negotiates the transaction for payment.

brownfield
An abandoned commercial or industrial site or under-utilized neighborhood where redevelopment is complicated by actual or perceived contamination.

building manager
A person employed by a property manager or directly by an owner, and usually manages a single large building or office complex.

building paper
Waterproof paper used between sheathing and roof covering.

bulk transfer law
The law concerning any transfer in bulk (not a sale in the ordinary course of the seller's business).

bundle of rights
An ownership concept describing all the legal rights that attach to the ownership of real property.

Business and Professions Code
The statute regulating the conduct of real estate brokers and establishing the Department of Real Estate.

business opportunity
Any type of business that is for lease or sale.

buyer's agent
A broker employed by the buyer to locate a certain kind of real property.

C.L.T.A. standard policy
A policy of title insurance covering only matters of record.

calendar year
Starts on January 1 and continues through December 31 of the same year.

California Fair Employment and Housing Act
State law that prohibits discrimination in the sale, rental or financing of practically all types of housing.

California Land Title Association
A trade organization of the state's title companies.

CAL-VET Program
A program administered by the State Department of Veterans Affairs for the direct financing of farm and home purchases by eligible California veterans of the armed forces.

"CAN-SPAM" laws
Federal and state law regulating commercial e-mail messages.

capital *("capital")*
Money and/or property owned or used by a person or business to acquire goods or services.

capital gain
At resale of a capital item, the amount by which the net sale proceeds exceed the adjusted cost basis (book value). Used for income tax computations. Gains are called short or long term based upon length of holding period after acquisition. Usually taxed at lower rates than ordinary income.

capitalism
An economic system in which most of the economy's resources are privately owned.

capitalization *(capitalización)*
(1) The process that can be employed to convert income to value. (2) An economic system in which most of the economy's resources are privately owned.

capitalization rate *(tasa de capitalización)*
(1) The rate of interest which is considered a reasonable return on the investment, and used in the process of determining value based upon net income. It may also be described as the yield rate that is necessary to attract the money of the average investor to a particular kind of investment. (2) It is sometimes call the "cap rate".

carryback financing
Financing by a seller who takes back a note for part of the purchase price.

cash flow
The net income generated by a property before depreciation and other non cash expenses.

caveat emptor *("caveat emptor")*
"Let the buyer beware".

CC&Rs
(See *covenants, conditions, and restrictions*)

GLOSSARY

certificate of eligibility
Issued by Department of Veterans Affairs-evidence of individual's eligibility to obtain VA loan.

certificate of reasonable value *(certificado del valor razonable)*
The Federal VA appraisal commitment of property value.

certificate of title *(certificado de título)*
A written opinion by an attorney that ownership of the particular parcel of land is as stated in the certificate.

chain of title *(cadena de título)*
A chronological history of property's ownership.

change, principle of
Holds that it is the future, not the past, which is of prime importance in estimating value. Change is largely the result of cause and effect.

chattel
Personal property.

chattel real
An item of personal property which is connected to real estate; for example, a lease.

chattels
(1) Personal property. (2) This term is sometimes used in law to describe any interest in real or personal property other than a freehold.

client *(cliente)*
The person who employs an agent to perform a service for a fee.

closed sheathing
Foundation for exterior siding; boards nailed to studding.

closing *(cierre)*
(1) Process by which all the parties to a real estate transaction conclude the details of a sale or mortgage. The process includes the signing and transfer of documents and distribution of funds. (2) Condition in description of real property by courses and distances at the boundary lines where the lines meet to include all the tract of land.

closing costs
The miscellaneous expenses buyers and sellers normally incur in the transfer of ownership of real property over and above the cost of the property.

closing statement
An accounting of funds made to the buyer and seller separately. Required by law to be made at the completion of every real estate transaction.

cloud on title
Any condition that affects the clear title of real property or minor defect in the chain of title which needs to be removed.

"COALD"
The mnemonic for the five duties an agent owes a principle: Care, Obedience, Accounting, Loyalty, and Disclosure.

Code of Ethics *(código de ética)*
A set of rules and principles expressing a standard of accepted conduct for a professional group and governing the relationship of members to each other and to the organization.

codicil
A change in a will before the maker's death.

cold calling
The practice of making unsolicited calls to people you do not know in order to get new business.

collateral
Something of value given as security for a debt.

color of title
That which appears to be good title but which is not title in fact.

commercial acre
(1) The area remaining from an acre of newly subdivided land after deducting the area devoted to streets, sidewalks, alleys, curbs, etc. (2) Also known as a buildable acre.

commercial e-mail message
Any electronic mail message whose primary purpose is the commercial advertisement or promotion of a commercial product or service.

commingling
The illegal practice of depositing client's funds in a broker's personal or general business account.

commission
A fee for services rendered usually based on a certain percentage of the sales price of a property.

commission split
The previously agreed upon division of money between a broker and sales-associate when the brokerage has been paid a commission from a sale made by the associate.

common area
An entire common interest subdivision except the separate interests therein.

common interest development
A common-interest development combining the individual ownership of private dwellings with the shared ownership of common facilities of the entire project.

common interest subdivision
Individuals owning a separate lot or unit, with an interest in the common areas of the entire project. The common areas are usually governed by a homeowners association.

common law dedication
When a property owner implies through his or her conduct, the intent that the public use the land.

common law
A body of unwritten law that was developed in England from the general customs and usage that was adopted in the United States.

community property
All property acquired by a husband and wife during a valid marriage (excluding certain separate property).

community property with right of survivorship
A law allowed a husband and wife to hold title to their property.

compaction
Extra soil that is added and compressed to fill in the low areas or raise the level of the parcel.

company dollar
The amount a broker has left after all commissions have been paid.

comparable sales
(1) Sales which have similar characteristics as the subject property and are used for analysis in the appraisal process. (2) Commonly called "comps", they are recent selling prices of properties similarly situated in a similar market.

comparative market analysis *(análisis del mercado comparativo o competitivo)*
A comparison analysis that real estate brokers use while working with a seller to determine an appropriate listing price for the seller's house.

comparison approach
(1) A real estate comparison method which compares a given property with similar or comparable surrounding properties. (2) Also called market comparison.

compensating balance
When a borrower deposits funds with the bank in order to induce the lender into making a loan.

competent
Legally qualified.

competition, principles of
Holds that profits tend to breed competition and excess profits tend to breed ruinous completion.

complete escrow
All terms of the escrow instructions have been met.

compound interest
Interest paid on original principal and also on the accrued and unpaid interest which has accumulated as the debt matures.

comps
A term used by real estate agents and appraisers to mean comparable properties.

concurrent ownership
(1) When property is owned by two or more persons or entities at the same time. (2) Also known as co-ownership.

condemnation
(1) The process by which the government acquires private property for public use, under its right of eminent domain. (2) The proceeding to exercise the power of the government to take private property from an owner for the public good, paying fair market value. (3) The proceeding to exercise the power of eminent domain.

condition
Condition similar to a covenant, a promise to do or not to do something. The penalty for breaking a condition is return of the property to the grantor.

condition precedent
A condition which requires something to occur before a transaction becomes absolute and enforceable; for example, a sale that is contingent on the buyer obtaining financing.

condition subsequent
A condition which, if it occurs at some point in the future, can cause a property to revert to the grantor. For example, a requirement in a grant deed that a buyer must never use the property for anything other than a private residence.

conditional use permit
Allows a land use that may be incompatible with other uses existing in the zone.

condominium *(condominio)*
A housing unit consisting of a separate fee interest in a particular specific space, plus an undivided interest in all common or public areas of the development. Each unit owner has a deed, separate financing and pays the property taxes for their unit.

conduit
A flexible pipe in which electrical wiring is installed.

conformity
When land uses are compatible and homes are similar in design and size, the maximum value is realized.

consideration
Something of value—such as money, a promise, property or personal services.

constructive fraud
A breach of duty legally declared fraudulent because it deceives others despite no dishonesty nor deceptive intent.

construction loan
An interim loan made to finance the actual construction or improvement on land. Funds are usually disbursed in increments as the construction progresses.

GLOSSARY

constructive eviction
Conduct by a landlord that impairs tenant's possession of the premises making occupancy hazardous.

constructive notice
Notice given by recording a document or taking physical possession of the property.

Consumer Credit Protection Act
A federal law that includes the Truth-in-Lending Law.

consumer goods
Goods sold or purchased primarily for personal, family, or household purposes.

contiguous
In close proximity.

contour
The surface configuration of land. Shown on maps as a line through points of equal elevation.

contract *(contrato)*
A legally enforceable agreement made by competent parties, to perform or not perform a certain act.

contract date
The date the contract is created. The contract is created when the final acceptance was communicated back to the offeror.

contract of sale *(contrato decompraventa)*
(1) A contract for the sale of real property where the seller gives up possession but retains title until the total of the purchase price is paid off. (2) Also called installment sales contract, a contract of sale, an agreement of sale, a conditional sales contract, or a land sales contract.

contract rent
The amount actually paid by a renter for use of the premises.

contribution, principle of
The worth of an improvement and what it adds to the entire property's market value, regardless of the actual cost of the improvement. Holds that maximum values are achieved when the improvements on a site produce the highest (net) return, commensurate with the investment.

conventional loan
Any loan made by lenders without any government guarantees (FHA insured or VA guaranteed).

conversion
The appropriation of property or funds belonging to another; as in a broker using a client's money.

convey
To transfer ownership or title.

conveyance *(escritura de traspaso)*
The transfer of title to land by use of a written instrument.

cooperating agent
A selling agent who assists another broker by finding a buyer.

cooperative
(1) Ownership of an apartment unit in which the owner has purchased shares in the corporation that holds title to the entire building. (2) A residential multifamily building.

corner influence
Commercial properties benefit from more exposure on a corner lot.

corner lot
A lot found at the intersection of two streets. It may be desirable because of its accessibility, but may also be noisy and expensive to maintain because of the increased frontage.

corporation *(corporación)*
A legal entity whose rights in business are similar to that of an individual.

correlation
(1) A step in the appraisal process involving the interpretation of data derived from the three approaches in value (cost, market and income) leading to a single determination of value. (2) Also frequently referred to as "reconciliation".

cost
The expenses in money, labor, material or sacrifices in acquiring or producing something.

cost approach *(acer camiento del coste)*
An appraisal method whereby a value estimate of a property is derived by estimating the replacement cost of the improvements, deducting the estimated accrued depreciation, then adding the market value of the land.

cost basis
Original price paid for a property.

counteroffer *(contraoferta)*
(1) The rejection of an original offer that becomes a new offer. (2) The rejection of an original purchase offer and the submission of a new and different offer.

covenant
A promise to do or not do certain things.

Covenants, Conditions, and Restrictions (CC&Rs)
Restrictions are placed on certain types of real property and limit the activities of owners. Covenants and conditions are promises to do or not to do certain things. The consequence for breaking those promises may either be money damages in the case of covenants, or the return of the property to the grantor, in the case of conditions.

crawlspace
Exterior or interior opening permitting access underneath a building, as required by building codes.

credit *(credito)*
A bookkeeping entry on the right side of an account, recording the reduction or elimination of an asset or an expense, or the creation of an addition to a liability or item of equity or revenue.

credit reporting agency
A company that researches the credit records of consumers and summarizes the findings in a factual credit report.

credit scoring
An objective, statistical method that lenders use to quickly assess the borrower's credit risk.

credit unions
An association whose members usually have the same type of occupation.

cripple
Stud above or below a window opening or above a doorway.

cubic-foot method
Similar to the square-foot method, except that it takes height as well as area into consideration. The cubic contents of buildings are compared instead of just the square footage.

cul-de-sac lot
A lot found on a dead-end street with the same way for ingress and egress.

curable depreciation
Items of physical deterioration and functional obsolescence which are customarily repaired or replaced by a prudent property owner.

customer
A prospective buyer of real estate; not to be confused with a property seller, who is the listing broker's client.

debt service
The sum of money needed for each payment period to amortize the loan or loans.

debtor *(deudor)*
A person who is in debt; the one owing money to another.

"DEC"
The mnemonic for the three disclosure requirements: Disclose, Elect, and Confirm.

deciduous
Plants and trees that lose their leaves seasonally in the fall.

decimal point
The period that sets apart a whole number from a fractional part of that number.

Declaration of Homestead
The recorded document that protects a homeowner from foreclosure by certain judgment creditors.

Declaration of Restrictions
A written legal document which lists covenants, conditions and restrictions (CC&Rs). This document gives each owner the right to enforce the CC&Rs.

dedication
The giving of land by its owner to a public use and the acceptance for such use by authorized officials on behalf of the public.

deed *(escritura de propiedad)*
A formal transfer by a party.

deed in lieu of foreclosure
A deed to real property accepted by a lender from a defaulting borrower to avoid the necessity of foreclosure proceedings by the lender.

deed of trust
(See *Trust Deed*)

deed restrictions *(limitaciones en la escritura)*
Limitations in the deed to a property that dictate certain uses that may or may not be made of the property.

default
Failure to pay a debt on a contract.

defeasible
Capable of being defeated. A defeasible estate is one that has a condition attached to the title, which if broken causes the termination of that estate.

deferred maintenance
Negligent, postponed, care of a building.

deficiency judgment
A judgment against a borrower for the balance of a debt owed when the security or the loan is not sufficient enough to pay the debt.

defined channel
Any natural watercourse, even if it is dry during a good portion of the year.

definite and certain
Precise acts to be performed are to be clearly stated.

delivery (of a deed)
The unconditional, irrevocable intent of a grantor immediately to divest (give up) an interest in real estate by a deed or other instrument.

demand *(demanda)*
The desire to buy or obtain a commodity.

demise
(1) To convey as an estate by will or lease. (2) To transmit by succession or inheritance.

demographics
Information from a variety of sources used to create a broad profile of any community.

demography *(demografía)*
The statistical study of human populations.

deposit receipt

Contract that acts as the receipt for earnest money given by the buyer to secure an offer, as well as being the basic agreement, between the buyer and seller.

depository institution

An institution that accepts deposits in the form of savings accounts, and makes loans using their depositors' monies.

depreciation *(depreciación)*

(1) Loss in value from any cause. (2) A tax advantage of ownership of income property.

depth table

A statistical table that may be used to estimate the value of the added depth of a lot.

deregulation

A process whereby regulatory restraints are gradually relaxed.

desk cost

(1) Profitability measure calculated by dividing the total operating expenses of the firm by the number of licensed sales associates. (2) Shows how much each sales associate must earn to cover expenses.

devise

A gift of real property by will.

directional growth

The location or direction toward which the residential sections of a city are destined or determined to grow.

discharge of contract

The cancellation or termination of a contract.

disclosure statement

The statement required by the Truth-in-Lending Law whereby a creditor must give a debtor a statement showing the finance charge, annual percentage rate, and other required information.

discount *(rebaja)*

(1) To sell a promissory note before maturity at a price less than the outstanding principal balance of the note at the time of sale. (2) Also an amount deducted in advance by the lender from the nominal principal of a loan as part of the cost to the borrower of obtaining the loan.

discount points

The amount of money the borrower or seller must pay the lender to get a mortgage at a stated interest rate. This amount is equal to the difference between the principal balance on the note and the lesser amount which a purchaser of the note would pay the original lender for it under market conditions. A point equals one percent of the loan.

discount rate

The interest rate that is charged by the Federal Reserve Bank to its member banks for loans.

discounting a note

Selling a note for less than the face amount or the current balance.

disintermediation

The process of depositors removing funds from savings.

dividend

A number to be divided by another number.

divisor

A number by which another number is divided.

"do not call"

Federal ad state regulations regarding unsolicited telephone calls.

Doctrine of Correlative Use

Owner may use only a reasonable amount of the total underground water supply for his or her beneficial use.

documentary transfer tax

A state enabling act allowing a county to adopt a documentary transfer tax to apply on all transfers of real property located in the county. Notice of payment is entered on face of the deed or on a separate paper filed with the deed.

document *(documento)*

Legal instruments such as mortgages, contracts, deeds, options, wills, bills of sale, etc.

dominant tenement

The property that benefits from an easement.

downzoning

A zone change from a high density use to a lower density use. For example, a commercial zone to a light industrial zone.

drywall

Gypsum panels used in place of wet plaster to finish the inside of buildings.

dual agency

An agency relationship in which the agent acts concurrently for both principals in a transaction.

dual agent

A broker acting as agent for both the seller and the buyer in the same transaction.

due-on-sale clause

An acceleration clause granting the lender the right to demand full payment of the mortgage upon a sale of the property.

duress *(coerción)*

The use of force to get agreement in accepting a contract.

"DUST"

The mnemonic for Demand, Utility, Scarcity, and Transferability.

18-month conditional license
Initial license issued to real estate salesperson who has only completed the Real Estate Principles course.

earnest money *(adelanto)*
(1) Down payment made by a purchaser of real estate as evidence of good faith. (2) A deposit or partial payment.

easement
(1) The right to use another's land for a specified purpose, sometimes known as a right-of-way. (2) The right to enter or use someone else's land for a specified purpose.

easement appurtenant
An easement that enhances land; usually a right of way.

easement by prescription
Created by continuous and uninterrupted use, by a single party, for a period of five years. The use must be against the owner's wishes and be open and notorious. No confrontation with the owner is required and property taxes do not have to be paid. The party wishing to obtain the prescriptive easement must have some reasonable claim to the use of the property.

easement in gross
An easement that is not appurtenant to any one parcel; for example, public utilities to install power lines.

eaves
The part of roof that hangs over the exterior walls.

economic age *(vida económica)*
Age of a building determined by its condition and usefulness.

economic life *(valor económica)*
(1) The estimated period over which a building may be profitably used. (2) Also known as effective life.

economic obsolescence
(1) A type of depreciation occurring because of forces outside the property. (2) Changes in the social or economic make-up of the neighborhood, zoning changes, over-supply of homes, under-supply of buyers, recession or legislative restrictions can cause economic obsolescence.

economic rent
What a leased property would be expected to rent for under current market conditions if the property were vacant and available for rent.

effective age
The age of a building based on its condition and usefulness.

effective demand
The desire coupled with purchasing power.

effective gross income
The amount of net income that remains after the deduction from gross income of vacancy and credit losses.

effective interest rate
The percentage of interest that is actually being paid by the borrower for the use of the money, distinct from nominal interest.

effective life
The estimated period over which a building may be profitably used.

egress
The right to exit from a property using an easement.

elevation sheet
Drawing that shows front and side exterior views of a building as it will be when finished.

emancipated minor
Someone who is legally set free from parental control/supervision.

emblements
Growing crops that are cultivated annually for sale.

eminent domain
(1) The right of the government to take private property from an owner, for the public good, paying fair market value. (2) Also known as condemnation or a "taking".

employee
Someone who is under the control and direction of a broker.

encroachment
The unauthorized placement of permanent improvements that intrude on adjacent property owned by another.

encumbrance
An interest in real property that is held by someone who is not the owner.

energy efficient ratio
(1) A measurement of the efficiency of energy; used to determine the effectiveness of appliances. (2) Also known as EER.

Environmental Impact Report *(declaración de impacto ambiental)*
(1) A study of how a development will affect the ecology of its surroundings. (2) Also known as EIR.

Equal Credit Opportunity Act
Federal act to ensure that all consumers are given an equal chance to obtain credit.

equitable title
The interest held by the trustor under a trust deed.

equity
The difference between the appraised value and the loan.

equity buildup
The gradual increase of the borrower's equity in a property caused by amortization of loan principal.

equity of redemption
(1) The right of a debtor, before a foreclosure sale, to reclaim property that had been given up due to mortgage default. (2) Also known as the right of redemption.

erosion
The gradual wearing away of land by natural processes.

escheat
A legal process where property reverts to the state because the deceased left no will and has no legal heirs. The state must wait five years before trying to claim the property. (Pronounced "es-cheat")

escrow *(en custodia de tercero persona)*
A small and short-lived trust arrangement.

escrow agent
The neutral third party holding funds or something of value in trust for another or others.

escrow holder
Acts as a neutral agent of both buyer and seller.

escrow instructions
Written directions, signed by a buyer and seller, detailing the procedures necessary to close a transaction and directing the escrow agent how to proceed.

estate
(1) The ownership interest or claim a person has in real property. (2) A legal interest in land; defines the nature, degree, extent and duration of a person's ownership in land.

estate at sufferance
A tenancy created when one is in wrongful possession of real estate even though the original possession may have been legal.

estate at will
The tenancy that may be ended by the unilateral decision of either party. There is no agreed upon termination date, and either party must give 30-days notice before ending the tenancy.

estate for life
A possessory, freehold estate in land held by a person only for the duration of his or her life or the life or lives of another.

estate for years
(1) A leasehold estate with a definite end date that must be renegotiated. (2) Commonly used for commercial leases.

estate from period to period
(1) A leasehold estate that is automatically renewed for the same term; a conveyance for an indefinite period of time. This does not need to be renegotiated upon each renewal. (2) Commonly a month-to-month rental.

estate in fee
(1) The most complete form of ownership of real property. (2) A freehold estate that can be passed by descent or by will after the owner's death. (3) Also known as estate of inheritance or fee simple estate.

estate of inheritance
(1) An estate which may descend to heirs. (2) Also known as perpetual estate.

estate tax
Federal tax on the transfer of assets owned by the estate of a person who has died.

estoppel
(1) A legal doctrine which prevents a person from denying something to be true or a fact which is contrary to previous statements made by that same person. (2) Also known as an implied or ostensible agency.

estuary
Where sea water and fresh water mix together.

et al
And others.

et ux
(1) Abbreviation for et uxor. (2) Means "and wife."

ethics
A set of principles or values by which an individual guides his or her own behavior and judges that of others.

eviction *(evicción)*
The legal process of removing a tenant from the premises for some breach of the lease.

eviction notice
Written notice from the landlord to the tenant requesting that he or she move out of the property within three days or meeting the landlord's requirements.

evidence of title
Proof of property ownership.

exclusive authorization and right-to sell listing
An exclusive contract where the seller must pay the listing broker a commission if the property is sold within the time limit by the listing broker, any other broker, or even by the owner.

exclusive listing *(listado exclusivo)*
An exclusive contract where the seller must pay the listing broker a commission if any broker sells the property.

execute
(1) To perform or complete. (2) To sign.

executed contract
All parties have performed completely.

execution sale
The forced sale of a property to satisfy a money judgment.

executor/executrix *(albacea)*
A person named in a will to handle the affairs of a deceased person.

executory contract
A contract in which obligation to perform exists on one or both sides.

expedientes
Land grants recorded by the Mexican government in California.

expenses
Certain items which appear on a closing statement in connection with a real estate sale.

express agreement
A written agreement, usually in the form of a listing contract which authorizes the broker to represent the seller in finding a ready, willing, and able buyer.

express contract
Parties declare the terms and put their intentions in words, either oral or written.

extended policy
An extended title insurance policy.

external obsolescence
Any influence negatively affecting a property's value that falls outside of the specific property site (i.e., a property located under an airport flight pattern).

fair market value
(1) The price the property would bring if freely offered on the open market with both a willing buyer and a willing seller. (2) Also known as market value and objective value.

false promise
A false statement of fact.

farm
A specific geographical location in which an agent walks every month in order to obtain listings.

fault creep
Movement along an earthquake fault caused by stress and/or earthquake shaking.

Federal Deposit Insurance Corporation (FDIC)
An agency of the federal government which creates a secondary market in conventional residential loans, FHA and VA loans by purchasing mortgages.

Federal Fair Housing Act
This law, amended in 1988, was created to provide fair housing throughout the United States.

Federal Home Loan Mortgage Corporation
A shareholder-owned corporation that purchases, secures, and invests in home mortgages.

Federal Housing Administration
A federal government agency that insures private mortgage loans for financing of homes and home repairs.

Federal National Mortgage Association
"Fannie Mae" a quasipublic agency converted into a private corporation whose primary function is to buy and sell FHA and VA mortgages in the secondary market.

Federal Reserve System *(Systema de la Reserva Federal)*
The federal banking system of the United States under the control of a central board of governors (Federal Reserve Board) involving a central bank in each of twelve geographical districts with broad powers in controlling credit and the amount of money in circulation.

fee
See *estate in fee* or *fee simple absolute*.

fee simple
The greatest possible interest a person can have in real estate.

fee simple absolute
(1) The largest, most complete ownership recognized by law. (2) An estate in fee with no restrictions on its use. (3) Property transferred or sold with no conditions or limitations on its use.

fee simple defeasible
Also known as fee simple qualified.

fee simple estate
The most complete form of ownership.

fee simple qualified
(1) An estate in which the holder has a fee simple title, subject to return to the grantor if a specified condition occurs. (2) Also known as fee simple defeasible.

fictitious business name
(1) A business name other than the name of the person who has registered the business. (2) Also known as assumed name. (3) A name that does not include the last name of the owner in the name of the business. (4) Also known as DBA or "doing business as."

fictitious trust deed
Recorded trust deed containing details which apply to later loan documents.

fiduciary
A relationship that implies a position of trust or confidence.

fiduciary duty
That duty owned by an agent to act in the highest good faith toward the principal and not to obtain any advantage over the latter by the slightest misrepresentation, concealment, duress of pressure.

fiduciary relationship
A relationship that implies a position of trust or confidence.

final tract map
A map indicating any changes required by the planning commission and is recorded in the county where the property is located.

finance charge

The dollar amount the credit will cost and is composed of any direct or indirect charge as a condition of obtaining credit.

financial intermediary

(1) An organization that obtains funds through deposits and then lends those funds to earn a return such as savings banks, commercial banks, credit unions and mutual savings banks. (2) Lenders that make real estate loans.

financing statement

(1) A written notice filed with the county recorder by a creditor who has extended credit for the purchase of personal property; establishes the creditor's interests in the personal property which is security for the debt. (2) A document used to record debt.

finder's fee

(1) Money paid to a person for finding a buyer to purchase a property or a seller to list property. (2) Also known as a referral fee.

fire stop

Boards nailed between studs to block the spread of fire in the walls.

first trust deed

A legal document pledging collateral for a loan (see *trust deed*) that has first priority over all other claims against the property except taxes and bonded indebtedness. This trust deed is superior to any other.

fiscal year

Starts on July 1 and runs through June 30 of the following year (used for real property tax purposes).

fixed rate full amortized loan

A loan with two distinct features. First, the interest rate remains fixed for the life of the loan. Second, the payments remain level for the life of the loan and are structured to repay the loan at the end of the loan term.

fixed rate loan

The most common type of loan. The principal and interest are calculated for the term of the loan. Payments are determined by dividing the total by the number of payments in the term of the loan. Regular payments of fixed amounts, to include both interest and principal are made. This payment pays off the debt completely by the end of the term.

fixture

(1) Personal property that has become affixed to real estate. (2) Real property that used to be personal property.

flag lot

A lot that looks like a flag on a pole. The pole represents the access to the site, which is usually located to the rear of another lot fronting a main street.

flashing

Sheet metal or other material that keeps the water from seeping into a building.

flood (100-year)

Boundary indicating areas of moderate flood hazards.

flood hazard boundary maps

Maps that identify the general flood hazards within a community.

floodplain

Low land adjacent to a river, lake or ocean.

floodwater

Water that overflows a defined channel.

footing

(1) The spreading part at the base of a foundation wall or pier. (2) A footing is an extended part of the foundation at the base or bottom of a foundation wall, pier or column.

forbearance

(1) Refraining from action by a creditor against a debt or after the debt has become due. (2) Forgiving a debt or obligation.

foreclosure

A legal procedure by which mortgaged property in which there has been default on the part of the borrower is sold to satisfy the debt.

foreclosure action

After a mechanic's lien is recorded, the claimant has 90 days to bring foreclosure action to enforce the lien. If he or she does not bring action, the lien will be terminated and the claimant loses the right to foreclose.

foreclosure sale

A sale where property is sold to satisfy a debt.

formaldehyde

A chemical organic compound found in building materials which may be a carcinogen.

foundation

The base of a house; usually concrete.

foundation plan

Drawing that shows foundation, sub-floors, footing, and pier placement.

franchise *(franquicia)*

A right or privilege awarded by law to operate a business using another company's name and products. In real estate, there are franchised brokerages such as Century 21 and ERA.

fraud

An act meant to deceive in order to get someone to part with something of value.

freehold

The full use of real estate for an indeterminate time. It differs from leasehold, which allows possession for a limited time.

freehold estate

An estate in real property which continues for an indefinite period of time.

front foot
The width of a property on the side facing the street.

front money
The minimum amount of money necessary to initiate a real estate venture, to get the transaction underway.

frontage
The length of a property along a street.

fructus industriales
Crops produced by human labor such as lettuce and grapes.

fructus naturales
Naturally occurring plant growth such as grasses.

fully amortized note
A note that is fully repaid at maturity by periodic reduction of the principal.

functional obsolescence
A type of depreciation stemming from poor architectural design, lack of modern facilities, out-of-date equipment, changes in styles of construction, or changes in utility demand.

functional utility
The combined factors of usefulness with desirability.

gable roof
A pitched roof with two sloping sides.

gambrel roof
Typically seen in Dutch colonial architecture, is a curbed roof, with a steep lower slope with a flatter one above.

general agent
A person authorized by a principal to perform any and all tasks associated with the continued operation of a particular project.

general lien
A lien on all the property of a debtor.

general plan
A master plan of long-term physical development adopted by cities and counties.

gift deed
Used to make a gift of property to a grantee, usually a close friend or relative.

gift tax
Tax that can be due when you give property or other assets to someone.

gold rush
A large migration of people to a newly discovered gold field.

good consideration
Gifts such as real property based solely on love and affection.

goodwill
An intangible, salable asset arising from the reputation of a business; the expectation of continued public patronage.

Government National Mortgage Association
(1) An agency of HUD, which functions in the secondary mortgage market, primarily in social housing programs. (2) Also known as Ginnie Mae.

government survey
A method of specifying the location of parcels of land using prime meridians, base lines, standard parallels, guide meridians, townships, and sections.

grace period
An agreed-upon time after the payment of a debt is past due, during which a party can perform without being considered in default.

graduated payment mortgage
(1) A loan with partially deferred payments of principal at the start of the term, increasing as the loan matures. (2) Also known as the flexible rate mortgage.

grandfather clause
An expression used in law that permits the continuation of a use or business to proceed because the current law denies permission.

grant
(1) A technical legal term in a deed of conveyance bestowing an interest in real property on another. (2) The words "convey" and "transfer" have the same effect.

grant deed
A type of deed in which the grantor warrants that he or she has not previously conveyed the property being granted, has not encumbered the property except as disclosed, and will convey to the grantee any title to the property acquired later.

grantee
The person receiving the property, or the one to whom it is being conveyed.

grantor
The person conveying or transferring the property.

gratuitous agent
A person not paid by the principal for services on behalf of the principal, who cannot be forced to act as an agent, but who becomes bound to act in good faith and obey a principal's instructions once he or she undertakes to act as an agent.

gross domestic product
The measure of goods and services produced by the nation during any one calendar year.

gross income
Total income from property before any expenses are deducted.

gross income multiplier
A figure which, when multiplied by the annual gross income, will theoretically determine the market value. A general rule of thumb which varies with specific properties and areas (industrial and commercial).

gross lease
A gross lease is also called a flat, fixed or straight lease. The tenant pays an agreed-upon sum as rent and the landlord pays any other expenses such as taxes, maintenance, or insurance.

gross national product (GNP)
The total value of all goods and services produced in an economy during a given period of time.

gross rent
Income (calculated annually or monthly) received from rental units before any expenses are deducted.

gross rent multiplier
A method used by real estate agents and appraisers to quickly convert gross-rent into market value. It is used for income-producing properties and is an easy way to get a rough estimate of the value of rental units.

ground lease
A lease for only the land.

ground rent
(1) Earnings of improved property credited to earnings of the ground itself after allowance is made for earnings of improvements. (2) Also called economic rent.

growing equity mortgage
A mortgage that has a fixed interest rate of increasing monthly payments.

guarantee of title
An assurance of clear title.

habendum clause
The "to have and to hold" clause which may be found in a deed.

handicap
Any physical or mental impairment which substantially limits one or more major life activities.

hard money loan
Any loan made on real property in exchange for cash.

hazard insurance
A property insurance policy that protects the owner and lender against physical hazards to property such as fire and windstorm damage.

hazardous household waste
Consumer products such as paints, cleaners, stains, varnishes, car batteries, motor oil, and pesticides that contain hazardous components.

hazardous waste
Materials—chemicals, explosives, radioactive, biological—whose disposal is regulated by the Environmental Protection Agency (EPA).

header
The horizontal, load-bearing, board over a doorway or window opening.

hedge against inflation
Real property appreciation keeps pace or exceeds inflation rates.

heir *(heredero)*
One who inherits property at the death of the owner or if the owner has died without a will (intestate).

highest and best use
An appraisal phrase meaning that use which at the time of an appraisal is most likely to produce the greatest net return to the land and/or buildings over a given period of time; that use which will produce the greatest amount of amenities or profit. This is the starting point for appraisal.

hip roof
A pitched roof with sloping sides and ends.

hold harmless clause
Protects the broker from incorrect information.

Holden Act
(1) A law designed primarily to eliminate discrimination in leading practices based upon the character of the neighborhood in which real property in located. (2) Also known as Housing Financial Discrimination Act of 1977. (See *redlining*)

holder
The party to whom a promissory note is made payable.

holder in due course
A person who has obtained a negotiable instrument (promissory note, check) in the ordinary course of business before it is due, in good faith and for value, without knowledge that it has been previously dishonored.

holographic will
Written in the maker's own handwriting, dated and signed by the maker.

home equity loan
A cash loan made against the equity in the borrower's home.

homeowners' association *(asociación de los dueños)*
A group of property owners in a condominium or other subdivision neighborhood, who manage common areas, collect dues, and establish property standards.

homeowners exemption
A $7,000 tax exemption available to all owner-occupied dwellings.

homestead
A piece of land that is owned and occupied as a family home.

Hoskold Tables
A method used to value an annuity that is based on reinvesting capital immediately; used by appraisers to valuate income property.

houseboat
A barge that is designed and equipped for use as a dwelling.

housing inventory
Housing units that are available for sale or in the process of being made ready for sale.

"HVAC"
The mnemonic for Heating, Ventilation, and Air Conditioning.

hypothecation
A process which allows a borrower to remain in possession of the property while using it to secure a loan.

I

intestate *(intestado)*
Dying without leaving a will.

implied contract
An agreement shown by acts and conduct rather than written words.

implied warranty of habitability
The property will be maintained to meet bare living requirements.

impound account
A trust account set up for funds set aside for future costs relating to a property.

improvements *(hacer reformas)*
Valuable additions made to property to enhance value or extend useful remaining life.

income approach
Estimates the present worth of future benefits from ownership of a property.

independent contractor
A person who is hired to do work for another person but who is not an employee of that person.

infill development
The development of vacant parcels in existing urban and suburban areas.

inflation
The increase in the general price level of goods and services.

ingress
The right to enter onto a property using an easement.

inheritance tax
A tax levied by states on inherited property and paid by the person receiving the property.

injunction *(requerimiento judicial)*
A court order forcing a person to do or not do an act.

innocent misrepresentation
When a person unknowingly provides incorrect information.

installment note
A note which provides for a series of periodic payments of principal and interest, until amount borrowed is paid in full. This periodic reduction of principal amortizes the loan.

installment sales
Where payments are made, by the buyer, to the seller, over a period of more than one year.

institutional lenders
A financial intermediary, such as a savings and loan association, commercial bank, or life insurance company, which pools money of its depositors and then invests funds in various ways, including trust deed and mortgage loans.

instrument *(instrument)*
A formal legal document such as a contract, deed or will.

insurance company
Major supplier of money for large commercial loans to developers and builders.

interest *(interés)*
The charge for the use of money.

interest only loan
A straight, non-amortizing loan in which the lender receives only interest during the term of the loan and principal is repaid in a lump sum at maturity.

interest rate
The percentage charged for the use of money.

interim loan
A short-term, temporary loan used until permanent financing is available, e.g., a construction loan.

interim use
(1) When the highest and best use is expected to change. (2) A short-term and temporary use of a property until it is ready for a more productive highest and best use.

interior lot
A lot that is surrounded by other lots, with a frontage on the street. It is the most common type lot and may be desirable or not, depending on other factors.

intermediation
The process of transfer capital from those who invest funds to those who wish to borrow.

interpleader action
A court proceeding initiated by the stakeholder of property who claims no proprietary interest in it for the purpose of deciding who among claimants is legally entitled to the property.

intestate succession *(sucesión intestada)*
When a person inherits property as a result of someone dying without a will.

inverse condemnation
When a private party forces the government to pay just compensation, if the property value or use has been diminished by a public entity.

involuntary lien
When the owner does not pay taxes or the debt owed, a lien may be placed against his or her property without permission.

Inwood tables
Means by which an income stream can be converted into present value; used by appraisers to valuate income property.

irrigation districts
Quasi-political districts created under special laws to provide for water services to property owners in the district; an operation governed to a great extent by law.

joint and several liability
A legal term used in reference to a debt or a judgment for negligence, in which each debtor or each judgment defendant is responsible for the entire amount of the debt or judgment.

joint tenancy
When two or more parties own real property as co-owners, with the right of survivorship.

joint venture *(contrato de asociación en participación)*
When two or more individuals or firms join together on a single project as partners.

joists
Parallel boards supporting floors or ceilings. The boards supporting them are girders, beams or bearing walls.

judgment
The final legal decision of a judge in a court of law regarding the legal rights of parties to disputes.

judgment lien
The final determination of the rights of parties in a lawsuit by the court.

judicial foreclosure
Foreclosure by court action.

junior mortgage
A second mortgage; one that is subordinate or has an inferior priority to the first mortgage.

junior trust deed
Any trust deed that is recorded after a first trust deed, whose priority is less than that first trust deed.

just compensation
Fair and reasonable payment due to a private property owner when his or her property is condemned under eminent domain.

key lot
A lot that resembles a key fitting into a lock, is surrounded by the back yards of other lots. It is the least desirable because of the lack of privacy.

kiosk
A free-standing small booth, such as a jewelry stand or a news-stand.

laches
Delay or negligence in asserting one's legal rights.

land
Includes airspace, surface rights, mineral rights, and water rights.

"LAND"
The mnemonic for the four elements of a valid lease: Length of time, Amount of rent, Names of parties, and Description of the property.

land contract
(1) A contract for the sale of real property where the seller gives up possession, but retains the title until the purchase price is paid in full. (2) Also known as a contract of sale or agreement of sale.

land project
Subdivisions located in sparsely populated areas (fewer than 1,5000 registered voters within the subdivision or within two miles of its boundaries), made up of 50 parcels or more.

landlocked
Property surrounded by other property with no access to a public road, street or alley.

landlord *(arrendador)*
(1) Lessor. (2) Property owner.

lateral support
The support which the soil of an adjoining owner gives to a neighbor's land.

lease *(arrendamiento)*
(1) A contract between owner, (lessor or landlord) and a lessee (tenant) which gives the tenant a tenancy. (2) Also known as a rental agreement. (3) A contract between an owner and tenant. (4) A movable document describing the temporary possession and use of the property.

leased-fee estate
The interest of the lessor in property.

leasehold
(1) An agreement, written or unwritten, transferring the right to exclusive possession and use of real estate for a definite period of time. (2) Also known as a rental agreement or lease.

leasehold estate
A tenant's right to occupy real estate during the term of the lease. This is personal property interest.

legacy
A gift of personal property by will.

legal description
(1) A land description recognized by law. (2) A description by which property can be definitely located by reference to government surveys or approved recorded maps.

legal title
Title that is complete and perfect regarding right of ownership.

lessee
(1) Tenant. (2) The one to whom property is rented or leased.

lessor
(1) Landlord. (2) Property owner. (3) The person who owns the property and signs the lease to give possession and use to the tenant.

less-than-freehold estate
(1) The lessee's interest. (2) An estate owned by a tenant who rents real property. (3) Also known as a leasehold estate.

leverage
Using a lender's money to finance a sale.

license *(licencia)*
(1) A permission granted by competent authority to engage in a business or occupation. (2) Permission to use a property, which may be revoked at any time.

license law
Another term for the real estate law.

lien *(gravamen)*
(1) A claim on the property of another for the payment of a debt. (2) A legal obligation to pay.

"LIEN$"
The mnemonic for the dollar sign and to show that lien$ involve money.

life estate
An estate that is limited in duration to the life of its owner or the life of another designated person.

limited liability company (LLC)
An alternative business that has characteristics of both corporations and limited partnerships.

limited partnership
A partnership of at least one general partner and one limited partner.

linear foot
A measurement of length rather than area (square foot) or volume (cubic feet).

liquidated damages clause
Clause in a contract that allows parties to the contract to decide in advance the amount of damages to be paid, should either party breach the contract.

lis pendens
(1) A recorded notice that indicates pending litigation affecting title on a property. (2) Also called a pendency of action. (Pronounced "lis pendenz")

listing
A contract between an owner of real property and an agent who is authorized to obtain a buyer.

listing agent
A broker who obtains a listing from a seller to act as an agent for compensation.

listing agreement
A written contract by which a principal, or seller, employs a broker to sell real estate.

littoral
Land bordering a lake, ocean or sea as opposed to land bordering a stream or river (running water). (Pronounced "lit-to-ral")

loan assumption
A buyer assumes the existing loan when a property is sold. The buyer takes over primary liability for the loan, with the original borrower secondarily liable if there is a default.

loan-to-value ratio (LTV)
The percentage of appraised value to the loan.

lot, block and tract system
(1) A process where developers divide parcels of land into lots. Each lot in a subdivision is identified by number, as is the block in which it is located; each lot and block is in a referenced tract. This process is required by the California Subdivision Map Act. (2) Also known as lot and block system, subdivision system or recorded map system.

love and affection
Consideration used in a gift deed.

maker

The borrower who executes a promissory note and becomes primarily liable for payment to the lender.

management contract

A contract that shows the terms of the agreement between the owner and the property manager.

mansionization

A new trend of home remodeling and construction that is emerging in older neighborhoods with small to medium-sized homes.

manufactured home

A home built in a factory after June 15, 1976 and must conform to the U.S. government's Manufactured Home Construction and Safety Standards.

"MARIA"

The mnemonic for the five tests of a fixture: Method of attachment, Adaptation, Relationship of the parties, Intention, and Agreement of the parties.

market comparison approach

(1) An appraisal method using the principles of substitution to compare similar properties. (2) A means of comparing similar type properties, which have recently sold, to the subject property. (3) Also called market data approach.

market price

The price paid regardless of pressures, motives or intelligence.

market rent

The rent a property should bring in the open market.

market value *(valor de mercado)*

(1) The highest price a property would bring if freely offered on the open market, with both a willing buyer and a willing seller. (2) Sometimes called objective value.

marketable title

Good or clear saleable title reasonably free from risk of litigation over possible defects.

material fact

Any fact that would seem likely to affect the judgment of the principal in giving consent to the agent to enter into the particular transaction on the specified terms.

maximum allowable rent

The maximum legal rent that a landlord may charge for a controlled rental unit.

mechanic's lien *(gravamen de una constructora o de un constructor)*

A lien placed against a property by anyone who supplies labor, services, or materials used for improvements on real property and did not receive payment for the improvements.

median home price

The price that is midway between the least expensive and most expensive home sold in an area during a given period of time.

megalopolis

A large densely populated metropolitan area consisting of a number of major urban areas and smaller surrounding cities.

Mello-Roos Act

Allows developers to make improvements (roads, parks, schools, fire stations) while making each homeowner pay for the improvements. These improvements are listed in the property taxes.

Mello-Roos District

An area where a special tax is imposed on those real property owners within a Community Facilities District. Public services such as roads, sewers, parks, schools and fire stations in new developments may be financed under this law.

menace

Using the threat of violence to get agreement in accepting a contract.

meridian

A survey line running north and south, used as a reference when mapping land.

metes and bounds

Land description that delineates boundaries and measures distances between landmarks to identify property.

minerals

Land elements found beneath the ground such as gold and coal and owned as real property. Fugitive substances that are not solid such as oil or gas must be taken from the ground. Once these elements are taken from the ground, they become the personal property of whoever removed them.

mineral rights

The legal interest in the valuable items found below the surface of a property (i.e., gold and coal).

minor *(menor de edad)*

A person under 18 years of age.

misplaced improvements

Improvements on land which do not conform to the most profitable use of the site.

misrepresentation

(1) Making a false statement or concealing a material fact. (2) A false statement of fact.

mistake

(1) An agreement was unclear or there was a misunderstanding in the facts. Mistake does not include ignorance, incompetence or poor judgment. (2) An error or misunderstanding.

mnemonics

The following memory aids may be found alphabetically in

this Glossary: "ADAM E. LEE", "COALD", "DEC", "DUST", "LAND", "LIEN$", "MARIA", "NDFA", "NIMBY", "PANCHO", "PEPS", "PETE", "PITI", "SCI", "TIMMUR", "T-TIP", and "UPTEE".

mobile home
A factory-built home manufactured prior to June 15, 1976, constructed on a chassis and wheels, and designed for permanent or semi-attachment to land.

mobile home park
Any area or tract of land where two or more mobile home lots are rented or leased or held out for rent or leased to accommodate manufactured homes or mobile homes used for human habitation.

monetary policy
The actions taken by the federal government to influence the availability and cost of money and credit as a means of promoting national economic goals.

money encumbrance
An encumbrance that affects the title.

month-to-month tenancy
A tenant rents property for a month at a time, under a periodic tenancy that continues for successive months until terminated by proper notice.

monument
A fixed landmark used in a metes and bounds land description.

mortgage *(hipoteca)*
A legal document used as security for a debt.

mortgage banker
A person whose principal business is the originating financing, closing, selling, and servicing of loans secured by real property for institutional lenders on a contractual basis.

mortgage loan disclosure statement
A statement that informs the buyer of all charges and expenses related to a particular loan.

mortgage yield
The amount received or returned from an investment expressed as a percentage.

mortgage-backed securities
Pools of mortgages used as collateral for the issuance of securities in the secondary market.

mortgagee *(acreedor hipotecario)*
The lender under a mortgage.

mortgagor *(deudor hipotecario)*
The borrower under a mortgage.

multiple-listing service
A cooperative listing service conducted by a group of brokers (usually members of a real estate association) to provide an inventory of all available properties in the area.

mutual assent
(1) An agreement between the parties in a contract. (2) The offer and acceptance of a contract.

mutual consent
(1) The offer by one party and acceptance by another party. (2) Also known as mutual assent or "meeting of the minds".

mutual mortgage insurance
A fee for an insurance policy charged to the borrower to protect lender under an FHA loan, in the event of foreclosure on the property.

mutual rescission
When all parties to a contract agree to cancel an agreement.

mutual water company
A water company organized by or for water users in a given district with the object of securing an ample water supply at a reasonable rate; stock is issued to users.

naked legal title
Title lacking the rights and privileges commonly associated with ownership may be held by trustee under a trust deed.

narrative appraisal
A summary of all factual materials, techniques, and appraisal methods used by the appraiser in setting forth his or her value conclusion.

"NDFA"
The mnemonic for No Darn Fooling Around.

negative amortization
Occurs when monthly installment payments are insufficient to pay the interest, so any unpaid interest is added to the principal due.

negligent misrepresentations
Untrue statements made without facts to back them up.

negotiable
Capable of being negotiated, assignable or transferable in the ordinary course of business.

negotiable instrument
Any written instrument that may be transferred by endorsement or delivery.

net lease *(arrendamiento neto)*
The tenant pays an agreed-upon sum as rent, plus certain agreed-upon expenses per month (i.e., taxes, insurance and repairs).

net listing
A listing agreement in which the commission is not definite. The broker receives all the money from the sale of the property that is in excess of the selling price set by the seller. The broker

must disclose the selling price to both buyer and seller within 30 days after the transaction.

net operating income (NOI) *(ingreso neto de operación)*
The balance remaining after deducting gross receipts of all fixed expenses.

net worth
The value of all assets minus all liabilities.

neutral depository
An escrow business conducted by someone who is a licensed escrow holder.

"NIMBY"
The mnemonic for Not In My Backyard.

"no fault" eviction
A lawful eviction in which the tenant is not at fault. This includes whether the owner wants to occupy the apartment or to get out of the rental housing business.

no notice of completion
If the owner does not record a notice of completion when work is finished, all claimants have a maximum of 90 days from the day work was finished to record a mechanic's lien.

nominal interest rates
The interest rate that is named or stated in loan documents.

non-conforming use *(uso no conforme)*
Legal use of property that at one period was established and maintained at the time of its original construction but no longer conforms to the current zoning law.

notary public
A licensed public officer who takes or witnesses the acknowledgement.

note
An evidence of a debt.

notice of completion
A notice filed by the owner or general contractor after completion of work on improvements, limiting the time in which mechanic's liens can be filed against the property.

notice of default
A notice to a defaulting party that there has been a nonpayment of a debt.

notice of non-responsibility
When an owner discovers unauthorized work on the property, he or she must file a notice. This must be recorded and posted on the property to be valid. The notice states the owner is not responsible for work being done, and releases the owner from the liability for work done without permission.

notice of trustee's sale
Notice given, and published, that a trustee's sale will be held to sell a property to satisfy a debt.

notice to pay rent or quit
(1) A written notice from the landlord to the tenant informing him or her to move out of the property within three days or meet the landlord's requirements. (2) Also known as an eviction notice.

novation *(novación)*
The substitution by agreement of a new obligation for an existing one.

null and void
Of no legal validity or effect.

1 month
For escrow purposes, 30 days.

1 year
For escrow and proration purposes, 360 days, 12 months, or 52 weeks.

1031 exchange
(1) A method of deferring tax liability. (2) Also known as a "tax-free" exchange.

obligor
(1) One who is bound by a legal obligation. (2) A person, delinquent in paying child support, whose name is listed by the Child Support Services.

obsolescence *(obsolescencia)*
Loss in value due to reduced desirability and usefulness of a structure because its design and construction became obsolete; loss because old-fashioned and not in keeping with modern needs, with consequent loss of income. May be functional or economic.

offer
A presentation or proposal for acceptance to form a contract.

offer to purchase
The proposal made to an owner of property by a potential buyer to purchase the property under stated terms.

offeree
The party receiving an offer.

offeror *(oferente)*
The party making an offer.

open end loan
A loan where the borrower is given a limit up to which may be borrowed, with each advance secured by the same trust deed.

open house *(casa abierta)*
A common real estate practice of showing listed homes to the general public during established hours.

open housing law
Congress passed the Federal Fair Housing Act in April 1968

which prohibits discrimination in the sale of real estate because of race, color, or religion of buyers. Its amendment in 1988 added: Those physically and mentally handicapped and those children under 18 years of age.

open listing
A listing agreement that gives any number of brokers the right to sell a property.

open sheathing
Boards nailed to rafters to form foundation for the roof.

option *(opción)*
(1) A contract to keep open, for a set period of time. (2) An offer to purchase or lease real property.

optionee
The person who wants to purchase or lease (lessee) the property.

optionor
The person who owns the property (seller, lessor).

"or more" clause
A clause in a mortgage or trust deed that allows a borrower to pay it off early with no penalty.

orientation *(orientación)*
The placement of a building on its lot in relation to exposure to sun, prevailing wind, traffic, and privacy from the street.

ostensible agency
An agency relationship created by the actions of the parties rather than by an express agreement.

ownership
(1) The right of one or more persons to possess and use property to the exclusion of all others. (2) A collection of rights to the use and enjoyment of property.

ownership in severalty
Property owned by one person or entity.

package loan
A type of loan on real property used in home financing covering land, structures, fixtures, and other personal property.

"PANCHO"
The mnemonic for the six requirements for adverse possession: Possession, Adverse, Notorious, Continuous, Hostile, and Open.

paramount title
Title which is superior or foremost to all others.

parcel map
Map showing a parcel of land that will be subdivided into less than five parcels or units, and shows land boundaries, streets, and parcel numbers.

parol evidence rule
(1) Oral or written negotiations made prior to a dispute about an executed contract and brought forward to influence the executed contract. Parol mean oral or by word of mouth but in this case means any evidence outside of the written agreement. (2) Prohibits introducing any kind of outside evidence to change or add to the terms of deeds, contracts or other writing once they have been executed.

partial reconveyance
A clause in a trust deed or mortgage permitting the release of a parcel or part of a parcel from the lien of that security instrument. The release usually occurs upon the payment of a specified sum of money.

partially amortized note
A promissory note with a repayment schedule that is not sufficient to amortize the loan over its term.

partition action
A court action to divide a property held by co-owners.

partnership
A form of business in which two or more persons join their money and skills in conducting the business.

party wall
A wall erected on the line between two adjoining properties, which are under different ownership, for the use of both parties.

patent
The legal document that transmits real property from the state or federal government to a person.

"PEPS"
The mnemonic for the four forces influencing value: Physical characteristics, Economic Influences, Political (governmental) regulations, and Social ideals.

percentage lease
The tenant pays a percentage of gross monthly receipts in addition to a base rent.

percolating water
Underground water not flowing in a defined channel.

percolation test
Test used to determine the ability of the land to absorb and drain water and is frequently used when installing septic systems.

personal property
Anything movable that is not real property.

"PETE"
The mnemonic for four types of government controls: Police power, Eminent domain, Taxation, and Escheat.

physical deterioration
(1) A type of depreciation caused by wear and tear, negligent care, damage by dry rot or termites or severe changes in temperature. (2) Also known as deferred maintenance.

GLOSSARY

pier
A column of masonry used to support other structural members.

pitch
The slope, incline, or rise of a roof.

"PITTI"
The mnemonic for Principles, Interest, Taxes, and Insurance.

planned development
(1) A planning and zoning term describing land not subject to conventional zoning to permit clustering of residences or other characteristics of the project which differ from normal zoning. (2) Sometimes called a planned unit development (PUD).

planning commission
An agency of local government charged with planning the development, redevelopment or preservation of an area.

plat map
Map of a subdivision indicating the location and boundaries of individual lots.

pledge
The transfer of property to a lender to be held as security for repayment of a debt. The lender takes possession of property.

pledged savings account mortgage
A borrower has a large amount of money in a savings or thrift account, and uses this money to maintain the account as security for a lender. The lender requires a certain ratio of the new loan amount to the balance in the account. The borrower must keep that amount in the account for a specified length of time. The lender can release the pledge account when the property has acquired enough equity to qualify under normal loan-to-value ratios.

plottage increment
Putting several smaller, less valuable parcels together under one ownership to increase value of total property.

pocket listing
A list that is kept by the listing broker or salesperson, and is not shared with other brokers in the office or other multiple listing service members. This is discouraged by the real estate profession and is prohibited by many broker's offices.

points
Charges levied by the lender based on the loan amount. Each point equals one percent of the loan amount; for example, two points on a $100,000 mortgage is $2,000. Discount points are used to buy down the interest rate. Points can also include a loan origination fee, which is usually one point. (See *Discount Points*)

police power
The power of the state to enact laws within constitutional limits to promote the order, safety, health, morals and general welfare of our society.

potable water *(agua potable)*
Fresh water that is safe and agreeable for drinking.

power of attorney *(energía del abogado)*
A legal document that gives another person the legal authority to act on his or her behalf.

power of sale
A clause in a trust deed or mortgage that gives the holder the right to sell the property in the event of default by the borrower.

preliminary notice
A written notice that must be given to the owner within 20 days of first furnishing labor or materials for a job by anyone eligible to file a mechanic's lien.

preliminary title report
An offer to issue a policy of title insurance in the future for a specific fee.

prepaid items of expense
Prorations of prepaid items of expense which are credited to the seller in the closing escrow statement.

prepayment clause
A clause in a trust deed that allows a lender to collect a certain percentage of a loan as a penalty for an early payoff.

prepayment penalty
(1) Penalty for the payment of a note before it actually becomes due. (2) A fee or charge imposed upon a debtor who desires to pay off their loan before its maturity.

prescription
The process of acquiring an interest, not ownership, in a certain property.

price
What the property actually sold for.

prima facie
Latin meaning first sight, a fact presumed to be true until disproved.

primary mortgage market *(mercado de hipote primario)*
Lenders make mortgage loans by lending directly to borrowers.

principal
(1) In a real estate transaction, the one (seller) who hires the broker to represent him or her in the sale of the property. (2) The amount of money borrowed.

priority
The order in which deeds are recorded.

private grant
The granting of private property to other private persons.

private mortgage insurance *(seguro hipotecario privado)*
Mortgage guarantee insurance available to conventional lenders on the first part of a high risk loan.

private restrictions
Created at the time of sale or in the general plan of a subdivision.

pro rata
In proportion; according to a certain percentage or proportion of a whole.

probate
The legal process to prove a will is valid.

probate sale
A court-approved sale of the property of a deceased person.

procuring cause
A broker who produces a buyer ready, willing and able to purchase the property for the price and on the terms specified by the seller, regardless of whether the sale is completed.

progression, principle of
The worth of a lesser valued residence tends to be enhanced by association with higher valued residences in the same area.

promissory note *(nota promisoria)*
The evidence of the debt.

promulgate
To publish or make laws known.

property
Anything that may be owned and gained lawfully.

property management *(administración de propiedad)*
(1) A specialty in which real estate brokers manage homes and large real estate projects such as industrial complexes, shopping centers, apartment houses and condominiums. (2) The branch of the real estate business involving the marketing, operation, maintenance and day-to-day financing of rental properties.

property taxes
Taxes used to operate the government in general.

proprietary lease
The lease used in co-op apartment buildings.

prorate *(proratear)*
(1) The division and distribution of expenses and/or income between the buyer and seller of property as of the date of closing or settlement. (2) The process of making a fair distribution of expenses, through escrow, at the close of the sale.

prospecting
The process of identifying potential customers.

public dedication
When private property is intended for public use. There are three types of public dedication: common law dedication, statutory dedication, or deed.

public grant
The transfer of title by the government to a private individual.

public record
(1) A document disclosing all important facts about the property, its marketing and the financing of the subdivision. (2) Also known as public report.

puffing
(1) A statement of opinion about property that is not factual. (2) Exaggerated comments or opinions not made as representations of fact, thus not grounds for misrepresentation.

pur autre vie
(1) For another's life. (2) A life estate created on the life of a designated person.

purchase money mortgage or trust deed
A trust deed or mortgage given as part or all of the purchase consideration for real property. In some states the purchase money mortgage or trust deed loan can be made by a seller who extends credit to the buyer of property or by a third party lender (typically a financial institution) that makes a loan to the buyer of real property for a portion of the purchase price to be paid for the property. In many states there are legal limitations upon mortgages and trust deed beneficiaries collecting deficiency judgments against the purchase money borrower after the collateral hypothecated under such security instruments has been sold through the foreclosure process. Generally no deficiency judgment is allowed if the collateral property under the mortgage or trust deed is residential property of four units or less with the debtor occupying the property as a place of residence.

quantity survey method *(estudio de costas)*
A detailed estimate of all labor and materials used in the components of a building. Items such as overhead, insurance and contractor's profit are added to direct costs of building. This method is time consuming but very accurate.

quiet enjoyment
Right of an owner or tenant to the use of the property without interference from the acts or claims of third parties.

quiet title action
(1) A court proceeding to clear a cloud on the title of real property. (2) Also known as action to quiet title.

quitclaim deed
Transfers any interest the grantor may have at the time the deed is signed with no warranties of clear title.

radon
Colorless, odorless, gas that is a carcinogen detected by a spectrometer.

rafters
Slanted boards of a roof that are designed to support the roof boards and shingles. To strengthen the load bearing factor of a roof, the rafters should be placed closer together.

range
A land description used in the U.S. government survey system consisting of a strip of land located every six miles east and west of each principal meridian.

range lines
Government survey imaginary vertical lines six miles east and west of the meridian to form columns.

rate
The percentage of interest charged on the principal.

ratification
The approval of a previously authorized act, performed on behalf of a person, which makes the act valid and legally binding.

ratified
Approved after the fact.

"ready, willing, and able" buyer
A person who is prepared to enter into a purchase contract, really wants to buy, and meets the financing requirements of purchase.

real estate *(bienes raices)*
Land and whatever physical property is on it, including buildings and structures. Current usage makes the term real estate synonymous with real property.

Real Estate Advisory Commission
A 10-member commission to offer advice to the Commissioner on matters pertinent to the Department of Real Estate.

real estate agent
A broker licensed by the Department of Real Estate who negotiates sales for other people.

real estate broker
Someone holding a broker license issued by the Department of Real Estate and permitted by law to negotiate real estate transactions between principals to employ persons holding salesperson or broker licenses.

Real Estate Commissioner
A person appointed by the governor to determine administrative policy and enforce the provisions of the real estate law and the Subdivided Lands Law.

Real Estate Investment Trust *(Fideicomiso de Inversiones en Bienes Raíces)*
A special arrangement under federal and state law whereby investors may pool funds for investments in real estate and mortgages and yet escape corporation taxes, profits being passed to individual investors who are taxed.

real estate law
(1) The law that affects the licensing and conduct of real estate licensees. (2) Another name for the Business and Professions Code, Part 1 entitled Licensing of Persons.

Real Estate Recovery Fund
A separate account funded through collection of a fixed amount from each license fee. It was established to pay judgments against real estate licenses.

real estate salesperson
A person with a real estate license who must be employed by a real estate broker in order to perform any of the activities that requires a license.

Real Estate Settlement Procedures Act
A federal law requiring disclosure to borrowers of settlement (closing) procedures and costs by means of a pamphlet and forms prescribed by the United States Department of Housing and Urban Development.

real estate syndicate
An organization of investors usually in the form of a limited partnership who have joined together to pool capital for the acquisition of real property interests.

Real Estate Transfer Disclosure Statement
A document that the seller must provide to any buyer of residential property (one-to-four units).

real property *(biene inmueble)*
Land (air, surface, mineral, water rights), appurtenances and anything attached, and immovable by law. Also included in real property are the interests, benefits and rights inherent in owning real estate, i.e., the "bundle of rights." Current usage makes the term real property synonymous with real estate.

real property loan law
Article 7 of Chapter 3 of the real estate law under which a real estate licensee negotiating loans secured by real property within a specific range is required to give the borrower a statement disclosing the costs and terms of the loan and which also limits the amount of expenses and charges that a borrower may pay with respect to the loan.

real property sales contract
An agreement to convey title to real property upon satisfaction of specified conditions which does not require conveyance within one year of formation of the contract.

Realtist
A member of a national organization, generally composed of African-American real estate brokers, known as the National Association of Real Estate Brokers (NAREB).

REALTOR®
A real estate broker holding active membership in a real estate board affiliated with the National Association of Realtors (NAR).

reconciliation

(1) The adjustment process of weighing results of all three appraisal methods to arrive at a final estimate of the subject property's market value. (2) Also known as correlation.

reconveyance deed

Conveys title to property from a trustee back to the borrower (trustor) upon payment in full of the debt secured by the trust deed.

recording

The process of placing a document on file with a designated public official for public notice. This public official is usually a county officer known as the County Recorder who designates the fact that a document has been presented for recording by placing a recording stamp upon it indicating the time of day and the date when it was officially placed on file.

rectangular survey system

(1) A process that uses imaginary lines to form a grid to locate land. (2) Also known as the U.S. Government Section and Township Survey.

red flag

Something that alerts a reasonably observant person of a potential problem.

redemption period

A period of time established by state law during which a property owner has the right to recover real estate after a foreclosure or tax sale by paying the sales price plus interest and costs.

redlining

(1) The illegal lending policy of denying real estate loans on properties in older, changing urban areas, usually with large minority populations, because of alleged higher lending risks, without due consideration being given by the lending institution to the credit-worthiness of the individual loan application. (2) The illegal use of a property's location to deny financing.

refinancing

Paying off an existing obligation and assuming a new obligation in its place. To finance anew, or extend or renew existing financing.

rehabilitation

The restoration of a property to its former or improved condition without changing the basic design or plan.

reinstate

To bring current and restore.

release clause

A provision found in many blanket mortgage or trust deeds enabling the borrower to obtain partial release from the loan of specific parcels.

reliction

When land covered by water becomes uncovered because of alluvial deposits along the banks of streams.

remodeling

Changes the basic design or plan of the building to correct deficiencies.

renegotiable rate mortgage

A type of loan in which the interest rate is renegotiated periodically.

rent *(alquiler)*

Payment for the use of a property, generally under a lease agreement.

rent control

(1) Laws in some communities that limit or prohibit rent increases. (2) Also known as rent stabilization.

rental agreement

Another name for lease.

replacement cost *(costo de reposición)*

The cost of replacing improvements with modern materials and techniques.

reproduction cost *(costo de reproducción)*

The current cost of building a replica of the subject structure, using similar quality materials.

request for notice

A notice that is sent, upon request, to any parties interested in a trust deed, informing them of a default.

rescission

Legal action taken to repeal a contract either by mutual consent of the parties or by one party when the other party has breached a contract.

resident manager

A person employed to manage an apartment building on a part or full-time basis.

residential ceiling height measurements

Minimum - 7.5 feet; normal - 8 feet

residential lease

A lease used for single family homes and duplexes.

restricted license

A type of probationary license issued when a license has been suspended, revoked or denied after a hearing.

restriction

A limitation placed on the use of property and may be placed by a private owner, a developer or the government. It is usually placed on property to assure that land use is consistent and uniform within a certain area.

retaliatory eviction

An eviction that occurs in revenge for some complaint made by the tenant.

return

(1) Profit from an investment. (2) The yield.

GLOSSARY

reverse annuity mortgage
A loan that enables elderly homeowners to borrow against the equity in their homes by receiving monthly payments from a lender to help meet living costs.

reversionary interest
(1) The right of the landlord to reclaim the property. (2) A future interest.

revocation
The canceling of an offer to contract by the person making the original offer.

revoke
Recall and make void.

ridge board
The highest structural part of a frame building.

right of replevin
The tenant has a legal right to recover personal property unlawfully taken by the landlord.

right of survivorship
(1) The right of a surviving tenant or tenants to succeed to the entire interest of the deceased tenant. (2) The distinguishing feature of a joint tenancy.

riparian rights
The rights of a landowner whose land is next to a natural watercourse to reasonable use of whatever water flows past the property.

rollover mortgage
A loan that allows the rewriting of a new loan at the termination of a prior loan.

R-value
A rating that measures how well insulation resists heat.

S corporation
A corporation that operates like a corporation but is treated like a partnership for tax purposes.

safety clause
Protects the listing broker's commission, if the owner personally sells the property to someone who was show the property or made an offer during the term of the listing.

sale-leaseback
A financial arrangement where at the time of sale the seller retains occupancy by concurrently agreeing to lease the property from the purchaser. The seller receives cash while the buyer is assured a tenant and a fixed return on buyer's investment.

sales associate
(1) A licensed real estate salesperson or broker whose license is held by an employing licensed broker. (2) Also known as associate licensee.

sales contract
A contract by which buyer and seller agree to terms of a sale.

sales tax
Collected as a percentage of the retailing sales of a product, by a retailer, and forwarded to the State Board of Equalization.

sandwich lease
A lease agreement created when a tenant sublets the property to another person, thus creating a sublessor-sublessee relationship. The person in the "sandwich" is a lessee to the owner and a lessor to the sublessee.

satisfaction
Discharge of a mortgage or trust deed from the records upon payment of the debt.

savings and loan association
A lending institution created as a mutual organization or as a stock institution. Deposits are insured by the Federal Deposit Insurance Corporation (FDIC).

scarcity
(1) The availability of a commodity in the marketplace. (2) A lack of supply of some type of real property resulting in increased value when demand exceeds supply.

schematics
Preliminary drawings and sketches by an architect, such as site plans and elevations.

"SCI"
The mnemonic for three approaches to value: Sales comparison approach, Cost approach, and Income approach.

second trust deed
The evidence of a debt that is recorded after a first trust deed; a junior trust deed.

secondary mortgage market *(mercado de hipote secundaria)*
The buying and selling of existing mortgages.

secret profit
Undisclosed profit made by a broker at their principal's expense.

section
An area of land, one square mile, or 640 acres; 1/36 of a township.

security *(garantía)*
Evidence of obligations to pay money.

security agreement *(contrato de garantía)*
A document commonly used to secure a loan on personal property.

security deposit
Money given to a landlord to prepay for any damage other than just normal wear and tear.

security interest
The interest of a creditor (lender) in the property of a debtor (borrower).

seller's market
The market condition which exists when a seller is in a more commanding position as to price and terms because demand exceeds supply.

seller's permit
Allows a retailer to buy the product at wholesale prices without paying sales tax. The retailer must then collect the proper sales tax from customers and pay it to the State Board of Equalization.

selling agent
The broker who finds a buyer and obtains an offer for the real property.

semiannual
Twice per year at six month intervals.

semimonthly
Twice a month.

separate property
Property owned by a married person in his or her own right outside of the community interest, including property acquired by the spouse (1) before marriage, (2) by gift or inheritance, (3) from rents and profits on separate property, and (4) with the proceeds from other separate property.

septic tank
A sewage settling tank which must be at least five feet away from the improvements.

servicing loans
Supervising and administering a loan after it has been made. This involves such things as collecting the payments, keeping accounting records, computing the interest and principal, foreclosure of defaulted loans, and so on.

servient tenement
The property that is burdened by an easement.

setback
The distance a building must be set back from the property line, street, or curb usually determined by local building codes.

severalty
Ownership of real property by one person or entity.

shared appreciation mortgage
Lender and borrower agree to share a certain percentage of the appreciation in market value of the property.

sheriff's deed
A deed given to a buyer when property is sold through court action in order to satisfy a judgment for money or foreclosure of a mortgage.

shoreline
The intersection of the land with the water (mean high water line).

short fund
When a home is sold and the homeowner's insurance policy is cancelled, the seller or owner of the policy receives a refund which is less than the credit they would receive if the buyer were to take over the existing homeowner's insurance.

side yard setback
The distance a building must be set back for the lot line at the side of the property.

sill (mud sill)
The lowest part of the frame of a house. It is fastened with bolts to the foundation and supports the upright studs of the frame.

simple interest
Interest computed on the principal amount of a loan only as distinguished from compound interest.

single agency
The representation of only one party in a real estate transaction.

sinking fund
A fund set aside from the income from property which, with accrued interest, will eventually pay for replacement of the improvements.

site
The position, situation or location of a piece of land in a neighborhood.

smart growth
Reconciling the needs of development with the quality of life. Smart growth focuses on revitalizing older suburbs and older city centers.

soil pipe
A pipe that carries waste from the house to the main sewer line.

Soldiers' and Sailors' Civil Relief Act (SSCRA)
A federal law designed to protect persons in the military service from loss of property when their ability to make the payment has been affected by their entering military service.

sole plate
(1) A board, usually 2" x 4", on which wall and partition studs rest. (2) A support for studs.

sole proprietorship
A business owned and operated by one person.

special agent
A person employed to perform a specific task.

GLOSSARY

special assessments
Taxes used for specific local purposes.

special power of attorney
A written instrument where a principal confers limited authority upon an agent to perform certain prescribed acts on behalf of the principal.

specific lien
A lien placed against a certain property, such as a mechanic's lien, trust deed, attachment, property tax lien or lis pendens.

specific performance
An action brought in a court to compel a party to carry out the terms of a contract.

specific plan
A particular development site or area of the general plan.

square-foot method
The most common method used by appraisers and real estate agents to estimate the cost of construction.

standard depth
Generally the most typical lot depth in the neighborhood.

standard policy
A policy of title insurance covering only matters of record.

standard subdivision
A land division with no common or mutual rights of either ownership or use among the owners of the parcels created by the division.

standby commitment
A letter that promises to deliver a takeout loan in the future.

State Housing Law
Outlines the minimum construction and occupancy requirements for dwellings.

statute of frauds
A state law which requires that certain contracts must be in writing to prevent fraud in the sale of land or an interest in land.

statute of limitations *("ley de prescripción")*
The period of time limited by statute within which certain court actions must be brought by one party against another.

statutory
Regarding laws created by the enactment of legislation as opposed to law created by court decisions.

steering
The illegal practice of only showing clients property in certain areas.

stigmatized property
(1) Property buyers or tenants may avoid for reasons unrelated to physical conditions or features. The most common are those in which there have been murders, suicides, or criminal activity. (2) Also known as psychologically impacted property.

stock cooperative
A corporation formed for the purpose of owning property.

straight-line depreciation
A method of depreciation under which improvements are depreciated at a constant rate throughout the estimated useful life of the improvement.

straight note
(1) A promissory note in which payments of interest only are made periodically during the term of the note, with the principal payment due in one lump sum upon maturity. (2) This may also be a note with no payments on either principal or interest until the entire sum is due.

Street Improvement Act of 1911
A law that empowers cities and counties to levy a special assessment to repair streets.

studs
Vertical supporting 2" x 4" boards in the walls spaced 16" on the center.

subagent
A broker delegated by the listing agent (if authorized by the seller) who represents the seller in finding a buyer for the listed property.

Subdivided Lands Law
A state law protecting purchasers of property in new subdivisions from fraud, misrepresentation or deceit in the marketing of subdivided property.

subdivision *(subdivisión)*
The division of land into five or more lots for the purpose of sale, lease, or financing.

Subdivision Map Act
The law that authorizes a city or county to control the orderly and proper development of the community.

subdivision system
Also known as a recorded map system.

"subject to" clause
A buyer takes over the existing loan payments, without notifying the lender. The buyer assumes no personal liability for the loan.

subjective value
Value given for personal reasons.

sublease *(subarrendamiento)*
Transfers less than the entire leasehold, with the original lessee being primarily liable for the rental agreement.

subleasee
The new person who has possession of a leased property.

sublessor
The original tenant of a leased property. They are still primarily liable for paying the rent to the owner for the sublease.

subordination clause
A clause in which the holder of a trust deed permits a subsequent loan to take priority.

subrogation *(subrogación)*
Replacing one person with another in regard to a legal right or obligation. The substitution of another person in place of the creditor, to whose rights he or she succeeds in relation to the debt. The doctrine is used very often where one person agrees to stand surety for the performance of a contract by another person.

substitution, principle of
Affirms that the maximum value of a property tends to be set by the cost of acquiring an equally desirable and valuable substitute property, assuming no cost delay is encountered in making the substitution.

succession
The legal transfer of a person's interest in real and personal property under the laws of descent.

supply and demand, principle of *(oferta y demanda)*
In appraising, a valuation principle stating that market value is affected by intersection of supply and demand forces in the market as of the appraisal date.

surplus productivity, principle of
The net income that remains after the proper costs of labor, organization, and capital have been paid, which surplus is imputable to the land and tends to fix the value thereof.

surrender
When a tenant voluntarily gives up a lease before the expiration of its term.

suspend
(1) Temporarily make ineffective. (2) The Real Estate Commisioner may suspend a real esate license for a violation of the licensing law.

swing loan
(1) A short-term loan used to enable the purchaser of a new property to buy that property on the strength of the equity from the property the purchaser is now selling. (2) Also known as a bridge loan.

syndicate
(1) Two or more individuals who come together for the business purpose of managing an investment. (2) Also known as a real estate syndicate.

takeout loan
The permanent loan that pays off a construction loan.

tax deed
A deed given to a successful bidder at a tax auction.

tax-deferred exchange
The trade or exchange of one real property for another without the need to pay income taxes on the gain at the time of trade.

tax delinquent property
Property that has unpaid taxes.

tax lien *(gravamen de tributación)*
When income or property taxes are not paid.

tax sale
Sale of property after a period of non-payment of taxes.

tenancy
(1) The interest of a person holding property by any right or title. (2) A mode or method of ownership or holding title to property.

tenancy in common
When two or more persons, whose interests are not necessarily equal, are owners of undivided interests in a single estate.

tenancy in partnership
Ownership by two or more persons who form a partnership for business purposes.

tenant *(arrendatorio)*
A renter.

tender
An offer by one of the parties to a contract to carry out his or her part of the contract.

tentative tract map
A map of the proposed subdivision that is submitted to a planning commission for approval or disapproval. It is used to make sure that the improvements, such as lot layouts, sizes, and configurations; grading plans; traffic access and street alignments; storm drainage, sewers, and water facilities; and other project features have been designed to conform to city or county general plans. The approval or disapproval of the planning commission is noted on the map. Therefore, a final map of the tract embodying any changes requested by the planning commission is required to be filed with the planning commission.

testate
A person who dies leaving a valid will.

testator / testatrix *(testador / testadora)*
A person who has made a will.

third party *(terceros)*
A person who may be affected by the terms of an agreement but who is not a party to the agreement.

tidelands
Lands that are covered and uncovered by the ebb and flow of the tide.

tight money
An economic situation in which the supply of money is limited, and the demand for money is high, as evidenced by high interest rates.

GLOSSARY

time
The duration of a loan.

timely manner
An act must be performed within certain time limits described in a contract.

"time is of the essence" clause
A clause in a contract that emphasizes punctual performance as an essential requirement of the contract.

time-share project
A form of subdivision of real property into rights to the recurrent, exclusive use or occupancy of a lot, parcel, unit, or segment of real property, on an annual or some other periodic basis, for a specified period of time.

"TIMMUR"
The mnemonic for Taxes, Insurance, Management, Maintenance, Utilities, and Reserves.

T-intersection lot
A lot that is fronted head-on by a street. The noise and glare from headlights may be detractors from this type of lot.

title *(título)*
Evidence that the owner of land is in lawful possession.

title companies
Companies that perform a title search on the property and issue a title policy for the lender and the purchaser to ensure that there is a valid mortgage lien against the property and title is clear.

title insurance *(seguro de título)*
An insurance policy that protects the named insured against loss or damage due to defect in the property's title.

title plant
The storage facility of a title company in which it has accumulated complete title records of properties in its area.

title report
A report which discloses condition of the title, made by a title company preliminary to issuance of title insurance policy.

"to let", "to demise"
These phrases mean the same as "to rent".

topography
Nature of the surface of land; topography may be level, rolling, and mountainous.

tort
A violation of a legal right, or a civil wrong such as negligence, libel, or nuisance.

townhouse
One of a row of houses usually of the same or similar design with common side walls or with a very narrow space between adjacent side walls.

township *(municipio)*
A grid of squares-each six miles by six miles (36 square miles).

township lines
Imaginary lines drawn every six miles north and south of the base line to form a horizontal row or tier of townships.

trade association
A voluntary nonprofit organization of independent and competing business units engaged in the same industry or trade, formed to help solve industry problems, promote progress, and enhance service.

trade fixture
An item of personal property, such as a shelf, cash register, room partition or wall mirror, used to conduct a business.

transferability
The title must be marketable with an unclouded title.

trust account
An account separate and apart and physically segregated from broker's own funds, in which broker is required by law to deposit all funds collected for clients.

trust deed
A security instrument that conveys naked legal title of real property.

trust funds
Money or other things of value received from people by a broker to be used in real estate transactions.

trustee *(fideicomisario)*
Holds naked legal title to property as a neutral third party where there is a deed of trust.

trustee's deed
A deed given to a buyer of real property at a trustee's sale.

trustee's sale
The forced sale of real property, by a lender, to satisfy a debt.

trustor
The borrower under a deed of trust.

Truth in Lending Act *("ley de Veracidad en los Préstamos")*
(1) A federal law that requires borrowers to be informed about the cost of borrowing money. (2) Also known as Regulation Z.

"T TIP"
The mnemonic for the four unities of joint tenancy: Time, Title, Interest, and Possession.

turnkey projects
Investors purchase projects that are ready for occupancy.

two-year grace period
A period of time after the expiration of a license that renewal is allowed as long as all real estate activity has ceased during that time and a late fee is paid at the time of renewal.

underwriting
The process of evaluating a borrower's risk factors before the lender will make a loan.

undivided interest
The buyer receives an undivided interest in a parcel of land as a tenant in common with all the other owners.

undue influence
Using unfair advantage to get agreement in accepting a contract.

unearned increment
An increase in value to real estate that comes about from forces outside the control of the owners, such as a favorable shift in population.

unemployment rate
The percentage of the people classified as unemployed as compared to the total labor force.

unenforceable contract
A contract that was valid when made but either cannot be proved or will not be enforced by a court.

Uniform Commercial Code (UCC)
A code that establishes a unified and comprehensive method for regulation of security transactions in personal property.

unilateral contract *(contrato unilateral)*
A contract where a party promises to perform without expectation of performance by the other party.

unilateral rescission
Legal action taken to repeal a contract by one party when the other party has breached a contract.

unit-in-place method
Cost of units in the building as installed is computed and applied to the structure cost. The total costs of walls in place, heating units and roof are figured on a square-foot basis, including labor, overhead, and profit. This is the most detailed method of estimating value.

unity
Equal right of possession or undivided interest. For example, each tenant has the right to use the whole property. None of the owners may exclude any co-owner from the property, nor claim any portion of the property for exclusive use.

unjust enrichment
The situation where a person has received and keeps money or goods that belongs to another. A lawsuit may be necessary to get back the property.

unlawful detainer action
(1) The legal remedy to remove a tenant. (2) Also called an action in ejectment.

Unruh Civil Rights Act
State law that prohibits discrimination by businesses.

"UPTEE"
The mnemonic for the five ownership rights in the Bundle of Rights: Use, Possess, Transfer, Encumber, and Enjoy.

urban sprawl
The unplanned and often haphazard growth of an urban area into adjoining areas.

useful life
The time frame when an asset (e.g., a building) is expected to remain economical to the owner.

usury *(usura)*
The act of charging a rate of interest in excess of that permitted by law.

utility *(utilidad)*
The ability of a property to satisfy a need or desire, such as shelter, income or amenities.

utility value
The usefulness of the property to its owner.

vacancy factor
Loss of income because of a vacant unit.

VA loan
A loan made to qualified veterans for the purchase of real property wherein the Department of Veterans' Affairs guarantees the lender payment of the mortgage.

valid
Legally binding

valid contract
(1) A binding and enforceable contract. (2) A document that has all the basic elements required by law.

valuable consideration
Each party to a contract must give up something to make the agreement binding.

valuation
The process of estimating market value.

value
(1) The present and future anticipated enjoyment or profit from the ownership of property. (2) Also known as worth.

variance *(variación)*
An exception granted to existing zoning regulations for special reasons.

vendee
The buyer under a contract of sale (land contract).

vendor
The seller under a contract of sale (land contract).

vested
Owned by.

vesting
The way title will be taken.

veterans' exemption
Entitles a resident of California who has been in the military during wartime to take a $4,000 real estate tax exemption. Because the homeowners exemption of $7,000 is greater, most California veterans choose the homeowners exemption.

void
An agreement which is totally absent of legal effect.

void contract
A contract that has no legal effect due to lack of capacity or illegal subject matter.

voidable
An agreement which is valid and enforceable on its face, but may be rejected by one or more of the parties.

voluntary lien
When an owner chooses to borrow money, using the property as security for the loan.

wainscoting
The bottom portion of a wall that is covered with wood siding; the top part is treated with another material.

waive
(1) To abandon. (2) To relinquish a right to enforce or require anything.

waiver
The relinquishment or refusal to accept a right.

walk-up
An apartment of more than one story with no elevator.

warehousing
The process of assembling into one package a number of mortgage loans, prior to selling them to an investor.

warranty deed
No longer used in California; a deed used to transfer title to property, guaranteeing that the title is clear and the grantor has the right to transfer it.

"WASTO"
The mnemonic for five ways to acquire or convey property: Will, Accession, Succession, Transfer, or Occupancy.

water
Water on the surface flowing in a stream or underground (percolating) is real property. If it is taken and bottled, then it becomes personal property.

water pressure test
Water pressure can be tested by turning on all faucets and flushing all toilets at the same time.

water table
The natural level at which water will be found, either above or below the surface of the ground.

wear and tear
Depreciation of an asset due to ordinary usage.

wetlands
Areas where water covers the soil, or is present either at or near the surface of the soil all year or for varying periods of time during the year, including the growing season.

will *(testamento)*
A written instrument whereby a person makes a disposition of his or her property to take effect after their death.

witnessed will
Will usually prepared by an attorney and signed by the maker and two witnesses.

wraparound loan
(1) A method of financing where a new loan is placed in a secondary position; the new loan includes both the unpaid principal balance of the first loan and whatever sums are loaned by the lender. (2) Sometimes called an All-Inclusive Trust Deed (AITD).

writ of execution
A legal document issued by a court forcing the sale of a property to satisfy a judgment.

writ of possession
A legal action granted by the court to the landlord if the tenant does not move out or answer a lawsuit.

"X"
A person who cannot write may execute a document by placing an "X" (his or her mark) where the signature is normally placed. Beneath the mark a witness then writes the person's name and signs his or her own name as a witness.

yield *(rédito)*
(1) The interest earned by an investor or an investment (or by a bank on the money it has loaned). (2) Also called return.

yield rate
(1) The yield expressed as a percentage of the total investment. (2) Also called rate of return.

zoning
The regulation of structures and uses of property within selected districts.

zoning ordinance
Regulates land use for individual projects.

GLOSSARY

Index

INDEX

M